T0329803

State or Merchant?

Political Economy and Political Process in 1740s China

Harvard East Asian Monographs 273

State or Merchant?
Political Economy and Political
Process in 1740s China

Helen Dunstan

Published by the Harvard University Asia Center
Distributed by Harvard University Press
Cambridge (Massachusetts) and London, 2006

© 2006 by the President and Fellows of Harvard College

Printed in the United States of America

The Harvard University Asia Center publishes a monograph series and, in coordination with the Fairbank Center for East Asian Research, the Korea Institute, the Reischauer Institute of Japanese Studies, and other faculties and institutes, administers research projects designed to further scholarly understanding of China, Japan, Vietnam, Korea, and other Asian countries. The Center also sponsors projects addressing multidisciplinary and regional issues in Asia.

Library of Congress Cataloging-in-Publication Data

Dunstan, Helen.

State or merchant? : political economy and political process in 1740s China / Helen Dunstan.

p. cm. -- (Harvard East Asian monographs ; 273)

Includes bibliographical references and index.

ISBN 0-674-02262-9 (cl : alk. paper)

1. China--Economic policy—1644–1912. 2. China--Politics and government—1644–1912. 3. China--History--Qing dynasty, 1644–1912. I. Title. II. Series.

HC427.7.D864 2006

330.951'032--dc22

2006000349

Index by the author

♾ Printed on acid-free paper

Last figure below indicates year of this printing

15 14 13 12 11 10 09 08 07 06

Acknowledgments

The archival research on which this book is based was funded by a Special Opportunity for Archival Research grant from the National Endowment for the Humanities, an independent federal agency, and a Special Studies Program travel grant and Sesquicentenary Research and Development Scheme grant from the University of Sydney. I thank both institutions and the staffs of the First Historical Archives in Beijing, the National Palace Museum library in Taibei, and the Institute of History and Philology and the Institute of Modern History at Academia Sinica, Taibei. I am especially grateful to the Institute of Qing Dynasty History at Renmin University of China for the repeated warm welcomes that it has extended to me, and to the Institute of Taiwan History (Preparatory Office) at Academia Sinica for its hospitality in 2001 and 2003. In particular, I thank those who arranged my invitations and accommodation: Kong Xiangji, Cheng Chongde, Xia Mingfang, and (in Taibei) Liu Ts'ui-jung.

Friends who have commented on earlier drafts and/or who have remained loyally encouraging and helpful throughout the years of preparation of this book include Mark Elvin, Antonia Finnane, Susan Naquin, Peter Perdue, and Pierre-Étienne Will. Lai Hui-min provided important advice about the resources available at the Institute of Modern History, Academia Sinica, and drew my attention to categories of palace memorials whose relevance I had overlooked. Remarks by Philip Kuhn, the late Gordon Dunstan, and Robert Tannenbaum have helped me to improve my writing style. Finding time to work on the manuscript while running a Chinese language and studies program at a metropolitan university has not been easy. I therefore thank those colleagues and former colleagues, particularly Derek Herforth, Maghiel van Crevel and David Bray, whose willingness to serve as acting departmental chair freed me to take the spells of leave that helped me to complete the book. The annual Christmas–New Year holiday and the special shutdown during the 2000 Sydney Olympics also deserve a thankful mention. My deepest debt is still to those—above all, the late Piet van der Loon—who taught me Classical Chinese at the University of Oxford. It is humbling to reflect that future progress in premodern Chinese history depends most fundamentally on teaching students to "apply your grammar," as Piet repeatedly enjoined us. I am deeply grateful for the exacting standards that we encountered in his classes.

I have been aided in the revision of the manuscript by substantial and constructive comments by two anonymous readers. I regret that considerations of space have prevented me from adopting all the referees' suggestions. Julia Perkins, Cheryl Tucker and Malcolm Skewis made valuable contributions to the final stages of the preparation of the manuscript. Of course, I alone am responsible for the remaining errors and infelicities in the text of this book.

My renderings of Sino-Manchu official titles generally follow those in Charles Hucker's *A Dictionary of Official Titles in Imperial China*.[1] However, I have not hesitated to make exceptions when these seemed justified. Two other invaluable works that I have used more often than my footnotes suggest are Qian Shifu's chronological table of senior Qing officeholders, and the relevant volume, compiled by Guo Chengkang, of the annalistic summary of Qing history prepared by the Institute of Qing Dynasty History at Renmin University.[2] I am indebted to the latter work for many references to the *Shilu* (Veritable records) located in the final stages of my research, as well as to a few other sources. While I have generally cited only the original sources (provided that I have personally examined them), I would like here to make special acknowledgment of my use of Guo's excellent work.

H.D.

---

1. Charles O. Hucker, *A Dictionary of Official Titles in Imperial China* (Stanford: Stanford University Press, 1985).

2. Qian Shifu, comp., *Qingdai zhiguan nianbiao* [Chronological tables of high officeholders in the Qing dynasty] (Beijing: Zhonghua shuju, 1980); Guo Chengkang, comp., *Qingshi biannian* [An annalistic history of the Qing dynasty], vol. 5, *Qianlong chao, shang* [The Qianlong reign, part 1] (Beijing: Zhongguo Renmin Daxue chubanshe, 1991).

Contents

Tables, Map, and Figures

Tables

Map

Figures

The Provinces of China Proper Under the Qing Dynasty (reprinted from *Conflicting Counsels to Confuse the Age*, by Helen Dunstan. Ann Arbor: University of Michigan, Center for Chinese Studies, 1996. Reprinted by permission).

Weights, Measures, and Units of Currency

Note: the equivalents stated below refer to the official standards. Local variation was considerable.

Capacity

1 *shi* = approximately 103.6 liters

Weight

1 *liang* = approximately 37.3 grams
1 *jin* = 16 *liang* = approximately 0.597 kilogram

Area

1 *mu* = approximately 0.0615 hectare
1 *qing* = 100 *mu* = 6.15 hectares

Distance

1 *li* = approximately 0.576 kilometer

Currency

The principal means of exchange in wholesale and other large transactions was silver, which circulated by weight. The *liang* (see above) of silver was the main unit of value. It was notionally supposed to exchange for a full "string" of 1,000 "copper" (actually brass) coins. In monetary contexts, *liang* is conventionally rendered "tael," while brass coins are called "cash." I follow these conventions here.

Abbreviations and Citation Conventions

The following abbreviations are used in the notes to the text and tables.

Bd. Rev.	Board of Revenue
Cat. no.	Catalog number
CC	First Historical Archives, *Zhupi zouzhe, Caizheng, Cangchu*
D.r.	Date of rescript
DQHDSL	*Qinding Da Qing huidian shili*
DQHDZL	*Qinding Da Qing huidian zeli*
Doc. no.	Document number
Grd. Coun.	Grand Council
Grd. Secs.	Grand Secretaries
GCQXLZ	*Guochao qixian leizheng*
GZD/KX	*Gongzhong dang Kangxi chao zouzhe*
GZD/QL	*Gongzhong dang Qianlong chao zouzhe*
HCJSWB	*Huangchao jingshi wenbian*
HHCC	First Historical Archives, *Huke hongben, Cangchu*
HQZY	*Huang Qing zouyi*
Int.	Intercalary
JF	First Historical Archives, *Zhupi zouzhe, Caizheng, Jingfei*
JS	First Historical Archives, *Zhupi zouzhe, Caizheng, Juanshu*

KC	First Historical Archives, *Zhupi zouzhe, Caizheng, Kuchu*
KX	Kangxi
KYQRFDZ	*Kang Yong Qian shiqi chengxiang renmin fankang douzheng ziliao*
LFZZ	National Palace Museum, *Junji dang, Lufu zouzhe*
LFZZQZ	*Qingzhe* or *qingdan* (statistical statement) included in the LFZZ collection
Mem.	Memorial
MQDA	*Ming Qing dang'an*
NGDKDA	Digitized document from the *Neige Daku dang'an*, Institute of History and Philology, Academia Sinica
NMA	Nine Ministries Assembly
PDJCFL	Lai Bao et al. *Pingding Jinchuan fanglüe*
Pr.	Print (from microfilm)
PYTOCG	Chen Hongmou, *Peiyuan Tang oucun gao: wenxi*
QCWXTK	*Qingchao wenxian tongkao*
QL	Qianlong
QSL/KX	*Da Qing Shengzu Ren Huangdi shilu*
QSL/QL	*Da Qing Gaozong Chun Huangdi shilu*
QSL/YZ	*Da Qing Shizong Xian Huangdi shilu*
Repr.	Reproduced in
TF	First Historical Archives, *Zhupi zouzhe, Caizheng, Tianfu*
Tl.	Tael
Transc.	Transcribed in
YFD	First Historical Archives, *Yifu dang*
YZ	Yongzheng
ZPYZ	*Yongzheng zhupi yuzhi*

Full details of all works and archival classifications listed above will be found in the Bibliography, pp. 491–504. The Bibliography also contains full details of all items cited by short title in the footnotes.

Basic Citation Conventions for Archival Sources

For memorials, classification details/abbreviation, then bundle number if applicable, submitter's name, and traditional date of memorial. Catalog/document numbers are supplied for undated copies, other documents whose date is in doubt, and materials from the Grand Secretariat Archives.

For detached statistical statements in the LFZZ collection, LFZZQZ followed by presumed traditional date in parentheses and National Palace Museum LFZZ document number.

For Grand Council record books, classification details or abbreviation followed by traditional date of record, document, or rescript, with microfilm reel and volume (*ce*) number in parentheses.

State or Merchant?

Political Economy and Political

Process in 1740s China

Introduction

Let us begin with four disjointed glimpses of the government of the Qing dynasty (1644–1911) at work.

In 1743, the governor-general of the central China "ricebowl" provinces of Hunan and Hubei, a Manchu called A'ersai, proposed new arrangements to smooth the annual process by which local officials restocked the antifamine granaries of which each county had one. If too many grain-buying missions converged at once on places where grain was in surplus, markets were upset and prices rose. A'ersai therefore advocated secret consultations between the top administrators of provinces with grain to spare and provinces that could not buy enough grain within their own borders. Where appropriate, the officials of jurisdictions in the former category would buy on behalf of those in the latter, taking account of local grain supply conditions as they did so. The emperor perceived a flaw in this move for improved coordination: the consultation process would involve delays. His own Grand Council, on the other hand, was in a position to obtain an overview of harvest and storage conditions throughout the realm. It would be more sensible for the Grand Council to have someone compare the harvest and grain-reserve reports from all the provinces. Should there be need for interprovincial cooperation, the center could direct the relevant provincial chiefs to take appropriate action.[1]

In 1760, the governor of Henan province in north China, a Chinese called Hu Baoquan, gave the emperor precise figures, drawn from the brokers' records of forty-one counties, on his jurisdiction's exports of

---

1. CC, A'ersai, QL 8/8/10; YFD, QL 18/4/11 (d.r.) (9:1624-1).

grain during about nine months from late July 1759. To be sure, the figures were incomplete: they represented only those stocks that were large enough to have passed through the hands of wholesalers and had thus been liable to oversight by brokers. In any case, Henan comprised about one hundred county-level jurisdictions. Nonetheless, Hu had access to details on 1,158,004 *shi* of grain that had been drawn out of Henan by poor harvests in adjacent provinces. He could have calculated, for example, that up to 918,992 *shi* had gone north, 163,669 *shi* southeast, and 75,343 *shi* west. He knew (and, indeed, reported to the emperor) exactly how much of this grain had originated in each of the thirteen larger administrative units to which the forty-one counties belonged. He also knew the approximate routes by which the grain had travelled. Had he wanted to find out the names of the exporting merchants, the brokers' records would have yielded this information.[2]

In 1736, the provincial administration commissioner of remote Yunnan, a Chinese called Chen Hongmou, issued a threat to anyone so wicked as to buy up wheat and beans as they were harvested and put them into hoards. This was a year of dearth; to hoard the newly ripened wheat and beans was callously to deprive the hungry poor of the relief that these crops should have brought. Offenders were to be beaten to death immediately.[3]

In late 1747, the governor-general of the southeast coastal provinces of Fujian and Zhejiang, a Manchu called Kaerjishan, confided to the emperor his worries about some Catholic, presumably Spanish, merchants from the Philippines. Their present trading visit to Xiamen (Amoy) was being managed successfully, with their ship's cannon and other military equipment placed in official custody until their departure. Their religion, however, was cause for concern. If they made a habit of such visits, might they not rekindle the embers of the subversive doctrine among the unstable Fujian populace? Would it not be best to give them the sort of farewell that, although munificent, would make it clear that they should not return? The grand councillors, charged by the emperor to consider Kaerjishan's memorial (letter to the

---

2. Hu Baoquan, mem. of QL 25/5/10, transc. Ye, comp., "Qianlong chao miliang maimai shiliao," part 2, pp. 32–33; cf. Rowe, *Hankow*, p. 187.

3. PYTOCG, *juan* 4:13a–b; cited also in Kishimoto, *Shindai Chūgoku no bukka*, p. 300.

throne), disagreed. Although several months later they would be assiduously passing on their monarch's orders to have four Catholic missionaries killed secretly in jail, they foresaw nothing but embarrassment should the state abruptly override a permission of thirty years' standing or renege on the well-established principle of keeping commerce open.[4] European imperialism might link Christianity and commerce, but, in terms of policy, the councillors put them asunder. Trade was no great problem.

The first three of these glimpses fit well with common images of the late imperial Chinese state. Most fundamentally, the government presided over an agrarian economy in which subsistence issues were of outstanding importance and in which private trade was well-developed. There was a rationally ordered bureaucracy with great potential for coordinated management. Manchu and Chinese officials cooperated to govern China in the Chinese way. The state was ambitious; its servants understood that information is control and pursued both diligently. In implementing the paternalist policies recommended by Confucianism, however, the state might resort to brutal violence to enforce its moralistic view of economics. It might also, perhaps, be sometimes tempted into overcentralization by the prospects of greater administrative rationality. These perspectives probably command most credence in nonspecialist circles, but historians of Qing-dynasty China would be more likely to qualify than to dismiss them. They are not basically unsound.

The fourth glimpse challenges persistent stereotypes while fitting with recent advances in scholarship.[5] The Sino-Manchu state of the Qing dynasty was not inveterately anticommercial. To the contrary, key policies were premised on recognition of the crucial functions of commerce. In the mid-eighteenth century, even the fear of subversion from an alien, heterodox religion was not permitted to disrupt a status quo allowing controlled foreign trade. But what of the domestic grain trade, which is the topic of this book? The eighteen provinces of "China proper" constituted a geographically diverse territory, several

---

4. YFD, QL 12/12/21 (d.r.) (7:1615-2), QL 13/9/3 (7:1616); Gao Xiang, *Kang Yong Qian san di*, p. 301.

5. E.g., Metzger, "The State and Commerce"; Will, *Bureaucracy and Famine*, pp. 212–15; Pomeranz, *Great Divergence*, pp. 157–61, 203–5; Rowe, *Saving the World*, pp. 197–204.

times the size of France, that was crisscrossed with roads and navigable waterways and that was vulnerable to local food shortages as well as large-scale famines. It had major urban populations, not to mention regional specializations in, for example, the cultivation of nonfood crops, rural handicraft production, and mining.[6] Even food-growing peasants could find themselves at least partly dependent on the market for their household grain (for most people, the staple food). Given these conditions, it is surprising neither that the interregional and local grain trades played a vital role, nor that sensible officials understood this fact.[7] However, recognition that the grain trade was important did not necessarily entail its being thought sufficient to ensure that all were fed in times of dearth. Nor did it necessarily imply that merchants would be left to pursue profit by whatever means they chose.

Let us return to Hu Baoquan and his provincial export figures. As mentioned, Hu knew that the total figure that he gave the throne for Henan's grain exports was incomplete. It did not include the loads of petty traders, borne on carts or donkeys. Hu opined that, in their "unbroken processions," such traders had exported more grain alto-gether than had the great merchants. If so, the minimum outflow of grain from Henan to its neighbors in 1759–60 exceeded 2.3 million *shi*, or 2.38 million hectoliters—probably, in large part, of wheat. This would have been a vast amount. Precision as to its food value is impossible because, in the absence of information from Hu, one cannot be certain of the mix of types of grain or even whether all of it was husked. However, if we take Fernand Braudel's estimate of three hectoliters for per capita annual consumption of dryland cereals in early modern Europe, 2.38 million hectoliters of grain was enough to feed nearly 800,000 north Chinese consumers for one year (or 9.5

---

6. For a detailed survey of regional diversity in China's eighteenth-century economy, see Naquin and Rawski, *Chinese Society*, chap. 5. For patterns and estimated rates of urbanization in late imperial China, see the seminal essays by Skinner in Skinner, ed., *The City in Late Imperial China*. Other important studies of Qing cities include Rowe, *Hankow*; Naquin, *Peking*; Johnson, *Shanghai*; and the remaining essays in the Skinner volume.

7. Surveys of the Qing grain trade and grain market include Abe, *Shindai shi*, chap. 6, and Xu and Wu, *Zhongguo ziben zhuyi*, vol. 1, pp. 272–77. Regional case studies include Shigeta, *Shindai shakai keizai shi*, part 1, chap. 1; Wang Yeh-chien, "Food Supply"; Marks, "Rice Prices, Food Supply, and Market Structure"; and Wong and Perdue, "Grain Markets and Food Supplies."

million for one month). Moreover, 2.38 million hectoliters represents almost one-third of the 7.45 million hectoliters (6 million quintals) that Braudel estimated as the maximum yearly volume of the entire international grain trade of seventeenth-century Europe.[8]

Could Henan's consumers afford to lose 1 or 2 million *shi* of grain to exports in those particular nine months? After all, although most of the land tax had been commuted into silver, the province had to meet an annual quota exceeding 200,000 *shi* for uncommuted land tax and for "tribute grain" (a supplementary grain tax earmarked for Beijing). In theory, also, a minimum of some 690,000 *shi* (unhusked) was needed every year to restock the province's main antifamine granaries. However good the 1759 and 1760 harvests, would there still be enough grain (allowing for the deduction of seed corn) to supply Henan's own population, at affordable prices, until 1761? Hu himself appears not to have worried, but he had ordered vigilance against any disruption of exports, presumably by local groups who might have been concerned about the incessant drain of cereals.[9] In other words, whether at any given time the pull of market forces threatened the food security of an exporting province was a matter of opinion. But this was not the only latent issue. Given that merchants were notorious for "scheming only for profit," could one be sure that all the grain was duly flowing towards markets, as opposed to being placed in hoards for speculative gain? Granted the paternalist credo that peasants were short-sighted, could one be confident that they had not been tempted into selling too much grain, thus jeopardizing their own subsistence during the lean months immediately before the following year's harvest? Given the combined risks of merchant selfishness, peasant improvidence, and climatic inconstancy, could one be certain that the current antifamine

---

8. Braudel, *Structures*, p. 127. An estimate of 3.0 hectoliters for per capita annual grain consumption in eighteenth-century north China may strike specialists as high. However, equivalent to about 2.9 *shi*, this figure is not quite midway between the "national average" of 2.5 *shi* proposed for eighteenth-century China by Wang Yeh-chien ("Food Supply," p. 88), and the indigenous official assumption of 3.65 (0.01 *shi* per day).

9. Hu Baoquan, mem. of QL 25/5/10, transc. Ye, comp., "Qianlong chao miliang maimai shiliao," part 2, pp. 32–33. For the figures cited in this paragraph, see QCWXTK, vol. 1, *juan* 4, p. 4,888; Will, *Bureaucracy and Famine*, table 13 (p. 193); and table 2 in chap. 4 below.

storage target for Henan (some 2.3 million *shi* for the main network of state-run granaries) would be sufficient? Conversely, if one increased storage levels in the antifamine granaries, what would be the effect on market prices in Henan and, indeed, on that province's ability to export grain to needy neighbors?

Hu did not raise these other issues in his report to the emperor. However, they were taken very seriously in mid-eighteenth-century China. While one recent estimate suggests that, nationwide, mid-Qing China should have enjoyed a huge grain surplus, official policies were premised on the assumption that shortage was never distant.[10] Not only had concern about the risk of famine been a hallmark of Confucian statecraft through the ages, but population was rising and grain prices with it. As Pierre-Étienne Will sums up the cumulative impression given by countless official documents, "Generally speaking, supply was never able to meet demand or, more precisely, the stimulation of demand on supply always threatened to stretch supply beyond its capacity."[11] Although the vast volume of the annual trade in staple foodstuffs—a relatively modest estimate is 30 million *shi* for the long-distance trade alone[12]—reflected large regional surpluses, there was frequent anxiety lest the lure of prices elsewhere transform surplus into deficit. These fears were sometimes well-founded.[13] So, sometimes, were fears that substantial stocks (tens of thousands of *shi*, or even more) were being hoarded. Such concerns, of course, were not unique

---

10. Guo Songyi ("Qingdai liangshi shichang," p. 47) estimates China's total cereal output in 1753 as approaching 138 million metric tons of unhusked grain (I have converted his "market *jin*" to kilograms). While conversion ratios between weights and volumes of unknown mixtures of grain types inevitably involve guesswork, this may have been equivalent to some 2,000–2,500 million *shi* unhusked, which may have yielded about 1,300–1,625 million *shi* husked. If we take Wang Yeh-chien's population estimate for 1750 (200–250 million people) and his estimated "national average" grain consumption for the eighteenth century (2.5 *shi*, presumably husked), the total annual husked grain requirement would have been 500–625 million *shi* only. See Wang, *Land Taxation*, p. 7, and n. 8 above.

11. Will, *Bureaucracy and Famine*, p. 209.

12. Xu and Wu, *Zhongguo ziben zhuyi*, vol. 1, p. 277. Cf. Wang Yeh-chien's estimate ("Secular Trends of Rice Prices," p. 38) of 12 to 17 million *shi* (I deduct 3 million *shi* of tribute grain) for the "annual volume" of the late eighteenth-century long-distance Yangzi River rice trade.

13. For examples, see Will, *Bureaucracy and Famine*, pp. 210–11.

to China in the preindustrial world. What made the Chinese case distinctive was, first, the sheer scale of the perceived problems, and, second, the specific way in which the state entered the grain market.

The late imperial Chinese state's attempts at direct regulation of the grain trade seem much less systematic than the French "police of grain" could sometimes be, despite the examples with which this chapter started. It was in buying and storing grain that Chinese practice was systematic while French efforts, in the mid-eighteenth century, were tentative and experimental.[14] The Qing state's main approach to popular subsistence policy was to control vast stocks itself, not so much through the tax system—uncommuted land tax and grain tribute quotas in the mid-eighteenth century totalled only 8.4 million *shi* per year[15]— as in the network of antifamine granaries. Known as "ever-normal" (that is, price-stabilizing) granaries, these granaries were expected, as of 1750, to hold a nationwide total of almost 33.8 million *shi* of unhusked grain when full, implying (according to somewhat notional guidelines) that a minimum of about 10 million *shi* should be bought annually for restocking.[16] In 1735, the nationwide storage target had been some 28 million *shi*; in 1740, some 58 million; and in 1745, some 48 million. This great instability suggests major shifts in central-government thinking about how much antifamine insurance the predominantly peasant population needed, and whether there was any such thing as over-insurance. The government's approach to private-sector stockpiling was also actively reviewed in the late 1740s. These episodes of heightened attention to the problems of subsistence policy took place under the young Qianlong emperor (reigned 1735–96), a Manchu known for his attempts to project an image of Confucian sagehood to his Chinese subjects.

What did it mean to run (or strive to be perceived as running) a large, commercialized agrarian polity according to the best Confucian

---

14. On the French "police of grain," see Kaplan, *Bread*, chaps. 1 and 2; on *ancien régime* attempts to build precautionary grain reserves, see Miller, *Mastering the Market*, pp. 53–56.

15. QCWXTK, vol. 1, *juan* 4, p. 4,888.

16. The best short introduction to the Qing ever-normal system is Will, *Bureaucracy and Famine*, pp. 182–99. Other important studies include Will and Wong, *Nourish the People*; Hoshi, *Chūgoku shakai fukushi seisaku*; and Yamamoto, "Shindai zenki no heichō seisaku."

principles? Confucianism was a doctrine that, while offering reluctant justification for wars that took the form of punitive or liberative expeditions, bade rulers place supreme importance on the well-being of their subjects. The population's moral well-being was the prime desideratum, but material security was seen as a prerequisite for goodness among the childlike masses. The ideals were high. According to one Confucian scripture, a sage in government would cause basic foodstuffs to be as readily available as fire and water—and what the scriptures said still mattered in Qing China.[17] In the eighteenth century, it was all too obvious that the stability of popular existence was not to be taken for granted. To quote Will again, tackling the related challenges of growing population pressure, migration, inflation, unrest, and litigiousness "required intervention, initiative, discipline, and above all an enormous amount of commitment."[18] Whatever the mixture of motives behind the edicts in which, as Will points out, the high Qing emperors "constantly hammer[ed] out" these values, the edicts were, implicitly, reiterating the standards by which the alien rulers' own performance as Confucian monarchs should be judged.[19]

This book is intended as a contribution to both intellectual and political history. It is partly a study of how Confucian-trained officials thought about the grain trade and the state's role in it. Disagreement was possible, even among the committed, about the wisdom of certain forms of intervention and as to how much intervention was desirable. There was, in mid-eighteenth-century China, a parallel of sorts to the "grain-centered liberalism" (Steven Kaplan's term) that inspired radical experiments in 1760s France.[20] Exploring the context and dimensions of the Sino-Manchu version of "grain liberalism" is one project undertaken in this book. However, although, as I show, the articulation of economically liberal arguments slightly preceded (and then overlapped with) the moderation or revocation of certain interventionist approaches, this does not necessarily entail that these changes were motivated chiefly by a conscious will to liberalize. As Pamela Crossley, Mark Elliott and others have compellingly reminded us, the

---

17. *Mengzi*, 7A/23.
18. Will, "The 1744 Annual Audits," p. 3.
19. See ibid. for the quotation.
20. Kaplan, *Bread*, pp. 97, 685–88; chaps. 3–11.

Manchu sovereigns were not simply converted aliens playing ideal Confucian rulers. The young Qianlong had inherited a multiethnic empire and the strategic need to be a Manchu among Manchus, defender of the minority rule of an occupying elite. He would himself soon prove to be a militarist empire-builder. With hindsight, one could hardly have relied on him to base every domestic policy decision on impartial consideration of what was best for the Chinese masses. He was not a Confucian for all seasons.[21]

This book tells an ordinary story about an extraordinary governmental system. Its message is complex, as is the story. Part I focuses on state action against hoarders. The first two chapters illustrate the range of techniques marshalled against hoarders on the assumption that grain speculation harmed the public interest. These techniques included cut-price sales of the kind that gave the ever-normal granaries their name; however, the topic of "[price-]stabilizing sales" is represented here by a case study of the "banner grain bureaus," grain-trading offices founded by Qianlong's predecessor and used to keep grain prices stable in Beijing. Chapter 3 surveys critiques of various interventionist practices before analyzing the defences of the speculator that were provoked by moves in 1745–48 to reassert the illegality of hoarding. Part I ends with an interim attempt to determine the scope and limits of belief in market forces among those who adumbrated theoretical justifications for their opposition to specific forms of intervention. This section offers a more systematic treatment of themes raised in other recent work on market consciousness in the Qing bureaucracy.[22] It establishes that rationales, expressed in terms of rudimentary economic theory, for major state withdrawals from involvement with the grain trade were available by 1750.

Part II explores challenges, from within the ruling apparatus, to the state's claim that its own stockpiling served the public interest. It provides a detailed account of a debate, which lasted from 1738 to 1753, about the question: how much grain should be withheld from the market in the ever-normal granaries? Based largely on archival sources,

---

21. Cf. Elliott, *Manchu Way*, introduction and passim; Crossley, *Translucent Mirror*, esp. part 3.

22. E.g., Will, "Discussions about the Market-Place"; Dunstan, *Conflicting Counsels*, chap. 7; Rowe, "State and Market" and *Saving the World*, chaps. 5 and 6.

this reconstruction more fully reveals the debate's complexity than, to my knowledge, any of the existing treatments.[23] Chapter 4 explains the issues as mid-eighteenth-century officialdom perceived them. Chapter 5 explores reactions to the Qianlong emperor's decision of 1738–39 to try to meet dramatically raised storage targets by selling titular state studentships for contributions to the granary reserves. Chapter 6 unravels the strange twists of policy surrounding a second resetting of the targets in 1743–44; and chapters 7 and 8 examine the discussions that preceded the decision, finalized in early 1749, to revert, in principle, to the low-level targets in force before 1738. It is shown that, between 1738 and 1749, many officials submitted arguments of principle against excessive government stockpiling. Beginning in chapter 6, however, grounds emerge for sensing motivations of another order behind two decisions to suspend (1745) or cut (1748–49) state buying for the granaries. I argue that the need to fund successive military campaigns was part of the background to both decisions and cannot be ignored in attempts to explain them. In particular, I suggest, the well-known target cut of 1748–49 was justified by economic arguments but motivated partially by fiscal needs. Herein lies the story's ordinariness.

As a study of Confucian government in action, this book describes a mode of public policy discussion that was far less dominated by the Confucian scriptures than some authors lead one to expect.[24] As a study of Confucian governance under Manchu imperial domination, the book illustrates, perhaps, a turning-point in the Qianlong emperor's political investments. In 1738, he tried to play the Chinese-style sage; by 1748, he had embarked on that pursuit of military glory for which he hoped posterity would honor him. As is well known, some important Chinese-style public welfare institutions such as the ever-normal granaries endured throughout his reign, and yet, from the vantage-point of the mid-eighteenth century, one sees a relative decline in his commitment to "nurturing the people." I substantiate the notion of relative shifts from state welfare activism to something between *laissez-faire* and *laissez-aller* in chapter 9, which uses case studies to set the cutback in the storage targets in a broader context. In the early stages of his career as a militarist, the Qianlong emperor abolished the

---

23. Listed in nn. 1 and 2 of chap. 4 below.
24. Cf., for example, Elman, *Classicism*, pp. 74–75.

banner grain bureaus and state support for able-bodied fugitives from famine, while hardening his heart—not to mention the law—against food rioters.

Whether one approves of such transitions depends on one's politics, but a theme of part II as a whole is the young Qianlong's undistinguished performance as leader of the government. We can observe with respect and sympathy the struggles of mid-eighteenth-century Chinese and Manchu bureaucrats to grapple with key economic issues of their day. Their opinions varied, but many of them made highly creditable efforts to apply their inadequately processed information and limited theoretical understanding to the problems of subsistence policy. The emperor, however, will be shown repeatedly as a rash decision-maker who was both easily led and more autocratic than some recent scholarship has argued.[25] He was capable of silly blunders that the best endeavors of his talented assistants could not always turn into magnificent, successful gambles. Whether he grew out of his early weaknesses or whether they matured into the failings of his later years awaits research, but his role in the ever-normal granaries debate does not inspire confidence. At least from a Confucian standpoint, the Qianlong emperor was perhaps, all along, unworthy of his capable officials.

I will conclude by clarifying what the reader can and cannot expect from this book. It is not intended as a work of economic history, although it presents occasional information and suggestions that should interest economic historians. Nor is it intended as an institutional study of the ever-normal system, although future scholars of that system would, I think, be unwise to ignore it. Although the research was partially inspired by Kaplan's work on French "grain liberalism," I postpone systematic comparison between the French and Chinese cases. This is partly because the parallel is after all a limited one, as illustrated by the fact that mid-Qing "liberalism" focused on consumer interests and viewed grain price inflation as an evil, whereas the French version emphasized the utility of higher prices as an incentive to production.[26] More important, however, is a question of priorities. Much that took place during 1738–53 is easily misread without close

---

25. Cf. Bartlett, *Monarchs and Ministers*, pp. 269–78.
26. Kaplan, *Bread*, pp. 102–4. I return to this point in chap. 3.

attention to nuance and detail. A fully-fledged comparison between Chinese and French political economy is premature until the documentary record on the Chinese side has been examined carefully. I undertake such an examination here.

As a contribution to intellectual history, this book embodies the assumption that, if we want to know how Qing officials thought, we must be prepared to spend time with them (or perhaps, in some cases, with their ghostwriters; whose thought precisely we are reading may be an unsolvable problem). While memorials, like all other texts, have obvious limitations as guides to their authors' beliefs, they at least show what could be conceived and argued by persons of the time and place in which they were written. We shall often slow down to capture the precise points made by (or in the name of) individual officials. However, it would be naive to understand the early Qianlong shifts in popular subsistence policy simply as reflections of a battle of opinions. Rather, the story is one of conflicting ambitions, interests, and ideas involving various sectors of the government establishment as well as, very possibly, a grain trade lobby. It must therefore be approached, in part, as a case-study in Qing politics. The reader is offered a close-up view of members of an ostensibly Confucian government pursuing divergent agendas around the question "state or merchant?" If the narrator's tone occasionally seems negative, as if to cast doubt on the merits of the Qing ("the greatest dynasty in Chinese history," according to enthusiasts), the goal is only to be realistic.[27] The story, I repeat, is ordinary.

---

27. The quotation is from Rawski, *Last Emperors*, p. 299.

PART I

Private-Sector Stockpiling:
State Versus Hoarder

I

Legal Ambiguity, Coercive Practice

During the Qing dynasty, it was generally accepted that redistributing grain surpluses was primarily the task of merchants. And yet it was the common knowledge of the age that merchants, if not all literally "wicked" (*jian*), were at best suspect. It is the common sense of our age too that traders must be watched—at least by the consumer—for signs of profiteering. University instructors who accuse their campus bookstores of burdening the students with outrageous textbook prices can readily identify with premodern officials to whom the issue was, potentially, one of life or death. Could the poor survive the greed of grain merchants?

It should not be surprising that Confucian-trained officials conventionally perceived the subsistence of the urban poor and other market-dependent groups as threatened by the profit-mindedness of merchants. For most people who did not grow the grain that they consumed, fluctuations in the marketed grain surplus meant perpetual food insecurity. For grain wholesalers, brokers, and retailers, these fluctuations spelled financial opportunity. Consumers needed low prices; it was the merchants who often charged high ones, whether or not these represented profiteering and deliberate manipulation of the market. In China as in *ancien régime* France, the servants of an ostensibly caring monarchy saw the distribution of the prime necessity of life controlled by people who could not be credited with normal consciences.[1] In paternalist eyes, it would have been an abnegation of responsibility to leave vulnerable consumers at the mercy of monopolists or specu-

---

1. On the stigmatization of grain merchants in *ancien régime* France, see Kaplan, *Bread*, pp. 53–56.

lators. Even if the hoarders were not merchants but landowners, diligent officials still felt duty-bound to take some action.

In Qing China, the approach to checking profiteering that consumed the most administrative effort was the system of state buying and selling most commonly implemented through the ever-normal granaries (*changping cang*, literally "granaries [for maintaining] constant price stability"). As mentioned in the introduction, the objectives of the Qing ever-normal system were broader than controlling merchant speculation. The granaries also served as antifamine stockpiles, and, for many Qing officials, this was probably their most important function. However, even if the main point of the annual cut-price sales of ever-normal grain was stock rotation, it remains true that these sales, made in the lean preharvest season, were also intended to force private-sector retailers to lower their prices so as to compete. Operations of the ever-normal type will be discussed in the next chapter, as well as in part II. The purpose of this chapter is to examine other, generally more direct approaches used by Qing officials to counteract perceived abuses by controllers of commercial grain supplies. Direct, as we shall see, could mean coercive.

The chapter begins with an examination of the status of speculative hoarding and other grain-trade "abuses" in Qing law. This is followed by discussion of three early and "high" Qing approaches to dealing with mercantile hoarders: control through information, forced sales of stocks identified as hoards, and deterrent punishment. To ascertain how far any of these approaches was typical is beyond the scope of this enquiry. The main purpose of this chapter and the next, which covers noncoercive methods, is to establish that, in spite of reservations, the belief that speculative hoarding called for action of some kind was strong in the Sino-Manchu bureaucracy in both halves of the eighteenth century. By showing this, I provide necessary context for the exploration, in chapter 3, of dissenting views about the desirability of measures against hoarding. In addition, these first two chapters propose tentative explanations for the wide variety of antihoarding practices depicted in their pages. The poorly defined status of speculative hoarding as an offense under Qing law left the way open for diversity of practice. Prudential considerations, having to do with respect for the vital role of commerce or for the social functions of the rural rich, determined that hoarders would not always be prosecuted with the maximum rigor permitted by the unclear law.

As the present chapter focuses on government control of merchant hoarding, there will be occasional opportunities to illustrate the amount and kind of information that conscientious authorities might possess about the grain trade as it operated in their jurisdictions. One would expect a reciprocal relationship between information gathering and processing on one hand and the content of public policy on the other. A state that, as shown in the introduction, had equipped itself with the capacity to monitor the volume of commercial grain in transit presumably took a close interest in the grain trade, even if the monitoring was not consistent or ubiquitous. The nature of the policies that government authorities pursued presumably conditioned the types of information that they sought to gather and the ways in which they used it. However, the accumulation and interpretation of information had potentially destabilizing effects on public policy. Men of the intellectual caliber of leading Qing civil servants might not be content with the mere filing of data gathered for the purpose of controlling trade, but might reflect upon the implications of those data. The destabilization of old certainties by mid-Qing market consciousness will be a theme of later chapters of this book, where I address the ways in which an emergent theoretical understanding of how the market worked combined with other factors to moderate the interventionism of the early Qianlong reign. In this chapter, however, I treat the topic of the Qing state's information in the context of its efforts at control.

What the Law Had to Say

In a broad sense, from the earliest years of the dynasty, Qing central-government policy favored free circulation of grain surpluses. As in *ancien régime* France, however, preference for free circulation was far from being the same thing as espousal of a *laissez-faire* approach to grain-trade policy. Circulation should be free, in the Qing governmental view, in the sense that no self-interested parties should be permitted to impede it, whether by hoarding grain for personal enrichment or by imposing trade embargoes to reserve supplies for the communities that had produced them. Because there was good reason to believe that many people were susceptible to one or the other of these two temptations, it made sense to assume that government must stand ready to prevent improper violation of free-circulation principles. Although, in China as in France, actual practice often showed a preference for moderate approaches, the upholding of free circulation could logically be seen as necessitating recourse to restraints and prohibitions.[2]

Policy, of course, is not the same as law. Identifying law is less easy in the case of late imperial China than in contemporary democracies in which laws are by definition passed by legislative assemblies. Thomas Metzger argues that discussion of Qing law should be confined neither to the penal code, with its largely inherited framework of penal statutes (*lü*) and more recent supplementary articles (*li*), nor to the collection of fundamental laws and institutions (*dian*) seen as providing permanent guidelines for the conduct of government. Included also should be imperial pronouncements having "the explicit character of law in that they were phrased as a rule, not just as a command on a particular occasion," and similar generally-applicable decrees promulgated by officials "on their own authority." Metzger further suggests that any imperial command, even one originally applying to a specific situation, could be used in subsequent law-making if adduced as precedent or analogy by officials seeking a new ruling. Much Qing law thus originated in "executive commands." Actions rendered criminal by such commands could be punished under the Statute on Violating Imperial Pronouncements (*zhishu you wei lü*) or the Statute on Violating Imperial Orders (*wei ling lü*) if no other basis for sentencing was specified.[3]

Broad though the scope of these two statutes was, it was a serious matter to fall foul of the first of them, for the penalty that it prescribed, while mild by Qing standards, was far from trivial. While violation of an imperial "order" was nominally punishable by 50 strokes of the light

---

2. Cf. Miller, *Mastering the Market*, pp. 10, 50–51. For discussion of the compatibility, in the minds of pro-regulation French officials, of "liberty" (as the best foundation for commerce) with regulation (as the only adequate means of defending the public from merchants' immoral proclivities), see Kaplan, *Bread*, pp. 62–63, 99–101. Further on the paradox that commitment to free circulation could result in policies that were the opposite of *laissez-faire*, see Dunstan, *Conflicting Counsels*, pp. 257–58. It is odd that Rowe (*Saving the World*, pp. 214 and 506 n. 149) ignores this crucial exposition in accusing myself and unidentified others of "suggest[ing]" that "the [which?] mid-Qing credo was . . . that of *laissez-faire* liberalism."

3. Metzger, *Internal Organization*, pp. 167–68. For Metzger's discussion of the penal code, see ibid., pp. 84–88, 207–9, 423–30. For explanation of the difference, in theory, between the two statutes on violating imperial commands, see ibid. p. 176 n. 9 and pp. 431–32.

bamboo, violation of an imperial "pronouncement" made the culprit liable to 100 strokes of the heavy bamboo. Because of the exceptional girth of Qing instruments of correction, nominal corporal punishments were converted into actual beatings according to a sliding scale. A nominal punishment of 100 strokes of the heavy bamboo meant, in practice, 40 blows with a bamboo rod some 6.4 centimeters (2 Chinese inches) in diameter at its wider end, and weighing "not more than" some 1.19 kilograms (2 Chinese pounds, or "catties").[4]

Already before the Manchu conquest of China proper (1644), a series of at least three decrees in the name of the Manchu ruler Hong Taiji (1626–43) forbade speculative hoarding. These decrees were presumably addressed, in large part, to the conquered Chinese population of Liaodong (southern Manchuria). Initiated, written, or translated by Chinese collaborators, they may have reflected Chinese economic assumptions and Ming bureaucratic practice, perhaps made more commandist by the circumstances of Manchu military occupation and a mounting economic crisis caused largely by warfare-related overcrowding.[5] The first decree was issued in 1636, the year in which Hong Taiji adopted the dynastic name of Qing and a time of acute subsistence difficulties in Liaodong.[6] It expressed indignation at those who "insist[ed] on waiting until the market price ha[d] soared" before they sold their grain. This violated the principle that "grain is the wherewithal for sustenance, and grain sales are the means of circulation." Not only were the "grain-possessing households" ordered to determine the amount that they themselves would need and "go forthwith to the market and sell" any surplus; the decree also specified a quota of grain that each group of eight grain-holding households must release for sale immediately. A further directive ordering that hoards be put on sale was issued the next year. In 1641, according to a late eighteenth-century official compila-

---

4. DQHDSL, vol. 18, *juan* 723:2a (p. 14,429); vol. 19, *juan* 749:20a (p. 14,698); vol. 20, *juan* 829:12b (p. 15,456). For the corporal punishment conversion system, see Bodde and Morris, *Law in Imperial China*, pp. 77, 80–81. As Bodde and Morris suggest (p. 178), the Statute on Violating Imperial Pronouncements was used for a much wider variety of offenses than one might expect from a literal reading of its text and the appended commentary.

5. On the Manchus' problems and policies in occupied Liaodong, see Roth, "Manchu-Chinese Relationship," pp. 22–31; Perdue, *China Marches West*, pp. 118–21.

6. Roth, "Manchu-Chinese Relationship," p. 27.

tion, Hong Taiji's approval of a memorial whose chief signatory was the Chinese defector Zu Kefa became the basis for a *li* outlawing hoarding.[7]

What can have been the long-term status of a *li* (a word that could mean "precedent" or "regulation" as well as "supplementary article") promulgated half a decade before the first edition of the Qing penal code, which was finalized in 1646, and half a century before the first edition of the Qing *Collected Statutes*, published in 1690?[8] No trace of legislation against speculative hoarding can be found in the most clearly relevant sections of the 1646 code, which are silent on the matter.[9] In 1709, during an episode discussed below, the Kangxi emperor (reigned 1661–1722) wrote in a way that may imply that no established rule (*li*) against speculative hoarding existed at that time.[10] I have been unable to find any eighteenth-century material that unambiguously specifies a punishment for hoarding in later editions of the penal code. The lack of explicit provision for the sentencing of hoarders would explain why one Henan governor wrote in 1748 that he had ordered persistent hoarders threatened with the punishment for "violating prohibitions."[11] Only one clause, incorporated into a rewritten supplementary article as late as 1806, forbids the speculative hoarding of grain by shopkeepers (an offence made punishable under the Statute on Violating Imperial Pronouncements). This article is found under the

---

7. QCWXTK, vol. 1, *juan* 34, p. 5,169.

8. Metzger, *Internal Organization*, p. 423.

9. See, in the reprint of the 1646 *Da Qing lü* (Penal statutes of the great Qing dynasty) in *Gujin tushu jicheng*, "Jingji huibian" / "Xiangxing dian" / "Lüling bu," the categories (1) Revenue (*hu*, *juan* 44–45), esp. the subcategory on market (*shichan*) offences, and (2) Justice (*xing*, *juan* 47–49), esp. the subcategory on miscellaneous offences.

10. QSL/KX, *juan* 238:12a.

11. CC, Shise, QL 13/1/23; and, e.g., Shen Zhiqi, comp., *Da Qing lü jizhu* (1715; 1746 revised edition by Hong Gaoshan), vol. 1, "Da Qing lü xuzuan tiaoli," vol. 2, *juan* 10, and vol. 3, *juan* 26; Yao Yuxiang and Hu Yangshan, comps., *Da Qing lüli xing'an* (1873), vol. 2, *juan* 13 and 14, and vol. 4, *juan* 32. Hoarding is not mentioned in Jing Junjian's brief survey of Qing commercial law, where discussion is confined to the provisions of the penal code. Jing, "Legislation," pp. 59–66; cf. Qiu, "You shichan lüli," pp. 327–31. An 1841 article prescribes punishments for a specific abuse that arguably fell within the category of hoarding, but the applicability of this article was very narrow. DQHDSL, vol. 19, *juan* 765:6a–7b (pp. 14,853–54).

archaically-named Statute on Valuing of Goods by Market Superintendents (*shisi ping wujia lü*); it dealt with the abuse by which traders, including would-be speculators, allegedly bought up large portions of the cut-price grain that the authorities would sell at times of high grain prices.[12] The clause, presumably intended to strengthen the legislation against this abuse, provided that shops might not store more than 160 *shi* of each kind of grain in which they dealt.

Similar ceilings had been set in Beijing before (50 *shi* in 1737, 50 *shi* in principle in 1787) but were apparently not codified. The limit prescribed by the 1806 clause had first been set in 1800, when it was fixed at 80 *shi*, but it was raised to 160 *shi* in 1801, partly as a concession to the moral frailty of shopkeepers, and partly as a prudential gesture during a subsistence crisis caused by flood. A rider to the 1806 clause explains that the measure was directed solely against speculation: where the purpose was not speculation but "circulation and sale" (*liutong tiaomai*), the ceiling did not apply.[13] The clause, like the whole article, was meant specifically for Beijing; it may have been invoked as a precedent by regional administrators who wished to impose analogous restrictions in the towns and cities under their authority. It is, however, equally possible that regional or local administrators already had rules of their own, such as the regulation cited by Robert Marks that limited each rice shop in the town of Foshan (Guangdong) to storing 100 *shi* at

---

12. Cf. Will, *Bureaucracy and Famine*, pp. 185–86. The Statute on Valuing of Goods by Market Superintendents deals with the activities of brokers. Bodde and Morris, however, claim that a system of "market supervisors" (*shisi*) still existed in Qing times, and that these "supervisors" were leading merchants whose functions included licensing the other merchants who plied the same trade in a particular city. See their *Law in Imperial China*, pp. 265–66.

13. DQHDSL, vol. 19, *juan* 765:4a–b (p. 14,852), vol. 22, *juan* 1,038:21b, 22b–23a (pp. 17,462–63); Yao Yuxiang and Hu Yangshan, *Da Qing lüli xing'an*, vol. 2, *juan* 14, pp. 1,364–65; QSL/QL, *juan* 56:9a–b; L. M. Li and A. Dray-Novey, "Guarding Beijing's Food Security," p. 1,020. There is nothing corresponding to the 1806 clause in the simpler version of the article that is included in the nineteenth-century Japanese copy-cum-translation of Shen Xiangnan's 1793 private edition of the Qing code, the *Da Qing lüli huizuan* (Ritsurei kenkyūkai, ed., *Shin ritsurei isan*, vol. 2, *juan* 11, p. 420). Cf. Shen Zhiqi, *Da Qing lü jizhu* (1746 revised ed.), vol. 2, *juan* 10, pp. 591–92, which also includes nothing resembling the 1806 clause.

a time (200 *shi* after 1790), on pain of being charged with hoarding.[14] But these were local ordinances, not national codified law.

It is conceivable that in the eighteenth century, an obscure passage, inherited from the Ming code, in the first clause of the Statute on the Coinage (*qianfa lü*) was interpreted by astute magistrates as providing a basis for sentencing speculative grain-hoarders. The clause as a whole is concerned with maintaining the smooth circulation of the legal coinage at officially determined exchange values. The passage in question shifts the focus by requiring that in private transactions, the prices (expressed in coin) of commodities such as precious metals, grain, and textiles should accord with the current (that is, market) rates. There then appear the words *ting cong min bian* (literally, "it is permitted to follow the convenience of the people"). The authors of the Qing official commentary copied their Ming predecessors in adding the word *shi-yong* ("to use"), so that the whole sentence was made to mean "Let [it or them] be used according to the people's convenience." In both codes, Ming and Qing, the main text of the statute continues: "If [it or they] is [are] obstructed and not promptly used (*xingshi*), [the offender] shall be beaten with sixty strokes of the heavy bamboo." The Ming and Qing commentators each dealt in their own way with the ambiguity of this wording, the former inserting additional small characters to the effect that the punishable behavior that might lead to such "obstruction" was disregard of the official exchange values for coin of different denominations, resulting in distorted commodity prices.[15] Perhaps being no more able than the present author to grasp the logic of the Ming interpretation, the influential early-eighteenth-century private commentator Shen Zhiqi turned it upside down. His main commentary represented the word "obstruct" (*zuzhi*) as referring to the coinage system and suggested, still somewhat ambiguously, that the offence lay in arbitrarily raising or lowering commodity prices, thereby causing the coinage to be "obstructed."

Would the logic of this reading be clear to all users of Shen's commentary? Sensing that more explanation was desirable, he used the supplementary annotation space above the text of the statute to point out that "a wicked man does not dare to raise or lower the value of coin

---

14. Marks, *Tigers*, p. 245.
15. Yao Siren, *Da Ming lü fu li zhujie* (1585 or later), *juan* 7, p. 378.

[directly], but . . . exorbitantly raising the price of goods is [tantamount to] lowering the value of coin, while underpricing goods is [tantamount to] raising it. It is this that leads to the obstruction [of the coinage system]." In other words, alterations of the market value of coin wrought by arbitrary commodity pricing would jeopardize the smooth circulation of the Qing official currency.[16] Shen's commentary was widely reproduced in later editions, one of which rewrote his primary explanation in such a way as to make a little clearer that it was the inappropriate pricing of goods that was the crime.[17] Since successful speculative hoarding would lead naturally to the charging of artificially elevated prices, it should theoretically have been possible (especially in a legal system with underdeveloped rules of evidence) to sentence hoarders under the Statute on the Coinage. Far-fetched as such reasoning must seem, we should note that Shen Zhiqi mentioned in the preface to his commentary that he had abundant experience of poring over judicial documents at the county and regional levels of government. His clarification may have shown local administrators a way of coping with the lack of explicit statutory provision for the punishment of hoarders.[18] It is also possible, however, that this passage was a legal embarrassment, seldom or never invoked in practice.

The above-mentioned abuse by traders of government-sold grain frustrated the intention of official cut-price sales; perhaps for that rea-

---

16. Shen Zhiqi, *Da Qing lü jizhu*, 1998 punctuated ed., vol. 1, p. 295; cf. 1746 revised ed., vol. 2, *juan* 7, pp. 433–34.

17. Ritsurei kenkyūkai, ed., *Shin ritsurei isan*, vol. 2, *juan* 8, p. 216. By contrast, the 1873 edition by Yao Yuxiang and Hu Yangshan reproduces Shen's original commentary. Yao and Hu, *Da Qing lüli xing'an*, vol. 2, *juan* 10, p. 1,102.

18. Shen Zhiqi, *Da Qing lü jizhu*, 1998 punctuated ed., vol. 1, p. 8. In both the Kumamoto copy of the 1793 edition and the 1873 edition (but not the 1746 edition of Shen's *Da Qing lü jizhu*), the top margin of each page is ruled off to create space for cross-references. Each of these two later editions supplies a cross-reference to the Statute on the Coinage either on the page containing the Statute on Valuing of Goods by Market Superintendents, or on the following page with the supplementary article about private traders dealing in official cut-price grain. The cross-reference consists of an abbreviated version of the sentence specifying that commodity prices should accord with current rates, followed by *ting cong min bian*. Presumably, the compiler was telling readers where to look for information on how to sentence price-manipulators. Ritsurei kenkyūkai, ed., *Shin ritsurei isan*, vol. 2, *juan* 11, p. 419; Yao Yuxiang and Hu Yangshan, *Da Qing lüli xing'an*, vol. 2, *juan* 14, p. 1,364.

son, it seems to have attracted more legislative attention than did the hoarding of grain that had never entered official hands. This may be seen if we turn to law in a broader sense, as the cumulative record of authoritative pronouncements (including imperial approvals of proposals from senior officials) that established general rules or might be relevant as precedents.[19] The earliest (1763) edition of the massive appendix to the *Collected Statutes* presenting such accretions to the basic laws (that is, the *Qinding Da Qing huidian shili* or, in this case, *zeli*) does contain a section called "Prohibition of Hoarding and Yeast-making." This includes a record of measures taken in 1716 to monitor shipments of Beijing-bound commercial wheat in an attempt to prevent hoarding. These measures, discussed below, included an explicit prohibition against hoarding; they were followed, in 1721, by an edict clarifying which authorities were responsible for forbidding the hoarding of rice or other types of husked grain in Beijing.[20] However, in the corresponding section in the final (1899) edition, there is only one eighteenth-century expression of imperial disapproval of hoarding in general that is later than the 1721 edict (which itself may have been inspired by abuse of official grain). This is an edict of 1760 invoking merchant speculation as the likely cause of rising grain prices in Beijing. The prohibition with which it concludes was probably directed primarily against speculative buying of stipendiary grain (the grain component of metropolitan official salaries) that the government had issued early as an emergency means of boosting the supply of food available on Beijing's markets. Thus it was like the prohibitions listed immediately below in addressing the problem of commercial exploitation of the state's well-meaning efforts to help poor consumers.[21]

The 1899 edition of the *Qinding Da Qing huidian shili* records pronouncements seeking to prevent the passage of large quantities of official cut-price grain into the hands of merchants for the following years: 1693, 1726, 1737, 1750, 1761, and, probably, 1796. There was one further

---

19. For the legislative status of imperial approvals of proposals ("appellate cases," to use Metzger's terminology), see Metzger, *Internal Organization*, pp. 176–77.

20. DQHDZL, *juan* 40:27b–28b. On efforts in the first few years of Qianlong's reign to ban yeast preparation as an indirect way of suppressing grain-based liquors, see Dunstan, *Conflicting Counsels*, pp. 208, 211–15, 217–19 and 234–40.

21. DQHDSL, vol. 9, *juan* 191:29a–b (p. 7,621); an abridged version appears also at ibid., vol. 22, *juan* 1,038:20b–21a (pp. 17,461–62).

prohibition, dated 1769, of the hoarding of stipendiary grain that had been bought by shopkeepers. While most of the pronouncements referred to Beijing, its vicinity, or Zhili as a whole, the rules of 1726 and 1796 seem to have been intended for nationwide application.[22] It was in 1775 that the above-mentioned supplementary article against abuse of cut-price grain was added to the penal code. Referring specifically to Beijing, it provided severe penalties for trafficking even in small amounts of grain intended for the public welfare.[23] A late nineteenth-century edition of the code includes as commentary to this article (as amended in 1806) an item from the *Hubu zeli* (Regulations of the Board of Revenue) covering infringements in the provinces.[24]

By contrast, not only is the penal code unclear as to the illegality of ordinary speculative hoarding (hoarding of purely commercial grain supplies), but in the last authoritative register of law made by imperial commands (the 1899 *Qinding Da Qing huidian shili*) there is no new precedent or regulation that unambiguously deals with this kind of hoarding dated between 1716 and 1814. The 1814 entry is an edict ordering determined action against some merchants in Anhui who clung to their vast hoards of grain during a time of dearth. The Anhui governor was ordered to have the exact size of the hoards investigated and to have them sold forthwith at a fair price set by the authorities. Only if the merchants resisted or were caught concealing stocks were they to incur criminal punishment including confiscation of their grain. As we shall see, these measures drew on an established repertoire and were theoretically standard practice, but it was only the 1814 authorization that was codified as a precedent in the *Qinding Da Qing huidian shili*.[25]

---

22. Ibid., *juan* 191:25b–30b (pp. 7,619–21). The DQHDSL list is not exhaustive; cf. QSL/QL, *juan* 40:9a and 41:12a–b (further pronouncements of 1737), and *juan* 64:10b–11b (1738). The wording of the 1796 rule is vague (as quoted), but the most likely interpretation is that it refers to the same abuse as the other pronouncements. As explained below, the 1737 pronouncement recorded in DQHDSL was a relaxation of the existing rules; however, the concern to prevent large-scale trafficking in official cut-price grain remained unchanged.

23. E.g., Ritsurei kenkyūkai, ed., *Shin ritsurei isan*, vol. 2, *juan* 11, p. 420; DQHDSL, vol. 19, *juan* 765:4a (p. 14,852).

24. Yao Yuxiang and Hu Yangshan, *Da Qing lüli xing'an*, vol. 2, *juan* 14, p. 1,364.

25. DQHDSL, vol. 9, *juan* 191:30b–31a (pp. 7,621–22). While acknowledging the ambiguous (part-authoritative, part-historical) status of the great appendices to the Qing *Collected Statutes* (Metzger, *Internal Organization*, pp. 220–22), I assume that

One cannot infer too much about eighteenth-century legislative tendencies from the choices made by nineteenth-century compilers. It is easier to find evidence that post-Kangxi-period officials assumed that speculative hoarding was illegal than it is to identify the documentary basis for their assumptions. For example, a memorial of 1744 cites an unidentified *li* (presumably meaning precedent or regulation) by which "there is a strict prohibition against *tunhu* [speculative hoarders]."[26] The reference may have been to the 1716 prohibition, perhaps understood as the particular "executive command" that definitively outlawed speculative hoarding. More likely, however, is that any official who referred to the illegality of hoarding had in mind a series of such commands that he had read during his career and that, although not codified, served to renew and reinforce a ban whose original promulgation date was of no practical importance. And yet there clearly were some written regulations specifying definite procedures for dealing with detected hoarders. In 1764, for instance, the Gansu provincial administration commissioner cited a *li* providing that if "rich households" (apparently meaning merchants) accumulated stocks as vast as 100,000 *shi* in the post-harvest period and did not immediately sell them, the local authorities were to force them to sell, as well as subjecting their operations to surveillance. This rule surely had other origins than the ban of 1716, and it cannot be explained as a provincial regulation, applicable only in Gansu, because the commissioner seems to have believed that it applied throughout the realm.[27] Unless subsequently repealed, this *li* should have sufficed to justify the action taken in 1814. Indeed, we may probably assume that the principle that hoarders could, and in some circumstances should, be forced to sell goes back not only to the time of Hong Taiji, but also to previous dynasties.[28]

---

the compilation of the *Qinding Da Qing huidian zeli* and *shili* was a process of what Metzger calls "derivative law making" (ibid., p. 168) inasmuch as it involved the perpetuation, in authoritative print, of *selected* precedents and regulations only.

26. QSL/QL, *juan* 215:24a. Further examples include QCWXTK, vol. 1, *juan* 36, p. 5,189 (1738); CC, Gao Bin, QL 8/12/19, and Fang Guancheng, QL 11/12/8.

27. Wang Jian, QL 29/2/24, repr. GZD/QL, vol. 20, pp. 643–44; also transc. HQZY, *juan* 55:30a–32a. Cf. CC, Huang Tinggui, QL 13/4/24 for a 1748 denial that large-scale grain speculators operated in Gansu.

28. Cf., for the Song dynasty (960–1279), Oberst, "Chinese Economic Statecraft," pp. 202, 211–13.

In eighteenth-century China, then, limits on permitted stockpiling could be imposed on dealers at both ends of the grain market. Local shopkeepers no less than powerful commercial magnates might be given a ceiling, appropriate to their scale of operation, beyond which any further storage would render them liable to official intervention. Given the strength of official concerns about the dangers of unbridled private hoarding, it is reasonable to ask why, even so, ordinary speculative hoarding was not definitively criminalized via the penal code, while hardly any eighteenth-century orders against this putatively antisocial practice were codified as precedents applicable throughout the realm. It is easy to explain such legislative reticence as far as landlord hoarding is concerned. As discussed in chapter 2, firm legislation against landlord hoarding would have implied the criminalization of members of an elite social class with whom local officials normally sought good relations. It would have meant requiring officials to take action against strategies that were perhaps not dissimilar to those by which, back home, their own kinsmen advanced their fortunes. With merchant hoarding, such considerations of prudence and class sympathy were assuredly much weaker, as witness the coercive measures that I illustrate below. Nonetheless, the suggestions in the late 1740s (discussed in chapter 3) that private hoarding had its beneficial side cast doubt on the wisdom of clear-cut legal prohibitions of the practice. Such reservations can only have reinforced a broader unease about the practicalities of surveillance and the likely consequences of dealing harshly with those very merchants who, as one scholar-official put it, controlled the people's fates.[29] In short, the paucity of codified legislation against ordinary hoarding no doubt reflects the common wisdom of the territorial bureaucracy. It was often best not to insist upon the illegality of hoarding unless the imminence of widespread hunger aggravated popular resentment of the "wickedness" of hoarders to such a pitch that the state would have lost moral legitimacy by failing to act.[30]

---

29. Hui Shiqi (1671–1741) in HCJSWB, vol. 3, *juan* 41:3a, quoted in Will, *Bureaucracy and Famine*, p. 213 and chapter 3 below. For early eighteenth-century French pragmatic caution about strong-arm methods, see Miller, *Mastering the Market*, p. 51.

30. Such a pattern of toleration of "illegal" hoarding until hunger threatened is shown in the background to the 1814 Anhui precedent. The 1814 incident involved some "grain merchants by the name of Lü" who allegedly controlled twenty-eight

As I have shown elsewhere, Qing territorial administrators were not without resources when confronted with perceived antisocial practices of ambiguous legal status. Whether a particular instance of such a practice was treated as a violation of the law might depend on how local administrators chose to interpret it. Normally, the Qing state upheld the right of merchants to transport grain away from the communities where they had bought it, even if such "export" inflamed the anxieties of local people. However, if the merchants in question could be portrayed as wicked monopolists, involved in conspiracies to buy up stocks and hoard them for delayed export to other regions, all in callous disregard of local needs, then coercive measures to prevent them might be authorized.[31] It seems likely that Qing officials similarly took advantage of the theoretical distinction between, on one hand, holding stocks off the market until prices rose, and, on the other, deliberately trying to induce a price rise by withholding stocks. The former was mere opportunism, the latter antisocial market manipulation. In reality, the major difference between the two kinds of activity lay only in the awareness and intentions of the speculators, although some hoarders were in a better position to influence price movements than were others. Power over prices was not necessarily a function of the scale of individual hoards: the specter of a city's lowly retailers acting in concert to raise prices was enough to worry interventionist officials.[32] Whether fairly or not, commercial operators were more likely to be accused of deliberate market manipulation than were rural landowners; the former were therefore more likely to be the targets of confident prohibition backed by threat of punishment. At the same time, however, the option of regarding hoarders as guilty only of opportunism may have been convenient for officials who suspected that determined action against speculators might backfire.

I will end this section with a story illustrating how mid-eighteenth-century policy advisors might even be prepared, on the basis of their

---

granaries and some subsidiary stockpiles along a seventy-*li* stretch of river in the Luzhou region of Anhui. Here they had "annually accumulated more than a million bushels of unhusked grain, buying cheap but selling dear." Officialdom must have turned a blind eye for at least a few years; it was the 1814 dearth that brought the call for action. DQHDSL, vol. 9, *juan* 191:30b–31a (pp. 7,621–22).

31. Dunstan, *Conflicting Counsels*, pp. 249–53.

32. See, e.g., ibid., p. 58 (translated memorial of 1733).

understanding of the structure of the retail grain market, to recommend relaxation of the rules about that unambiguously illegal practice, trafficking in official cut-price grain. This story provides our first example of the availability of detailed information on the grain trade to assist in policy formation. It also sounds cautionary notes about the administrative culture within which an ambitious new emperor (Qianlong) was shortly to launch visionary initiatives to improve his subjects' well-being.

In the early summer of 1737, high grain prices in Beijing led to the opening of eighteen venues for selling cut-price grain to the city and suburban populations. But how closely should the venue administrators monitor their customers to ensure that the grain was bought only in small amounts, according to the rules, to meet the short-term consumption needs of individual households? A supervising censor, Ma Hongqi, complained that would-be purchasers were being subjected to such exacting questioning that they preferred to buy from ordinary retailers to avoid the long waits at the venues. By slowing down the sales in this way, the administrators could restrict the daily volume sold to one or two *shi* per venue. Ma interpreted such action as an easy method of avoiding censure for letting large amounts of cut-price grain fall into the hands of grain dealers or liquor manufacturers.

Ma's strictures may not have been entirely fair. The venue administrators were under pressure to be vigilant. They were probably confronted with the cunning of dealers who (according to later allegations) used numbers of poor people to buy cut-price grain on their behalf.[33] Such a tactic may legitimately have suggested to administrators the desirability of close questioning of customers. Ma, however, favored a relaxed approach to the whole problem. In his view, petty trafficking in official cut-price grain need not be a bad thing. If poor people were allowed to sell any surplus from their purchases of cut-price grain, this would not only mean a little extra income for them, but it should also help with spreading the official grain down through the lanes and alleyways. The positive effect of competition on the market price would

---

33. Cf. DQHDSL, vol. 9, *juan* 191:30a (p. 7,621: pronouncement of 1761). For the edicts ordering, first, vigilance during the 1737 Beijing cut-price grain sales, and, later, penalties for administrators who had allegedly let abuses occur, see QSL/QL, *juan* 40:9a and 41:12a–b.

thereby be extended. Ma's proposal was that only such "wicked persons" as accumulated quantities of ten *shi* and more for trading should be prosecuted. The poor should be allowed to sell up to a total of one *shi* (presumably per household for the duration of the sales).

In their joint response to Ma's memorial, the grand secretaries and Nine Ministries Assembly not only endorsed his ideas but also recommended more generous limits on the amounts of cut-price grain that could be traded. This was because of two considerations. One was the predicament of weak and elderly women who lived far from the cut-price sales venues. They were dependent on the hawkers who brought grain to their doors to sell. The other was the crucial role of the thousand and more petty hulling shops (*duifang*) existing in the capital. These daily purchased grain to hull and sell along the streets from shoulder carrying-poles; their ability to operate was a precondition for Beijing's price stability. All the hulling shops had only petty capital and were not in a position to engage in hoarding and speculation. In the assembly's judgment, forbidding the resale of official cut-price grain meant seriously reducing the flow of grain to the hulling shops and therefore pushing up prices in the door-to-door trade. In future, they opined, punishment should be incurred only by those traders who accumulated quantities of "forty to fifty *shi*" or more, or diverted cut-price grain to liquor preparation. Those dealing in only "a few *shi*" should be left alone.

This recommendation was adopted.[34] However, there was a hiccup in its implementation. Apparently without informing the venue ad-

---

34. QCWXTK, vol. 1, *juan* 36, pp. 5,187–88; QSL/QL, *juan* 41:29b–30a; DQHDSL, vol. 9, *juan* 191:27a–b (p. 7,620). The relaxed approach adopted in 1737 contrasts sharply with the harshness of the new supplementary article of 1775. The latter set a nominal punishment of 80 strokes of the heavy bamboo (in practice, 30 strokes) for shopkeepers who bought *up to ten shi* of official cut-price grain, and 100 strokes (in practice, 40) plus one month in the cangue ("portable pillory") for the dealers who sold it to them. DQHDSL, vol. 19, *juan* 765:4a (p. 14,852). On the other hand, Li and Dray-Novey find that the Beijing authorities sometimes deliberately used commercial channels to make official cut-price grain available to consumers. This was, perhaps, especially likely when the type of grain was wheat, which the participating shopkeepers converted into flour before reselling it. L. M. Li and A. Dray-Novey, "Guarding Beijing's Food Security," pp. 1,014–15 (earliest example 1759). Such measures may have exacerbated the temptations that culminated in the stiffening of the law.

ministrators of the change of policy and its rationale, the Board of Revenue published notices announcing that small traders were permitted to buy "up to ten *shi* or so" of cut-price grain. One administrator understandably found the Board proclamation "contradictory," in light of the existing rules and the good reasons for them. He argued that even when one allowed each customer to buy only one or two pecks, "wicked traders" still found ways of building hoards from these small allocations. The consequences of the tiff were minor (the administrator was granted discretion to sell grain in the quantities he thought appropriate), but it has a significantly familiar ring.[35] Such instances of poor communication weaken bureaucratic morale and increase cynicism towards higher authority. On the positive side, however, the recommendations of the grand secretaries and Nine Ministries Assembly show the Qing ruling establishment at its most sensitive and thoughtful. Here was a deliberative body comprising fifty or so of the bureaucracy's most senior dignitaries drawing on a sympathetic understanding of the humblest level of the Beijing grain trade in formulating policy advice.[36]

Controlling Merchant Speculators Through Statistics

As we have seen, ordinary speculative hoarding (hoarding that did not involve official cut-price grain) was somewhat ambiguously illegal. Not only was it illegal in a way that normally allowed local administrators a great deal of discretion in deciding whether to prosecute offenders; its ambiguous illegality also invited considerable variation, or even vacillation, in central government policy about enforcement. This section shows how, in the last third of his long reign, the Kangxi emperor

---

35. QSL/QL, *juan* 43:14a–b.

36. The membership of the Nine Ministries Assembly (literally, "Nine Chief Ministers," *jiu qing*) consisted of the senior officials of the nine major central government departments: the six administrative boards, the Censorate, the Office of Transmission, and the Court of Judicial Review. For valuable information on the Assembly's deliberative procedures in Ming times, see Hucker, "Governmental Organization," pp. 65–66. Research on the conduct of Assembly meetings under the Qing is badly needed, as Beatrice Bartlett's remarks (*Monarchs and Ministers*, pp. 154 and 188) leave many unanswered questions. Cf. Elliott, *The Manchu Way*, p. 217.

experimented with using the collection and transmission of information as a technique of control. Although this method was intended as an alternative to coercion, it still involved deterrence and intimidation. Its targets were not local engrossers but interregional grain merchants whose indispensability posed the dilemmas of policed free circulation at their most acute.[37]

Granted conventional assumptions, one could hardly take no action to control the mobile operators on whose undeveloped social consciences hung the subsistence of entire populations. Yet crude surveillance by official underlings who were perceived as no less greedy than the merchants would have meant subjecting the latter to financial pressures that, at best, would be passed on to the consumer. The more severe the punishments threatened for commercial offences, the larger the bribes that could be extorted by those with power to make arrests. Such harassment might persuade the victims that the routes where they encountered it were best avoided; making good on threats of heavy punishment might, at the extreme, eliminate resourceful merchants from the grain trade altogether. While the available evidence is insufficient to show that the Kangxi emperor had fully worked out these implications, his reservations about straightforward coercion reflected the common sense of a bureaucracy that conducted most of its direct business with the governed through a despised subaltern staff. On the most charitable view, except in very recent scholarship, Qing official underlings were underpaid (if paid at all) and ill-socialized in the values of benevolent Confucian governance.[38]

In the late summer of 1709, it struck Kangxi as odd that although plenty of grain was reportedly passing into the Yangzi River artery from Jiangxi and the Huguang region (Hunan and Hubei), rather little was entering the downstream markets of Jiangsu and Zhejiang, which he took to be the proper destination of the shipments. Grain prices were still rising in the latter provinces (instead of falling, as would have

---

37. On the role of long-distance rice merchants in Kangxi times, see Chen Dongyou, "Kangxi chao mijia."

38. For some generalities about the economic position of Qing clerks and runners, see Ch'ü, *Local Government*, pp. 44–49 and 64–67. For an important re-examination of the conventional wisdom on these groups, see Reed, *Talons and Teeth* (esp. pp. 69–75 and 155–59 on ethical aspects).

been expected after harvest).[39] He blamed the phenomenon on "rich and influential houses broadly buying up the rice of Huguang and Jiangxi and hoarding it while waiting for their price, extracting profit in the middle." He directed the grand secretaries and Nine Ministries Assembly to consider countermeasures, but when, five days later, their joint advice arrived, he found it unsatisfactory. The deliberators had recommended ordering the provincial governors and governors-general concerned to choose honest, capable officials to implement strict surveillance at all the well-known river ports. "If there are any rich or influential persons who hoard market rice, they should require them to put it on sale at the current price at the place where it was hoarded. Hoarding should not be permitted." Any infringements should be punished according to the Supplementary Article on Scoundrels (*guanggun li*)—a piece of legislation that, by 1709, prescribed immediate decapitation for the principal offender.[40]

Likely as it is that these proposals reflected (or intensified) time-honored principles for dealing with hoarders, the emperor thought them impractical. His concern was precisely that the suggested procedure would give menial underlings a pretext for making inspections and extorting money. He ordered a subtler system that would not involve explicit prohibition, but would instead exploit the government's capabilities in data collection and communication. It would guide the merchants into socially responsible behavior rather than policing their activities; and it would, in the emperor's view, tackle the problem at its root. The first step would be to find out which merchants had the grain that was at risk of being hoarded.

Kangxi suggested that it would be simple for appropriately selected officials to discover the names of all persons, whether visiting merchants from the Lower Yangzi or local people, who bought commer-

---

39. Cf. Wang Yeh-chien, "Secular Trends of Rice Prices," table 1.1 (p. 41), which suggests that the emperor was referring to a seasonal fluctuation rather than an ongoing crisis. The Suzhou annual rice price had peaked in 1708. Although still rather high in 1709, it was on the way down.

40. On the identity, history, and analogical application of the *guanggun li*, see Sommer, *Sex, Law, and Society*, pp. 99, 327–28. Originally a law against extortion, this article was applied to "an increasingly wide range" of offences, as illustrated in the 1707 ruling on the punishment for sexual violation of young girls. DQHDSL, vol. 20, *juan* 825:8b (p. 15,417).

cial quantities of rice at "well-known [river] ports or great market-towns" in the Middle Yangzi provinces.[41] The Middle Yangzi governors and governors-general were to have this information collected, together with the names of the sellers and the amounts of grain involved. Besides reporting the collected information monthly to the central government, the Middle Yangzi governors and governors-general were to send it to their opposite numbers in Jiangsu and Zhejiang. When this was done, opined the emperor, "if the rice of Huguang and Jiangxi does not make its way to Jiangsu or Zhejiang for sale, where else will it go? The knowledge of this rice being the property of all [*ci mi zhong suo gong zhi*], buying and selling will proceed without the need for orders, and rice aplenty will arrive [in the two provinces]."[42]

To whom does this *zhong* ("all") refer? A possible interpretation is the general public, who could have been informed through notices. According to Metzger, one indirect means by which the central government could put pressure on territorial officials to comply with imperial orders was to require the display of "yellow posters" communicating the imperial decision to society at large. In Metzger's judgment, "there was enough literacy and gossip in the society to make these [posters] an effective means of communication."[43] It is just conceivable that the emperor imagined that publicizing the names of merchants who were expected to arrive in Lower Yangzi cities with

---

41. The terms (1) Upper Yangzi, (2) Middle Yangzi, and (3) Lower Yangzi are used in this book to refer to the three great subdivisions of the Yangzi Valley corresponding, roughly, to (1) Sichuan; (2) Hunan, Hubei, and Jiangxi; and (3) southern Jiangsu, southern Anhui, and northern Zhejiang. The terms—used here for convenience only—derive from G. William Skinner's influential division of China proper into "physiographic macroregions." I ignore the subsequent refinement by which an additional Yangzi-valley macroregion, roughly corresponding to Jiangxi, has been identified, because mid-Qing writers on the grain trade typically referred to Jiangxi and Huguang together as the major grain-exporting region of the central Yangzi Valley. For maps identifying the physiographic macroregions as originally conceived, see Skinner, "Regional Urbanization," pp. 214–15. For the additional (Jiangxi) macroregion, see, e.g., Leong, *Migration and Ethnicity*, p. 22 (map by Skinner).

42. QSL/KX, *juan* 238:10a–b and 11b–13a; see also QCWXTK, vol. 1, *juan* 34, p. 5,174, and DQHDSL, vol. 9, *juan* 191:25b–26a (p. 7,619).

43. Metzger, *Internal Organization*, p. 163 n. 1.

substantial stocks of grain would serve to unleash comparable social pressure on these merchants. He was playing with fire, if so. The year before, a memorial from Ningbo (Zhejiang) had painted him a vivid picture of the barely restrained fury of an urban mob demanding punishment for some merchants and others who were thought to have conspired to bleed the local market of grain.[44] Even if he hoped only to deter would-be speculators through fear that similar fury might be turned on them, such use of the potential for mob action would have been most adventurous. In any case, it is not obvious how a mob could have intimidated merchants who had failed to arrive, and who had placed their hoards in distant warehouses, of whereabouts unknown.

All in all, I think we must abandon this interpretation in favor of the less interesting alternative: that zhong refers only to the group of Middle and Lower Yangzi chief provincial administrators plus those of their subordinates to whom they would pass the collected information—most probably, the magistrates of jurisdictions that lay along the Yangzi.[45] Presumably, the emperor supposed that if the merchants were aware that their names and grain holdings were known to the bureaucracy, they would not dare to fail to keep their stocks in motion until arrival at a Lower Yangzi market. The plausibility of this reading is strengthened by consideration of the procedure adopted on a similar occasion a few years later. In that episode, examined below, the governor of the recipient province was instructed to gather independent data on the quantity of grain arriving from two supplier provinces. If the amounts reported to be arriving in his jurisdiction were significantly lower than those reported to have been bought and dispatched in the supplier provinces, this was presumably to be seen as indicating that some grain had vanished into hoards and must be brought to light.

Attempts were made to implement at least the data-collection part of the new policy of 1709. This was probably not difficult, given that the emperor had envisaged such collection only at the "well-known [river] ports [and] great market-towns." Recourse to state-licensed brokers was

---

44. Wang Shichen, KX 47/8/22, repr. GZD/KX, vol. 1, pp. 888–92. The offence of the conspirators, in the public's eyes, lay in preventing Ningbo from enjoying a rare episode of low grain prices by buying up large quantities of grain for shipment elsewhere.

45. For examples of the use of zhong to refer to the members of a limited collectivity, see Fu, Ming Qing nongcun, pp. 6–7, 15.

compulsory in wholesale grain transactions, and the brokers were expected to keep records of their clients' names, merchandise and places
of origin, as well as of each individual transaction. The registers were to
be submitted to the local authorities monthly for inspection.[46] Wherever this system functioned as it was supposed to, the task of the specially deputed data-collectors must have been simply to extract the
required information from the brokers' records, recompile it, and
forward it to the provincial government.

Whether all significant sales of grain destined for shipment on the
Yangzi could be "captured" by these means is another matter. Zhao
Shenqiao, the Hunan governor, had reservations. In a memorial that he
drafted in about October 1709, he duly presented the names of buyers
and sellers, detailed figures for the quantities involved, and statements
of the place of sale for wholesale grain transactions at the two major
river ports of Xiangtan and Hengzhou plus another eight riverine
county-level jurisdictions with rice markets. Such was presumably the
easy part of the research, but Zhao seems to have thought it insufficient.
He pointed out that rice was to be found all over Hunan, and a comprehensive investigation would therefore be necessary.[47]

Whether or not such ostensible conscientiousness led to fuller statistics, the monitoring of the Yangzi Valley grain trade continued at
least into the summer of 1710. Indeed, after receiving one of the
monthly reports from Jiangxi, the emperor began to take an interest in
the larger picture, asking for information about how the volume exported from Jiangxi since monitoring began compared with that in
previous years. The answer of the governor, Lang Tingji, may not reflect much sophistication in the handling of statistics, but it does confirm that quantitative data were already available through brokers'

---

46. Rowe, *Hankow*, p. 187; Jing, "Legislation," pp. 59–60. The requirement that
brokers record the name, place of origin, travel permit (*luyin*) number, and quantity and type of goods of visiting merchants and boat-owners, and submit the register monthly for inspection, is specified in the Ming and Qing penal codes under
the Statute on Setting Oneself up as a Broker or Shipping Agent without Authorization. See, e.g., Shen Zhiqi, *Da Qing lü jizhu* (1746 revised ed.), vol. 2, *juan* 10,
pp. 587–88. Presumably, the goods purchased by the visitors were recorded as well
as those that they had brought to sell.

47. See Zhao's "Draft Palace Memorial on the Movement of Rice in Hunan
Reporting the Names of Buyers and Sellers and the Quantities Involved," cited in
Shigeta, *Shindai shakai*, pp. 14–15.

records in the early eighteenth century. It also suggests that actually using these records as a source of data was an innovation, at least in Jiangxi. Lang did not attempt to provide figures for 1708 or earlier, stating only that before the monitoring system started, the quantities of grain changing hands among the people had not been investigated. However, he did supply aggregate figures for the amount of husked and unhusked rice "sold by brokers to merchants" in Nanchang, the provincial capital, from the beginning of (lunar) 1709 until September, when the monitoring system had started; and then both for the whole province and for Nanchang alone for the ensuing period in which data had been reported monthly.[48]

Converting his figures into common units (a refinement that Lang neglected), we find that over the former, seven-month period a quantity equivalent to 314,107 *shi* of unhusked rice (44,872 *shi* per month on average) was sold through Nanchang, presumably into the downstream Yangzi River grain trade. During the following, ten-month period the corresponding total was 514,440 *shi* (51,444 *shi* per month on average). Lang explained the increase, which looked smaller on his arithmetic, by

---

48. His figures were as follows. For the sake of comparability with other data in this book, they are presented here in *shi* of unhusked rice, although most of this grain had been sold by the brokers in husked form. I have used the Qing official conversion ratio: one *shi* of husked rice represented two *shi* unhusked (cf. Will, *Bureaucracy and Famine*, p. 131). *Units:* shi *of unhusked rice*

Place and dates	Rice sold in husked form	Rice sold in unhusked form	Total
In Nanchang, 1st to 7th months (approx. Feb. to Aug.) 1709	306,280	7,827	314,107
In Nanchang, 8th month (approx. Sept.) 1709 to 5th month (approx. June) 1710	502,640	11,800	514,440
In whole province (including Nanchang), 8th month 1709 to 5th month 1710	1,170,898	12,410	1,183,308

pointing out that present price conditions (high in the Lower Yangzi, low in Jiangxi) would normally be expected to produce a large trade flow. As an additional factor, he mentioned his own sternness in forbidding local people in some regions of the province to place embargoes on the "export" of their rice to the outside community.[49] The Jiangxi report reflects the rudimentary competence in economics and statistics of one early eighteenth-century official. However, it does not tell us whether the monitoring strategy was successful in preventing Middle Yangzi grain from disappearing into hoards while supposedly *en route* to Lower Yangzi markets.

We may perhaps infer that satisfaction was not total from the fact that when similar measures were adopted in northern China seven years later, they were reinforced with a strict and explicit ban on merchants buying up and hoarding grain in the region of production or *en route* to the final market. This time, provision was made for the disciplining of "unworthy" official underlings who took advantage of the prohibition to commit extortion. This second episode, which began in the summer of 1716, was otherwise roughly parallel to the first. The cue at which the central government took action was again a perceived mismatch between the quantity of grain available in a supplying region (this time, Shandong and Henan) and the behavior of grain prices in a market (that of the imperial capital) to which commercial stocks were expected to flow. When the price of wheat in Beijing failed to fall in a manner deemed commensurate with the abundance further south, the explanation was assumed to lie in the activities of speculators. Again, the major strategy adopted was monitoring of waterborne commercial grain. The Shandong and Henan governors were to find out "the quantity of wheat and [other] grain coming north by water and being sold to merchants," report it monthly to the emperor, and at the same time notify the governor of Zhili (the quasi province in which Beijing lay). The Zhili governor was to ascertain the quantity of grain arriving in his jurisdiction from these provinces and report it monthly likewise.[50]

---

49. Lang Tingji, KX 49/7/4, repr. GZD/KX, vol. 2, pp. 615–18.

50. DQHDZL, *juan* 40:27b–28a; quotation from edict transcribed in GZD/KX, vol. 6, p. 489; QCWXTK, vol. 1, *juan* 34, p. 5,175.

The second round of data-collection (that taking place in Zhili) was a refinement, but a memorial of April 1717 calls into question its effectiveness in revealing speculation. The Zhili governor drew the emperor's attention to a 69,481-*shi* discrepancy between the total amount of grain reported to have left Henan and Shandong during the half-year following the start of data-collection in late July 1716 (some 666,836 *shi*), and the total reported to have arrived in Zhili over presumably the same period (some 597,355 *shi*). However, he saw no problem in accounting for this discrepancy with the supposition that there had been sales *en route*.[51] Would the emperor have been satisfied with such a hypothesis had the discrepancy been larger? It was the fact that the total amount of grain in transit had been a mere six-digit figure that enabled the governor to defuse the issue. The emperor had expressed renewed concern that the continuing high prices in Zhili during the spring of 1717 spelled the activity of hoarders, but that had been on the assumption that Zhili's 1716 imports of grain from Henan and Shandong had exceeded 2 million *shi*. From the work of the investigators in all three provinces, it now appeared that this estimate was far too high. Indeed, after mid-September there had been so little grain leaving Shandong that the Shandong governor had stopped reporting.[52]

Pierre-Étienne Will has written that the above two episodes suggest that large-scale "interregional trade was a relatively easy target for administrative action, subject as it was to control in the major ports, at

---

51. This was not the first time that he had offered such an explanation. Already in September 1716, he had noticed that the amount that his subordinates reported to be entering Zhili from Shandong was less than that which the Shandong governor had reported to be coming north from "Jining and elsewhere." He commented that, on one hand, as Jining was a long way south of the Shandong-Zhili border, it was quite possible that the merchants had made sales *en route*, while on the other, the Shandong officials might have included in their statistics grain from Henan that was passing through Shandong. Zhao Hongxie, KX 55/8/11, repr. GZD/KX, vol. 6, p. 545.

52. The governor nonetheless covered himself by stating that he was reiterating the antihoarding prohibition. Zhao Hongxie, KX 56/2/25, repr. GZD/KX, vol. 6, pp. 829–33. For further reports containing monthly figures on grain movements from Shandong and Henan to Zhili between July 1716 and April 1717, see ibid., pp. 489–90, 495–98, 513–14, 544–46, 873–75. The first of these memorials refers to a separate document reporting daily figures.

customs barriers, and along the great trade routes."[53] If my interpretation is correct, the point of the monitoring system as introduced in 1709 was to intimidate the merchants. If merchants who regularly plied the Yangzi knew that they were expected to arrive with grain cargoes at the "obligatory points of passage"[54] *en route* to Jiangnan, they would not dare, for the sake of their future operations, to stockpile their supplies instead. However, the memorials that I have seen suggest neither that the monitoring was effective nor that it was particularly thorough. It is not even clear whether the measures adopted in 1716–17 emphasized the systematic collection of exporting merchants' names by the Henan and Shandong authorities.[55] The lack of clarity suggests that this latter exercise was possibly intended only to indicate whether the ban on hoarding was being defied, and, as we have seen, the data gained were not necessarily convincing even for that purpose. Also significant, in comparative perspective, is the absence of any unambiguous indication, for either episode, that the data collected in the producer provinces were to include each exporting merchant's intended place of sale.

Requiring grain merchants to specify an intended place of sale was not an unknown practice in China two or three decades after these two episodes. In one case in 1738, merchants arriving at their declared destinations were required to obtain evidence that they had duly sold their grain in the appointed markets by having the local authorities stamp the permits with which they had been supplied *en route*. They were then expected to return to the internal customs stations that had issued the permits so that their compliance with their declared intentions could be verified. In another case ten years later, merchant compliance

---

53. Will, *Bureaucracy and Famine*, p. 212.

54. Ibid.

55. The name of one merchant appears in a 1716 monthly report from the Henan governor as part of the formula ". . . the amount of *mi* [husked grain, probably millet], wheat and miscellaneous cereals bought by the visiting merchant [name] and others . . . totalled . . ." In this case, as the total purchased was over 50,000 *shi*, the author was probably citing one representative name out of a longer list of merchants (or partnerships) operating independently of each other. Formulae of this kind are common in Qing official documents. The other merchants may have been named in the more detailed report to which the author refers; in this and the other memorials that I have seen, however, the focus seems rather to be on determining the amounts of grain that were supposed to be in transit. Li Yang, KX 55/7/7, repr. GZD/KX, vol. 6, pp. 489–90.

was to be assured partly by the involvement of brokers, who were required to guarantee that their clients would sell at agreed destinations, but also through an exchange of documents between the permit-issuing authorities and the authorities of the agreed places of sale.[56] In both these cases, there were special circumstances, but in *ancien régime* France, it was a matter of routine to use documentary control procedures to hold merchants to selling stocks at destinations that they had reported in advance.[57] Compared with such quasi escorting of each load or cargo, the measures adopted at Kangxi's instance in 1709 and 1716 seem loose and incomplete. One sees here in Kangxi the intelligent amateur of government, overruling his advisors, whose punitive approach to hoarders may have reflected standard bureaucratic practice, and instead designing an experiment that may have needed better bureaucratic underpinning if it was to work (that is, assure the prompt delivery of cargoes to the markets that the emperor deemed proper for them).

Beatings and Forced Sales

The data-collection exercises of 1709–10 and 1716–17 addressed perceived problems in the interregional grain trade. They required interprovincial cooperation, and it is therefore not surprising that they were initiated by the central government. They were also aimed at large-scale commercial operations: what interested the emperor in 1716 was the waterborne long-distance trade, not the vigorous cart and pack-horse traffic that provided vital supplementary foodstuffs for Beijing.[58] Let us now turn to regional and local measures that did not involve interprovincial cooperation, that targeted operations of varying size, and that were not necessarily based on orders from the central government.

---

56. Dunstan, *Conflicting Counsels*, pp. 266 and 324–25.

57. When grain merchants in *ancien régime* France registered with the police (as was compulsory), they were required to specify the town or city in which they usually sold. When buying stocks, they were expected to report "the amount, price and quality"; they were then issued with a certificate that was to be submitted for inspection at the "destined market" (Kaplan's phrase). French police authorities at the place of purchase would sometimes send a copy of the certificate to their counterparts at the intended place of sale. Kaplan, *Bread*, vol. 1, pp. 66–67, 69.

58. Dunstan, "'Orders Go Forth,'" p. 80.

The theme throughout this section is coercion, or at least deterrence. Merchants could be threatened with dire punishments, thrashed, or forced to sell their grain at controlled profits or without profit at all.

Unfortunately, many administrative texts speak only of the need for strict prohibition of mercantile hoarding or related misdoings, without providing details of the methods of enforcement or the punishments incurred. However, offenders were probably assumed to have rendered themselves liable to severe corporal punishment under some applicable statute, most likely that on Violating Imperial Pronouncements. The threat of a heavy (perhaps even fatal) beating was probably the standard harsh form of deterrent with which Qing territorial officials confronted mercantile hoarders. The other common way of dealing with such hoarders—forcing them to sell the hoarded grain under official supervision—could serve both as a milder deterrent and as a short-term means of addressing the problem of supply.

One can have the impression that beatings and forced sales were alternatives in the minds of some administrators. Several sources seem to show officials planning to use one of the two methods, but not both. On closer consideration, the following pattern not only makes sense, but also fits the evidence that I present below. While any mercantile hoarder laid himself open to the risk of severe corporal punishment, the likelihood that he would in fact be so treated depended partly on the responsible official's view as to the depth of his iniquity, and partly on the extent to which he himself resisted orders to part with his grain. Practical considerations probably led the more experienced territorial officials not only to give priority to ensuring that the hoarded grain was released swiftly onto local markets, but also to prefer that this be done without ruining the hoarders, still less beating them to death. The mercantile hoarders most likely to be beaten as common criminals in an experienced official's jurisdiction were, I suspect, those who were so refractory as to refuse to take advantage of an offered "second chance."

To experienced officials, in other words, the main value of the availability of harsh sentences for hoarders may have been its potential to deter detected hoarders from noncooperation with orders to sell their grain. When harsh beatings were threatened as a punishment for the primary offence of hoarding, this may, of course, reflect a situation in which hoarding was unusually prevalent and callous, and the need for deterrence thus especially clear. It is, however, equally likely to reflect a lack of sophistication or experience on the part of the official issuing the threat. As I show below, at least one Qing provincial governor recognized that the harshest deterrents are not always the most effective. We cannot hope to find consistent principles determining how territorial officials chose between coercive options: when firm direction from above was not provided, not only the objective circumstances but also the experience, temperament, and relative sophistication of the individual official would influence his choices. While the wisest practice may have been to use the mild and the harsh approaches in tandem, some hastier and less experienced officials probably saw no further than the need to sound determined and inflict deterrent punishments—without such signs of weakness as offering a second chance.

I begin with an example of a provincial governor's ingenuity in using the standing prohibition of hoarding, whose status he considered firm, to check merchant exports of food from a dearth-stricken area, an activity that the emperor could not be relied on to prohibit.[59] This example tells us nothing about methods for suppressing hoarding; however, it will serve as a corrective to the image of interventionist simplism given later in this section. It demonstrates that not every official who assumed that hoarding could and should be banned was blind to the operation of what we would call market forces. In certain circumstances, banning hoarding (or at least, banning an activity that it was convenient to call "hoarding") could be seen as a way of freeing market forces from improper interference by self-interested middlemen. I shall then present available evidence on the subject of enforcement, focusing on the two approaches (beatings and forced sales) and the probable relationship between them. The chapter will end with consideration of a late eighteenth-century episode that illustrates a fundamental problem with the legalistic handling of hoarders. It was easier to check every entry in a merchant ledger than it was to prove intent.

During an appointment as acting Shandong governor in January 1747, Fang Guancheng was confronted with a spate of requests from his subordinates for a temporary ban on the seaborne export of food to

---

59. A few years earlier, a request from the same province for a similar ban in similar circumstances had reportedly been dismissed with the imperial comment that if there were indeed no grain to spare for export, exports would have ceased without the need for prohibition. Dunstan, *Conflicting Counsels*, p. 256.

southern provinces.[60] Despite the grain shortage and high grain prices, Fang did not feel that he could authorize such a ban, because it would have gone against the spirit of repeated edicts against selfishly "blocking the purchase of grain [for communities elsewhere]" (*edi*). Nor did he propose to risk the emperor's rebuke by seeking exceptional permission to prohibit exports. Instead, he requested approval for a strategy of indirectly halting exports by enforcing the existing ban on hoarding. His rationale combined, on one hand, the simple commandist logic that clearly illegal behavior should be suppressed, and, on the other, an invocation of the efficacy of a certain market mechanism. This mechanism was thought able to protect the food supply of grain-exporting regions.

According to Fang, investigation had revealed that at all the Shandong ports there were brokers (*hanghu*) who bought up "miscellaneous cereals" (*zaliang*) and sold them to merchant vessels from the south. His informant had said that normally this did no damage, but in years of dearth it was "extremely harmful to the people's food supply." Fang chose to regard these brokers as hoarders, an interpretation presumably based on the fact that they withheld grain from the market until their preselected customers arrived. He inveighed against the illegality of their behavior, and he represented them as driven by an antisocial and incessant lust for profit. In future, he declared, they should be required to keep to their proper role as brokers. This role did not include accumulating stocks for clients in advance of their arrival, so that these supplies bypassed the market. Once the "hoarders" were no longer able to distort the normal distribution of supplies via the market, one of two outcomes would occur. If grain were plentiful and cheap, the fact that visiting merchants were buying on the market rather than from "hoarders" would provide opportunities for ordinary traders to make

---

60. The Qing normally maintained a ban on the seaborne export of food, even when the destination was another Chinese province, but among the many exceptions was a standing authorization of the southward export of soybeans from Shandong (Will, *Bureaucracy and Famine*, pp. 216–18). According to Will, the exception granted for soybeans did not extend to grain. Fang, however, does not seem to have thought that he could invoke the ban on grain shipments to take action against the export of "miscellaneous cereals." It is clear from Fang's memorial that officialdom had come to tolerate the seaborne export of at least these relatively low-grade cereals from Shandong ports.

the modest profits needed to support their livelihood. If, on the other hand, grain were scarce and prices high, the visitors would be deterred and would stop exporting of their own accord.[61] The idea that high prices, by serving as a disincentive to exporters, acted to protect the stocks of dearth-stricken communities was not new in 1747.[62] The originality of Fang's memorial lies in its implied suggestion that the "hoarders" had impeded the operation of this market mechanism by reserving stocks for the exporters, presumably at prices that did not fully reflect the current grain shortage.

In proposing his solution to the emperor, Fang failed to discuss means of enforcement. Examination of a sample proclamation against misdemeanors that included hoarding may clarify why he and others saw no need to spell out how they planned to make their bans effective. Official proclamations constituted an established genre whose minatory formulae had only to be recombined for individual occasions. An administrator who was envisaging a prohibition knew that it would be simple to have one of these texts composed and promulgated in his name—unless he wanted to write it himself. Thus, in the mid-1730s, Zhao Hong'en, as governor-general of Jiangsu, Anhui, and Jiangxi, perceived a need to ban "hoarding, putting prices up exorbitantly (*gaotai*), and obstructing the delivery of rent grain." The text preserved in the published collection of his proclamations duly mentioned examples of the behavior that had driven him to action—forestalling (*jiemai*, that is, buying grain up before it reached the market) and engrossing by traders in southern Jiangxi, "combining to fix prices" (*qihang yijia*) by urban retailers south of Lake Boyang.[63] The proclamation treated the Jiangxi provincial bureaucracy to a brief homily on its responsibilities for guiding popular behavior. Then came the orders:

---

61. CC, Fang Guancheng, QL 11/12/8. Fang reported that he was also ordering more general vigilance against any speculative activity that might be contributing to the high price of grain. His memorial was approved.

62. It had been expressed on more than one occasion since the late 1730s. Dunstan, *Conflicting Counsels*, pp. 256 and 322.

63. The retailers had allegedly taken advantage of protracted rainfall to create fears of shortage that could be translated into price rises. Zhao wrote that "they halt their hulling implements, sprinkle the rice with water, adulterate it with husks and sand, and monopolistically raise the price to exorbitant levels (*longduan gaotai*)." For examples of such misbehavior elsewhere, see Dunstan, *Conflicting Counsels*, p. 58 (Guangzhou); Will, *Bureaucracy and Famine*, p. 212 (Hankou, Suzhou).

the province's circuit and prefectural authorities were to institute constant surveillance in town, city, and countryside against these kinds of misconduct. Offenders were to be arrested and prosecuted.

Direct threats to "wicked traders," "wicked brokers," and other potential violators were placed at the end of the proclamation. Such individuals were advised to "turn back" immediately and thus preserve their own lives and those of their families (*baoquan shen jia xingming*). The recalcitrant could expect to be delivered to the authorities "in chains," to be sentenced according to the relevant statute. It is not clear that grain dealers with sufficient literacy to manage their own businesses would necessarily have known all the characters that Zhao used in his concluding rhetoric, which was crafted with greater elegance than seems functional for communicating with tradespeople. But whether the average grain dealer could understand the characters for "bite one's navel [in useless remorse]" is perhaps not the crucial issue. Standard formulae (such as "each should comply in fear") were regularly used at the end of prohibitions and could probably be recognized well enough by the half-literate.[64] Presumably, they would have been taken seriously only if the tradespeople were able to link the threats of punishment "according to the statute" with images of the broken bodies of people in their own or neighboring communities who, for no worse crime, had fallen foul of the brutality of the Qing judicial system.[65]

How literally should we take Zhao Hong'en's hint that infraction of his prohibition could lead to the death of the offender? It is true that, as we saw in the preface to this book, a relatively inexperienced Chen Hongmou once threatened the extralegal punishment of immediate beating to death for "lawless and wicked" persons who, during a year of dearth, built hoards out of the newly harvested beans and wheat crops. But this was intended as an extreme sanction for an extreme outrage. Chen did not specify the punishment that lay in store for tradespeople arrested for the more ordinary malpractice of taking advantage of

---

64. On "functional literacy" in Qing China, see Rawski, *Education and Popular Literacy*, esp. p. 140 for estimated male and female literacy rates in nineteenth-century China (with knowledge of "a few hundred characters" taken as the minimum criterion for literacy).

65. For an illustrated account of the physical damage that Qing courts might inflict even on unconvicted suspects, see Kuhn, *Soulstealers*, pp. 14–17. For Zhao's proclamation, see Zhao Hong'en, *Yuhua Tang*, 70a–71a.

widespread hoarding to charge exorbitant prices.[66] Our only means of judging whether routine punishments for mercantile hoarding are likely to have been life-threatening is investigation of the penalties prescribed by the statutes under which offenders could be sentenced legally.

As we have seen, to be punished under the multipurpose Statute on Violating Imperial Pronouncements meant suffering forty strokes of a bamboo rod with a diameter of 6.4 centimeters (at the wider end) and a weight supposed not to exceed some 1.19 kilograms. The milder punishment of twenty strokes of a bamboo rod 4.8 centimeters in (wide-end) diameter and weighing up to about 0.9 kilogram awaited those so fortunate as to be sentenced only under the Statute on Violating Imperial Orders. If the Statute on Doing What Ought Not To Be Done (*bu ying wei lü*) was ever used for grain hoarding or price manipulation, the punishment would have been either fifteen strokes of the lighter rod, or thirty strokes of the heavier rod, depending on the seriousness of the offence. To turn to the three statutes on economic crimes that might have been applicable, it should theoretically have been possible to sentence an offender to death by strangulation (after the assizes) under the provisions of the Statute on Valuing of Goods by Market Superintendents, but beatings of between five and forty strokes must have been much more common. The relevant part of the Statute on the Coinage prescribes a punishment of twenty strokes of the heavier rod, while the harshest sentence normally available under the Statute on

---

66. PYTOCG, *juan* 4:13a–b. Beating to death was extralegal in the sense of not being one of the standard death sentences (listed in Bodde and Morris, *Law in Imperial China*, p. 78) but not necessarily in that of violating imperial pronouncements (see chap. 9 below). Suzuki Hidemitsu argues that its principal attraction was that its nonstatutory status exempted it from the mandatory review of death sentences that was supposedly a principle of premodern Chinese justice (ibid., pp. 131–34; Suzuki, "Jōhei kō," esp. pp. 150–54). Summary execution "under the heavy bamboo" must have been especially tempting in contexts in which swift deterrent punishment appeared expedient and the offence was deemed unusually reprehensible. Other cases in which beating to death might be inflicted include miscellaneous derelictions of duty or abuses of power by official underlings, a group stigmatized as reprobate (see, e.g., Zhao Hong'en, *Yuhua Tang*, p. 40b; Dunstan, *Conflicting Counsels*, p. 295).

Restraint of Trade was thirty strokes of the heavier rod.[67] In 1738, when the central government issued its own prohibition against price-fixing combinations of shopkeepers, it ordered that future infractions should be punished under the Statute on Restraint of Trade, but with the penalties increased by one degree.[68] It is therefore likely that this was the statute that, a few years earlier, Zhao Hong'en had had in mind for grain retailers convicted of such commercial conspiracy.

It is probably safe to assume that most grain merchants whose speculative hoarding, engrossing, and/or price manipulation were deemed worthy of criminal punishment were beaten with between twenty and forty strokes of the heavier rod. Such beatings were not, in principle, death sentences. Thus, in warning potential offenders to protect their lives, Zhao was arguably pursuing intimidation at the expense of strict regard for truth. However, it is not impossible that, whatever the intention of the law, some felons beaten with a full forty strokes died of their wounds. The potentially lethal nature of the rods resulted not only from their weight but also from their length: 1.76 meters (5.5 Chinese feet) was standard for both the lighter and the heavier kinds.[69] Brought down with might, such rods would have inflicted severe damage on bare buttocks. A combination of a weak constitution, loss of blood, and insufficiently hygienic treatment of the wounds could have been fatal in some cases. A late seventeenth-century handbook for county magistrates pointed out that beatings inflicted during judicial torture could cause death if the person delivering them were so minded. Penal beatings carried out with maximum intent to harm were probably not different. Chen Hongmou's threat of beating to death for persons who built new hoards in the middle of a food

---

67. In all cases, I have cited the actual (as opposed to nominal) number of strokes. See Bodde and Morris, *Law in Imperial China*, pp. 77 and 81, and, e.g., Shen Zhiqi, *Da Qing lü jizhu* (1746 revised ed.), vol. 1, *juan* 1, p. 4; vol. 2, *juan* 7, pp. 433–34, *juan* 10, pp. 591–93 (for relevant cross-references, see ibid., vol. 2, *juan* 18, pp. 965–67; vol. 3, *juan* 23, pp. 1,354–57; vol. 3, *juan* 26, p. 1,489. Application of the Statute on Restraint of Trade would theoretically have made possible a sentence of death by strangulation (after the assizes), because this statute indirectly provided for a scale of sentences culminating in that penalty. However, stay of execution until after the assizes made commutation to a noncapital sentence highly likely (Bodde and Morris, *Law in Imperial China*, pp. 138–42).

68. DQHDSL, vol. 19, *juan* 765:13b–14a (p. 14,857).

69. Shen Zhiqi, *Da Qing lü jizhu* (1746 revised ed.), vol. 1, *juan* 1, p. 4.

shortage becomes easier to understand if we see it as the next step up from beatings from which some victims did not recover—in the context of a legal system in which the power to order fatal beatings may have been surprisingly diffused.[70] And Zhao Hong'en's appeal to think of the lives of "self and family" should not seem far-fetched if we recall that severe injury to a breadwinner could jeopardize the livelihood of his entire household.

The fact remains, however, that by no means all persons caught with stocks of hoarded grain during food shortages were subjected to criminal punishment. As we have seen, another principle was available: forced sale of hoarded grain, under official supervision and, in some cases, at a "reduced" price. For example, in 1748, during a mild dearth, the Manchu official Kaitai, as Jiangxi governor, reported that he had had the stocks of "some tens" of hoarders in the Nanchang area impounded. He had ordered the local authorities to make the hoarders sell them off piecemeal, under supervision, at a price 0.1 tael per *shi* below the current market rate. This, and not corporal punishment, was Kaitai's idea of a deterrent with a chance of success. He argued that these hoarders were small-time offenders whose profit-seeking instincts were stronger than their fear of breaking the law, and whose hearts would not necessarily be changed by severe sanctions. He had seen a proposal, rejected three years earlier by the Board of Revenue, for the imposition of a 30 percent price cut on merchant hoarders. Kaitai thought this rate too high but wanted to adopt the principle. A milder warning, in the form of forced sales that would leave the hoarders without profit but not seriously erode their capital, was the strategy of choice.[71]

Kaitai was determining his policy *ad hoc*, but forced sales of large hoards in drought-stricken Shaanxi in 1753 were carried out in the name of an existing regulation (*li*). The governor Zhongyin, confronted with reports of merchants "accumulating hoards in the full thousands and heaped tens of thousands of *shi* for export to Shanxi," invoked a regulation that empowered provincial chief administrators to declare export bans when there had been poor harvests in their jurisdiction and there

---

70. Suzuki, "Jōhei kō," pp. 157–59, 162–65; Huang Liu-hung, *Complete Book*, pp. 276, 309.

71. CC, Kaitai, QL 13/3/28. The emperor's response was "Noted." On the proposal for a 30 percent price cut, see chap. 3 below.

was "not sufficient grain for the folk's sustenance." It is not clear whether it was the same regulation that Zhongyin cited as prescribing that the hoarders should be made to sell their grain, under supervision, at the place where the hoards had been found.[72] Nor, indeed, is it clear whether the fact that the would-be exporters had been hoarding was what determined that they should be forced to sell their grain. Five years earlier, Chen Hongmou, likewise faced with the need to ban grain exports from Shaanxi, had ordered that travelling grain merchants caught without permits authorizing their participation in the province's internal grain trade should be made to put their grain on sale, at a reduced price, either on the spot, or (if that was not feasible) in the vicinity of the place of detection. His directive was concerned only with grain in transit, not grain immobilized in hoards. However, although the exact significance of Zhongyin's measures is uncertain, it is noteworthy that he showed even more concern than Kaitai for the hoarders' continuing ability to function as grain merchants. In the event, he had their stocks bought up by the authorities for cut-price sales to prevent mass hunger, but so far from forcing them to take a loss *pro bono publico*, he ordered that the price that they received be set in such a way as to allow them a gross profit of 0.2 to 0.3 tael per *shi*. He also indicated that an advantage of having officialdom buy the grain in bulk was that it would spare the merchants from having their capital "held up" by slow sales on a market that would have been glutted by the sudden dissolution of the hoards.[73]

Zhongyin's approach exemplifies the sensible official's instinct for constructive alternatives to inflicting the harsh beatings that would have marked merchant hoarders as common criminals. It also suggests awareness that grain merchants had a vital job to do and might need consideration to help them do it efficiently. Zhongyin planned coercion but not punishment. While the possibility of corruption should not be excluded, his leniency, or indeed generosity, was easily justifiable in terms of public policy considerations. However, the vast dif-

---

72. Probably not, as the slightly fuller version of the regulation allowing for provincial export bans quoted in LFZZ, Xu Qi, QL 12/12/3 (d.r.) contains no such provision.

73. PYTOCG, *juan* 27:16a–18a, and Zhongyin, memorial of QL 17/8/10 reproduced in GZD/QL, vol. 3, pp. 576–77 (cited and translated in Dunstan, *Conflicting Counsels*, pp. 251–54, 264–71).

ference between his treatment of hoarders and that threatened by Zhao Hong'en arouses curiosity as to what, other than the experience and personality of individual officials, determined whether merchants and shopkeepers were merely made to sell their grain under conditions not of their own choosing, or whether they were arrested, interrogated, and sentenced to harsh beatings.

Two possible principles are reflected in the sources, although there is little to suggest consistent application. First, as in the Anhui case of 1814, "the sentence they deserve" (*ying de zhi zui*) could be kept in reserve for hoarders who resisted official orders that they sell their stocks or who hid stocks from officials sent on missions of inspection. Another example comes from early 1744, when a vice-president of the Board of Military Affairs urged that the Zhili governor-general be told to have the authorities of jurisdictions south of Beijing take action against local hoarders. The measures he envisaged were closely parallel to those ordered in Anhui in 1814: the authorities should determine a fair price, the hoards should be sold locally and promptly, and, "as a warning to the [growing] tendency towards greed" (*tanfeng*), punishment should be meted out to any hoarders who resisted or concealed stocks.[74] The sources are not explicit as to whether the punishment would be for obstructing the implementation of official orders, or whether it would be a sentence appropriate to the crime of speculative hoarding but made more severe because of the resistance. Given that hoarding, as a violation of imperial commands, was in itself a punishable offence, I suspect the latter. "The sentence they deserve" was essentially the sentence the Anhui merchants deserved for hoarding large amounts of grain during a food shortage. The threat that it might be inflicted would deter resistance and concealment.

The second possible principle has to do with the degree of criminality. In some cases, it appears, this was a matter of the individual official's perception of degree of wickedness, and here consistency is not to be expected. Chen Hongmou threatened beating to death for persons so depraved as to deny consumers access to newly harvested crops during a food shortage; Zhongyin called the Shaanxi hoarders "wicked" (*jian*) several times but still sought to ensure that they would make a

---

74. DQHDSL, vol. 9, *juan* 191:31a (p. 7,622); CC, Gao Bin, QL 8/12/19. As we shall see in chap. 3, the governor-general resisted this proposal.

profit. In other cases, there may have been legal distinctions, the documentary basis for which is unclear, determining when criminal punishment should and should not be applied. It may have been because the southern Jiangxi hoarders were also forestalling grain and colluding with brokers to corner supplies that Zhao Hong'en mentioned them in a proclamation vaguely threatening a death sentence for future offenders. The purpose for which stocks of grain had been accumulated could also serve as grounds for a distinction. In the Tongzhou case of 1778 with which I end this section, the reported reason for not bringing criminal proceedings against merchants who were clearly speculating was that their stocks had been warehoused in accordance with a standard commercial routine. However, as I have suggested, it is likely that evidence of intent deliberately to manipulate grain prices was often used as a criterion determining whether a hoarder should be treated as a criminal. Lack of such evidence may have been the leading factor in the Tongzhou decision.

During the summer of 1778, the merchant clients of the four great wheat warehouses (*duifang*) of Tongzhou (near Beijing) incurred government scrutiny by having what seemed an inordinately large amount of grain in storage during the period of insecurity that followed a dry spring. As was found by the detailed official inquiry, merchants from Henan, Shandong, Zhili, and northern Jiangsu were in the habit of bringing wheat for the Beijing market north as far as Tongzhou every year, beginning in the second (lunar) month. They deposited it in the Tongzhou warehouses for a flat fee of 0.01 tael per *shi*, before selling it gradually to Beijing and Tongzhou retailers. They disposed of the greater part within the same year, and of the rest the following year as soon as their new wheat arrived. In 1778, however, 210,980 (37 percent) of the 564,800 *shi* originally deposited were still lying in the warehouses as late as the beginning of July. Of the latter amount, only some 25,800 *shi* had been brought north during the spring and early summer of 1778; the rest was all grain deposited (by a total of more than 220 merchants) during 1777. The size of the aggregate amount still left in store created the suspicion that the merchants were responding to the recent lack of rain by withholding stocks deliberately in order to push up the price.

On the basis of a collective denial from eighty or so wheat merchants who were in Tongzhou at the time, a close examination of the warehousers' books for that and the preceding years, and corroboration of the merchants' statement by some retailers, the high-ranking central government officials leading the inquiry concluded that in following the normal practice of placing their goods with Tongzhou warehousers, the merchants had not been guilty of hoarding. It followed that their stocks were not liable to confiscation, nor were they themselves liable to criminal proceedings. The investigators nonetheless assembled the merchants for an exhortation session, and the report of their address to the merchants casts further light on the legal distinction they may have been making. The merchants were not guilty of *tunji juqi*, a phrase usually translated as "hoarding and speculating," but their action in not promptly releasing their accumulated stocks still constituted *guanwang* behavior. The normal connotation of *guanwang* in Qing official texts is "opportunistically watching developments before committing oneself or one's resources," but in this context it could just as well be translated as "speculation." There is a very fine line between consciously delaying sales of warehoused stocks in the hope of increasing one's profit margin and doing the same with hoards deliberately built for speculative gain.[75] Given that the merchants had been suspected of trying to raise prices, it is permissible to suggest that they were let off lightly because of lack of proof of a conspiracy to manipulate the market price of wheat in Tongzhou and the capital. Of course, corruption may have contributed to the lenient reading of their behavior.

In the event, the merchants suffered the noncriminal penalty of selling their stocks somewhat more quickly than they might have wished and at a price below the market rate. The investigators' report represents this as a voluntary undertaking on their part. The merchants offered to sell the rest of their wheat within two months at a price 0.2 tael per *shi* below the market rate; the investigators recommended that this offer be accepted, and the emperor reduced the merchants' sacrifice by halving their self-imposed price cut and giving them a four-month deadline.[76] If, for the moment, we confine our thinking within the in-

---

75. The investigators had evidence that the wheat deposited in Tongzhou warehouses in 1775 had all been sold by the early summer of 1776 (their report does not specify exactly when in 1777 the last of the 1776 deliveries were sold). Thus the delay in selling large amounts of wheat in the lean summer months of 1778 could easily have been deemed an abuse tantamount to hoarding.

76. 1879 *Tongzhou zhi, juan* 10:23a–27a (reference from Sasaki, "Shindai kanryō," pp. 38–39).

terventionist frame of reference discussed in this chapter, the Tongzhou episode may be said to reflect a certain paradoxical impotence (or
was it only lack of will?) on the part of the Qing state. Obtaining detailed quantitative information was no problem. This inquiry, headed
by no lesser personages than a vice-president of the Board of Justice and
a vice-president of the Board of Revenue, meticulously examined individual ledger entries to verify the merchants' claim that some 10,000 *shi*
of the aggregate stockpile represented wheat already ordered by retailers but not yet delivered to them.[77] However, the terms of the investigation (as reported to the emperor) apparently did not go beyond
confirming the merchants' statements as to the amounts of grain that
had entered or left (or were about to leave) the Tongzhou warehouses.
The investigators were defeated by the difficulty of distinguishing
between warehousing and hoarding, or, in other words, by the problem of establishing deliberate intent to make improper profits by
withholding grain from sale.

   This is not to say that the investigators' handling of the case was
necessarily unwise. To the contrary, if we step outside the interventionist mentality, we can observe that the Qianlong emperor's sof-
tening of the terms on which the merchants were to sell may have
reflected more than the "grace" (*en*) mentioned in his rescript. His
generosity was perhaps motivated by considerations of the best way of
managing commercial supplies during a year of shortage, and by some
recognition of the need to make the flow of grain continuous by limiting its speed. The public might be better served by sales spread over a
four-month period than by sales completed in two months. That in
eighteenth-century China there could be awareness of these issues, and
of the potential role of hoarders in managing shrunken supplies, is a
major theme of chapter 3. Before embarking on it, we have two more
aspects of the interventionist tradition to consider. Both fall generally
within the category of noncoercive practice.

---

77. 1879 *Tongzhou zhi, juan* 10:23a refers to one of the chief investigators as
President of the Board of Justice, but the person in question, Hu Jitang, was not
promoted to this position until 1779. Qian, comp., *Qingdai zhiguan nianbiao*, vol. 1,
pp. 239–40, 627.

2

The Subtler Ways of Handling Hoarders

The previous chapter explored some basically coercive means by which the Qing state and its servants sought to ensure merchant compliance with the indeterminate laws forbidding hoarding. However, there was a noncoercive strand in Qing interventionist practice, and no account of Qing interventionism would be complete without discussion of it. In this chapter, I identify two kinds of basically noncoercive antihoarding practice. These are, first, state selling on the ever-normal principle, and, second, the exhortatory techniques that prudent officials tended to prefer when dealing with landlord speculative hoarders.

Ever-normal cut-price (that is, "[price]-stabilizing") sales may be seen as the Chinese counterpart of the "simulated sales" of eighteenth-century France—although this statement could with greater justice be reversed. The principle that state-run, competitive cut-price sales could moderate high market prices was understood by eighteenth-century officials in both countries.[1] However, while pre-eighteenth-century antecedents for simulated sales may possibly be reflected in one French official's confidence (expressed in 1709) that such competitive selling had been "in all times, the most sure and efficient means to bring down the price of grain,"[2] both the theory and the practice of the Chinese "[price-]stabilizing sale [of grain]" (*pingtiao*) drew on a tradition that was two millennia old by the Qing dynasty. French practitioners of

---

1. On French "simulated sales," see Miller, *Mastering the Market*, chap. 2.
2. Words of one Daguesseau translated in ibid., p. 57.

simulated sales were refining this technique experimentally in a context in which large-scale direct management of commercial grain supplies was an unfamiliar role for government—indeed, one likely to arouse suspicion. Consequently, French practice stressed secrecy, and the government's involvement was often disguised. Working through merchants or other "intermediaries," French officials typically let the public think that market prices were being drawn down through or-dinary commercial processes.[3] In China, by contrast, socially respon-sible manipulation of the price of grain—or, when occasion demanded, of charcoal or even "copper" coin—was a time-honored technique of "Confucian" statecraft (albeit with ancient origins in the rival "Legalist" tradition). Despite (presumably) a hiatus in the Ming dynasty, when the government did not maintain the granary reserves to underpin an ever-normal system, the sight of servants of the state performing cut-price sales in times of dearth was nothing untoward in Chinese cities.[4] In principle, such sales were an expected service.

It will be necessary to discuss the Qing state's ordinary stabilizing sales in part II, for this topic is inseparable from that of the ever-normal granaries. Here, therefore, I introduce instead one variation on the ever-normal theme, the Yongzheng-reign (1722–35) attempt to regulate Beijing grain prices through the "grain bureaus of the Eight Banners." This initiative, whose original purpose was to assure the food supply of improvident bannermen, involved coercion towards the intended beneficiaries, who were, in principle, forbidden to sell spare stipendiary grain to other buyers. Towards the speculator, however, the new program was no more coercive than were ordinary stabilizing sales. Although it came to be perceived as an important means of counter-acting profiteering among Beijing's grain dealers, this program has re-ceived little scholarly attention.[5] Appreciation of the effort that Qing administrators put into such schemes may clarify why, despite pater-nalist concerns that were no less intense than those that drove the

---

3. Ibid., pp. 53–58, 61–71.

4. See, e.g., Will and Wong, *Nourish the People*, pp. 3, 8–11; Hartwell, "Cycle of Economic Change," pp. 132–34; Dunstan, "'Orders Go Forth,'" pp. 73–74.

5. The major study is Hosoya Yoshio, "Hakki beikyoku kō," which offers a different interpretation from mine. See also L. M. Li and A. Dray-Novey, "Guard-ing Beijing's Food Security," pp. 1,008–9; Wu Jianyong, "Qingdai Beijing de liang-shi gongying," pp. 179–81. I thank Lillian M. Li for sending me a copy of Wu's essay.

French "police of grain," Qing recourse to direct monitoring and regulation of the ever-suspect grain merchants seems attenuated compared with *ancien régime* French practice.[6] Heirs to a venerable technique whose French equivalent was an innovation of the "Age of Reason," Qing officials could busy themselves protecting poor consumers without constantly harassing would-be speculators. Study of this particular version of the ever-normal model will also nicely frame the overall transition recounted in this book. The banner grain bureaus represented an ingeniously crafted, finely focused piece of interventionism by the Yongzheng emperor. For reasons discussed in chapter 9, they were abolished by his son in 1752.

In the second part of this chapter, I illustrate a probably common preference for noncoercive approaches when the problem was hoarding on the part of landlords. Moral exhortation was the usual centerpiece of such approaches. An exploration of the reasons for the preference is followed by a case study in which I revisit the deeds of Chen Hongmou in a subsistence crisis in Jiangxi in 1742–43. While previous scholarship has been appreciative of Chen's efforts, my point is that his commitment to noncoercion must have become strong indeed if he persisted in it despite evidence that it was not working. To conclude the chapter, I point out that disinclination to assert state power was less than universal among officials who were faced with widespread landlord hoarding. Not only could the more interventionist envisage extending the state's supervisory capacities into the private granaries of landowners; it is also likely that real pressure, amounting even to coercion, was sometimes exerted against landlord hoarders. Thus in both halves of this chapter, the theme of coercion is not completely absent even though the focus is on subtler methods. Noncoercive techniques could have coercive aspects or contrast with strong-arm methods used by less patient practitioners. The general thesis of these first two chapters is thus amply confirmed. No matter whether the approach was basically coercive or noncoercive, punitive or suasive, the inter-

---

6. While the French "police of grain" should not be represented as rigid or perennially enforced, comparison of chapter 1 above with Kaplan's exposition of the characteristic features of the French "police" approach strongly suggests that Sino-Manchu practice was less systematically coercive and regulatory than was French practice. Kaplan, *Bread*, pp. 66–78, 85–86.

ventionist tradition was strong in eighteenth-century China. The development of the banner grain bureaus reflects that tradition at its most robust.

Enter the Banner Grain Bureaus

In 1728, the Yongzheng emperor established twenty-four state grain-trading offices in Beijing, ostensibly as an act of economic paternalism towards the rank-and-file members of the so-called Eight Banners who were domiciled in that city. The twenty-four actual banners (nominally, eight each for persons of Manchu, Mongol and Chinese ethnicity) constituted the quasi-military structure in which descendants of the mid-seventeenth-century Manchu conquering forces (including Mongol and Chinese adherents) had their lives organized.[7] The economic well-being of the lowlier bannermen frequently required imperial attention, for bannermen were expected to live on stipends, plus the income from any land they might retain from postconquest allocations that had disproportionately favored officers. As banner landholdings shrank into irrelevance, survival on stipends alone became ever more difficult.[8] The Yongzheng emperor's original intention in creating the twenty-four grain-trading offices, or banner grain bureaus (*Baqi miju*, literally "Eight Banner husked-grain bureaus," also known as *guan miju*, official husked-grain bureaus), was to rescue the bannermen from what he represented as their lack of economic sense. However, as the bureaus began to operate somewhat like ever-normal granaries, they were soon acclaimed for their success in checking speculation and thus stabilizing Beijing grain prices.

The edict that founded the bureaus addressed the bannermen's alleged ineptitude in selling part of the grain component of their stipends at low prices, only to be forced to purchase high-priced grain when their supplies ran out. According to the edict, once the bannermen had collected their periodical rice (or, in a minority of cases, millet) allocations from the state granaries in Beijing or nearby Tongzhou, they

---

7. On the Eight Banners, see Elliott's superb recent study, *Manchu Way*. On bannerman residence in Beijing, see ibid., pp. 98–105; Naquin, *Peking*, pp. 372–81, 397–405.

8. Elliott, *Manchu Way*, pp. 191–93, 196–97; Naquin, *Peking*, p. 378; Crossley, *Orphan Warriors*, pp. 48–51.

would sell some of the grain to meet the cost of transporting the rest back to their residences.[9] Those who were "unskilled in matters of contriving livelihood" were selling at low prices without considering the need to make their ration last until the next grain issue. The emperor's proposed solution was not to grant the bannermen subsidies for "porterage," but rather to set up bureaus that would buy and store the grain they wished to sell, releasing grain to them "at an equitable price" when they needed to buy it. He envisaged that there would be profit (the difference between the current prices at which the bureaus would buy and their consumer-friendly resale prices), but ordered the Princes and Grand Ministers in Charge of Banner Matters to deliberate on how the profit should be used to benefit the bannermen.

Is the edict's representation of Yongzheng's motives convincing? It gives the impression that the rank-and-file bannermen were selling grain from their own allocations, but in fact the captains (*zuoling*) or other officers were responsible for collecting the stipends for their whole companies from the state granaries. Some captains were allegedly not above fraud and misappropriation.[10] The point of establishing the bureaus was possibly to bring the marketing of stipend grain under the control of senior banner administrators, thereby ending rackets that it might have been impolitic to mention in an edict. The fact that the Princes and Grand Ministers recommended that the bannermen be strictly forbidden to sell their grain to buyers other than the bureaus is consistent with such an interpretation. Also relevant may be the deliberators' alleged slowness in obeying the emperor's orders to make detailed recommendations as to how his idea should be implemented, and the fact that their initial response utterly failed to satisfy Yongzheng.[11]

---

9. On stipendiary millet, cf. mem. by Grd. Secs., YZ 10/6/8 (d.r.), excerpted in *Yuxing qiwu zouyi*, YZ 10:4a–b (pp. 691–92). The word *mi*, as used in Qing documents, can mean husked grain of any kind. Here, I translate it as "grain," unless the context requires that the type of grain be specified.

10. Dang Guli, YZ 2/8/5, as summarized in E'ertai, *Baqi tongzhi chuji*, vol. 13, *juan* 70:10b (p. 4,516); cf. Hosoya, "Hakki beikyoku kō," pp. 182–84.

11. See the imperial harangue transcribed in E'ertai, *Baqi tongzhi chuji*, vol. 13, *juan* 69:12a–13a (pp. 4,473–75). The emperor demanded that the responsible Grand Ministers return their *yanglian* allowances (salary supplements "for nourishing integrity"), presumably as a punishment for sloth. He seems, however, to have

Whatever the reason for the foot-dragging, the Princes and Grand Ministers eventually devised a scheme under which twenty-six bureaus would be created. There would be two bureaus at Tongzhou, called after the two "wing" divisions of bannermen garrisoned there, as well as twenty-four within the capital. The metropolitan bureaus would be provided with a starting grant of 5,000 taels each, and the Tongzhou bureaus with 8,000 taels each. The difference in capitalization no doubt reflects the fact that the Tongzhou granaries especially served high-status payees, and the Beijing granaries low-ranking officers and ordinary bannermen. The emperor approved the recommendations and ordered that the Board of Revenue find the necessary monies. Several years later, at the beginning of the Qianlong reign, three separate bureaus for the Imperial Household Department bondservants were added.[12]

In 1729, the bureau of the Tongzhou "right-wing" division reported a profit in excess of 400 taels (5 percent) for its first twelve months of operation. The Princes and Grand Ministers had deferred making a recommendation on how profit should be used, and the Tongzhou division now asked leave to retain it as capital for further grain purchases. The emperor's reply that, in future, reports on grain bureau affairs should be presented triennially no doubt constituted tacit consent. A sample triennial report studied by Hosoya Yoshio shows that between 1728 and 1734, the bureau of the Manchu Bordered Red Banner was realizing profit at an average rate of 7.3 percent per annum (with the highest profits in the first three years).[13] Given such business success, it is not surprising that the court soon found it possible to draw upon the banner grain bureaus for other functions. In 1731, for instance, a censor pointed out that letting the brass coins accepted from the people during official cut-price sales accumulate at the Board of

---

thought them guilty of lack of vision and commitment, rather than of collusion or corruption.

12. Ibid., *juan* 69:11b–14b (pp. 4,472–78); *Shangyu qiwu yifu,* YZ 6:1a–3b (pp. 283–88); QCWXTK, vol. 1, *juan* 35, pp. 5,181–82; Hosoya, "Hakki beikyoku kō," pp. 182, 193–94 (cf. QSL/QL, *juan* 64:18b).

13. QCWXTK, vol. 1, *juan* 35, p. 5,182; Hosoya, "Hakki beikyoku kō," pp. 190–93. The Bordered Red bureau's initial capital of 5,177 taels (including a 177-tael bonus from the above-standard purity of the silver provided) earned a net profit of 2,276.5 taels between 1728 and 1734.

Revenue was likely to provoke a rise in the exchange value of coin relative to (unminted) silver. He proposed that, in order to provide an outlet for the coin to flow back to the market, the bannermen be paid an increased proportion of the monetary component of their stipends in coin (instead of silver) for the duration of the sales. The emperor suggested that the Eight Banners open "coin bureaus" (*qianju*) at which the public could obtain the coin released in stipend payments at a better rate than that offered by private coin-shops. The final decision was, however, that this business should be undertaken by the banner grain bureaus, which would bear the cost of transporting the coin from the Board of Revenue and of employing assayers (one per bureau) out of their profits on normal transactions.[14]

Similarly, in the summer of 1732, a rise in the price of beans led to a decision to use the grain bureaus to channel a secure supply of fodder to the bannermen to feed their horses. To cope with the immediate problem, deteriorating *suomi* (an inferior kind of rice) and millet from the Bejing and Tongzhou granaries were to be sold to the bannermen through the bureaus. The famous E'ertai, newly established as one of Yongzheng's two most trusted "inner deputies," did not, however, rest content with such a makeshift solution.[15] Evidently thinking the capital's supply of beans vulnerable as long as it relied on nearby state farms (*zhuang*) plus commercial deliveries from Henan and Shandong, he proposed that these two provinces each be required to provide 50,000 *shi* of beans per year in lieu of part of their grain tribute quota. Here too, the bureaus would be used to sell the fodder to the bannermen. The emperor assented.[16] As one final example from the beginning of the Qianlong reign, in 1738–39 the bureaus featured in plans for special cut-price sales of grain and beans bought north of the Great Wall. The

---

14. *Shangyu qiwu yifu*, YZ 9:4b–8a (pp. 444–51); E'ertai, *Baqi tongzhi chuji*, vol. 13, *juan* 69:19b–23a (pp. 4,488–95); Dunstan, "'Orders Go Forth,'" pp. 73–74.

15. The term "inner deputy" (or "inner-court imperial deputy") is Beatrice Bartlett's. See her *Monarchs and Ministers*, chap. 3, and esp. pp. 90 and 93 for the rise of E'ertai.

16. Mem. by E'ertai and other Grd. Secs., YZ 10/6/8 (d.r.), excerpted in *Yuxing qiwu zouyi*, YZ 10:4a–5a (pp. 691–93); cf. QCWXTK, vol. 1, *juan* 43, p. 5,252. On *suomi*, see Will, *Bureaucracy and Famine*, p. 153.

bureaus were to store the beans and such grain as would be sold within the so-called Inner City, where the bannermen resided.[17]

Not even this last case, however, suffices to explain why, in discussions held in 1751, it was assumed that the key purpose of the bureaus was to help to keep grain prices stable and to counter speculation. Nor does it explain why, in his 1733 proposal that civilian husked-grain bureaus be set up in the major cities of distant Guangdong, the governor-general Emida took the operation of the Beijing bureaus as the model for a price-stabilizing mechanism that would function all year round.[18] To resolve this problem, we need two more pieces of information. First, there was an understanding that the surplus rations of the bannermen made a significant contribution to the subsistence of the general Beijing population and, therefore, to keeping down grain prices on the city's markets. This may be seen in the response to a 1723 proposal for preventing merchant exploitation of stipendiary grain. To the supervising censor Batu, a simple ban on selling stipend grain would put the most effective check on shopkeepers and dealers who flocked to buy the newly-issued rations and withheld them until prices rose. Commenting on his suggestion, the banner commanders-in-chief and the metropolitan prefect pointed out that, although the grain was being bought up by commercial interests, it was at least being kept within the capital. All the city's residents depended on the grain from the state granaries, and if sales by the bannermen were stopped, price rises would be likely. Less sweeping measures were therefore advisable. In future, bannermen who thoughtlessly sold all their grain should be disciplined, while dealers who charged extortionate grain prices during times of shortage should be forced to sell at prices set by the authorities.[19]

---

17. CC, Bd. Rev., QL 3/11/20 and QL 4/3/28; QCWXTK, vol. 1, *juan* 36, p. 5,190. The first of these sources shows that the famous Imperial Household Department merchant Fan Yubin was involved in the grain procurement work on this occasion. Cf. Dunstan, "Safely Supping" and the studies therein cited.

18. QCWXTK, vol. 1, *juan* 37, pp. 5,197–98; Dunstan, *Conflicting Counsels*, pp. 32–33, 59–60.

19. Banner Commanders-in-Chief and Metropolitan Prefect, YZ 1/5/8 (d.r.), excerpted in *Yuxing qiwu zouyi*, YZ 1:1a-b (pp. 509–10); QSL/YZ, *juan* 7:8a-b. Although the emperor accepted this advice, controls were instituted one year later to ensure that only genuinely surplus grain was sold. Captains were to have their subordinate group heads calculate the amount of grain each household would require per stipend period. They were to order that this quantity be retained.

It is not quite clear whether the stipend grain sold by bannermen was thought to be important to the residents of Beijing as a whole, or only to the predominantly banner population of the Inner City.[20] However, the balance of the evidence supports the former view, although it was probably only certain groups within the city's population who ate such grain. Admittedly, a literal reconstruction of the court's early intentions for the bureaus might make one wonder whether enough stipend grain was being sold by rank-and-file bannermen to have much impact in the Outer City. The court had provided for up to 120,000 *shi* to be bought from the bannermen, probably three times per year, and reserved for them to purchase later.[21] Thus the maximum amount that it expected to be purchased for the bureaus was presumably 360,000 *shi* per year. As the bannermen were not to be allowed to sell to buyers other than the bureaus, the court should logically have been assuming that their marketable surplus ought not to exceed this total. In view of the bureaus' original purpose, it is reasonable to assume that Yongzheng envisaged that the grain they stocked would be resold in the Inner City, where it would not necessarily have been in surplus compared with the population's food needs. In itself, the amount of 360,000 *shi* probably represented the annual grain requirement of more than one-fifth of the Inner City population,

---

Before a sale could proceed, the group head was to guarantee in writing that the grain was surplus to the household's needs. He was also to notify the captain. Banner Commanders-in-Chief, YZ 2/5/27 (d.r.), excerpted in E'ertai, *Baqi tongzhi chuji*, vol. 13, *juan* 70:7a-8b (pp. 4,509–12). For 1727 prohibitions of the "reckless" mortgaging and sale of stipend grain, see Hosoya, "Hakki beikyoku kō," pp. 184–85.

20. On the zonal structure of eighteenth-century Beijing, see Dray-Novey, "Spatial Order," pp. 890–91; Elliott, *Manchu Way*, pp. 98–105. According to Dray-Novey, the Inner City was home chiefly to banner families plus some Chinese shopkeepers. For general discussions of the provisioning of Qing Beijing, see L. M. Li and A. Dray-Novey, "Guarding Beijing's Food Security," esp. pp. 996–1,012; Wu Jianyong, "Qingdai Beijing de liangshi gongying"; Li Wenzhi and Jiang Taixin, *Qingdai caoyun*, pp. 59–72, 77–86.

21. A 1751 memorial mentions an "original target" of 5,000 *shi* per bureau (QCWXTK, vol. 1, *juan* 37, p. 5,198). 5,000 *shi* is the amount that could be bought with an initial capital grant of 5,000 taels at the notionally standard grain price of one tael per *shi*. For evidence that, in the Yongzheng period, the stipend grain of rank-and-file bannermen was issued only thrice per year, see Hosoya, "Hakki beikyoku kō," p. 187; L. M. Li and A. Dray-Novey, "Guarding Beijing's Food Security," p. 1,006.

a proportion high enough to give credibility to the new scheme's reported effectiveness in stabilizing market prices. However, if the bannermen were selling only 360,000 *shi* per year at most, and if, as the emperor believed, this total included grain that they would need to replace later for their own subsistence, it is not obvious that, prior to 1728, the bannermen's sales would have made a major contribution to supplying the 350,000 or more Outer City and suburban residents.[22]

Such a view of the metropolitan grain market in the eighteenth century is certainly too narrow. 360,000 *shi* constituted only a minor proportion of the annual total of stipend grain issued to metropolitan bannermen, and it is not clear to what extent the bannermen were really selling grain that was required for their own subsistence.[23] In 1751, it was estimated that, while between 60 and 70 percent of the bannermen's stipend grain was being sold, the bureaus were purchasing only between 20 and 30 percent of it. "The rest all circulates outside, and the common folk rely on it to make ends meet."[24] While it would be unwise to assume that such percentages applied in the late 1720s, there may well have been some spillage between the amounts that the bureaus were designed to buy and those that bannermen found ways of selling. The grain sold may have exceeded 360,000 *shi* per year; it joined that alienated by government officials, banner office-holders, and other high-status payees in a redistribution that was geographical, ethnic, and social.

---

22. The population estimates used in this paragraph (including a figure of at least 500,000 for the Inner City population in the 1720s) are based on Han, *Beijing lishi renkou dili*, pp. 124–28; cf. L. M. Li and A. Dray-Novey, "Guarding Beijing's Food Security," pp. 995–96; Elliott, *Manchu Way*, pp. 117–19. In calculating numbers fed, I have used Wang Yeh-chien's proposed "national average" per capita grain consumption rate of 2.5 *shi* per year ("Food Supply," p. 88).

23. Wu Jianyong states the annual total of stipend grain issued to ordinary metropolitan bannermen in the high Qing era as over 2.4 million *shi* ("Qingdai Beijing de liangshi gongying," p. 170). This is supported by a source of 1752—YFD, QL 17/2/10 (d.r.) (8:1622-1)—which quotes over 600,000 *shi*/quarter. However, 2.4 million may be too high for the Yongzheng reign if indeed stipend holders in 1720s Beijing numbered only about 100,000 (Elliott, *Manchu Way*, pp. 117–19), and if the rates for the two lowest-paid groups were only 11 and 23 *shi* per year (E'ertai, *Baqi tongzhi chuji*, *juan* 29:3b). Han's figures suggest a larger number of stipend holders in the metropolitan area as a whole (Han, *Beijing lishi renkou dili*, pp. 124, 126).

24. QCWXTK, vol. 1, *juan* 37, p. 5,198.

To be sure, food preferences probably limited the demand for stipend grain outside the Inner City. The market for grain sold by rank-and-file bannermen was probably a "lower-orders" one that featured sojourners and migrants, both Chinese and Manchu. Another source of 1751 described the customers for the "old rice and *suomi*" paid out in banner stipends as "bannermen from near and far who have migrated to the capital plus loafers, artificers, and subaltern civil service staff from other areas."[25] This suggests that it was lower-middle-class and under-class outsiders who were prepared to tolerate the low-grade fare imported, in the form of tribute grain, from southern China. As to the habits of the original recipients, Lillian Li and Alison Dray-Novey have argued plausibly that a customary preference for northern dryland crops, combined with distaste for frankly stale rice, was a major reason why so much stipend grain was sold.[26] Perhaps, however, poverty constrained many bannermen to put up with the "old rice" or indeed to buy it when the stocks that they had kept ran out. "Old rice," as issued to bannermen, should still have been "sound rice" (*hao mi*)—as opposed to the leftover "rice of uncertain purity" (*chengse mi*) whose status as a low-priced foodstuff made it especially suitable, in official eyes, for use in relief sales to the nonbanner populace outside the Inner City.[27] Nor should it be assumed that bannermen ate just any northern crop in preference to stale rice. In December 1738, the Board of Revenue proposed final arrangements for the special sales of grain and beans planned for the following spring. It noted that the bannermen domiciled in Beijing tended to eat "old rice," while the city's nonbanner residents ate "miscellaneous cereals," that is, the standard dryland crops of northern China. The bannermen were not accustomed to eating *gaoliang* and the like, and probably would not buy much of such cereals. Consequently, although the millet and *gaoliang* delivered to date should be sold in the

---

25. Ibid., p. 5,197. On the migration of impoverished bannermen to Beijing in the mid-eighteenth century, see Crossley, *Orphan Warriors*, p. 19.

26. L. M. Li and A. Dray-Novey, "Guarding Beijing's Food Security," pp. 1,007–8.

27. QSL/YZ, *juan* 101:5b–6a (reference from Hosoya, "Hakki beikyoku kō," p. 190). On price-stabilizing sales outside the Inner City and the disposal of *chengse mi*, see L. M. Li and A. Dray-Novey, "Guarding Beijing's Food Security," pp. 1,012–13.

Inner City, all further consignments of "miscellaneous cereals" should be placed in extramural depots closer to their likely markets.[28]

It would be rash to assume that, in the 1720s, there was great enthusiasm to buy stipend grain on the part of nonbanner Beijing residents who had grown up in northern China. However, a memorial of 1731 envisaged that grain from the banner bureaus might properly be sold to residents of both the Inner and the Outer City. The author presumably believed that there was some demand for old rice in the Outer City; indeed, his concern was to prevent commercial exports of such rice beyond the city's borders.[29] "Old rice and *suomi*" were marketable commodities even in northern China. In Beijing, they were probably eaten by rank-and-file bannermen, by impecunious southerners, and by other groups that could not afford to be fastidious about their daily fare. Admittedly, we should perhaps not take the claim that all the city's residents relied on grain from the state granaries completely literally, even allowing for the use of *chengse mi* to feed the least fastidious of all. It seems safe to conclude, however, that, like the alienated salary grain of government officials, the grain sold by the bannermen played an important role in the provisioning of Beijing as a whole already in the Yongzheng period.[30]

The second piece of information that shows why the banner grain bureaus came to be seen as tools for year-round price stabilization is that, by the early 1730s, they were being used for exactly this purpose. They did not represent the sole approach to price stabilization, but complemented other sales venues that were intended for nonbanner residents. The 1731 memorial mentioned above explained the principle of bureau stabilizing sales thus: "Should the price of grain go up to some extent, [a portion of the grain in store] is immediately brought out and sold, the wish being to keep the price forever stable."[31] In other

28. CC, Bd. Rev., QL 3/11/20; cf. Hosoya, "Hakki beikyoku kō," p. 197.

29. Aqitu, YZ 8/11/27 (d.r.), excerpted in *Yuxing qiwu zouyi*, Yongzheng 8:13a–b (pp. 679–80).

30. For examples of the impact that alienated official salary grain was seen to have upon the Beijing grain market, see CC, Bd. Rev., QL 4/3/28 and Sanhe et al., QL 8/8/4; QSL/QL, *juan* 566:4a.

31. Aqitu, YZ 8/11/27 (d.r.), in *Yuxing qiwu zouyi*, Yongzheng 8:13a (p. 679). Together with the other evidence cited below, this suggests a need to qualify

words, the bureau administrators were selling grain, presumably at submarket prices, in the manner of the ever-normal granaries, but without the seasonal constraints of ever-normal operations. Although, when faced with actual subsistence crises, county magistrates might make stabilizing sales of ever-normal grain at any time of year, the usual expectation was that ever-normal stabilizing sales would take place in the lean preharvest months. The assumption of a once-yearly, preharvest release of ever-normal stocks corresponded with the principle of once-yearly, post-harvest replenishment (although the fickleness of the post-harvest market often made restocking problematic). By contrast, not only were the banner bureau stocks drawn from stipends paid in fixed, thrice-yearly installments, but the bureaus were originally given monopsony rights over the portions of these stipends that recipients wished to sell. Rebuilding the reserves three times per year was thus comparatively simple. In short, ingenious administrators under the Yongzheng emperor's leadership had taken advantage of an institutional, nonmarket allocation process to invent a mechanism more flexible and responsive than the ever-normal system to smooth price fluctuations on the Beijing grain market. The decision, probably in 1737, to increase the frequency of stipend payments to four times per year no doubt enhanced the bureaus' operations.[32]

Even in the early 1730s, success was not perceived to be complete. According to the 1731 memorialist, since the bureaus' establishment all grain prices in Beijing had been "very stable," except that in the past twelve months they seemed to have crept up again. Secret enquiries had revealed that the explanation lay in purchases by outside merchants, who were transporting grain out of the capital in quantities of up to "a few hundred *shi*" per merchant. This view of causes and effects may not have tallied fully with reality. A reference, in an edict of early 1730, to very low grain prices in recent years (prices so low, indeed, that grain stocked in the bureaus was not selling) must raise questions as to how big the upward fluctuations would have been if there had been no bu-

---

Hosoya's view that there was no serious emphasis on using the grain bureaus for stabilizing sales until the early Qianlong period. "Hakki beikyoku kō," pp. 196–97.

32. For the introduction of quarterly payment, see Hosoya, "Hakki beikyoku kō," p. 187; L. M. Li and A. Dray-Novey, "Guarding Beijing's Food Security," p. 1,006.

reaus.[33] Such doubts, however, are not reflected in the 1731 memorial. This recommends that bureau grain be sold exclusively to Inner and Outer City residents, and that large purchases by outside merchants be explicitly forbidden. The emperor approved this. Whatever his original objectives, by now the monarch was in favor of the bureaus as price-stabilizing tools. When, in 1731, he congratulated himself on their success, his satisfaction was at the stability not of the bannermen's household economies, but of grain prices over the past three years.[34]

Two years later, Emida, as chief administrator of Guangdong, gained Yongzheng's approval for a plan to create similar year-round price-stabilizing institutions in Guangzhou (Canton) and other Guangdong cities without the backing of banner stipends. He relied instead on the volume of grain circulating in the efficient waterborne trade network of the Lingnan provinces (Guangdong and Guangxi). The ready availability of commercial grain outside Guangzhou would enable bureau officers to go, "as convenient, to places where grain is cheap" and spend the proceeds of recent stabilizing sales "so that there is continuous replenishment." The success of the banner grain bureaus in Beijing had inspired Emida to design imitations using the resources available in his own jurisdiction. "*Perceived* success," says the cautious historian—but indeed, Emida claimed to have witnessed the bureaus' effectiveness in the Inner City with his own eyes, and to be in a position to appreciate it, as a native of the capital.[35]

The banner grain bureaus still had their advocates in the early Qianlong period. In 1744, Yong Xing, a Chinese banner commander-in-chief who had been sent to Tongzhou to make stabilizing sales, proposed a revival of the Tongzhou banner bureau system. The two original Tongzhou bureaus had had total capitalization of 16,000 taels, but they had been amalgamated in the mid-1730s, when their total capitalization was cut to 6,000 taels. The result, as Yong Xing described it, was that the single post-amalgamation bureau could buy too small a

---

33. QSL/YZ, *juan* 90:17b–18a (reference from Hosoya, "Hakki beikyoku kō," p. 190); cf. L. M. Li and A. Dray-Novey, "Guarding Beijing's Food Security," p. 1,009.

34. Aqitu, YZ 8/11/27 (d.r.), in *Yuxing qiwu zouyi*, Yongzheng 8:13a–b (pp. 679–80); edict transcribed in *Shangyu qiwu yifu*, Yongzheng 9:11b–12a (pp. 458–59).

35. See memorial translated in Dunstan, *Conflicting Counsels*, pp. 58–60. On the Lingnan grain trade, see Marks, "Rice Prices, Food Supply, and Market Structure."

proportion of the salary grain sold in Tongzhou to compete effectively with the forty to fifty "private bureaus" (*minju*—presumably ordinary grain businesses). The private bureaus, having bought the rest of the salary grain, acted in concert to raise prices even as the banner bureau strove to influence the market in the opposite direction with its cut-price sales. The private bureaus won. Invoking the successful record of the banner bureaus in Beijing, Yong Xing asked that a second banner bureau be re-opened in Tongzhou, that the total capitalization of the Tongzhou banner bureaus be raised to 20,000 taels, and that they be given preemption rights over the salary grain sold in Tongzhou. His proposal was approved.[36]

Both in its resourcefulness and in its premises concerning the proper role of government in the economy, the banner grain bureau experiment was typical of the Yongzheng-period approach to statecraft. As the investigating censor Ma Chang'an explained the value of the banner bureau system two years after Yongzheng's death, "the authorities controlled the power of determination (*quan*) over the current price of husked grain. Wicked merchants and selfish traders were [thus] unable to hoard privily or raise prices in an arbitrary way." For Ma, as for Yongzheng's advisors, it was proper to forbid the sale of stipend grain to any buyer other than the bureaus, for once all the alienated grain was channelled to those agencies, "with the authorities controlling the power of determination, the price of husked grain will naturally be unable to keep rising to high levels."[37] The state thus triumphed over market forces for the good of the consumer. As will be seen, such discourse lost part of its hold over imperial statecraft during the next fifteen years. The robustness of the interventionist tradition in the Yongzheng reign was not to be maintained.

Civility in Place of Chastisement

What of local officials' treatment of landlord hoarders—those who waited to release their large stocks of rent grain until the market offered the best price to be expected before the grain's perishability or their

---

36. CC, Yong Xing, QL 9/6/12; QSL/QL, *juan* 218:12b–13b.
37. CC, Ma Chang'an, QL 2/10/3. For an example of similar state-centered economic rhetoric from Yongzheng's own brush, see Dunstan, "'Orders Go Forth,'" p. 74.

own financial circumstances necessitated sale? Grain sold locally might be consumed in the same neighborhood or region, or it might be bought by interregional trading interests and transported far away. Whether resident or absentee, landlords who hoarded grain while the local peasantry went hungry were already courting resentment, if not violence and looting. However, the export of grain from communities whose subsistence for the coming months seemed insecure was perhaps even more inflammatory.[38] If a landlord hoarded grain in anticipation of a price rise in response to the demand from other provinces, or if he withheld his stocks until external buyers visited his home locality, he arguably added betrayal to callousness. Whatever the reality behind the notion that landlords had customary duties to ensure their tenants' welfare, a man who, for the sake of profit, sent away grain that could have saved the local poor might well seem to be flaunting his indifference to the claims of human solidarity.[39]

There is little reason to doubt that the conventional position among socially-conscious eighteenth-century officials was that hoarding by landlords was immoral. Like popular collective action to block the export of local grain supplies, such hoarding also violated the Qing state's general commitment to free circulation of available grain surpluses. One sometimes finds these two kinds of behavior condemned in the same document, no doubt because they often occurred at the same time and could be seen as interrelated. To Chen Hongmou, writing as Jiangxi governor during the early 1740s food shortage discussed below, the rise in prices caused by hoarding after a poor harvest gave "local ruffians" a pretext for trying to block exports. The "ruffians" ' blockades in turn offered the hoarders an excuse for shutting their granaries tighter than ever. Hoarders, Chen suggested, could fear to sell their

---

38. On the forms taken by subsistence crisis violence, see Will, *Bureaucracy and Famine*, pp. 56–59, 215. Popular hostility towards the export (or re-export) of grain from vulnerable communities is a major theme of Wong, "Food Riots."

39. For the view (based on northern Chinese evidence) that the concept of tenant rights to specific forms of consideration from landlords persisted into the twentieth century, see Thaxton, "On Peasant Revolution," p. 27. By contrast, Will draws on scholarship on the Lower Yangzi region to argue that the rhetoric of a landlord–tenant bond, involving mutual obligations, had ceased to correspond to socioeconomic reality by the mid-Qing, although invocations of the mutual responsibilities of rich and poor still featured in official discourse. Will, *Bureaucracy and Famine*, pp. 68–73.

grain because of the blockades and the generally ugly mood prevailing in the countryside.[40]

It was probably in part because famines tended, in such ways, to sharpen latent class antagonisms that officials commonly preferred to treat landlord speculative hoarders gently and considerately. To force landlords to sell their grain as if they had been merchants would have meant seeming to side with the unruly poor. Unruliness in this context could mean threatening landowners by demonstrating outside their homes, or intercepting merchant boats whose cargoes, from another point of view, were vital grain supplies for urban populations. Again, tenants might refuse to let rent grain out of their villages, thereby depriving the landlords of the wherewithal to pay their taxes.[41] Too clear an expression of sympathy for the perpetrators of such actions would have risked destabilizing the balance of power in the countryside, as well as ignoring the broader implications for state finance and the claims of populations elsewhere. It was more prudent for officials to try to cajole the group closest to them in socioeconomic background into some kind of cooperation than to run such risks.[42] Appeals to the hoarders' true self-interest might be as ineffective as appeals to their moral sense, but at least they would not vindicate the disobedient lower orders. Class solidarity apart, the gamble taken by officialdom was that refraining from alienating the wealthy, literate, and influential members of rural communities would prove more important for preserving the social fabric than adopting strong-arm measures in support of popular demands.

I must enter one caveat before proceeding further. Documentary sources often refer to hoarders by such vague terms as "local rich households" (*difang fuhu*) without differentiating between landlord hoarders, merchant hoarders, landlords who supplemented their rent grain with speculative buying, landlords maintaining hoards in rural areas, and absentee landlords whose stockpiles were kept at urban

---

40. PYTOCG, *juan* 15:26a–b and *juan* 16:4a, 6a, 7a. For another example, see the 1726 memorial by He Tianpei quoted in Abe, *Shindai shi*, p. 495.

41. On the social-order problems accompanying Qing subsistence crises, see Will, *Bureaucracy and Famine*, chap. 3.

42. For a vivid nineteenth-century illustration of the potential for class hatred and violence in the Chinese countryside even (or perhaps especially) where the position of tenants was rather strong, see Bernhardt, *Rents*, pp. 63–66.

residences. Although context or explicit indication sometimes shows that it is mainly landlords whom the author has in mind, in other cases one knows only that the topic is hoarders who are not explicitly identified as merchants. It would be rash indeed to claim that a cajoling strategy was never applied to grain merchants and dealers. To the contrary, local officials may sometimes have found it wiser to use a positive, persuasion-based approach with businesses, especially those thought to be hoarding with intent to sell on local markets, than to threaten or coerce them. However, I have found no explicit eighteenth-century evidence of such behavior, apart from the ambiguous case of the wheat merchants exhorted at Tongzhou in 1778 after being cleared of hoarding.[43] The rationale for a lenient, suasion-based approach is clearest in the case of landlords, as they were conventionally seen as pillars of the social order, and it was obviously important not to undermine them. In what follows, I take the lenient approach as that whose classic application was to landlords, whether resident or absentee. In some cases, however, the "local rich households" targeted by a suasion-based approach probably included commercial interests as well as landlords speculating in the grain from their own fields.

An example of Qing official concern about the risk that interclass relations would be violated during famine is found in Huang Liuhong's famous handbook for local magistrates, the *Fuhui quanshu* [Comprehensive Treatise on Felicity and Kindness] (1699). Huang discusses the problems caused by persons who, being "rich in grain reserves," "shut up their granaries in their greed for generous profits" during famine years. He envisages that such behavior may provoke the hungry to "surround their homes demanding grain, and, if denied, to join together to break down their granaries, [so that], intimidated by their numbers, [the owners] can do nothing." So far from suggesting that the action of the hoarders is illegal, Huang recommends that they be saved from the consequences of their greed without suffering physical violence or material loss. All that he advises magistrates to do is issue exhortations to the "rich families" in good time, urging them on moral grounds to sell or lend their surplus grain. The magistrate should be present when the rich open their granaries, for fear that the hungry people will get out of hand, and he should secure "a slight reduction in the price" at

---

43. See chap. 1 above.

which the grain is sold. Where the owners opt for lending, the magistrate should recognize each contract by adding his official stamp. He should return the contract to the creditor with the promise that his staff will ensure repayment of the loan after the autumn harvest. "If this is done, the rich families will avoid [actual] loss, while the tendency to plunder [stocks of] grain will die down of itself, without [the need for] prohibition."[44]

Other authors focused on the risk that members of the lower orders would take advantage of official prohibitions to put pressure on controllers of large grain stocks. For Chen Hongmou, writing amid the central-Shaanxi drought of 1748, the fear was that "feckless and disreputable persons" would be tempted into such behavior by the fact that he had put the province's internal grain trade under surveillance to ensure that no supplies passed into other provinces. Given that exportation was forbidden, the owners of supplies could be expected to respond to the high prices by selling grain within Shaanxi; however, the "feckless and disreputable" might first take advantage of the posted surveillance warnings to accuse merchants and other grain-owners of hoarding, to attempt to buy or borrow their supplies by force, or, if frustrated, to intimidate them by denouncing them to the authorities. Besides having county magistrates warned not to be hoodwinked by such denunciations, Chen authorized the victims of forced sale or loan attempts to have their local security representative (*xiangbao*) report their tormentors immediately to the authorities, who were to arrest the malefactors.[45]

Chen was not alone in fearing lest official controls on grain trade activities provoke unruly persons to "form gangs, make demands [of grain-owners], and harass [them]."[46] An imperial edict of July 1743 alleged that if, during subsistence crises, public notices were posted ordering "rich households" to make rent concessions or to sell off their surplus grain, the wicked would regard such actions not as voluntary expressions of community awareness, but rather as the grain-

44. Huang, *Fuhui quanshu, juan* 27:19a–b. Cf. Djang Chu's rendering of this passage in Huang, *Complete Book*, pp. 567–68.

45. PYTOCG, *juan* 28:3a–4a. On the 1748 Shaanxi export ban, see chap. 1 above and Dunstan, *Conflicting Counsels*, pp. 251–53 and 264–67.

46. PYTOCG, *juan* 28:4a.

controllers' legal obligations. The depraved lower-class wretches would see any reluctance to fulfill these "obligations" to their satisfaction as justifying them in taking the law into their own hands. "If [the grain-controllers] slightly fail to meet their wishes, they promptly [start to] harbor thoughts of robbery." The emperor claimed that "such cases" (presumably meaning raids on private granaries that had originated in official notices ordering the rich to sell their surplus grain) had recently been reported from several southern provinces.[47]

The vice censor-in-chief Fan Can took up the refrain some eighteen months later in an important memorial that will be discussed in the next chapter. Advocating that exhortation to the rich to sell their grain be done in secret, he drew up a litany of ways in which the "wicked and refractory" might take advantage of publicly posted notices forbidding the prolonged storage of grain. A quotation will best serve to give the flavor:

[The wicked and refractory will be likely to] spread talk about how much the Court loves and cares for the masses of the poor, deluding the respectable and good, and forming bands and gathering crowds. They may go up to the gates [of wealthy households] and jostle and insult [the owners]; or they may indulge in fights and commit crimes of violence; or they may brazenly label as great households [families] that have [only] a modest competence; or they may accuse [families] that have retained small quantities of food [for their own] use of having surplus stocks. . . . Worst of all, they [may] take advantage of the fact that there exists a basis [in the shape of the official prohibition] for their putting pressure [on grain-holders] to give free rein to their evil habᵗ ; of plundering and robbery.[48]

Partly in order to avoid such disturbances, Fan recommended the wider adoption of a method that he had found successful during his recent governorship of Anhui. When subsistence crises threatened, holders of relatively modest stocks should be quietly persuaded to sell them off in small amounts; those with "full thousands and heaped tens of thousands" of bushels should be encouraged to set up "bureaus for the sale of grain" (*tiaoju*) under their own management in nearby villages. There should be no compulsion to sell below the current price,

---

47. QSL/QL, *juan* 193:13b–14a.

48. QSL/QL, *juan* 230:24a, emended by reference to the version of Fan's text quoted in Kishimoto, *Shindai Chūgoku no bukka*, p. 313.

but hoarders who did should be publicly honored in proportion to their sacrifice.[49]

The idea of exhorting landowners to sell their grain was far from being new with Fan Can. Robert Hymes has described this approach as "a commonplace" of famine relief administration in the Song dynasty (960–1279), when it was known as "exhorting [the rich] to share [their grain]," *quan fen*.[50] The effectiveness of the approach depended on the power of appeals to moral sentiment, coupled with the strength of belief that there was social capital to be gained from public tokens of official approbation, or social peril in incurring visible expressions of official disapproval. Fan may have been unusual in his insistence on discretion. Will cites the (possibly apocryphal) case of a nineteenth-century magistrate whose mixture of incentives to the local gentry to contribute to a privately-run famine relief bureau included the threat of moral pillorying. Noncontributors would be required to display a door plaque identifying them by name as "inhumane in spite of being rich." As the magistrate forbade the local people to take advantage of the plaques to "persecute" despicable rich neighbors, he must have been aware of the danger.[51] The risk, however, was well calculated. A wise magistrate tried to win over to the path of conscience all local members of his class who could be won. As long as popular feelings against hoarders were running high, it could be prudent for him to dissociate himself from the recalcitrant, in order to ward off the hostility that might have been turned against him for not taking stronger action.

At the time of Fan's memorial, the use of moral suasion against landlord hoarders was imperial policy. It had been asserted as such by the 1743 edict cited above, a pronouncement that seems motivated largely by the state's need for a stronger rhetorical position from which to invoke the law's full rigor against those who looted private grain bins in subsistence crises. Of course, a faster flow of private stocks to local markets would, in the short term, have soothed the feelings of potential looters, thereby making robbery less likely. Thus a desire constructively to mitigate the social tensions in the countryside was no doubt also present in the thinking of the court. County magistrates

---

49. QSL/QL, *juan* 230:23a–b.
50. Hymes, "Moral Duty," p. 281.
51. Will, *Bureaucracy and Famine*, pp. 59–60.

were to be secretly instructed that, during acute food shortages, they should urge the local wealthy to release their grain. So skilful and resourceful should their exhortations be that the rich would comply with pleasure, understanding that it was not morally permissible to try to influence the market price by clinging to one's surplus. If this seems a simple order that magistrates use their full persuasive powers to free incarcerated grain, the main thrust of the edict as a whole is insistence on the need to repress looting. Looting is represented as a more serious matter than being "inhumane in spite of being rich," and it is to incur severe chastisement. Looting is a violation of the law; if hoarding is as well, the fact goes without mention.[52]

Chen Hongmou's Jiangxi experience with landlord hoarders. The territorial bureaucracy had not uniformly waited to be told that landlord hoarders should be urged, not forced, to sell their stockpiled grain. To the contrary, for several months before the 1743 edict, Chen Hongmou had been using just such an approach as governor of Jiangxi, which suffered a food shortage in 1742–43. Although his policy on this occasion has been discussed by others, it is worth scrutinizing his experience to clarify nuances that previous scholarship has missed.[53] Specifically, R. Bin Wong has written of the mix of crisis management activities undertaken in Jiangxi in 1743 that "The state successfully met the challenge of harvest scarcities," while William Rowe claims that "Ultimately, the bountiful harvest of 1743, in conjunction with Chen's own dearth-management policies . . . , brought the crisis to a successful end."[54] My reading of Chen's series of directives from the spring and summer of 1743 is, by contrast, that any successes he may have enjoyed did not include the strategy of cajoling wealthy landlords to sell hoarded grain. My point here is not so much that the persuasion-based approach was ineffective, but rather that Chen persisted with it despite its poor results. Landlord speculative hoarders could be triumphantly successful in manipulating prices on the local grain market, and still the state did not use force against them.

---

52. QSL/QL, *juan* 193:13b–14b.

53. Cf. Wong, "Food Riots," pp. 772–74; Rowe, "State and Market," pp. 12–13 and, more recently, *Saving the World*, pp. 180–83.

54. Wong, "Food Riots," p. 774; Rowe, *Saving the World*, p. 177.

Chen professed to regard the landlord hoarders' behavior as immoral.[55] Nonetheless, in the delicate and complex situation that he faced in 1742–43 Jiangxi, he showed a consideration for their interests that is no less remarkable for being chiefly tactical. While harvests had been bad in 1742, private reserves of grain were not entirely depleted, and Chen tended to blame the prevalence of high grain prices on the twin forces that, as mentioned earlier, he thought were keeping available stocks off the market. As he summarized the situation at the time of the 1743 summer harvest,

> While there has still been grain within each neighborhood, [its owners] have either been wholly given over to securing a high price, and have not been prepared to let their grain go lightly, or else have only planned on distant sale, and have not been willing to sell near at hand. The poor and needy households of the district have not been without a certain tendency to take advantage and to block the passage [of the grain], not permitting distant sale, while the wealthy households have grown even more unwilling to lend or sell because of these obstructions. The reason for which grain has become daily scarcer while its price has daily risen is, in reality, the obstinate wrangling between rich and poor.[56]

While this passage suggests that, in many cases, grain was being withheld from the local market because its owners believed that they could secure higher prices by selling it for interregional export, Chen's earlier directives seem to reflect an assumption that the typical hoarder was speculating, rather, on the local market. The local market was understood to be susceptible to pressure from outside demand; the resulting higher prices on the local market would reward the speculator who waited long enough before he sold, no matter where his grain was eaten.[57] As we shall see, Chen cast part of his appeal to the hoarders in

---

55. PYTOCG, *juan* 16:3b–4a. For Chen, even hoarding limited amounts of grain as insurance for one's own household subsistence was in the category of actions that "do not deserve severe reproach." Ibid., *juan* 15:21a.

56. Ibid., *juan* 16:14a.

57. Cf. the first half of an earlier version of Chen's explanation for the high grain prices in Jiangxi. Close to the beginning of 1743, Chen wrote that the *cherté* (dearness) "actually results from [the action of] the local rich households, [who] on first hearing that grain was dear in other provinces, and that there [would be] a great deal of buying [on the Jiangxi market], formed the opinion that later on the price of grain would naturally be bound to increase daily, and for this reason were

terms of their own financial interests. In his admonitory rhetoric, he addressed hypothetical hoarders whose calculations focused on the rising prices of the local market, and he tried to convince them that there was nothing to be gained by further obstinacy.

Perhaps Chen's problem was partly that he had misconstrued the intentions of much of his intended audience. As a relative newcomer to the Middle Yangzi provinces, he may not have allowed for the attractions, for some wealthy landowners, of selling their grain directly to exporting merchants or to brokers servicing the export trade.[58] Two passages quoted by Shigeta Atsushi provide virtually contemporaneous evidence, from adjacent Hunan, that such attractions were important. The first text, dated 1745, describes "great traders" going with their silver to the rice brokers of the Changsha region straight after harvest. The brokers would take the merchants on buying tours of the countryside to stock up with grain for export, in response to which "the very wealthy [would] exorbitantly raise the price [that they asked for their grain]." The second text, defending the liberty of "grain-possessing families" to sell onto the export market, argues that their convenience demands that they be allowed to dispose of stocks in bulk, whether by placing them with brokers or by selling them to "outside merchants."[59] If, in early 1743, major Jiangxi landlords were still awaiting visits from rich merchants to whom they could name their price, or if they too saw in the export trade the best opportunity for selling their stocks smoothly, Chen's economic homilies were misdirected.

Chen's policy during the first half of 1743 had three interwoven strands. He tried to ease the crisis by making grain supplies available from the ever-normal and community granaries. He used admonition and prohibition, backed by the threat of punishment, to discourage popular attempts to frustrate would-be grain-exporters, not to mention rent resistance, forced loans, forced cut-price sales, and other misdemeanors of the anxious poor. At the same time, he sought to allay popular fears by coaxing hoarded grain onto the market. His initial

unwilling to release their grain for sale" (PYTOCG, *juan* 15:20b; for a different interpretation of this passage, see Wong, "Food Riots," p. 772).

58. Chen, a native of Guangxi, had been in Jiangxi only since the early autumn of 1741. Qian, comp., *Qingdai zhiguan nianbiao*, vol. 3, p. 1,827; vol. 2, p. 1,594.

59. Shigeta, *Shindai shakai keizai shi*, p. 43.

efforts to induce the wealthy hoarders to release their stocks relied entirely on exhortation. His first directive on this crisis, issued near the beginning of 1743, includes a proclamation to "the denizens of the entire province, military or civilian, scholar or commoner," of which the parts addressed to hoarders appeal to their consciences, invoke the superstition that immorally gained wealth will not endure, and try to make the speculator's judgment for him. Chen told the hoarders that "By now the price [that one might wait for] is already to be had; those houses that have grain ought precisely to be selling it so as to make substantial profit." He advised them that, because large-scale, official stabilizing sales would soon take place (reinforced by loans from the community granaries), "there is definitely no reason to expect the price to go up further than its present level." If the hoarders sold now, they would gain higher prices than in previous years, besides contributing substantially to community well-being.[60]

It is surely not surprising that the hoarders remained unconvinced by such a rash and premature prediction as to price behavior. About four months later, with at best several weeks to go until the summer harvest, Chen was exclaiming: "High prices such as these have hitherto been seldom seen. If these people are still not selling, whenever are they going to do so?"[61] He had already made it easier for them to sell by taking measures of the kind advocated by Huang Liuhong to ensure their security. He had ordered that local authorities issue special notices to protect those grain owners who were deterred from selling by fear of crowd action. The local officials were also to send personnel to keep order at the sales. Chen had sought to make lending more attractive by ordering the offer of official guarantees that loans of grain would be repaid with interest.[62] At this point, however, he changed tactics

---

60. PYTOCG, *juan* 15:20a–23a. Chen's appeal to the hoarder's interests is in marked contrast to the hyperbolical moralism that dominates the thirteenth-century antihoarding exhortation translated by Hymes ("Moral Duty," pp. 305–6). It may not have been significantly less naive, however.

61. PYTOCG, *juan* 16:4a. This directive is dated QL 8 (1743), fourth moon. The summer harvest was in the fifth moon, but there was an intercalary (second) fourth moon in 1743.

62. Ibid., *juan* 16:7a and 14a. Chen noted that the interest should be at the usual rate. He had earlier forbidden the wealthy to value loans according to the current, elevated price of grain and then charge compound interest on them. Ibid., *juan* 15:22b.

somewhat, ordering more intense measures of persuasion including a program of officially-sponsored and official buying. Besides saving hoarders the embarrassment and possible danger of dealing directly with the public, this program would challenge them with the awkwardness of a refusal to sell even to the government or its appointed agents.

The plan was conceived as one that could be implemented anywhere in the province, with flexibility to accommodate diverse local conditions. The broad objective was simply to have grain acquired for depleted local markets. The program was, however, also to serve the more specific purpose of dissolving hoards. In the directive that announced the scheme, Chen admitted that he lacked full information as to the prevalence of hoarding over the whole province. It was possible that in some jurisdictions "there is really not much grain," and the holdings of the wealthy were only for their own consumption. He mentioned that he had reports of socially responsible rich people and local gentry who had bought grain especially for nonprofit (or low-profit) sale to poorer neighbors. However, such semi-philanthropy had a major limitation. "Those willing to make outlays do not necessarily possess much silver, while those who have the silver are not necessarily prepared to lay it out. To bind them with official law would be close to harassment and the imposition of forced contributions."

Faced with the reality that those with rich reserves of silver were unlikely to be more public-spirited than were those with rich reserves of grain, Chen envisaged supplementing the limited private initiatives with a program financed from official coffers. Public funds should be entrusted to selected prosperous and well-motivated elders or local gentry, who would buy grain for resale to the public on a cost-recovery basis. The grain should be acquired in the first instance from local grain-owners, who should be paid "in ready silver at the market price." If it was necessary to buy outside the county, the authorities should issue their agents with safe-conducts and "notify the civil and military officials along the route that they are not to be impeded." The agents should recycle the capital as many times as the market situation in their home community demanded, before returning the original sum to the county treasury at the end of the operation. "If this is done, it will be possible for all the grain available in each locality to reach the market, and the grain of other places, near and far, will also be allowed to circulate." Hoarders who wished to sell or lend their grain themselves should be helped in the ways already indicated, but "those who do not wish to lend must not be forced."[63]

Another directive issued a little later specifically addressed the application of the plan to "wealthy hoarding households." Here, Chen modified his earlier orders that agents buying grain from local grain-owners should pay the market price. This was now to apply only as long as the market price did not exceed one tael per *shi* (presumably of unhusked rice).[64] If the market price had surged above one tael per *shi*, a compromise price was to be paid for hoarders' stocks. Although this would be lower than the market price, it should be set high enough to gratify the hoarders, "in the hope that they will be prepared to sell, vying only to be first. All that should not be permitted is further, opportunistic, large price increases." We may perhaps infer that some of the hoarders, noting that the official-sponsored purchases were to be at the market price, had done their very best to jack the latter up before they took advantage of the deal Chen had offered.

Chen also gave new instructions for dealing with major hoarders. County magistrates, he said, were sure to know who were the big grain-owning households in their jurisdictions. If there were any hoarders who had "full thousands and heaped tens of thousands of *shi*," the magistrate should ask them to visit him, or he should call on them in person. He should appeal to their consciences and help them to a clearer understanding of their own self-interest in the matter. He should propose that the county administration buy their grain and sell it locally, thereby securing them against the risk of interference by the

---

63. Ibid., *juan* 16:6a–7a.

64. In July, the Jiujiang customs superintendent reported recent (husked) rice prices of 2.6 to 2.7 tls./*shi* in three northern Jiangxi prefectures, with still higher levels (3.3 to 3.4 tls./*shi*) at Jingde Zhen (CC, Tang Ying, QL 8/5/22). These prices, consistent with Chen's remark that "High prices such as these have hitherto been seldom seen," confirm that Chen's ceiling of one tl./*shi* must have referred to unhusked rice. In a producer province like Jiangxi, one tl./*shi* for husked rice (a level that Qing bureaucrats took as the general norm) may still have been a relatively high price in the early 1740s, but it was not a famine rate. Cf. Chuan and Kraus, *Mid-Ch'ing Rice Markets*, table D–6, pp. 141–43; Will, *Bureaucracy and Famine*, pp. 133 n. 12, 184 n. 23. Although Chen did not say explicitly that the ceiling of one tl./*shi* was for unhusked rice, he consistently used the word *gu* (unhusked grain) to refer to the stocks that he hoped would be bought from hoarders. PYTOCG, *juan* 16:3b, 6b.

crowd or actual violence. Chen suggested that refusal of such an offer would be an act of sheer irrationality, because the summer harvest was not far away, and popular blockades prevented grain-owners from sending grain to any market other than the local one. Recalcitrant hoarders risked being left with a devalued stock on their hands, having incurred popular ill-will for nothing.

Such *tête-à-têtes* with brazen hoarders were apparently as far as Chen instructed his subordinates to go. The man who had, in frontier Yunnan in 1736, threatened summary beating to death for those hoarders whom he thought most callous did not order coercion against the wealthy grain-controllers of the heartland province of Jiangxi. The last substantial order in this same directive is that local officials inform him whether or not any individual hoards within their jurisdictions exceeded 1,000 *shi*. However, they were not to send personnel to ascertain the exact size of the large hoards, because that would be "akin to searching."[65] We may surmise that there was nothing further from Chen's mind than coercion.

In these later directives, Chen made some concessions to local demands that grain not be removed from the communities that had produced it. He ordered, for example, that whereas crowds could not be allowed to obstruct the passage of commercial grain that was merely in transit, "it should be permitted for the grain of a given locality to be sold preferentially within it." If there were any surplus, it could be transported to help neighboring counties. As Chen went on to specify that persons who impeded the export of surplus grain should be duly arrested, we may say that he maintained a prudent emphasis on discipline for lower-class offenders. Nonetheless, it is likely that the wording I have quoted was carefully formulated to give his subordinates tacit approval for declaring county-level export bans if necessary. Officially-declared grain-export bans were controversial, and there was no guarantee that imperial authorization, if sought, would be granted. In the tense weeks before the summer harvest in 1743 Jiangxi, it would have been sensible for the provincial governor to give county magistrates to understand that no action would be taken against

---

65. PYTOCG, *juan* 16:3a–5b. On Chen's tough stance in Yunnan in 1736, see above, introduction.

them should they prevent the export of grain that was not clearly surplus.[66]

This subtle shift of policy, combined with Chen's incidental acknowledgment (cited above) that the popular blockades were working, raises the question whether his approach, tested by a half-year of crisis, can really be considered a success. It would, of course, be unreasonable to deny that "Without the distribution of granary reserves, it is likely that the number of riots that took place in the spring of 1743 would have been far greater than the 160 that actually occurred."[67] Yet the figure of 160 is not small. On this occasion, did the authorities "lead" and "guide" the "stupid people," or were they led by them? One is forced to suspect the latter. Chen issued his first directive against speculative hoarding and popular export blockades in approximately January; both were still rampant in approximately May. If the speculators did sell during the next month or so before the summer harvest, they had probably been intending to do so all along. If they did not, it would seem likely that, as discussed earlier, they had been keeping their stocks for the interregional grain market, in which case Chen's appeal to their economic rationality was misapplied. In the meantime, they had surely been gratified by continuing rises in the market price. They were ultimately to have the pleasure of extracting, albeit indirectly, some of their highest prices of the season from the very authorities whom they had driven to allot funds to buy up their stock. If the original plan was followed, these prices will have been recouped from ordinary consumers.

It would be careless to assume that all premodern Chinese landlords were unscrupulous profit-maximizers. To the contrary, displays of landlord social responsibility in contributing to and organizing local

---

66. PYTOCG, *juan* 16:9a; see also pp. 4a and 5a in the same *juan*. On the uncertain prospects of gubernatorial requests for export-ban approval, see Will, *Bureaucratie et famine*, pp. 186 n. 78, and 187–88 (or pp. 215–16 of the English translation, in which the paragraph in question has been changed); Dunstan, *Conflicting Counsels*, pp. 254–56.

67. Wong, "Food Riots," p. 773. Wong's quotation (ibid.) of a list of meritorious types of action gives the impression that official exhortations to grain-owners had borne fruit. In fact, Chen's purpose in making the list was only to specify actions that should be rewarded.

famine relief are well attested for the Jiangnan region.[68] Nonetheless, the conclusion drawn above reinforces similar findings by Kathryn Bernhardt and Richard von Glahn. Landlords and investors whose priority was gain would not be greatly swayed by bureaucratic exhortation drives.[69]

When the Strong Arm Menaced Landlords

It is therefore not surprising that one occasionally finds suggestions of more-or-less coercive means being adopted against landlord hoarders. To be sure, in some of these cases landlord status was a background factor, the activity that provoked government wrath being of a commercial or even industrial nature. In 1743, for example, an edict ordered the Jiangsu authorities to take effective action against a form of speculative hoarding called *zhantun*, "warehouse hoarding," that was reportedly carried out by "landed families" of the Suzhou area. While the only measures specified in the edict are exhortation and secret investigation, the emperor referred to his "repeated" previous prohibitions of the practice, which presumably implies that firmer action was expected.[70] Earlier, in the poor-harvest year of 1737, the emperor ordered severe action against hoarding by (primarily) "distilling houses throughout the region south of the capital," some of which were probably rich landowning families. This was a special case: three months earlier, in an attempt to save grain for famine-prevention, the emperor had "perpetually" banned liquor distillation in northern China. The distilleries had allegedly responded by "hoarding grain in the hope that the interdiction [would] be lifted, or waiting until the price of grain [had] soared in expectation of substantial profit." The recommendation on which the court was acting had envisaged that the liquor makers (and other hoarders) be merely admonished to set aside the grain needed by their own households and to put the rest on

---

68. E.g., Wu Tao, "Qingdai Jiangnan shequ zhenji." For a history of philanthropy in late imperial China, see Liang, *Shishan yu jiaohua*.

69. Cf. Bernhardt, *Rents*, pp. 62–63; von Glahn, "Community and Welfare," p. 233. Rowe, *Saving the World*, pp. 182–83, recognizes the inadequacy of Chen's assumptions but manages to end on a positive note.

70. QSL/QL, *juan* 189:17b–18a.

sale at the market price. The emperor found this idea too mild. In his view, offenders were so reprobate as to justify punishment without warning. Local administrators must therefore not content themselves with posting proclamations but must act promptly and decisively to stamp out hoarding.[71]

A case of potential recourse to coercion against ordinary landlord hoarders may be cited from the earlier career of Chen Hongmou. In the 1736 proclamation in which he threatened beating to death for people who built hoards with newly ripened beans or wheat, Chen had cautioned the "grain-possessing families" of Yunnan that if they did not respond to his appeal to release grain hoarded from the previous year's harvests, they would not only be forced to sell under official supervision at a reduced price, but would also see some of their grain confiscated and distributed to the needy. This would be a lesson to those who were "inhumane in spite of being rich." The context suggests that this threat was addressed to landowners, for it is followed by a separate message for merchants and brokers, who were warned that arrest and criminal proceedings would be their lot if they charged exorbitant prices.[72]

Even without the central or provincial government mandating actual coercion, it was possible for the state to put more pressure on landlord and other local hoarders than Chen envisaged in Jiangxi in 1743. There was the most orthodox of precedents for state intrusions into private storage areas. While prefect of Nankang (in present-day Jiangxi), the high priest of Song Neo-Confucianism, Zhu Xi (1130–1200), had ordered "systematic" investigations of the size of rural household grain reserves, thus enabling the authorities to identify those families that could "make private relief sales" to their less fortunate neigh-

---

71. QSL/QL, *juan* 48:17b–18a. On the 1737 distillation ban, see Dunstan, *Conflicting Counsels*, pp. 203–6. That some of the liquor manufacturers were rich landowners is suggested by a reference, in a dissenting memorial, to "prominent and wealthy families with their high walls and deep courts, where search and arrest reach not," who would dare to defy the liquor prohibition. Sun, *Sun Wending Gong zoushu, juan* 8:20a, translated in Dunstan, *Conflicting Counsels*, pp. 228–29.

72. PYTOCG, *juan* 4:13a–b; see also Shigeta, *Shindai shakai keizai shi*, p. 41. Shigeta refers, with inadequate substantiation, to examples of bans (presumably entailing threats of coercion) against landlord speculative hoarding in Hunan.

bors. Such identification would itself have been a form of pressure, whether Zhu intended to force the richer families to sell or not.[73]

Somewhat similarly, in 1744 the Fujian governor Zhou Xuejian designed a voluntary incentive scheme under whose guise local administrations would have monitored the size of private grain reserves while seeking to promote social responsibility among their owners. Although probably not implemented, his proposal shows what one high regional official thought worth trying. Zhou suggested that, following good harvests, prosperous farming families and wealthy landowners be directed to report the amount of grain that they had put in store, apart from that set aside for their own household consumption. At the same time, they should be asked whether they would be willing to save their surplus for the assistance either of their own community or of some other jurisdiction that might find itself in shortage. The next year, participants would be expected to report where, in the preharvest season of high prices, they had sold their grain and how much they had charged. Their selling price was to be the current market price or lower. Tokens of official recognition would be given to those who had sold for less than the market price, the highest award (for sellers of over 3,000 *shi* at cut-price rates) being the right to wear the hat button of an eighth-rank (very junior) official. Presumably to facilitate verification of the amounts sold, the monitoring of the amounts held prior to sale was to be exact and bureaucratic. Between making their original, post-harvest report and the end of the old year, participating households were to report any sales that they might make to meet their "urgent needs." These amounts would be deducted before a year-end register of reported holdings was made for the perusal of the magistrate's superiors.

Zhou's scheme was one proposed solution to that central problem of mid-Qing political economy, how to encourage the maintenance of private grain reserves (to supplement the limited holdings of state and state-sponsored granaries) without multiplying the number of potential

---

73. Hymes, "Moral Duty," p. 303; cf. von Glahn, "Community and Welfare," pp. 232–33 for further detail. Von Glahn states that Zhu "did endorse coercive measures to compel the wealthy to sell grain during times of famine" (p. 233), while Zhihong Liang Oberst has argued that coercion was a feature of many *quan fen* schemes in the Song dynasty, including Zhu's. See her "Chinese Economic Statecraft," pp. 202, 209–13, 231–42.

speculative hoarders. Although he presented his plan as one that used incentives, not coercion, the registration of participants' reserves might have tempted local officials to try to supervise the use that landed grain controllers (including holders of a mere 100 *shi*) made of their private property. It is not surprising that, in his noncommittal reply, the emperor reminded Zhou of the unsuitability of legislative, regulatory approaches in matters of this kind. "The folk's convenience" (that is, the freedom of landed grain owners) was to be respected.[74] Zhou had dreamed the eighteenth-century administrator's dream of state-directed private hoard formation. Although theoretically captivating, such deep state penetration of the agrarian economy would have fitted poorly with the characteristic late-imperial policy of sensitivity to landed interests as the mainstay of the social order.

Zhou Xuejian's plan was perhaps only elaborate wishful thinking. There was greater real likelihood of pressure being put on hoarders when official funds were allocated to buy hoarded stocks. When a subsistence crisis was developing in Shaanxi in 1737, for instance, the governor-general asked permission to issue a temporary ban on hoarding by the rich, along with all grain buying by merchants or neighboring provinces, so that the authorities could secure the grain needed for relief sales and loans. While his main concern was presumably to ensure that local markets had enough stocks to sustain official buying, direct official contacts with the hoarders may have involved thinly disguised coercion. Similarly, an edict of 1723, in ordering firm action to address a worsening subsistence crisis in Henan, directed the governor to "make plans in advance so that the grain of the rich families"—constantly wont to "store up grain in order to reap speculative profits"—"may all circulate [or] be sold to the authorities for relief purposes." Although this edict prescribed no specific means, its main utility was no doubt to strengthen the position of the Henan territorial bureaucracy in putting pressure on the hoarders.[75]

---

74. QSL/QL, *juan* 219:16a–17a.

75. QSL/QL, *juan* 49:18a–b; QSL/YZ, *juan* 7:17b–18a and QCWXTK, vol. 1, *juan* 35, p. 5,177. In 1721, the Kangxi emperor had allotted 500,000 taels from the Imperial Household Department treasury (presumably for buying hoarded stocks) and sent two high metropolitan officials to Shaanxi to "exhort rich households to sell their [hoarded] grain according to the market price." Exhortation by imperial

It was probably inevitable, given the unclear status of speculative hoarding in Qing law, that there would be diversity of practice among officials dealing with hoarders of any kind, landlord no less than merchant. As shown in the next chapter, a Manchu governor-general called Celeng alleged in an anti-interventionist tirade that a good deal of coercive practice took place under the name of "exhortation." To suggest that it was usually the less experienced, more hot-headed territorial officials who were prone to forcing wealthy landed families to sell their grain is not to claim that resort to such measures was uncommon. Other things being equal, the use of coercion against landlord hoarders was more likely in jurisdictions where there were few influential landlord hoarders who had personal connections to officialdom. Thus the experience and temperament of the local magistrate (or his superiors) were not the only factors. It would be rash to speculate as to the relative frequency of coercive and noncoercive actions against landlord hoarders over the whole of mid-Qing China. What can be said is that there was an articulate body of opinion in favor of genuinely noncoercive exhortation, which had been commended to local officials in an administrative handbook published in 1699 and which was declared imperial policy in 1743.

In 1745, a reversal of the policy of 1743 began a three-year episode of heightened prohibitionism towards both mercantile and landlord hoarding. That this could happen underscores the indeterminacy of the Qing state's position on hoarding. It is also consistent with other radical and sudden shifts of economic policy in the early Qianlong reign.[76] A major purpose of the next chapter is to refine our understanding of mid-Qing bureaucratic views on antihoarding prohibitionism by examining some responses to the events of 1745–48, among other midcentury texts by senior officials.

I conclude the present chapter with three observations. First, in discussing the variety of antihoarding measures that prevailed in eighteenth-century China, chapters 1 and 2 have confirmed that speculative hoarding was commonly regarded as a harmful practice that demanded governmental intervention of some kind. This was the

---

envoys was surely harder to resist than that by mere local officials. QCWXTK, vol. 1, *juan* 34, p. 5,175.

76. Cf. Dunstan, "'Orders Go Forth,'" esp. pp. 75–86, 131–34; chaps. 5–8 below.

conventional position; chapter 3 will assess how radically it was challenged in the later 1740s.

Second, chapter 1 in particular has illustrated the amount of information on the grain trade that eighteenth-century administrators and policy advisors had at their disposal. Potentially, senior officials had access to highly detailed information, both on quantitative aspects and on specific market networks. However, some problems remained. For example, the available data collection mechanisms did not capture all small-scale movements of commercial grain. Given that much grain moved in small consignments, this limitation left a cumulatively vast amount outside the purview of the state. Perhaps of more practical consequence were the ambiguities involved in the notion of "hoard." The sensible official would have stopped short of so designating every large accumulation of unsold commercial grain. Unfortunately for the less sensible (and for perplexed judicial investigators), criteria for distinguishing between illegally hoarded and innocently warehoused grain were lacking. The scale of the difficulties that this lack could cause is shown in a midcentury fiasco whose story and significance will be addressed in chapter 3.

Finally, to pass from knowledge to ideology, material in chapters 1 and 2 has illustrated the polarity in mid-Qing approaches to political economy that is one main theme of this book. On one hand, a 1737 exposition of the rationale for Yongzheng's banner grain bureaus stresses the desirability of the state's "controlling the power of determination" over market prices. By contrast, a 1747 memorial by Fang Guancheng shows that even within the interventionist tradition, arguments could be framed partly in terms of the efficacy of market forces.

To find an invocation of the efficacy of market forces in a memorial proposing action against so-called "hoarders" is unexpected, at least at first sight. It is not unduly Eurocentric to suppose that the more natural context for discourse about market mechanisms is opposition to state interventionism. One question to be examined below is how far mid-Qing discussions of state grain trade policy reveal a market-mechanisms discourse taking place "on home ground," as Braudel might have said.[77]

---

77. Cf. Braudel's distinction between "capitalism away from home" (in production) and "capitalism on home ground" (in trade, preferably long-distance trade). Braudel, *Wheels of Commerce*, chaps. 3 and 4.

Chapter 3 begins an exploration of the links between, on one hand, mid-Qing claims of the utility of profit-motivated grain transactions and the efficacy of market forces, and, on the other, arguments that specific manifestations of state interventionism were superfluous if not harmful.

3

Interventionism Questioned

Chapters 1 and 2 have shown that, while methods of dealing with offenders differed, there was a strong and persistent belief that speculative hoarding was an evil that demanded official countermeasures of some kind.[*] This chapter shows how a temporary shift of policy towards harsher action even against landlord hoarders provoked contrary arguments stressing the utility of hoarding. These arguments were reinforced by some of the responses to an imperial questionnaire issued in January 1748. While the interventionist tradition proved resilient in the face of these challenges, the counterarguments were also echoed later in the eighteenth century.

High-Qing anti-interventionist discourse had both seventeenth-century antecedents and other targets besides antihoarding action. The early sections of this chapter set the 1740s discussions in context by illustrating other aspects of Qing anti-interventionism, particularly opposition to the setting of price ceilings and to what I elsewhere call "supply protectionism" (attempting to retain supplies for a particular community or region by coercively preventing exports).[1] Robert Hymes has shown that arguments of the kind I discuss here were far from new in China in Qing times. Already in the Southern Song (1127–1279), an official called Dong Wei had anticipated some of them, particularly in his discussion of the ill-effects of setting price ceilings for

---

[*]A few short passages of translation in this and subsequent chapters appeared in my 1996 book, *Conflicting Counsels*, published by the Center for Chinese Studies, University of Michigan.

1. Dunstan, *Conflicting Counsels*, pp. 248–49.

grain. Hymes persuasively suggests that Dong conceived of market response to subsistence crises as a "self-regulating process" (although, as he points out, Dong did not advocate leaving the market entirely alone).[2] Yet even if some of the key ideas of high-Qing anti-interventionism had been expressed five centuries before, to dismiss it on these grounds as unworthy of study would betray a naively linear approach to history. The high-Qing version must be documented before its significance can be assessed, and its political context must be explored if the assessment is to be a realistic one. In this chapter, I embark upon these tasks.

Perhaps more controversial may be my use of the term "*anti-interventionist.*"[3] Kishimoto Mio, pioneering here as in much else, published an article in 1987 on "the tone of mid-Qing economic policy" as reflected in the debates of the 1740s. One substantial section of this study is entitled "The *Non*interventionist Position [*fukanshō ron*] in Qing Economic Policy" (emphasis mine).[4] Kishimoto noted that Qing "noninterventionism" was not linked with the historically dynamic concepts of individual rights that contributed to Western economic liberalism. Unlike its European counterpart, it was *only* a matter of choice of techniques for maximizing the common good of society. Within the Chinese context, its framework was therefore traditional.[5] In accordance with this finding, Kishimoto proposed the thesis that mid-Qing economic policy was dominated by a search for the golden

2. Hymes, "Moral Duty," pp. 294–99, 302; cf. Will, "Discussions about the Market-Place," pp. 356–57. For further examples of Song respect for commercial processes and/or opposition to specific forms of intervention, see Oberst, "Chinese Economic Statecraft," pp. 213–23, 238–40; for late Ming examples, see Liu Shijiao, *Huangzhu lüe* (1608), p. 496, and Cai Maode's "Eight guidelines for attracting merchant rice," transc. Lu Zengyu, *Qinding kangji lu* (1740), p. 420. Oberst finds a reconsideration of the conventional negative appraisal of the social role of merchants already in some Song writings (ibid., pp. 275–79, 311–17, 328–32).

3. For the case for a careful, discriminating use of the term "economic liberalism" to represent thought of the kind discussed in some parts of this chapter, cf. Dunstan, *Conflicting Counsels*, pp. 8, 257, 327–33.

4. Kishimoto, "Shinchō chūki keizai seisaku," pp. 27–32. A revised version of this article is included in Kishimoto, *Shindai Chūgoku no bukka*, and it is to this 1997 book that references are given hereafter.

5. Kishimoto, *Shindai Chūgoku no bukka*, pp. 314–15.

mean between too much and too little intervention, between excessive harshness and excessive leniency.[6] She wrote almost as though Qing government was itself set up in such a way as to permit a self-correcting mechanism to operate. The commitment to the golden mean, coupled with the practice of supplying territorial officials with "guidelines" as opposed to detailed orders, made reversal of direction easy whenever it was clear that a particular approach had reached its limits (or indeed exceeded them, presumably).[7]

The image of Qing economic policy perpetually "zigzagging" (*dakō sitsutsu*)[8] within a basically closed system of political economy is an alluring one and not to be lightly dismissed. It fits many of the facts discussed below and would seem strengthened by Hymes's above-mentioned discovery. However, it would be regrettable if scholars were deflected by the genuine originality of Kishimoto's insight from undertaking close empirical research into the shifting ground of mid-Qing economic policy. It is true that, early in his reign, the Qianlong emperor stressed the importance of taking the middle course (*zhong* or *zhong dao*) in governmental matters.[9] It follows neither that his own policy decisions consistently eschewed extremism nor that investigation of extremism in mid-Qing governance is labor lost. A blandly cyclical view of mid-Qing public policy would be reductionist; it would ignore not only the causes and consequences of specific swings but also the impulsions that drove individuals to argue as they did. While these impulsions were too various to be captured by a simple dichotomy between interventionist and anti-interventionist leanings, the expressions of anti-interventionist views are interesting in their own right. Some of them appear opinionated, partisan. To claim that Qing economic policy was essentially a search for middle ways amounts to a suggestion that, despite excesses on the part of individuals, it was under the control of sensible and moderate men. As part II below illustrates, these sensible men (of whom there were more than a few) must be identified before their moderation is assumed.

---

6. Ibid., pp. 315–17.
7. Ibid., p. 317.
8. Ibid.
9. Ibid., pp. 315–16.

Referring to debates of the kind discussed here, Pierre-Étienne Will has written, in somewhat the same vein as did Kishimoto, that "Rather than between government intervention and non-intervention (between *police des grains* and market principle), these debates, it seems to me, are between *more* and *less* governmental intervention and control—for in such circumstances [subsistence crises] complete *laissez-faire* was out of the question."[10] To say this is to side with the moderates, while dismissing the extremists from the historical record. It is true that "complete *laissez-faire*" was neither a practical nor a political possibility, but it does not follow that no Qing official would have thought it the ideal. To my knowledge, it cannot be claimed that any Qing official articulated a fully worked out, comprehensive vision of a grain market operating for the greatest good of all without any governmental intervention whatsoever. Most anti-interventionist memorials addressed a specific aspect of the interventionist tradition, and their arguments were shaped by the particular provocation (typically, a change in central government policy or the perverse results of literal-minded compliance) that had inspired them. However, many of them are rhetorical and breathe a real animus against the interventionist practice in question, if not state interference generally. Some of them either discuss how a market mechanism could solve the given problem or invoke abstract principles upholding the superiority of commerce, the profit motive, and the pursuit of self-interest over state attempts to regulate the market.

It would be unreasonable to decline to call such documents "anti-interventionist" simply because their authors typically envisaged the continuation of state intervention in some form (or because authors who were "anti-interventionist" in one context made interventionist assumptions in another). Radical employees of bureaucratic organizations usually have to make concessions to the dominant paradigms both in their actions and in written expressions of their views. To be sure, we have no reliable way of determining what any given author "really thought"; intuition based on the tone of each memorial is the best that we can do, and it is insufficient. My choice of emphasis, however, can be justified in terms of the evidence as it exists. What is

---

10. Will, "Discussions about the Market-Place," p. 353.

striking about the most anti-interventionist documents discussed in this book is not the residual interventionist practice that the authors typically espouse, but rather the stridency of their denunciations and the radicalism of their proposals by the standards of mid-eighteenth-century Chinese mainstream political economy. While some of their pronouncements were provoked by interventionist excesses, these authors were not looking for a golden mean. Rather, they challenged the foundations of normal mid-Qing practice and tried to steer policy towards minimal state intervention of a more market-conscious kind.

The true radicals of the 1740s will mostly be encountered in part II of this book. I introduce their views not with approval, but because they are part and parcel of the historical record and must not be ignored. In this chapter, I explore the high-Qing anti-interventionist position on issues other than the ever-normal granaries, which are the topic of part II. I thus endeavor to determine the range of arguments and understandings that were available for synthesis into a coherent vision of a radically liberalized grain market, had anyone seen fit to construct such a vision systematically.[11] The purpose here is not to measure Chinese understandings against the principles of European classical economics as an exercise in transcultural comparative evaluation. My focus is squarely on the mental world of Qing bureaucrats confronting real-life problems of grain stockpiling and distribution. As some of these bureaucrats had anti-interventionist ideas, assessing the potential of their insights is an altogether reasonable venture, and I undertake it in the final section of this chapter. From an economically liberal perspective, the results are rather positive.

A 1748 Manifesto Against the Busybody State

Let us seek a preliminary overview of mid-Qing anti-interventionism by examining one of its more broad-ranging expressions. This was the response of the Manchu Celeng, governor-general of Guangdong and Guangxi, to an imperial command of January 1748 that the provincial chief administrators suggest explanations for the recent upward trend in grain prices. As discussed in chapter 7, the imperial circular is

---

11. Will addresses similar issues in the first half of his "Discussions about the Market-Place," albeit with significant differences of emphasis.

probably best viewed as a hint, first, that the court now deemed "excessive" stockpiling of grain in the state granaries to be the prime inflationary factor, and, second, that it would like the governors and governors-general to indicate support for this position. Celeng obliged, as will be shown in chapter 7. Here I discuss his vehement yet quite sophisticated attack on other aspects of the interventionist tradition.

Celeng denounced four types of state interference that, he claimed, intensified the ill-effects of the granary system as currently operated. He blamed the four practices (which he seems to have thought common among county magistrates) on the excessive impatience of territorial officials, including provincial chiefs, to see grain price stability attained within their jurisdictions. All four had the opposite effect, in Celeng's opinion.

The first object of his disapproval was "forcing down the price" (*yi jia*), that is, the imposition of price ceilings. This, he claimed, had a double-acting negative effect. The officious inspection methods commonly in use entailed extra business costs, passed on to the consumer in the form of higher prices. They also meant gross inconvenience to both middlemen and merchants, which served only to deter those who would otherwise have brought fresh grain supplies into the county. Prices, therefore, did not come down. Celeng described the official meddling in graphic terms:

Now I have heard that in areas where grain is dear, the authorities invariably begin by setting prices, not permitting any further rise [beyond these ceilings]. They may even be arresting speculators one day and investigating grain brokers the next. They insist on [the grain dealers] coming in person to submit the receipts from each day's grain transactions; this apart, they set up circulating registers (*xunhuan bushan*) [in order to permit] continuous inspection. Orders are issued that the grain boats of passing merchants be escorted under guard [to the administrative seat]; brokers in the marketplace are kept daily scurrying to the official chambers. It is not just that the subaltern personnel will unavoidably make difficulties [for these people] and practice extortion [at their expense]; it is also to be feared that all the charges will be passed into the price [asked for the] grain (*guan ru mijia zhi zhong*). While the wish was to seek lower prices, the actual result is higher ones, on top of which the merchants, hearing what is going on, arrest their steps.

Celeng did not think that local officials should do nothing when grain prices rose. He indicated that he understood that they could not remain indifferent on such occasions. What they should do was make some unobtrusive "adjustments" while they calmed the populace. Commercial rice (*sic*) would then "catch wind [of the high prices] and arrive," gradually exerting the predictable, oft-demonstrated stabilizing effect on local grain prices.

The second item in Celeng's list of counterproductive practices was that of "exhorting [hoarders] to release [their stocks] for sale," in other words, taking the standard non-coercive approach to landlord speculative hoarding. Celeng's objection was partly on the grounds that the word "exhortation" often masked coercive practice. More interesting is his opening defence of speculation. Not only does this uphold the morality of small-time landed speculators; it also hints that even capitalist speculation fulfills a positive function for the community in which the grain is hoarded. Celeng argued as follows:

In [any given] village there will necessarily be one or two persons of substance. With farming as their livelihood, how could they be without small quantities of surplus grain? The reason for which they possess their meager family estates is that these have all been accumulated out of tiny parcels. From the state's point of view, [such folk are] decent people who keep to their proper place; within each rural area, they represent solidity and soundness (*yuanqi*). If they do have grain stored in their homes, they are only seeking [the right] price before they sell. Even [actual] hoarders are weighing up profit and capital (*jiquan zi mu*); they sell as soon as the lean preharvest period arrives, in order to devise some other operation [for their capital]. Even should they fail to do this, they will still sell off their old stocks to buy new; they will definitely not be prepared to store them long. Besides, if the region has chanced to suffer a poor harvest, one does not fear an increase in the price of grain; one fears a lack of grain to save the situation. [This makes it] still more unobjectionable to give these grain-possessing households time to bring their stocks out of their own accord, in order also to provide against contingencies.

In other words, speculative hoarding resulted in the existence of genuinely local grain reserves that, although maintained for private profit, could nonetheless help save village communities during subsistence crises.

At least, the private stockpiles could have produced public benefits if only local administrators had left their owners in peace. Celeng went on to detail ways in which official interference either deterred stockpile formation or, arguably, encouraged a persistence in withholding stocks that was at variance with the normal behavior patterns of economically rational hoarders who were planning to sell locally. He claimed that as soon as grain became at all expensive, local officials would compel grain-owning households to sell at a "reduced" price, or would actually impound their grain in their own granaries.[12] "Although in name it is [a question of] voluntary action in response to exhortation, the reality is forced compliance with compulsory assignments." Those who failed to cooperate were regarded as "hoarders" (*tunhu*), presumably of the capitalistic kind, and criminal proceedings were begun against them. As a result, the rural rich perforce became so cautious that they did not even dare keep enough grain to lend to poorer neighbors. At the same time, the sight of the authorities browbeating wealthy households was likely to tempt the disorderly into violent collective actions whose aim was to despoil the rich. The heightened tensions in the countryside aggravated the tendency to see grain as a "rare commodity [worth holding on to]" (*qi huo*), that is, as an object of speculative hoarding.

At this point, Celeng left his rhetoric to speak for itself. It is worth noticing, however, that his point was probably not only that measures intended to suppress hoarding indirectly provoked hoarder intransigence. Taken in conjunction with his earlier defence of speculation, his allegations also suggest that he saw the retention of hoarded grain long after prices had risen as abnormal behavior for the rational hoarder. That is, he probably saw it as behavior to which speculators would normally resort only if driven by extra-economic forces such as the threat of popular violence engendered by official meddling.

Celeng's third complaint was principally against official connivance at, if not cooperation in, popular supply protectionism. He prefaced his allegations with a conventional exposition of the need for swift-flowing and efficient commerce if subsistence difficulties were to be relieved. Unfortunately, however, local officials, misled by an unduly particularistic conception of their duty, did what they could—without openly

---

12. Celeng may have misunderstood the motivation of some of these impoundings. Will cites an early seventeenth-century case in which the official sealing of private granaries was done as an incentive. Grain-owners "who agreed to sell part of their reserves to the administration at a designated price" were granted this symbol of government protection against the pillaging to be expected in a famine year. Will, *Bureaucracy and Famine*, pp. 60–61.

violating "repeated" imperial prohibitions of unauthorized grain export bans—to stop grain flowing out to other jurisdictions. They deliberately held up departing merchant vessels on the pretext that inspection was required, and they dealt leniently with "troublemakers" who instigated popular export embargoes. The popular embargoes, allegedly fomented "as soon as" grain became dear in a neighboring county, involved crowd actions to detain by force those who had bought local grain but planned to sell it on external markets. If the victims were permitted to leave with their grain, this would be only after they had made a substantial payment to their captors. For the local officials to tolerate such treatment of would-be exporters was tantamount, Celeng suggested, to forbidding their return on future buying expeditions.[13]

Particularly interesting in Celeng's denunciation is his proposed distinction between the "good" (reliable and socially responsible) merchants who would be deterred by such ill-treatment, and the unscrupulous adventurers who might continue to operate despite it. After reminding the emperor that all commerce in grain was motivated by the hope of "tiny profits," he pointed out the likely effects on merchant behavior of a combination of supply protectionism and artificial price controls. This time, he was not arguing that the main object of his criticism (supply protectionism) was counterproductive for the communities in whose supposed interest it was undertaken; rather, he was considering the impact of this practice in light of the wider society's need for unimpeded commerce. He posited a scenario in which grain merchants were first delayed by official and private obstruction at their place of purchase, and later greeted, on arrival at their intended place of sale, with the discovery that the authorities, having heard rumors of the level of grain prices in the region of production, had set the price at which they were to sell. A "good" merchant who therefore could not recoup his capital would avoid that route in future. The only people who would trade in such circumstances were "perverse and wicked profit-seekers, adventurers who ship and sell by stealth and who can speculate at will."

---

13. For other descriptions of popular supply protectionism, see, e.g., Wong, "Food Riots," pp. 775–76 and passim; Quan, "Qianlong shisan nian," pp. 551–52; Abe, *Shindai shi*, pp. 495, 499, 513.

Celeng's fourth and final objection was to recent measures to control the depositing of grain with pawnshops. He claimed that these measures had upset a traditional and not particularly exploitative rural mechanism for assisting poor people to avoid having to sell the grain that they had harvested. He described an annual cycle in which needy tenant farmers pledged their winter clothes for grain when spring arrived, and then redeemed them after harvest with new grain deposits, with the result that it would not be clear to an outsider which was the security and which the loan.[14] However, Celeng's peasants knew exactly what they were doing. He explained the motivation of both parties thus:

The petty folk cherish [grains of] rice as they would pearls. They truly fear that if they lightly sell the rice left over once their rent is paid, they will later face the worry of [having to] buy [rice] at a higher price than they received [for their own crop]. . . . The pawnbrokers benefit from the circularity [of this process] through which they pursue their tiny profits; the tenant farmers, for their part, are happy with the ease with which [their rice] can be redeemed, so that their work of cultivation is not jeopardized.

This was why, according to Celeng, all the household effects of such peasants lay in the pawnshops throughout the busy farming seasons. In fact, his use of the word "redeem" (*shuqu*) was inexact. Interest was payable on the grain issued in spring, implying that the peasants did surrender ownership rights over the grain that they deposited and were borrowing that or other grain in spring. Nonetheless, the system may have met their needs. The busy farming seasons coincided, roughly, with the annual lean preharvest—that is, *soudure*—periods. The farmers were protected from the high grain prices that were typical of *soudure* periods as long as they retained cheap access to the grain that they had harvested, or to an equivalent amount.

Needless to say, it was official interference that had disturbed these finely-tuned arrangements, in Celeng's view. Close surveillance in recent years had deterred pawnbrokers from accepting pledges (or re-

---

14. For a late nineteenth-century description of Canton Delta village pawnshops as "safe store-house[s] for everybody's property," especially out-of-season clothes, see Whelan, *Pawnshop in China*, p. 19. For a reference to north-China pawnshops "serving as summer storage" for winter clothes, see Naquin, *Millenarian Rebellion*, p. 226.

payments) in the form of grain, because they feared that they would be accused of hoarding. There was now (since 1747) an imperially-approved, presumably nationwide ban on the commercial malpractice of stockpiling grain in pawnshop storehouses by repeatedly recycling loans of capital received from pledging grain straight after harvest, buying more grain, and pledging each successive load of grain acquired. Pawnbrokers were to be held responsible for ensuring that no hoards were built in this way on their premises.[15] It is therefore understandable that, according to Celeng, village pawnbrokers, men of modest means, were more unwilling than ever to take the risk of accepting grain from farmers. Thus were the peasant clients forced to sell their grain in order to redeem their winter clothes; this left them dependent on the *soudure* market for their food the following spring. Whereas hitherto their interest payments had been only about 0.1 tael per *shi* borrowed, now they were paying prices 0.3 to 0.7 tael/*shi* above those for which they had sold during the autumn season of abundance. Moreover, the increased pressure on the *soudure* market meant an even higher level of grain prices at that difficult time of year.[16]

We have just observed one mid-eighteenth-century regional administrator explaining what he considered the most egregious examples of official interference hampering market forces (as we would say) and pushing prices up instead of down. It may seem that what concerned him was not state intervention *per se*, but rather the misguided efforts of overzealous local officials, acting in ways that would not necessarily have won central government approval. Let us therefore try more systematically to relate each of the four kinds of intervention to imperial policy and law. In the case of official connivance with supply protectionism, local authorities were indeed violating the spirit of imperial policy. Unless food availability in the exporting area was low enough to justify exceptional treatment, or unless the merchant exporters could be convincingly accused of hoarding, conspiracy, or other wrongdoing, supply-protectionist embargoes were not allowed. "Forcing down the price" may not have been explicitly forbidden, but

---

15. On "hoard pawning" and the bans against it, see below and Dunstan, *Conflicting Counsels*, pp. 258–59, 273–76.

16. CC, Celeng, QL 13/3/28 or, for an unusually full summary, QSL/QL, *juan* 311:40a–44a.

it was probably regarded as less than best practice in the upper echelons of the bureaucracy. I have never seen it advocated in high-level policy discussion documents, nor have I seen it ordered from the throne.

With the new constraints on the activities of village pawnshops, the picture becomes more complex. The central government prohibition had been intended to suppress a capitalistic abuse of the facilities offered by pawnbrokers. More could perhaps have been done to make clear that the new ban was not directed at pledges of subsistence grain by peasants. In 1745, the Jiangsu governor, ordered to implement an earlier version of the ban, had ordered the posting of notices to this effect.[17] If his counterparts elsewhere had failed to show such forethought, or if notices were not enough to convince village pawnbrokers that their innocent activities would escape the attentions of proverbially rapacious *yamen* underlings, we can say that the ban's unintended consequences at village level reflected the deficiencies of the territorial bureaucracy. And yet the assumption underlying the prohibition was that speculative hoarding was a harmful practice. It was not only harmful but, in principle, illegal. Advocates of bans on "hoard pawning" (*tundang*), as the abuse was called, were trying to do in one context what officials who put pressure on landlord speculators were trying to do in another: suppress the illegal activity of hoarding. As will be shown below, a "zigzag" of policy in 1745 had left the territorial bureaucracy under orders to adopt a tough stance against landlord speculative hoarders, with threats and coercion to be used as required. Thus those local officials who compelled hoarders to sell had not necessarily been violating central government policy. Even had the moral suasion policy of 1743 still been in force, officials who imposed forced sales would only have been taking an unauthorized shortcut to the accepted goal of freeing hoards to restock undersupplied markets.

It is therefore reasonable to give critiques of antihoarding action special status among Qing anti-interventionist discussions. Like the radical arguments against the ever-normal system introduced in part II, they challenged conventional assumptions as to the best ways of realizing Confucian ideals of monarchical responsibility towards the humble. This is much less true of the arguments against supply pro-

---

17. CC, Chen Dashou, QL 10/1/8; Dunstan, *Conflicting Counsels*, pp. 259, 278.

tectionism or artificial price controls. Yet among the arguments against all four kinds of intervention, there are some that invoke the notion that existing institutions of society, supported by the profit motive and market mechanisms, can produce satisfactory outcomes with no, or little, contribution from the state. In what follows, I survey a few more writers' arguments against supply protectionism and official price controls, before turning to the defences of grain speculation that were provoked by the stern antihoarding policies of the late 1740s.

Contra *Price Controls and Grain Export Embargoes*

Distinctively sophisticated and vituperative among Qing arguments against official price controls were those of the seventeenth-century intellectual Wang Fuzhi (1619–92), whose stance as a Ming loyalist kept him from taking office under the Manchus.[18] In commenting on two historical episodes in his *Du* Tongjian *lun* (On Reading the *Comprehensive Mirror for Assistance in Government*), he expressed unequivocal opposition to government attempts to regulate the price of grain by fiat. The first passage quoted below comes from Wang's response to a fifth-century attempt to boost agricultural prices through official intervention buying. This discussion, whose concern is consistently with the producer interest, and which is underpinned by a simple quantity-theory understanding of money and the price level, may well reflect late seventeenth-century anxieties about low grain prices and a perceived money-shortage.[19] The drift of Wang's argument is that intervention buying and selling are preferable to trying to set floors or ceilings for the market price of grain. However, intervention selling would be unnecessary if those taxes that were payable in kind were commuted, because the rich would then be forced to sell their grain in order to obtain the necessary money. Intervention buying would be unnecessary if the state rapidly disbursed the funds it had collected, because a plentiful supply of money could counteract the effects of an

---

18. On Wang's philosophy, see Black, *Man and Nature*.

19. On the Kangxi depression, its reflection in economic thought, and its connection with a perceived silver shortage, see Kishimoto, "Kōki nenkan." The belief that a decline in silver imports was largely responsible for the depression is questioned in von Glahn, *Fountain of Fortune*, pp. 224–45.

abundant harvest. Cheap money was the key to the material, and therefore moral, well-being of the farming population.

It was in the middle of this discussion that Wang made the following concise statement about price controls:

When [grain and silk] are dear, it is not possible to make them cheap [by fiat]. If officialdom forbids their being dear, and accumulators of grain shut their doors to purchasers [in consequence], this will [only] exacerbate the dearness. When they are cheap, it is not possible to make them dear [by fiat]. If officialdom forbids their being cheap, and holders of precious metal [i.e., silver] decline to pay it out [in consequence], this will [only] exacerbate the cheapness. Officialdom would, therefore, do better not to make such prohibitions.[20]

Price ceilings, by lowering the rewards to sellers, encourage persistence in hoarding; price floors deter commercial spending on agricultural products. If less money comes onto the market, the exchange value of money will rise, which is tantamount to saying that there will be a further fall in commodity prices.

Wang's support for the producer interest was matched, in a second piece of commentary, by a dismissive lack of sympathy for indigent consumers. This time, Wang was reflecting on a ninth-century civil provincial governor's resistance to a subordinate's desire to "force down" the price of grain. Wang briefly put the technical case against such "forcing." If grain prices were artificially reduced at a time of plenty, grain would flow out of the community, leaving it without reserves against a famine year. If, on the other hand, such action were (more understandably) taken at a time of shortage, there would be nothing to attract trade from elsewhere to rescue the community as its own supplies ran out. As the point that price ceilings deterred life-saving imports had already been argued by Dong Wei of the Southern Song, it may not be surprising that Wang saw no need to elaborate on it (beyond noting, later in his discussion, that by repelling imports one played into the hands of local speculators, who would fully exploit the aggravated scarcity).[21] Rather, he devoted the bulk of

---

20. Wang Fuzhi, *Du* Tongjian *lun*, vol. 2, *juan* 16, pp. 537–38; quoted in Hu, *Zhongguo jingji*, vol. 3, p. 509.

21. Cf. Hymes, "Moral Duty," p. 295. On the availability and likely influence of Dong Wei's writings from the late Ming on, see Will, *Bureaucracy and Famine*, p. 9; Rowe, *Saving the World*, p. 184.

his remarks to denigration of the character of those to earn whose praise "commonplace" officials allegedly set price controls.

In Wang's eyes, those who cheered at news of official action to reduce grain prices could only be vagabonds and followers of "parasitic occupations," people who did not devote themselves to agriculture and did not know how to save. Any peasant couple who were diligent in cultivation and textile production, maintained their ponds, and took care over harvesting and storage should be able to avoid starvation in a famine year. So also should craftsmen and petty traders who ate moderately, worked tirelessly, and were "free of the habits of drinking and gambling, singing and beating on the drum, sleeping in the daytime, sitting in the early morning, and general profligacy." Even if very needy, they could still gather wild food plants or find employment with the rich; "they will be urgently contriving [how they may procure] gruel for their eight-mouth families, and will certainly not be clamorously [waiting] on the banks of rivers or at corners of the roads and hoping for the price to be brought down, inciting the crowd with their uproar." And yet, continued Wang, there were in fact large numbers of such people, only too ready to chime in when one of them struck up a plaintive whining, but blind to the consideration that if, as they desired, the authorities imposed a lower price, they still had not the wherewithal to pay it. "If one thus humors their crazed fantasies and thereby keeps [importing] merchants at a distance of a thousand *li*, the powerful enjoyers of abundance [i.e., wealthy speculators] will intensify their sway over the fates of men, effortlessly reaping in the profit of the surging prices. If not only do the feckless people do themselves to death, but the authorities show them the quickest way thereto, alas, how sad it is that commonplace officials gain a splendid reputation while the bodies of the starving fill the ditches."[22]

No doubt Wang spoke for many who preferred to attribute vagabondage to personal defects of character rather than to external causes such as invasion or civil war. However, few of his works were published before 1840, which makes it unlikely that great numbers were influenced by his rhetoric or had the opportunity of building on his

---

22. Wang, *Du* Tongjian *lun*, vol. 3, *juan* 25, pp. 885–86. This text is excerpted in Hu, *Zhongguo jingji*, vol. 3, p. 509.

rather fine theoretical reflections.[23] The two texts examined below, by Huang Liuhong and Hui Shiqi respectively, seem insipid in comparison with Wang's. Devoid of invective and concerned with practicality, they show no particular originality in stating the argument that price ceilings deter imports and/or prolong hoarding. They deserve a glance partly because they clarify what Celeng may have had in mind when calling for "adjustments" in the interval before grain merchants, attracted by high prices, import the price-lowering supplies. Each author proposed a plan by which the state could expedite this process.

Huang Liuhong, in his handbook of local administration (published seven years after Wang's death), adopted the viewpoint of the county magistrate who aspired to restore price stability in his own jurisdiction and who suffered no undue qualms about the needs of populations elsewhere. Like Wang, he opined that "forcing down the price" would be counterproductive because it would deprive the county's markets of both local stocks and imports. He did, however, recommend a scheme by which the sharp administrator could attract supplies into his county at the expense of other jurisdictions where the magistrates were less enlightened. The magistrate who followed Huang's advice would start to buy grain at an elevated price while publicizing his intent to purchase "so many tens of thousands of *shi*" at current market rates for retail to the local population. When distant merchants learned that he was offering a high price whereas many of his counterparts had imposed price restrictions, they would hasten "day and night" to bring grain to his county. Once plenty of grain had arrived, the magistrate should withdraw from the market and leave the people to make purchases, "which being done, the market price will be as stable as [it is] after an abundant harvest."[24]

---

23. See Ch'i Ssu-ho's biography of Wang in *Eminent Chinese*, ed. Hummel, vol. 2, p. 818.

24. Huang, *Fuhui quanshu, juan* 27:19b–20a. There is nothing corresponding to this passage in the Djang translation (Huang, *Complete Book*, p. 568). Somewhat similar was the scheme of "forceless forcing down" (*buyi zhi yi*) recommended in a handbook of historical famine relief measures published with imperial sponsorship in 1740. Popular confidence should be secured by publicizing the total amount of grain available within the jurisdiction and requiring its controllers to sell it at the current (that is, market) price; merchants would then be attracted by the fact that sale at the market price was still permitted. Lu, *Qinding kangji lu*, p. 330.

Another kind of import incentive was advocated by the Suzhou classicist and, at one time, Hanlin Academy reader-in-waiting Hui Shiqi (1671–1741), in an essay on famine relief written probably before 1738. Hui objected to price ceilings because they halted the mechanism that would otherwise have kept grain flowing into markets like those of his own, exceptionally urbanized, home region:

Whenever things are plentiful, their value will be low; whenever they are scarce, their value will be high. It was because of this that, in times of plenty, the statesmen of antiquity gathered [things] in to make [those remaining on the market] valuable and, in times of scarcity, dispersed [what they had previously gathered] to make [the commodity in question] cheap. The reason why one never hears of any [ancient statesman] having forced prices down is indeed that prices cannot be stabilized by forcing. As Jiangnan is without stored grain, the populace of more than twenty upper-level jurisdictions all depend upon [the grain] trade for their food, which means that the rice merchants are truly the controllers of the people's fates.[25] When prices are high, [the merchants] congregate, and when prices are low, they turn and go elsewhere. . . . When orders forcing prices down are issued, the rice merchants do not come because [they are afraid] of selling at a loss. I fear that rice will be still scarcer, and prices will surge up still more.

Hui also expressed law and order concerns similar to those discussed in chapter 2. In his view, the imposition of price controls encouraged the people to be disputatious, provoking incidents in which consumers took the law into their own hands and either forced grain-owners to sell or simply plundered them.

Hui recommended an approach that was tried sporadically during the late Kangxi and Yongzheng periods and became nationwide policy in 1737–38. This was to try to stimulate merchant enthusiasm for transporting grain to famine-stricken areas by remitting the transit taxes normally payable whenever a cargo passed through an internal customs station. The remissions would be selective, applying only at those stations that lay on the route to a disaster-stricken zone.[26] Evi-

---

25. In saying that Jiangnan lacked stored grain, Hui referred to household reserves. He had claimed that Jiangnan families did not store significant amounts of rice still in the husk—the only form in which it would keep for more than a year.

26. Kōsaka, "Kenryū-dai zenki," pp. 47, 49; He, "Qianlong nianjian," pp. 89–91; Will, *Bureaucracy and Famine*, pp. 213–14; cf. QSL/QL, *juan* 43:11b–12a, *juan* 73:4b.

dently, proponents of this measure cannot have been particularly strong believers in the efficacy of market forces. Indeed, as I have shown elsewhere, the officials of the Board of Revenue, concerned lest the remissions be abused, in 1737 set up a battery of precautions that would tempt one to believe that they had no idea of market forces whatsoever—for which they were ridiculed by the classicist Fang Bao the following year.[27] Hui Shiqi's position was that a better remedy for scarcity than arbitrary price controls was "to set commerce flowing" (*tongshang*), and the way to swell the flow of trade into afflicted regions was to attract grain merchants with at least a 50 percent transit tax reduction. He conjured up vivid, if hyperbolic, images of the Huguang shipping that would stream to Jiangnan (which was drought-stricken at the time) if only this were done.[28]

If there was a wide readership in mid-Qing China for Huang's handbook, not to mention famine relief manuals that reproduced Dong Wei's work, the argument that price controls were counterproductive must have been familiar in many a county *yamen*.[29] Was it commonplace? Had the average magistrate anything to learn from expositions such as Hui Shiqi's? Celeng, in 1748, gave the impression that resort to price ceilings was rife among local officials; were his strictures justified? These questions must remain open for the time being. After all, magistrates who were aware of the theoretical argument against price ceilings may occasionally have bowed to pressure from urban consumers and imposed them notwithstanding. Unrest was a widespread and serious problem in the 1740s, a decade of rising grain prices. The near riot that broke out in Suzhou in 1748 in support of a commoner's demand for action on rice prices suffices to explain why early compliance with popular feeling would have been tempting to a timid local official (as one report suggests was so on that occasion).[30] It is also

27. Dunstan, *Conflicting Counsels*, pp. 305–6, 324–26.

28. HCJSWB, vol. 3, *juan* 41:3a–b. Hui's discussion is cited in Will, *Bureaucracy and Famine*, p. 213.

29. Cf. Will, *Bureaucracy and Famine*, p. 9; Rowe, *Saving the World*, p. 184.

30. Wu Renshu, "Chengshi liangshi baodong," p. 349; see also Santangelo, "Urban Society," pp. 104–5, and chap. 9 below. I thank Dr Wu for giving me a copy of his article.

possible that some magistrates were familiar with the argument but were not persuaded by it.

Uphold the rightful liberties of sellers: no supply protectionism here! The orthodox line against grain export embargoes was that they arose from selfish disregard for greater need elsewhere (as reflected in the higher prices that were drawing stocks away). This much is already clear from previous scholarship.[31] Here, I introduce examples that address the problem from a different angle, that of the interests and, indeed, what we would call the rights of sellers. This will serve to make the point that although the concept of individual economic rights, undeveloped and implicit, did not play a role in China similar to that of the Enlightenment discourse of rights in Europe, it was neither alien to Confucian-trained Qing literati nor divorced from Qing anti-interventionism. The formulaic expressions of economic individualism that I mention in part II, while few in number, are thus shown to be less isolated than they might otherwise have seemed.

Between 1678 and 1698, Tang Menglai, a native of north China who once reached a low rank in the Hanlin Academy, wrote an essay on the evils of supply protectionism.[32] Noting the harm that export embargoes did to consumers in dearth-stricken regions, he suggested that complacent perpetrators of such bans were like doctors who claimed world-saving expertise for causing total blockage of their patients' circulation. However, his main purpose was to argue against supply protectionism from the viewpoint of grain sellers in the community that was the object of protection. Adopting this perspective enabled him to argue that export embargoes were counterproductive in terms of their own aim, that is, to stop grain flowing out to other areas. His essay arguably reflects the concerns of landowners in the aftermath of the early Kangxi depression, when there had been complaints of low grain prices even during shortage, and when many landowners had reportedly had insufficient monetary income to pay their land tax.

---

31. Existing discussions of Qing opposition to supply protectionism include Will, *Bureaucracy and Famine*, pp. 215–16, and Dunstan, *Conflicting Counsels*, pp. 254–57, 271–73.

32. The former year is mentioned in Tang's essay, and he died in the latter. For basic biographical information, see HCJSWB, *Xingming zongmu*, 2a.

While the cogency of Tang's argument is not dependent on this context, his essay would have seemed most compelling to landowners who had experienced thrashing for tax delinquency caused by a depressed grain market.[33]

At first sight, it is tempting to accuse Tang of representing the interests of the more substantial landowners, while disregarding the anxieties of poor consumers. However, Tang's home province was Shandong, where the concentration of landownership was relatively low. His claim that almost everyone sold grain, and that the great majority were payers of the land tax, may not have been a gross exaggeration in the context of a predominantly agricultural north-Chinese environment with little tenancy or cash-cropping, low demand for labor, and limited urban populations that were still recovering from the demographic crises of the Ming–Qing transition. Tang's seeming assumption that, apart from the demand from speculators, there was no significant local market for grain surpluses was also consistent with these circumstances. Even his claim that everyone, throughout the rural social scale, bought cloth (as opposed to wearing homespun) does not necessarily betray him as a spokesman for the better-off landowners.[34]

---

33. Concern about low grain prices accompanying poor harvests is expressed in Ren Yuanxiang, *Minghe Tang wenji, juan* 2:37b (an early Kangxi model examination essay on taxation policy; edited version in HCJSWB, *juan* 29:11b–12a). On a 1676 essay by Tang Menglai that discussed the depression from a monetary perspective, see Kishimoto, "Kōki nenkan," pp. 265–67. The beating of depression-stricken taxpayers is mentioned by Tang's contemporary Gao Heng (a fellow-native of Zichuan county, Shandong): HCJSWB, *juan* 53:21a–b.

34. Admittedly, Francesca Bray's account of the diffusion of cotton weaving in northern China raises the possibility that, by the late seventeenth century, peasant self-sufficiency in cotton textiles had been established in much of Shandong. Bray, *Technology and Gender*, pp. 217–21. However, geography may have militated against the rapid participation of Tang's home county (Zichuan) in the trend towards cottage cotton-cloth production in north China. I also suspect that Bray's interpretation of a passage by Xu Guangqi (1562–1633) tends to overstate the swiftness of the change (cf. Xu, *Nongzheng*, vol. 2, *juan* 35, pp. 969–70; Naquin and Rawski, *Chinese Society*, p. 143). Although the Kangxi depression would have been a stimulus to self-sufficiency, most Zichuan households may still have been buying cloth in the late seventeenth century.

Tang addressed those situations in which grain export bans (here meaning bans on exportation by outsiders) were imposed on behalf of communities that were enjoying favorable supply conditions, but whose administrators feared that overbuying for other areas would at best send prices soaring, and at worst deplete the local stocks entirely. To Tang, forbidding merchants from elsewhere to buy was unrealistic. Sellers sold their grain because they had no choice, and they would go on selling whether outside purchasers were barred or not. "If one owes one tael of tax, one cannot settle with a payment of five-tenths because there is a ban on [outside] purchasing," any more than one could suddenly stop buying cloth and wadding or fulfilling social obligations. Grain therefore continued to flow out of the community despite the prohibition; it left in the hands either of local people or of outside merchants who possessed the necessary connections. Some marketed grain stayed in the community, but only because it had been bought by powerful families that were rich enough to hoard. In the meantime, the declaration of the export ban would have depressed the local price of grain, so that farmers needed to sell more of their crop to realize the same sum of money.

In a depressed market onto which extra grain was being poured, it took longer than usual for farmers to complete their sales. Tang painted a vivid, perhaps hyperbolic, picture of the distress caused by this and other unintended consequences of the prohibition:

In the official sphere, uncompleted tax payments mean many days of beating [the delinquents]; among the public, unbought clothing also means long days of cold and hunger. [The sufferers] look at each other and cry aloud, but there is nothing they can do. . . . Besides, those who sell grain are not the rich households; the rich buy grain, not sell it. All [propertied] households, exalted and humble, rich and poor alike, are taxpayers, and even those poor people who work as hired laborers or rent land from others [and are therefore not responsible for paying tax] all use their limited receipts of grain in order to acquire cloth.[35] Whereas hitherto they could obtain more than enough from sale of a small [proportion], now on the contrary they have been put in a position in which selling a large [proportion] will not suffice [to meet their needs]. Where is the benefit to poor people?

---

35. I take the second *zu* ("rent") in this sentence to be an error.

During the recent, frequent natural disasters, Tang went on, the last thing anyone had wanted to do was to sell grain unnecessarily. People did not need export bans to prevent them from alienating their own vital reserves, besides which they would have to sell more if exports were banned than if unrestricted outside buying kept the price up. Tang had now made the case that export bans were counterproductive: they caused an aggravated drain of cereal food from the community, and they channelled grain into the hoards of speculators.

They also showed distressing blindness to celestial providence. Tang mentioned another recent period in which good harvests had been accompanied by a total lack of effective demand for grain. The heaped-up stocks had lain unwanted in household granaries, and some families had fled their homes because they could not pay their taxes.[36] If this grain could have been bought for hungry people elsewhere, the local crisis could have been avoided, for "if one region has an abundant[37] harvest, and there are those who come to buy from the four quarters, this is Heaven wishing to bring slight relief to the afflictions of the people's lives in this one region, and great deliverance to the afflictions of the people's lives in the four quarters." Tang finished by disposing of the argument that there was still one group that might need the protection of grain export bans, that is, vagabondish types "without a foot of soil or inch of homestead" who were entirely dependent on the market for their food. Such people, averred Tang, would be glad to make a living by trading tiny quantities of grain, and export bans would only hinder them.[38]

Tang's discussion focused on the needs and interests of grain sellers, but it mentioned nothing corresponding to what we might call their rights. I conclude this section by considering two passages by Chen Hongmou in which he set out, for the benefit of ordinary Jiangxi people who might be tempted to impose illegal export bans, the legitimate liberties of grain owners regarding their own property. It is obvious that these sources must be used with caution.[39] In another

---

36. Cf. the texts by Tang and Gao Heng cited in n. 33 above.

37. Emending *shao* ("a little," "scant") to *feng* ("abundant").

38. HCJSWB, *juan* 42:4b–5a.

39. Cf. Rowe, *Saving the World*, pp. 180–81, where closer attention to context would perhaps have been desirable.

context, Chen might have discussed the problem of profit-maximizing landlord behavior very differently. He found it expedient to warn the poor that the rich were entitled to sell at a time and in a manner profitable to themselves, but it does not follow that, among his peers, he would have argued for an abstract concept of rights that license conduct independently of moral dictates.

These passages constitute the preambles to two of Chen's administrative documents from the 1742–43 Jiangxi subsistence crisis. The first is a proclamation of early 1743 exhorting the wealthy to stop hoarding, and the poor to stop encroaching on the proper liberties of grain-controllers. The second is a directive, issued some four months later, in which Chen advised his subordinates as to the considerations that they should use to dissuade would-be participants in supply protectionist blockades, forced sales, and other popular collective actions. The preambles were followed by more admonitions and assurances. For example, Chen told the popular supply protectionists that official buying in Jiangxi for other provinces had ceased, and that the Jiangxi ever-normal granaries stood ready to make major cut-price sales as soon as spring arrived. He warned them that anti-export blockades only exacerbated the situation, and that by engaging in such actions they risked criminal punishment. However, it is the preambles that are of interest here.

In the first preamble, the poor were directed to accept that they lived in an inegalitarian commercialized agrarian economy in which the disposal of grain was determined by market logic:

As for the poor, they ought to consider that it is fated whether one is rich or poor, and that for harvests to be bad and grain dear is a normal [hazard] of the seasons. Their one recourse is to be diligent and frugal and to exert themselves; how can it be tolerated if they gratuitously disturb and obstruct the wealthy households? That [the latter] have grain is either because of what their fathers and grandfathers built up and handed down to them, or else arises from their own frugality and diligence. To harvest grain from one's own land and sell it when [the right] price can be had is altogether natural and proper, and there is nothing presumptuous (*feifen*) about it. How could one let the grain-possessing families contrariwise be ruled by the poor people? Not only is it inevitable that there will be some trading within the home jurisdiction; even if the merchants of neighboring provinces come with the price and buy, this too is a normal phenomenon of commerce (*maoyi zhi chang*) and has been so from year to year.

In conclusion, Chen invoked two recent edicts that, he suggested, manifested such great imperial concern with popular subsistence and the need for grain to circulate efficiently that it was it doubly unthinkable to let "local perverse people" block grain exports from their home districts.[40]

The second preamble, which is shorter, re-emphasized the naturalness and permissibility of landowners seeking a good price for their grain:

As to [those] poor people who invariably obstruct the grain, they fail to consider that those who possess grain, in every case, possess it either because it comes to them from their own land, or else by virtue of their past frugality and diligence. If one has surplus grain, to sell it with an eye to price is altogether natural and normal, and it is absolutely not a question of expropriating other people. Whoever would be content simply to give his grain away?[41]

In the context of the 1742–43 Jiangxi subsistence crisis, Chen's message was that the poor must recognize that the rich enjoyed legitimate ownership rights over their grain. The poor must therefore desist from the blockades that not only inhibited the rich from selling but also implicitly challenged their right to sell for the best price the market offered. As we saw in chapter 2, Chen also had a message for the rich: it was immoral to decline to sell while waiting until prices peaked. The rich had a moral duty to think of the needs of the community; it was the duty of the poor to wait peaceably for the rich to start to give moral considerations precedence over full enjoyment of their rights of ownership.

Did Chen really believe that, irrespective of morality, the Jiangxi landlord hoarders were within their rights? It would be rash to reply affirmatively, not least because he used no word that corresponds to our term "rights." There was, in any case, a tension: if, technically, hoarding was illegal, how could landlords have a right to hoard their grain? Or should this question be reversed? If landlords arguably had

---

40. PYTOCG, *juan* 15:21b–22a; cf. Rowe, "State and Market in Mid-Qing Economic Thought," pp. 12–15. For the background to Chen's homily, see chap. 2 above.

41. PYTOCG, *juan* 16:4b.

some right to delay the sale of their grain, how could the state simply treat "hoarding" as, in principle, illegal? Perhaps, as we look at the shifts of policy on speculative hoarding, we should recognize not merely an example of the Qing state "zigzagging," but rather a case of law being in partial conflict with consensual attitudes among the class from which Chinese officials were predominantly drawn. The legislative institutions of late imperial China offered limited provision for addressing conflicts between law and (sectional) social attitudes. Chen's extraordinary persistence with the ineffective exhortation strategy in Jiangxi in 1742–43 may not have been motivated entirely by craven fears about the social fabric, but also by informal recognition of the ownership rights even of obdurate landowning hoarders.

"Laws Should be Obeyed"

The last section surveyed arguments against one interventionist practice that, in most circumstances, contravened imperial policy, and another that was not usually encouraged by the central government. The arguments against coercive antihoarding action to be introduced later in this chapter were, to the contrary, articulated mostly in the wake of explicit central government mandates for determined action against speculative hoarding, including, in one case, hoarding by landowners. This section examines these mandates, focusing on the ban on landlord hoarding (1745) and two other bans of ca. 1745 and 1747 and their interpretation at provincial level. The next section introduces the arguments of critics.

Likely as it is that Chen Hongmou voiced the feelings of many landowners in insisting on their right to make self-interested choices about the sale of their grain, Confucian-trained civil servants were expected to transcend their own class viewpoint in framing policy proposals. Wang Pilie, a man of Qingpu county in the Lower Yangzi, did this magnificently (if indeed his background was a landed one) in a memorial that he submitted on 1 December 1744 as provincial surveillance commissioner of Henan. Wang requested firm measures against the two layers of hoarders through which, he suggested, grain had to pass before it reached the retail market: first landlords and then merchants. It was his memorial that inspired the tough new stance on landlord speculative hoarding.

Wang's proposals regarding merchants were rejected as too harsh, although they were not draconian by eighteenth-century standards. Wang asked that, in order to give teeth to a previous prohibition, merchants should be expected to "sell as soon as they [had] bought" (*sui măi, sui mài*); those whose infringements caused price rises "to the people's detriment" should be forced to sell at a 30 percent discount compared with the "current price." Wang apparently expected this to be a serious deterrent; perhaps, therefore, by "current price" he meant the observed seasonal price before alleged merchant misdoing forced it up. If so, there is nothing surprising in the Board of Revenue's objection that a 30 percent price cut would harm the merchants' capital. The Board recommended that effective action to check merchant hoarding be left at the discretion of local authorities, who should devise appropriate surveillance measures in the light of circumstances, avoiding laxity and undue harassment.

In an odd reversal of usual practice, the Board was more amenable to a toughening of measures against big-time landlord hoarders. Its stated rationale leaves doubt as to the real reason: had senior Board officials always thought the 1743 policy of relying upon exhortation too indulgent, or had Wang written in such alarmist tones as to make it politically unwise to dismiss his proposal? The former seems more probable, as Wang had shown himself to be an economic fundamentalist who could normally have been ignored as a crank. His preamble stressed the desirability of limiting, or preferably equalizing, landholdings, on the grounds that otherwise, food would inevitably be in short supply. Then he came to the point: nowadays over half the nation's arable belonged to rich households, who invariably waited for the market price to be "extremely high" before they began to sell their stockpiled grain. Next came some arithmetic. A poor household's annual grain requirement did not exceed 10 *shi* or so. If one rich household stockpiled some 1,000 *shi*, some 100 poor households would be deprived; if 10,000 *shi*, some 1,000 poor households would be deprived—and so on, to the level of the county, then the province, and then finally the realm. The more grain rich households accumulated, the less food there was for the poor, which meant that price stability was not a realistic prospect. It was, in short, the kind of document that usually receives short shrift unless it is perceived as furnishing an opportunity for doing something thought desirable for other reasons, or unless it appeals to a naive power-holder.[42]

Crank or not, Wang showed admirable concern for social justice. He claimed that various acts of bounty by the present emperor had benefited only the rich. As those he listed all concerned agrarian taxation (paid only by landowners), this would have been true for areas where landlordism was so highly developed as to shut out the small peasant proprietor entirely. Let no churlish historian ask exactly where in 1740s China such areas were found. The felicity of rich landowners had been further enhanced, said Wang, by a tightening of discipline that freed them from predation by official personnel and local hoodlums; and yet they still despoiled society in their quest for profit. Determined action by the state was therefore justified. Local officials—sure to know how many rich households lived in their jurisdictions and how much grain each stored—should require such households to release their grain for sale gradually after putting it in store, and to refrain from withholding stocks deliberately to push up the price. Persons who accumulated stockpiles of 1,000, or, still worse, 10,000 *shi* and did not promptly sell them should be forced to contribute to local public works projects; Wang did not say how. Were the antisocial wealthy to be shamed by taking part in manual labor along with the lower orders? Or were they to organize substantial maintenance or construction projects at their own expense? The latter interpretation may be more consistent with Wang's wording, and it makes good sense. Transferring public sector burdens to the shoulders of the guilty rich would force the latter to make restitution to society for the wrong of hoarding.

The Board of Revenue balked at the public works proposal, but not at compulsion for those rural magnates who were cynical and ruthless in exploiting the grain market. Responding to Wang's memorial on 2 January 1745, the senior Board officials restated the existing policy of relying on exhortation to combat landlord hoarding, but then signalled

---

42. Cf. the Qianlong emperor's earlier decision to refer a similar memorial by Wang for consideration by the Nine Ministries Assembly. This memorial expounds what Wang perceived as a vicious cycle between unequal distribution of land ownership, landlord hoarding, and land and grain prices. The analysis was acute (even if not soundly based in fact), but the proposed remedy was little more than wishful thinking. CC, Wang Pilie, QL 7/4/8.

their acceptance of the notion that there were rich commoner landlords so unscrupulous that coercion was the only way. It is not clear on what evidence the Board depicted landlords who, controlling stockpiles in the "full thousands and heaped tens of thousands" of *shi*, refused to sell until they could reap "tenfold profit," their tenacity increasing as the market price rose higher. Nor did the Board pronounce on what coercive measures should be considered justified or what penalties should be inflicted on recalcitrant offenders. What was unambiguous was its endorsement of coercion. Governors and governors-general should be instructed to have local officials post notices, "ensuring without fail that the wealthy households respectfully observe the prohibition and sell [their stocks] off gradually, thereby stabilizing the market price." Should there be landlords who ignored these warnings, the authorities should "force [them] to sell" (*leling chutiao*). The Board prudently added the formula "after weighing up the circumstances," thus allowing local officials some discretion and a possible escape route, but the change of policy was clear.[43]

An objection from the vice censor-in-chief Fan Can did not greatly weaken the Board's resolve. As we saw in the last chapter, Fan claimed that lawless elements would be likely to take advantage of official anti-hoarding proclamations to oppress landowners great and small. He therefore argued for a strategy of confidential suasion backed by positive incentives. The emperor took the unusual step of expressing agreement with Fan's memorial in his rescript ordering the Board to "deliberate [on it] secretly and report swiftly." Put in a difficult position, the senior Board officials had little choice but to find merit in Fan's proposals. It was his insistence on the need for secrecy in exhortation that they rejected. This rejection gave them the opportunity to reinstate legalistic diction where the language of morality might otherwise have reigned supreme. It was, they said, essential that the state's "prohibitions and commands" should be plain for everyone to understand and follow, while the public-order problems that Fan feared could only be reflections of mismanagement. They therefore reiterated that, in years of dearth, clear notices should be posted as a first step, "so that the rich may know that laws should be obeyed, and

---

43. CC, Bd. Rev., QL 9/11/30; this quotes Wang's memorial, which is dated QL 9/10/28.

that for offenders there awaits the governmental interdiction, while those who are obedient will receive the honor of rewards." The emperor approved this. Rich landowners were now to be warned publicly that the law applied to them.[44]

At first sight, there seems to have been no similarly marked shift in policy towards mercantile hoarders. After all, officials were probably less likely to hesitate before threatening merchant hoarders with forced sales or beatings than was the case when they confronted wealthy, well-connected landlord hoarders. There was, therefore, less scope for major escalation in the rigor of the state's response to merchant hoarding. What did take place, however, was a series of explicit bans on the practice of "hoard pawning." There is some evidence that the last of these bans was interpreted—at least in Zhejiang—as mandating unusually determined action not only against any kind of merchant hoarding, but also against anything that arguably resembled it. Thus by the end of 1747, some Lower Yangzi grain dealers were experiencing unusually systematic controls on their activities.

The abuse known as hoard pawning was described in a handful of memorials; these represent it as a phenomenon primarily of the Lower Yangzi provinces, especially Jiangsu and Zhejiang. The main features of the practice, and the case against it, may be summarized in the words of the investigating censor Tang Pin. Having mentioned the attractively low interest rates normally imposed on loans secured by grain deposits, Tang went on:

Suppose a man has only 1,000 taels of capital. He buys a certain quantity of rice, pawns it for 700 to 800 taels, and then, with the utmost dispatch, buys more rice and pawns it for 500 to 600 taels. Purchases and pawnings follow each other in quick succession; at a rough estimate, the cycle does not stop until one portion of capital has bought four or five portions' worth of rice. Then in the *soudure* periods of the following spring and from late summer into early autumn, the price of rice is bound to rise. The merchants, putting together principal and interest, gradually redeem and sell their grain. This means that what the little folk have harvested in one year begins by falling at a low price into merchant hands, and ends by reverting at a high price to the people. The pawnbrokers and hoarders enjoy handsome profits without stirring from their

---

44. QSL/QL, *juan* 230:24b–26a.

seats, while the small folk bear the hardship. The harm done by the hoard pawning of rice is thus extremely serious.[45]

Tang Pin and others succeeded in persuading the emperor that hoard pawning was an evil to be eliminated. Each memorial of complaint about the practice led to approval of coercive action, if not a more general prohibition. Fan Can, as Anhui governor, wrote to the emperor about this matter in June 1744. He mentioned that offending merchants saw hoard pawning as a way of "avoiding the name of *tunhu*"—not necessarily a futile stratagem, since Fan agreed that, technically, the term did not apply to them. He reported that he was prohibiting all pawnbroking transactions that involved significantly more than 100 *shi* of grain, or grain "bought for trading purposes by wicked merchants." The emperor approved this.[46] By early February 1745, the Jiangsu governor had probably received two sets of orders to suppress hoard pawning. The first must have been pursuant to a ban, applying to Jiangsu and Zhejiang, that had been approved before Wang Pilie wrote his memorial; this ban was issued in response to a complaint about hoard pawning by the investigating censor Ma Jing. The second set of orders was probably a clarification of the policy on mercantile hoarding in response to Wang Pilie's memorial.[47]

It was in the spring of 1747 that Tang Pin submitted his denunciation of hoard pawning. Aware that raw silk, raw cotton, and, probably, kinds of grain other than rice were also subject to hoard pawning, he feared that the abuse would spread to other provinces. He therefore proposed measures not only for the Lower Yangzi provinces, but for the whole nation. Tang wanted the onus for eliminating hoard pawning to be placed on pawnbrokers, who he suggested should be punished under the Statute on Violating Imperial Pronouncements (forty strokes of the heavy bamboo) if they persisted in storing "hoard-pawned" grain or other primary products. Pawnshops should be required to declare any such hoards that they were holding; the hoards would then be

---

45. HQZY, *juan* 44:10b–11a; quoted from the integral translation of Tang's memorial in Dunstan, *Conflicting Counsels*, pp. 273–76. For an alternative account, see Yang, *Money and Credit*, p. 74.

46. CC, Fan Can, QL 9/4/26; QSL/QL, *juan* 215:24a–b.

47. CC, Chen Dashou, QL 10/1/8, and Bd. Rev., QL 9/11/30; the latter summarizes Ma Jing's account of the evils of hoard pawning.

compulsorily purchased by the local authorities. Subsequently, the pawnbrokers should be required to submit quarterly bonds vouching that no grain or other primary products had been pledged with them for hoard-formation purposes. The emperor, concurring with Tang's views, ordered that the provincial chief administrators implement his proposals.[48]

About a year later, an edict stated that "last year, the censor Tang Pin set out the case for a severe prohibition against speculative hoarders (*tunhu*), and [an order to this effect] was circulated to all provinces."[49] In view of the specificity of Tang's proposals, the looseness of this wording is surprising. After all, Fan Can had thought that there was a distinction between hoarders and persons who hypothecated the constituents of hoards to pawnbrokers. Moreover, at least one senior territorial official, the Zhejiang provincial administration commissioner Tang Suizu, grasped that the 1747 instructions referred to hoard pawning, as can be seen from his request for an exemption for poor silk producers.[50] And yet his superior, the Zhejiang governor Chang'an, reportedly took action, in the name of this same prohibition, against mercantile hoarding generally. In his zeal, he made it impossible for warehousers to accept consignments of grain for storage.

Exactly what happened is unclear. It is conceivable that Chang'an was scapegoated for a diversion of commercial supplies whose cause lay in a completely different area of state activity, as I explain in chapter 8. For now, I take at face value the retrospective sources that seemingly enable us to reconstruct the story. In his edict repudiating Chang'an's "bad implementation" of the "severe prohibition against speculative hoarders" supposedly initiated by Tang Pin, the emperor (or his ghostwriter) observed that the result of the Zhejiang ban on warehousing had been that "The merchants have nowhere to lay up [their grain]; the region has no grain supplies in store." The main purpose of this edict, issued on 28 May 1748, was to instruct Chang'an's successor, Fang Guancheng, to assess the situation and determine how best to

---

48. HQZY, *juan* 44:11b–12b; QSL/QL, *juan* 286:24a–25a; Dunstan, *Conflicting Counsels*, pp. 258–59, 275–76; cf. Tang's biography in GCQXLZ, *juan* 177:20b.

49. QSL/QL, *juan* 314:6a.

50. The memorial is excerpted in *Qingshi liezhuan*, *juan* 22:42b; reference from Wu Qiyan, "Qingdai qianqi yahang zhi," p. 44.

reduce the market price of grain, which the edict described merely as higher than before, but which another, perhaps more candid, source claims to have "soared daily higher [throughout the area] from Suzhou to Hangzhou since hoarding was forbidden."[51] In his mid-June reply, Fang assured the emperor of his own grasp of the issues by discussing the ways in which Chang'an's interpretation of the ban had been mistaken. This exposition provides some details of the crisis while suggesting a rationale for Chang'an's eccentric action.

Fang noted that, on his way to take up office (probably in late April or early May), he had learned that grain prices were very high from Shandong south as far as Hangzhou. In Shandong's case, bad harvests provided a likely explanation. While opinions differed as to why prices were high in "Suzhou, Songjiang, Hangzhou, and Huzhou," many people blamed the paucity of grain merchants now arriving in these Lower Yangzi cities. This, in turn, was thought to be because warehouse proprietors no longer dared to store their cargoes. Fang had verified that the Hangzhou warehousers had stopped storing grain. He reported that in that city there were twenty-four warehouses serving the waterborne grain trade, and that, until recently, these had held about 200,000 *shi* of husked rice (presumably in aggregate) when full. Now, however, they were mostly empty, and "there is nothing in which the population can have confidence."

Even granting the ill repute of the Hangzhou rice-warehousers, which might have made them ready targets of a ban, how could Chang'an and his two immediate successors, Guzong and—very

---

51. QSL/QL, *juan* 314:6a–7a; memorial by Chen Zhaolun, transc. his *Zizhu Shan Fang shiwen ji, juan* 5:17a–18a (for edited version, see HCJSWB, *juan* 40:6a–b). The date of this memorial is not available, and there is no internal evidence to clinch the assumption that the ban whose effects it denounces was that of 1747. However, Chen was a native of Hangzhou, and the points he makes are consistent with the more dispassionate accounts elsewhere. His implicit explanation for the surge in prices is (a) that grain merchants had lost interest in the northern Zhejiang market because the unavailability of warehousing services prevented their disposing of their grain in bulk; and (b) that there were now extra costs being passed on to consumers—the costs, for the remaining merchants, of being forced to stay in cities like Hangzhou to sell their grain piecemeal.

briefly—Aibida, have allowed such a dangerous situation to develop?[52] In stating the dimensions of Chang'an's error, Fang offered one possible clue. He noted that there was a distinction between the pawning of locally-grown grain, which was the intended object of the bans inspired by Ma Jing's and Tang Pin's memorials, and the reception of grain imported from other regions, which Chang'an had prevented from being temporarily amassed in warehouses. Commercial warehousing was akin to brokerage, Fang pointed out, and could not be likened to pawnbroking. "Even if there are [some long-distance merchants who] pledge rice for silver at the warehouse and then seek to buy more rice, they will still be buying it from rice-growing regions such as Huguang and Anhui. This means that the rice will be arriving from outside, enabling the area to have abundant supplies and low prices, which is quite different from pawning local [grain] to the detriment of popular subsistence."[53] In other words, the warehouses may have been extending credit to the interregional grain merchants, with the cargoes that were placed with them for storage serving as security. Thus, however mistaken, Chang'an's action in (presumably) making the warehousers liable to the measures recommended by Tang Pin may not have been completely arbitrary.

What could Fang have meant by saying that commercial warehousing was akin to brokerage? A passage in the edict to which he was responding suggests an explanation. The edict observed that northern Zhejiang depended for more than half its rice supply on boats coming down via Suzhou from Jiangxi and Huguang. When these boats arrived, it was standard practice for the brokers to unload their cargoes into warehouses and to release the grain for sale gradually. "Local markets" (*xiangshi*), that is, markets outside the major cities, were dependent on this process. Even when few boats arrived from the Middle Yangzi, the fact that such opportunities induced the sale of warehoused stocks

---

52. An editorial discussion in a work published with imperial sponsorship in 1740 singles out the Hangzhou rice-warehousers as the most "detestable" of profiteers and hoarders. Lu, *Qinding kangji lu*, p. 330. For the rapid turnover in Zhejiang governors after Chang'an's dismissal in the autumn of 1747, see Qian, comp., *Qingdai zhiguan nianbiao*, vol. 2, pp. 1,598–99.

53. CC, Fang Guancheng, QL 13/5/19.

meant that there was no cause for fear.[54] In other words, the brokers who now controlled the stocks (and presumably owned the warehouses as well) operated in much the same way as speculative hoarders did, keeping stocks in reserve until the market offered an incentive to sell. This suggests another possible rationale for Chang'an's action. Like the investigators in the 1778 Tongzhou case, he may have fallen foul of the difficulty of distinguishing between normal, legitimate commercial arrangements and the illegal activity of hoarding.[55] For a governor who was "not overwise," it was, perhaps, enough that the warehousers held stocks of grain, some of which may have been security for advances to interregional grain merchants, and that they took their time to sell.

Why, given that Chang'an's jurisdiction did not extend to Suzhou and Songjiang, were prices high in these two southern Jiangsu prefectures as well? The northern Zhejiang cities were "downstream" of Suzhou in the extended Yangzi Valley distribution network; thus a near cessation of rice-boat arrivals in northern Zhejiang should not have had any great impact on Suzhou. Unless the southern Jiangsu *cherté* was due entirely to the adverse weather conditions mentioned in a local security report, or to yet other causes, there are two possible explanations.[56] One is that territorial officials in the Suzhou-Songjiang region had made the same kind of mistake as had Chang'an; the other is that Chang'an's blunder was even more deeply disruptive of the Yangzi Valley grain trade than Fang described. If the transactions that Chang'an identified as "hoard pawning" were in fact credit arrangements that contributed significantly to the financing of the Yangzi Valley grain trade, it is natural that much of this trade would have been paralyzed by an abrupt suspension of the system.[57] Deliveries of grain to Suzhou would have been affected.

---

54. Literally, "the warehoused stocks are sold, taking advantage of the occasion." QSL/QL, *juan* 314:6a–b.

55. Cf. chap. 1 above.

56. The 1748 Jiangsu wheat harvest was affected by flooding in March followed by hailstorms on 30 April and 1 May. KYQRFDZ, vol. 2, p. 583; cf. Santangelo, "Urban Society," p. 104.

57. A hint in a work published in 1740 that the Hangzhou warehousers exercised power over *wealthy*, presumably long-distance merchants makes better sense if the former were creditors of the latter, although the complaint is only that the ware-

The upshot of the northern Zhejiang fiasco was indeterminate, reflecting, I think, something more than the fundamental ambivalence of Qing policy on hoarding. Let us look chronologically at developments of the first half of 1748. At the beginning of the year, outright prohibition of speculative hoarding was still in vogue, although the emperor was beginning to have doubts. Xu Qi, the Shaanxi governor, had reported that he was implementing selective controls on grain exports from Shaanxi in response to mediocre harvests and grain price increases. Believing that ruthless stock accumulation was often preparatory to large-scale exportation, he used the same memorial to complain about engrossers (some of them "merchants from outside") amassing grain either through futures transactions or by "buying piecemeal but hoarding wholesale" (*lingdi zhengdun*) when the new grain reached the market. The hoarders allegedly sold only when the price had doubled. Concerned both to relieve existing pressures on Shaanxi prices and to prevent abuse of grain sold cheaply from the ever-normal granaries, Xu had ordered measures to stop the engrossers from exporting grain, as well as to curb hoarding. The emperor broadly endorsed his memorial on 3 January, but he also referred the part about grain futures and engrossing to the Grand Council for comment. Reporting on 11 January, the Council both agreed that buying grain futures from peasants should be strictly banned, and invoked the favorable decision on Wang Pilie's memorial to point out that firm action against hoarding was already the policy in force. The entire territorial bureaucracy should be reminded that active vigilance against hoarders was required. While the emperor approved this on 12 January, an edict of the same date expressed reservations about the decision.[58]

The 12 January edict was that in which the emperor asked provincial chief administrators why grain prices had been rising over recent years. He listed hoarding as one possible cause, thereby inviting comment on this issue. In fact, as discussed in chapter 7, he had an agenda that had not much to do with private-sector hoarding—at least, not directly. The skepticism, expressed in passing, about the recommendations that he

housers withhold stocks from the market "if the rich merchants slightly fail to comply with their wishes." Lu, *Qinding kangji lu*, p. 330.

58. LFZZ, Xu Qi, QL 12/12/3 (d.r.); YFD, QL 12/12/12 (d.r.) (7:1615-2); QSL/QL, *juan* 304:14b–15a, 16a; cf. Wang Xianqian, comp., *Donghua xu lu, juan* 26:11b.

had just approved was partly a matter of lack of faith in the diligence of the bureaucracy. He also commented, however, that it remained to be seen whether, even if local officials did implement any serious enforcement measures, these would actually have a salutary effect upon the level of grain prices.[59] It would be going too far to call this remark prophetic; however, when Chang'an's serious enforcement efforts sent grain prices "soaring," the court should not have been taken unawares. In his edict of 28 May, the emperor enunciated a principle that, had it been followed consistently, would have inaugurated a *volte-face* on policy on hoarding, as well as encouraging retreat from other interventionist approaches. However, although the edict used some vocabulary of a Chinese economic liberalism, present in almost equal measure were expressions of distrust of the bureaucracy. As a result, the message was not that market forces can be trusted to realize the best possible outcomes for society, but rather that the inherent flaws of the bureaucracy are likely to vitiate any governmental measures. In view of the Zhejiang fiasco, this emphasis is perhaps understandable.

As is well known by now, in the May edict, the emperor eschewed governmental management of "the affairs of the market-place" in favor (in most cases) of "let[ting] the people carry out the circulation for themselves" (*ting minjian zi wei liutong*).[60] The edict cited the discovery, after an unsuccessful regulatory experiment in 1744–45, that the best way of controlling the "price" (exchange value) of coin in Beijing was in fact to "govern it by nongovernance" (*yi buzhi zhi zhi*);[61] and the instructions to Fang Guancheng (at least in the version that Fang actually received) specified that he was to "cause the market price to come down *naturally* day by day" (emphasis added).[62] The activities of "brokers and verminous bullies" were to be subjected to secret surveillance, but society was to be spared the laying down of yet further vexatious rules and regulations. In short, governmental intervention should be mini-

---

59. QSL/QL, *juan* 304:16a–b.

60. Naquin and Rawski, *Chinese Society*, pp. 25–26; Dunstan, "'Orders Go Forth,'" p. 134; Dunstan, *Conflicting Counsels*, p. 260.

61. Dunstan, "'Orders Go Forth,'" parts 1 and 3, esp. pp. 132–34.

62. The word "naturally" (*ziran*) does not occur in the *Shilu* version of this edict. However, it was included both in the court letter that transcribed the edict for Fang and the other chief Jiangnan administrators, and in the re-transcription of the edict in Fang's reply. *Qianlong tingji*, vol. 1, p. 96; CC, Fang Guancheng, QL 13/5/19.

mal, both in this case and as a larger principle, but the reason for this was only that if government began to take a managerial role, "what was originally intended to be beneficial to the people [would], with unsatisfactory implementation, turn out full of hindrances." Fang was specifically instructed not to make unrestrained use of menial subaltern personnel, who were a byword for harassment in official discourse.[63]

There was thus no imperially-sanctioned positive economic principle or theory to direct future action. Within the guidelines that the emperor had established (and that were communicated not only to Fang, but also to the governors and governor-general for Jiangsu and Anhui), all could proceed according to the dictates of common sense. The measures Fang proposed for dealing with the crisis in Zhejiang embodied this approach precisely. He would still enforce the prohibition on hoard pawning insofar as it referred to locally-grown grain; and, in order to attract long-distance merchants back to northern Zhejiang markets, he would publicize the fact that there was no indiscriminate ban on warehousing. The emperor endorsed this with a simple "noted."[64] So far, so good, but common sense, it seems, also prompted the Board of Revenue to recommend, and the emperor to approve, within two weeks of the 28 May edict, a renewed ban on "wicked merchants seizing opportunities to buy and store, engaging privily in hoarding."[65] Society was not to be left in any radical sense to manage the commercial distribution of grain for itself.

It is not usually a good thing when governments base economic policy on doctrinaire adherence to a theory. It is possible, although not obvious, that mid-eighteenth-century Chinese society was better served by its theoretically naive and inconsistent monarchy than was 1760s France by the resolute *économistes* who advised Louis XV. Even so, it is worth pausing to emphasize the limitations of the 28 May edict, which, despite its liberal rhetoric, is best not cited as an expression of "faith . . . in the responsiveness of market forces to supply and demand."[66] While there were numerous rudimentary expressions of such faith by senior

---

63. *Qianlong tingji*, vol. 1, pp. 95–96; CC, Fang Guancheng, QL 13/5/19; cf. QSL/QL, *juan* 314:6b–7a.
64. CC, Fang Guancheng, QL 13/5/19.
65. QSL/QL, *juan* 314:36b.
66. Naquin and Rawski, *Chinese Society*, p. 26.

Chinese and Manchu civil servants in the "long 1740s," these were not the inspiration for the 28 May edict but part of its context. In particular, various arguments of principle against antihoarding bans were submitted to the throne in the late 1740s, as I show in the next section. Potentially, and in combination with points made elsewhere, on other issues, these offered a coherent theoretical rationale for a consistent policy of nonintervention in the grain trade. What the May edict reflects is not the emperor embracing such a policy, but, arguably, the court being distracted from any serious engagement with the vision of "governing by nongovernance" by the folly of a senior administrator.

Does this episode in turn reflect a larger problem? Was preoccupation with bureaucratic failings one factor militating, for better or for worse, against imperial support for the development of disciplined, innovative, and consciously theoretical approaches to political economy in mid-Qing China? The limited development of theory was not without significance. That the Qianlong emperor in 1748 did not anticipate the 1760s French experiment with a radical, ideologically-inspired liberalization of the grain trade is perhaps not remarkable, given the rather different circumstances in China.[67] What is important is that mid-Qing economic policy, being guided only by the elements of theory, was inevitably at the mercy of empiricism. It is probably the lack of a replacement for empiricism, more than any imperial commitment to the golden mean, that explains the "zigzagging" in mid-Qing public policy.

The Speculator Vindicated

Reacting—probably—to the northern Zhejiang crisis, the Hangzhou-born official Chen Zhaolun intimated that he wished someone would have the courage to say openly that hoarding should be encouraged.[68] What could he have meant? This section explores the defences of the hoarder that were put forward in the later 1740s in a policy context that

---

67. On the 1760s French experiment, see Kaplan, *Bread*, vol. 1, pp. 90–96 and chap. 3. The rest of Kaplan's book discusses the controversial implementation of the liberalization, its reception by society, and the subsistence crises that tested its theoretical rationale.

68. Chen Zhaolun, *Zizhu Shan Fang shiwen ji, juan* 5:18a.

was, as we have seen, increasingly hostile to hoarding. The defences were of three kinds. First, some attention was paid to the function of hoarding in stock conservation, across time, within the individual community. Here, the argument was akin to that of Adam Smith's classic vindication of the speculator, although much less developed.[69] More prominent in the Chinese discussions was, second, recognition of the speculator's role in doing what consumers and officials were not allowed to do coercively: retain marketed stocks for the future consumption of the home community (rather than letting them be sucked into the interregional or interlocal grain trade). Third, some authors also drew attention to the needs of sellers, which, they argued, could be better met if speculation were at least partially tolerated. A majority of the texts introduced below stressed the importance of private grain reserves in the event of famine or acute preharvest food shortage; a key assumption, explicit or implicit in most of the discussions, was that the self-interest of hoarders ensured that stocks were not withheld indefinitely, but were brought forth by price incentives. The remaining question, given such perceptions, was how much, if anything, the state should do to hasten the predicted sales. The consensus was that exhortation, if not pressure, was needed in times of shortage; however, there are signs that even this consensus was not fully firm.

I do not claim that no hint of such defences can be found before the pendulum swung towards decisive antihoarding proclamations in 1745. Already in the late 1730s, during a debate over the desirability of banning yeast production (as a step to eliminating the grain-based liquor industry), Nasutu, the governor-general of Jiangsu, Anhui, and Jiangxi, had remarked that buying up and hoarding wheat represented "the people's normal practice in buying cheap and selling dear." As long as it was not a preliminary to large-scale yeast production, there was no need to ban it. At about the same time, the Shaanxi governor Zhang Kai suggested that speculative hoarding, which was, he said, ubiquitous in Shaanxi, supplemented official buying in keeping prices up for wheat growers, thereby averting any risk of glut.[70] Also not new was Celeng's

---

69. Adam Smith, *Wealth of Nations*, vol. 2, pp. 30–31 and 40–41.

70. Memorial by Nasutu, QL 3/10/12, transc. Ye, comp., "Qianlong nianjian Jiangnan," p. 16; memorial by Zhang Kai, QL 3/9/15, transc. idem, "Qianlong

argument that controls on the pawning of grain and textile raw materials were liable to harm peasant producers. In 1728, Li Wei, as Zhejiang provincial chief, had countered a proposal that Huzhou pawnbrokers be forbidden to accept pledges of grain by describing arrangements similar to those Celeng outlined two decades later. The main difference was that the peasants of the Huzhou-Jiaxing region in the 1720s could apparently redeem their rice with the proceeds of the wheat and raw silk harvests, rather than by pledging their winter clothes. This meant that the transactions were, unambiguously, secured money loans. Li admitted that the terms initially seemed somewhat unfavorable to the borrower, with rice valued at 1.0 tael securing a loan of only 0.6 to 0.7 tael; however, as the monthly interest rates were only 1.0 or 1.5 percent, the redeemed grain was still "cheap rice" compared with that available upon the *soudure* market. Li also pointed out that grain placed with a pawnbroker was thereby fixed in the community of its production and preserved from being carried off elsewhere.[71]

Finally, in February 1744, less than a year before the Board of Revenue endorsed coercive action against landlord hoarding, the Zhili governor-general, Gao Bin, opposed the regimen of forced sales that a central government official, Wang Chengyao, had proposed for the disaster-stricken region south of the capital. Wang, a vice-president of the Board of Military Affairs, had expressed concern about the "wicked, mean" behavior of rich merchants and "local people who have surplus wealth"; having made large speculative purchases while grain was cheap, they were disinclined to sell as prices rose. Wang recommended that the responsible county magistrates be ordered, through Gao, to make the hoarders sell their stocks locally, on pain of punishment, at a

---

nianjian Jiangbei," part 1, p. 32; cf. Dunstan, *Conflicting Counsels*, pp. 208–15, 234–40.

71. Sasaki, "Shindai kanryō," p. 36. In the 1740s, Celeng was not the only official to express a sympathetic understanding of why peasants pawned primary products. Fan Can likewise noted that farmers pawned grain out of fear to sell it. When Tang Pin's proposed ban on hoard pawning was approved, Tang Suizu worried that it would prevent poor northern Zhejiang sericulturists from pawning their raw silk at times of low demand, while waiting for a favorable market opportunity. Their pressing need for monetary income would force them to rely on "wicked" brokers who would underpay them for their produce. CC, Fan Can, QL 9/4/26; *Qingshi liezhuan, juan* 22:42b.

fair price determined by the authorities. Gao conveyed his disagreement in a memorial that, once or twice, bordered on the theoretical.

Much of Gao's counterargument amounted to a claim that there was little mischief against which to take action. He had already done about all that was necessary, for market incentives and a sense of social responsibility within the landlord class had done most of the rest. Early in the disaster, he had ordered conscientious surveillance in the two stricken prefectures, as well as an investigation of the activities of grain dealers in the Baigou valley area on the margin of the disaster zone. As the waterborne commerce down the River Baigou was believed to tempt local shopkeepers to buy up grain and beans, Gao had ordered the local authorities to find out how much grain each shopkeeper was holding. The total had turned out not to exceed 3,000 *shi*, and the shopkeepers had submitted bonds attesting that they were moving their grain to two specified counties that were in the grip of drought. Gao pointed out that no official ban on hoarding had been needed to achieve this. As "the merchants were already able to make profit," they were "naturally disinclined to store their grain for long, but indeed vied to go to the disaster zone." Systematic enquiries in the disaster-stricken prefectures, meanwhile, had shown that there were no local rich people with unduly large bought stocks of grain. There were large landowners with surplus stores that they were loath to sell, but moral exhortation in accordance with the policy of 1743 had brought results. Gao was receiving reports of landlords providing their tenants with grain or voluntarily cooking gruel to supplement official relief efforts.

Towards the end of his discussion, Gao declared faith in the same scenario that had beguiled Chen Hongmou the year before.[72] However the owners of large stocks had come by them, now, with grain scarce and its price high, they were bound to seize the opportunity to sell, motivated by an "urgent quest for generous profit." The imminence of official measures to stabilize the price of grain would give further encouragement, for such people were too astute to let their plans be ruined by official cut-price sales or subsistence loans to poor people. They would sell in time, without being forced to do so; forcing them would only make them hide their grain away more deeply. However, Gao did

---

72. Chap. 2 above.

not propose to test this hopeful doctrine through experiment. To the contrary, officials in the disaster zone would be enjoined to maintain "stern surveillance and effective prohibition."[73]

It is thus not permissible to claim that the harsh antihoarding policies of the late 1740s provoked a breakthrough based on radically new conceptions. What may have been distinctive was the rather systematic and somewhat more abstract nature of the discussions generated when the antihoarding measures, followed, some time later, by imperial doubts about their wisdom, brought the topic of grain speculation to the forefront of attention. Faced with demands for outright bans in 1745, Fan Can, as a vice censor-in-chief, and Chen Dashou, as Jiangsu governor, wrote reasoned objections. In 1748, four other provincial chief administrators (one Chinese and three Manchu), having been asked to assess hoarding as one possible inflationary pressure, submitted reflections that were thoughtful and had interesting implications. One of the six contributions was Celeng's, discussed above; the other five will be examined closely in what follows.

Celeng and, possibly, Chen Dashou apart, these authors did opine that limited official action to restrain hoarders was necessary in some circumstances. Not one of the six could be described as a pure anti-interventionist on all aspects of subsistence policy. However, not only were their opinions far removed from the notion that hoarders should be beaten to punish their own wickedness and to deter stockpiling by others; their combined arguments logically imply the possibility that official intervention might, in fact, not be necessary at all.

Fan Can worried that the Board of Revenue's coercive policy would have unintended economic, as well as law and order, consequences. He therefore found it an imprudent way of counteracting landlord hoarding, an objective that he did not see as problematic in itself. Fan, a native of Jiangsu, argued that famine-preparedness in rural communities was crucially dependent on the stockpiles of the local rich. The real fear for poor folk was that the grain of the wealthy would be carried off by merchants who, coming from distances of hundreds or thousands of *li*, had nothing to do with the communities where they bought supplies.

---

73. The emperor's rescript was "Noted," implying tacit acceptance. CC, Gao Bin, QL 8/12/19. On the 1743–44 Zhili subsistence crisis, see Will, *Bureaucracy and Famine*.

If wealthy stockpilers were ordered to sell their grain, communities that lay on water routes would be especially vulnerable to depletion through the export trade. In such circumstances, the stockpilers would naturally opt for the convenience of bulk sales onto the external market. They would, Fan thought, all be in contact with some trusty broker who could have their stocks removed in no time. "The popular indigence that, to this point, had been an object of concern was a matter of depleted [households] without a hundredweight or bushel of reserves already occupying half [the population]. Once the wealthy are entirely bereft of surplus, the depletion [that will be experienced on] that day will be true depletion."

The implication of Fan's views so far is that hoarding was useful because it guaranteed that there would be reserves of grain scattered around the countryside to supplement the stocks of the official granaries. It did not follow that, in his opinion, officialdom could leave hoarders entirely alone, knowing that they would put their stocks on sale in their own good time. In Fan's experience, it was in years when an abundant harvest seemed assured that grain poured onto the preharvest market, its owners vying to dispose of it before the price fell. In the preharvest period of bad years, recalling landlord hoarders to their moral duty was an urgent task, although, as we have seen, Fan thought it should be accomplished confidentially.[74] Thus, in his views as to the proper state response to hoarding, Fan still thought within the conventional framework discussed in the previous two chapters. A self-interested hoarder, left to himself in a bad year, would be likely to persist in starving the market; the resulting aggravation of popular misery demanded governmental action, although a legalistic approach was not the right one.

Chen Dashou, Jiangsu governor since 1741, had adopted the practice of issuing annual instructions that grain-owners be exhorted to sell their stocks off gradually in the *soudure* period, but there is reason to question how far he really thought this necessary. The purpose of his memorial of 8 February 1745 was to submit an argument of principle against bans on hoarding. Chen had been ordered, as we have seen, to

---

74. QSL/QL, *juan* 230:21b–23a; text checked, where possible, against the fuller version excerpted in Kishimoto, *Shindai Chūgoku no bukka*, p. 310. Cf. chap. 2 above.

implement a prohibition on hoard pawning. He reported that he had previously instructed magistrates to collect signed bonds from local pawnbrokers renouncing all such business, but his main concern was to argue that hoarding served a useful purpose. One has the impression that he reported action chiefly because he was expected to. He claimed that speculators sold once prices were high, and in any case before the autumn harvest; it was, presumably, only to the extent that some individuals responded slowly to the market's message that there was a real role for exhortation. As Chen arguably showed signs of insecurity about the speed with which some hoards were sold, we cannot presume that he thought exhortation useless. His emphasis, however, was different from Fan Can's. *Merchant* hoarding, although motivated by self-interest, was useful; self-interest prompted socially beneficial sales. Chen was concerned not with the nature of the state's response but with the protection of the hoarder's contribution.

Chen made a couple of common-sense points tending to ridicule advocates of bans on hoarding. The high prices of *soudure* periods were part of an annual cycle of fluctuations driven, ultimately, by conditions in the countryside. It was not the case that they were caused entirely by hoarding. Wang Pilie had urged that merchants be required to sell their grain as soon as they had bought it; probably with Wang's memorial in mind, Chen pointed out that such a policy would cause post-harvest grain prices to fall even lower than normal, which would hurt the farmers. The nub of his argument, however, concerned the function of speculation in conserving stocks. The merchant's self-interest caused him to accumulate (possibly through transactions of the hoard pawning type) reserves that he would keep until local shortage offered him an incentive to sell them. The fact that he had the reserves to sell would then be in the local people's vital interests.[75] So far, Chen's point seems to have been, like Fan's, only that hoarding keeps supplies within the

---

75. "There are . . . recurrent cases of those whose capital is somewhat more substantial [than that of petty shopkeepers] accumulating stocks through minor purchases and awaiting a good price. Although this is [the working of] the merchant's profit-seeking heart, once the price is high, the rice is sold, and [thus] is still consumed within the local area. The market does not run short of rice; the price is kept from rising even higher." Translation adapted from Dunstan, *Conflicting Counsels*, p. 277. This and other key passages from the memorials under examination are quoted in the original in Deng (Dunstan), "Tunhu yu jihuang," pp. 228–31.

home community; indeed, Chen noted that a further disadvantage of forcing merchants to resell immediately would be that the resulting glut would inevitably provoke a flight of stocks to more favorable markets. However, Chen also argued that "Only a certain given total is produced. Rather than rushing to have it sold cheaply, taking no account of the deficiency to come, would it not be closer to the mark to keep it stored within the population, and let it come onto the market in an unbroken flow?"[76] Here he clearly referred to the role of speculators in managing the timed release of available stocks within the local context.

What exactly had he in mind? There is no warrant for assuming that he had arrived at Adam Smith's belief that speculators, with conscious calculation and entirely in pursuit of their own interests, assisted society with an exact rationing of the available food supplies in years of dearth.[77] One may more modestly suggest that he would have understood Richard Leftwich's textbook argument that speculators "smooth out both prices and quantities sold over the entire period" of the agricultural year;[78] however, it is not clear exactly how he thought their operations helped grain to "come onto the market in an unbroken flow." He may have believed the mechanism to be that which the Qianlong emperor discerned in the activities of the Hangzhou grain brokers, or, for that matter, that on which the deliberate price-stabilization efforts of the banner grain bureaus depended: the controllers of reserves released a portion of their stocks whenever upward price fluctuations signalled that the market was short of grain. Such an understanding would clearly have been within reach of an eighteenth-century Chinese observer, and it may also have been closer to reality,

---

76. Translation from Dunstan, *Conflicting Counsels*, p. 278.

77. For Smith, "When the scarcity is real, the best thing that can be done for the people is to divide the inconveniencies [*sic*] of it as equally as possible through all the different months and weeks, and days of the year. The interest of the corn merchant makes him study to do this [as] exactly as he can: and as no other person can have either the same interest, or the same knowledge, or the same abilities to do it so exactly as he, this most important operation of commerce ought to be trusted entirely to him. . . ." Adam Smith, *Wealth of Nations*, vol. 2, p. 41; for further elaboration, including an analogy with rationing aboard ship, see ibid., pp. 30–31.

78. Words from Leftwich, *Price System*, quoted in Chuan and Kraus, *Mid-Ch'ing Rice Markets*, p. 25.

for Europe as well as China, than Smith's model of the precisely calculating ration-master.[79]

Huang Tinggui and Aligun, as governors of Gansu and Shandong respectively, belonged to a small group of provincial chief administrators who noted the positive functions of hoarding in their responses to the 1748 imperial questionnaire about the recent rise in grain prices. These two respondents drew attention to the needs of sellers. If we compare their views on hoarding with their opinions on the ever-normal granaries, we find a pattern that at first looks paradoxical. While both thought hoarding socially useful, both supported the same ever-normal granaries whose *raison d'être* included confounding the schemes of hoarders. The paradox is quickly resolved when one appreciates their logic.

It was the commercial isolation of Gansu communities that, in Huang's opinion, made the role of speculation benign in that province. Not only were the risks of famine in Gansu exceptionally severe because of the difficulty of bringing in supplies from elsewhere in the empire or indeed the province; the lack of effective external demand for Gansu grain also exposed Gansu farmers to unusually high risks of glut. Gansu therefore needed speculative activity for the same reason as it needed ever-normal operations. Peasants who urgently required cash income after harvest benefited from the activities of small-time speculators (many of them from Shanxi or Shaanxi) who accumulated hoards of up to some hundreds of *shi* during the autumn while the price was low. Forbidding this small-scale hoarding, even if feasible, would both drive poor peasants into the moneylender's clutches and deprive Gansu communities of necessary extra grain reserves in case of harvest failure. Huang thus painted an unexpected picture of petty profit-motivated hoarding supplementing state stockpiling in the latter's role of furnishing demand in time of plenty and supply in time of shortage. He denied that there were any big-time speculators operating in Gansu. He did, however, assume that local officials could put hoarders under pressure to sell their grain without delay at a reduced price in subsis-

---

79. CC, Chen Dashou, QL 10/1/8. For further discussion of this text and a partial translation, see Dunstan, *Conflicting Counsels*, pp. 259–62 and 276–79.

tence crises; in this, he was closer to the interventionist position even than Fan Can.[80]

The risks of peasant farming in Shandong were surely less extreme than those that stalked the Gansu countryside, yet Aligun's account of the utility of speculation was very similar to Huang's. After the autumn harvest, Aligun suggested, the interests of the farmers who needed to sell grain were matched by those of speculators who wanted to buy it; in the *soudure* period, the community was rescued from the annual shortage by the speculators' sales. Strict prohibition would mean driving the farmers to sell their grain to merchants serving other markets. Aligun shared the opinion that speculators, being in business only with a view to making sales, might wait for the right price before they sold but would not hoard their grain indefinitely. He even resorted to sophistry, twisting ancient definitions to suggest that hoarders qualified as regular merchants of the non-travelling type (*gu*), and that the state's handling of them should not violate its traditional, supportive stance towards the legitimate commercial sector. Intervention should be limited to encouraging speculators to sell in timely fashion and forbidding deliberate manipulation of the *soudure* market.[81] Aligun and Huang Tinggui could thus reasonably have argued that the roles of speculation and of the ever-normal system were complementary: the former reinforced the latter, while the latter was available to check the possible excesses of the former. They could logically have seen official cut-price sales as a delicate arrangement to maximize social utility by restraining profiteering without deterring hoard formation.

Celeng and Aligun were not the only 1748 respondents to point out that speculators did eventually sell and/or to mention the importance of their sales for vulnerable communities.[82] Let us move on, however, to the more radical ideas of Kaerjishan, governor-general of Fujian and Zhejiang. Kaerjishan had been Chang'an's superior when the latter is-

---

80. CC, Huang Tinggui, QL 13/4/24.

81. LFZZ, Aligun, QL 13/8/6 (d.r.); QSL/QL, *juan* 323:47a–b.

82. See, e.g., CC, Chen Hongmou, QL 13 (cat. no. 1143-013), and Tuerbing'a, QL 13/6/9. Undated archived memorials such as Chen's are copies; in these cases, I supply catalog numbers from the "Treasury and Granary Reserves" volume of the published catalog of palace memorials on fiscal matters held by the Beijing archives (Zhongguo Diyi Lishi Dang'an Guan, comp., *Zhongguo Diyi*, vol. 3).

sued his unfortunate orders on suppressing hoarding. He may not have known much about the crisis, as the governor-general's official residence was in Fuzhou, and the emperor probably did not involve him when he ordered Fang Guancheng to remedy the situation.[83] If, however, Kaerjishan did have Chang'an's actions in mind when writing his remarks about the role of hoarding, he must have thought that his subordinate's approach could not have been more undesirable.

Kaerjishan argued that prohibitions against speculative hoarding should be discriminating. While they should be severe in times of shortage, policy should recognize that wealthy merchants who accumulated hoards in good years were building reserves whose value would be seen when shortage struck. The merchant stocks would then be needed, for otherwise the population would become wholly dependent on the inadequate supplies of the official granaries. Alone among the authors discussed here, Kaerjishan specifically mentioned how valuable the private stocks would be if they were kept at population centers or at nodes on land or water routes.[84] Whether Kaerjishan was conscious of the fact or not, this notion mimicked thinking that was sometimes influential in the planning of the ever-normal system.[85] His suggestion that merchant hoarding could, in the right circumstances, be regarded as precautionary antifamine stockpiling was a large extension of the more common position that hoarding served local consumer interests by keeping stocks at home. His view had potentially far-reaching implications, for it could have been further extended to suggest at least partial privatization of the state's role in precautionary grain storage. If one could be sure either that the state could make private stockpilers sell in times of dearth, or that their interests would prompt them to do so of their own accord, why not let merchants provide a higher proportion of the stock conservation services needed by society, and save the state the bother?

---

83. Kaerjishan was not included in the distribution list for the court letter giving Fang the imperial view about the crisis and its management. *Qianlong tingji*, vol. 1, p. 93. On the location of the Min-Zhe governor-general's headquarters, see Zhao Ersun et al., comps., *Qingshi gao*, vol. 8, *juan* 65, p. 2,127; vol. 9, *juan* 70, p. 2,242.

84. CC, Kaerjishan, QL 13/6/26 (fragment).

85. See, e.g., the 1731 decision to build supplementary prefectural granaries at nodal points on the water-transport network in four especially populous prefectures of Jiangsu province. QCWXTK, vol. 1, *juan* 35, p. 5,184.

How Market-Conscious Qing Officials
Thought the Market Worked

Despite the 1740s vindications of the speculator, the interventionist tradition in policy on hoarding proved resilient. [86] But the anti-interventionist tradition, and a disposition to accept hoarding as normal, were robust as well. In 1759, Tang Pin, of all people, listed criteria for grading brokers (presumably those of Jiangxi, where he was provincial administration commissioner at the time) into three divisions. One criterion was whether their businesses involved *tunfa*, literally "releasing [for sale goods previously] amassed," that is, warehousing goods prior to selling them for merchant clients. He was evidently using the word *tun* (usually, "to hoard") without any connotation of immorality or illegality. [87] In 1764, the Gansu provincial administration commissioner, Wang Jian, advocated greater respect for the letter of a regulation that set the ceiling for the amount of grain that could be hoarded with impunity as high as 100,000 *shi*. Beyond that limit, "rich households" who did not sell immediately of their own accord were to be forced to do so. Emphasizing the importance of private purchases of grain, which helped the growers and created stockpiles that could be used to relieve shortage, Wang complained that local officials were indiscriminately banning all such buying, with the result that crafty persons were colluding with subaltern bureaucratic staff to set up local grain monopsonies, which depressed the price received by farmers. He suggested that popular talk of a "disaster caused by plenty" (*shuhuang*—an expression that normally referred to glutted grain markets) was actually a reflection of the monopsonies' impact. Wang asked the court to clarify to territorial officials nationwide that persons buying grain futures or accumulating a full 100,000 *shi* of grain and refusing to sell were liable to punishment, but otherwise "the people should be left to do as suits them." [88] In view of Huang Tinggui's 1748 denial that large-scale

---

86. See, for example, the 1778 investigation of warehoused wheat at Tongzhou, and the 1814 decision against large-scale hoarders in Anhui (chap. 1 above).

87. Wu Qiyan, "Qingdai qianqi yahang zhi," p. 32.

88. Wang Jian, QL 29/2/24, repr. GZD/QL, vol. 20, pp. 643–44. The transcription in HQZY, *juan* 55:30a–32a, inserts a *wu* (five) between *shi* (ten) and *wan*

hoarding took place in Gansu, it is interesting that it was a Gansu senior official who drew attention to a rule implying that no action need be taken against persons who withheld up to 100,000 *shi*. Perhaps, by 1764, the need for bulk grain shipments to support the conquest and colonization of the empire's far western New Borderlands (Xinjiang, reached through the Gansu corridor and appropriated during 1755–59) had influenced the level of commercial stockpiling that the Gansu provincial authorities thought desirable.[89]

It is beyond the scope of the present study to determine whether official policy on hoarding zigzagged for the remainder of the eighteenth century, and whether there was nonetheless a long-term tendency to raise the threshold at which coercive action was mandated. Rather, I conclude this chapter by attempting to construct a model of how the grain market functioned, based on the expressed beliefs of (mainly) eighteenth-century Chinese and Manchu officials. The purpose is to determine what a market-conscious mid-eighteenth-century Chinese or Manchu official might have said if asked to explain how the grain market worked, or would have worked without state intervention. This exercise involves drawing together fragmentary assertions, many of them culled from expositions of the ways in which state intervention allegedly prevented what we call market forces from operating as they should have. The resulting composite is an elementary but coherent model with one incompletely resolved tension and a few uncertainties. We cannot say that it reflects the actual thought of any given Qing official; it does, however, represent the level of economic understanding that was demonstrably within reach of mid-eighteenth-century Chinese and Manchu bureaucrats, as far as the grain market was concerned.

The most basic axiom was that scarcity (shortage of staple food grains relative to need for them) was reflected in high prices and abundance in low ones. A community, urban or rural, whose prices at a given time were higher than the local norm could be viewed, sche-

---

(ten thousand), thereby making Wang appear to have proposed that the ceiling for legitimate stockpiling be raised to 150,000 *shi*.

89. Cf. Perdue, *China Marches West*, pp. 272–91, 394–95. Commercialization and state harnessing of merchant capital play a major role in Perdue's account of popular-subsistence policy in Gansu in the 1750s (ibid., pp. 366–75).

matically, on two planes: a horizontal (spatial) plane, in which it was one of many communities, each with its own temporary supply conditions reflected in its current price level; and a vertical (temporal) plane, in which attention focused on the privately-owned reserves that had been generated by the local agriculture or had been imported earlier (typically through commercial activity or the payment of rent in kind to nonresident landlords). To take the horizontal plane first, the key issue was whether commercial stocks would be attracted to the community in question; this depended primarily on the local price level relative to price levels elsewhere, and secondarily on the purchasing power of the local people relative to achievable price levels in their own community. Evidence of mid-eighteenth-century recognition of the importance of what we call purchasing power and effective demand is presented in chapter 5; this aspect is therefore ignored for now.

For many officials, it sufficed to note, as Hui Shiqi did, that high prices attracted merchants while low prices repelled them. However, a more sophisticated understanding is shown in a 1738 memorial by Fang Bao, who argued first that differing price levels reflected the relative severity of food shortages in different communities, and second, that trade would naturally gravitate towards the highest prices and, therefore, the areas of greatest need. It was a commonplace that the arrival of merchant cargoes led to an abatement of high prices; Fang added the idea that a place in which this process had just taken place would probably have ceased to be the area of greatest need, so that trade would forsake it in favor of more undersupplied markets. Like most mid-eighteenth-century Chinese political economists, Fang wrote in terms of merchant responsiveness to price incentives. However, it was possible to describe the workings of the market in depersonalized terms (as with Celeng's striking prediction that "commercial rice [would] catch wind [of the high prices] and arrive," *shangmi wenfeng er zhi*), or even abstract ones (as with the law that "where goods mass together, prices fall," *huo ji jia luo*, invoked in a 1738 memorial by Emida and Wang Mo).[90]

---

90. See above and Fang Bao, *Fang Bao ji*, vol. 2, p. 554, discussed and translated in Dunstan, *Conflicting Counsels*, pp. 306 and 325; QCWXTK, vol. 1, *juan* 36, p. 5,190, cited in Dunstan, ibid., pp. 31–32.

On the vertical plane, the key issue was the eventual disposal of the reserves held by the given community, or, to be more exact, in the case of rural communities, the disposal of the grain that, having passed from the control of the households that had grown it, might or might not remain in their community in the form of reserves. Let us first assume that privately-owned reserves exist, that the only ones with significant potential to assure community survival are those sizable ones held by landlords and merchants, and that the controllers of reserves act only to maximize their monetary income; in other words, philanthropy and a sense of social responsibility do not affect decisions as to whether or when to release private stocks. Market-conscious mid-eighteenth-century officials could probably have reached consensus that, although their motivation was entirely selfish, the controllers of reserves were in effect managing them in the interests of the local community. They (the owners or their agents or brokers) did this by ensuring that a suitable proportion of the available grain was saved for the *soudure* period; in addition, in situations in which food supply depended on continuous replenishment from outside (the case of major cities), they were able to protect consumers from occasional price fluctuations. Although they tended not to sell as rapidly as consumers might have wished, the key fact was that they sold when the need was greatest.

But when exactly did their sales take place? Here was the first area of uncertainty. Even if one ignored the possibility of downright unethical behavior such as creating purely artificial price increases, there still seems to have been insufficient evidence to convince every writer on the subject that, as Adam Smith believed, a skilful speculator's disposal of his stocks provided the community with the best outcome possible, given the particular supply constraints that faced it. Several authors thought that hoarders sold before the end of the *soudure* period, whether because their only motive had been to await the rise of prices, because they would need capital to restock in the autumn, or because they wanted to turn their capital over as fast as possible.[91] But it was only the most optimistic of these writers, Celeng and, conceivably, Chen Dashou, who seem to have believed that administrators should normally be able to wait for the hoarder's untutored perception of his

---

91. For the clearest statement of this view, see CC, Tuerbing'a, QL 13/6/9.

interests to result in sales. Others were presumably more concerned about the distress that the community would undergo meanwhile, and it does not seem to have occurred to them that the delay might be in the community's best interests. We lack unambiguous accounts of hoarders selling stocks off gradually in response to *soudure* price incentives. It is, moreover, possible that the minority of writers, such as Kaerjishan, who stressed the role of speculation as precaution against harvest failure did not believe that all hoarded grain was sold before the end of the *soudure*, but rather that some would be retained into the new agricultural cycle. While Kaerjishan may have thought that carrying stocks forward represented better service to society than selling out within the *soudure* period, the fact remains that we cannot be sure that all agreed that hoards were never carried forward.

The major tension in the model was that between, on one hand, the need of producer and recipient communities to retain reserves for local, vertical disposal, and, on the other, the need of understocked communities elsewhere to draw supplies in through the horizontal mechanisms of the interregional grain market. No mid-eighteenth-century Chinese or Manchu political economist, to my knowledge, tried to argue that the market would ensure the most rational distribution of available stocks overall, that is, taking into account both vertical and horizontal usage. To be sure, there were ideas of checks and balances believed to work in rough and ready fashion. An answer to supply protectionism, put forward before 1740, was that communities in real danger of subsistence crisis would be protected by the resulting high prices, which would deter would-be exporters.[92] This offered no assurance that, by the time that local price rises signalled to external buyers that they should now stop, too much would not already have been bought to leave the host community facing the coming *soudure* without worse hardship than its grain would help prevent elsewhere. Alternatively, local speculators might effectively impound security reserves for their home communities, but what assurance was there that enough grain would then flow to relieve greater need in neighboring or distant settlements? Fang Bao's argument (summarized above) suggests

---

92. Yan Sisheng, *Chumeng shanfang ji, Shu* [Letters], *juan* 2:37a, cited and translated in Dunstan, *Conflicting Counsels*, pp. 300, 304, 322. For further examples and discussion, see ibid., pp. 256–57 and 261.

that the notion of the market as optimizing allocator of resources may not have been beyond the intellectual reach of members of the eighteenth-century Sino-Manchu bureaucracy, but it does not follow that they could or should have applied such an idea beyond the horizontal plane. Fang's model, after all, was not directly applicable. Cast in terms of the choices made by mobile grain controllers, it said nothing about those confronting sedentary ones, who, even if they sold onto the interregional market, could not expect the full price that awaited grain importers in disaster-stricken zones.

The chief role of the speculator, in "enlightened" mid-Qing economic discourse, was arguably to counterbalance the lure of external markets by checking the outflow of grain to them. Unperturbed, as far as we can see, by the difficulty of arriving at a theoretical resolution of the tension between vertical and horizontal, the vindicators of the hoarder took the opportunities offered by the discursive memorial *genre* to emphasize his uses to society. Given the typical assumption that hoarders would sell once the price was right, it was logically possible to suggest that they ought simply to be left alone, and one official (Celeng) did so.[93] As far as the vertical plane was concerned, total *laissez-faire* was not an unthinkable approach in mid-eighteenth-century China, although it was decidedly a minority position.[94] But what of the horizontal plane? Pure *laissez-faire* would logically have been possible here too, but whether it could have been thought sensible depended on the answer to a quantitative question. Could price incentives in severely disaster-stricken areas always (or indeed ever) draw in enough grain to bring the price down to a level such that even poor peasants in remote country villages could buy the food to keep themselves alive

---

93. "Besides, if the region has chanced to suffer a poor harvest, one does not fear an increase in the price of grain; one fears a lack of grain to save the situation. *[This makes it] still more unobjectionable to give these grain-possessing households time to bring their stocks out of their own accord*, in order also to provide against contingencies" (emphasis added). CC, Celeng, QL 13/3/28.

94. Cf. the late Ming official Cai Maode's advice, in his "Eight guidelines for attracting merchant rice," that "When the rice arrives, one should in all things respect the folk's convenience, the officials not so much as asking whether it is stockpiled or sold." The guidelines, which are very brief, were transcribed in an imperially-sponsored compilation published in 1740. Lu, *Qinding kangji lu*, p. 420; fuller text in Li Chainong, *Huangzheng zheyao*, pp. 553–54.

until there was a harvest? Part II of this book explores not only the answers that were implicit in the antifamine institutions of the high Qing state, but also those offered by the most radical 1740s critics of the ever-normal granaries.

For now, let us note the sophistication of the model for which a number of mid-eighteenth-century officials unwittingly created the components. Whether one approves of economic liberalism or not, these Chinese and Manchu officials, unfettered by the supposed pre-occupations of Confucian scholar-gentry, had started to explore the possibilities of an amoral conception of the market—one in which self-interest, refigured as the vehicle of market forces, was not to be naively thwarted in its normal paths. In this sense, their ideas bear comparison with those of the *économistes* in eighteenth-century France. But let us also note a key difference with French "grain liberalism." There was no explicit interest in robust grain prices as an incentive to growers. While what Will might call "productivism" was both a craze in mid-eighteenth-century France and a persistent tradition in eighteenth-century Chinese official and imperial discourse, the idea that strong agricultural prices might draw more food from the soil was part of French "grain liberalism" but not of its 1740s Chinese counter-part.[95] Does this suggest a certain lack of dynamism in the Chinese model, reflecting pessimism about subsistence and the ecological margin for growth? The Chinese earth was indeed to be "exhausted" to sustain the teeming population, and the price to growers must indeed be high enough for them to meet their basic needs; but no 1740s Chinese or Manchu official, to my knowledge, advocated *laissez-s'éléver* for grain prices in general.

While the secular trend of grain prices was mostly upward in the eighteenth century in both China and France, the years immediately preceding the radical liberalization of the French grain trade in 1763–64 were ones of low grain prices.[96] In 1740s China, to the contrary, it was high grain prices that absorbed government attention. Sino-Manchu imperial and official reactions—almost consistently negative—to the

---

95. Kaplan, *Bread*, pp. 94–95, 102–4, 111–12, 116, and, on French "agromania," 119–20; Will, "Clear Waters," p. 309. I return briefly to Chinese "productivism" in chap. 7 below.

96. Kaplan, *Bread*, pp. 122–23, 145.

fact of rising grain prices are discussed in part II below. Suffice it here to note one sociopolitical aspect of the difference between French and Chinese "liberal" views as to the right direction for grain prices. In France, articulate and powerful agrarian interests joined what Kaplan calls the "liberty lobby" to press for, and then celebrate, measures (such as qualified approval for the international export of grain) that, by boosting prices, would have augmented their own wealth.[97] By contrast, in Sino-Manchu governmental discourse, tillers of the soil were a subaltern class, morally estimable in theory, but childlike in practice. Their prosperity was desired, but not their monetary affluence. A dynamic vision of peasant consumerism as a spur to productivity should not have been inconceivable in the late traditional East Asian world, for it was not everywhere remote from reality.[98] But I know of no market-conscious 1740s Chinese or Manchu official who conceived it.

---

97. Ibid., pp. 94, 121–24, 164–65.

98. Cf. Thomas C. Smith's suggestion that a long list of "useful and attractive things to buy" may "go some way toward explaining why" the farmers of a southern Japanese district in the 1840s "worked 'night and day'"—admittedly, at "by-employments" rather than grain production. T. C. Smith, *Native Sources*, p. 90.

PART II

Private-Sector Stockpiling:

The State As Hoarder

4

The Issues in the Ever-Normal

Granaries Debate

The next five chapters explore a fifteen-year debate about the proper scope of government attempts to assure popular subsistence through the nationwide ever-normal granary network.* This debate began with a quixotic decision, in 1738–39, to increase the national grain storage target at least twofold. On the surface, the central issue was whether, and if so how, the state could keep large grain reserves without incurring excess grain-price rises as a consequence of its own buying. In the 1740s, imperial policy went through several twists and turns in an attempt both to determine a high-level storage target that would not prove inflationary, and to find a noninflationary way of drawing grain into the state reserves. However, the alleged effect of public-sector storage on the market price of grain may not have been the fundamental point at stake. Close reading suggests that certain interests underlay the arguments at various points in the debate. A number of officials radically questioned both the principle and practice of the ever-normal system. Their attacks clarify our vision as to the fundamental issue, thereby informing speculation as to one type of interest that may have helped to shape events.

The story to be unravelled here is of a length and complexity to which even the most detailed account available so far—a study by Gao

---

*Two short passages of translation in this chapter appeared in my 1996 article, "The 'Autocratic Heritage,'" published by *East Asian History*.

Wangling—does less than complete justice.[1] Both Gao's specialized study and the brief references to the debate in other works on Qing popular subsistence policy tend understandably to focus on the events of 1748–49. In 1748, the court made what looks like a deliberate attempt to elicit negative assessments of the price impact of current storage policy from all provincial chief administrators, with a view, presumably, to cutting the grain storage targets—a step finally taken in early 1749. The reduction was by almost 30 percent, which was no insignificant proportion.[2] Although most of the provincial governors-general and governors obliged the court with at least qualified indictments of the ever-normal system, they also examined many other possible causes of the recent rise in grain prices. Their responses, taken as a group, thus furnish an unusually rich source for investigating the economic consciousness of mid-Qing regional officials.[3]

The interest and importance of the developments of 1748–49 are undeniable, and due attention will be paid to them in chapters 7 and 8. However, failure to examine these developments in the context of a long controversy involving several policy shifts has led previous authors to overlook one noteworthy fact. The global target (48,110,680 *shi*) from which the revised target of early 1749 (33,792,335 *shi*) was a 29.76 percent reduction was actually a compromise figure finalized as recently as 1744 and unlikely ever to have been reached. To speak,

---

1. Gao Wangling, "Yige wei wanjie de changshi"; a revised version of this article appears in chaps. 6 and 7 of the same author's *Shiba shiji Zhongguo*. The longest previous accounts in English are Rowe, "State and Market," pp. 26–31; Rowe, *Saving the World*, pp. 259–67; Marks, *Tigers*, pp. 234–36; and (for the debate's first phase) Dunstan, "The 'Autocratic Heritage,'" pp. 83–102. The best short account of the debate as a whole is Kishimoto, *Shindai Chūgoku no bukka*, pp. 301–4.

2. For references to these events, see, e.g., Gao, *Shiba shiji Zhongguo*, pp. 141–48; Rowe, *Saving the World*, pp. 259–62; Will, *Bureaucracy and Famine*, pp. 191–94; Will and Wong, *Nourish the People*, pp. 142–43; Yamamoto, "Shindai zenki no heichō seisaku," pp. 63–64; and Liu Ts'ui-jung, "A Reappraisal," pp. 306–7.

3. Nonarchival versions of this material were first introduced to modern scholarship on eighteenth-century China as a contribution to price history. See Quan, "Qianlong shisan nian," pp. 552–64. The two best-known memorials from the ever-normal granaries debate (CC, Yang Xifu, QL 13, cat. no. 1142-025 and Zhu Lunhan, QL 6/7/20) have usually been cited in a price history context without reference to their origin in the controversy. See, e.g., Zelin, *Magistrate's Tael*, pp. 294–97.

therefore, of an almost 30 percent cut from the existing storage level in 1749 would almost certainly be incorrect. It is, moreover, impossible to gauge the political significance of the 1748 discussions if one is unaware that by then the debate was ten years old, and most of the arguments were probably well known to most of the participants. It is especially important not to miss the radical hostility to the whole ever-normal system expressed initially during 1739–43. An undertone of radical challenge persisted right up to the end of the debate, which, as Will has noted, extinguished itself after a last blaze of extremism in the early 1750s.[4]

The story told below is perhaps not hugely significant for the long-term history of the Qing ever-normal granaries, which may explain the scant attention paid to the debate in Will and Wong's otherwise definitive *Nourish the People: The State Civilian Granary System in China, 1650–1850* (Michigan, 1991). The limits of feasible grain storage in state-managed granaries were surely more influential than the meanderings of imperial ambition. The practical difficulties that beset the ever-normal system are analyzed, with masterly command of detail, in Will's chapters of *Nourish the People*; they probably did more to shape the evolution of the ever-normal system than the policy debate examined here.[5] Close study of this debate is, however, necessary for a deepened understanding of the terms in which mid-eighteenth-century Chinese and Manchu officials discussed political economy. Better than any other topic, it illustrates the cleavage between diehard advocates of interventionist techniques in popular subsistence policy and partisans of a "hands-off" approach. As a contribution to research on the Yongzheng–Qianlong transition, it reveals the relatively young Qianlong retreating from an escapade that took his father Yongzheng's interventionism to incongruous excess. It not only shows how, but also suggests why, the early Qianlong court shifted towards a strong if temporary preference for minimizing state involvement in provisioning activities.

The present chapter first provides essential information on the ever-normal system. It then explores the issues involved in the debate, both as identified by historian's hindsight and as reflected in contem-

---

4. Will and Wong, *Nourish the People*, pp. 143–47.
5. Ibid., part 2, "Structural Problems," all of which is by Will.

porary critiques, particularly the first radical attacks of 1739–43. Chapters 5 through 8 offer a detailed narrative account of the debate, including the policy shifts and the discussions that directly influenced them. Finally, chapter 9 discerns consistencies, in certain other areas of public policy, with the court's drift of opinion away from grain trade activism.

Storage and Rotation Quotas

The availability of *Nourish the People* renders superfluous any detailed examination of the workings of the ever-normal system.[6] In what follows, I provide only the minimum of information necessary for understanding the debate, while regretting any oversimplification. Although I depict the granaries as sources of important services to vulnerable populations, it should be kept in mind that not only did the granaries not always function quite as the rules envisaged, but there were also times when their intended beneficiaries were given cause to curse them. On one hand, stories of the indigent joining disturbances when frustrated in their expectations of timely relief from the granaries suggest that such aid played a welcome and important role in the life of the poor. These stories are, however, balanced by complaints of ordinary peasant households being forced to sell grain to the granaries, or to buy stale grain that was no longer worth storing.[7]

The principle of ever-normal operations was simple and of ancient origin.[8] The state would buy up stocks of grain after the autumn harvest, thereby (theoretically) helping the farmers, who might otherwise

---

6. For a more concise introduction, see Will, *Bureaucracy and Famine*, pp. 182–99, to which my account below is heavily indebted. Also useful, despite its negative tone, is chap. 5 of Hsiao, *Rural China*.

7. See, e.g., KYQRFDZ, vol. 2, pp. 562–86; Will and Wong, *Nourish the People*, p. 169. While official sources commonly represent the instigators of grain riots as "disreputable persons" or unworthy holders of state "student" status, and while rioters were in many cases urban, not rural residents, a disturbance report of 1747 (KYQRFDZ, vol. 2, pp. 568–69) suggests vividly the importance that grain loans from the ever-normal granaries could have for the poor of rural towns and villages.

8. For a sophisticated ancient exposition of ever-normal theory (albeit from a manipulative, Legalist perspective), see Ma Feibai, ed., *Guanzi Qingzhong pian*, vol. 1, pp. 225–41. For the pre-Qing history of the ever-normal and related systems, see Will and Wong, *Nourish the People*, pp. 1–14.

suffer from low prices and inadequate demand. It would store the grain over the winter, until the arrival of the *soudure* period. At that point it would start to sell the grain at a price lower than the current market rate, thereby (theoretically) undercutting shameless profiteers as well as boosting supply. The market price would therefore fall, to the advantage of poor consumers. Such was the idea of the "[price]-stabilizing sale"; the ever-normal granaries were, in principle, depositories for the price-stabilizing grain.

In the Qing period, however, the ever-normal granaries doubled as precautionary reserves against subsistence crises. Preparedness in case of famine—or, to quote an oft-used slogan, "having precautions and being free of worry" (*you bei wu huan*)—was a responsibility taken very seriously by the early high Qing state, and the elaborate guidelines for maintaining the reserves reflect the government's commitment. There was a range of ways in which granary stocks could be deployed, depending on the circumstances. Stocks could be lent, distributed free, or sold in special "stabilizing sales"; they could be used to help the local population through a minor crisis, or to enable it to hold out until relief supplies arrived from elsewhere; and they were available for transfer to assist dearth-stricken populations elsewhere in the province or indeed beyond it.[9]

There is considerable evidence that routine stabilizing sales in the annual *soudure* period were still thought important by many if not most territorial officials in the mid-eighteenth century.[10] Indeed, even in this era of generally high demand for grain and high commercialization, the demand-supplementation function of state post-harvest buying was not redundant everywhere.[11] However, the role of the

---

9. Will, *Bureaucracy and Famine*, pp. 186–87, 204–6, 277–79.

10. For examples of careful official thinking about how to use stabilizing sales to the best effect, see the 1738 documents by Nasutu, Emida, and Wang Mo summarized in QCWXTK, vol. 1, *juan* 36, pp. 5,189–90 (cf. Dunstan, *Conflicting Counsels*, pp. 31–32).

11. Will and Wong, *Nourish the People*, p. 143 n. 3, and, e.g., QCWXTK, vol. 1, *juan* 35, pp. 5,183–84 (Huguang, 1730); CC, Huang Tinggui, QL 6/11/28 (Gansu, 1742); QSL/QL, *juan* 223:32a (Gansu, 1744). By the 1740s, post-harvest demand supplementation was most likely to be needed in the relatively uncommercialized northwestern provinces. However, even in a heartland province like Jiangxi, the farmers of remote mountain counties might sometimes depend substantially on official custom for their grain. CC, Peng Jiaping, QL 8/5/27.

ever-normal granaries in the Qing state's overall famine relief system was arguably more important than their role in counteracting seasonal price instability, which was not ubiquitously and invariably severe. The annual springtime sales thus served a second function, which Will suggests was actually more basic than their price-stabilization role. This second function was rotation of the stock to prevent mildewing and rotting.[12]

In the eighteenth century, ever-normal granaries were, in principle, expected to sell 30 percent of their reserves each spring. However, higher rates of 50 or even 70 percent were specified for certain regions to take account of higher humidity or the greater perishability of the type of grain being stored.[13] A decree of 1742 instructed granary administrators (in most cases, county magistrates) to make no bones about exceeding the 30 percent rotation norm when especially harsh *soudure* conditions warranted the sale of extra grain. Yet Will and Wong have questioned, using sample data from the 1740s, whether granaries were typically voided of even 30 percent of their reserves per year (including such grain as was lent, not sold).[14] In spite of this and other evidence of flexibility (or noncompliance), mid-Qing complaints about the tyranny of the rotation rule give the impression that, unless officially excused, administrators felt under pressure to meet the 30 percent quota, although the *soudure* market was sometimes sufficiently well-stocked to render stabilizing sales a positive embarrassment.[15] The

---

12. Will, *Bureaucracy and Famine*, pp. 183, 186–87.

13. Will, *Bureaucracy and Famine*, p. 183 n. 22; Will and Wong, *Nourish the People*, p. 53; QCWXTK, vol. 1, *juan* 34, pp. 5,172–73 and *juan* 36, p. 5,187; DQHDSL, vol. 9, *juan* 189:17b–19a (pp. 7,585–86).

14. QCWXTK, vol. 1, *juan* 36, p. 5,191; Will and Wong, *Nourish the People*, pp. 54–56 and 135; Will, *Bureaucracy and Famine*, p. 183. I have some reservations about the appropriateness of generalizing from 1740s figures because, as shown below, there was much experimentation in the ever-normal system in that decade. For pre-1742 authorizations to exceed the 30 percent norm, see QCWXTK, vol. 1, *juan* 35, p. 5,185 (Zhili, 1733, granaries stocking less than 10,000 *shi* only) and p. 5,186 (northern China, 1735); *juan* 36, p. 5,187 (Sichuan, 1736).

15. E.g., Will and Wong, *Nourish the People*, pp. 56–57; and, for central government concessions on the need to meet the annual rotation quota, e.g. QCWXTK, vol. 1, *juan* 36, p. 5,187 (1736, Hunan) and 5,192 (1742, general). See also CC, Shuai Nianzu, QL 9/1/8 for an acting governor's initiative in proposing a one-time 20 percent rotation target for his province. The percentage had been carefully selected

grain sold in the spring, or distributed for relief purposes, was supposed to be replaced through the autumn post-harvest purchases. At least in theory, therefore, every county-level jurisdiction in China (since each such jurisdiction was supposed to have an ever-normal granary) was replacing a minimum of 30, or in variant cases 50 or 70 percent of its reserves each autumn, and in some years considerably more.

What were the quantities involved? This question is inseparable from that of the size of the storage targets, or "quotas," to use the conventional translation of the Chinese term (*e*).[16] The basic principle informing the setting of targets was that the quantity stocked in each ever-normal granary should reflect the population size that it was meant to serve. Targets were usually expressed in *shi* of unhusked grain, for grain kept better if stored in that form, a practice systematically adopted after 1725. The simple schedule of quotas generally in force at the beginning of the eighteenth century was 10,000 *shi* for a large county, 8,000 *shi* for a medium-sized county, and 6,000 *shi* for a small county. The amounts to be sold off each year, assuming a 30 percent rotation norm, were therefore 3,000, 2,400, and 1,800 *shi* respectively.[17]

Given the vast regional differences in population density in late imperial China, a single basic schedule could not have lasted long. Already in the first years of the eighteenth century, variant schedules were introduced for certain provinces. As this process continued, other

---

to take into account both a recent run of good harvests and the likelihood of pressure on the province's grain markets because of poor harvests in the adjacent province. But for the latter consideration, it might have been thought necessary to repeat the previous year's rotation rate of less than 10 percent.

16. In principle, the translation "target" is appropriate when the stated figure represents an aspiration to whose realization officials are expected only to commit their best endeavors. A "quota" is a figure that the central government has reasonable grounds for considering normally attainable in a defined period, and to which officials expect to be held unless they can show cause otherwise.

17. QCWXTK, vol. 1, *juan* 34, p. 5,173. This states that one-third of the stock was to be sold each year, but the difference between one-third and 30 percent is not significant for the amounts in question. The source also notes that the quotas refer to "husked and unhusked" grain. In principle, two *shi* of unhusked grain were deemed equivalent to one *shi* of husked (with variations depending on the type of grain). It is likely that the units are correctly read as *shi* of unhusked grain or husked equivalent. Cf. QCWXTK, vol. 1, *juan* 34, pp. 5,170–71 and *juan* 35, pp. 5,177–78; Will, *Bureaucracy and Famine*, pp. 131, 190 n. 41, and 193 n. 50.

criteria besides population size began to influence grain storage targets. For example, some strategically located granaries were designated as supplementary depots for their regions and given higher targets. Although the available data are incomplete, it seems safe to say that, over the first four decades of the eighteenth century, provincial storage schedules showed a tendency towards both higher storage levels and greater complexity.[18] To illustrate this complexity, table 1 reproduces the finely differentiated schedule approved for Shaanxi in 1744, as part of the process (discussed in chapter 6) of determining compromise targets, that is, targets reduced from the unrealistic levels set in the late 1730s, for all provinces. Shaanxi's county-level jurisdictions were divided into ten groups according to three criteria: size, population density, and special characteristics. Although, in this case, the Shaanxi authorities were under orders to adopt the total amount of regular ever-normal grain that happened to be in store in the first half of 1743 as the revised provincial storage target, their schedule epitomizes the care associated with pursuit of the preparedness ideal at its most conscientious.[19]

Complete information on provincial and national aggregate targets is not available for any date before 1748. However, authoritative central government documents of the early 1740s refer to the nationwide target in force at the beginning of the Qianlong reign as approximately 28 million *shi*.[20] An incomplete set of pre-1738 provincial targets (or actual Yongzheng-period storage levels retrospectively taken as the targets for that reign) is provided in a list originally appended to the early 1749 report advising the emperor on how to make further reductions from the compromise targets that had been finalized in 1744. The recommendation was, in principle, to restore the "Yongzheng-period targets" of all but six provinces, whence the importance of listing these old figures. The list is torn towards the end, removing the data for five of the six exceptions. However, figures for Shaanxi, Guangdong, Fujian,

----

18. QCWXTK, vol. 1, *juan* 34, p. 5,173, and *juan* 35, pp. 5,183–86; Will, *Bureaucracy and Famine*, pp. 189–90.

19. HHCC, Bundle 93, Bd. Rev., QL 8/6/3; CC, Shuai Nianzu, QL 8/12/7.

20. CC, Grd. Secs. and NMA, QL 8/int.4/6; QSL/QL, *juan* 189:2a. Both these sources imply that the target was between 28 and 29 million *shi*; however, CC, Bd. Rev., QL 6/5/2 puts it at between 27 and 28 million.

Table 1
The Schedule of Ever-Normal Storage Targets Adopted for Shaanxi in 1744
(Units: *shi* of unhusked grain)

Group	Target for each CLJ*
1. The two highly populous CLJs in which Xi'an (the provincial capital) was situated	75,000
2. Seven frontier CLJs with significant troop concentrations and poor transport facilities	50,000
3. Twelve CLJs "near the frontier" with barren soil, steep mountain roads, and populations that "have few reserves"	40,000
* * * * * * *	
4. Seven large CLJs with dense populations	50,000
5. Eight " " " sparse "	45,000
6. Eleven medium " " dense "	40,000
7. Seven " " " sparse "	30,000
8. Seventeen small " " dense "	17,200+
9. Seven " " " sparse "	8,000
* * * * * * *	
10. Seven CLJs that lie close to the River Han, where the prevailing dampness makes grain stockpiles liable to rot. Targets to be determined by the amount of "old grain still in store." Implied *average* target per CLJ	(6,362.86)
Total Target for the Province	2,733,010

*CLJ = county-level jurisdiction
SOURCES: CC, Shuai Nianzu, QL 8/12/7; QCWXTK, vol. 1, *juan* 36, p. 5,193.

Gansu, and Guizhou are supplied in table 2 from the provincial reports used by the list's compilers.

Table 2 presents the "Yongzheng-period targets" in rank order and shows the minimum amount theoretically to be sold each spring, assuming a 30 percent rotation norm. It also includes (as does the list) the Kangxi-period data that were available in 1749. Parentheses are used to show cases in which documentation that I have seen—either the list or one of the reports on which it was based—clearly indicates that the

Table 2
The So-Called "Yongzheng-Period Targets"
(Units: *shi* of unhusked grain. Rounding has been avoided where the compilers of the 1749 list ignored decimals exceeding 0.5. Recorded totals supplied entirely from other sources are correct to nearest integer.)

Province	Kangxi-period target or reported total	Yongzheng-period target or reported total	Minimum theoretical annual rotation target (approx.)
Shandong	—	2,959,386[a]	888,000
Zhejiang	1,504,551[1,2]	2,800,000[1,2]	840,000
Henan	(1,265,787)	(2,310,999)	(693,000)
Shaanxi	(1,212,722)[3i]	(2,061,741)[i]	619,000
Zhili	—	1,996,216[4,b]	599,000
Guangdong	(1,678,383)[ii]	(1,925,685)[ii]	(578,000)
Anhui	480,000[1,5]	1,884,000[1,5,c]	565,000
Fujian	(1,725,434)[iii]	(1,690,168)[d,iii]	(507,000)
Jiangsu	—	1,528,000	458,000
Jiangxi	1,341,248[6,7]	1,370,713[e]	411,000
Shanxi	(1,052,253)[8]	(1,315,837)[f]	(395,000)
Guangxi	1,599,120	1,274,378[g]	382,000
Gansu	1,228,571[9]	1,228,571[9,iv]	369,000
Fengtian	—	1,080,000[1,4]	324,000
Sichuan	(414,027)	1,029,800[10]	309,000
Hunan	(360,726)	(702,133)	211,000
Hubei	216,763	520,935[h]	156,000
Yunnan	(445,853)	(508,699)	(153,000)
Guizhou	(180,903)[6,v]	(181,657)[6,j,v]	(54,000)
TOTAL		28,368,918	8,511,000

[1] Figure stated in *shi* husked, and converted here to *shi* unhusked by doubling.
[2] Target set in 1710 (KX) or 1727 (YZ); to be reached through supplementary grain contributions. Reported actual storage levels in 1722 and 1735 were 369,554 and 1,504,508 *shi* (unhusked) respectively. LFZZQZ (QL13), 2939 and 2941.
[3] Figure for 1724 taken as representing KX levels because annual reporting had been suspended between 1715 and 1724.
[4] Excludes CLJs for which quotas had not yet been set.
[5] The YZ target comprises a 480,000 *shi* quota set in 1704 (KX), a 1,204,000 *shi* contributions target set in 1726, and a separate 200,000 *shi* contributions target for three prefectures. Appendix to LFZZ, Namin, QL 9/9/23 (d.r.).
[6] Figure includes a small subtotal for husked grain converted to *shi* unhusked by doubling.
[7] Figure for 1699. Appendix to LFZZ, Kaitai, QL 13/8/24 (d.r.).
[8] Figure for 1719. LFZZQZ (QL 13), 3660.

Table 2, cont.

[9] Converted from the stated KX target of 860,000 *shi* (assumed to be northwestern "granary *shi*"). Source notes explicitly that no change to this target was recommended in YZ. Cf. Perdue's finding that the actual storage level in Gansu in 1735 was 750,000 *shi*, which perhaps means 1,071,429 *shi* by standard measure. Perdue, "The Qing State," p. 105.

[10] Target set in 1731. Appendix to LFZZ, Bandi, QL 13/9/26.

Variant figures

[a] For Shandong, 3,530,000+ *shi*. This figure seems to include over 570,000 *shi* of community granary and other special category grain. HHCC, Bundle 87, Yan Sisheng, QL 8/1/24.

[b] For Zhili, 2,006,216 *shi*. The difference is accounted for by the 10,000-*shi* target for Guang-chang county, which was transferred from Shanxi to Zhili in 1733. CC, Sun Jiagan, QL 6/9/14; Zhao Ersun et al., comps., *Qingshi gao*, vol. 8, *juan* 54, p. 1,920.

[c] For Anhui, 1,832,000 *shi* (figure stated in *shi* husked, and converted here to *shi* unhusked by doubling). Mem. by Nasutu, QL 3/5/24 (d.r.), transc. Lü Xiaoxian, comp., "Qianlong san-nian," part 1, p. 6.

[d] For Fujian, 1,848,800 *shi*. JS, Zhou Xuejian, QL 10/7/16 (also copied as Zhou Xuejian, QL 10/8/15 (d.r.), transc. Lü, comp., "Qianlong sannian," part 2, pp. 22–24). See also CC, Kaerji-shan and Pan Siju, QL 13/10/28, which gives the YZ figure as 1,690,551.

[e] For Jiangxi, 1,377,000 *shi*. CC, Peng Jiaping, QL 8/5/27.

[f] For Shanxi, 1,550,000 *shi*. CC, Kaerjishan, QL 6/7/26.

[g] For Guangxi, 1,413,398 *shi*. The figure includes 139,020 *shi* of army rations grain turned over to the ever-normal granaries. HHCC, Bundle 93, Bd. Rev., QL 8/6/20.

[h] For Hubei, 650,000 *shi*. QSL/QL, *juan* 189:23b.

[j] For Guizhou, 185,000 *shi*. HHCC, Bundle 93, Zhang Guangsi (fragment, n.d., sent to Bd. Rev. QL 8/6/28). Citing the 1741 provincial gazetteer, James Lee quotes 226,304 *shi* as the total ever-normal holdings of Guizhou in "ca. 1735." Will and Wong, *Nourish the People*, table 12.6.

SOURCES: Unless otherwise stated, CC, "Ge sheng changping cang gu ding'e qingdan" [List of Established Provincial Targets for Ever-normal Granary Grain Holdings] (fragment, n.d., dated 1749 by present author; cat. no. 1132–016); cf. QCWXTK, vol. 1, *juan* 36, p. 5,195.

[i] Appendix to LFZZ, Chen Hongmou, QL 13/9/20.

[ii] Appendix to LFZZ, Yue Jun, QL 13/9/13.

[iii] LFZZQZ (QL 13), 3257 (originally appended to CC, Kaerjishan and Pan Siju, QL 13/8/28).

[iv] CC, Huang Tinggui, QL 13/9/20.

[v] Appendix to LFZZ, Aibida, QL 13/9/12.

figure in question is a reported actual storage level, usually from 1722 or 1735 (the last years of Kangxi and Yongzheng). Other dates, where specified, are indicated in notes to the table. In five more cases, the Yongzheng figure, even if presented as a "target," lacks the right-hand zeros that bespeak planning and must have originated, at least in part, as the actual storage level of an unstated year.[21] This logic, however,

---

21. As Will points out, a ragged actual storage figure for even one county added to a rounded provincial target would give the latter a ragged appearance. Will and Wong, *Nourish the People*, p. 278.

does not apply to the Gansu figures, where I have assumed that the Kangxi-period target of 860,000 *shi* was expressed in northwest China's extra-large "granary *shi*," of which the standard *shi* was seven-tenths. Converting the Gansu target on this assumption yields a ragged figure.[22] Appended to the table are several variant figures; while some may be the elusive actual targets of the Yongzheng period, most probably reflect revisions to those targets after Qianlong's accession.

Whatever the value of the figures in table 2, they indeed total some 28.3 million *shi*, implying a minimum theoretical annual rotation target of about 8.5 million. It is probable that, according to the consensus of the midcentury bureaucracy, these were manageable storage and rotation norms. The ever-normal granaries debate was, among other things, the product of central government experiments to determine whether higher storage and rotation levels could be realized and sustained. The first of these experiments began in 1738, when the recently-acceded Qianlong emperor decided to let titular studentships in the Imperial Academy (that is, *jiansheng* titles) be sold in exchange for in-kind contributions to the granaries. The provincial chief administrators were required to set contribution targets, a process that reportedly resulted in a nationwide total contribution target of about 32 million *shi* of unhusked grain. As this was to be added to the "original" or basic target of 28 million *shi*, the total target was about 60 million *shi*.[23] At roughly the same time, provincial administrations were tightening and systematizing the rules and procedures governing the annual buying, selling, and lending of ever-normal grain.[24] Under imperial leadership, the territorial bureaucracy was preparing to run a vast stockpiling and social welfare enterprise with maximal effectiveness.

---

22. Cf. ibid., pp. 236–38, 285–87. The assumption that the 860,000 figure is not rather a granary *shi* target of 602,000 *shi* expressed in standard *shi* is justified by (a) Gansu's strategic importance and vulnerability to glut and famine, and (b) an explicit statement in a source of early 1752. The statement refers to the Kangxi target, which was unchanged in the Yongzheng period. Wu Shiduan, QL 16/11/22, repr. GZD/QL, vol. 2, pp. 25–26.

23. These totals are derived from the first two sources cited in n. 20. The rough figures given in the third source suggest a total target of only 57 to 58 million *shi*.

24. Hoshi, *Chūgoku shakai fukushi seisaku*, pp. 96–102.

For 60 million *shi* was a stupendously high target. It probably exceeded even the peak storage levels achieved later in the century.[25] As the emperor apparently envisaged that the contributed stocks would be rotated at the same rates as the basic stocks, the minimum theoretical annual rotation target would have risen from 8.5 million *shi* to 18 million. To territorial officials with experience of the problems of maintaining ever-normal granary reserves, the implications of high contribution targets must have been frightening indeed. Soon widespread, moreover, was the notion that official stockpiling harmed consumers' short-term interests by pushing up grain prices. To those who gave this idea credence, 60 million *shi* must have been an unconscionably large amount for the state to hope to impound in its granaries.

However, let us consider the 60-million *shi* target in relative terms. If we divide both 28 million and 60 million *shi* by the 1741 official population total of some 143,411,560 persons—chronologically, the closest official population figure available—we find that the court was, at most, aspiring to increase an emergency reserve of about 0.195 *shi* unhusked per person to about 0.418 *shi* unhusked per person. By the famine relief standards formalized in 1740, the former figure represented adult survival rations for 19.5 days, the latter rations for 41.8 days.[26] Given the relatively limited incidence and severity of famines in eighteenth-century China, and the fact that supplementary grain from other sources could usually be brought in when local granary reserves proved insufficient, a 0.418 *shi per capita* storage target may have represented overinsurance. However, transporting relief supplies could be expensive, especially in northern China. It was not necessarily stupid to regard the maintenance of large local stockpiles as a more cost-efficient

---

25. Cf. Will and Wong, *Nourish the People*, appendix, tables A.1 and A.2. The figures in these tables are thought generally to represent granary holdings in the period of maximum depletion in the annual cycle (ibid., pp. 255–56, 264–68). Holdings in the months of greatest fullness were presumably higher. Unfortunately, the theoretical 30 percent rotation norm does not constitute a solid basis for calculating the holdings of the granaries when full. Caution as to the height of peaks is thus advisable.

26. These calculations are inspired by similar ones in Liu Ts'ui-jung, "A Reappraisal," p. 317 and have rough indicative value only. See QSL/QL, *juan* 157:30b for the 1741 official population figure; Will, *Bureaucracy and Famine*, pp. 130–31 on the 1740 relief standards.

way of managing the risk of famine than relying on interregional grain transfers whose feasibility could not be guaranteed.

Of greater importance for the discussion that follows is the relation that the 60-million *shi* target bore to the total amount of grain (a) produced, and (b) available for commercial distribution. The implication of a somewhat rhetorical estimate offered by the censor Wan Nianmao in 1745 is that a target of that magnitude would have been, at most, only about 3 percent of annual grain output.[27] Unscientific though this finding is, it corresponds remarkably closely with the result of calculations based on a modern estimate by Guo Songyi. Guo has estimated China's total grain output in 1753 as some 137.87 million metric tons of unhusked grain. While conversion between weight and volume is perilous when the mix of types of grain cannot be known, this amount may have been equivalent to some 2,000–2,500 million *shi* unhusked.[28] Sixty million *shi* unhusked would, then, have been between 2.4 and 3 percent of the 1753 grain output, and a slightly higher proportion of the (no doubt lower) average yearly output of the late 1730s. More to the point, if we assume that the state would have replaced, on average, 20 million *shi* per year (allowing for relief distributions as well as variant rotation norms), it would have claimed only about 1 percent of the 1753 output figure for its granaries each year.

Let us now compare this 20-million *shi* estimated annual state purchasing requirement with the estimated amount of grain that annually entered mid-Qing markets. The results of this comparison likewise suggest that, while perhaps higher than was prudent, the 60-million *shi* target should not have implied outrageous pressure on the marketed grain surplus. In 1985, Xu Dixin and Wu Chengming published an estimate of 30 million *shi* for the amount of staple foodstuffs (grain and beans) annually distributed via the private-sector, long-distance trade in

---

27. Wan estimated annual output per province at over 100 million *shi* and pointed out that the pre-1738 target of 28 million *shi* was not large in comparison. HCJSWB, vol. 3, *juan* 40:3b. One could—rashly—extrapolate a nationwide annual output figure of 1,900 million *shi* by taking his estimate as a genuine average for all nineteen provinces.

28. Guo Songyi, "Qingdai liangshi shichang," p. 47 ("market *jin*" converted here to kilograms). For proposed conversion ratios between *shi* and market *jin* of husked grain, see ibid., p. 46, and Xu Dixin and Wu Chengming, eds., *Zhongguo ziben zhuyi*, vol. 1, pp. 277 and 320.

pre–Opium War China. In 1994, however, Guo Songyi proposed the higher estimate of 46.5 to 57.5 million *shi* per year for private-sector grain traded over long or medium distances in mid-Qing times. Since most of the grain was probably transported in husked form, the un-husked equivalent would have been considerably higher. As Guo pointed out, however, even his higher estimate did not allow for the large quantities of grain that were traded within regional and local networks. He suggested that, in order to derive a global estimate in-cluding locally traded grain, 10 to 15 percent of total output could be taken as the actual amount traded in the average year. This would im-ply, for 1753, a marketed grain total of between 200 million and 375 million *shi* unhusked per year.[29] The 20-million *shi* annual state pur-chasing requirement would have been 10 percent of the lower figure and about 5.3 percent of the higher.

Guo's estimate for China's grain output in 1753, implying a large surplus compared with consumption needs, is hard to reconcile with the conventional mid-eighteenth-century perception that grain was perennially in short supply.[30] Perhaps, therefore, it is too high. How-ever, even had actual output in ca. 1740 been only 1,000 million *shi* unhusked, and even had the state realized the 60-million *shi* target, it would still have been a wild exaggeration to suggest (as the Qianlong emperor once did) that "half the people's output goes into the grana-ries." Replenishing the granaries would still not have taken more than one-fifth of each year's marketed grain surplus, granted the assump-tions made above. And yet, supposing that population growth and the unreliability of harvests indeed exerted constant pressure on grain markets in mid-eighteenth-century China, an ambitious state stock-piling policy would have brought trading interests unaccustomed and unwelcome levels of official competition, especially in those markets that attracted the most buyers. Whether for this or for some other reason, it was not long before the policy was challenged. Its first few critics were mostly not part of the territorial bureaucracy that ran the granaries and was directly charged to promote popular well-being. The critics' cry was that excessive storage in the ever-normal granaries was

29. Xu Dixin and Wu Chengming, *Zhongguo ziben zhuyi*, vol. 1, p. 277; Guo, "Qingdai liangshi shichang," pp. 45–47.
30. Cf. Introduction, n. 10 above.

causing an undesirable rise in market grain prices. The next section investigates on what reasonable grounds, if any, this complaint could have been made.

Granary Restocking and Grain Price Inflation

In July 1743, shortly after the grand secretaries and Nine Ministries Assembly had reported that the total holdings of the granaries still stood at only about 31 million *shi*, the superintendent of the Jiujiang internal customs station, Tang Ying, alleged a connection between heavy official buying for the granaries and a recent surge in grain prices in Jiangxi province. As we saw in chapter 2, 1742–43 was a bad year in Jiangxi, and there were other possible explanations for the *cherté*. Tang, however, did not discuss the vicious cycle of supply protectionism and hoarding that so worried the provincial governor. He merely drew attention to the strange fact that Jiangxi was facing crisis-level prices even though the 1742 fall harvest had not been particularly bad.[31] In the famous pottery town of Jingde Zhen, for instance, rice prices had generally been 3.3–3.4 taels per *shi* so far in 1743, compared with a normal range of 0.7–1.3 tael/*shi* over the eight years that Tang had lived there.

Tang showed no hesitation in tracing the crisis to the successive arrivals of official buyers for the granaries of several neighboring provinces: "Huguang," Jiangsu, Zhejiang, and Fujian. Such depletion of the Jiangxi markets had these buyers caused that a reversal of normal trade flows had ensued. Merchants who had originally set out to ship grain downriver to Jiangsu, in the usual way, had been turning round, attracted by the higher prices at which they could sell in Jiangxi and the Huguang provinces. It was unprecedented, thought Tang, to have at least 1,000 commercial grain boats going backwards through the Jiujiang customs station in their eagerness to supply Middle Yangzi rice markets. Tang did not need to remind the emperor that Jiangxi, Hunan,

---

31. Further on Jiangxi's climatic problems in 1742, see CC, Peng Jiaping, QL 8/5/27. Peng, the Jiangxi provincial administration commissioner, seems to have been sympathetic to the view that buying for the granaries was the leading inflationary pressure. However, he also referred to floods in 1742 in some ten county-level jurisdictions, plus bad harvests elsewhere in the province.

and Hubei were normally assumed to be grain-surplus, grain-exporting provinces.[32]

This is one of many documents from the 1740s linking high grain prices with official buying for the granaries. Some texts, including Tang's, express concern about grain prices on specific markets, while others seek to link the granary-restocking process with an increase in the general level of grain prices. It is now well established that grain price inflation was both real in 1740s China and part of a long-term process lasting until ca. 1820. This inflationary trend had causes other than experiments in boosting granary reserves. Traditional explanations stressed population pressure; in the mid-twentieth century, Quan Hansheng proposed a monetary explanation focusing on the influx of New World silver. Subsequent analyses by Wang Yeh-chien examine the interrelation between population growth and money-supply increase (including the rising output of indigenous brass coin), while drawing in additional factors such as "unprecedented commercialization" and, at the turn of the eighteenth century, extraordinary government spending to suppress rebellion.[33]

Debates as to the reasons for price movements in premodern China are important and, as the work of Richard von Glahn illustrates, by no means over.[34] What follows here, however, is not a contribution to these debates but rather an analysis, both critical and sympathetic, of the mid-eighteenth-century belief that state stockpiling in the ever-normal granaries caused high grain prices. The analysis is pursued

---

32. CC, Tang Ying, QL 8/5/22, and Grd. Secs. and NMA, QL 8/int.4/6. Tang's account of trade flows was perhaps oversimplified. According to Peng Jiaping, Jiangxi's *cherté* had been aggravated by high grain prices in all the adjacent provinces; these had kept grain merchants from importing grain to Jiangxi, which suggests that such imports were normal, at least in bad years. It thus corroborates Zhu Lunhan's testimony, cited below, that the self-sufficiency even of Jiangxi had become problematic. CC, Peng Jiaping, QL 8/5/27.

33. On the reality of the inflation, the pioneering work of Quan Hansheng must be supplemented with more recent regional studies that use archival data. The most important references include Quan Hansheng, "Meizhou baiyin" and "Qing zhongye yiqian"; Wang Yeh-chien, "Secular Trends of Rice Prices"; L. M. Li, "Grain Prices in Zhili"; and Marks, "Rice Prices, Food Supply, and Market Structure." For Wang's revisions of Quan's bullionist interpretation, see his "The Secular Trend," pp. 361–65, and "Secular Trends of Rice Prices," pp. 54–65.

34. von Glahn, *Fountain of Fortune*, pp. 224–45.

in terms of the situation that faced eighteenth-century administrators as they understood it, including not only the dilemmas that paternalist assumptions posed, but also, more importantly, the practicalities of annual granary restocking. I do not use "paternalist" as a term of abuse. Much Qing paternalism was motivated by recognition of the vulnerability of peasant farmers not only to the vagaries of climate and the effects of population growth, but also to the greed of landlords, moneylenders, and grain merchants.

Let us start with population growth, because by the end of the 1740s there were signs of a consensus that this was the fundamental problem. Official awareness of the pressure that population growth placed on grain prices found expression early in that decade. In 1741, the investigating censor Zhu Lunhan suggested that the Middle Yangzi provinces, although known hyperbolically for their ability to feed the entire realm, were no longer even self-sufficient. Jiangxi was now exporting population; the Huguang region was importing rice from Sichuan. "If . . . official and commercial grain-buyers these days invariably set their sights upon the Huguang provinces, this is because they do not realize that to-day's Huguang is not the same as that of yesteryear."[35] The perceived issue regarding the ever-normal granaries was whether, given this background of rising pressure upon limited supply, the state could responsibly exacerbate the situation by expanding its precautionary reserves, or even maintaining them at present levels.

In view of the calculations presented in the previous section, we may give short shrift to those less thoughtful contemporaries (including the Qianlong emperor) who suggested that the mere quantity of grain in store was the leading cause of the inflation. It is, furthermore, inevitable that in a large country with substantial urban and cash-cropping populations, significant amounts of grain will be withdrawn from the post-harvest market and warehoused for sale later in the annual cycle. The resulting increase in post-harvest prices has been seen as socially desirable by thinkers as diverse as the theoreticians of the classical ever-normal system and Adam Smith. The former were concerned primarily with the cash income of farmers; the latter saw high post-harvest prices as a check on society's propensity to imprudent

---

35. CC, Zhu Lunhan, QL 6/7/20, or HCJSWB, vol. 3, *juan* 39:10a.

consumption.[36] The autumn price rise must be greater if society is to be insured against crop failure in the following annual cycle, no matter whether the insurers are self-interested grain merchants or the agents of a paternalistic state. Thus, theoretically, there should have been no objection when official purchases were followed by price rises, unless it could be argued either that the interests of consumers were being harmed through overinsurance, or that buying for the ever-normal granaries caused larger price rises than the same amount of buying for commercial stockpiles. The latter possibility is examined below. First, however, it is necessary to say more about the granary system's *raison d'être*.

If all peasants could have kept their own reserves (an idea that imperial policy ostensibly favored), immediate post-harvest prices would have fallen less than merchants and consumers were accustomed to expect, but no-one could have blamed the state. With storage by the growers, furthermore, effective conservation might have been less problematic than with bureaucratic management (except, perhaps, in flood-prone areas).[37] However, an assumption behind Qing granary policy was that most households, including peasant households, were unable to store grain for themselves. To quote Zhu Lunhan again, "the principle behind [official] storage is properly that, because the common people are not able to maintain domestic grain reserves (*gaicang*), one copiously stockpiles grain on their behalf, in preparation for relief and special sales."[38] This may have been an exaggeration, at least as far as peasant households were concerned. Referring to eighteenth-century Lingnan, Marks claims, with much supporting evidence, that "After [the main autumn] harvest, peasant families stored more than enough grain to get them through to the next harvest"—enough, indeed to let them survive a partial harvest failure. To be sure, some of these reserves may have been deposited with pawnshops, as Celeng described, rather than being kept in peasant storage baskets.[39] The reason for the discrepancy between Marks's evidence and Zhu's generalization may have been regional variation, or it may have had to do with official percep-

---

36. Adam Smith, *Wealth of Nations*, vol. 2, pp. 30, 40–41.

37. Cf. Will and Wong, *Nourish the People*, p. 110 (which cites recent experience in developing countries).

38. CC, Zhu Lunhan, QL 6/7/20, or HCJSWB, vol. 3, *juan* 39:10a.

39. Marks, *Tigers*, pp. 240–42; cf. chap. 3 above.

tions of the amount of antifamine insurance that peasants needed, or with bureaucratic ignorance of the realities of peasant life. The fact remains, however, that Zhu voiced a widespread consensus.

Explanations for imputed peasant inability to maintain grain reserves were basically of two kinds: those that charged the peasant with improvidence, and those that pointed out the practical difficulties in the way of peasant storage. The perception of the peasant as improvident was implicit in the Qianlong emperor's early campaign against liquor distillation and explicit in some of his edicts.[40] It may be further exemplified by the following words of Yaertu, the Henan governor in 1743, who was seeking permission to continue buying for the Henan granaries despite a moratorium. "If [the peasants] do not sell [their surplus wheat] to the authorities, one cannot be certain that they will not sell it on the market. Once the silver or coin has entered their hands, it will most easily be spent. When all their grain is gone, where will their reserves be?"[41] As illustrated in chapter 6, this image left peasants potentially vulnerable to withdrawals of government sympathy. Such withdrawals were likely to be justified by rhetoric urging self-reliance for the poor.

Chen Dashou, writing in 1745, explained the need for Lower Yangzi peasants to market their grain in loose, but less derogatory terms. All the farming household's annual expenses, whether tax payments or the costs of "serving their parents and bringing up their young," and indeed "all their operations and activities," must be met out of the proceeds of the harvest. Other commentators would have added debt repayment. Peasant indebtedness could be represented as a symptom of improvidence, as it was by Yang Xifu in 1748, but there were other ways of looking at this problem. Debt could be unavoidable precisely when farmers were unable to raise sufficient monetary income from the sale of grain—perhaps because of low post-harvest prices. A debt incurred because of insufficient farming profits in Year A became a charge on Year B's harvest.[42] There was also the problem of rent, especially in the

---

40. For examples, see Will, *Bureaucracy and Famine*, p. 181.

41. CC, Yaertu, QL 8/int.4/25, and, for another example, Yaertu, QL 6/4/29. On Yaertu's role in the liquor suppression campaign, see Dunstan, *Conflicting Counsels*, pp. 217–19.

42. CC, Chen Dashou, QL 10/1/8; CC, Yang Xifu, QL 13 (cat. no. 1142-025); CC, Huang Tinggui, QL 13/4/24; Dunstan, *Conflicting Counsels*, pp. 277 and 283.

southern provinces where tenancy rates were highest. In Yang Xifu's opinion, the obligation to pay rent could force tenant farmers to part with grain that was needed for the current year's consumption. Still worse, grain that could have kept the tenants self-sufficient filled the granaries of speculating landlords, enabling the latter to manipulate market prices. Even in Henan, according to Yaertu, "As for the gentry and rich households who have spare grain in their homes, if [their grain] is not bought by the authorities and stored in the [official] granaries, [the owners] will inevitably hoard it and use it for speculation, increasing the price and afflicting the people."[43]

Some might have objected that, however wantonly ordinary peasants sold their grain, at least such irresponsibility supplied the market. Yaertu, however, did not take this cheerful view. Not only had he to contend with gentry and landlord hoarders, but, if ordinary farmers were left alone to sell their grain, "rich merchants and great traders . . . will engross the whole amount, and later on the market price will be theirs to put up or down at will."[44] Here Yaertu touched on the ancient premise of the ever-normal system and a *leitmotif* of Chinese political economy: merchants were suspect. However, he was writing at a time when most regional administrators understood full well that the services of grain merchants were vital to society. Ever-normal theory, moreover, had originated in northern China, and its natural target was the sedentary speculator. It did not provide an adequate framework for state-market interactions in the post-Tang world of large-scale interregional grain trade, which was supported by southern Chinese surpluses and borne largely on southern water-routes. The possibility of restocking local granaries from an interregional grain market destabilized the neat schema of the classic ever-normal system. It also raised the specter of state purchases undermining an otherwise functional commercial distribution system.

From the viewpoint of mid-Qing officials, there were three possibilities for the management of grain that was required neither for in-kind tax payment nor for immediate consumption by the farmer: retention by the agrarian community, commercial management, and

---

43. CC, Yang Xifu, QL 13 (cat. no. 1142-025); CC, Yaertu, 8/int.4/25; Dunstan, *Conflicting Counsels*, p. 284.
44. CC, Yaertu, 8/int.4/25.

governmental management. Some grain would stay, unmarketed for the time being, within local communities, but there was a risk that it would be in the hands of landlords who would use it for speculation. Hence the attraction of such schemes as the state-supervised "community granaries" (*shecang*) that were actively promoted in the early Qianlong reign. These would (theoretically) retain the advantages of decentralized, community-controlled storage, but be dedicated to the whole neighborhood's well-being.[45] The rest of the grain, however, would enter the market soon after harvest. The fundamental question underlying the ever-normal granaries debate was who should manage this marketed surplus, state or merchant? The conventional Qing answer was "both." Of necessity, merchants would warehouse and redistribute the greater part of the marketed surplus, but the state would equip itself (a) to take over where the profit motive left off, by feeding famine victims who could not afford to pay; and (b) to provide a check on antisocial profiteering through its "stabilizing sales." However, the late 1730s attempt to double the granaries' share of the gross surplus potentially implied unprecedented state encroachment on the merchants' customary share. In these circumstances, certain policy advisers (possibly representing mercantile interests) started to raise basic questions about the state's involvement in the grain trade even at existing storage levels.

As Zhu Lunhan observed, the diminishing surpluses available on Middle-Yangzi markets were subject to extensive buying by both merchants and officials serving other provinces. Local consumers, urban and rural alike, no doubt resented the higher prices that they therefore had to pay. However, to judge by their collective actions to prevent export of grain, ordinary people seem to have assumed that commercial buying was at least as much to blame as buying for the granaries.[46] Why, then, could officials like Tang Ying plausibly single

---

45. On the promotion of community granaries under Yongzheng and Qianlong, see Will and Wong, *Nourish the People*, pp. 37–40, 63–69. According to this account, although theoretically the *shecang* were to draw stocks from the holdings of the local rich, in fact the state contributed substantially to the formation of *shecang* reserves.

46. Cf. the Jiangxi case discussed in chap. 2 above. That anxiety had been aroused in Jiangxi by the large-scale official purchases of which Tang Ying com-

out state buying as inflationary? The rest of this section examines the technical difficulties that made state buying vulnerable to such criticism.[47]

Theoretically, the grain sold in a given county to stabilize prices in the *soudure* period was to be replaced by buying on that same county's post-harvest market. Unfortunately, local post-harvest prices were not always low enough for grain that had been sold at less than market rates to be replaced without a loss. The guidelines laid down to address this problem allowed considerable flexibility, given the constraint that buying could not be postponed indefinitely. Some rules of 1738, for instance, provided that if after the autumn harvest local prices were still high, the restocking purchases should be carried out in nearby areas where prices were normal. If prices were high throughout the region, restocking should be postponed at least until the next year's summer wheat harvest, and possibly until that autumn. If a granary's stocks were badly depleted, arrangements should be made to buy in an adjacent province where prices were low, with a provincial subsidy if necessary.[48] These regulations, besides helping to keep the system solvent, gave local markets some protection from heavy buying by the state at times when they were poorly stocked. However, the provision that major shortfalls from the storage quotas could be made good by interprovincial buying created the risk of state demand being concentrated on regions known for their high cereal production, especially the Middle Yangzi. Such concentration would be particularly intense after subsistence crises that had depleted granary reserves over large areas.

This problem had been recognized already in the 1720s. In 1727 Fumin, as acting Huguang governor-general, had noticed that merchant and official buying on behalf of other provinces (not necessarily for granary restocking) was keeping up grain prices in Huguang. He, however, accepted the elevated prices as an implication of the Qing state's traditional free-circulation policy.[49] In the 1720s, the balance of

---

plained can probably be inferred from reassuring words in one of Chen Hongmou's directives. PYTOCG, *juan* 15:20b and 22a.

47. For broader discussion of the problems of buying for the granaries, see Will and Wong, *Nourish the People*, pp. 142–78.

48. QCWXTK, vol. 1, *juan* 36, p. 5,189; cf. Will and Wong, *Nourish the People*, pp. 148–50.

49. ZPYZ, Fumin, p. 49b; reference from Abe, *Shindai shi*, p. 499.

economic interests in the region was perhaps still favorable to such *sang-froid*. As late as 1731, the governor of neighboring Jiangxi could argue that the in-kind grain "tribute" tax was necessary to maintain demand for Middle Yangzi surpluses within the other tribute-paying provinces.[50] However, during the next decade of population growth and urban expansion within and outside the Middle Yangzi, the balance appears to have shifted, at least in official discourse. By the early 1740s, the region's chief officials may have had reason to be ostensibly more sympathetic to those whose interests were best served by low grain prices than to those who wanted high ones. The self-sufficiency of the Middle Yangzi was now incomplete, and a hungry populace was an administrative problem. However, although 1740s discussions of high prices consistently argue in terms of consumer hardship, consumers cannot have been the only interest group that liked grain to be cheap. Cheap grain in supplier provinces suited long-distance merchants, whose profit margins could be realized most smoothly when there was no need to protect them by passing on high acquisition costs. More simply, low acquisition costs increased potential profit margins.

The 1740s expositions of why official rather than merchant buying should be blamed for high grain prices generally address one or both of the following: the special characteristics of bureaucratic buying, and the response of other participants in the grain trade. As to the former, although the annual rotation quotas and restocking rules were less than rigid, frequent pleas for greater flexibility suggest that the system showed only limited sensitivity to market fluctuations. Officials could feel under pressure to fill their large purchase quotas quickly because of constraints that would not have applied in business. In 1748, for instance, the Shandong governor Aligun alleged that officials tended to do all their buying at one time because they thought it inadvisable to let different cost prices appear on the accounts. Presumably, to the bureaucratic auditors such discrepancies would have indicated possible

---

50. ZPYZ, Xie Min, pp. 41a–b (reference from Abe, *Shindai shi*, p. 441). Xie was opposing the idea of temporarily commuting the tribute on the grounds that such action would leave the other tribute-paying provinces with their own grain surpluses. Demand for Middle Yangzi grain would then be weakened, making it harder for the producers to obtain the monetary income needed for their main tax payments.

malfeasance.[51] It was, moreover, clearly plausible that bulk purchases by officials who needed to meet quotas by fixed deadlines could overstrain local markets.[52] However, the more interesting contemporary discussions are those that stress the response of grain wholesaling brokers to the governmental buyers' plight.

For Aligun the point was that the brokers, knowing that their official clients would try to do all their buying in one swoop, "vie[d] with each other to put up the price." More developed was the argument of Zhang Yunsui, who wrote as follows of the granary restocking process, also in 1748.

[The process] is constrained by a predetermined price as well as quotas that must be fulfilled. . . . When the home locality has insufficient for their purchases, [the responsible officials] buy afar in neighbor jurisdictions. There are the costs of freight and porterage; there are the cares of loss amidst the waves. . . . Besides, . . . whenever new grain comes upon the market, its price originally is low. As soon as word arrives that there is buying for the granaries afoot, this price goes up immediately. For with commercial purchasing, when the price is low the merchants buy, and when it has gone up they stop: they are able to operate at will. But when officials buy stocks to refill the granaries, there is a fixed deadline laid down by the regulations, and even though the price be high, it is not open to them not to buy up to the quota level. The wicked brokers, with their long experience, know that this is so, and can thus give full play to their manipulative arts. This makes the places where abundance reigns suffer the same affliction as disaster zones.[53]

---

51. LFZZ, Aligun, QL 13/8/6 (d.r.); QSL/QL, *juan* 323:46b. Such concerns about the tunnel vision of bureaucratic auditors may have been justified. For example, the Board of Revenue was suspicious when different porterage and shipping rates appeared on the accounts for an interprovincial transfer of grain from different parts of Jiangxi in 1739. It even demanded that the officials who had arranged the transport be held personally responsible for refunding the expenditure it deemed excessive. The issue was still unresolved in 1741. HHCC, Bundle 61, Bao Gua, QL 6/7/9.

52. E.g., CC, Tian Mao, QL 8/6/21.

53. CC, Zhang Yunsui, QL 13 (cat. no. 1142-024); QSL/QL, *juan* 311:45a. By "predetermined price," Zhang presumably meant the maximum price set for each province by the Board of Revenue for replacing grain that had been used for emergency relief or interprovincial transfers. Will and Wong, *Nourish the People*, pp. 152–53. For an earlier complaint about the ill-effects of "Board prices," see CC, Peng Jiaping, QL 8/5/27.

For further insights as to how markets may have reacted to the presence of official buyers, we may turn an earlier (1743) account by the Huguang governor-general A'ersai. According to A'ersai, the cause of recent grain price rises "even in Hunan" was the convergence of official purchasers from other provinces.

Once the assigned personnel arrive, their [purchase] quotas invariably exceed thousands and tens of thousands, while as to the price, no matter whether it be low or high, they throng to purchase widely, intent upon assuring their supply. The long-distance merchants, fearing only that [the price] will rise still higher, join the fray to buy; the rich households, by contrast, calculating that the price must rise, hold on to their stocks firmly. On this, the price is gradually put up, and, in the circumstances, it is hard for it to fall again.

The somewhat similar account by the central government official Tian Mao stressed the publicity attending bureaucratic buying. He complained that, because the impending arrival of buyers from other provinces was openly announced,

As soon as the ordinary people of the region hear the news, they are afraid that [such official] purchasers will come hard on each other's heels. On this, those houses that lack grain vie with each other to buy stores, while houses that have grain indulge in reckless hoarding.

In short, consumers panicked, speculators hoped, and the price of grain surged upwards.[54]

Other officials drew attention to the likely consequences of the grain merchants' frustration for the end consumer. Ji Huang, one of the radical critics of the ever-normal system, suggested in 1741 that merchant buying did not start until official purchasing was over. "The merchants, having waited a long time, buy at high prices. How could they be willing to sell at lower ones?" Finally, in 1744 Anning asked whether the customers of long-distance traders could expect to be served at all. His account of why official buying pushed up prices in producing regions introduced another factor: the inexperience and lack of probity at least of those who travelled with official buyers and did their work for them. As Anning saw it, the friends and "permanent

---

54. CC, A'ersai, QL 8/8/10, and Tian Mao, QL 8/6/21. For other references to the problem of publicity, see, e.g., Anning's account discussed below, and CC, Yinjishan and Chen Hongmou, QL 8/12/16.

attendants" (*changsui*, that is, bondservants) of these officials were "bearing funds that do not matter to them personally and doing something in which they are not practiced, in both of which respects they are greatly inferior to merchants." Wishing to ensure a margin for their own enrichment, such people made a point of spreading talk that grain was dear. This may have persuaded the officials to entrust more funds to them, but it hardly disposed the brokers to sell cheaply. When grain prices had been artificially pushed up in the producing region, merchants serving other markets were deterred from buying. It stood to reason that prices in the "neighboring" (consumer) provinces would remain high too.[55]

It is not easy to judge the merits of these criticisms, plausible though they appear. Then as now, it was easier to create a climate of suspicion by invoking images than to publicize the lengthy and uninteresting record of actual practice, which might tell a different story.[56] Certain chief administrators of Middle Yangzi provinces could have testified that official buyers did not always insist on buying their full quotas irrespective of the price. Chen Hongmou, as Jiangxi governor, claimed in early 1743 that, contrary to popular report, the current high grain prices were protecting Jiangxi consumers from further official buying for other provinces. The year before, Xu Rong, his Hunan counterpart, had mentioned that, on one hand, personnel from Guangdong had arrived with orders to buy their assigned amounts no matter what the price. On the other hand, however, Hubei's buyers had been recalled because of Hunan's high rice prices, while Fujian's emissaries were loath to take responsibility for buying in a market that, if one allowed for transport costs, was now less favorable even than Fujian's. They were, therefore, awaiting further orders.[57] Admittedly, such situations

---

55. CC, Ji Huang, QL 6/7/16, and Anning, QL 9/2/10.

56. See, e.g., HHCC, Bundle 61, Yuan Zhancheng, QL 6/2/10, which shows the Gansu authorities taking care not to overstrain local markets even in a year of plenty. One quoted memorandum explains that, although rough guidelines had been set for the amount each jurisdiction was to buy, local officials were being given the discretion to buy more if prices remained low, or less if rising prices warned them that they risked "harming the people's food supply." In 1742, the new Gansu governor introduced a rule by which official buying would take place only after midday, so as to let private purchasers buy all they needed in the mornings. CC, Huang Tinggui, QL 6/11/28, 13/4/24.

57. PYTOCG, *juan* 15:20b and 22a; CC, Xu Rong, QL 7/2/18.

could be invoked in arguments against official buying. Liu Fang'ai, in early 1744, observed that official buying had to be stopped short when the limited funds did not suffice to pay sharply increasing market prices, but, for him, the surging prices would have been induced by the official buying in the first place. The price increase burdened the folk, and all for nothing since the granaries could not be filled.[58]

It would be arbitrary for a historian to decide that the whole problem was imaginary. A more reasonable view might be that the short-term impact of large-scale official buying could be roughly as many contemporaries described it, but that the important issues are the significance of this impact and its implications for government policy. By no means everyone who saw the problem claimed that the solution was radically to reduce official intervention. For example, A'ersai, whose concerns about market responses to official buying have been quoted, went on to argue that granary reserves remained important because of the risk of natural disasters, the perennial problem of the *soudure*, and the stubborn greed of speculators, who were deaf to moral reasoning and could not be constrained to sell by force of law.[59] For A'ersai and others like him, the point was to adjust the existing procedures.

Proposals for adjustment went beyond calls for more flexibility. One underlying problem was a lack of coordination to prevent official buyers from converging blindly upon the same markets. This problem was addressed to some extent. In the early 1740s, for example, Xu Rong and A'ersai, as chief administrators for Hunan, proposed measures to enhance coordination. Already, by the rules of 1738, the purchasing authorities were required to inform the authorities of the host jurisdiction, in advance, of the amount that they intended to buy. Xu Rong's proposal, made in 1742, was that the Middle Yangzi provincial authorities send monthly reports on grain prices in counties that were close to river ports to their counterparts in six southern and southeastern provinces, including Anhui and Guangdong. The reports, which would cover the whole period from the autumn harvest until the last month of the lunar year, would allow the purchasing authorities to make informed decisions as to where to send their buyers. In addition,

---

58. CC, Liu Fang'ai, QL 8/11/26.
59. CC, A'ersai, QL 8/8/10.

Xu envisaged that if another province needed to buy grain urgently, but prices in the Middle Yangzi were too high, the Middle Yangzi authorities should make the best arrangements possible to sell the needed grain from their own granary reserves. [60] These proposals were adopted. [61]

A'ersai, for his part, asked the emperor to institute a system of secret consultations between the chief administrators of grain-surplus provinces, including Sichuan, and those of any other provinces that happened to need grain. The authorities of the grain-surplus provinces would themselves do any buying, and they would buy only as much as seemed advisable in light of local grain supply conditions. Although A'ersai's proposal was made at a time (in 1743) when interprovincial buying had been halted, it could have inspired a better coordinated system of official redistribution of provincial surpluses. Unfortunately, as mentioned in the introduction to this book, the emperor decided to centralize the allocation process in order to enhance efficiency. The Grand Council would survey harvest and storage conditions nationwide and mastermind any interprovincial cooperation that it found to be necessary. The result, to judge from the two survey reports that I have inspected (both, admittedly, from the early 1750s, by when the context had changed) was routinization and inaction—inevitably, because the surveys were completed months after any need for them had passed. [62] Still, A'ersai's initiative had been a worthy one.

Another problem that seemed remediable to some senior officials was that of the excessive publicity surrounding interprovincial buying missions. Here the solution was simple: the official buyers should travel

---

60. This part of Xu's proposal was no innovation. By 1742, Hunan and Hubei had extra quotas totalling about 900,000 *shi* that were set aside for purchase by "neighboring provinces." Will and Wong, *Nourish the People*, p. 409; CC, Fan Can, QL 6/12/8.

61. QCWXTK, vol. 1, *juan* 36, p. 5,189; CC, Xu Rong, QL 7/2/18, and Grd. Secs. and Bd. Rev., QL 7/4/12; QSL/QL, *juan* 164:30b–31a; cf. Will and Wong, *Nourish the People*, p. 144 n. 6. That Xu did not develop his idea into a plan for coordinated buying was perhaps because he did not stress the need to protect Middle Yangzi markets. The problem, as he represented it, was to avoid wasting government funds on abortive buying missions, or (costlier still) on persisting in buying despite overhigh prices.

62. CC, A'ersai, QL 8/8/10; YFD, QL 16/4/3 (d.r.) (8:1618-1) and QL 18/4/11 (d.r.) (9:1624-1).

incognito and come to market in the guise of ordinary merchants. In 1743, the Fujian authorities adopted this tactic not only for buying on Taiwan, but also for a secret buying mission in the Lower Yangzi provinces. This mission violated a recently adopted moratorium on interprovincial buying; whether or not the tactic was effective in preventing sudden price rises, the assurance that they would attempt it probably helped the Fujian authorities to gain imperial approval for the trip. Perhaps the sense that it was expedient to disguise official buying goes some way to account for the practice, perceived as an abuse, of entrusting the task to brokers or even real merchants.[63]

Unfortunately, secrecy in interregional buying could be associated with delinquency in communicating with the authorities of the host jurisdiction. For instance, when in 1737 the acting Guangdong governor instructed Guangdong personnel buying on Guangxi markets to do their buying "merchant-style," he was concerned that, if he notified the Guangxi authorities of the impending mission, the news would reach the markets, and prices would be raised. Secret buying, in this case, replaced communication.[64] One would have thought that the prescribed intrabureaucratic communication needed only to be done in secret if it was to be compatible with incognito buying. However, advocates of incognito buying were presumably most exercised by the problem of market response to open bureaucratic buying. They may have seen this problem as acute enough to justify full secrecy. In 1748, for instance, one senior administrator emphasized the need for officials from the Lower Yangzi region, who had to buy upriver and perhaps as far away as Sichuan, to prevent news of their intentions from reaching target markets in advance. Sending beforehand to notify the relevant authorities was the wrong thing; instead, they should instruct their deputies to wait until they had acquired the grain "openly and fairly, exactly as in [ordinary] market exchanges," and only then contact the local administration with a statement of the prices paid. It could then be verified that current market prices had been used, and the higher-level auditing procedures could be completed.[65]

---

63. CC, Zhou Xuejian, QL 8/8/9; Will and Wong, *Nourish the People*, pp. 146–47; and, for an example of expressed concern about the use of brokers, QSL/QL, *juan* 323:48a.

64. QSL/QL, *juan* 53:20a–b.

65. QSL/QL, *juan* 323:47b–48a.

Finally, if the objection to publicity was that it put information in the hands of profit-maximizing brokers, one crude but obvious solution was tighter control on brokers. Hu Baoquan, who as a probationary investigating censor enjoyed the luxury of detachment from grassroots administration, claimed in 1743 that the high prices associated with official buying resulted entirely from broker selfishness. The important thing, therefore, was to monitor the moral caliber of brokers. Those whose intent was antisocial profiteering should not be allowed to practice.[66]

It is important to recognize the willingness of officials such as those cited above to grapple with the difficulties of the ever-normal system. It is only against the background of such commitment that we can grasp the radicalism of the handful of people, mainly junior censors, who pushed opposition to the ever-normal system as far as was politically thinkable towards proposing outright abolition. As shown in chapters 5 and 6, although these critics met with continuing resistance from the responsible central and provincial authorities, their arguments not only had a slow erosive power, but also directly influenced policy at important junctures. The present task is to introduce their point of view, focusing on the founders of the debate in 1739–42. The following profile of the pioneer critics of the ever-normal system opens the story of the great controversy.

The First Extreme Opponents of Official Buying

The criticisms of the ever-normal system examined here had much in common with the concerns discussed above. The shared starting point was the notion that official buying caused rises in grain prices that harmed consumer interests. In both cases, it was market conditions in the Yangzi Valley trading system on which attention centered. The early radicals created rhetoric that others, extreme and moderate alike, would later parrot. The characteristics that distinguished their memorials from those of most concerned administrators in the 1740s may be listed as follows. First, an emphasis on the alleged dichotomy between beneficial commercial and harmful official management of marketed grain surpluses; second, proposals that buying for the state granaries be

---

66. CC, Hu Baoquan, QL 8/6/28.

cut back if not discontinued altogether (with at best limited interest in alternative arrangements); third, allegation that the harm done by official buying outweighed any good that consumers might derive from stabilizing sales; fourth, denial that stabilizing sales did any good at all, or representation of them as pernicious; and fifth, lack of attention to the complexities of actual practice (not to mention shameless exaggeration). Although these characteristics were not all present in each memorial, they typify the early radical discussions as a set.

I begin with a 1739 memorial by Lu Zhuo—only marginally a radical and, not coincidentally, the only radical with territorial administrative responsibilities at the time of his critique. Lu wrote as Zhejiang governor. Like Ji Huang, Lu suggested that merchants visiting the Middle Yangzi provinces had to wait until the many official purchasers had all been served before they could start buying. "Before one province has finished buying, another comes hard on its heels. [Meanwhile, the merchants], arriving with substantial funds after long journeying by lake and river, wait day after day without buying a single grain." The result, claimed Lu, was that these wealthy merchants lost interest in visiting Middle Yangzi grain markets. The Lower Yangzi provinces, therefore, went short of grain even in years of plenty. The general level of grain prices in the Lower Yangzi provinces had risen, and the Middle Yangzi provinces were suffering from higher prices because of the response of speculators and "wicked brokers" to official buying. In fact, the whole realm was afflicted when the higher cost prices caused by official purchasing were passed on to consumers.[67] Given that local authorities resorted to interprovincial buying only when they had no choice, what was really happening was that "in order to build precautionary reserves for populations that have [just] experienced bad harvests, one is first depriving populations that have had good harvests of their morning and evening meals."

Variants of this last complaint, with its gratifying suggestion that the fortunate were bearing unfair burdens, were repeated throughout the

---

67. Literally, "Given that [dealers] can sell dear to officials, how could they be willing to sell cheap to merchants? Since the merchants have spent much capital, they extract still heavier profits, which means that there are none of the empire's people who do not share the tribulation caused by [bureaucratic] buying." Did Lu mean to suggest that the irritated merchants were extracting larger profit margins, or was he writing carelessly?

debate. However, Lu's proposed solution was unique. He suggested that the Middle Yangzi authorities be told to introduce a complex quota system by which 70 percent of the grain on the market in a given county at a given time would be allotted for commercial purchase, and 30 percent for official buying. All arriving merchants and officials would have to report their intended purchases to the magistrate of the host county. This magistrate would issue permits showing the local brokers how much the bearers were allowed to purchase in each round of buying. The 30 percent reserved for officialdom would be divided equally among the buying provinces, but no such artificial allocation would be imposed on the merchants' share. Lu claimed that eliminating the official-versus-merchant competition would ensure that Middle Yangzi grain spread freely, leading to a general fall in grain prices. Despite his confidence, the grand secretaries and Board of Revenue advised rejection of the plan. They agreed that measures were required to stop merchant purchases being delayed by official ones, but they found Lu's quota system both impractical and conducive to malpractice by brokers and government clerks. Merchants would still be held up, and they would still have extra costs to pass on to consumers.[68]

Lu's criticism of official buying was quite radical, but his proposed solution was probably not intended greatly to reduce the quantity officials bought. About six months earlier, however, Wu Wei, a middle-rank official in a Board of Works department, had made a frontal attack on the routine operations of the ever-normal system, in a context of rising grain prices. His proposals amounted to a plea at least to discontinue buying for the granaries until harvests improved, and preferably to sell the reserves off altogether. His memorial was ostensibly occasioned by concern that Jiangsu and Zhejiang were trying to restock their granaries, even though the Lower Yangzi had been suffering from natural disasters. Trying to restock in bad years was inappropriate,

---

68. CC, Lu Zhuo, QL 4/6/12, and Grd. Secs. and Bd. Rev., QL 4/7/16. Lu envisaged that the province of intended sale would be stated on each merchant's permit. The authorities of that province would be notified so that they could verify the grain's arrival. The reason given for rejecting this part of the plan suggests that the deliberators had taken note of Fang Bao's 1738 argument of principle against a similar control procedure (see chap. 3 above). The proposed checks would have deprived merchants of the flexibility to respond to price signals, thereby deterring them from continuing to ply their trade.

suggested Wu, because of the resulting strain for Middle Yangzi markets, where supplies were purchased to the detriment of Jiangxi and Huguang consumers. This much would soon be conventional, but Wu struck a distinctive note where he addressed the ever-normal system's underlying principles. Specifically, he argued that the results of merchant and official buying went in opposite directions:

> With commercial buying, the accumulated stocks of one region are taken and distributed in all directions, for which reason grain is daily observed to flow more freely. However, with official buying, stocks from the four directions are taken and accumulated in one place, for which reason grain is daily seen to be more insufficient.

However, official storage had a still worse consequence, Wu argued. If the authorities merely stockpiled grain bought at the current elevated prices, this meant leaving an expensive asset where it could do no one any good. If they did dispose of it in stabilizing sales, they would "not necessarily" be willing to sell at low prices grain that they had bought for high ones. On the contrary, they would insist on charging the full market rate. Merchant "monopolists," noting what a high price the (supposedly cheap) official grain was fetching, would then feel justified in trying to outdo the state. "In other words, [official] stockpiling of grain will have created an excuse for merchant speculation. With what security does it provide the folk?"

Wu made three proposals, of which the first two should perhaps be taken as alternatives. Ideally, existing stockpiles should be sold off at less than market prices; failing that, counties whose current reserves fell short of their basic (pre-1738) targets should acquire no more grain until good local harvests enabled them to purchase on their own home ground. Wu's third proposal was for a temporary suspension of the campaign to sell *jiansheng* titles for grain contributions to the granaries. He claimed that the response, while very poor, was still enough to have an adverse impact on grain prices. The rich were paying "double prices" for the grain with which to purchase *jiansheng* titles, causing a "daily" increase in the general level of grain prices. Future contributions should be accepted only in jurisdictions where the harvests had been good, he argued. The grand secretaries and Board of Revenue were unsympathetic to all three proposals. Having intimated that Wu's criticisms did not take account of actual practice, they concluded: "It would not be expedient to halt grain buying altogether just because of poor harvests at one point in time, or to have the existing stocks sold off completely. [If this were done], the storing up that [is appropriate in] normal times could not continue, and the relief bestowed in years of dearth would be deficient."[69]

Thus was the issue joined. The years 1739 to 1741 saw a series of four memorials echoing Wu's call for a halt to buying; each was referred to a full session of the Nine Ministries Assembly. First, in the fall of 1739, came a memorial from Bulantai, a high-ranking military official from the Manchu Plain White Banner who was based in northern Zhili and had served rather briefly (and not to the Yongzheng emperor's satisfaction) in the 1720s as governor first of Hunan and then of Jiangxi. Bulantai suggested use of stocks from the community granaries to replenish the ever-normal granaries, thereby obviating the need for purchase. That same winter, the investigating censor Xu Yisheng proposed a halt to opportunistic interprovincial buying on the grounds that "it is to be feared that the official shipments impede commerce." The young Ji Huang, who would rise to eminence later in Qianlong's reign, argued in 1741, as an expectant advisor to the Heir Apparent, that official buying did not only harm consumers, waste government resources, and inflict unwelcome personal liability on county magistrates; it was also ultimately useless because the stabilizing sales did no good. He wanted a complete cessation of buying by the Lower Yangzi provinces, the urgent cancellation of efforts to increase reserves beyond the pre-1738 targets, and a redefinition of the policy of selling *jiansheng* titles, which he thought should replace official buying as a means for routine granary restocking. Finally, towards the end of 1741, a supervising censor called Yang Eryou claimed that half the people's grain was being bought by the authorities. His suggestion for obviating this shocking (and fictitious) state of affairs was that, wherever possible, community granaries should replace ever-normal granaries as sources of famine relief grain. Where this was not possible, ever-normal reserves should be rotated in the same way as community ones: the stocks should be lent in spring and reclaimed in new grain after the fall harvest. Only when grain was actually cheap need there be any worry about

---

69. CC, Grd. Secs. and Bd. Rev., QL 4/2/5. This quotes Wu's memorial. My interpretation of his first proposal—ambiguous in his text as quoted—is guided by the grand secretaries' and Board of Revenue's response.

price support for farmers; post-harvest buying could therefore become a special intervention measure, not an annual procedure.[70]

Not one of these memorials found favor with the Nine Ministries Assembly. Their responses variously cited the flexibility that already existed; the overriding need to ensure adequate reserves in case of natural disaster; and the fact that post-harvest repayment of grain loans presupposed adequate harvests. Only Xu and Yang elicited any concessions, that to Xu being merely that provincial chief administrators should be ordered to ensure that buying was done only as long as the market was favorable. Officials were to stop buying as soon as prices rose, but they were still to make sure that reserves did not become depleted. Yang was somewhat more successful. In January 1742, in a foretaste of things to come, the emperor assented to the Nine Ministries Assembly's recommendation that provincial chief administrators be ordered to survey their existing reserves and determine which granaries still needed further replenishment, and which were full enough to justify a temporary halt to buying.[71]

The January decision set a potential precedent for deeming granaries sufficiently well-stocked even when they contained less than their basic (pre-1738) targets. However, it cannot have made much immediate difference, since the annual buying should have been largely completed by the time of the imperial pronouncement. Yang Eryou, therefore, returned to the attack. In May 1742, he denounced two alleged abuses, the second of which, he claimed, completely vitiated the ever-normal system. His memorial, while not always entirely clear, evinces the exu-

---

70. Mem. of January 1742 by the Nine Ministries Assembly quoted in HHCC, Bundle 93, Bd. Rev., QL 8/6/3; the 1742 memorial quotes Yang Eryou's and briefly summarizes those of Bulantai, Xu Yisheng, and Ji Huang. See also GCQXLZ, *juan* 284:47a–53a; Kishimoto, *Shindai Chūgoku no bukka*, pp. 302–3, 312; CC, Ji Huang, QL 6/7/16. Ji claimed that stabilizing sales were useless on two grounds: that the price asked was virtually identical with the market price, and that even were it significantly lower, antisocial dealers would still make corrupt arrangements to buy large stocks of the official grain and sell them at a profit. Furthermore, official supplies were limited and would eventually run out. This would give merchants the opportunity they had been waiting for to raise their prices, and local speculative activity would be intensified.

71. Mem. of January 1742 by the Nine Ministries Assembly quoted in HHCC, Bundle 93, Bd. Rev., QL 8/6/3.

berantly deadly neatness of expression that is the hallmark of Qing *exposé* rhetoric.

Yang first drew attention to the plight of those low-ranking people— from county magistrates down to village officers—who, he said, were charged to carry out official buying but not issued with funds enough to pay prevailing market prices. The consequence, he claimed, was that they had to make the shortfalls good from their own pockets. His second criticism was bolder, amounting to an accusation that the state was the biggest antisocial speculator, market-manipulator, and monopolist of all. In Yang's account, the county magistrates relentlessly continued buying grain on local markets, thereby pushing up the price, right up to the time of greatest scarcity in the *soudure* period. They then began to sell, but a handy regulation required them to limit the price cuts to a mere 0.05 tael per *shi* from the current price in normal years, or 0.1 tael per *shi* in years of dearth. There was, in fact, a cogent rationale for using such small cuts, and, in any case, the official prices were not supposed to be static, but to continue moving downwards step by step, drawing the market prices down behind them.[72] But Yang had no time for these subtleties. The point for him was that, given the seasonal price rises that they had themselves exacerbated, the local authorities would now be selling at an unconscionable profit. Merchants, meanwhile, would not bother to supply the market. In short:

Officialdom, with its buying, has hitherto been burdening the people's food supply with price increases, and is now, through its stabilizing sales, successfully competing for sources of profit that should be the people's. The virtuous intention of the Court has, in the last analysis, become no different from the speculative hoarding of the wealthy. How can we wonder that the people fail to perceive the virtue but regard it as a grievance?

Yang's proposal was that, in future, stabilizing sales be at cost price, supplemented as necessary to cover wastage and transport.[73] Unfortunately, his information was out of date. The rule limiting the price

---

72. Dunstan, *Conflicting Counsels*, pp. 31–32. For an apparently successful early twentieth-century reinvention of this incremental approach to price reduction, see Elvin, "Gentry Democracy," pp. 171–73.

73. CC, Yang Eryou, QL 7/4/18; or Grd. Coun. copy transc. Ye, comp., "Qianlong chao miliang," part 1, pp. 25–26. For a full translation, see Dunstan, *Conflicting Counsels*, pp. 85–88.

reductions to 0.05 to 0.1 tael per *shi* (a rule that had, in any case, existed in that form only since 1739) had just been revised. An edict of early April had expressed concern that such restrictiveness would not allow the poor to benefit substantially in years of real dearth. In future dearths, therefore, the price cut should be set *ad hoc*, with the provincial chief administrators recommending rates according to the circumstances. Although Yang may not have known this, the Jiangsu authorities had already gained imperial approval for an initial cut of 0.2 tael per *shi* in stabilizing sales in the disaster-stricken regions of their province. Their memorial cited one of the main arguments against excessive price reductions: that it was when officialdom severely undercut private sellers that the latter withdrew from the market or (in the case of travelling merchants) took their grain elsewhere. In these circumstances, Yang's proposal had no chance of acceptance. In any case, as the grand secretaries and Board of Revenue implied in their response, it would have undermined the financial viability of the ever-normal system. Yang's way of looking at that system was nonetheless embarrassing. It may have had something to do with the promulgation of a second edict, also in 1742, restating the new policy at greater length and stressing the duty of provincial chiefs to recommend reductions large enough to ensure real public benefit.[74]

Yang Eryou's memorial is stimulating as rhetoric, but it is not exactly philosophical. The last words in this section are therefore given to Anning, although he was not among the most extreme opponents of the ever-normal system. In the 1744 memorial cited above, we find the following short passage, in which commercial, profit-motivated distribution is represented as "natural," and official intervention in the grain trade as going against nature:

> In sum, the flowing of grain should [be permitted to] accord with nature. When merchants make their calculations, it is not that they are not actuated by [the thought of] profit, and yet, when they converge on Jiangxi and the Huguang provinces, the market price does not go up. The fact that, even though

------

74. QCWXTK, vol. 1, *juan* 36, pp. 5,191–92; CC, Nasutu, Zhou Xuejian, and Chen Dashou, QL 7/3/20; CC, Grd. Secs. and NMA, QL 8/int.4/6; and (for the grand secretaries' and Board of Revenue's response to Yang's memorial), CC, Grd. Secs. and Bd. Rev., QL 12/10/25.

official purchases do not amount to one per cent of mercantile ones, they promptly cause a rise in grain prices, is not a natural outcome.[75]

Was There a Grain Trade Lobby?

Thought about economic policy does not develop in a socioeconomic vacuum but is susceptible to influence from sectional and private interests. It was understood, in Qing central government circles, that a provincial chief administrator might advocate the sectional interests of "the people" of his jurisdiction, even if the morally superior governor was one who gave due weight to the conflicting needs of people elsewhere. A debate driven by concern to protect the Middle Yangzi grain consumer would have been seen as legitimate, although the morally correct resolution that the court was duty-bound to seek would have balanced Middle Yangzi interests with those of less fortunate consumers in the rest of south and central China.[76] The odd thing about the debate examined here is that the concern professed for Middle Yangzi interests seems not to have come primarily from officials with formal responsibility for the well-being of Middle Yangzi residents. It is reasonable to ask whether sectional or private interests other than those that could be openly acknowledged were at work.

In general, two kinds of private interest might have influenced discussions of the ever-normal system: the interests of local and regional officials as individuals, and commercial interests. Both were likely to go against the ever-normal system. It is true that some officials may have been disposed to defend the granary system because they were exploiting it for private gain. For example, a Guangdong prefect was impeached in 1743 for allegedly shipping grain from the prefectural granary to Vietnam and "[realizing] a high price for his own enrichment" from its sale there.[77] On balance, however, the interest of the average local official was probably in reduced central government commitment to the ever-normal system. It was not comfortable to be financially responsible for large stocks of a perishable foodstuff, for the rotation procedures were sometimes hard to implement, and they were subject to thorough audit when a magistrate left office. Will has sug-

---

75. CC, Anning, QL 9/2/10.
76. Cf. Will, *Bureaucracy and Famine*, p. 215.
77. CC, Jiang Pu, QL 8/5/1; cf. Will and Wong, *Nourish the People*, pp. 160–61.

gested that professed concern that granary restocking might deplete the local food supply could be a smokescreen for the magistrate's aversion to the risk of personal embarrassment that went with storing grain.[78] It is unlikely that the whole attack on the ever-normal system was a vicarious expression of local officials' resentments and fears. However, magistrates who were not zealots in the cause of "nourishing the people" might well have wished success to the attackers.

More interesting, but even harder to substantiate, is the idea that the system's most vocal opponents were speaking for commercial interests. Admittedly, some of these opponents did not hesitate to allege that antisocial merchant conduct followed in the wake of state attempts to buy grain for the granaries. However, if their goal was to defend the merchants' market share, the central point would have been to make a persuasive case against official buying, not to challenge the conventional image of merchant morality. Given the strength of this image, an argument that was consistent with it should have had some prospects of imposing on Confucian-trained official readers. It was, however, the arguments for the greater social utility of commercial distribution that went to the matter's heart. Here, the opponents of official purchasing were making claims that merchants would have welcomed without reservation.

Examination of basic biographical information about the radical opponents of the ever-normal system confirms Kishimoto's observation that a number of them had Zhejiang connections, while further establishing a link with Huizhou (Anhui), famous as the ancestral home of major merchant lineages. Yang Eryou, admittedly, was from Shanxi, and the investigating censor Wei Tingpu, who proposed a moratorium on buying for the granaries in 1743, was from Guangdong. However, Wu Wei and an equally outspoken radical called Sun Hao had passed the metropolitan examination as residents of Hangzhou (city or vicinity), while Xu Yisheng was from the nearby county of Deqing. As we have seen, Lu Zhuo, a Chinese Bannerman, wrote his critique of ever-normal buying as the Zhejiang governor. Ji Huang,

---

78. Will and Wong, *Nourish the People*, pp. 147–48, and, on the difficulties of storage, the liability of county magistrates, and the audit and inspection process, pp. 103–5, 110–25, 196–218.

although from Wuxi in Jiangsu, was the son of Ji Zengyun, who would have been based in Hangzhou during 1736–38 while governor-general (and governor) of Zhejiang. Lu Zhuo was Ji Zengyun's immediate successor as Zhejiang provincial chief. Wu Wei, Sun Hao, and Ji Huang were all graduates of the same metropolitan examination, that of 1730, while Ji Huang once wrote a biography of a cousin of Xu Yisheng (Yisheng's own *jinshi* date being 1723). Wu Wei, moreover, was claimed as a Huizhou man by ancestry or origin; his name is found among the records of illustrious native sons of Shexian, seat of Huizhou prefecture.[79] It is, therefore, possible that there were personal links at least among the four more junior officials (Wu, Sun, Ji, and Xu), that the similarity of their opinions reflects conversations and/or correspondence that had taken place among them, and that Wu's Huizhou background inclined him to understand the merchant viewpoint. It may also be relevant that, although Huizhou and Hangzhou were separated by a provincial boundary, they are not very far apart and were linked by a trade route.

Evidence of possible grain-trade connections in the late-Ming ancestry of Xu Yisheng notwithstanding, it would be hard to prove an actual conspiracy between the radicals and Lower Yangzi grain trade interests.[80] The historian lacks the resources of the investigative journalist for exposing clandestine discussions between government officials and members of sectional interest groups within society. I have argued elsewhere that the evidence is (at best) suggestive of surreptitious arrangements "to give Lower Yangzi grain-trade interests political representation that by the standards of the day was illegitimate," and

---

79. Dunstan, "The 'Autocratic Heritage,'" pp. 100–1 and references there cited; 1923 *Hangzhou fu zhi, juan* 111:17a; 1937 *Shexian zhi, juan* 4:40a, 6:63b–64a; cf. Kishimoto, *Shindai Chūgoku no bukka,* p. 302. Further on Wu Wei, see Zhaolian, *Xiaoting za lu,* pp. 479–80. For the roles of Sun, Wei, and Wu in the events of 1743, see chap. 5 below.

80. To judge by his recorded philanthropic deed, the son of the Deqing Xu descent group's founding ancestor may have had grain-trade connections or been a grain merchant for part of his life. The founding ancestor had migrated to Deqing from coastal Yuyao county (Shaoxing prefecture) in the sixteenth century. See Min Erchang, comp., *Beizhuan ji bu, juan* 11:3a; Dunstan, "The 'Autocratic Heritage,'" p. 101 n. 87.

that, whether such arrangements existed or not, the arguments and proposals of the radicals were such as to suit the Yangzi Valley grain merchant community.[81] The reader can assess the justice of the latter claim by following the progress of the ever-normal granaries debate in 1742–43, as told in the next chapter.

81. Dunstan, "The 'Autocratic Heritage,'" pp. 100–2.

5

A Sage and His Advisors:

1738–1743

This chapter explores the unfolding of the ever-normal granaries debate from the adoption of the high-level storage targets in 1738–39 to the limited victory of the granaries' radical critics in 1742–43. It examines the rationale for the high-level storage policy, shows that the sale of *jiansheng* titles for grain contributions to the granaries proved inadequate as a means of reaching the high targets, and discusses the success of two further attacks by investigating censors in 1742 and 1743. Influenced by these critiques, the court did more than discontinue the high-level storage policy. It declared a moratorium on buying for the granaries—only to find itself caught between the radicals' cries for further dismantling of the ever-normal system, and the concerns of those who feared depletion of the state's precautionary reserves. In these circumstances, the court compromised, made *ad hoc* arrangements, and clutched at straws.

Two straws—that is, alternative approaches—were offered, one by the radicals and their supporters, the other by certain senior provincial officials. The radicals proposed increased use of the expedient of giving famine relief partly in the form of silver; the bright idea from Jiangxi and Fujian was a reformed *jiansheng*-title sales policy as—ideally—the sole major path to granary restocking. This chapter examines the terms in which the first of these approaches was put forward. An account of how the second came to be attempted is reserved for chapter 6.

Fanfare for an Innovation

Attempting to stock ever-normal granaries by selling *jiansheng* titles was nothing new in 1738. Nor was the setting of grain contribution targets. Although the normal way of selling *jiansheng* titles was to have the buyers pay in silver at the Board of Revenue, sales in exchange for direct grain deliveries to the ever-normal granaries had been in use since 1681. Indeed, they had long been accepted as a standard way of building granary reserves. Reported success had varied greatly between provinces, but the basic idea was not absurd.[1] Adult males of sufficient means could be attracted to the purchase of a *jiansheng* title by the advancement opportunities thereby obtained, not to mention certain legal, fiscal, and social privileges.

Officials in the 1740s wrote as though the chief inducement to *jiansheng*-title purchase should have been the short cut it provided to eligibility to sit the provincial examinations for the *juren* degree. Purchasers thus motivated were trying to improve their chances in a quasi lottery whose custom from educated males was little diminished by the mediocre prospects of success. The *jiansheng*-title holder could also attempt the *juren* examinations with reduced competition in Beijing, taking advantage of a special quota (for the number of successful candidates). Perhaps more to the point, he gained eligibility to buy various medium- and low-ranking posts in the bureaucracy. Even if he did not want to invest further in advancement, merely by virtue of being a *jiansheng* (titular Imperial Academy student) he enjoyed a limited tax exemption, the entitlement to certain marks of status, and legal immunities that, while incomplete, could nonetheless be useful. In principle, the *jiansheng* studentship was therefore salable.[2]

---

1. Will and Wong, *Nourish the People*, pp. 28–30. For examples of pre-Qianlong contribution targets, see the annotated figures for Zhejiang and Anhui in table 2 above.

2. Ch'ü, *Local Government*, pp. 173–75; Chang, *The Chinese Gentry*, pp. 5–6, 22, 29–30, 32–43; Ho, *Ladder of Success*, p. 34. It was presumably to the legal immunities that the supervising censor Huang You referred in mentioning applicants who were in a desperate hurry for certificates of *jiansheng* status to use as "protective talismans." Huang You, QL 3/7/13 (d.r.), transc. Lü Xiaoxian, comp., "Qianlong sannian," part 1, pp. 7–8.

More dubious was the realism of the early Qianlong-period attempt to use studentship sales to double granary reserves that were already sizable. Problematic issues include not only the size of the effective demand for *jiansheng* titles, but also the sustainability of that demand, given that privileges tend to lose value as the number of their holders rises. It is true that provincial chief administrators discussed other impediments to the sale of *jiansheng* titles for grain at considerable length. However, it was not, to my knowledge, until 1745 that any senior official undertook a systematic exploration of the variables affecting the demand for *jiansheng* titles, or, to be more exact, the differential effect on demand of the required means of payment in various circumstances.[3] There was much theoretical naivety behind the policy of trying vastly to increase reserves by selling *jiansheng* titles.

The immediate antecedents of this poorly thought-out notion lay in the Yongzheng period. In 1733, the Hubei surveillance commissioner, Wang Rou, proposed *jiansheng* title sales as an effective, noncoercive means of drawing grain out of the speculative hands of "wealthy merchants and great households," and placing it under the socially responsible control of ever-normal granaries. Wang argued that paying for *jiansheng* titles locally in grain would be much more convenient for the buyers than having to arrange for the delivery of silver to a distant office. So great would be the eagerness to purchase that "It may confidently be predicted that whenever there befalls a year of plenty, half the grain will be in the hands of the authorities, and half among the people." The increased size of the reserves would permit buying from the granaries by missions from other provinces, thus reducing pressure upon markets (presumably those of the Middle Yangzi) that, although originally well-stocked, were at risk of overstrain from bulk official purchases for emergency relief elsewhere.

The Yongzheng emperor endorsed Wang's idea in principle. After all, if Yamamoto Susumu is right, promoting storage as a substitute for emergency buying was Yongzheng's own policy.[4] The emperor indi-

---

3. See the discussion of CC, Qin Huitian, QL 10/6/25 in chap. 6 below.
4. Yamamoto portrays the Yongzheng build-up of reserves as a response to the problems caused by buying relief grain *ad hoc*. In particular, in 1727–28, large official purchases for downstream provinces appeared to have provoked a high-price crisis in Sichuan. Yamamoto suggests that Yongzheng hoped to cut the need for emergency buying by boosting local reserves and encouraging certain provinces

cated, however, that the time was not ripe for a great build-up of stocks through sale of *jiansheng* titles.[5] Unfortunately, circumstances were altered by his death in 1735. In the late 1730s, the throne was occupied by a young man (the Qianlong emperor) who was expected, by rhetorical convention, to establish himself as a sagely ruler. But in which direction might sagehood be found? Self-appointed guides were not slow to come forward. Making original suggestions might advance their career prospects. A new ruler's advent could also encourage previously silenced idealists to proffer advice out of conviction, and previously unsuccessful statesmen to express pent-up dissatisfaction with the policies of the last reign. By the summer of 1737, the senior court scholar Fang Bao had prevailed on Qianlong to launch a campaign to wipe out liquor distillation in north China, thereby conserving, estimated Fang, at least 10 million *shi* of grain per year.[6] In late 1737, the investigating censor Chang Lu proposed that sales of *jiansheng* titles be used to double the nation's granary reserves.

Chang was not the only official to make innovative suggestions about the granaries during Qianlong's inaugural years. In 1737, Gan Rulai urged that voluntary grain contributions be solicited because official stocks were limited, and "to have the people nourished by officialdom is not as good as having them nourish each other." Two years later, the investigating censor Shen Maohua advocated that granary endowment lands be established so that the harvests could provide a secure basis for the annual restocking process. In his famous memorial of 1741, Zhu Lunhan, also as an investigating censor, suggested that one year's tribute grain be retained in the provinces where it had been collected in order to restock their granaries. Although tribute grain had been used for popular subsistence before, the idea of occasionally substituting tribute retention for official buying was new, or so Zhu be-

---

(especially the Middle Yangzi ones) to build stocks that could be used elsewhere. Yamamoto, "Shindai zenki no heichō seisaku," pp. 50–53.

5. ZPYZ, Wang Rou, pp. 85b–87a (reference from Abe, *Shindai shi*, p. 496); cf. Will and Wong, *Nourish the People*, p. 49.

6. Dunstan, *Conflicting Counsels*, pp. 205–6. For the reservations about Yongzheng's fiscal policies expressed soon after Qianlong's accession, see Zelin, *Magistrate's Tael*, pp. 266–68. On the young Qianlong's understanding of excellence in ruling, see Kahn, *Monarchy*, chap. 9.

lieved.[7] None of these ideas remotely approached Chang's for sheer grandeur of vision.

Chang proceeded from two premises: first, that the nation's vast but indigent population "must, of necessity, rely upon the court to keep reserves on its behalf"; and second, that the limited existing grain stocks might suffice either for free distribution during famine or for stabilizing sales, but not both. Indeed, when famine came, stocks that looked large in normal times would start to seem extremely small. The larger the afflicted area, the greater the likelihood that there would be enough neither for free distribution nor for stabilizing sales. Bringing in extra stocks from other regions, as one then had to do, was very wasteful because of the high transport costs.[8] The solution, nay, "the task of most importance at the present time," was to double granary reserves throughout the nation. In effect, Chang was suggesting that to store enough grain in each region to meet all probable contingencies would be more cost-efficient than the normal eighteenth-century approach of using local stocks for stop-gap relief only, and supplementing them with external supplies as need dictated.[9] Although this implicit claim of Chang's was probably mistaken, several provincial chief administrators would have agreed with him thus far, to judge by their behavior during 1743–44.

Chang proposed that all the nation's county-level jurisdictions be classified into three grades by size and population. In general, "large" counties should stock about 60,000 *shi*, "medium" counties about 50,000 *shi*, and "small" counties about 40,000 *shi*. These very substantial stocks (respectively 6.0, 6.25, and 6.66 times as large as the quotas in force in 1700) would be maintained according to the 30 percent stock rotation principle. Chang's plan provided for two types of harvest

---

7. CC, Gan Rulai, QL 2/6/6, Shen Maohua, QL 4/3/27, and Zhu Lunhan, QL 6/7/20 (or HCJSWB, vol. 3, *juan* 39:9b–11a); cf. Will and Wong, *Nourish the People*, pp. 31–32 and 46–49.

8. Referring to such transport costs, Chang used a phrase roughly translatable as "billions." For more exact figures, see, e.g., Yamamoto, "Shindai zenki no heichō seisaku," p. 44; HHCC, Bundle 61, Bao Gua, QL 6/7/9; Will, *Bureaucracy and Famine*, p. 279 n. 10. Sample rates mentioned in these sources are 0.422 tl./*shi* between Hunan and Zhili in 1723–24, and over 1.0 tl./*shi* between Henan and Shaanxi in ca. 1720.

9. Will, *Bureaucracy and Famine*, p. 277; cf. Will's study of the provenance of relief supplies in the 1743–44 Zhili famine (ibid., chap. 8).

only: positively good and positively bad. In years of abundance, 30 percent of the existing stocks would be replaced; in years of natural disaster, the amounts issued from the granaries would be determined by need. They would be replaced, by purchase, after harvest.

How were the new storage targets to be realized? Since the cost of buying the extra reserves would be prohibitive, the best plan would be sales of *jiansheng* titles. The practice of selling the titles for silver at the Board of Revenue would be suspended, and the required form of payment would be a grain contribution to the ever-normal granary of the applicant's home county. Once a given county's grain stocks had reached the new target, its native sons would be permitted to "contribute" (*juan*) elsewhere in the prefecture. They would be allowed to "contribute" in other prefectures and, in due course, other provinces once their own prefecture and province had reached the new target. Each province would convert the silver price per *jiansheng* title into an equivalent amount of grain according to the normal grain prices prevailing in the region. Once set, the valuation rate would not be changed. When the reserves of the whole nation had reached the new target, the central government would revert to selling the titles for silver. In the meantime, regular tax funds would be needed for building extra granaries and supplementing the reserves of any counties that did not attract sufficient contributions.[10]

In a memorial drafted by the Board of Revenue, the body ordered to consider Chang's idea advised against it. This body was no less than a joint conference of the Regency Council, appointed to "superintend the affairs [of government]" during the new emperor's statutory mourning period, and the large Nine Ministries Assembly. However, despite the "sweeping powers" that Beatrice Bartlett has attributed to Qing regency councils, the deliberators failed to dissuade Qianlong from trying Chang's experiment.[11] Not that they rejected the whole concept of a nationwide increase in storage levels. After all, they had recommended that the Zhili authorities be permitted to buy extra grain to supplement that province's reserves. However, the procedure that

---

10. Chang Lu's memorial (d.r. QL 2/int.9/29) is quoted in Regency Council and NMA, QL 2/10/21, transc. Lü Xiaoxian, comp., "Qianlong sannian," part 1, pp. 3–4.

11. Bartlett, *Monarchs and Ministers*, p. 139.

they had envisaged for Zhili was market-sensitive, with buying to take place only when grain supplies were ample. Their concern about Chang's proposal was that aspirants to *jiansheng* status could not be trusted to respect market conditions in the way that local officials could be told to do. The aspirants, in their impatience, would not await a year of plenty before buying the grain they needed to obtain the title. They would "buy all at once, competing to be first, with the inevitable result that grain prices will rise, and the people's food supply will suffer." Local variations in grain prices, meanwhile, would make uniform provincial silver-to-grain conversion rates unrealistic, yet setting local rates would be too complicated and might provoke abuses. It would be better to extend the policy already recommended for Zhili. Provincial chief administrators should be directed to estimate the storage levels needed in each county of their jurisdictions, report, and wait for years of plenty before buying grain with public funds.[12]

Responding thus to Chang's proposal might have been calculated to provoke an ambitious, inexperienced ruler to adopt it. If public funds were used, where would be the scope for conspicuous achievement? Although at first Qianlong indicated that he was accepting the recommendation of the highest deliberative council in the land, a subsequent edict showed him overriding it. On 7 March 1738, he ordered all provincial chief administrators to consider whether their jurisdictions would benefit from a program of selling *jiansheng* titles for grain. If so, they should submit detailed proposals regarding implementation. Qianlong did not explicitly suggest that they aim at doubling reserves; he merely ordered them to determine whether present storage levels were adequate or not. However, those governors and governors-general who favored a title sales program were instructed to advise on "setting quantities" (*ding shu*). It was implied that the extra grain would be subject to the annual 30 percent rotation rule. While the phrase "setting quantities" was vague, the Board of Revenue endorsed a subsequent memorial from the Zhili governor-general advocating county-level targets as barriers to the play of market forces, which would otherwise channel contributions to the granaries of jurisdictions with low grain

---

12. Regency Council and NMA, QL 2/10/21, transc. Lü Xiaoxian, comp., "Qianlong sannian," part 1, pp. 3–5.

prices.[13] The proposals from the provinces would indeed feature contribution targets.

Although figures for three provinces are not available, surviving
records show that the provincial contribution targets set in 1738–39
were generally very high (see table 3). Some were higher than the quotas
already in force. A later policy discussion document mentions proposed increases in individual granary targets of up to 80,000–100,000 *shi*
in extreme cases (probably for prefectural granaries in major cities). We
can therefore agree that a passage in a 1743 edict that seems to mean that
an original nationwide target of over 28 million *shi* had been raised to
over 32 million must instead be read as indicating that the revised global
target implied by the new policy of 1738–39 was over 60 million *shi*, that
is, the sum of the two figures. That the two figures must be added has
already been noticed by Gao Wangling; it can be confirmed, in principle, from archival sources dated 1742 and 1743.[14]

At provincial level, adding the available 1738–39 contribution targets
to the so-called "Yongzheng-period targets" shown in table 2 is problematic because, as we have seen, the majority of these look like reported actual storage levels only. Fortunately, the requirement to set a
supplementary contribution target forced administrators to define an
"original" (*yuan*) or—for a translation that better fits this context—
"basic" target in relation to which the new stocks would be extra. Although I cannot be sure that all the figures in column A of table 3 are
those taken as basic targets in 1738–39, documentary evidence makes it
possible to say this of some of them. Several of the column A figures are
different from the table 2 "Yongzheng-period targets," reflecting either
subsequent revisions or, perhaps, in one or two cases, the real targets of
the Yongzheng period. The uncertain status of some column A figures
leaves column C (in principle, putative basic targets plus recorded
contribution targets) as a preliminary, indicative guide to the actual
total targets of 1738–43. The same is true of table 4, which presents the
column C totals in rank order. Although there is some documentary

---

13. Edict of QL 3/1/17 transc. Lü Xiaoxian, comp., "Qianlong sannian," part 1,
p. 5, or QSL/QL, *juan* 61:1b–3a; JS, Bd. Rev., QL 3/2/12; cf. Will and Wong, *Nourish
the People*, p. 49.

14. QSL/QL, *juan* 189:2a; Gao, "Yige wei wanjie de changshi," pp. 15–16; mem.
by Grand Secretaries and Nine Ministries Assembly, QL 7/5/9, transc. HHCC,
Bundle 87, Zhang Yunsui, QL 8/2/28; CC, Grd. Secs. and NMA, QL 8/int.4/6.

basis for assuming that the Gansu figures are expressed in the large "granary *shi*" of northwest China (and must therefore be converted, as in table 3, to yield standard *shi* equivalents), they are rendered problematic by two ambiguously worded, mutually inconsistent variants.[15] Yet even if, as is conceivable, the figure that in 1748 was represented as the 1738 total target in fact originated as the contribution target of the latter year (expressed in standard *shi*), the total Gansu target during 1738–43 would still have been at least 4 million standard *shi*, and probably some 4.5 million.

The sum of the sixteen available provincial contribution targets is about 26 million *shi*. Even assuming that the three missing provincial targets account for the last 6 million *shi* needed to bring the total above 32 million, how literally should we take the notion that, in 1739–43, the Sino-Manchu territorial bureaucracy aimed at a total ever-normal storage target of over 60 million *shi*? There are indications that the total of the targets that provincial administrations actually envisaged meeting was a somewhat lower figure, perhaps about 58 million *shi*. A 1741 archival document that is no less authoritative than the slightly later texts implying over 60 million *shi* mentions the following nationwide aggregates: over 27 million *shi* for the basic target, and over 30 million *shi* for the extra contribution target.[16] Such a discrepancy invites investigation. Various possible explanations suggest themselves; here, I confine myself to the only one that I can document. I present the evidence in detail, as it foreshadows a method adopted by more than one province in the 1740s to deflect the title-selling policy from its high-minded goal of boosting ever-normal grain reserves (and, therefore, local administrators' worries). Instead of offering the people added food security, the title-selling policy was to reduce the burdens of officialdom—through a subversion strategy that almost triumphed during 1745, as chapter 6 will tell.

Chang Lu's innocent idea of using *jiansheng* title sales as an alternative to massive extra buying was the thin end of a rather useful wedge. All Chang had suggested was that, as the state could not afford to double the stockpiles through purchase, it should try to realize this

15. See notes to table 3; and cf. Wu Shiduan, QL 16/11/22, repr. GZD/QL, vol. 2, pp. 25–26.
16. CC, Bd. Rev., QL 6/5/2.

Table 3
The Provincial High-level Storage Targets, 1738–43
(Units: *shi* of unhusked grain. In principle, the figure in column C should be the sum of those in columns A and B. Use of bold type indicates cases in which, to the contrary, the column C figure is *less* than the sum of the columns A and B figures. These cases are discussed in the text.)

Province	A Basic target (from table 2 unless otherwise indicated)	B 1738–43 contribution target	C 1738–43 total target (in principle, A + B)	D C as a percentage of A (to nearest integer)
Shandong	**2,959,386**	**1,100,000**[i,ii,vi]	**3,806,386**[1,a]	129%
Henan	2,310,999	1,992,400[iii]	4,303,399	186%
Shaanxi	2,061,741	3,292,000[ii,vi]	5,353,741	260%
Guangdong	1,925,685	3,500,000[i]	5,425,685	282%
Fujian	1,848,800[2]	1,045,000[b,vi]	2,893,800	157%
Anhui	**1,832,000**[3,4,i]	**966,130**[5,i,vi]	**1,832,000**[3,4,i]	100%
Jiangsu	1,568,000[6,ii,v]	571,000[c,ii,v]	2,139,000[ii,v]	136%
Shanxi	1,550,000[4]	1,490,000	3,040,000[iv,v]	196%
Guangxi	1,413,398[4]	1,274,020[ii,vi]	2,687,418	190%
Jiangxi	**1,370,713**	**2,098,021**[7,d,i,ii]	**3,290,000**[i,v]	240%
Gansu	1,228,571[8]	(3,457,143)[8]	4,685,714[8]	381%
Hunan	1,202,133[9]	1,565,000[iii,v]	2,767,133	230%
Sichuan	1,100,000 + [10,v]	1,774,600[iii,v,vi]	2,874,600 + [10,v]	(261%)
Hubei	1,070,000[9,iv,v]	1,200,000[v]	2,270,000	212%
Yunnan	701,600[11,ii,iii,vi]	701,000[i–iii,vi]	1,402,600	200%
Guizhou	395,200[11,ii]	247,000[ii,iii]	642,200	163%

NOTES: No data on the 1738–43 high-level targets for Zhili, Zhejiang, or Fengtian.
[1] This figure is the sum of the columns A and B figures minus 253,000 *shi*. The 253,000 *shi* represents a shortfall from the basic target that had been incurred in 1737 and was to be made good through contributions (see text).
[2] Table 2 variant.
[3] Figure stated in *shi* husked, and converted here to *shi* unhusked by doubling.
[4] Table 2 variant used here for the sake of consistency, as it is from the same source as that in column B and/or C.
[5] Contribution target represents the difference between the basic target and the actual level of reserves in 1738.
[6] The Jiangsu "Yongzheng-period target" (1,528,000 *shi*) had been increased by 40,000 *shi* (20,000 *shi* each for Chongming and Nanjing).
[7] A trivial discrepancy between the sources has been resolved in favor of the version in HHCC, Bundle 89, Bd. Rev., QL 8/3/19.
[8] These figures represent a basic target of 860,000, a contribution target of 2,420,000, and a total target of 3,280,000 granary *shi*. The contribution target is calculated from the other two figures and attested in no documentary source that I have seen. The 3,280,000 *shi* figure was represented in 1748 as a total target set in 1738 and reaffirmed in 1743. CC, Huang Tinggui, QL

13/9/20, QL 13/10/24. Reports of 1740 (JS, Bd. Rev., QL 5/10/20) and 1743 (CC, Huang Tinggui, QL 8/4/3) mention the higher figure of 3,380,000 *shi* with phraseology permitting the interpretation that this is the total target, but in contexts that lead one to expect citation of the contribution target. An edict of 1741 (QSL/QL, *juan* 136:7b–8b; Lü, comp., "Qianlong sannian," part 1, p. 13) cites 3,800,000 *shi*, apparently as the contribution target. Given these ambiguities, and the lack of explicit evidence that the Gansu targets were expressed in granary *shi* in 1738–43, one can experiment with the implications of taking each figure of 3+ million *shi* as a standard-*shi* contribution target set in 1738. But no possible combination of the available figures, assumed to be in either granary or standard *shi*, then offers a clearly convincing reading. It is simplest to believe that 100,000 *shi* were later added to a 1738 *total* target of 3,280,000 *shi*, and that the 3,800,000 *shi* figure is erroneous.

[9] Figure comprises the basic target plus an extra quota (grain for selling to other provinces) established in the late 1730s: 500,000 *shi* for Hunan, 420,000 *shi* for Hubei (Will and Wong, *Nourish the People*, p. 409; QSL/QL, *juan* 189:23b–24a; CC, Fan Can, QL 6/12/8). For Hubei, the table 2 variant is here adopted as the basic target.

[10] Column A: 1738 actual holdings figure treated like a basic target. Column C: sum of columns A and B; the source cited gives a rounded figure.

[11] New, early Qianlong target. For Yunnan, minor discrepancies between the sources are resolved in favor of the information in the earliest source located. For Guizhou, the column A figure is based on the assumption that the 210,200 *shi* of extra grain on which the provincial authorities had decided previously were added to a basic target of 185,000 *shi* (table 2 variant).

Variant 1738–43 target figures not noted above (omitting mere roundings)
[a] Shandong total target, 4,380,000+ *shi*. This figure seems to include over 570,000 *shi* of community granary reserves and other special category grain (see text). HHCC, Bundle 87, Yan Sisheng, QL 8/1/24.
[b] Fujian contribution target, 1,064,000 *shi*. E.g., QSL/QL, *juan* 185:12b; CC, Nasutu and Zhou Xuejian, QL 9/4/24. Will and Wong (*Nourish the People*, p. 50) quote 2,000,000 *shi*, but, as shown in chap. 6 below, this target was set in 1745. While the primary sources are mutually inconsistent, it is safe to say that the 1738–39 Fujian contribution target was below 1,100,000 *shi*, and that it was raised in stages. On the basis of the earliest source located (JS, Wang Shu, QL 6/8/5), I suspect that while 1,064,000 *shi* was regarded as the original target by 1744, it replaced 1,045,000 *shi* in 1741 as a result of the proposal made in that memorial.
[c] Jiangsu contribution target, 569,000 *shi*. This was the figure mentioned in the Liang-Jiang governor-general's original (1738) proposal for implementing the *jiansheng* title sales policy (Lü, comp., "Qianlong sannian," part 1, p. 6).
[d] Jiangxi contribution target, 1,920,000. Will and Wong, *Nourish the People*, p. 50. This is the approximate figure obtained by subtracting the pre-1738 target from the new total target, but it differs from that explicitly stated in two documentary sources. The discrepancy is explained below.

SOURCES *(other than those already noted)*
[i] Mems. transc. Lü Xiaoxian, comp., "Qianlong sannian," part 1, pp. 6, 10–11, 15–17.
[ii] HHCC, Bundle 87, Yan Sisheng, QL 8/1/24, Zhang Yunsui, QL 8/2/28; Bundle 88, Chen Dashou, QL 8/3/10; Bundle 89, Bd. Rev., QL 8/3/19; Bundle 93, Bd. Rev., QL 8/6/3 and 8/6/20, and Zhang Guangsi (fragment, n.d., forwarded to Bd. Rev. QL 8/6/28).
[iii] Will and Wong, *Nourish the People*, pp. 49–50, 397, 435–36 (table 12.1), and 439.
[iv] QSL/QL, *juan* 91:15a–b, 148:10a, and 189:23b–24a.
[v] CC, Bao Gua, QL 6/6/7; Xu Shilin, QL 6/6/8; Kaerjishan, QL 6/7/26; Fan Can, QL 6/12/8; Xu Rong, QL 8/3/22; Shise, QL 8/7/4; and Chen Dashou, QL 9/4/24.
[vi] JS, Qing Fu, QL 3/5/7; Qing Fu and Zhang Yunsui, QL 5/2/16; Yang Xifu, QL 5/2/28; Hao Yulin and Chen Dashou, QL 5/4/25; Wei Dingguo, QL 5/5/24; Shise, QL 5/11/16; Wang Shu, QL 6/8/5; and Qing Fu, QL 12/3/15.

important goal by selling *jiansheng* titles. The grand secretaries perhaps meant something more when they wrote in 1739, in response to Wu Wei's objections, that if the wealthy paid for *jiansheng* titles with grain, this saved officialdom "the trouble of buying" (*caimai zhi fan*). In 1739–40, the Gansu authorities had to argue with the Board of Revenue for permission to take advantage of good harvests to do some not very major buying. To their dismay—for the rate of contributions in Gansu was sluggish and uneven—the Board claimed that the *jiansheng* title sales policy (and a special dispensation allowing aspirants from other provinces to "contribute" in Gansu) made the projected purchases unnecessary. These purchases may have been intended to fill shortfalls from the basic targets as opposed to building the reserves to higher levels. The episode suggests that, for the Board, studentship sales could now be preferable to buying grain even when market conditions were favorable and funding was not a problem.[17] There is, moreover, evidence from Jiangxi, Shandong, and Anhui that, from the time when they proposed their contribution targets, some provincial administrations planned to use *jiansheng* title sales to replace grain that was theoretically held under the basic targets, and that would normally have been replaced by purchase.

Table 3 embodies the assumption that each province's new total target (column C) should be the sum of its basic target (column A) and contribution target (column B). This is demonstrably so in the cases of Jiangsu and Sichuan, where all three figures are found in at least one source. It is also a safe inference in cases where, in principle, the basic target was doubled; this applies to Yunnan and Guangxi.[18] In the cases of Jiangxi, Shandong and Anhui, however, the new total target is less than the sum of the basic and contribution targets. In Jiangxi's case, the recorded total target (3,290,000 *shi*) is the sum (after rounding) of the

---

17. CC, Grd. Secs., QL 4/2/5; HHCC, Bundle 61, Yuan Zhancheng, QL 6/2/10. The Board professed concern that the combined impact of official buying and buying by aspirants to *jiansheng* status would cause a sudden rise in prices.

18. JS, Qing Fu, QL 3/5/7; HHCC, Bundle 93, Bd. Rev., QL 8/6/20. Guangxi's contribution target was virtually identical with its "Yongzheng-period target" (table 2). It differs from the column A figure only because the latter includes 139,020 *shi* of army rations (apparently incorporated into the basic target). In Yunnan's case, in doubling the targets the provincial authorities ignored the last 600 *shi* stored in the provincial capital.

contribution target (2,098,021 *shi*) and the amount actually in store when the contribution target was proposed (1,192,121 *shi*), minus an untidy extra-quota amount held by one county (about 143 *shi*). Thus the Jiangxi authorities must have been hoping to use contributed grain to fill over 150,000 *shi* out of their basic target (in principle, some 1,371,000 *shi*, but a lower figure may have been assumed in 1738).[19]

The records for Shandong are complicated by the apparent inclusion of over 570,000 *shi* of community granary reserves and other special category grain in the stated basic and total targets. For consistency, the Shandong figures used in table 3 are based on the "Yongzheng-period target" of table 2, which is presumably for ever-normal grain alone. However, the Shandong authorities in 1738 did their sums with the inflated figures. The stated total target (over 4,380,000 *shi*) comprised the contribution target (1,100,000 *shi*) plus the amount (over 3,280,000 *shi*) that should have been in store in 1738, given that over 253,000 *shi* of the inflated basic target (over 3,530,000 *shi*) had been used for disaster relief in 1737. This shortfall was to be made good through contributions, within the contribution target. Thus only 847,000 *shi* of the contribution target would be an addition to the Shandong basic target. In terms of the uninflated figures used in table 3, a total target that, at first sight, one would have calculated as 4,059,386 *shi* was in fact only 3,806,386 *shi*. It was later decided that 100,000 *shi* that had been transported to Zhili should also be replaced within the contribution target; this implied further shrinking of the total Shandong target. Finally, in the extreme case of Anhui, the governor-general saw no point in increasing reserves beyond the basic target. With Anhui's reserves still being kept largely in husked rice, he opined that extra stocks might simply rot. The contribution target he proposed (966,130 *shi* unhusked) was the exact amount by which Anhui's reserves were then short of their basic tar-

---

19. HHCC, Bundle 89, Bd. Rev., QL 8/3/19. The Jiangxi basic target was unusually fluid. The "Yongzheng-period target" recognized in 1749 was 1,370,713 *shi* (table 2). However, in a report transcribed in the above source, the Jiangxi provincial administration commissioner, Peng Jiaping, suggested that the actual holdings reported in 1736 (1,346,682 *shi*) could be regarded as the "old target." In another 1743 memorial, Peng wrote that in 1742, Jiangxi's provincial target had been somewhat over 1,377,000 *shi*. CC, Peng Jiaping, QL 8/5/27.

get. In Anhui, the sole purpose of *jiansheng* title sales would be replenishment of the existing stocks.[20]

Adding up the amounts of shortfall from basic target that the authorities of Jiangxi, Shandong, and Anhui alone proposed to make good out of contributions, we find that over 1,469,000 *shi* must be subtracted from the theoretical 60-million *shi* nationwide storage target. No doubt the full amount that should be subtracted is still higher. In other words, there was between the global basic target of 28 million *shi* and the global contribution target of 32 million *shi* an overlap whose size cannot be ascertained precisely. This overlap probably increased with time, through decisions some of which may not have been reported to the central government. Whether or not the figure of 30 million *shi* mentioned in 1741 reflects deliberate deduction of known overlap, we may be sure that the real global target of 1738–43, while unprecedentedly high, was less than 60 million *shi*. Meanwhile, one can readily picture any cynics there may have been among provincial top officials as they undertook the target-setting process. Such people would have judged (correctly) that the whole project was chimerical. Their hope would have been that the contributions would at least suffice to bring stocks up to basic target level, with minimal expenditure of administrative effort and none at all of silver.

Table 3 shows that the provinces that set the highest contribution targets were at the nation's extremities: Guangdong in the south, and Shaanxi and Gansu in the north. To judge by the incomplete and possibly misleading information on new total targets, Guangdong and perhaps Zhejiang apart, northern China (China north of the River Huai) was now more clearly the region where the largest granary reserves were thought desirable.[21] Table 4 suggests that the Middle and Upper Yangzi regions belonged to a second tier, which also included Fujian and Guangxi. As we have seen, the Middle Yangzi provinces were those on whose markets official buyers from other provinces were most likely to draw. Jiangxi was already becoming a regular supplier of

---

20. HHCC, Bundle 87, Yan Sisheng, QL 8/1/24; Nasutu, QL 3/5/24 transc. Lü Xiaoxian, comp., "Qianlong sannian," part 1, pp. 5–7.

21. Zhejiang's contribution target is unknown. However, as its basic target was 2,800,000 *shi* (table 2), a modest 1,000,000-*shi* contribution target would have brought this southeastern province almost to shared fifth place in table 4.

Table 4
The 1738–43 High-level Storage Targets in Rank Order
(Units: *shi* of unhusked grain)

Province	Total storage target	Province	Total storage target
Guangdong	5,425,685	Sichuan	2,874,600+
Shaanxi	5,353,741	Hunan	2,767,133
Gansu	4,685,714	Guangxi	2,687,418
Henan	4,303,399	Hubei	2,270,000
Shandong	3,806,386	Jiangsu	2,139,000
Jiangxi	3,290,000	Anhui	1,832,000
Shanxi	3,040,000	Yunnan	1,402,600
Fujian	2,893,800	Guizhou	642,200

NOTES: Total storage targets from table 3, column C. No data on the 1738–43 high-level targets for Zhili, Zhejiang, or Fengtian.

stocks from its own granaries to other provinces; Hunan and Hubei gained special quotas for that purpose in 1738–39; and Sichuan would no doubt be called upon to play a larger role in future.[22] Whether hoping to protect their provinces' own markets from outside official buying or simply aiming for enlarged capacity both to serve other provinces with emergency grain shipments and to provide crisis relief at home, the authorities of the Middle and Upper Yangzi provinces envisaged storage levels that were not only quite high, but also more than double the corresponding basic targets (see table 3, column D). Even in Hubei, a "Yongzheng-period target" of about 521,000 *shi* (table 2) was raised by over 300 percent, allowing for the special extra quota as well as the contribution target.

Also noteworthy in the list of total targets (table 4) is the fall in Jiangsu's relative position. Jiangsu was the nation's most urbanized and densely populated province, but also the most highly commercialized. It had had the ninth highest of the "Yongzheng-period targets" (table 2); its revised total target during 1738–43 was the fourth lowest of those shown in table 4. To a traditionalist administrator, Jiangsu, with its

---

22. Will and Wong, *Nourish the People*, pp. 303–4; Yamamoto, "Shindai zenki no heichō seisaku," pp. 53–54 and ff.; n. 9 to table 3 above.

large nonagrarian population, would have seemed a very vulnerable province—one in which capacity to carry out large-scale stabilizing sales was vital. Its "downgrading" during 1738–43 seems a landmark in the transition towards the late eighteenth-century distribution of grain stocks, which favored frontier and relatively uncommercialized provinces, but left highly commercialized ones substantially reliant on the interregional grain market.[23]

From Zeal to Disappointment

R. Bin Wong's overview of the studentship sales system between 1738 and the late 1760s acknowledges that its record was checkered, but still gives the impression that, at least before 1750, the sales made a positive contribution to "mobilizing" grain for the reserves.[24] By the summer of 1742, however, the grand secretaries and the Nine Ministries Assembly were ready to declare that the experiment had largely failed. The reason for the difference between the two assessments lies in the choice of yardsticks, and the yardsticks used by central government policy advisors in the 1740s underwent two changes, as I show below. In 1742, the yardsticks applied to the accumulated proceeds were the targets set in 1738–39.

Compared with these targets, the results to date in 1742 seemed pathetic indeed. Ten out of the eighteen provinces of China proper had not met even 10 percent of their respective targets. Three more (Guangdong, Yunnan, and Shaanxi) had met "10 or 20 percent," while Fujian and Gansu had achieved "30 or 40 percent." Only for Anhui, Sichuan, and Jiangsu were there moderate success stories to be told. Anhui and Sichuan had achieved 60 and 70 percent respectively, while Jiangsu had overfulfilled its exceptionally low target. Jiangsu, however, had been given an advantage because of repeated dearths. It had been permitted not only to sell *jiansheng* titles at a 30 percent discount, at

---

23. Cf. Perdue and Wong's analysis in Will and Wong, *Nourish the People*, pp. 296–98. The governor-general who proposed a low contribution target for Jiangsu was Nasutu, whose realism about the varying demand, in Jiangsu, for routine springtime sales of ever-normal grain is described by Wong (ibid., pp. 53–54; cf. QCWXTK, vol. 1, *juan* 36, p. 5,189). Nasutu, QL 3/5/24 transc. Lü Xiaoxian, comp., "Qianlong sannian," part 1, pp. 5–7.

24. Will and Wong, *Nourish the People*, pp. 49–52.

least in the stricken areas, but also to accept payment in silver as an alternative to grain. Less than one-third of the contributions had been made in grain. Meanwhile, as the silver payments remained unspent, continuing disasters were leaving Jiangsu's granaries depleted. In the spring of 1743, the Jiangsu authorities were still urgently trying to attract more in-kind contributions.[25]

It was not only in Jiangsu that silver had been accepted instead of grain. In 1740, the governor-general for Guangdong reported that the county granary of the Chaozhou prefectural seat had collected only about 70 percent of its *jiansheng* title sales proceeds in the form of grain. Another county in the same prefecture had collected a mere 20 to 30 percent of the payments in that form. The governor-general suspected that such a state of affairs was not confined to Chaozhou. He blamed it on the local officials, who would rather be responsible for silver than for perishable grain. A year later, the central government was showing that it understood this point of view. As stocks increased, it might prove impossible to observe the rotation norms, and county magistrates would indeed be liable for the rotting grain. The question then became what spoilage rates should be declared allowable, so as to reassure the magistrates without tempting them to negligence. There were also allegations of abuses—using oversized measures, charging unauthorized fees, and so on—even when grain was collected. Such behavior would have tended to deter contributors, which may have been its purpose. As a slightly later Jiangsu governor put it, "When *shengyuan* [government students] and 'men of promise' [here, ordinary commoners] make their contributions, [the county magistrates] are thinking not so much of practicing extortion to enrich themselves, but rather of applying pressure to make men afraid to come forward."[26]

Even without sabotage by local magistrates, the "in-kind" studentship sales policy encountered crippling problems. The numerous provincial reports of slow or negligible progress reflect two main issues. In

---

25. Mem. by Grand Secretaries and Nine Ministries Assembly, QL 7/5/9, transc. HHCC, Bundle 87, Zhang Yunsui, QL 8/2/28; CC, Depei, QL 8/3/27.

26. Maertai, QL 5/4/3, and Haiwang, QL 6/2/8 transc. Lü Xiaoxian, comp., "Qianlong sannian," part 1, pp. 12, 14–15 respectively; Chen Dashou, QL 9/4/24 transc. ibid., part 2, pp. 14–15; CC, Bd. Rev., QL 6/5/2 (cf. Will and Wong, *Nourish the People*, p. 120), and Liao Biqi, QL 6/10/19. The translation "men of promise" is Chang Chung-li's.

the earlier memorials, provincial chief administrators are predominantly seeking concessions on the rule requiring applicants to buy the title within their home county (that of their official registration). The authorities of several provinces quickly realized that they could accelerate the flow of contributions if permitted to accept them from outsiders such as merchants. To be sure, such concessions provoked a conflict of interests with the outsiders' home provinces, sometimes resulting in appeals for their limitation.[27] Yet some of the cases made for special treatment were compelling. In provinces like Gansu, Yunnan, and Sichuan, the inhabitants of remote, mountainous, frontier territories could not be persuaded to buy *jiansheng* titles—especially when these people were not Han Chinese and had no reason to appreciate the system. In provinces (such as Sichuan) that had received major flows of immigrants, confining sales to officially registered inhabitants could mean excluding large proportions of a county's population, or even the majority. The only hope of meeting the contribution targets was to open the sales to settlers, visiting merchants, and other sojourners. Even a province as well endowed as Jiangxi could have difficulty in meeting its target with contributions from native sons alone. Jiangxi's native sons with grain to spare were interested mainly in the rising prices that external demand brought. They preferred a tangible return in silver to the dubiously valuable opportunities conferred by *jiansheng* status.[28]

Several provinces received at least temporary permission to open title sales to outsiders, but this was no panacea.[29] In March 1741, the Manchu president of the Board of Revenue, Haiwang, argued that it was time to stop experimenting. At the very beginning of Qianlong's reign, while studentships were being sold for silver at the Board of

---

27. In early 1742, the Hubei governor claimed that since 1739, when Hubei started selling *jiansheng* titles, only about thirty men had bought the title in Hubei, whereas over 700 Hubei natives had bought it in other provinces. CC, Fan Can, QL 6/12/8. For appeals for protection against concessions favoring one or more other provinces, see, e.g., JS, Yue Jun, QL 5/10/15, and Shise, QL 5/11/16.

28. Li Rulan, QL 4/11/11, Yue Jun, QL 5/1/28, Qing Fu and Zhang Yunsui, QL 5/2/16 transc. Lü Xiaoxian, comp., "Qianlong sannian," part 1, pp. 9–12; JS, Yang Xifu, QL 5/2/28. For a still useful overview of migration flows in late imperial China, see Ho, *Studies*, chap. 7.

29. See, e.g., JS, Shise 5/11/16 (Shaanxi and Gansu), and Yang Xifu, QL 5/2/28 (Fujian, temporary; Guangxi).

Revenue, the sales had yielded up to 1.3 million taels per year, all earmarked for famine relief. Now, however, the annual value of the grain delivered by *jiansheng* purchasers was only 300,000 to 400,000 taels. Except in the case of Sichuan, the one notably successful province, it would be only sensible to revert to collecting silver at the Board, and use the silver to enable provinces to buy grain towards their contribution targets. Half convinced, the emperor ordered that, for all provinces, the option of paying silver at the Board be fully restored to *jiansheng* buyers. However, the attempt to sell some *jiansheng* titles locally for grain was not to be abandoned. The two approaches were to be pursued concurrently.[30] This ruling shifted the attention of provincial chief administrators to a second issue. Given rising grain prices, would paying in grain at 1738–39 valuation rates be the rational choice of persons who could pay in silver?

The consensus was that it would not. In 1738, while the in-kind title-sales policy was still at the planning stage, the senior supervising censor Huang You had warned that it could not succeed if the option of paying silver at the Board were not removed. Apart from the fact that county magistrates would obstruct applicants who wished to pay in grain, thereby diverting them towards the Board, the procedures involved in paying locally in grain would be too cumbersome and time-consuming compared with a simple monetary transaction in Beijing. There were even special couriers to make the purchase on behalf of clients.[31] Huang had worried that, even were the price per title

---

30. Haiwang, QL 6/2/8 and edict of same day, transc. Lü Xiaoxian, comp., "Qianlong sannian," part 1, pp. 14–15, and QSL/QL, *juan* 136:8b–10a. Haiwang's idea of letting provinces buy grain towards their contribution targets was not wholly discarded. In September 1741, with a good harvest in prospect, the Shanxi governor was authorized to expedite progress towards the target by buying 250,000 *shi* of grain (about 17 percent of Shanxi's contribution target) and 30,000 *shi* of beans. CC, Kaerjishan, QL 6/7/26; QSL/QL, *juan* 148:10a–b.

31. Huang You, QL 3/7/13 (d.r.) transc. Lü Xiaoxian, comp., "Qianlong sannian," part 1, pp. 7–8. Real conflicts of interest were involved here. A junior Hanlin compiler had opposed the suspension of sales at the Board, citing the inconvenience that return to their home counties would cause Beijing's literati sojourners, and an exception was made for them. In response to objections, the Board confirmed that the exception was for sojourners who hoped to take the special *juren* examinations held triennially in Beijing; such aspirants would be able to buy their *jiansheng* titles

Table 5
Discrepancy between Grain Valuation Rates and
Reported Actual Grain Prices in Four Provinces, 1742–43
(Prices are stated in taels per *shi* of unhusked grain.)

Province	Valuation rate	Actual market price
Shandong	0.5	0.7–0.8 +
Jiangsu	0.5	0.7–0.9
Hubei	0.4 (+)	0.5–0.6 +
Hunan	0.32–0.5[1]	Annually rising

[1] Hunan's county-level units had been divided into five groups, depending on local grain prices. The valuation rates ranged from 0.32 to 0.5 tael per *shi*.
SOURCES: CC, Bao Gua, QL 8/2 (cat. no. 1123-021); CC, Depei, QL 8/3/27; CC, Fan Can, QL 6/12/8; CC, Xu Rong, QL 8/3/22; cf. Wong and Perdue, "Grain Markets and Food Supplies," fig. 4.1 (p. 133).

converted into grain at a rate slightly favorable to applicants, more people would pay in silver than in grain; by 1743 in many provinces, titles were on sale for amounts of grain whose current value exceeded the set price in silver (108 taels for applicants with no academic qualifications).[32]

In Shandong, for example, the established valuation rate being 0.5 tael per *shi* (unhusked), the 108-tael price was converted to 216 *shi* of grain. By 1743, the market value of 216 *shi* of grain in Shandong was at least 150 to 170 taels.[33] As table 5 suggests, comparable situations existed

---

at the Board in the three months immediately preceding the examinations. This exception—retained until the general reopening of sales at the Board in 1741—was allegedly abused on a large scale. JS, Grd. Secs. and Bd. Rev., QL 3/6/27, Bd. Rev., QL 3/7/21, QL 5/10/20; Haiwang, QL 6/2/8, transc. Lü Xiaoxian, comp., "Qianlong sannian," part 1, p. 14.

32. 108 taels is represented as the standard price, reflecting the assumption that most buyers would have no academic standing. Lower rates were available for the different categories of *shengyuan*, the lowest being for stipendiary students (presumed to have the greatest academic merit). Persons deemed to be of less than ordinary social status could buy *jiansheng* titles at an exceptionally high rate. See, e.g., CC, Xu Rong, QL 8/3/22.

33. Calculated from data in CC, Bao Gua, QL 8/2 (cat. no. 1123-021).

in other provinces (albeit not everywhere).[34] Matters could be still worse if applicants were charged "wastage" (extra grain to compensate for the likely accidental waste) and a granary construction fee. The Liang-Jiang governor-general claimed that, if one allowed for these two items, the true cost of a *jiansheng* title in Jiangsu (except where modified by the 30 percent discount mentioned above) could actually exceed 200 taels.[35]

Some provincial chief administrators obtained permission to reduce the prices charged in grain. Proposing a simple percentage discount, as did the Hubei governor, was deemed an acceptable evasion of the problem that the valuation rate was not supposed to be adjustable. However, the central government even countenanced departures from the latter principle. Hubei was authorized to accept payment at a 10 percent discount, while Jiangxi was allowed to raise its valuation rate from 0.4 to 0.5 tael per *shi*, and Fujian from 0.54 or 0.6 to 0.9 tael per *shi*. Jiangsu, in April 1743, wished to combine the two approaches: the valuation rate should be increased from 0.5 to 0.733 tael per *shi*, and disaster-stricken regions should be allowed to give a temporary 20 percent discount on the adjusted price of 150 *shi* per title. Jiangxi had meanwhile gained permission to forbid its natives to buy *jiansheng* titles both in other provinces and at the Board of Revenue itself. Jiangsu and Shandong requested the same privilege. The Shandong governor even suggested that such a concession was all that his province needed. Were there no alternative to paying locally in grain, he argued, applicants would naturally "leap" with enthusiasm to do so, even if the price were not adjusted.[36] But all these valuable perspectives came too late. The emperor was now ready to give ear to other counsels.

---

34. In Gansu, the governor sought to cut the valuation rate in April 1743, because low grain prices were enabling applicants to buy the title for grain worth only some 40 to 70 taels. CC, Huang Tinggui, QL 8/4/3.

35. CC, Depei, QL 8/3/27.

36. CC, Fan Can, QL 6/12/8; CC, Bd. Rev., QL 7/2/14; CC, Bao Gua QL 8/2 (cat. no. 1123-021); CC, Xu Rong, QL 8/3/22; CC, Depei, QL 8/3/27; cf. CC, Nasutu and Zhou Xuejian, QL 9/4/24.

The First Retreat

In March 1741, the emperor had still maintained that one could not have too much grain in local reserves (*difang ji gu bu yan qi duo*).[37] As we saw in chapter 4, however, the challenges to such assumptions had already begun. Admittedly, the early radical criticisms of the ever-normal system focused on the problems caused when grain within the basic targets was replaced by purchase, especially purchase in the Middle Yangzi region. Presumably, however, dissatisfaction that had smoldered in the 1730s, as the grain trade adjusted to the limited pre-1739 expansion of reserves, was kindled by the adoption of a policy that implied eventual doubling of the pressure of official buying upon Middle Yangzi markets. The 1738 regularization of the practice of interprovincial buying for badly depleted granaries was an added provocation, but it would have been the threat implicit in the 1738–39 title sales policy that galvanized any Lower-Yangzi grain-trade lobby.[38]

From 1741, the critics of the annual purchase system began to influence policy. The first proposals to sway the emperor were from moderate officials who were concerned about the impact of official buying but did not radically attack the ever-normal system. Zhu Lunhan's appeal to use tribute grain for granary restocking has been mentioned above. It was intended to give the tribute-paying provinces a one-year respite from official buying, whose ill-effects, given population increase and merchant competition for available grain surpluses, Zhu expounded at length. His proposal coincided with a broadly similar request from Emida, who had been appointed as a vice-president in the Board of Military Affairs after a decade in top provincial posts, and whom there was as yet no reason to suspect of antigranary opinions. Overruling the assigned deliberators, the emperor decided that altogether 800,000 *shi* of tribute grain (presumably husked, and thus

---

37. Edict of QL 6/2/8, transc. Lü Xiaoxian, comp., "Qianlong sannian," part 1, p. 15.

38. On the 1738 rule on interprovincial buying as codification of existing practice, see Will and Wong, *Nourish the People*, p. 45. A 1737 memorial mentions the habitual restocking of northern Zhejiang granaries through purchases in "neighboring provinces or neighboring counties." QSL/QL, *juan* 46:21a–b, quoted in Yamamoto, "Shindai zenki no heichō seisaku," p. 60 n. 38.

equivalent to 1.6 million *shi* unhusked) should be held back in Jiangsu, Zhejiang, and Anhui in 1742 to restock the depleted granaries of these three provinces. As his edict put it, "Since they will have the retained tribute grain, they can naturally refrain from going to neighboring territories to buy." Price rises in Jiangxi and the Huguang provinces would therefore be averted, he opined.[39]

As noted in chapter 4, in January 1742, the court responded to Yang Eryou's first radical memorial by ordering a survey in each province to determine which granaries still needed replenishment, and which were full enough for buying to be halted temporarily. A sample reply, that from Jiangxi, written in the summer of 1742, confirms that this was understood to mean that granaries could be deemed to need no more restocking even if short of their basic targets. The Jiangxi report conceded little. Of Jiangxi's present total shortfall (some 165,000 *shi*), about 125,700 *shi* (over 75 percent) should be replaced, while purchase of the remaining 39,300 *shi* could be delayed for the time being. On determining that 24,500 *shi* of the total shortfall were superfluous in the granaries that were supposed to hold them, the Jiangxi chief administrators proposed not to excise this overstock from the provincial target, but to redistribute it to granaries where it could be more useful.[40] Such a response would hardly have satisfied Yang. Given the difficulties of granary restocking, reconciling oneself to the existence of shortfalls, some longer-lasting than the rules allowed, must have been a routine experience of most regional administrators.[41] The January decision

---

39. CC, Zhu Lunhan, QL 6/7/20; QSL/QL, *juan* 150:3a–4b. A more moderate, 1742 memorial by Zhu Lunhan justifies excluding him from the ever-normal system's radical opponents. In 1742, Zhu recognized the boldness of "requests to put an end to stockpiling" but said that they ignored the indispensability of official grain reserves. He recommended increased flexibility in buying for the granaries. CC, Zhu Lunhan, QL 7/9/28.

40. HHCC, Bundle 92, Chen Hongmou, QL 8/5/10, which quotes the 1742 report (prepared by Peng Jiaping and forwarded with Chen's endorsement). A major criterion used by Peng in determining how much was needed in each granary was the ease of moving stocks elsewhere. It was the granaries of the remoter counties (those from which grain was not easily transported) whose full restocking Peng saw as less urgent or redundant.

41. On shortfalls that persisted beyond the permitted year, see Will and Wong, *Nourish the People*, pp. 150–51. The Jiangxi shortfalls were a case in point: accounting

suggests a weakening of imperial commitment to increased stockpiling, but it was not the drastic change of policy that Yang and others sought. When the *volte-face* came, it took place in two stages, of which the first was certainly, and the second possibly, provoked by a memorial from an investigating censor. The first of these radical censors was Sun Hao, from Hangzhou or its immediate vicinity. His ostensibly quite moderate memorial was considered by the grand secretaries and the Nine Ministries Assembly in early June, 1742. Citing alarming data, Sun pointed to the "daily rising" price of rice as the greatest hardship besetting the "southeastern" provinces. "For some decades," he wrote, rice in Zhejiang had cost 0.8 tael per *shi* (husked), but now it was nothing out of the ordinary for it to cost 1.5 to 1.8 tael per *shi*.[42] Sun did not blame the granaries alone; he also lamented the ill-effects of population pressure and the high "price" (exchange rate relative to silver) of brass coin. However, he did cite the previous attacks on the granary system by Bulantai, Xu Yisheng, Ji Huang, and Yang Eryou, referring to their "very full" discussions of the "mischiefs" caused consumers by the granary restocking process. He mentioned Qianlong's response to Zhu Lunhan's memorial as evidence that the emperor "deeply understood" the problem. He then made two suggestions. First, a ceiling should be set for the amount of grain that other provinces could buy in Jiangxi, Hunan, or Hubei. Second, "in cases where the newly added contribution targets combined with the old ever-normal quotas come to excessively large quantities that it will be extremely difficult to realize," appropriate reductions should be made, with a view to establishing "realistic targets" (*shizai ke xing zhi shu*). That much might seem common sense, but Sun argued in conclusion, "If official buying takes place on a large scale, it will certainly be impossible to stabilize the

---

for 12 percent of Jiangxi's basic target, they had originated in major shipments to Jiangsu and Fujian in 1738-39 (HHCC, Bundle 92, Chen Hongmou, QL 8/5/10).

42. Cf. the 1684-1802 annual prices for Xiaoshan county, near Hangzhou, tabulated from lineage records by Wang Yeh-chien ("Secular Trends of Rice Prices," table 1.1, pp. 41-44). These suggest that Sun was selecting data in such a way as greatly to exaggerate the sharpness of the price rise.

price of rice; if the targets for the granaries are high, it will, equally certainly, be impossible to reduce the scale of official buying."[43]

The grand secretaries and Nine Ministries Assembly resisted Sun's first suggestion and partially side-stepped his argument. Defending his first proposal, Sun had dismissed the notion that all that was needed was "good management" under the policy of flexible response to price conditions. All thoughts of careful management went overboard, Sun charged, when interprovincial buyers with their predetermined buying quotas, fixed sums of public funds, and "intentions set on swift completion" made for the Middle Yangzi provinces. However, the grand secretaries and Nine Ministries Assembly sought to preserve the concept of "good management" by building on current progress towards improved coordination of interprovincial buying. As we saw in chapter 4, about a month earlier the central government had accepted Xu Rong's proposal that the Middle Yangzi chief administrators send their counterparts in other southern provinces monthly reports on post-harvest grain prices in those of their subordinate counties that were easily accessible by water. The grand secretaries and Nine Ministries Assembly now suggested adding the requirement that the chief administrators of the buying and selling provinces communicate about the size of proposed purchases. The chief administrators of selling provinces would have the power to cut purchase targets that were too high relative to harvest conditions in their jurisdictions. Even the revised targets would not authorize blind buying. If prices rose excessively after the buying personnel arrived, the amounts to be bought should, if possible, be supplied out of the selling province's own granaries, as Xu Rong had proposed. Otherwise, the chief administrators of the selling province would have to make the best discretionary arrangements that they could.

On the issue of the storage targets, the deliberators found it difficult not to agree with Sun. Nationwide, they said, grain contributions of only some 6 million *shi* had so far been reported, which left the realm about 26 million *shi* short of the total contribution target. The plan was to rotate contributed grain just like grain within the basic targets, but it

---

43. HQZY, *juan* 35:33a–38a; reference from Zelin, *Magistrate's Tael*, p. 361. Internal evidence confirms that the date given by the HQZY compilers (1739) is incorrect. For alternative transcriptions, cf. n. 45 below.

was already proving hard enough to restore stocks to basic target level. The registers for the end of the preceding lunar year (which would have arrived recently) showed a shortfall of 4 million *shi* from the total basic target.[44] With grain dear in "all" provinces, this was not the time for major growth in granary reserves. The deliberators rehearsed some of the *clichés* that would soon be standard fare in justifications for granary retrenchment. There was only "so much" arable, only "so much" grain produced; if grain were not stockpiled "above" (that is, by the state), it would be free to flow "below" (that is, within society), which would "naturally" conduce to lower prices. Great famines did not happen regularly; stocks held under the basic targets had not been found inadequate in regional subsistence crises. In unusually bad disasters, distributing relief partly in silver had been as effective as giving victims grain alone. In short, the high-level storage policy had been unnecessarily ambitious. It was time to think again.

The grand secretaries and Nine Ministries Assembly recommended that the provincial targets be reset. The governors and governors-general should be ordered to propose new targets for each county in their jurisdiction, taking into account size, population density, and distance from navigable waterways. If a county's basic target were found adequate, it should be kept as the new target; if supplementary grain contributions were desirable, some lower figure than the 1738–39 contribution target should be added to the basic target, and the total adopted as the new, compromise target. Once the new county-level targets had been approved by the Board of Revenue, they would be permanent. They should be set with feasibility in mind; they were to be not only attainable, but also sustainable—low enough, that is, for annual stock rotation to be manageable, or even easy. This being the case, serious efforts should be made to realize them, though not through all-out buying. Buying should be done where shortfalls from the new targets were due to sale or distribution of stocks already held. However, where the new targets were higher than the highest level previously reached by actual reserves, the gap should be filled gradually through contributions. Jurisdictions that had already exceeded the new targets

---

44. The provincial year-end reports of granary reserves were due at the Board of Revenue in the second quarter of the following lunar year. Will and Wong, *Nourish the People*, pp. 253–54.

should not maintain reserves of "extra-quota grain" but use these surplus stocks as needed for replacing grain within the targets. Only when
the "extra-quota grain" was all absorbed into the regular reserves were
normal guidelines for restocking to be followed.[45]

The emperor accepted these proposals, and the provincial chief
administrators embarked upon preparing revised target schedules for
their jurisdictions. This process was not far advanced when, on 9 May
1743, the emperor implicitly aborted it with a new edict. This edict,
which halted not only the attempt to boost reserves by selling *jiansheng*
titles, but also the contentious practice of interprovincial buying, was
the court's first actual capitulation to the opponents of the ever-normal
system. Target resetting continued, with results to be discussed in
chapter 6, but the policy confusion ensuing from the emperor's initiative produced surprising complications.

Initiative or response? A memorial dated 8 May had requested a
one-year moratorium on buying for the granaries. This was, essentially,
the policy adopted by the end of May, although the edict mentioned
suspension only of interprovincial buying, while the recommendations
that guided its implementation did not mention a one-year term. This
limitation may have been added later, as the implications of the policy
struck home.[46] The author of the moratorium request was the investigating censor Wei Tingpu, from Guangzhou (Canton) or its vicinity.
Wei noted that, as grain prices were continually rising, the approved
expenditure rates for replacing stocks used in emergency relief were
growing insufficient. When the Board of Revenue rejected pleas to
approve higher rates, the provincial authorities might hand the problem down to the county magistrates, who could be made to pay the
shortfall personally. So far, this was roughly the issue to which Yang
Eryou had drawn attention one year earlier, but Wei's account had a

---

45. Mem. by Grd. Secs. and NMA, QL 7/5/9, transc. HHCC, Bundle 87, Zhang
Yunsui, QL 8/2/28. This is one of a series of 1743–44 *tiben* (routine memorials) by
provincial chief administrators proposing compromise targets under the heading
"Memorial in connection with the daily rising price of rice in the Southeast, and
related matters." Any of these *tiben* is likely to include the text of Sun's memorial
and the deliberators' response.

46. The earliest reference to the one-year limit that I have seen is in CC, Bd. Rev.,
QL 8/11/3, which quotes instructions given to the Sichuan governor-general in an
interview with the emperor in August 1743.

new twist. The magistrates in turn were tempted to pass the burden on to "wealthy families" or merchants, who would obligingly supply grain to the authorities at less than market prices, but then recoup themselves at the public's expense. The resulting higher prices would leave consumers paying "at least two years' resources" for a one-year food supply (in other words, the cost of living would double at best). In such a situation, and given the ubiquity of high grain prices, worrying about the risk of localized subsistence crises was beside the point. The best plan was to suspend buying for the granaries until the "health" (*yuanqi*) of the economy was somewhat restored.[47]

It would not have been unthinkable for Qianlong to refer an investigating censor's memorial to the Nine Ministries Assembly (as he did with Wei's), but act on it (the day after it was written, in this case) without awaiting the assembly's response. The May edict does not refer to the specific complaint that Wei had raised, but it does reflect acceptance of the argument that, in present circumstances, bringing prices down must take priority over preparedness for harvest failures. It may have been Wei's memorial that impelled the emperor to a decision. He had recently received complaints that the studentship sales policy was being ruinously undermined by rising grain prices. The monthly price statistics that arrived routinely may have hit home less forcibly than the Hunan governor's remark that prices in that province had been higher in 1741 than 1740, and higher still in 1742, and that they did not fall much even after harvest.[48]

The May edict's rhetoric seems indebted to points made earlier by other critics of official purchasing, especially Zhu Lunhan. Having raised objections to population increase and bad harvests as possible explanations for the prevalent high prices, it asserted that the true cause lay in "all the provinces adding to their granary reserves and vying with each other to buy." So far, only some 6 million *shi* had been received from *jiansheng* title sales, "and yet the price of grain is rising everywhere." The state bought for the granaries out of concern that if the folk retained their surplus grain, "they [would] not have the sense to exercise frugality, so that it [would] be squandered." However, given high popular demand, overassiduous official buying entailed the risk of

---

47. CC, Wei Tingpu, QL 8/4/15; cf. CC, Yang Eryou, QL 7/4/18.
48. CC, Xu Rong, QL 8/3/22.

starving the commercial sector and deterring merchant distribution. Besides, each province should be able to produce enough for its own needs. "If now because one province grows exceptionally large amounts of grain, the others flock to buy from it, the province that had much grain will inevitably be reduced to scarcity before they finish with it." Finally, the grain used to acquire *jiansheng* titles was all part of the limited output of the applicants' home region; it was either drawn from household grain reserves or bought on the local market. In other words, there was a loss either to domestic storage or to the amount available for commercial distribution. This being so, "it is no wonder that grain grows still scarcer while its price rises still higher."

While indicating that no shortfalls should be permitted from the basic targets (those totalling 28 million *shi*), the emperor ordered a moratorium both on interprovincial buying and on accepting grain as payment for *jiansheng* titles. When, at some future date, there had been good harvests, and grain prices were back to normal, these practices could be resumed cautiously.[49] The grand secretaries and Nine Ministries Assembly, ordered to work out the details of the new policy, presented their proposals on 29 May in a memorial drafted by the Board of Revenue. Using, without explanation, essentially the same figures as they had used the year before, the deliberators pointed out that, given that over 24 million *shi* of the 28-million basic target were in stock, and that over 6.7 million *shi* had been received from sales of titles, the present level of reserves was over 31 million. This was at least an increase over the old target.[50] Without posing the awkward question

---

49. Edict of QL 8/4/16 transc. Lü Xiaoxian, comp., "Qianlong sannian," part 2, p. 12; QSL/QL, *juan* 189:1b–3a.

50. Cf. Will and Wong, *Nourish the People*, table A.1, p. 528, which shows total holdings according to the *minshu gushu zouzhe* (annual statistical reports on population and ever-normal grain holdings) of about 31.7 million *shi* in 1741, and 29.6 million *shi* in 1742. The 1743 *minshu gushu* total is identical with that reported for 1742 (although every 1743 *provincial* total differs from the corresponding 1742 figure). Will opines that, in general, *minshu gushu* figures represented granary holdings at the point of maximum depletion in the annual cycle, while year-end figures such as those cited by the deliberators represented post-restocking holdings (ibid., pp. 253–56 and 264–65). In theory, therefore, *minshu gushu* totals should normally be less than 70 percent of the corresponding year-end totals. However, the 1742 *minshu gushu* total is over 92.5 percent of the 1742 year-end total cited by the deliber-

whether so small an increase could have seriously affected grain prices, they assured the emperor that 31 million *shi* would suffice for any probable contingency. If need be, one could always transfer grain from other provinces or divert tribute grain. The deliberators summarized the case against interprovincial buying, echoing the edict's phraseology in places and adding the allegation that merchants tended to start withholding stocks and charging higher prices as soon as they heard that official buying was imminent. Selling titles for grain could be an aggravating factor, reducing supply on the market just as the edict had suggested. But with the moratorium in effect, "each province's output will suffice for its own needs, besides which, with grain among the people circulating freely, prices will naturally and necessarily come down, and the people will be spared the worry of problems in procuring food."

This rhetoric suggests a notable reversal of conventional assumptions. While the deliberators reiterated that granary reserves must be kept up to basic target levels, their detailed proposals would have entailed the perpetuation and worsening of existing deficits, at least in the short term. They envisaged that grain held in excess of the basic targets be not replaced when it had been distributed or sold. If it were necessary to draw on stocks within the basic target, or indeed *if the basic stocks were used in their entirety*, the proceeds of any sales were to be deposited in the provincial treasury, where they would stay unless or until conditions on the local markets were suitable for granary replenishment. Conditions would be suitable when "there has been an abundant harvest, the price of grain has fallen, and the farmers have surplus grain." Thus even local buying was to be suspended unless market conditions were positively good; when buying resumed, it was not to be driven by fixed quotas. In-kind title sales could be allowed when harvests had been good, and applicants were to pay at the old rates (presumably because these reflected the low prices whose return would justify resumption of the in-kind sales).[51]

The moratorium, then, while general, was not to be complete. Several contemporary sources nonetheless refer to a "halt to buying"

---

ators, and as much as 85 percent of the 1742–43 theoretical maximum holdings (total basic target plus total received through sale of *jiansheng* titles).

51. CC, Grd. Secs. and NMA, QL 8/int.4/6.

(*tingzhi caimai*), as if the moratorium were total. Partly a matter of abbreviation, this may also reflect ambiguity in the deliberators' wording. To what level must grain prices fall before local buying should be permitted? The interpretation that the radicals would have preferred was that buying could resume when annual prices in a given region had returned to a more "normal" level, undoing the past years' inflation.[52] However, the stipulation could equally have been taken to mean that buying was permissible when a good harvest led to prices that were low compared with those of the most recent *soudure* peak, but still above the level of a few years earlier. Deliberate or not, the ambiguity gave all parties room to manoeuvre. The emperor would be able to determine which interpretation should be followed in the light of circumstances and of reactions from the bureaucracy. He would be able to blame provincial chief administrators who had "misunderstood" the policy's intent if its results proved unfortunate. The provincial chief administrators could use the discretion with which the recommendations explicitly entrusted them, pursuing agendas that might stress preparedness, relief for markets, or (if the emperor's later allegations are to be believed) a respite from the yearly headache of restocking granaries.

The recommendations were duly adopted, but with one exception. The emperor disagreed with his advisors as to whether Jiangxi and Fujian should be permitted to continue their studentship sales programs. These two provinces, as we have seen, had been authorized to revise their valuation rates, thus lowering the price in grain per *jiansheng* title. In an early response to the May edict, the investigating censor Li Qingfang had questioned whether in-kind title sales could be blamed for recent price rises, given that the province that had collected the most grain was Sichuan, and one did not hear of high grain prices there. The policy had generally failed because of the unrealistic valuation rates, a flaw that Jiangxi and Fujian had now corrected. Li asked not only that Jiangxi and Fujian be allowed to continue selling titles for

---

52. In the mid-1740s, the "normal" price for husked rice in Lower Yangzi cities could still have been assumed to be not much above 1.0 tael per *shi*, a level last experienced in Suzhou (as an annual average) in 1735 and 1736. Since 1736, the annual price at Suzhou had trended upwards, peaking at 1.6 tael per *shi* in 1743. Wang Yeh-chien, "Secular Trends of Rice Prices," table 1.1; cf. Will, *Bureaucracy and Famine*, p. 184 n. 23.

grain, but also that other provinces be told to follow their example. Most importantly, he held out the alluring notion that a continued program of in-kind title sales could be used, instead of buying, to make good deficits within the basic targets. The deliberators dismissed Li's ideas on formalistic grounds; the emperor, however, overruled them. Jiangxi and Fujian were to continue sales until the end of an experimental year and then report. Thus were the details of the first retreat concluded.[53]

Even granted that the moratorium was not to be complete, the policy reversal was radical in the extreme. To imply that empty granaries should be tolerated if market conditions were unfavorable would have seemed wildly irresponsible by the usual standards of mid-Qing public policy.[54] Who was behind this startling departure? Given that the grand secretaries and Nine Ministries Assembly went farther than the May edict's instructions, perhaps there were adherents of the extreme antigranary position who were influential in that body. However, the only known antigranary extremist among the fifty quasi signatories to the report was Ji Huang, author of one of the first attacks on the annual purchase system. In his early thirties, Ji was junior among the deliberators in both rank and age.[55] On the other hand, also present in the assembly were six grand (that is, privy) councillors, including the senior statesmen E'ertai and Zhang Tingyu, and the rising star Nuoqin. Their closeness to the emperor would have enabled such men to indicate the latest imperial thinking to "outer court" colleagues. If the emperor wanted to influence the drift of the recommendations whose preparation he had ordered, he had the means to do so.[56] Such action at a distance would have helped him to evade responsibility.

---

53. CC, Li Qingfang, QL 8/4/26, and Grd. Secs. and NMA, QL 8/int.4/6; QSL/QL, *juan* 189:4b.

54. The deliberators referred vaguely to the possibility of redistributing stocks between granaries but did not make such expedients central to the new policy.

55. Ji Huang had been appointed as a vice commissioner (rank 4a) in the Office of Transmission, which gave him a place in the assembly.

56. On the closeness to Qianlong of his right-hand men among the grand councillors, see Bartlett, *Monarchs and Ministers*, pp. 174–76, 217–19. Bartlett suggests that the grand councillors led, organized, and managed the Nine Ministries Assembly's deliberations (ibid., pp. 154 and 188). Haiwang, a grand councillor with concurrent responsibility as Manchu president of the Board of Revenue (cf. ibid., p. 181), would have been ideally placed to embody Qianlong's wishes in the report

What was Qianlong's motivation, if indeed he was the force behind the Assembly's proposals? One might surmise alarm about price trends, coupled with a psychological drive to overcompensate for the naive excess of the title sales policy through instant punditry in the doctrine of the opposition. Such speculations rapidly encounter complications that deter the historian from dwelling on them long. The emperor did not draft his own edicts, and, as the upshot showed, he was not firmly committed to the opposition's doctrine.[57] "The Qianlong emperor" as we "know" him from his edicts was no more a single individual than the Nine Ministries Assembly. More obscure yet is the role, if any, of a grain-trade lobby and the intellectual blandishments of those—the junior Ji Huang?—who may have spoken for it. Nonetheless, the implication of the moratorium was to reserve the nation's richest after-tax grain surpluses for merchant distribution. Any grain-trade lobby would have been delighted.

Resistance to the 1743 Retreat

The moratorium announcement generated a number of formal responses from individual civil servants, whom we may classify into three groups. First were those central government officials, such as Li Qing-fang, who remonstrated with the emperor about the moratorium, suggesting policy adjustments or alternative approaches. Second were provincial chief administrators, whose reactions were mixed, but who were sure that their own jurisdictions' granaries must be restocked. Third were the radicals, who saw the moratorium as a positive initiative that must be upheld for long enough to yield results—or even taken further. At least three of them (two censors and a senior Hanlin academician) contributed to the debate at this stage, advocating a change of emphasis from issuing relief in grain to the market-oriented strategy of partial use of silver.

The radicals did not carry the day. Their ideal would no doubt have been suspension of official buying even where grain was abundant so as to let prices fall to a putative normal level. The emperor, presumably

---

that his Board drafted. Whether the grand councillors were in the habit of manipulating assembly deliberations to meet the emperor's preferences is, however, far from clear (cf. ibid., p. 154).

57. Ibid., pp. 217–18, and below.

trying to compromise, took steps to minimize the need for buying, but he did not resist the arguments of governors to whom it would have seemed perverse not to restock badly depleted granaries when harvests had been good (or even satisfactory). The ban on interprovincial buying was retained, but the emperor made arrangements for interprovincial transfers. He allowed several governors to have buying done within their own provinces.

Among the remonstrating central government officials, two investigating censors wrote before the grand secretaries and Nine Ministries Assembly reported. These were Chen Qining, from Jiangning (Nanjing) or its vicinity, and Li Qingfang, from Anxi in Fujian. Both opined that a general moratorium on buying would have unacceptable effects; they agreed, however, that there were problems with the ever-normal system as recently operated. They concurred with the court's view that interprovincial buying should be stopped but were concerned about the implications of postponing buying nationwide. As Chen pointed out, if buying were halted and no substitute adopted, not only would the stocks begin to dwindle, but when a good year came and purchasing resumed, the extra buying needed to make up the aggravated shortfalls might annul the good done by the moratorium.

Chen favored the moratorium provided that a substitute for buying was put into practice. He suggested that, for a year or two, until reserves had been restored to basic target levels, a limited proportion of the land tax be collected in grain (instead of silver). After that, restocking should be done through cautious buying, on local markets only. However, officialdom should realize that buying for the granaries was not, in itself, the cause of the high prices. These arose from population growth, poor harvests, and the fact that increased official purchases were not being matched by corresponding rises in stock levels. The population problem was already very grave, with output "insufficient to supply requirements," but territorial officials could still strive to expand production, in the faith that "man can assuredly overcome the skies" when faced with ordinary natural disasters. Chen's allegation that "much is bought but little is added to the reserves" probably referred to the failure of the studentship sales policy, which Chen considered almost total. Of the 6 million or so *shi* supposedly contributed, one-fifth at most had been delivered by the applicants; the rest had been purchased by local officials, using the silver in which payment for *jiansheng* titles had more commonly been made. Moreover, some officials had pretended that grain already in stock had been collected in return for *jiansheng* titles, while misrepresenting the silver paid by applicants as the proceeds of past sales of grain. In short, the title sales policy had fuelled official buying without increasing actual reserves by even 6 million *shi*. Chen therefore advocated that this policy be discontinued permanently, with no exceptions made for years of plenty.[58]

Li Qingfang, as we have seen, thought otherwise. For him, in-kind title sales should be promoted realistically as a potential alternative to buying. Li was, indeed, more of an outright opponent of the court's new policy than Chen. He conceded that the granary system was vitiated by the abuses pointed out by Yang Eryou and Wei Tingpu but argued that there was an ancient principle at stake: state reserves were necessary to keep the power of manipulating prices out of private hands. "If grain is stockpiled by the wealthy, they will invariably speculate and take advantage of the folk's exigency. Their prices will inevitably be double." Paternalism demanded action. "Within society, rich and poor are extremely far apart. To carry out redistribution [literally, 'draw on excess to supplement paucity,' an expression from *The Book of Changes*] is a responsibility involved in being parent to the people. In governing the people, there is no justification for leaving things to follow their own course (*wu ren qi ziran zhi li*)." As if to emphasize the timelessness of these truths of political economy, Li used the hyperbole of a Han-dynasty classic of social criticism: "The paths between the fields of the rich stretch on and on, while the poor lack space enough on which to stand an awl."[59]

Li's memorial shows that, in a decade in which a handful of policy advisors argued, with increasing influence, that "leaving things to follow their own course" was precisely the approach to be preferred in economic matters, at least one censor was prepared to articulate a "classical" justification for the opposite position. Writing more as moralist than as economist, Li decried the (alleged) practices that separated the contemporary ever-normal system from its ancient model. It was wrong that officials sold ever-normal grain at market prices during

---

58. CC, Chen Qining, QL 8/4/23.
59. The allusion (a cliché) is to a memorial by Dong Zhongshu (ca. 179–ca. 104 B.C.) calling for land reform, reduction of fiscal pressures on society, and other measures to alleviate the sufferings of the poor. Ban Gu et al., *Hanshu, juan* 24A: 1,137.

the *soudure*, just like "wealthy people," and that by buying at sub-market prices after harvest they provoked their suppliers to charge higher prices to the ordinary consumer. However, the correct response to such abuses was to eliminate them, not to disable an institution whose importance had been shown once more in last year's natural disasters. Replacement stocks should be bought locally, with purchase duly postponed after bad harvests; above all, official buyers should eschew thoughts of profit and abide by the market price, so that "for grain-possessing houses, selling to the authorities will be no different from selling to the public." Talk of a total moratorium thus overshot the mark. Ever-normal operations should, much as the edict had suggested, follow the principle of local self-sufficiency, but provided that they were conducted fairly, it would be a mistake to interrupt them.[60]

The role of granary reserves in recent natural disasters was invoked also by the director of the Court of State Ceremonial, the mathematician Mei Gucheng. In a memorial submitted a few days after the grand secretaries and Nine Ministries Assembly reported, he reminded the emperor that, had the latter not authorized the restocking of Jiangnan's granaries with tribute grain the previous year, it might have been impossible to save 7 million lives when central Jiangsu underwent disastrous floods. Concerned, like Chen Qining, to find a substitute for buying while the moratorium lasted, Mei proposed that, until prices fell and buying was resumed, up to one-fifth of each year's tribute grain should be held back in order to restock the more strategic granaries. Jurisdictions that were distant from water routes and whose tribute grain had therefore been commuted should be ordered to collect the tax in kind until their granaries had been restocked. Playing the elder statesman, Mei assured the emperor that, after thirty years of court and other central-government service, he understood full well the vital function of the tribute grain in sustaining the metropolitan establishment. But granary restocking in the provinces was necessary too. The major part of his proposal fell upon deaf ears. For now, the emperor was willing only to order consideration of the idea of levying commuted tribute grain in kind for restocking the granaries of landlocked

---

60. CC, Li Qingfang, QL 8/4/26.

jurisdictions—a notion that received short shrift from the deliberators to whom it was referred.[61]

The view from the provinces (expressed in memorials written mostly in the autumn) was that buying must be done that year, in view of major shortfalls. Despite the ambiguity of the new policy, provincial spokesmen generally understood their task to be to argue that, in their jurisdiction, the combination of at least reasonably good harvests and depleted granaries justified careful local buying. Recent relief activities had typically contributed much to the depletion of reserves, and provincial chiefs were anxious for permission to restock before the next emergency. The provincial memorials do, however, vary somewhat in approach, reflecting differences both in circumstances and in perceptions as to how far argument was needed.

The senior administrators of Jiangxi and Hunan assumed that, provided that harvests were at least satisfactory, they were allowed to buy. The issues raised in the memorials from crisis-ravaged Jiangxi were how much of the province's abnormally large shortfall it was feasible to buy that year, what prices the central government must permit official purchasers to pay, and what to do about the probably excessive shortfall that would remain after the limits of prudent buying had been reached. The acting Fujian governor wrote as if there were no moratorium even on interprovincial buying. His problem was that, at best, Jiangsu, Zhejiang, and Anhui markets would not be able to supply a very large proportion of Fujian's substantial shortfall.[62]

In Henan, by contrast, two successive governors, Yaertu and Shise, assumed that they must make a case in order to have local buying authorized. The former, indeed, saw fit to argue at some length, despite Henan's good wheat harvest. As Yaertu's was the earliest provincial response, it may reflect the most uncertainty as to how the new policy would be interpreted at central government level. As we saw in chapter 4, he argued in June that if the local surplus were not bought by the authorities, it would only fuel peasant improvidence, landlord speculation, and merchant engrossment. Shise wrote in November, by which time parts of Henan had suffered poor harvests and would therefore

---

61. CC, Mei Gucheng, QL 8/int.4/10; QSL/QL, *juan* 190:11b–13a.

62. CC, Peng Jiaping, QL 8/5/27; Chen Hongmou, QL 8/7/20; Jiang Pu, QL 8/7/20; Zhou Xuejian, QL 8/8/9; QSL/QL, *juan* 193:18b.

have seemed subject to suspension of restocking. Accordingly, Shise's argument was that if the Henan authorities cleaved blindly to the proscription on buying while prices were high, in a few years' time the granaries would be completely empty. Shise and Yaertu were among several governors who declared their willingness to meet the moratorium halfway by buying less than was required for full replenishment. Yaertu assured the emperor that buying in Henan would be confined to rebuilding the more depleted stockpiles and would not be quota-driven or deadline-driven. Chen Dashou, for Jiangsu, wanted to let local officials buy up to half the grain required to restore stocks to basic target level, subject to a maximum purchase of 3,000 *shi* per county and an undertaking that buying would cease if the market price reached 0.6 tael per *shi* unhusked, which he took as the "normal" price for Jiangsu.[63]

The emperor's responses to the provincial memorials show no zeal to uphold a total moratorium in the face of protestations that harvests were good and buying essential. It is true that he did not openly rescind the moratorium on interprovincial buying. In late June or July, he dismissed the acting Hunan governor Jiang Pu's plan to notify the neighboring provincial governments, in the spirit of the coordination policy agreed in 1742, that Hunan was expecting a good harvest and should be able to welcome official buyers from other provinces that year. Qianlong's comment was that to allow such buying would provoke high prices in Hunan. However, already in June he had been indicating that, as far as local buying was concerned, provincial governors should be guided by the circumstances. In August, having intimated that he would be inclined to favor buying for the Shaanxi granaries should that province have a good harvest, he remarked, in a general way, that buying should "naturally" be done (although not to excess) where crops had been abundant and prices were normal. In September, Chen Hongmou suggested that, in those Jiangxi counties in which *jiansheng* title sales were poor and market conditions unsuitable for official buying, landowners be given the option of paying their land tax with grain deliveries to the granaries. This produced an imperial assurance that ". . . the suspension of buying basically refers to places where grain

---

63. CC, Yaertu, QL 8/int.4/25; Chen Dashou, QL 8/7/22; Shise, QL 8/10/3; QSL/QL, *juan* 197:22a–b and 202:17b–18b.

is expensive. Assuming that this year Jiangxi has harvests, it can in principle restock its granaries to target levels." The emperor also authorized Chen Dashou's suggested program of limited grain purchases. He expressed strong satisfaction with the Hubei governor's plan for careful buying to help build that province's reserves, which stood at about 30 percent of the augmented basic target (see table 3, column A). He was equally pleased with the Shandong governor's undertaking to establish which jurisdictions should buy and which should wait. Shise, as Sichuan governor, even secured permission to continue his province's successful program of *jiansheng* title sales; after his transfer to Henan, he gained approval for limited buying despite the recent localized disasters.[64]

Interprovincial buying had been stopped, but was essential restocking really possible without some redistribution of provincial grain surpluses? His mind perhaps concentrated by the early signs of a severe subsistence crisis in a large area south and southeast of the capital, the emperor gave this question new attention in August. On 10 August he accepted a proposal, submitted that same day by Tian Mao (a vice-president of the Board of Personnel), that the newly-appointed Sichuan governor be secretly ordered to buy 100,000 to 200,000 *shi* of grain in Sichuan, where prices were low, and make them available for shipping down the Yangzi to restock granaries in provinces such as Jiangsu. He had earlier responded to the news of an abundant spring wheat crop in Shaanxi by ordering the Shaanxi governor to buy 100,000 *shi* of wheat and send them to restock the Henan granaries. In the event, 150,000 taels were allotted for the Sichuan buying program, with fixed purchase targets explicitly abjured.[65] Indeed, when the Sichuan governor re-

---

64. CC, Yaertu, QL 8/int.4/25, Shise, QL 8/7/4, Chen Hongmou, QL 8/7/20, Chen Dashou, QL 8/7/22, Yan Sisheng, QL 8/8/3, Bd. Rev., QL 8/11/3, Kaerjishan, QL 8/8/19, and Shise, QL 8/10/3; QSL/QL, *juan* 193:18b, 197:22a–b and 23a–24a, 199:14a–15a, and 202:17b–18b. The objection to Chen Hongmou's proposal need not have been its impact on tax revenue, as he envisaged compensation out of the unexpended proceeds of past grain sales.

65. On the progress of the 1743–44 Zhili subsistence crisis, see Will, *Bureaucracy and Famine*, pp. 25–32. The emperor approved the first allocation of external relief supplies for Zhili on the same day as he accepted Tian's proposal (ibid., p. 153). The speed of his response to Tian's idea was probably dictated by the imminence of the Sichuan governor's departure from the capital to take up his post. A messenger

ported termination of this program in early February 1744, it was on the grounds that purchase of the equivalent of over 173,000 *shi* of unhusked grain had left prices rising to a level that spelled unfair treatment for Sichuan consumers.[66]

It may be that Qianlong saw in such opportunistic measures a potential solution to the problem of restocking, as was suggested by Tian Mao and reinforced in late September in the memorial by A'ersai discussed in chapter 4.[67] However, given the rationale behind the moratorium, it made sense—with the annual restocking season fast approaching—to try to minimize the amount of grain bought locally in provinces where the state of markets arguably met the prescribed conditions for permitting buying. On 3 September, at the instance of the investigating censor Shen Tingfang, Qianlong finally instructed that 900,000 *shi* husked (equivalent to 1,800,000 *shi* unhusked) out of the tribute grain for 1743–44 be allotted to eight southern provinces to help with granary restocking. This was a large concession for the court to make, but it may have eased the situation in those provinces, even if it did not obviate the need for buying so much as postpone it. As all governors were well aware, rice that was already husked would not keep well in humid areas.[68]

In Jiangxi, admittedly, Chen Hongmou took advantage of the tribute grain diversion to order the suspension of buying to replace grain sold in 1742 and 1743. Cautious local purchasing was to take place only after the late harvest, and only in places where prices were low and there were still shortfalls in the reserves. In thus directing his subordinates, Chen acted largely as the moratorium's proponents would have wished. The responses of the Huguang governors were probably more realistic. The Hubei governor credited his province's share of the

---

delivered the confidential instructions to the new governor before the day was over. CC, Tian Mao, QL 8/6/21; CC, Bd. Rev., QL 8/11/3.

66. CC, Jishan, QL 8/12/24.

67. CC, Tian Mao, QL 8/6/21, and A'ersai, QL 8/8/10.

68. CC, Yan Sisheng, QL 8/8/28; QSL/QL, *juan* 196:18a–b. 200,000 *shi* of tribute grain were to be allocated to Fujian, and 100,000 to Guangdong. The six rice-growing tribute-paying provinces (Jiangsu, Anhui, Zhejiang, Jiangxi, Hubei, and Hunan) would each retain 100,000 *shi*. In December, Shandong was authorized to keep 80,000 *shi* of tribute grain; however, this was to provide for relief loans and sales in the new year, not to replace routine restocking. QSL/QL, *juan* 203:16a–b.

extra-perishable tribute grain to a supplementary target, established in the late 1730s, for grain to be available for sale to other provinces (see table 3, note 8). The integrity of the reserves intended for the Hubei populace would not be jeopardized. The acting Hunan governor not only planned to start selling the tribute grain soon after the lunar new year (before the onset of the springtime rains and the *soudure* price rises), but also envisaged using some of it to found or boost stocks in Miao territories that had been recently incorporated into Hunan. For him, the retained tribute rice was perhaps less a godsend than an embarrassment for which creative uses must be found.[69] It may have crossed his mind (and Mei Gucheng's) that the tribute grain diversion could have been much more useful, if only it had been declared in time for the retainable amount to be levied in unhusked form that year. One could not raise this kind of point in a memorial, however, any more than the Jiangxi authorities could note that what they really needed was permission to buy grain next-door in Hunan.

If there was truth in the belief that buying for the granaries of other provinces exerted undue pressure upon Middle Yangzi markets, the chief officials of the Middle Yangzi provinces should presumably have welcomed the ban on interprovincial buying for its promised protection of supplies for home consumers. Comments in their memorials suggest that this was partially the case. In September, Jiang Pu observed that although Hunan was enjoying its best harvest for some years, the granary shortfalls that were the legacy of previous poor harvests meant that Hunan indeed did not have enough for outside official buyers, given that its own people must be fed. Jiang wrote merely to accept the emperor's correction of his earlier gaffe, but his opposite numbers in Hubei and Jiangxi commented more positively on the improved market conditions to be anticipated now that buying by the emissaries of other provinces was halted. Before the autumn harvest, Peng Jiaping, the Jiangxi provincial administration commissioner, expressed hope that the ban would lead to at least somewhat lower grain prices in Jiangxi. However, while he represented the ban as offering Jiangxi's

---

69. PYTOCG, *juan* 16:24a–25a; CC, Yan Sisheng, QL 8/8/28, and Jiang Pu, QL 8/8/28. For an assessment of progress in restocking the Jiangxi granaries as of late November, see CC, Peng Jiaping, QL 8/10/15. Peng was anxious enough about the situation in some counties to warn that buying would have to be permitted even if the price were close to 0.7 tael per *shi* (unhusked).

people a lifeline, other Middle Yangzi senior administrators seem to have appreciated it mainly because the expected lower prices would enhance the prospects for successful buying for their own provinces' granaries. This was not quite the purpose of the moratorium.

And yet the moratorium had given the local price level heightened importance with regard to granary restocking. For example, it was because access to the Hunan surpluses had been denied that low grain prices in Jiangxi were now crucial for granary restocking; but was the ban indeed to be reflected in significantly lower prices? Peng himself was less than fully confident—a reservation that proved justified, for, after the late harvest, his superior Chen Hongmou noted that memories of exceptionally high prices earlier in the year were engendering reluctance to sell grain, with the result that prices had not greatly fallen. So far from praising the deep insights of the radicals, Peng also complained about the criticisms of officials who, lacking practical experience of buying for the granaries, did not understand the pressures shaping the behavior patterns that they found objectionable.[70]

Finally, it is striking that, in the Middle Yangzi, the strongest documentable approval for the ban on interprovincial buying came not from a territorial official with formal responsibility for popular well-being, but from Tang Ying, the Jiujiang internal customs superintendent whose denunciation of such buying was introduced in chapter 4. In the same memorial, written in July 1743, Tang Ying took it upon himself to act as spokesman for the Jiangxi people, arguing that the oft-cited canonical injunction to save grain (a passage from the *Book of Rites*) supplied no warrant for "buying the next-door neighbor's surplus in a year of dearth in order to contrive one's own reserves."[71] If only, Tang suggested, every province's officials would set grain aside properly (that is, through local purchase at the market price) and in the spirit of the ancient formula, the nation's granaries would all be filled. The people of those provinces that were blessed with abundance would then be spared the ill-effects of buying on their markets for the granaries of other provinces.

---

70. CC, Peng Jiaping, QL 8/5/27, Jiang Pu, QL 8/7/20, Chen Hongmou, QL 8/7/20, 8/10/22, Yan Sisheng, QL 8/8/3, and A'ersai, QL 8/8/10.

71. For full translation of the *Liji* (Book of Rites) passage, see Dunstan, *Conflicting Counsels*, p. 140.

Had the topic been commercial buying, Tang would have risked censure for thus pandering to the "selfish" instincts of Jiangxi consumers. However, since his rhetoric elaborated on the emperor's own recently enunciated doctrine of provincial self-sufficiency in government stockpiling, he was probably safe. It is an open question whether Tang's true loyalties were with Jiangxi consumers or grain trade interests. Appointed to his customs superintendency as a vice-director of the Imperial Household Department, he had lived for eight years at Jingde Zhen, presumably because of palace interests in its porcelain manufactories. Whether this background had encouraged any significant contacts with the commercial world is a matter for speculation. What is certain is, first, that in placing all the blame for Jiangxi's food crisis on interprovincial official buying, he was going farther than both Chen Hongmou and Peng Jiaping;[72] and, second, that in this memorial he offered a superb example of merchant responsiveness to price incentives swiftly, efficiently, and silently serving the public good. Official buying had drained grain from Jiangxi; private commerce, attracted by the famine prices, was undoing the damage.[73]

The Radicals Rebuffed

The middle course eventually adopted by the emperor must have disappointed Sun Hao, Wu Wei, and others of like persuasion. Sun had returned to the attack in a memorial read by the emperor on 7 July, about five weeks after the details of the moratorium were settled. Sun mentioned a continuing debate between defenders of reserves and advocates of a prolonged suspension of official buying. The former, he said, argued that, given the annual three-tenths sale norm, a three-year moratorium would lead to nine-tenths-empty granaries. The latter, by

---

72. While Chen's directives, used in chap. 2 above, cannot be taken wholly at face value, it is fair to say that, in the explanation of the Jiangxi crisis that he created for public consumption, he recognized a larger range of factors than did Tang. Chen even claimed, quite early in the crisis, that popular concern about official interprovincial buying could cease now that the high prices in Jiangxi had turned the outside purchasers away. PYTOCG, *juan* 15:20b and 22a. Peng, writing a few days after Tang, mentioned floods the previous year in some ten county-level units and bad harvests elsewhere in the province. CC, Peng Jiaping, QL 8/5/27.

73. CC, Tang Ying, QL 8/5/22.

contrast, held that as the trend of grain prices had taken time to rise, it must take time to fall. Short-term suspension would therefore be ineffective. Sun was aligned with the latter party. As he put it, "the most pressing, most important matter at the present time is simply to hold fast to the Sage Edict that commanded general suspension." He opined that, for the time being, keeping granaries full to basic target level should not be even a nominal policy objective.

In his discussion, Sun addressed not the substance of the moratorium policy as worked out by the grand secretaries and Nine Ministries Assembly, but the initial formulation in the edict of 9 May. He was thus able to argue that the policy be made more radical without explicitly adopting the extreme position that buying should be halted even where good harvests had seasonally lowered prices. The edict had suspended interprovincial buying and the attempt to boost reserves by selling *jiansheng* titles for grain. According to Sun, these measures had received widespread and joyful acclaim but still had fatal limitations. The title sales policy had never been the problem, since payment in grain had been "almost a matter of an empty name." The inflation had resulted rather from the incessant official buying inherent in the ever-normal system. The risk now was that suspending the attempt to build extra reserves would heighten zeal in the routine restocking process. The problem with halting interprovincial buying was, likewise, that it would encourage the assumption that buying in the home province was harmless. This assumption must be false, because Sichuan and the Middle Yangzi provinces were alone in having surplus grain. Officials who were forced to rely on inadequately stocked intraprovincial markets would resort to buying directly from local "households with much grain." Endless abuses would ensue; for example, merchants would be harassed when their boats were intercepted and detained. In short, intraprovincial buying would be as detrimental to the level of grain prices as interprovincial buying, and policy should recognize this fact.[74]

Sun Hao, at least, did not explicitly suggest acceptance of reserve depletion to below 60 percent of basic target level. By contrast, Wu Wei, now a supervising censor at the Office of Scrutiny for Works, repeated his call for the nation's ever-normal stocks to be sold off in

---

74. CC, Sun Hao, QL 8 (cat. no. 1125-032); text also in HCJSWB, *juan* 44:5b–6b. For the rescript date, see HHCC, Bundle 94, Bd. Rev., QL 8/6/13.

their entirety. Wu apparently saw things in clear-cut terms (and argued in highly rhetorical ones). The hardship being caused by grain price elevation was extreme, so much so that the challenge facing government was to "bring back Heaven and Earth's springtime and save the people's lives." A patient severely debilitated by illness needed to have the cause of the disease removed and then to be built up with tonics; so also with the present sickness of the whole society. Policy makers should stop wasting time with ineffective nostrums such as banning distillation and the growing of tobacco; such prohibitions, besides being uncanonically repressive, were peripheral to the task at hand. What better tonic could society receive than to have the source of its disease (the grain that had been bought for the granaries) restored to it as nourishment? All the ever-normal stocks should be sold at greatly reduced prices, with sales venues set up at all market towns. Jurisdictions with insufficient granary reserves to have much impact on high prices should be allowed, as an extraordinary measure, to use tribute grain instead (geography permitting, one assumes). Thus "what is collected from the people will be temporarily shared with them, while what is surplus to the state's requirements will temporarily supply the folk's deficiency."

As a means to reverse grain-price inflation, this subitism was radical to the point almost of madness, but if the real purpose was to rid the nation of the ever-normal granaries, there was a calculating rationality behind the simplism. Wu's proposal raised the question of how emergency relief could be provided once the granary reserves had disappeared. His answer was that silver should be distributed instead of grain.[75] In other words, the state would still stand by the people, but the task of provisioning would be left to merchants.

To suggest that doles of grain could be replaced entirely by money was extreme by 1740s standards, but partial substitution of silver for grain was an approved practice, and others had already argued that its possibility justified an easing of concern about grain storage levels. The evolution of official thinking as to the advisability of using silver largely paralleled that on the broader issue of the granaries themselves.

---

75. CC, Wu Wei, QL 8/7/2. Wu had noted the possibility of partial substitution of silver for relief grain in his early 1739 memorial (quoted in CC, Grd. Secs. and Bd. Rev., QL 4/2/5).

In the literalist late 1730s, the emperor expressed strong reservations about including distribution of silver in a famine relief plan for Shanxi, although he did assent. In a series of edicts, he raised the common-sense objection that the thing to give starving people was food, made the interventionist point that grain distributions deterred "wicked merchants" from hoarding, and emphasized the seriousness of the risk that silver would be misappropriated by corrupt official personnel. He even retorted that "If there is grain available for purchase, there is no need for the authorities to give relief."[76] A rationale for the strategy of *yin gu jian zhen* (issuing relief in a mixture of grain and silver) would have to be developed to avoid the risk of similar rebuttals in the future.

In fact, the Shanxi experiment became a precedent for recognition of *yin gu jian zhen* as an expedient. In 1738, the grand secretaries and Board of Revenue dismissed a proposal that ever-normal granaries store both grain and silver in a target ratio of 6:4. This, after all, was inconsistent with the court's initiative to boost stockpiles of actual grain. However, they took seriously a suggestion that the same ratio govern the content of future doles to famine victims. Their justification was a conservative one, reflected in their recommendation (which the emperor approved). Relief should be distributed entirely in kind when stock levels permitted; when they did not, the doles should be made partially in silver, using appropriations from tax revenues.[77] Thus although certain officials (including the Shanxi authorities in 1737)[78] saw positive virtue in *yin gu jian zhen*, in principle the several cases of its implementation during 1738–43 were stop-gap measures only. Indeed, to Shise, in November 1743, the mere fact that he had recently been unable to avoid seeking approval for recourse to this approach was "clear proof" that Henan's granaries were excessively depleted.[79]

---

76. QSL/QL, *juan* 54:9a–10a, 55:5a–6a, and 12a–b.

77. JS, Grd. Secs. and Bd. Rev., QL 3/6/27.

78. In late 1737, the Shanxi authorities pointed out that millet and "miscellaneous cereals" were available on local markets in the stricken jurisdictions. Reportedly, the clients of official relief efforts were positively willing to receive half of their doles in monetary form, as they would then be able to buy these relatively cheap cereals. Such an approach would permit local officials to conserve a portion of the granary reserves for the coming *soudure* period. QSL/QL, *juan* 55:5b.

79. CC, Shise, QL 8/10/3. On the use of *yin gu jian zhen* down to 1743, see HHCC, Bundle 94, Bd. Rev., QL 8/6/13, and Will, *Bureaucracy and Famine*, pp. 133 and (for fascinating details of distribution procedures) 146–47.

Already in 1741, however, Ji Huang had mentioned the *yin gu jian zhen* option to support his argument that buying for the granaries of Lower Yangzi provinces should be halted. In their 1742 report endorsing Sun Hao's proposal that the storage targets be reset, the grand secretaries and Nine Ministries Assembly also claimed that in the past, officials faced with unusually serious natural disasters had used *yin gu jian zhen* to overcome the difficulty of transporting grain to remote areas. As famine victims who were given silver could use it to "buy food at their convenience," it followed that "for benefiting the disaster-stricken, there is no difference between issuing relief in silver and dispensing it in grain." The intended implication was that this strengthened the case for abandoning the high-level targets.[80]

Sun Hao was pushing this argument farther when he suggested, in 1743, that, for the time being, local officials should not be disciplined for having only, say, 60 or 70 percent of the basic target actually in store, provided that silver corresponding to the rest remained available. As long as the silver was there, it could be used in *yin gu jian zhen* operations. Less extreme than Wu Wei, Sun envisaged that relief in kind would be given if the granaries had adequate reserves, or if transfers from other jurisdictions could be made. However, if the stocks available were insufficient, either silver should be given once the grain had been exhausted, or the allocations should be mixed from the beginning. If worst came to worst, it would not be unthinkable to give relief entirely in silver. Once *yin gu jian zhen* was established as a normal practice, there would be no reason for hurrying to restore reserves to target level. Replenishment could be done at a relaxed pace, as market conditions permitted.

Listing five "advantages" of issuing relief in silver, Sun wrote: "Though there may be a famine year, there will certainly not be exhaustion of all grain supplies. One may have grain and fear the want of silver, but if only one has silver, how will one fear the want of grain?"[81]

---

80. CC, Ji Huang, QL 6/7/16; mem. by Grd. Secs. and NMA, QL 7/5/9, transc. HHCC, Bundle 87, Zhang Yunsui, QL 8/2/28.

81. The first three advantages identified by Sun were the relative convenience, for both authorities and people, of doles in lightweight silver; the fact that stored silver did not rot, while embezzlement could be detected promptly; and the greater flexibility that silver gave recipients. The fourth advantage is discussed below. My

This observation was perhaps an overstatement, but it represented reality up to a point. Especially in the Yangzi Valley, it would be at a late stage in the development of a subsistence crisis that there was no more grain available for purchase, and many crises ended before that point was reached. To distribute the wherewithal to buy instead of grain was not, in principle, an irresponsible idea.[82] To be sure, Sun's off-hand assurance hardly constituted a developed rationale for a policy that seemed counter to common sense. Conspicuously absent was articulation of the principle that peasants with sufficient "market power" or "market command" would be able to draw in external stocks that would otherwise have gone (or stayed) elsewhere.[83] This component had, however, been supplied in a memorial shortly predating Sun's by the junior supervisor of the Household Administration of the Heir Apparent and academician expositor-in-waiting Li Qingzhi. Having acknowledged Li as the original proponent of wider use of silver distributions, Sun presumably did not feel obliged to repeat all his points.[84]

Li Qingzhi and Li Qingfang were cousins: both were from the Anxi (Fujian) descent group whose most famous forebear was the Kangxi-period advocate of Song Neo-Confucianism, Li Guangdi.[85] However, the two had little kinship of opinion. Qingzhi was more interested in reforming the ever-normal system than in echoing Qingfang's passionate defence of it. Qingzhi argued that excessive distrust of qualified local officials had led the central government to impose rigid stock rotation procedures that had proved inflationary and were at variance with the true principle of ever-normal operations (*changping benfa*). This principle was that intervention buying and selling should be undertaken only when market conditions so indicated, and to the precise

---

1986 translation of the full list of advantages (from HCJSWB, *juan* 44:6a) is reproduced in Marks, *Tigers*, p. 235.

82. Cf. Atwell, "Notes," pp. 20–21; Will, *Bureaucracy and Famine*, pp. 289, 295.

83. The terms "market power" and "market command" are borrowed from Amartya Sen. See his analysis of the Ethiopian famine of 1972–73, in which he argues that the people of a certain province starved because they had insufficient market power (or command) to "pull food into" their region from the rest of the country, or indeed to keep all the food that was already there. Sen, *Poverty and Famines*, p. 96.

84. CC, Sun Hao, QL 8 (cat. no. 1125-032).

85. Li Yuandu, comp., *Guochao xianzheng shilüe*, vol. 1, pp. 200–1.

extent necessary to restore price equilibria. In Kangxi times, Li hinted, this principle had been respected. Not only had county magistrates had the discretion to tailor sales volumes and prices to the actual depletion level of the local market; they had also been immune from disciplinary action for letting granary reserves run down, as long as they retained the corresponding funds in silver. (Sun Hao quoted Li verbatim on this point.) In future, Li opined, the duration of official buying and selling operations should be governed by market conditions, as reflected in price movements vis-à-vis the local norm. Official prices should move flexibly with market prices, being somewhat higher than the market rate when the authorities were buying, and somewhat lower during stabilizing sales.

The intent of this main recommendation was to restore the (presumed) true ever-normal principle. Li's concluding idea, while duly provided with classical and scriptural justifications (from the *Guanzi* and the *Zhouli*), was more original. Sales of *jiansheng* titles should resume at provincial level, with payment collected in the form of silver. The silver should be earmarked for direct distribution to famine victims. This idea made sense because:

When it comes to food for the disaster-stricken, even the likes of yams and miscellaneous foodstuffs can all maintain life; the only thing to fear is to be empty-handed and so sit withering [to death]. If relief is given in silver, [the recipients] will naturally each be able to contrive plans for survival. Besides, if the disaster-stricken folk have money, merchants will assuredly come to do business (*shangfan bi yingyun er lai*), and it will naturally be possible to avoid the cutting-off of food supplies.

It is true that neither Li Qingzhi nor Wu Wei (who echoed him with a "Once the folk have money, it will be possible to sell [them] rice, on which merchants from near and far will all come running") used abstract concepts such as "market power," "market command," or even "effective demand." However, in their rudimentary fashion, they had articulated the principle that a local population's ability to compete for commercial grain supplies depends on its purchasing power. Wu rounded off his version of the argument by pointing out that once the merchants had assembled, the price of rice could not but fall.[86]

---

86. CC, Li Qingzhi, QL 8/5/3; Wu Wei, QL 8/7/2; cf. Will and Wong, *Nourish the People*, pp. 477–78.

It is by no means an inescapable conclusion that Li, Sun, and Wu proposed increased recourse to issuing relief in silver because they supported grain trade interests. In our own day, Amartya Sen has argued, at book length, that boosting "exchange entitlements" may be better famine relief strategy than following the literalist assumption that the key task is to counter "food availability decline."[87] We should notice nonetheless, with reference particularly to Wu's proposal, that the merchant community could have asked for little better than, on one hand, to be freed from state competition (and, perhaps, occasional forced sales to the granaries), and, on the other, to have indigent populations turned temporarily into paying customers. We may gain further insight into the ideology of the market-oriented radicals by noting two last themes in Sun's memorial: the encouragement of peasant microcapitalism as a famine relief strategy, and the related notion that society should be more self-reliant.

Wu (who cited the Northern Song statesman Zeng Gong in his support) and Sun were agreed that giving famine victims silver would enable them to find means to support themselves. As Sun put it: "The mean folk in their quest for profit have arts of the utmost subtlety. If one affords them some small quantity of silver, they will . . . be able to contrive some hawking trade and to go after drachms and scruples. Grain in its sluggishness (*zhi*) is not as good as silver in its penetration (*tong*)." Encouraging the use of relief silver as petty trading capital could have been justified as an attempt to make each tael distributed go farther (besides helping recipients to boost their own exchange entitlements over a longer period). The idea was possibly inspired by observation of petty craftsmen-vendors similar to the itinerants whose ingenuity so impressed Rudolf Hommel in the 1930s and whose figurative descendants still grace Chinese street-markets.[88] As a vision, it fitted the world of prosperous, commercialized Jiangnan, with which Sun was most familiar. It is nonetheless hard to see the notion as a realistic strategy for succoring a mass of peasant victims even at the early stages of a grave subsistence crisis. Behind it, one suspects, stood a normative

---

87. Sen, *Poverty and Famines*, pp. 3–8 and passim.
88. Hommel, *China at Work*, pp. 31–32, 36–39, 212–18, 309, etc. The craftsman typically applied his own labor and tools to materials (or broken objects) supplied by the customer. Thus little capital was needed.

idea that relief clients should, at most, be helped to stand on their own feet.

In his concluding discussion, Sun gave one hint that he thought the state should limit its commitment to providing for the poor. Referring to the moratorium edict, he wrote: "[This] had in view the circulation of the grain; it had in view storage of grain among the people; it had in view making the populace nourish itself (*shi min zi yang*); and the whole realm already feels the blessings of it."[89] Under Sun's preferred arrangements, while the state would not necessarily dismantle the granary system, it would accept the partial devolution of its functions to a private economy boosted by the public funds distributed to famine victims. The victims who were the most able to compete for commercial grain supplies would be those with the resourcefulness to stretch their doles by making petty profits. The large profits would go to the grain merchants who brought the supplies. Making society responsible for nourishing itself entailed recognition of society's own way of solving problems. Sun, apparently, regarded that way as satisfactory.

The opinion that relief in silver could replace relief in kind routinely and on a large scale did not become official policy in 1743. As A'ersai pointed out in his thoughtful memorial of late September (a memorial that was received well by the emperor), the doles given to victims would not necessarily suffice for them to pay the high grain prices provoked by bad harvests. In 1742, local authorities in Hubei had been commuting grain entitlements into silver at the rate of 0.5 tael per *shi* (unhusked) while the corresponding market price was 0.7 to 0.8 tael per *shi*. The victims had, therefore, gone short. Using silver remained an expedient to which one might be driven; nothing but serious misgivings could be aroused by claims that if the granaries were out of grain, "one [could] always rely on silver and be free of worry."[90]

The Board of Revenue had reached a similar conclusion in its deliberation on Sun Hao's memorial in early August. Sun's proposals were rejected largely because they ignored the details of the moratorium policy as formulated by the grand secretaries and Nine Ministries Assembly in late May. The Board argued that these details made Sun's central points redundant. However, his ideas also fell foul of the

---

89. CC, Sun Hao, QL 8 (cat. no. 1125-032).
90. CC, A'ersai, QL 8/8/10.

Board's insistence that the distribution of silver was an inferior form of famine relief, justified when there was no choice but not to be regarded as a panacea. Sun suffered the ultimate disparagement of having his long and eloquent discussion dismissed in a routine memorial (*tiben*). Two days later, similarly short shrift was given to Li Qingzhi's idea of "issuing relief in silver in lieu [of grain]" (*yi yin dai zhen*).[91]

Even had the central government accepted Sun's proposals, experience would probably have forced it to acknowledge the limitations of such a policy before long. In the spring of 1744, the authorities combatting the famine in Zhili found that there was little point in persisting with *yin gu jian zhen*, because, as Will puts it, "there was nothing left to purchase."[92] Presumably, the Zhili peasants were not being given enough "market command" to draw in stocks at a time of year when prices were high everywhere. Even if it were argued (as Emida did in 1745) that silver stored in place of grain could be used by the authorities to buy relief supplies, there remained the question, especially in northern China, whether large amounts of grain would be available, when need arose, on suitably located markets.[93] In the Yangzi Valley, where grain was more plentiful and topography more conducive to the efficient functioning of markets, experiments had better prospects of success; yet even in the Middle Yangzi provinces, experienced administrators could justifiably have regarded such departures as extremely risky. While Sun Hao's and Wu Wei's memorials remain important for the study of market consciousness among mid-eighteenth-century Confucian-trained officials, the ideas that they propounded were too daring for most responsible contemporary opinion.

However, refusal to adopt a notion formally does not necessarily imply its banishment from thought. As circumstances continued to make

---

91. HHCC, Bundle 94, Bd. Rev., QL 8/6/13; NGDKDA, Bd. Rev., QL 8/6/15 (archive copy, doc. no. 098714).

92. Will, *Bureaucracy and Famine*, pp. 133–34.

93. In the summer of 1744, the Henan governor expressed concern as to whether the Shandong authorities would be able to buy the relief grain they needed in Henan without excessively depleting Henan markets. Although, on this occasion, a solution was found, the episode was still a warning. QSL/QL, *juan* 217:35a–b; cf. Emida, QL 10/5/13 (d.r.), transc. Lü Xiaoxian, comp., "Qianlong sannian," part 2, p. 19.

granary replenishment difficult, apparently inflationary, or simply inconvenient, administrators at all levels must have consoled themselves with the reflection that issuing relief in silver was better than sheer helplessness. Awareness of the *yin gu jian zhen* option continued to underpin suggestions that granaries need stock only a given proportion of their targets in the form of grain. Meanwhile, the idea that famine victims should be helped to stand on their own feet—or might indeed be left to stand on their own feet—would become more influential as the decade wore on.

6

Overt and Covert: 1744–47

This chapter investigates the background to the second, more definitive retreat from stockpile aggrandizement in 1748–49. It explores the less familiar episode in which, in 1744–45, the court ordered the provinces to resume *jiansheng* title sales with a view to relying entirely on the in-kind proceeds to restock the granaries. This policy, although soon abandoned as a failure, was probably in part responsible for the granary reserves attaining, during 1745–46, their highest reported level for any year before the later 1760s.[1] It seems odd that a conservative restocking strategy, intended to minimize the state's activity in the grain market, was associated, *prima facie*, with record levels of government stockpiling. The key to this paradox was a change of direction in the resetting of storage targets, a process that had been inaugurated in June 1742 in response to Sun Hao's first memorial.

Scrutiny of the outcomes of target resetting in 1743–44 is essential for a correct understanding of the famous 30 percent cut in early 1749. In the second half of 1743, as a result of the moratorium policy formulated by the grand secretaries and Nine Ministries Assembly, the official nationwide storage target was basically the pre-1738 one of some 28 million *shi*. However, since the previous year, provincial chief administrators had been determining new, compromise targets to replace the chimerically high ones set in 1738–39. It was the compromise targets, established mainly in 1743–44, whose total approached 48 million *shi*; it was the 48-million *shi* target that was cut in 1749. The process by which the compromise targets emerged reflects the evolution of policy after

---

1. Will and Wong, *Nourish the People*, appendix, table A.1, p. 528.

the moratorium decision in May 1743. This evolution was probably even more confusing for territorial administrators at the time than it is for historians. It is important to be able to recognize the 1743–44 targets, for it is only by establishing which target a given provincial official took as operative that one can tell how he interpreted his orders from above. Previous scholarship, however, has failed to notice that a set of targets had been systematically drawn up.[2]

We can best clarify granary policy in the mid-1740s by addressing the target-resetting process before examining the rationale for the attempt to rely solely on *jiansheng* title sales to restock the granaries. The concept of "rationale" here is inadequate, for the distinction between surface rationale and underlying motives will henceforth be vital to our reading of developments in policy. Rationales were supplied by memorial writers with varying degrees of sincerity. The key issue is what mix of interests underlay the court's selection of specific rationales to justify specific policy departures. In chapters 4 and 5, suspicions of covert and not necessarily creditable motivations focused on the possibility of influence from grain-trade interests and the presumed reluctance of county magistrates to risk maintaining large stockpiles of grain. From the mid-1740s, covert fiscal considerations enter the story. They are discernible mainly on their home ground at the Board of Revenue, but may also have influenced the court itself.

1744 Versus 1743: The Patterns in the Reset Targets

Preserved in the First Historical Archives (Beijing) is a fragmentary "List of Established Provincial Targets for Ever-normal Granary Grain Holdings," originally appended to an unidentified policy discussion document.[3] Presumably because the latest date found in the list is 1744, the fragment is entered under that year in the published catalog of palace memorials on fiscal matters held by the Beijing archives. The content clearly shows, however, that the list was prepared as part of the

---

2. Cf. Will's claim that "A consistent list of provincial totals was drawn up for the first time in 1748," a date that should read "early 1749" (Will and Wong, *Nourish the People*, p. 277). The acceptability of this statement rests entirely on the interpretation of the word "consistent."

3. CC, "Ge sheng changping cang gu ding'e qingdan" (fragment, n.d., dated 1749 by present author; cat. no. 1132-016).

1748–49 deliberations about cutting the 48-million *shi* target. It includes not only the provincial targets set in 1743–44, but also province-by-province recommendations for implementing the storage reduction policy. We may confidently identify the list as the reference matter appended to the grand secretaries' definitive report of January 1749.

Data for only five provinces are absent from the list. The missing 1743–44 targets can be supplied from earlier documents, except in Fujian's case. Fujian had still not finalized an overall target as of July 1748; by that date, it had a contribution target of 2,150,000 *shi*, including a recently added 150,000 *shi* target for Taiwan.[4] Otherwise, table 6 provides a complete set of compromise provincial targets (column A). With the addition of 2,150,000 *shi* for Fujian, the targets total 47,894,806 *shi*—only 215,874 *shi* less than 48,110,680 *shi*, the figure generally accepted as the standing target before the cut of 1749. The discrepancy would widen to about 1.6 million *shi* if the available Gansu figure (3,280,000 *shi*) proved to be expressed in standard *shi*, invalidating the conversion I have done in table 6. I think this is unlikely, given that in 1752, the Gansu administration commissioner was complaining that Echang, provincial governor in 1749–51, had calculated the shortfall in Gansu's granary reserves on the *false* assumption that the total target was supposed to be in standard *shi*.[5] Depending on the size of the discrepancy (that is, whether it was 200,000+ or 1.6 million *shi*), it can probably be explained by one or more of the following: target increases or additional targets originating after 1744, a notional noncontribution target for Fujian, and figures for supplementary and special granaries of the sort that one governor-general decried in 1748. At least one such reserve, nominally accounting for 400,000 *shi*, had been created during 1744–48.[6]

---

4. LFZZQZ (QL13), 3258; see also CC, Pan Siju, QL 13/6/25, JS, Zhou Xuejian, QL 10/7/16 (also copied as Zhou Xuejian, QL 10/8/15 (d.r.), transc. Lü Xiaoxian, comp., "Qianlong sannian," part 2, pp. 22–24). On the complicated case of Fujian, see below.

5. The commisioner argued that granary *shi* were used when issuing grain from Gansu granaries and that the Kangxi-period target had been set in terms of this large measure. Wu Shiduan, QL 16/11/22, repr. GZD/QL, vol. 2, pp. 25–26. Cf. Will's evidence that granary *shi* were used for setting county-level targets in Gansu as late as 1831. Will and Wong, *Nourish the People*, pp. 285–87.

6. The 400,000 *shi* stockpile was to be held on Taiwan for the emergency relief of Fujian's coastal jurisdictions. CC, Kaerjishan and Pan Siju, QL 13/8/28, and its

Column B of table 6 presents the determinable total storage targets of 1738–43 in order to facilitate comparison (column C). As column C shows, in three cases (Henan, Anhui, and Sichuan) the "compromise" targets were somewhat higher (about 16, 9, and 2 percent respectively) than the high targets they replaced. In Gansu, there was probably no change (except, perhaps, cancellation of a 100,000-*shi* addition to the target set in 1738). It is only by reading the variants mentioned in note 8 to table 3 (and/or, indeed, the figure that in 1748 was represented as Gansu's 1738 *total* target) as standard-*shi compromise* targets from the years 1738–42 that we can posit a significant 1743 cut in the Gansu target—a cut probably by 20–30 percent, depending on assumptions. In all other cases, the compromise targets clearly meant reductions, as expected. The cuts ranged from about 1 percent (Jiangsu) through about 10 percent (Shandong, Shanxi) to a more substantial proportion somewhere between nearly one-quarter and just over one-half (in ascending order, Guizhou, Yunnan, Hunan, Guangdong, Guangxi, Shaanxi, Jiangxi, Hubei). It is, moreover, likely that the exceptionally high Henan target, which I have seen in no source other than the 1749 list, includes a figure for the tribute grain reserves founded in 1704 for emergency use originally in two adjacent provinces (Shanxi and Shaanxi). The best available source suggests that in early 1749, 1,436,200 *shi* was taken as the nominal target for these special granaries.[7] If we deduct this figure, the Henan compromise target becomes 3,573,800 *shi*, representing a cut of 729,599 *shi* (16.95 percent).

Incomplete as the data are, they suggest some partial patterns. Most of the provinces that took large proportional cuts lay, roughly speaking, in the southern part of what Wang Yeh-chien once called the "developing area" of Qing-dynasty China. A generally favorable ratio

---

appendix, LFZZQZ (QL13), 3257; Will, *Bureaucracy and Famine*, p. 196, table 14, note *g*, and p. 280; cf. QCWXTK, vol. 1, *juan* 36, pp. 5,195–96, and, for the governor-general's strictures, CC, Celeng, QL 13/3/28.

7. CC, Shise, QL 13/9/8. This memorial and its appendix, LFZZQZ (QL13), 3209, report on Henan's holdings of tribute grain as well as ever-normal grain in response to an edict issued in pursuance of the target reduction policy. Both documents would have been used in preparing the 1749 list. On the Henan tribute grain reserves, see Will, *Bureaucracy and Famine*, pp. 196, 280; Dunstan, *Conflicting Counsels*, pp. 23–26, 44–47.

Table 6
The Compromise Storage Targets of 1743–44
(Units: *shi* of unhusked grain)

Province (year when target finalized)	A 1743–44 target	B 1738–43 total target*	C A compared with B
Henan (1744)	5,010,000[1]	4,303,399	+706,601 (16.42%)
Gansu (1743)	4,685,714[2c]	4,685,714[2]	No change
Zhili (1744)	4,370,000	N.d.	—
Shandong (1743)	3,975,200[a]	4,380,000[3]	–404,800 (9.24%)
Zhejiang (1744)	3,480,000	N.d.	—
Guangdong (1744)	3,359,767[b]	5,425,685	–2,065,918 (38.08%)
Sichuan (1744)	2,929,459	2,874,600+	(+54,859) (1.91%)
Shanxi (1744)	2,736,000	3,040,000	–304,000 (10.00%)
Shaanxi (1743)	2,733,010[d]	5,353,741	–2,620,731 (48.95%)
Jiangsu (1744)	2,111,000	2,139,000	–28,000 (1.31%)
Anhui (1744)	2,000,000[4]	1,832,000[4]	+168,000 (9.17%)
Hunan (1743)	1,757,354	2,767,133	–1,009,779 (36.49%)
Jiangxi (1743)	1,606,000	3,290,000	–1,684,000 (51.19%)
Guangxi (1743)	1,413,398	2,687,418	–1,274,020 (47.41%)
Fengtian (1743)	1,120,000[4,5]	N.d.	—
Hubei (1743)	1,017,844	2,270,000	–1,252,156 (55.16%)
Yunnan (1743–44)	941,600[6]	1,402,600	–461,000 (32.87%)
Guizhou (1743)	498,460+[7e]	642,200	–143,740 (22.38%)
TOTAL	45,744,806[8]		

*Data in column B from table 3, column C.
[1]May include 1,436,200 *shi* for the tribute grain reserves located in Henan. If so, the Henan ever-normal compromise target was 3,573,800 *shi* (see text).
[2]Stated figure of 3,280,000 (presumably) granary *shi* converted here to standard *shi*.
[3]Although listed as a variant in table 3, this figure is used here because it was that from which the Shandong authorities intended the proposed compromise target to be a slight reduction. It probably includes over 500,000 *shi* of community granary and other special category grain.
[4]Figure stated in *shi* husked; converted here to *shi* unhusked by doubling.
[5]Figure is Yongzheng target plus target for a jurisdiction that had been raised to county status at the end of Yongzheng's reign (Zhao et al., comps., *Qingshi gao*, vol. 8, *juan* 55, p. 1,929).
[6]A small correction to the information in the 1749 list is made here.
[7]Actual amount in store, adopted as target by order of the Board of Revenue; includes a little husked rice and grain of other kinds. The Guizhou authorities had proposed a higher target (598,800 *shi*). HHCC, Bundle 93, Zhang Guangsi (fragment, n.d., sent to Bd. Rev. on QL 8/6/28); CC, Aibida, QL 13/9/12.
[8]If the stated 1743 Gansu target (3,280,000 *shi*) was already in standard *shi*, the total of the column A figures would be 44,339,092 *shi*.

Table 6, cont.

SOURCES FOR COLUMN A: Unless otherwise stated, CC, "Ge sheng changping cang gu ding'e qing-dan" (fragment, presumably 1749).
ᵃ HHCC, Bundle 90, Bd. Rev., QL 8/4/13. "Ge sheng changping cang . . ." quotes the rounded figure of 3,970,000 *shi*.
ᵇ QSL/QL, *juan* 214:9b.
ᶜ CC, Huang Tinggui, QL 13/9/20.
ᵈ HHCC, Bundle 93, Bd. Rev., QL 8/6/3.
ᵉ Appendix to LFZZ, Aibida, QL 13/9/12; cf. CC, Zhang Yunsui, QL 13/9/19.

between grain output (or indeed potential output) and population made these south-central and southwestern provinces unlikely to need especially large reserves for their own people. As to the exceptions, Jiangxi had more in common, in terms of eighteenth-century grain distribution, with its western neighbors in Wang's "developing area" than with the Lower Yangzi, while Guangdong and Shaanxi were the only provinces whose post-1738 total targets exceeded 5 million *shi*.[8] More importantly, however, it is noticeable that all but one cut by 20 percent or more took place in 1743, while—the problematic Gansu case apart—only two of the 1743 cuts (those for Shandong and Guizhou) were by less than 30 percent. Both target increases were made in 1744, as were three of the four cuts by less than 20 percent (including Henan's likely cut). Those compromise targets that were below 2 million *shi* were set in 1743; except in the cases of Shandong, Shaanxi, and Gansu, the higher targets, ranging from 2 to 4.37 million *shi*, were set in 1744.

A similar temporal pattern is discernible when we compare the compromise targets (minus the presumed tribute grain target in Henan's case) with the known basic targets (table 7). Apart from the probably uncut Gansu target, no target finalized in 1743 was more than 50 percent higher than the corresponding basic target. Among the 1743 targets, that for Guangxi was identical with the basic target, that for Fengtian was higher only by 40,000 *shi* (for a jurisdiction that was raised to county status after the basic target had been set), and that for

---

8. Wang Yeh-chien, *Land Taxation*, pp. 84–86. Sichuan, by contrast, was a "developing area" province whose target was raised slightly. Sichuan's administrators had capitalized on the low grain prices associated with the province's "developing" status to reap exceptional success in building stocks by selling *jiansheng* titles. In requesting the increase, they were continuing to push a policy that seemed to work.

Table 7
The Compromise Targets of 1743–44 Compared with the Basic Targets
(Units: _shi_ of unhusked grain; percentages correct to nearest integer)

Province (year)	A 1743–44 target	B Basic target*	C A compared with B
Gansu (1743)	4,685,714	1,228,571	+3,457,143 (281%)
Zhili (1744)	4,370,000	1,996,216	+2,373,784 (119%)
Shandong (1743)	3,975,200	2,959,386	+1,015,814 (34%)
Henan (1744)	3,573,800[1]	2,310,999	+1,262,801 (55%)
Zhejiang (1744)	3,480,000	2,800,000	+680,000 (24%)
Guangdong (1744)	3,359,767	1,925,685	+1,434,082 (74%)
Sichuan (1744)	2,929,459	1,100,000	+1,829,459 (166%)
Shanxi (1744)	2,736,000	1,550,000	+1,186,000 (77%)
Shaanxi (1743)	2,733,010	2,061,741	+671,269 (33%)
Jiangsu (1744)	2,111,000	1,568,000	+543,000 (35%)
Anhui (1744)	2,000,000	1,832,000	+168,000 (9%)
Hunan (1743)	1,757,354	1,202,133	+555,221 (46%)
Jiangxi (1743)	1,606,000	1,370,713	+235,287 (17%)
Guangxi (1743)	1,413,398	1,413,398	Figures identical
Fengtian (1743)	1,120,000	1,080,000	+40,000 (4%)
Hubei (1743)	1,017,844	1,070,000	**–52,156 (5%)**
Yunnan (1743–44)	941,600	701,600[2]	+240,000 (34%)
Guizhou (1743)	498,460	395,200	+103,260 (26%)

* Data in column B from table 3, column A, or table 2.
[1] If we use the higher figure stated in the 1749 list, this line reads: 5,010,000 (1744 target); 2,310,999 (basic target); +2,699,001, i.e., 117% (1744 target compared with basic target).
[2] By 1748, the Yunnan basic target was taken to be 701,500 _shi_, but this probably reflects careless rounding. CC, Zhang Yunsui, QL 13/9/19; KC, Tuerbing'a, QL 13/12/18.

Hubei was 5 per cent _lower_ than the augmented basic target of the early Qianlong reign (although this latter target was about twice as high as the so-called "Yongzheng-period target"). While the extent to which the targets set in 1744 were higher than the basic targets ranged from 9 percent (Anhui) to 166 percent (Sichuan), five of the eight known 1744 targets were over 50 percent higher than the corresponding basic targets. Of these five, four were over 70 percent higher, and two over 100 percent higher. The highest percentage increases were those for Sichuan, Zhili, Shanxi, Guangdong, and Henan, in that order.

As shown below, it is a change of policy that accounts for these temporal patterns. Although provincial chief administrators had been authorized, in 1742, to recommend moderate increases compared with the basic targets, after May 1743 the Board of Revenue directed the target-setting process in the spirit of the moratorium decision. Only a policy change would enable a significant number of provinces to gain approval for new targets that were only slightly lower (or indeed higher) than their high-level targets, and/or represented major increases compared with their basic targets. We cannot, in fact, assume that the reason why the compromise targets of the south-central and southwestern provinces were finalized in 1743 was that, aware that large reserves were not needed for the populations of these provinces, their chief administrators rushed to propose the 20 to 55 percent cuts shown in table 6. A sampling of the correspondence on this issue in routine memorials suggests that, while this is true of Jiangxi, the general tendency of provincial chief administrators north and south in 1743 was to propose higher compromise targets than the Board of Revenue would countenance. In most cases summarized below, this was mainly because the new targets were proposed either before the moratorium decision or in ignorance of its details. The Board of Revenue, responding after the decision, either dismissed requests for an increase vis-à-vis the basic target as now contrary to policy, or, at best, affirmed this principle with some concession.

From Obedient Modesty to Ambiguous Ambition

Jiangxi's new target was settled smoothly and quite early. The proposed 51 percent cut from the high-level target was considered by the Board of Revenue on 13 April 1743, before the moratorium decision. The report detailing the proposal was prepared (as was normal) by the provincial administration commissioner, Peng Jiaping, and endorsed by Chen Hongmou as governor. It was probably written in the autumn of 1742, and thus before the 1743 subsistence crisis, which might have made Peng more cautious. Peng did not identify Jiangxi's role in supplying other provinces as an especially relevant consideration. The important points, for him, were that Jiangxi people did "not greatly rely upon official grain," and that the high grain prices of recent years (themselves the result of increased official buying) had made it impossible to fill even 10 percent of the contribution target, which was thus rendered meaningless. Prefectural reports suggested that some county-level basic targets should be raised, others adjusted slightly, and others again lowered (typically those for isolated areas whence grain could not be easily transported). A systematic, county-by-county revision of all targets yielded a provincial total of 1,606,000 *shi*, which did after all exceed the basic target. The 1.6-million *shi* figure was approved; this was the target that the Jiangxi authorities took as operative thereafter.[9]

Systematic county-by-county revisions of all targets were of course expected from all provinces. Table 1 (in chapter 4 above) must suffice to illustrate the way in which provincial chief administrators applied the 1742 instructions to determine targets on the basis of each county's size, population density, and distance from navigable waterways. What matters here is the fate of the total recommended targets, and the principles on which they were determined. As we have seen, according to the 1742 instructions, compromise targets were expected to comprise the basic target plus, if necessary, a modest supplementary target to be filled through sale of *jiansheng* titles.

Among those provinces that clearly took substantial cuts in 1743, the cases of Yunnan, Guangxi, and Guizhou show the adoption of lower compromise targets than those initially proposed by the provincial authorities. In Yunnan, the provincial administration commissioner's original, pre-moratorium report envisaged that a high-level target produced, in principle, by doubling all the local basic targets should yield to one based on a 50 percent increase in the basic targets, unless there was reason to use a higher rate. A minority of jurisdictions, including some "newly opened" ones with growing populations, should keep their high-level targets; one "newly opened" jurisdiction that contained a prefectural capital should have its basic target raised by 275 percent. The resulting total compromise target would have been slightly over 1.1 million *shi*, representing a 21 percent cut from Yunnan's high-level target. However, the revised proposal that the Board of Revenue considered in June 1743 was that a reduced supplementary contribution target totalling 240,000 *shi* be added to the basic target. The Board obtained imperial permission to instruct the Yunnan governor to abide by the May edict that had halted all collection of grain contributions for the granaries, while intimating that Yunnan could be

---

9. HHCC, Bundle 89, Bd. Rev., QL 8/3/19, and, e.g., CC, Peng Jiaping, QL 8/5/27. Peng took the amount in store in 1736 as Jiangxi's basic target; this was some 24,000 *shi* lower than the figure shown in table 7.

allowed to try to fill the proposed contribution target at some future date when harvests had been good. When collection for this supplementary target was approved in 1744, Yunnan effectively acquired a compromise target of 941,600 *shi*, almost one-third lower than its high-level target.[10]

Guangxi's original proposal fared still worse. After a consultation process that went down to the county level, the Guangxi provincial administration commissioner agreed that the 1738 contribution target (1,274,020 *shi*) had been unrealistic. However, he identified numerous jurisdictions that, for military or other reasons, needed larger reserves than those prescribed by the basic targets. He therefore proposed a revised contribution target of 709,110 *shi*, just over half that set in 1738. Had this figure been accepted, Guangxi's high-level target (2,687,418 *shi*) would have been cut by 21 percent. But when the Board of Revenue replied in August 1743, it merely adduced the moratorium without drawing attention to the provision that collection of grain contributions could be resumed when conditions improved. The proposal for a 709,110 *shi* contribution target was dismissed, and the Guangxi authorities were told to retain their basic target as the "permanent" quota for Guangxi. Thus was Guangxi's high-level target cut by 47 percent.[11]

The same fate initially befell the Jiangsu authorities' attempt to keep their atypically modest high-level target (2,139,000 *shi* for the nation's most densely populated province). In 1738, Jiangsu had adopted a contribution target of 571,000 *shi*, representing a mere 36 percent increase over the basic target. As noted in chapter 5, this pulled Jiangsu down from its midway position in the list of "Yongzheng-period targets" (table 2) to a position fourth from bottom in the list of ascertainable high-level targets (table 4). With hindsight, this "demotion" seems to mark a stage in a transition from traditionalist thinking, according to which highly urbanized, populous Jiangsu would have needed large grain reserves, to the more market-oriented assumption that the most commercialized provinces were served efficiently by the interregional grain trade and needed limited assistance from state granaries. Writing

---

10. HHCC, Bundle 87, Zhang Yunsui, QL 8/2/28, Bundle 91, Bd. Rev., QL 8/int.4/18; CC, Tuerbing'a, QL 13/9/23.

11. HHCC, Bundle 93, Bd. Rev., QL 8/6/20; this quotes the Guangxi authorities' memorial, dated 7 June 1743. For the case of Guizhou, see table 6, n. 7.

not later than April 1743, Anning, as Jiangsu's provincial administration commissioner, showed awareness of the latter argument but thought it only partially compelling. He acknowledged that commerce circulated even in years of dearth through major cities at strategic points on land and water routes. He also pointed out, however, that such cities were by definition places of high population concentration and needed large amounts of grain for *soudure* stabilizing sales even in ordinary years. There were also the remoter jurisdictions that, although their needs were less extensive, could not necessarily rely on trade or swift delivery of supplementary relief grain. Jiangsu's existing contribution target was therefore not excessive, and since, given a return of good harvests, it could easily be met, there was no point in cutting it. So concluded Anning, with Chen Dashou's gubernatorial endorsement. On 16 June, however, the Board of Revenue invoked the moratorium decision to dismiss their opinion. Jiangsu, like Guangxi, was to be left with its basic target (1,568,000 *shi*) only. The cut from the high-level target that was now imposed was by nearly 27 percent. Only in 1744 would the Jiangsu authorities be able to secure a more favorable outcome.[12]

We may conclude this sampling of the target-setting process in 1743 by looking at two northern provinces, Shandong and Shaanxi, whose compromise targets were finalized that year. The Shandong proposal was written in February and considered by the Board of Revenue on 6 May, just before the moratorium edict—timing that no doubt explains the smallness of the cut imposed. Even so, this cut was slightly larger than the Shandong authorities had recommended. The Shandong figures are unusually complicated, but the gist of the provincial administration commissioner's deliberations was that the 1738 contribution target of 1,100,000 *shi* should be reduced to 754,400 *shi*. This revised target, which he later described as a *bi bu ke shao zhi shu* ("absolutely indispensable amount"), had been determined by consideration of the circumstances in each jurisdiction; for several reasons an excessive cut should be avoided, he opined. The Board, however, denied the need to give contribution targets to two jurisdictions that

---

12. HHCC, Bundle 88, Chen Dashou, QL 8/3/10; Bundle 91, Bd. Rev., QL 8/int.4/24; and below.

had previously lacked them, thereby removing 28,400 *shi* from the reduced target.[13]

As the Board's consideration of the Shaanxi proposal took place in July, it is not surprising that the ruling was similar to that for Guangxi and Jiangsu. The only difference was that the relatively low target that Shaanxi was directed to retain was not its basic target, but the amount actually held in the first half of 1743, excluding some 500,000 *shi* raised through contributions. The Shaanxi authorities had sought approval for a compromise target of 3,495,540 *shi*; the Board replied that the 2,733,010 *shi* of non-contribution grain already in store sufficed to meet the basic target and was to be adopted permanently. Shaanxi thereby acquired a target that, although one-third higher than the basic target, was almost 22 percent lower than the responsible authorities had recommended.[14]

Overall, the situation must have appeared dismal to any governor who believed that major state stockpiling was important. However, policy reversal was less than twelve months away.

Target-setting in 1744: the rebirth of ambition?   In late January 1744, the Yunnan provincial administration commissioner, the Mongol Alantai, appealed against the failure to adopt his original proposal of a 1.1-million *shi* compromise target. Referring to the special needs of Yunnan, with its mountainous terrain and large mining population, he pointed out the nightmare that the moratorium policy represented for responsible provincial government. Yunnan's targets were atypically low; given that both buying and the acceptance of contributions were suspended pending better harvests, what were the authorities to do when, as had happened during the past autumn, flood relief claimed almost two-thirds of one jurisdiction's basic target, and almost nine-tenths of another's? Alantai requested a more modest upward revision of the county-level basic targets than he had originally envisaged: while large jurisdictions should still have 50 percent increases, medium-sized jurisdictions should have 33 percent, and small ones 25 percent increases. But

---

13. HHCC, Bundle 87, Yan Sisheng, QL 8/1/24, Bundle 90, Bd. Rev., QL 8/4/13; CC, Bao Gua, QL 8/2 (cat. no. 1123-021).

14. HHCC, Bundle 93, Bd. Rev., QL 8/6/3. CC, Shuai Nianzu, QL 8/12/7, the source for table 1, presents the acting Shaanxi governor's January 1744 proposals for redistributing the 2,733,010-*shi* target among the province's county-level units.

Alantai was acting some two months too soon—even if the opening of contributions for Yunnan's supplementary target of 240,000 *shi* was approved as a concession to him.[15] If he had waited until after 7 April, he would have had a chance of more or less restoring the high-level target for his province, as his counterparts in Shanxi, Jiangsu, and Sichuan were shortly to do.

On 7 April 1744, the emperor announced a new policy that, while not necessarily ensuring granary restocking to basic target level, enabled the ambitious to resuscitate the dream of greatly increasing reserves. *Jiansheng* titles were once more to be sold for grain, but this time as a potential, noninflationary substitute for buying grain in order to restock the granaries. To make this policy effective, *jiansheng* title prices were to be converted into grain at rates that more realistically reflected current grain prices, while steps were to be taken to prevent abuses by official personnel. The original edict made no mention of the setting of new contribution targets, which would probably have signified (or been taken to signify) an aspiration to increase reserves beyond the basic target levels. However, the Board of Revenue's subsequent memorandum to provincial chief administrators included the instruction that such targets should be set. When several administrators proposed quite high targets, they were not told that they had failed to understand the emperor's intentions.[16]

Let us sample the provincial target proposals considered after the 7 April edict. In the second half of May, the Board of Revenue advised approval of Guangdong's proposal for a compromise target consisting

---

15. CC, Alantai, QL 8/12/15. While it is not possible to calculate the total by which Alantai proposed to raise the Yunnan target, a likely estimate is 289,000 *shi*—only 20 percent higher than the supplementary contribution target. He suggested that, in future, grain for Yunnan's granaries be bought directly from the wealthier households, thereby avoiding sudden price increases on local markets that were normally not amply stocked.

16. Edict of QL 9/2/25 transc. Lü Xiaoxian, comp., "Qianlong sannian," part 2, pp. 12–13, or QSL/QL, *juan* 211:16b–18a. For references to the instruction to set targets, see, e.g., Chen Dashou, QL 9/4/24 and Zhou Xuejian, QL 10/8/15 (d.r.), transc. Lü, comp., "Qianlong sannian," part 2, pp. 14–15, 22–24. The latter reference strongly suggests that the Board originated the idea that contribution targets should be set. Its motivation—if innocent—was probably concern to implement bureaucratic controls rather than desire to revive the chimera.

of "the old holdings" plus the cumulative amount raised through *jian-sheng* title sales by the time the moratorium came down. This gave Guangdong a target of some 3.3 million *shi*, 74 percent higher than its basic target.[17] The Guangdong proposal had probably been prepared in ignorance of the policy change, if not before the change was made, but its acceptance must have signalled that increases vis-à-vis the basic target could now be proposed with reasonable prospects of success. In early June, the Jiangsu governor, Chen Dashou, presenting (as instructed) proposals for implementing the new studentship sales policy, success-fully sought to reverse the Board's dismissal of his and Anning's 1743 request that the Jiangsu high-level target be not cut. That target had been 2,139,000 *shi*; Chen noted that 28,000 *shi*, the standard high-level target for a Jiangsu medium-sized county-level unit, should be sub-tracted because one such unit had been re-amalgamated with its neigh-bor. This left 2,111,000 *shi*, the figure shown in table 6 as Jiangsu's compromise target, set in 1744. To reach this target, Jiangsu would have to collect over 1 million *shi* by way of contributions. Its original (1738–43) contribution target had been only 571,000 *shi*.[18]

In early August, the Board responded favorably to the Zhili governor-general's proposal that Zhili's county-level basic targets, which ranged from 3,000 to 25,000 *shi*, should be replaced by its 1738–43 contribution targets, which ranged from 20,000 to 40,000 *shi*. When this was done, Zhili's compromise target was 119 percent higher than its basic target, as shown in table 7. Only somewhat less ambitious was the proposal of the Shanxi governor, Aligun, approved in November. He suggested that Shanxi's compromise target be determined on the basis of a 10 percent reduction from the high-level target. The difference between the new target (2,736,000 *shi*) and the amount in store was 853,400 *shi*; this latter was the quantity that Shanxi would aspire to fill by selling *jiansheng* titles.[19]

We may finally take the complicated case of Fujian, which was still wrestling with the Board over its compromise target in the autumn of 1745. Fujian's chief administrators had originally proposed a compro-

---

17. QSL/QL, *juan* 214:9b. For elucidation of this implied total holdings figure, see chap. 8 below.

18. CC, Chen Dashou, QL 9/4/24 (also transc. Lü Xiaoxian, comp., "Qianlong sannian," part 2, pp. 14–15); QSL/QL, *juan* 216:21a–b.

19. QSL/QL, *juan* 219:8b–10a, 227:2a.

mise target of 2,810,902 *shi*, which was not much lower than the province's revised high-level target (2,962,800 *shi*). The Board, dissatisfied with the figures they had cited, had instructed them to await the end of the experimental year of adjusted-rate studentship sales that Fujian, like Jiangxi, had been granted as an exception to the moratorium. When this year expired, which would be on 11 May 1744, Fujian's administrators were to propose a new target, taking into account the quantity of grain actually contributed. Perhaps because progress in attracting contributions had initially been slower than expected, the Fujian governor, Zhou Xuejian, waited until the spring of 1745 before making a proposal.[20] By then, the Board was more cautious about the feasibility of targets than it had been in 1744. Fujian's post-1738 contribution target had been 1,045,000 *shi*, a figure subsequently increased to 1,064,000 and then to 1,114,000 *shi*. When Zhou, in 1745, proposed a further increase of 886,000 *shi*, to bring the total to 2 million, the Board ordered reconsideration. This was partly because Zhou had proposed only a contribution target, and had not gone through the motions of determining an overall compromise target according to the policy of 1742. However, it was also because Fujian had attracted contributions to a cumulative total that fell short of 610,000 *shi*. It was premature to speak of raising the existing target by over 800,000 *shi* when 504,000 *shi* must be contributed before that target would be realized.

Zhou justified his expansionary proposal in a long memorial that the emperor read on 10 September 1745. This memorial gives important hints as to the likely thinking of provincial governors who recognized opportunities of manipulating the court's ever-changing policy to the advantage of their own administrations. He reported that he had not proposed a compromise target because the spirit of the 1742 policy, which called for reduced targets, was no longer operative. Meanwhile,

---

20. During the year that ended on 11 May 1744, the Fujian granaries received 158,140 *shi* through *jiansheng* title sales. While this figure showed a considerable increase in annual receipts compared with the first four years of the studentship sales policy, the absolute amount represented only 15 percent of Fujian's "original" contribution target. In early December 1744, Zhou was able to report the collection of a further 134,840 *shi* even before the autumn harvest ended—an improvement in the rate of contributions that he found encouraging. CC, Nasutu and Zhou Xuejian, QL 9/4/24; CC, Zhou Xuejian, QL 9/10/29.

filling the granaries with grain contributions was an approach that especially suited Fujian. Buying for the granaries, he claimed, was "ten times" harder in Fujian than in other provinces, given that Fujian did not produce enough grain for its population, while topography left the province commercially isolated. Fujian's cumulative total of grain contributions had reached 1,024,196 *shi* by summer's end. The time of writing (early autumn 1745) was, therefore, a very reasonable time at which to ask that the contribution target be raised to 2 million *shi*. If he waited for collection of the last 90,000 *shi* needed to meet the existing target, the inevitable delays involved in the approval process would halt the flow of contributions.

As to the basic target, Zhou acknowledged that Fujian had "originally" had a target of some 1,848,800 *shi*. If the proposed new contribution target had been added to it, Fujian's compromise target would have been the fourth-highest in the nation (3,848,800 *shi*). However, the tenor of Zhou's memorial suggests that his preferred strategy was to maximize contributions, in the hope that grain acquired in this way would replace purchased grain as completely as possible. The point of pushing up the contribution target was, presumably, to make it overtake the basic target, with a view to rendering the latter ever more redundant. Already in December 1744, Zhou had secured imperial approval for a short-term experiment with suspending purchases in Fujian's inland prefectures, so as to maximize the quantity of grain available in private hands for making contributions. His approach was in the spirit of the edict of 7 April 1744, but he was also subverting bureaucratic discipline, which required that every province specify a revised overall target to replace the high-level one of the late 1730s. Perhaps for this reason, Zhou temporized, rather than being fully explicit about his intentions. A substantial portion of the "original" target was held only in the form of silver and could not be easily replaced, he said; this made the whole question of the basic target problematic. The best plan would be to wait until the full 2 million *shi* had been contributed and then review the situation, buying grain only for those jurisdictions that still had inadequate reserves. A permanent target would be set at that stage; although Zhou said that it would combine the basic and the contribution targets, what he surely intended was that contributions would supply the lion's share. In the event, not only was the contribution target of 2 million *shi* approved, but subsequent reports suggest that Zhou's approach was largely successful in terms of his half-covert goals.[21]

Despite its complexity, the Fujian case was worth examining for what it implies about the likely motivations of provincial chief administrators during the target-resetting process. One is initially tempted to assume that in pressing for relatively and, later, very high compromise targets, most provincial chief administrators were actuated by their sincere judgment, as responsible officials, that food security for the people in their charge required significantly larger granary reserves than the basic targets prescribed. On this reading, one applauds those administrators of northern, western or far-southern provinces who, by waiting for the wind to change, managed to neutralize a policy that prescribed for the whole of China on the basis of conditions in the Yangzi Valley. Such an interpretation is probably valid in the case of certain governors, especially those who, in 1743, strove to retain higher targets than the Board was willing to endorse. However, the case of Fujian, combined, perhaps, with the extremism of the Zhili target, suggests that one must cast the interpretative net a little wider.

There are several possible explanations for any given high-target proposal other than the common-sense assumption that it reflects a conscientious official's responsible judgment. One is that the official, confused about the intent of current policy, or accustomed to associating commitment to the public good with larger grain stockpiles, acted on the belief that a high-level proposal was expected of him or would earn him credit. In March 1744, the emperor accused provincial chief administrators in general of having welcomed the moratorium (because it meant less bother) and let granary reserves run down.[22] After that, proposing a high contribution target would have been one way of protesting one's devotion to the goal of "nourishing the people." Per-

---

21. JS, Zhou Xuejian, QL 10/7/16 (or Zhou Xuejian, QL 10/8/15 (d.r.), transc. Lü Xiaoxian, comp., "Qianlong sannian," part 2, pp. 22–24); CC, Zhou Xuejian, QL 9/10/29, Pan Siju, QL 13/6/25; Will and Wong, *Nourish the People*, p. 50; and below. Reports of 29 December 1745 suggest the following rough breakdown of the Fujian ever-normal network's assets: 2.3 million *shi* of grain (of which perhaps about 1.1 million had been contributed since 1738); at least 400,000 taels of unspent purchase funds in the provincial treasury plus some 120,000 held at lower levels. KC, Maertai and Zhou Xuejian, QL 10/12/7, Zhou Xuejian, QL 10/12/7.

22. QSL/QL, *juan* 209:8a–9a.

sonal idiosyncrasy may also have been a factor. Until the summer of 1743, Henan had a strongly interventionist governor in Yaertu; thereafter, the Henan provincial government was in the hands of Shise, who was accustomed to successful *jiansheng* title sales in Sichuan. However, the case of Fujian draws attention to a third possibility: that some of those provincial chiefs who proposed high contribution targets after the 7 April edict were responding to the court's suggestion that well-run title sales could replace the vexatious process of buying grain for granary replenishment.

The orders sent out by the central government continued to apply the formula of 1742: there would be separate contribution targets that would, in principle, be supplementary to the basic targets, although a single total target figure was to be supplied, and although, in practice, permission might be given for contribution targets to encroach upon the sphere of basic targets (that is, the sphere of restocking through purchase). Some of those provincial chiefs who interpreted the Board's instructions in such a way as to produce very high targets perhaps knew quite well that these high targets could not be attained. They may nonetheless have hoped that if they were enabled to collect large quantities of contributions, they would be permitted to stop buying altogether in the next policy change. As the upshot shows, they had not entirely misjudged the emperor if such was their anticipation.

While we should not overlook the possibility of cynicism on the part of some provincial chief administrators, it is important to remember what a high contribution target meant for them as heads of provincial bureaucracies. Experience had shown that many county-level officials lacked enthusiasm for the studentship sales policy because they feared responsibility for extra grain. Presumably, the greater the central government's efforts to make the policy more realistic, the greater would be the interest of local officials in sabotaging it. In order to elicit their cooperation, provincial chiefs may have found it expedient to hint that, if only local officials could demonstrate the possibility of restocking the granaries by selling *jiansheng* titles, they might in future be allowed to use this administratively undemanding technique instead of buying. As the next section shows, in 1742 and 1743, exactly such a hint was given to Jiangxi's local officials by so ostensibly conscientious a governor as Chen Hongmou. On the issue of grain stockpiling, complicity, rather than wide goal divergence, may have characterized the relationship between superiors and subordinates more than the surface record indicates.

Studentship Sales, Once More the Panacea

To understand the rationale for the surprising change of policy in April 1744, we must revisit the previous winter. On 30 January 1744, the Liang-Jiang governor-general, Yinjishan, and the outgoing Jiangxi governor, Chen Hongmou, reported on the results of Jiangxi's one-year experiment with selling *jiansheng* titles at reduced prices (as expressed in grain). The experiment had probably been authorized in November 1742 and inaugurated the following month; thus the report was due. Chen and Yinjishan claimed noteworthy success, asserting that applicants were still coming forward in an unbroken stream, and that by the end of the lunar year (12 February 1744) the total raised would probably be about 200,000 *shi*.[23] We should notice that, even if this estimate had not been too optimistic, it was less than half of Jiangxi's annual purchase requirement, assuming (for the sake of argument) strict adherence to the 30 percent annual rotation norm and even Jiangxi's *basic* target. In fact, late in the first quarter of lunar 1744, reported contributions since the spring of lunar 1743 still totalled only 188,600 *shi*.[24]

Undeterred by such realities, on 30 January 1744, Yinjishan and Chen Hongmou submitted a second joint memorial reflecting on *jiansheng* title sales as a technique for routine granary restocking. They requested only that Jiangxi be permitted to pursue such an approach, with further adjustment of the grain valuation rate, and, therefore, of the price per title. However, parts of their argument were couched in general terms, tempting the emperor to assume that what applied in Jiangxi would apply elsewhere. They also mentioned a fiscal advantage to filling the granaries with grain contributions: the proceeds of stabilizing sales could then be diverted to military uses.

---

23. JS, Yinjishan and Chen Hongmou, QL 8/12/16; also quoted in CC, Grd. Secs., n.d., erroneously dated 1749 in catalog (cat. no. 1148-039). Cf. QSL/QL, *juan* 209:4a–b.

24. The new Jiangxi governor mentioned on 7 May 1744 that 28,600 *shi* of contributions had recently been added to 160,000 *shi* collected during lunar 1743. CC, Saileng'e, QL 9/3/25.

What military uses had they in mind? Alas, our sources are generally reticent about the fiscal aspects of the 1744–45 studentship sales experiment. The discussions were usually conducted as if the only task were to devise the best obtainable grain acquisition policy. However, as we shall see, in 1745 a censorial official expressed the suspicion that fiscal considerations lay behind the latest twist of policy. The hint in the second joint memorial by Chen and Yinjishan gives advance warning that his guess is to be taken seriously. Admittedly, the first major military campaign of Qianlong's reign was not to happen until 1747–49. Already in 1743, however, the Qing state had begun a military involvement that was to escalate, in 1745, into a costly expedition in the mountains west of that far-western Sichuan outpost, Dajian Lu.[25] In high-Qing China, subventions for campaigns were not necessarily issued from the central government treasury controlled by the Board of Revenue, but might be allocated from the tax revenues of nearby provinces under a fiscal system based on compromise between the principles of "tax sharing" and "grants-in-aid," as Wang Yeh-chien has put it.[26] There were, in principle, two categories of provincial tax funds: the "retained," provincial share, and a "deliverable" share allotted to the central government. A proportion of the latter might be allocated by the Board as subsidies to poorer provinces; the balance was to be remitted to Beijing. Under the post-1725 cross-provincial subvention scheme, Jiangxi, along with Hubei and Hunan, was a designated first-tier source of aid for Sichuan, Yunnan, and Guizhou, all of whose military establishments were seen to be perennially in need of subsidies from richer neighbors. Jiangxi could thus expect increased military activity in any of China's western or southwestern peripheries to lead to larger claims on its tax revenues.[27]

We should not jump to the conclusion that Chen and Yinjishan were thinking about saving funds for military purposes for the precise reason that higher expenditure on the Sichuan frontier was already

---

25. Guo Chengkang, comp., *Qingshi biannian*, vol. 5, p. 159; QSL/QL, *juan* 191:18a–19a; Dai Yi, *Qianlong di*, p. 169.

26. Wang, *Land Taxation*, p. 18.

27. DQHDSL, vol. 9, *juan* 169:15a (p. 7,308); cf. Luo, *Lüying bing*, pp. 368–69. For comprehensive accounts of military supply under the Qing dynasty, see Chen Feng, *Qingdai junfei* and Lai, *Qianlong zhongyao zhanzheng*.

expected. Other possibilities are that the military implications of the Sino-Manchu empire's increasing contact with, and "bureaucratization" policy towards, non-Han peoples elsewhere in southwestern China were creating extra fiscal pressures on Jiangxi, or that more funds were needed to maintain Jiangxi's own armed forces. References in two 1748 reports suggest that transfer to provincial military coffers may have been a standard use for stabilizing-sales proceeds that were deemed redundant.[28] Thus the Jiangxi chief administrators' idea of saving granary restocking funds for military purposes is far from inexplicable, although the empire was not openly at war.

Chen and Yinjishan's main arguments addressed issues that had been more central in the ever-normal granaries debate thus far. Their views are worth examining, as they probably influenced the policy change announced on 7 April. Chen and Yinjishan first claimed that sales of *jiansheng* titles had played a crucial role in the replenishment of Jiangxi's granaries to 70 to 80 percent of (compromise) target level after the crisis depletion of the first half of 1743. Had purchasing alone been used, they said, restocking would have been well-nigh impossible, but the combination of retained tribute grain, Sichuan grain diverted to Jiangxi, and title sales proceeds had enabled the authorities to rebuild stocks substantially.[29] Without mentioning that the amount bought so far approached 285,000 *shi* (about 18 percent of the compromise target, 23 percent of the amount in store by the late spring of 1744, and more than the total raised in contributions), Chen and Yinjishan went on to argue that the uncertainty of harvests would make total reliance on buying highly problematic in future years as well.[30] They then suggested that the policy of selling *jiansheng* titles for grain—which had been discontinued everywhere except in Jiangxi, Fujian, and Sichuan—was worth

---

28. CC, Yue Jun, QL 13/10/28; KC, Tuerbing'a, QL 13/12/18. On Yongzheng and early Qianlong policy towards southwestern aborigines, and its reflection in a Miao uprising in 1740, see Woodside, "The Ch'ien-lung Reign," pp. 252–57.

29. 50,000 *shi* of husked rice from Sichuan, originally destined for Jiangsu, had been retained in Jiangxi with the Liang-Jiang governor-general's concurrence. CC, Saileng'e, QL 9/3/25.

30. For Jiangxi's purchases in 1743, see ibid.; cf. Will and Wong, *Nourish the People*, p. 304, table 9.4. Additional purchases after Chen and Yinjishan wrote their memorial took the total bought to over 320,000 *shi*.

further consideration. The concern about this policy was, they said, that grain contributed to the authorities meant less "among the people" and thus higher market prices. However:

Those who contribute [grain to purchase] *jian*[*sheng* titles] are certainly rich households who put forth their surplus [grain] in order to pursue achievement and renown [through facilitated access to the examinations for the *juren* degree]. Even if there chance to be some families with little grain who must buy grain to pay to the authorities, this is still a matter of trading among the people. In a rice-producing region like Jiangxi, an incalculable amount of husked and unhusked grain is bought and sold among the folk after the autumn harvest. There is no question of grain becoming scarce and prices rising just because there are families making contributions [to buy] *jian*[*sheng* titles] within the locality. [Such activity] is hugely preferable to official buying, with which . . . the rumor spreads both near and far, making the market price rise suddenly, [so that] if the authorities pay less than the full price they harm the folk, while if they make up the sum [from other sources], they themselves suffer embarrassment.

Only after this did Chen and Yinjishan come to the point: to continue title sales in Jiangxi would be the only way to achieve both prompt replenishment of the granaries and freedom from "the burden of buying" (*caimai zhi lei*).

Chen and Yinjishan argued that reliance on grain contributions would be more likely to work if the grain valuation rate could be raised further, from 0.5 to 0.6 tael per *shi*, and if the option of paying for *jiansheng* titles in other provinces or with silver at the Board of Revenue could remain closed to Jiangxi applicants. With these conditions met, the increased flow of contributions would enable "the grain sold off each year in stabilizing sales to be replaced with that year's contributions." Arrangements would have to be made for counties in which nobody contributed, but Chen and Yinjishan did not foresee serious problems here. The proceeds of the annual stabilizing sales would all be sent to the provincial treasury for army pay, except where needed to buy grain (on well-stocked markets only) for granaries that had not received contributions. In conclusion:

In the future, when there are contributions every year, it will be possible to have the granaries constantly full and put a stop to buying. It is not only that the 0.6 tael per *shi* is in fact cheaper than [the price incurred in official] buying, [so that] there will be no loss to state finances.[31] At the same time, inasmuch as [stabilizing] sales in [each] locality will be provided for with local grain, there will not be the bother of porterage costs and transportation; inasmuch as the [stabilizing] sales [that serve] the poor will be provided for through contributions by the rich, there will be the subtle [action] of redistribution [literally, adjusting fullness so as to remedy depletion, *zhuo ying ji xu*]. [It will mean] nourishing society through society itself [literally, using the folk to nourish the folk, *yi min yang min*], while having precautions and [thus] being free of worry [*you bei wu huan*].

The true subtlety, it seems, was that the state would generate new funds for military purposes while cloaking its scheme in rhetoric about community self-reliance through adjustments of the inequality between rich and poor. The adjustments would be trivial and more apparent than real; but if they spared officialdom the burden of the annual grain purchases, they would have met their other main objective. In fact, pursuit of Chen and Yinjishan's preferred approach in Jiangxi was to produce a cumulative total of 100,177 taels of dispensable restocking funds, dispatched to Yunnan for military finance probably in 1746.[32]

Promoting *jiansheng* title sales as an alternative to buying grain was not a sudden inspiration on the part of Chen and his superior. From the inception of Jiangxi's one-year experiment, Chen had tried to use the notion that title sales could obviate the need for buying to gain cooperation from the richer sections of society as well as from the county

---

31. This presumably refers to the opportunity cost of converting *jiansheng* title prices into *shi* of grain at the relatively generous grain valuation rate (by Board standards) of 0.6 tl./*shi*. The claim about relative costs may not have been mendacious. In late November 1743, Peng Jiaping reported the prices being paid for granary replenishment supplies as 0.5–0.7 tl./*shi*, noting the risk that buying would continue in some counties at a price slightly above 0.7 tl./*shi*. CC, Peng Jiaping, QL 8/10/15. The following March, Anning claimed that the price of *husked* rice in the Middle Yangzi had risen from 0.7–0.8 tl./*shi* to 1.5–1.6 tl./*shi* in recent years, and still stood at 1.3–1.4 tl./*shi* despite almost one year of the moratorium (CC, Anning, QL 9/2/10). A mid-spring price of 1.3–1.4 tl./*shi* for husked rice may be compatible with the Jiangxi authorities having paid, on average, a little more than 0.6 tl./*shi* for unhusked in the previous restocking season.

32. CC, Yinjishan and Chen Hongmou, QL 8/12/16, Kaitai, QL 13/9/26 (cat. no. 1145-002); KC, Saileng'e, QL 10/10/25. The print of CC, Kaitai, QL 13/9/26 held by the Institute of Modern History, Academia Sinica has the biro-written date of QL 13/9/28 substituted for the brush-written original. Here, I follow the catalog.

magistrates. In announcing the reduced *jiansheng* title prices to the people of Jiangxi towards the end of 1742, he had suggested that if enough applicants came forward each year, it would be possible to abandon the grain purchase method permanently. That done, "the local poor could all be spared the hardship of high grain prices, while the rich, for their part, would escape the burden of forced sales." Chen had also hinted to local officials that it was in their interests to make the policy work, since every contribution would mean less to purchase. He had reasserted this inducement in a directive issued in the early autumn of 1743. In this latter document, he had told his subordinates that he was planning to ask the emperor, at the close of the experimental year, for permanent authorization for Jiangxi to sell studentships for grain, as a method for routine restocking of the granaries.[33]

On 4 March 1744, the Jiangxi authorities received permission to sell *jiansheng* titles for grain for one more year. At this point, the emperor was only reacting to the negative advice of the grand secretaries, who had opined that the sales should be terminated at the end of the experimental year, before the scheme's very success became a threat to grain prices on Jiangxi markets.[34] It is not clear that Qianlong was yet convinced by the broader argument that Chen and Yinjishan had submitted in late January. He had grown dissatisfied with the moratorium but had as yet no positive policy with which to replace it. Thus when, on 7 March, he repudiated the notion that there was a general moratorium on buying for the granaries, he ordered only that the future rule should be to "buy when buying is appropriate and cease when ceasing is appropriate." This, he indicated, was what provincial chiefs should have been doing all along. Referring, one hopes, to officials other than those whose insistence on the need for buying was noted in chapter 5, he alleged that provincial governors and governors-general had welcomed the moratorium because it spared them onerous responsibilities, with the result that granary reserves had been depleted.[35] Even if there were provincial chiefs who merited his strictures, one

---

33. PYTOCG, *juan* 15:9a–12b (esp. 12a); *juan* 16:18a–20b (esp. 19b–20a). For a more positive assessment of Chen's contributions to title-sales policy than that offered above, see Rowe, *Saving the World*, pp. 255–59.

34. Grd. Secs., n.d. [1744] (cat. no. 1148-039); QSL/QL, *juan* 209:4a–b.

35. QSL/QL, *juan* 209:8a–9a. Hsiao, *Rural China*, p. 161, errs in attributing this edict to Yongzheng and dating it to 1731.

cannot banish the suspicion that, in accusing his regional lieutenants of adopting one legitimate interpretation of the policy laid down the previous May, the emperor betrayed his own frustration and political resourcelessness.[36]

It was the Manchu Anning, provincial administration commissioner of Jiangsu, who rescued him. On 23 March, while about to leave office to mourn his mother, Anning submitted a memorial that offered an explicit justification for a policy of selling *jiansheng* titles as an alternative to buying grain. Anning's contribution to relieving Qianlong's scruples was that he addressed the conundrum that a successful title-sales program would, by definition, deplete grain markets just as much as did official buying. What needed to be argued was that the true objection to the purchase system was not the sheer quantity of grain that it took off the market, but rather the specific features of official buying that, allegedly, made it inflationary where commercial purchasing was not. The germ of such an argument was present in the Chen Hongmou and Yinjishan memorial of 30 January, but it was not well developed. Anning's role was to take the ideas submitted for Jiangxi by Chen and Yinjishan and re-present them in a more abstract, systematic form, thereby offering a rationale for a new policy that would apply to all of China. Internal evidence suggests that he had the text of the Jiangxi memorial.[37]

---

36. Had the moratorium seriously eroded granary reserves? The total stated at the end of the *Veritable Records* entries for 1743 is identical with that for 1742, while the available provincial totals do not show a consistent pattern. As these figures may reflect holdings at the beginning of the annual restocking season, they cannot settle the matter. However, the 1744 figures do not seem consistent with severe granary depletion by the end of 1743, unless one assumes extraordinary success in selling *jiansheng* titles over the summer of 1744. The territorial bureaucracy may be tentatively exonerated of gross negligence. Will and Wong, *Nourish the People*, appendix, table A.1, p. 528.

37. R. Bin Wong writes that "Criticisms against purchases were not necessarily well founded. If the grain mobilized through contributions or tribute represented grain that would otherwise have been on the market or would itself need to be replaced by market purchases, then the net effect on prices of granary purchases and nonpurchase mechanisms would be the same" (Will and Wong, *Nourish the People*, p. 52 n. 26). This underestimates the sophistication of officials like Anning. Wong's objection takes us to Anning's starting point.

Anning first reiterated the argument of Sun Hao and others that buying must be halted for a period of years if the potential benefit were to be realized. He also gave it a new twist. Enquiries of natives of the Middle Yangzi provinces had elicited a reason for the fact that, despite the moratorium, Yangzi Valley grain prices had so far only stabilized, rather than showing clear signs of reverting to the lower levels of past years. This reason was that grain-controllers, accustomed to the recent high prices, were withholding stocks from the market in the hope that the lucrative opportunities of pre-moratorium days would shortly be restored. Thus, "since the people have not yet forgotten the profits of selling dear [to official buyers and/or in a market influenced by official buying], it would, in the nature of the case, be unwise to propose [resumption of] official buying hastily." Indeed, it would be risky to resume such buying even after a couple of years in which grain prices fell. The suspension would have to be maintained for several years to be effective. Given that intraprovincial buying had been taking place in Yangzi Valley provinces despite the moratorium, it would be reasonable to interpret Anning's remarks as referring to interprovincial buying. The fact remains, however, that he wrote simply of "buying," thus subtly conditioning Qianlong to be receptive to the Jiangxi authorities' extreme idea of halting even local purchases.

Anning wrote nothing to suggest that he considered depletion of the granaries to be acceptable. Rather, he urged that the policy of selling *jiansheng* titles for grain be revisited, because an alternative to purchase must be found. Realizing the need to argue that a successful title-sales program would not be inflationary, he devoted many lines to showing that it was the process of official buying that raised prices, not simply the amounts bought. His exposition of the supposed inflationary aspects of the buying process was introduced in chapter 4 above, in juxtaposition with similar statements by other officials. Anning was saying nothing radically new, although he stressed different factors from some of his contemporaries and made the argument in a new context. He concluded this part of his discussion by claiming that merchants who normally served "consumer" provinces were unwilling to buy stocks on markets in which over-publicized official buying had artificially raised prices. "Therefore do I opine," he wrote, "that the high price of rice arises from the pomp and circumstance [*shengshi*, that is, noise and publicity] associated with official buying. It is not to be attributed only to the excessive quantities acquired."

Anning also needed a more rigorous and less province-specific argument than that of Chen and Yinjishan for accepting the title sales policy as noninflationary. Here he borrowed the structure of the opening of the Chen-Yinjishan argument and elaborated it, while omitting all explicit reference to conditions in a major rice-producing province. In the following translation, the parts that seem to be directly paraphrased from Chen and Yinjishan are in italics. With the making of grain contributions to buy studentships, Anning wrote:

In most cases it is a question of families with resources putting forth what they have surplus so as to contrive achievement and renown. This means there is no guarantee that if they did not deliver it to the authorities they would not hoard it in their homes, awaiting a high price. *Even if there are some few [applicants] who buy grain to deliver to the granaries,* they will still be sure to do their calculations carefully. They will certainly not be prepared to pay high prices for an empty name. Market prices will certainly not rise because of [such buying].

Anning argued, in short, that grain paid to the authorities directly from landlord granaries might otherwise have reached the market only after a period of antisocial hoarding. To the limited extent that grain already on the market might be withdrawn for buying *jiansheng* titles, there was no need for worry lest the consequence be shortage. High prices would deter prospective applicants from buying grain on ill-stocked markets.

Before concluding with the comparison of official and commercial buying quoted above in chapter 4, Anning predictably urged that the price in grain per title be reduced for the time being, and that the option of buying titles for silver at the Board of Revenue be suspended. The emperor referred his memorial to the grand secretaries for secret deliberation.[38] This may be why it took him as much as a fortnight to reveal his conversion to Anning's way of thinking. On 7 April, however, came the edict restoring the policy of selling *jiansheng* titles for grain throughout the nation, halting the sale of titles for silver at the Board, ordering that title prices as expressed in grain be lowered (at least temporarily), and holding out the possibility that if enough grain were thereby collected, the purchase system could be suspended indefinitely. The edict's rhetoric is clearly indebted both to Anning's

---

38. CC, Anning, QL 9/2/10.

memorial and to the earlier document by Chen and Yinjishan. It even shows some signs of plagiarism.[39]

The reliability of *jiansheng* title sales for routine granary restocking had not been empirically demonstrated when Qianlong proclaimed the change of policy. It may not be accidental that, in their eagerness to establish the noninflationary character of this approach, its advocates neglected to address its likely effectiveness (or lack thereof) in refilling the granaries. It was only in the following year that one central government official, in a most thoughtful memorial, seriously discussed the problem of effective demand for *jiansheng* titles, and even he did not address the prospects of sustaining that demand in the long term.[40] The policy was to be declared a failure and abandoned before the end of 1745 (although, by then, it showed signs of relative success). That so dubious a policy was so heedlessly embraced seems to bespeak a diminution of commitment to maintaining granary reserves even at basic target level. Such a lessening of commitment may have been compounded out of several factors: long-standing bureaucratic resentment of the burden of the granary system, and of the jeopardy in which it placed even conscientious magistrates; a new interest in examining the resources devoted to this system in a broader fiscal context; perhaps a growing sense of insecurity about the system's value, as the arguments of its opponents gained more credence; and frustration, on Qianlong's part, with the failure of his grand initiative of 1738, aggravated by a new impatience with a system whose *raison d'être* was only that the common people seemed somehow unable to save grain for themselves.

---

39. The edict echoed, recycled, and at one point amended some of Anning's wording. Its central exposition, which manifests a clear affinity with both memorials, reads: "We find upon consideration that if one wishes to keep purchasing suspended without allowing granary reserves to fall short [of their quotas], the only thing to do is reinstate the rule permitting in-kind contributions in the provinces. For dearness in the price of grain is attributable to official buying, and not to contributions [made by applicants for] *jian[sheng]* status]. With official purchasing, the merchant folk get wind of what is going forward and increase [their price], or clerks and petty functionaries wreak evil and engage in mischief, so that the folk are often burdened. In the case of contributions, each [applicant] puts forth his surplus to deliver it to the authorities, which basically does not interfere with market prices." QSL/QL, *juan* 211:17a–b.

40. This memorial, by Qin Huitian, is summarized below.

The last of these suggestions is supported by another, at first sight unrelated edict, issued about a month after that of 7 April. This homiletic, rhetorical pronouncement urged territorial officials to hold the people more responsible for their own subsistence. Its point of departure was a warning that imperial willingness to see a portion of the tribute grain retained for granary restocking (as in 1742 and 1743) was not to be taken for granted. Rather, there must be a campaign against the mentality, imputed to the populace, of assuming that state relief would always be available, and that there was therefore no need to attend to one's own family subsistence. The edict stopped well short of suggesting that the state would cease to intervene in serious subsistence crises. Its general drift, however, was that if only the people were properly busy with productive labor, they would be able to keep adequate reserves for ordinary contingencies; yet as things stood, the excessive readiness of territorial officials to provide famine relief was trapping the folk into "basking in the willingness of those above to make good what they lack and save and succor them, so that they depend upon it permanently as their strategy for the support of life." People so deluded were bound eventually to suffer cruel disappointment. It was surely not coincidental that Qianlong preached popular self-reliance while inaugurating an experiment that spelled less effort for officials, a retreat from planning, and a diminished guarantee that the state would have enough grain locally available to feed the hungry in emergencies.[41]

By early August 1745, Anning was writing as if the suspension of official buying had already been in force again for quite some time.[42] There is, however, considerable evidence to suggest that, after the edict of April 1744, the central government moved slowly towards requiring local officials to rely entirely on selling *jiansheng* titles and, therefore, to desist from buying grain. In early August 1744, the Board of Revenue, commenting on proposals from the Zhili governor-general, recommended that, beginning in 1745, Zhili officials should rely on *jiansheng* titles sales to replace grain that they had not yet been able to replace

---

41. *Shangyu dang*, QL 9/3/23; QSL/QL *juan* 213:10a–12b. For further discussion and a translation of this edict, see Dunstan, *Conflicting Counsels*, pp. 69–72, 89–92.

42. Anning, QL 10/7/6 transc. Lü Xiaoxian, comp., "Qianlong sannian," part 2, pp. 20–21.

through purchase. A similar guideline had probably been laid down for Guangdong in May. In October 1744, just before the late rice harvest, Peng Jiaping submitted a plan to combine the two approaches in restocking Jiangxi's granaries. He said that Jiangxi had the funds to buy 400,000 to 500,000 *shi* out of the total shortfall; this would leave less than a third to be made good through title sales. The harvest prospects being favorable, he seemed reasonably confident that the target could be met, perhaps with some redistribution of the contributions. It was Chen Hongmou, not Peng, who had pushed the idea that title sales could replace the annual buying process; Chen had now been transferred to Shaanxi, and Peng probably had reservations about his erstwhile chief's opinion.[43] Nonetheless, if any province was going to rush to give up buying, then (Fujian apart) it would surely have been Jiangxi. If, in the autumn of 1744, Jiangxi still planned to buy most of its acquisition target, it is unlikely that the territorial bureaucracy was yet under pressure to rely entirely on *jiansheng* title sales.[44]

The Fujian case was somewhat different, although it too tends to confirm that pressure to refrain from buying had not yet begun. By early December 1744, the Fujian governor, Zhou Xuejian, had hatched a scheme by which Fujian would temporarily suspend buying so as to clear the way for contributions. This was an ingenious, perhaps disingenuous, conception; my present point is that Zhou assumed that he must ask imperial permission for it. This would have been superfluous had cessation of buying been the promulgated policy.

Zhou's memorial—combined with the subsequent success of Fujian's title sales program—may have influenced developments in 1745 by encouraging the central government to hope that funds could be saved through reliance upon contributions to restock the granaries. He also offered a new rationale for ending purchases: they inhibited the growth of *jiansheng* title sales. Annual grain output being limited, he argued, if

---

43. Compare CC, Peng Jiaping, QL 8/10/15 with CC, Chen Hongmou, QL 8/10/22.

44. QSL/QL, *juan* 219:9a–b and 214:9b; CC, Peng Jiaping, QL 9/9/4. Peng hinted that this year official buying would benefit the Jiangxi grain market, because good harvests in neighboring provinces were likely to reduce demand for Jiangxi grain. If Peng had felt under pressure to refrain from buying, he would presumably have built an argument around the risk of glut, instead of merely mentioning it in passing.

title sales and official purchasing took place at the same time, "as the amount collecting in the official granaries doubles, that circulating among the folk will naturally diminish." But would stocks indeed double? Grain for sale to the authorities and grain used to purchase titles both emanated from "the spare grain of the wealthy." If official buying and a title sales drive were pursued simultaneously, the wealthy would "either crave the high prices [paid by official buyers], in which case contributors will naturally be few, or else be eager for achievement and renown, in which case no grain will be made available for purchase." It followed that it was necessary to choose between buying grain and selling studentships for grain. Zhou favored the latter option.

Zhou proposed that the authorities of Fujian's inland prefectures stop buying to replace the backlog of used grain, thereby encouraging "*shengyuan* and 'men of promise' [to] contribute in unbroken stream." If, by the following spring, the cumulative amount contributed in any given jurisdiction sufficed to meet its target, the unexpended proceeds of past stabilizing sales would be delivered to the provincial treasury for eventual reallocation. Otherwise, determined efforts should be made to meet the target either through purchase or by continued title sales. The emperor found these proposals "very satisfactory," and Fujian's title sales program was in fact markedly successful over the next several months.[45] Thus Zhou had offered the emperor an extra argument for suspending the purchase method, helped to create a "Fujian model" of effectiveness in using the alternative approach, and set a further precedent for saving granary-restocking funds for other purposes. Other provinces would no doubt soon be urged to follow suit.

---

45. CC, Zhou Xuejian, QL 9/10/29. Fujian's reported cumulative contributions total had risen from 383,420 *shi* in the spring of 1743 to 541,560 *shi* in May 1744, 676,400 *shi* by early November 1744, 775,696 *shi* by the end of January 1745, and 1,024,196 *shi* by the end of July 1745 (see also CC, Nasutu and Zhou Xuejian, QL 9/4/24, and JS, Zhou Xuejian, QL 10/7/16). Thus Fujian had gathered nearly 100,000 *shi* in the last quarter of lunar 1744, and 248,500 *shi* during the first two quarters of lunar 1745. Compared with progress prior to May 1744 (n. 20 above), the increased rate of contributions was impressive.

The Ever-Normal System on the Brink

It was not until the late summer of 1745 that the central government began to force the pace, although some had the impression that a general, if incomplete, suspension of buying for the granaries was already the policy before that.[46] By mid-August, however, the Board of Revenue had sent a firm memorandum to all provinces ordering that buying be not carried out this harvest season. This directive is quoted or excerpted in three dissenting memorials, two by provincial governors, and one by the censorial official Wan Nianmao. It apparently did not invoke the notion that suspending purchases might be required for success in selling *jiansheng* titles; rather, its emphasis seems unabashedly fiscal. After noting the effect of regional price difficulties in delaying annual restocking through the purchase method, the memorandum stated baldly that the revival of the title sales program provided amply for the gradual refilling of the granaries, so that "even if there should be an emergency, there will truly be enough [grain] to meet requirements." There was, therefore, no need for provinces to spend the proceeds of past stabilizing sales on buying grain. All provincial administrations must, without fail, send the Board an itemized statement of the unexpended purchase funds under their jurisdiction, so that the Board might plan how best to use these monies. As if to warn that comment was not desired, the Board concluded with the peremptory admonition that, this being a policy departure that had been studied thoroughly and cleared with the emperor, there must be no delay in complying.[47]

Requests to be allowed to buy grain in the usual way were submitted by at least five provinces from approximately mid-September onwards, while a sixth (Guangdong) asked for exemption for those places in which *jiansheng* titles were impossible to sell. Not all of these submissions mention the Board memorandum (and that from Gansu may have been written in ignorance of it); it would, therefore, be rash to repre-

---

46. Besides Anning's memorial cited in n. 42, see Li Qingfang, QL 10/5/23 (d.r.), transc. Lü Xiaoxian, comp., "Qianlong sannian," part 2, pp. 19–20.

47. CC, Chen Dashou, QL 10/8/16, and Yan Sisheng, QL 10/9/8; HCJSWB, *juan* 40:3b–4a. Chen noted that he had received the memorandum (in Jiangsu) on 18 August.

sent the whole set of memorials as provincial protest against crass fiscality. After all, the order to refrain from buying may have met the dearest secret wishes of a number of provincial chiefs; those who sought exemption from it were only showing greater conscientiousness than their counterparts elsewhere. Their requests reflect an understandable skepticism as to the reliability of title sales as the sole technique for granary replenishment.

While three of the five provinces were in northern China, the other two were Jiangsu and Hubei: two of those Yangzi Valley jurisdictions concern about the level of whose grain prices had ostensibly inspired the whole movement to suspend official buying. Chen Dashou (Jiangsu) and Yan Sisheng (Hubei) wrote explicitly to request exemption from the Board's directive; both mentioned the uncertain prospects for title sales, the relief needs of certain jurisdictions that had suffered natural disasters, and the favorable harvest conditions elsewhere in their provinces.[48] Yan, whose reproachful memorial was the more forthright in spelling out the implications of the Board's new orders, informed the emperor that he was ordering his subordinates to do their buying promptly, but that he would report any funds left over when the buying ended within the deadline laid down by the Board.[49]

It was left to the censor Wan Nianmao to criticize the idea of diverting granary restocking funds to other purposes, which he did in a memorial that showed that he was under no illusions. After politely admitting that he did not fully understand what the Board officials had in mind, he expressed the suspicion that they meant to allocate the unexpended purchase funds to military uses. As if to remind us how attractive these funds would have looked, he remarked that Jiangsu, Shandong, and Gansu currently held half of their (presumably basic) storage targets in the form of silver, while the proportion that was held in silver nationwide exceeded the 30 percent (perhaps some 4.2 million

---

48. Chen claimed that the Jiangsu jurisdictions that had had most success in selling *jiansheng* titles were Huai'an, Xuzhou, and Haizhou, all in the province's relatively poor north. It was these very jurisdictions that had now suffered floods, leading to dimmer prospects for title sales in the months ahead.

49. CC, Chen Dashou, QL 10/8/16 (Jiangsu), Huang Tinggui, QL 10/8/20 (Gansu), Yan Sisheng, QL 10/9/8 (Hubei), Qing Fu and Chen Hongmou, QL 10/9/27 (Shaanxi); QSL/QL, *juan* 247:14a (Jiangsu), 18b–19a (Shandong); *juan* 249:32b–33a (Guangdong).

taels) theoretically to be expected at the beginning of the annual buying season. Not only this, Wan claimed, but such was the unpopularity of grain storage among local magistrates that, on learning of the Board's orders, they would sell all the grain they had in store, adding the proceeds to the sums to be reported for reallocation. They would thus dispose forever of the obligation to buy grain. Wan gave short shrift to the idea that relying upon *jiansheng* title sales was a realistic option. He claimed (with questionable arithmetic and unclarified assumptions) that even if, nationwide, the provinces were annually able to match the sales record of the Board, it would still take more than a decade to restore granary stocks to basic target level. Fujian's success was exceptional; the progress being made by other provinces, while uneven, was much slower. It would not offset the annual 30 percent sales, which could empty the granaries completely after three more years (even if local magistrates did not deliberately speed the process). If the proceeds of the sales were all transferred to military uses, then, with neither grain nor unexpended purchase funds, the granary system would be defunct.

Wan devoted a few lines to the importance of the ever-normal granaries. He hinted astutely—and with extreme and prudent delicacy—at the potential for social disorder if throngs of the disaster-stricken went unfed. He then linked the idea of menacing mobs with that of interruptions to the normal flow of grain onto the market. Only if doles of grain from the ever-normal granaries kept the local situation quiet would the wealthy have the confidence to sell their grain; otherwise, "as they perceive the seething [mass of] poor people assembling like ants, they will fear that trouble may break out and not dare sell [their surplus] openly." For Wan, in other words, the granaries assisted market processes when they were under strain, rather than hindering their normal operation as the critics had alleged. Indeed, he turned the critics' central allegation upside-down. It was precisely because of the steeply rising food prices that granary reserves were crucial, and the real worry should be that they were not more substantial.[50]

---

50. HCJSWB, *juan* 40:3b–4b. I have rearranged the order of Wan's points to make the exposition smoother, as well as clarifying implications that he left unstated.

There was no doubt hyperbole in Wan's allegation that county magistrates would seize the chance that the Board memorandum offered them to deal the ever-normal system mortal blows. What, however, of his suspicions regarding the Board of Revenue? To put these suspicions into context, it is necessary to consider how the revival of the title sales program in April 1744 would have affected the central government fiscal interests represented by the Board. The word "revival" here is imprecise: the sale of *jiansheng* titles had never been suspended. What had been suspended in May 1743 was the attempt to increase granary reserves by selling the titles for grain. The abandonment of this attempt had meant that, apart from the continuing experiments in Jiangxi, Fujian, and Sichuan, there was nothing to divert title sales revenue from flowing, in the form of silver, to the coffers of the Board. Such a development can hardly have been unwelcome from a Board perspective.

Board reservations about the fiscal implications of selling *jiansheng* titles for grain had been expressed in 1741. During the first phase of the attempt to double granary reserves through title sales, payment in grain had been compulsory in principle, with the normal practice of accepting silver at the Board suspended for most applicants. In consequence, according to the 1741 report by Haiwang, the Board's Manchu president, an annual revenue of up to 1.3 million taels had shrunk by about 70 percent. In response to Haiwang's concerns, the option of paying in silver at the Board was restored in the spring of 1741.[51] This had been enough, in the eyes of some contemporaries, to end all prospects of success in raising large amounts of grain by selling *jiansheng* titles. When the attempt to do so was abandoned two years later, the Board had won the first round of the competition for direct control of *jiansheng* title revenues.

That the court removed the option of paying in silver at the Board when it revived the policy of selling *jiansheng* titles for grain in April 1744 shows that it was not incapable of learning from experience. However, from the Board's perspective, this prudent adjustment meant a loss of income. It was, indeed, because the 1744 initiative was fine-tuned for success that it challenged Board interests more strongly

51. Haiwang, QL 6/2/8, and edict of same day, transc. Lü Xiaoxian, comp., "Qianlong sannian," part 1, pp. 14–15 and QSL/QL, *juan* 136:8b–10a.

than its predecessor. Is it too cynical to suggest that tempting the provincial governors to set ambitious contribution targets after April 1744
was a deliberate Board ploy, aimed at establishing yardsticks against
which the promising new program could eventually be deemed a failure? After all, a source that could yield almost as much silver as a
third-class province's land tax had been taken from the Board and
parcelled out among the territorial bureaucracy—in an effort to deposit
unknown quantities of perishable grain in more than a thousand
county granaries.[52] The notion, implicit in the edict of April 1744, that
a successful title sales program would make granary restocking funds
redundant offered the Board a chance of compensation for the loss of
revenue; in August 1745, before the annual buying season started, the
Board moved to enforce its claim. Short-term as the compensation was
(a finite windfall would replace a perennial fount of silver), the chance
was not to be let slip.

Was compensation really such an urgent matter for the Board? In
principle, the silver gained from *jiansheng* title sales was earmarked for
famine relief.[53] Theoretically, this was a matter literally of life or death;
yet, from a treasury perspective, funds that are committed prior to
collection are generally less desirable than funds that can be allocated
flexibly. What made Wan Nianmao suspect that the Board planned to
divert the unexpended granary restocking funds to military uses was its

---

52. According to Haiwang, pre-1738 annual revenue from *jiansheng* title sales at
the Board had been 1.2–1.3 million tls., while Wan Nianmao, in 1745, cited 1.4–1.5
million at most (perhaps for post-1741). Haiwang, QL 6/2/8, transc. ibid.; HCJSWB,
juan 40:4a. 1753 provincial land-tax revenues (silver component only) fell within the
following bands: 3.5–4.5 million tls. (four provinces); 2.0–3.5 million (five provinces);
1.0–2.0 million (four provinces); and under 1.0 million (six provinces). In a good
year, *jiansheng* title sales yielded only somewhat less silver than the land tax of
Hubei (1.4 million tls.), Hunan (1.5 million), or Fujian (1.5 million). Wang, *Land
Taxation*, p. 72, table 4.2; p. 70, table 4.1, col. 5.

53. While new to the throne, Qianlong had retained a *jiansheng* title sales program while repudiating the sale of other ranks and titles. On the Nine Ministries
Assembly's advice, the proceeds were earmarked for famine relief, a principle still
cited in the early 1740s. It was presumably intended to help justify an expedient that
might otherwise have seemed to marr the sagely governance of the new era.
QSL/QL, *juan* 11:14a–15a (edict of QL 1/1/21); edict of QL 3/1/17, and Haiwang, QL
6/2/8, transc. Lü Xiaoxian, comp., "Qianlong sannian," part 1, pp. 5, 14–15; Xu
Daling, *Qingdai juanna zhidu*, pp. 39–40; Guo Chengkang, comp., *Qingshi biannian*, vol. 5, p. 4.

requirement that provincial governors forward their statements of these funds in time for the preparation of the annual "winter allocations" (*dongbo*) budget.[54] This not only implies that the restocking funds were to be drawn into the centralized revenue allocation process, but also makes it likely that they would be spent on the armed forces.[55] The fact that they could be represented as savings arguably justified presuming flexibility in their proper uses; from this point of view, they were superior to title sales revenue. The amount should also have been considerably larger than one year's income from title sales; in the short term, the Board was overcompensating itself. But why incur the odium of seizing public welfare funds for general budgetary purposes without more urgent cause than departmental pique at a reallocation of famine relief resources?

By August 1745, the Qing state had mobilized 15,000 men for a military operation to the west of Sichuan. While it may have been too soon for anyone in Beijing to realize that the financial cost would be much greater than originally thought, the Board now had a new potential source of worry.[56] In early July, meanwhile, the emperor, citing the existence of a surplus in the national exchequer, had announced a universal remission of the land tax due in 1746. The subsequent decision, on 23 July, to spread this munificent gesture over three years will have gone some way to ease the budgetary concerns that must have arisen at the Board. The fact remained, however, that in 1746 there was

---

54. HCJSWB, *juan* 40:3b–4a; cf. CC, Chen Dashou, QL 10/8/16.

55. The "year's-end major allocations" (*nianzhong dabo*) seem to have been based largely on the "registers of army supply estimates for the winter allocations" (*dongbo guxiang ce*: provincial estimates of military costs for the following year plus statements of available resources) as opposed to the more general financial statements required for the supplementary allocation processes in spring and autumn. Iwai, "Shindai kokka zaisei," pp. 141–42; Luo, *Lüying bing*, pp. 368–69.

56. Qianlong accepted the need for military action during February and March 1745, but the campaign was not formally launched until late May or begun in earnest before August. In mid-July, the emperor noted that the tax funds requested for the operation totalled "as much as" 500,000 taels. By the spring of 1746, the cost was at least twice that sum, the governor-general was requesting yet more funds, and victory remained elusive. Guo Chengkang, comp., *Qingshi biannian*, vol. 5, pp. 196–97, 200–1, 205, 208; Dai Yi, *Qianlong di*, pp. 169–71 (on p. 169, "1735" is a misprint); QSL/QL, *juan* 233:18b–19a, *juan* 235:18b–20a, *juan* 239:33a–b, *juan* 242:27a–28a, *juan* 245:28a–29a, *juan* 260:18a–b.

to be no land-tax revenue from Jiangsu (which had the second-highest basic annual quota for the silver component of the land tax), from the seven frontier (or semi-frontier) provinces of Shaanxi, Gansu, Sichuan, Yunnan, Guizhou, Fengtian, and Fujian, from Hunan (which was expected to help subsidize the military establishments of Sichuan, Yunnan, and Guizhou), or from Zhili (one of two reserve-tier provinces for subsidizing Shaanxi and Gansu).[57] In such circumstances, a prudent treasury department had to take precautions.

The principle that buying was a necessary technique for granary replenishment survived the August memorandum. Qianlong responded to five of the six provincial appeals for permission to buy with either some form of noncommittal "noted" (arguably, tacit consent) or explicit approval. He assured one petitioning governor-general that he need not see himself as fettered by the Board's ideas.[58] It is reasonable to hypothesize that the façade of central-government unity hid a tussle between Qianlong, who wanted his munificent intent upheld, and the Board's directors, whose habitually exacting sense of fiscal responsibility drove them to subvert it. The Board eventually won a victory that incidentally clinched the ever-normal granaries' salvation, although not all the granary restocking funds escaped reallocation. As late as 10 January 1746, the Board identified the "grain[-purchase] funds [released by] halting purchasing" (*ting mai gujia*) of provinces that were embarking on their tax-remission year as one source of stop-gap funds for those provinces' armed forces. Grain-purchase funds from heartland provinces sent to the troops of Yunnan and Guizhou respectively included at least the 100,177 taels of savings generated by Jiangxi's title sales program and 34,831 taels of Zhejiang stabilizing-sales proceeds. Guizhou was to use about 63,042 taels of local granary-restocking funds for paying its own troops, while the first

57. QSL/QL, *juan* 242:9a–10b, 243:13b–14a; Wang, *Land Taxation*, p. 70, table 4.1, col. 3; DQHDSL, vol. 9, *juan* 169:15a (p. 7,308). On reserve levels in the Board of Revenue's treasury, see Kishimoto, *Shindai Chūgoku no bukka*, p. 491, fig. 13.1; Lü Jian, comp., "Kang Yong Qian Hubu," pp. 20–21. Although, almost throughout the 1740s, central government reserves somewhat exceeded one year's projected basic income from the land tax (silver component only), this level was by no means high by eighteenth-century standards.

58. See rescripts to CC, Chen Dashou, QL 10/8/16, Huang Tinggui, QL 10/8/20, Qing Fu and Chen Hongmou, QL 10/9/27; also QSL/QL, *juan* 247:19a; *juan* 249:32b–33a. The Hubei governor's memorial was referred to the Board. CC, Yan Sisheng, QL 10/9/8.

call on Fujian's ever-normal savings (over 500,000 taels) was presumably the Fujian military.[59]

In early November, when sales of *jiansheng* titles were probably going fairly well, the emperor ostensibly accepted the grand secretaries' professed opinion that the campaign to sell titles for grain was "half a matter of an empty name devoid of substance." He thereupon restored the option of paying for the titles in silver at the Board. Although he did not simultaneously abolish the option of paying in grain at county granaries, there would no longer have been much credibility in claims that the granaries could be sufficiently restocked through *jiansheng* title sales.[60] Purchase would again have to be accepted as the norm. It is likely that, by this time, growing realization of the implications of the universal tax remission, coupled with new concern about the cost of military operations west of Sichuan, had weakened Qianlong's resistance to Board preferences.[61] He was now willing to let the Board resume control of *jiansheng* titles as a supplementary revenue source.

The Rebirth of Controversy

The fiscal situation in the autumn of 1745 probably provides an adequate explanation of an apparently perverse decision on the emperor's part. It is not normal to abandon policy experiments at the precise time when, as discussed in the next section, some measure of success is blessing them at last. Before examining the available data on the level of grain holdings in the second half of 1745, however, let us explore the

---

59. KC, Saileng'e, QL 10/10/25, Maertai and Zhou Xuejian, QL 10/12/7, Zhou Xuejian, QL 10/12/7; Bd. Rev. communication transc. NGDKDA, Zhang Guangsi, QL 11/5/26 (doc. no. 074841). Of the other provinces whose tax remission year was 1746, Sichuan and Yunnan identified some ever-normal sales proceeds as available to substitute for normal revenue (in Yunnan's case, 64,061.8 taels from the sale of "extra-target" grain). KC, Qing Fu and Jishan, QL 10/11/22, Zhang Yunsui, QL 10/11/17.

60. QSL/QL, *juan* 250:17a–b (edict of QL 10/10/10, also transc. Lü Xiaoxian, comp., "Qianlong sannian," part 2, p. 24).

61. In the autumn of 1745, Qianlong rejected an opportunity of ending the hostilities in the mistaken hope of a lasting military solution to the border problem. By late October, the court was thinking seriously about the revenue shortfalls that the universal tax remission would create. Dai Yi, *Qianlong di*, p. 170; QSL/QL, *juan* 249:18a–b.

minor spate of critical memorials that was unleashed by this experiment, from its inception in April 1744 until August 1745. These memorials, although less directly influential than some others that I have discussed, formed part of the environment in which the emperor made decisions. If it is not unfair to see him as more interested in grand gestures than in the minutiae of government, it is likely that the continuing controversy helped erode his zeal for positive initiatives.[62] He had enough to do without wasting mental energy on a policy that provoked endless debate without spectacularly enhancing the state's antifamine institutions, and whose potential fiscal benefits could not be realized without seeming contradiction of his oft-professed devotion to the people's welfare.

Wan Nianmao was not alone in his concern about the level of commitment to maintaining actual reserves of grain within the ever-normal system. Yaertu, ex-governor of Henan and a Mongol bannerman, expressed dismay at the trend of imperial policy in late May 1744, while acting vice-president of the Board of Military Affairs. Yaertu, as we saw in chapter 4, was thoroughly traditionalist in his approach to ever-normal policy. He asserted the necessity of the granary system, tracing it to the people's lack of thrift, which he took as a simple fact that policy must recognize. Consistent with Wan's dark prediction, Yaertu claimed that the moratorium on buying grain in 1743 had been "profoundly in conformance with the wishes of the county-level magistrates." The more recent (March 1744) command to buy or not according to the circumstances had only given magistrates a pretext for foot-dragging. Such local officials were not above submitting false reports as to their actual grain holdings. In fact, the granaries were "already mostly empty," and as grain continued to be used in relief operations and stabilizing sales, there would soon be none left.

What made Yaertu's jeremiad distinctive was his suggestion that a certain blindness to the objective requirements for the people's long-term welfare underlay all that the central government did out of professed concern about the impact of state grain buying. He voiced skepticism about the notions that official buying caused high prices, that its prolonged cessation would naturally bring prices down, and that the granaries would be spontaneously refilled now that the price in grain per *jiansheng* title had been lowered. In his view, the making of these claims reflected failure to realize that in government, long-term considerations must take precedence over avoiding short-term inconvenience for the people:

It is possible to rejoice with the petty folk over the fulfillment [of one's plans], but hard to enlist their cooperation in thinking out the early stages. If one forgets the trials ahead [in one's preoccupation with] avoiding temporary resentment, making preparations [only when] the trouble has arrived and guarding against disaster [only when] it has arisen, it is to be feared that the unhappy consequences will not be slight. If one buys [grain for the granaries] in a year of plenty, with the possible result that prices rise, although the people will be inconvenienced, at least their stomachs will not be [completely] empty.

Failure to keep the granaries well-stocked, by contrast, would lead to deaths in ditches in a famine year. The present rise in grain prices was due entirely to population increase, and the total failure of prices to fall despite a year of moratorium showed that suspending official purchases was ineffective.[63] As for title sales, the reduction in the price per title was not necessarily enough to attract buyers. The policy was too slow-acting.[64]

Yaertu was fighting back against the critics of the ever-normal system. What he may not have realized was that new voices could argue positions different from his while still laying claim to concern for disaster victims. This was the case with certain advocates of letting county magistrates accept silver in return for *jiansheng* titles. This idea, ad-

---

63. Does regional variation explain the discrepancy with Anning's perception, two months earlier, of a slight improvement in grain prices (CC, Anning, QL 9/2/10)? Wang Yeh-chien, "Secular Trends of Rice Prices," table 1.1, p. 42, shows the annual rice price at Suzhou, where Anning was based, falling from a high of 1.60 tl./*shi* in 1743 through 1.55 tl./*shi* in 1744 to 1.42 in 1745. While supply conditions in Zhili were not the sole determinant of grain prices in Beijing (Yaertu's base), it is worth noting that Zhili wheat prices climbed steadily throughout most of the 1740s, while a 1744–45 fall in millet and sorghum prices may not have been visible by May 1744. L. M. Li, "Grain Prices in Zhili," fig. 2.3, p. 79.

64. CC, Yaertu, QL 9/4/12. Yaertu proposed that jurisdictions that had good harvests in a given year buy extra grain for less fortunate units within the same province. It may be a measure of the depletion he perceived that he suggested that each province be required to have at least 60 percent of its target actually in store when it submitted its year-end report.

mittedly, was not quite new: it had been propounded by the investigating censor Xue Cheng in June 1743, in the wake of the moratorium announcement. Xue's worry was that making payment in Beijing compulsory for distant purchasers of *jiansheng* titles would expose them to unconscionable profiteering by the middlemen to whom they would entrust their silver. Rather than waste a valuable source of relief funds on a scheme crippled by this disincentive, it would be better to let local magistrates acquire silver to be saved for restocking the granaries when prices fell, or distributed to famine victims under the *yin gu jian zhen* formula.[65] When the Shandong provincial administration commissioner Qiao Xueyin proposed a similar plan on 5 July 1744, he made it seem common sense, at least for his own jurisdiction.

Qiao pointed out that Shandong had collected a cumulative total of only 13,900 or so *shi* of grain through title sales since 1738. He attributed this dismal record partly to repeated floods and droughts, which affected grain prices even beyond the smitten areas, and partly to the unfavorable transport conditions in this northern province. Even with Shandong's concessionary 20 percent reduction in the price in grain per title, continuing rises in the price of grain left applicants being charged grain worth 170 to 180 taels for a title whose fixed silver price was 108 taels.[66] Rather than persisting with a hopeless policy, it would be more sensible to let applicants pay in silver, while leaving payment in grain as an option. Granted the normal price (108 taels per title) and a mere 9-tael surcharge for various fees, the greater convenience of making the transaction locally (rather than in Beijing) would generate enthusiasm for purchase. Large quantities of silver would thus become available in local coffers, either for buying grain to restock the granaries, or for direct distribution under the *yin gu jian zhen* approach (of which Qiao wrote appreciatively). This experiment, he suggested, should be continued for a year. In the event, Shandong was authorized to proceed

---

65. JS, Xue Cheng, QL 8/5/3. Xue thought that title-purchase funds went through at least two intermediaries: the frequent travellers who accepted transport commissions from multiple applicants, and the "silver firms" (*yinhao*) that made the transaction at the Board. Thus was the official price of 108 tls. inflated into an actual cost of 130–170 tls.

66. For a summary of the provincial title-price reductions set by the Board of Revenue after the edict of 7 April 1744, see JS, Grd. Secs. and Bd. Rev., QL 10/6/11. The standard discount was 15 percent.

with *ben zhe jian shou*, "collecting payment both in kind and in commuted form," which proved somewhat successful. By the late autumn, Qiao was sufficiently encouraged to seek to expand this program in Shandong.[67]

Approving *ben zhe jian shou* for Shandong did not imply permitting it for the whole nation. Qiao had been able to cite a precedent: as noted in chapter 5 above, Jiangsu had once been authorized to sell *jiansheng* titles for silver after severe floods. This enabled him to claim that Shandong's recent natural disasters qualified it for the same privilege. For the remaining provinces, the form in which applicants should pay for *jiansheng* titles remained an issue in 1745. This situation generated a minor classic of traditional Chinese political economy, a memorial by Qin Huitian (a Board of Rites vice-president) advocating acceptance of payment for titles in either grain or silver, according to the buyer's wishes.

As I have translated and discussed this document elsewhere, a statement of the most important points will suffice here. Qin's memorial shows market-consciousness not only in defending the principle of using silver in relief distributions, but also in implicitly recognizing that the state, as seller, must understand that it is operating under market conditions. It must, therefore, consider the effective demand for what it offers. It can expect to be successful only when it both acknowledges the variables determining whether buyers will prefer to pay in grain or silver, and shows the flexibility to accommodate the buyer's preference. Allowing purchasers to choose the form in which they pay will also obviate the risk of problematic market conditions being aggravated by the title sales program. Such aggravation would take place either when nonfarmers, forced to pay in grain, bought it on markets that were poorly stocked, or when farmers, required to pay in silver, sold extra grain on oversupplied markets. The rational course of

---

67. CC, Qiao Xueyin, QL 9/5/25 (also transc. Lü Xiaoxian, comp., "Qianlong sannian," part 2, p. 16); Kaerjishan, QL 9/12/3 (d.r.), transc. ibid., pp. 16–17. The latter source reveals that Qiao had sought to restore the 1738 province-wide contribution target (1.1 million *shi*) and to extend the program to twenty-three jurisdictions that had not been assigned contribution targets in the 1743 target-resetting process. Kaerjishan (his superior) supported the second proposal only.

action for applicants who had a choice would also be that which was in society's best interests.[68]

Qin's memorial was written towards the end of July 1745. It may have fared less well than it deserved because debate had been stirred by a less impressive document by Emida, then acting governor-general of the Huguang provinces. Emida's memorial was initially considered by the court in mid-June and had been rejected by the time Qin wrote— which prompted Qin to clarify that his idea was different. Emida had proposed that county-level sale of *jiansheng* titles for silver *totally* replace the demonstrably vain attempt to raise significant amounts of grain through title sales. This eager interventionist of the 1730s was now suggesting that the state should limit its commitment to the granaries.[69] He invoked arguments associated with the antigranary position and pointed out that silver revenue from title sales might be spent on other purposes beyond grain storage—for example, the maintenance of city walls, water conservancy, or social welfare activities such as providing for orphans and the destitute. To this list he added, in a subsequent memorial, the systematic replacement of worn-out or otherwise substandard military equipment, such as bows and arrows.

Was Emida trimming his sails to the political wind, or was he was sincerely disillusioned with the granary system? He himself protested later that his point was only that 28 million *shi* represented an ample storage level, while there were better uses for *jiansheng* title sales than adding to the stockpiles. A surprising error in his original memorial suggests that he was possibly losing his grip as an administrator.[70] Be

---

68. CC, Qin Huitian, QL 10/6/25; HCJSWB, *juan* 39:12b–13b; Dunstan, *Conflicting Counsels*, pp. 296–300, 313–20. Qin, like Sun Hao, noted that one of the advantages of giving silver to disaster victims was that it could serve as petty business capital.

69. For Emida as erstwhile expositor of ever-normal theory and creative promoter of institutions operating on the ever-normal principle, see Dunstan, *Conflicting Counsels*, pp. 31–33, 58–62.

70. He wrote as if the 1738–43 total contribution target (some 30 million *shi*) were still in force. Despite all the policy confusion, a territorial official of his seniority would normally have been accurate on such a point. In 1746, he was relieved of the Huguang governor-generalship on grounds of incapacity for top-level regional administration. Yet he received further senior appointments, including a board presidency, before his death in 1761. Zhao et al., comps., *Qingshi gao*, vol. 36, *juan* 323, p. 10,810.

that as it may, this text has its own interest. There was iconoclasm in his rebuttal of the cliché that the government must save grain because otherwise the thriftless folk would waste it. In present circumstances, he pointed out, with the profits to be made on grain "double" those from other goods, "the folk are storing grain as they would gold."

Emida also cast the famous fiscal reforms of the previous reign in a quite different light from that suggested by Madeleine Zelin. Zelin argues, with much convincing detail, that an important achievement of Yongzheng's *huohao guigong* (regularization of the meltage surcharge) reform was to create regular budgetary appropriations and discretionary funds for the various needs of local and provincial government.[71] Emida opined in this memorial and his subsequent response to critics that the effect had been the opposite. The regularization of the meltage surcharge had deprived local magistrates of discretionary funds for a wide range of public purposes, such as those that could be financed with the income from a reformed title-sales scheme. In fact, part of Emida's quarrel was probably with some revisions to the *huohao guigong* reform made under Qianlong in 1740. These revisions, aimed at checking local overspending, had imposed central government controls on use of *huohao* funds, thereby removing a flexibility that may have been abused less often than the court believed. Emida's point, however, was that allowing local officials to sell titles for silver would potentially undo the harm that had arisen from the *huohao guigong* scheme.[72]

His proposal did not find favor with the grand secretaries and Board of Revenue, who considered it in light of a critical response by Li Qingfang. As in 1743, Li argued vigorously to defend the ever-normal system. His memorial represents another traditionalist reaction to the radical undermining of that system implied by the policies of 1744–45. Li's

---

71. Zelin, *Magistrate's Tael*, chs. 4 and 5, esp. pp. 169–83. The *huohao guigong* reform (1723–30) was intended to rationalize regional and local government finance, thereby freeing the taxpayers of illegitimate exactions. Legalizing the nonstatutory meltage surcharge made it possible to set up regular budgetary allocations for salary supplements, wages, and miscellaneous expenses, thus putting the previously underfunded territorial administrations on a relatively sound financial footing. Surplus funds generated by the reform became available for nonrecurrent public expenditures.

72. Emida, QL 10/5/13 (d.r.) and 10/8/6 (d.r.), transc. Lü Xiaoxian, comp., "Qianlong sannian," part 2, pp. 18–19, 21–22 (cf. JS, Emida, QL 10/4/24); QSL/QL, *juan* 242:23a–24b; Zelin, *Magistrate's Tael*, pp. 126–27, 270–72.

concern, in June 1745, was that however much Emida protested that "shortfall from the old [i.e., basic] targets cannot be allowed," in present circumstances his proposal meant a general depletion of all granary reserves in a few years. Present central government policy made it essential that local authorities collect grain for *jiansheng* titles, because title sales were now the only approved means of granary restocking, apart from the strictly local buying that Li took to be allowed when harvests had been good. Given the vagaries of climate, one could not depend on buying of this kind to avoid progressive erosion of reserves throughout the system.

Li devoted some space to elaborating his previous argument that social inequality necessitated ever-normal operations. He had claimed in 1743 that grain left in the hands of the wealthy would be used for speculation. Now he used this line of thought to fault the notion that famine victims could always be given silver. If all the grain were stockpiled by the local rich, the poor would not necessarily have access to it even once they had received state silver. If the wealthy did consent to sell, they would take advantage of the situation to charge exorbitant prices, which the poor would have to pay. In consequence, the real buying power of any given peasant's dole would be less than two- or three-tenths of what the court intended.

Li also had an answer to the cliché that "There is only so much grain, and if the authorities hold more, the people will hold less." Experience in his home province of Fujian suggested that the implications of this truism were not as the critics of the ever-normal system assumed. Li distinguished between two stages of Fujian's campaign to build reserves through title sales. First were the two years from (probably) the late spring of 1741 to that of 1743, in which, he incorrectly stated, "there was not yet provision for acquiring the *jiansheng* title by presenting grain"; the rate of contributions had, in fact, been slow during this period.[73] Second had been "these last two years," in which large numbers of titles had been sold for grain. Exactly contrary to what the cliché's rehearsers would have predicted, grain had been very dear in Fujian in the first period, but the price had come down greatly in the second, that is, at

---

73. During the first four years after Fujian began selling titles for grain in 1739, the cumulative total raised was 383,420 *shi* (CC, Nasutu and Zhou Xuejian, QL 9/4/24). This implies average contributions of only 95,855 *shi* per year.

the very time in which much extra grain had been withdrawn into the granaries. While the improvement was due partly to the weather, it was also the effect of widespread stabilizing sales. "That rice price stability depends upon official sales is therefore clear."[74]

Li's memorial illustrates yet again the tenacity with which the ever-normal system was defended. However, if he influenced the decision to dismiss Emida's proposal, this was perhaps mainly through his help in clarifying the implications of letting *jiansheng* titles be sold locally for silver. As the grand secretaries and Board of Revenue indicated on 10 July, Emida's idea was incompatible with the brave year-old attempt to phase out the annual grain-purchase system by selling titles for grain.[75] The incompatibility must also have struck Anning, who in early August wrote a memorial defending the experiment that he himself had advocated, attacking Emida, and urging the emperor to admonish the territorial bureaucracy. Emida had commented that, given the way in which county magistrates "daily agonized" over the risk that their existing stocks would rot, it was "truly hard to expect them to put solid effort" into acquiring yet more grain through title sales. As a point made many times by others, this must have seemed innocuous to Emida. Unfortunately, such complaints, when voiced by a provincial chief, could be taken to betray poor leadership. It was ostensibly for this that Anning attacked him.

Anning was back in provincial leadership, having returned to duty as Jiangsu provincial administration commissioner in February. He told the emperor all about those local officials who believed their personal interest to lie in deterring would-be title buyers, alleging that such indifference to duty was widespread in all provinces. Emida's memorial epitomized the negligence of provincial chiefs who failed to take their subordinates in hand. "Know[ing] full well" that local magistrates put difficulties in the way of applicants, Emida had in effect sought to accommodate their preferences, rather than checking their misconduct or taking measures to prevent the dreaded rotting of stored grain.

It was during this tirade that Anning stated his objection to Emida's proposal. Selling *jiansheng* titles for silver was a bad idea not because it

---

74. Li Qingfang, QL 10/5/23 (d.r.), transc. Lü Xiaoxian, comp., "Qianlong sannian," part 2, pp. 19–20.

75. JS, Grd. Secs. and Bd. Rev., QL 10/6/11.

spelled erosion of the granary reserves, but because it would undo the good of the renewed suspension of the annual grain-purchase system. Emida had noted the possibility of using the silver realized through title sales to buy grain to supplement available reserves as needed during famines. For Anning, the problem was not the unreliability of this approach, but rather that it would revive large-scale official purchasing. Emida's proposal showed "gross failure to realize that since the cessation of [official] buying, the price of grain has fallen day by day, and success is gradually becoming manifest. If, at this point, [officialdom forsakes the practice of] collecting grain in small amounts and reverts to purchasing in bulk, this will inevitably send prices up again, and the good results so far will all be thrown away."

Whether Anning's strategy was really working or not, he had political capital invested in it. It is understandable that he wanted to push the case for it for as long as possible. It may still have been a miscalculation to use his own jurisdiction as a case-study of what could be achieved if only senior officials showed their subordinates that they were personally determined to achieve results. Anning reported that, over Jiangsu as a whole, "within one year, over 200,000 *shi* of unhusked grain have already been collected." This figure could be expected to rise provided that the province's local officials "reform[ed] themselves completely of their long-accustomed habits." Anning could not have known that about six weeks later, his superior, the governor Chen Dashou, would use the fact that Jiangsu had so far collected "only" some 200,000 *shi* as one of his grounds for seeking exemption from the order to refrain from buying grain this autumn. Chen, it seems, did not share Anning's vision and was capable of undermining his subordinate's position by reporting the same information in a different light.[76]

In the short run, Anning still enjoyed the court's support. He requested an edict calling on governors-general and governors to give conscientious leadership and to report annually the amount of grain that title sales had yielded in their provinces. The emperor obliged him on 17 August with an edict summarizing his account of local magistrates' behavior and criticizing Emida. In his censure of Emida, the

76. JS, Anning, QL 10/7/6, transc. Lü Xiaoxian, comp., "Qianlong sannian," part 2, pp. 20–21 (cf. separate mem. JS, Anning, QL 10/7/6 for details of the situation in Jiangsu); CC, Chen Dashou, QL 10/8/16.

emperor again complimented Anning by borrowing his wording (with trivial changes). He issued the requested order that provincial chiefs perform their duty. What he did not mention was Anning's suggestion that they be required to supply the year-end figures that might indicate their diligence.[77]

Examining the Figures

The court's surprising lack of interest in statistical evidence of the progress of title sales persisted into November, when it was shown again in the decision to terminate the program. It will be recalled that, early in that month, Qianlong endorsed the allegation that the current approach was not working and authorized the Board of Revenue to resume its own silver-for-titles program. This would have been taken as the death knoll for attempts to raise significant amounts of grain through title sales, although the possibility was consciously left open. Thus perished the Anning experiment, abandoned by his master as a failure. What makes this verdict seem perverse is that if only the court had waited for the annual, early winter data on the nation's civil grain reserves and population, it would have received a crude statistical indication that the experiment was working rather well, at least as far as granary restocking was concerned.

These data—the *minshu gushu*, "population and grain figures"—were collected under a reporting system that Qianlong had established in late 1740 to monitor the adequacy of grain reserves for the actual population.[78] In the winter of 1745, the official *minshu gushu* total for current storage in the granary network was 35,586,613 *shi* of unhusked grain. This was almost 3.5 million *shi* higher than the 1744 figure, and the highest figure for any year from 1741 through 1749.[79] Although problematic (as discussed below), these data supply *prima facie* evidence that adjusted-rate title sales, supplemented with some purchases of grain, had not only kept the realm's reserves at more than basic target level,

---

77. Edict of QL 10/7/20 transc. Lü Xiaoxian, comp., "Qianlong sannian," part 2, p. 21; or QSL/QL, *juan* 245:8a–9a.

78. QSL/QL, *juan* 130:1a–3a; Will and Wong, *Nourish the People*, pp. 254–55.

79. The nationwide *minshu gushu* totals are stated in QSL/QL at the end of each year's entries, beginning in 1741. They are tabulated in Will and Wong, *Nourish the People*, appendix, table A.1 (pp. 528–37).

but also realized some initial progress towards the 48-million *shi* compromise storage target. As the rationale for the 1744–45 title sales policy implied indefinite postponement of any serious attempt to reach that target, one may reasonably claim that the policy's grain-acquisition goals had been exceeded.

It is, of course, likely that some of the figures from lower levels had been deliberately inflated, either to create a presumption of diligence on the part of the responsible official, or in hopes that a policy intended to eliminate the onerous annual buying process would be vindicated and renewed. Even if the figures are completely honest, the increase in holdings may be in part illusory, reflecting the fact that title sales could bring grain into the granaries earlier in the year than the post-harvest purchase system did. It is not necessarily that the granaries were drawing in more grain, but that they were drawing in a portion of the grain early enough for it to be included in statistics that would have omitted the same quantity if purchased in the autumn.[80] While recognizing these possibilities, we must also entertain the notion that the revised title sales program of 1744–45 was more successful than it suited central government interests to acknowledge in November 1745.

As argued above, the premature termination of Anning's experiment probably reflects Qianlong's capitulation, under the sway of fiscal problems that were largely of his making, to the Board's abiding preference for keeping title sales in its own income-maximizing hands. To be sure, there were additional contributory factors. As we have seen, although the Board had claimed that it had the throne's support for the attempted coup of ordering exclusive use of title sales for granary restocking, Qianlong's acquiescence in this radical departure had crumbled swiftly in the face of cogent provincial arguments that buying was essential. His connivance with the Board may have reflected continuing adherence to Anning's theories, but every exemption from the Board's decree lowered the prospects of a comprehensive vindication of the policy those theories had inspired. In the meanwhile, the persistent

---

80. As shown in note 45 above, the Fujian figures imply a slightly higher rate of contributions in the first half of lunar 1745 than in the last quarter of lunar 1744, which would normally have been the latter part of the official buying season. The stocktaking on which *minshu gushu* reports were based is thought to have been held in about the eighth moon, before the annual buying process.

controversy may have sapped the ruler's loyalty to the experiment. Indeed, this vacillating, easily-led monarch may have found the debate destabilizing of commitment to any positive approach at all. With one side sounding the alarm about total depletion of the granaries, while Emida and others kept alive the fear that more grain in the granaries would *of itself* raise prices, Qianlong may have grown uncertain whether general failure or outstanding success in gathering grain by selling titles would be more undesirable.[81] Better, perhaps, to embrace banality than to pursue adventures that might lead to empty granaries or worsening inflation.

Was it inertia that left the compromise targets in force until early 1749? *Prima facie*, the *minshu gushu* figures suggest no particular determination to reach them. While sample memorials from the late 1740s imply a mixed record as regards both success and commitment, they do not radically challenge this impression.[82] On the positive side, the Shaanxi provincial administration commissioner reported early in 1747 that since 1739, Shaanxi had raised a cumulative total of 810,000 *shi* by selling titles. Although this figure exceeded the level reached in 1743 by only some 305,000 *shi*, it would, if added to the basic target, have given Shaanxi theoretical reserves of 2,871,741 *shi*, 5 percent more than a compromise target that had originated as the actual amount in store in 1743 (excluding contributions). Fujian, with its exceptionally high grain valuation rate (0.9 tael per *shi*), was making steady progress, being reportedly over halfway to meeting ex-governor Zhou Xuejian's additional contribution target of 886,000 *shi*. This implies a cumulative total exceeding 1,557,000 *shi* at the time of writing (August 1747). Fujian was probably also advancing towards Zhou's ideal of definitive imperial approval for the substitution of title sales for restocking through purchase. The only major change its spokesmen wanted was the raising of Taiwan's low valuation rate. Figures discussed in chapter 8 further suggest that by 1748, Jiangxi, Guizhou, and Guangxi had either over-

---

81. Emida, QL 10/5/13 (d.r.) transc. Lü Xiaoxian, comp., "Qianlong sannian," part 2, p. 18.

82. It is, however, curious that two provincial memorials cite the 1738–43 contribution target as yardstick in calculating shortfalls. JS, Qing Fu, QL 12/3/15 (Shaanxi), Saileng'e and Chen Hongmou, QL 12/4/27 (Hubei).

fulfilled or very nearly met their relatively (or, in Guizhou's case, exceptionally) low compromise targets.[83]

The central government showed willingness to help those provinces whose stocks had been depleted by natural disasters. In 1747, Jiangsu was favored with an increase in its already generous price-per-title discount to 25 percent, permission to sell the more academic *gongsheng* (tribute student) title for grain, and, best of all, revocation of the option of *jiansheng* title purchase at the Board for Jiangsu applicants. This last privilege was subsequently extended to Anhui, which had likewise enjoyed a 20 percent title-price discount since 1744. Permission to sell *gongsheng* titles for grain and exemption from Board competition may also have been granted to Shandong, Sichuan, and, needless to say, Fujian. But were all these concessions everywhere effective? Yinjishan wrote in January 1748 that contributions were forthcoming in most parts of Anhui, but the severe depletion reported later in that year belies his optimism that the province's granaries would thus be refilled. A 1749 memorial noted that in Jiangsu, only 70,000 *shi* were raised by title sales in lunar 1747 (after the concessions took effect), and not quite 94,000 in lunar 1748. As relief operations reportedly consumed these proceeds as they were received, they probably did not effect much progress towards Jiangsu's compromise target (2,111,000 *shi*).[84]

At the opposite extreme from the Shaanxi experience was that of Hubei, whose chief administrators, Chen Hongmou and his superior Saileng'e, complained on 4 June 1747 that buying grain, whether locally or in Sichuan, was not a practical way of rebuilding Hubei's stocks from their perilously low level of some 589,000 *shi*. Having had experience of the Jiangxi title sales program, both officials were particularly frustrated that in lunar 1746, less than 10 percent of Hubei's nu-

---

83. JS, Qing Fu, QL 12/3/15, Kaerjishan and Chen Dashou, QL 12/7/6, Chen Dashou, QL 12/7/6; chap. 8 below, esp. table 14; cf. HHCC, Bundle 93, Bd. Rev., QL 8/6/3. Guangdong's case, which resembles that of Shaanxi, is discussed in chap. 8. Raoyang county, Zhili, probably exemplifies overfulfillment of a local compromise target. Raoyang's actual stocks in 1748 are stated as 33,608 *shi*. If, as seems likely, it had been classified as a medium-sized county, its compromise target will have been 30,000 *shi*. Will, *Bureaucracy and Famine*, table 15 (p. 198); cf. QSL/QL, *juan* 219:8b–9a.

84. JS, Saileng'e and Chen Hongmou, QL 12/4/27, Yinjishan, QL 12/12/26, Huang Tinggui and Yaerhashan, QL 14/4/30; chap. 8 below (table 10). On the *gongsheng* status, see Chang, *The Chinese Gentry*, pp. 4–5, 19–20, 27–29.

merous title-buyers had paid locally in grain. They asked for concessions similar to those granted Jiangsu, but with only a 20 percent discount on the price per title. They offered a fiscal incentive, made plausible again by the Jiangxi experience: saved grain-purchase funds accumulating in the provincial treasury would eventually yield a military subsidy of at least equal value to the forgone silver income. This may have been intended to interest a court that had just launched the war now known as the first Jinchuan campaign. If so, it missed its mark. Noting that his approach was to adopt a middle course between the Board preference for a centralized title-sales program and the provincial preference for a dispersed one, Qianlong rejected their submission.[85]

We shall have cause to revert to the Jinchuan campaign in chapter 8. This chapter concludes with an examination of available figures on total granary holdings in relation to Suzhou rice-price data over the fifteen years from 1741 to 1755. Problems with the granary statistics (*inter alia*) would make this a highly questionable exercise were the intention to discern patterns of real influence between reserve levels and Yangzi Valley market prices. My focus, however, is not so much on what was really happening as on the court's options in interpreting the data whose collection it had ordered. My contention is that officials who were conscious of the indicated trends both in granary reserves and in rice prices at the interregionally important market of Suzhou would have had no reason to suppose that increased granary reserves were a significant inflationary pressure. Those who expressed such a belief were ignoring data that were available, albeit neither fully reliable nor processed in such a way as to enlighten policy discussions.

The *minshu gushu* data for the quinquennium 1745–49 (see table 8 and figure 1 below) suggest that in 1746 an effort was made to maintain stocks at about 35 million *shi*, after which they were allowed to sink to some 32.7 million *shi* in 1747, and 31 million in 1748. Unfortunately, these figures cannot be taken at face value, as it is not clear to which stage of the annual cycle they refer. Will has argued plausibly that *minshu gushu* "actual" grain storage data generally reflect the phase of

---

85. JS, Saileng'e and Chen Hongmou, QL 12/4/27; QSL/QL, *juan* 289:42a. The orders for military action in the Jinchuan area were given in late April. Guo Chengkang, comp., *Qingshi biannian*, vol. 5, p. 256.

Table 8
Total Granary Holdings According to the *Minshu Gushu* Data,
Compared with Annual Rice Prices in Suzhou Prefecture, 1741–55

Year	A Reported granary reserves (millions of *shi*)	B Annual price of rice in Suzhou prefecture (taels per *shi*)
1741	31.7	1.34
1742	29.6	1.53
1743	29.6	1.60
1744	32.1	1.55
1745	35.6	1.42
1746	35.1	1.37
1747	32.7	1.61
1748	31.0[1]	2.04
1749	32.2	1.69
1750	33.2	1.64
1751	27.3	1.93
1752	26.7	2.31
1753	29.0	1.73
1754	32.1	1.64
1755	33.0	1.89

[1]The 1748 figure has been corrected to 31.0 million *shi* on the basis of QSL/QL, *juan* 331:66a, where it is stated as 31,018,751 *shi*. Will and Wong have copied the figure as 31,108,751 *shi*.
SOURCES: Will and Wong, *Nourish the People*, appendix, table A.1, the "*Shilu* total" row; Wang Yeh-chien, "Secular Trends of Rice Prices," table 1.1, the "annual price" column. The *minshu gushu* data have been checked against the original (year-end) entries in QSL/QL and are correct to one decimal place.

maximum depletion, that is, early autumn, before the annual restocking. Provincial governors were expected to send their figures to the
central government in the eleventh moon; for this to be possible, data
compilation must have begun a few months earlier, and there is some
evidence that this was typically in the eighth moon or thereabouts.[86]

It would be simple-minded to calculate holdings in the maximum
fullness stage on the assumption that the *minshu gushu* totals are 70
percent of them. Quite apart from Will's well-substantiated caveats

---

86. Will and Wong, *Nourish the People*, pp. 254–56, 264–65.

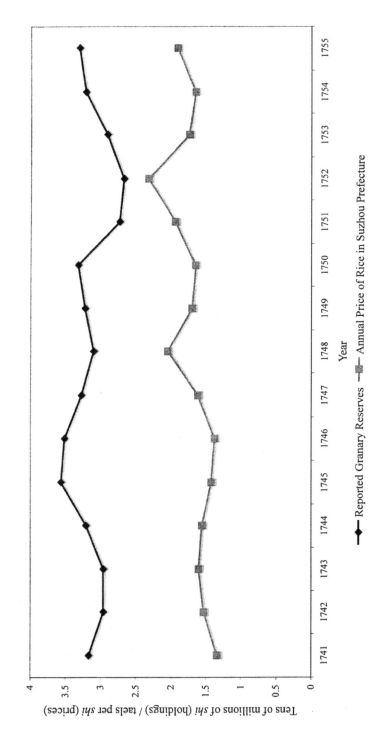

Figure 1 Total Granary Holdings According to the *Minshu Gushui* Data, Compared with Annual Rice Prices in Suzhou Prefecture, 1741–55

about the consistency and reliability of *minshu gushu* data, it is not at all the case that exactly 30 percent was replaced each year. It is also likely that the national totals include a certain amount of grain held by community and other non-ever-normal granaries, as do many of the provincial totals.[87] For a period of greater stability in storage policy, it might have been defensible to take the figure of which any given *minshu gushu* total is 70 percent as a very rough approximation to the maximum likely corresponding ever-normal post-restocking levels. Had this procedure been applicable for 1745, the peak early autumn figure of that year, 35,586,613 *shi*, would have implied that the corresponding figures for the early spring of 1745 and 1746 are unlikely to have exceeded 50.8 million *shi* but might have approached that level. If so, the compromise target (48 million *shi*) might well have been met, and the title sales policy could not plausibly have been dismissed as a failure. However, the story told above makes this calculation doubly unrealistic. Reported global storage peaked in 1745 because of regional successes (feigned or real) in selling *jiansheng* titles. The peak figure represents the partial replacement of a basically seasonal restocking process by one that was not necessarily concentrated in the annual post-harvest period and may have served to add to the reserves. The early autumn storage figures for 1745 should thus not even theoretically have constituted 70 percent of a full complement of grain held in each early spring. Preharvest contributions reduced the proportion of the pre-existing holdings that remained to be replaced after the data were compiled; new holdings, by definition, did not correspond to pre-existing ones.

It is probably best to leave the interpretation of the 1740s *minshu gushu* data open for the time being. It had been assumed since the beginning of the Qianlong reign that, if one ignored attempts to build up supplementary reserves through title sales, a "full" ever-normal system stored only 28 million *shi*. Estimates of 1741–42 total holdings by the grand secretaries and Nine Ministries Assembly based on the genuinely year-end *zouxiao an* or *zouxiao ce* figures (compiled early in the fol-

---

87. Ibid., pp. 54–56, 135, 233–76. The proportion of community granary stocks in a provincial total could, exceptionally, approach half, as with the 1748 Hubei figure (almost 1,070,000 *shi*, of which some 460,000—43 percent—were *shecang* grain). CC, Peng Shukui, QL 13/12/8.

lowing year) suggest that in the early 1740s, ever-normal holdings at the point of maximum fullness tended not greatly to exceed the corresponding *minshu gushu* totals. That body indicated in mid-June 1742 that, as of the end of 1741, grain actually in store under the basic targets totalled only "in excess of" 24 million *shi*, to which some 6 million *shi* had been added through title sales. While the year-end reports from the more distant provinces may not yet have arrived, the grandees seem to have taken these figures as not far from final, implying total holdings of perhaps some 31 million *shi*. The *minshu gushu* total for 1741 was 31.7 million *shi*. Including recorded receipts from title sales, even a fully replenished ever-normal network at that time would have contained only some 34 million *shi*. The 1742 *minshu gushu* total (29.6 million *shi*) was over 85 percent of that figure; it was over 92 percent of the total current ever-normal holdings (between 31 and 32 million *shi*) as estimated in late May 1743 on the basis of year-end reports—by implication, those for 1742.[88] Unfortunately, the year-end figures themselves are not available. We have only the *minshu gushu* series.

It is conceivable that the gap between the *minshu gushu* and the year-end figures widened during the decade. For 1748, we have both (1) explicit statements of the amount each province had in store before restocking, and (2) means of calculating the amount that could theoretically have been in store by early 1749 had all grain issued been replaced. I examine these figures in chapter 8. To avoid anticipating that discussion, I make only three observations here. First, the theoretically possible early 1749 total of about 39 million *shi* that I calculate compares with a 1748 *minshu gushu* total of only 31 million. Second, however, as Will has noted, figures of the former kind, which he calls "theoretical reserves," should not automatically be taken to correspond to real holdings at the point of maximum fullness in any given annual cycle. We should usually expect them to be larger—substantially larger, when nationally aggregated.[89] It follows that the ever-normal system probably did not hold as much as 39 million *shi* in early 1748; indeed, I estimate that it is most unlikely to have held more than, at most, 41 million

---

88. Grd. Secs. and NMA, QL 7/5/9, transc., e.g., HHCC, Bundle 87, Zhang Yunsui, QL 8/2/28; CC, Grd. Secs. and NMA, QL 8/int.4/6; and, on the *zouxiao an* or *zouxiao ce* (reports/registers of year-end results), Will and Wong, *Nourish the People*, pp. 253–55.

89. Cf. Will and Wong, *Nourish the People*, pp. 260–61.

at any point during the 1740s. Lastly, the uncertain referent of the *minshu gushu* figures is not so very relevant, after all, in the present context, given that the aim is only to determine what the court could have read from the data at its disposal. For present purposes, we need to assume only that Qianlong and his advisors would have accepted the national *minshu gushu* totals as a guide to the general trajectory of storage-level fluctuations. I am aware of no evidence that would invalidate this assumption.

The celebrated price report system of eighteenth-century China brought the court monthly data on prices for all major cereals for every prefecture throughout the nation.[90] What would the emperor's advisors have seen, had they systematically compared sample time series compiled from the price data with the *minshu gushu* figures? Table 8 and figure 1 suggest a partial answer to this question—cheating a little, because they draw on quantitative and representational techniques with which mid-Qing officials could not have been familiar. They compare the national *minshu gushu* totals, from their inception (1741) until 1755, with one set of subregional price data, those for Suzhou prefecture in the Lower Yangzi. Unbalanced as this comparison may be, its crudity does not exceed that of the antigranary clichés whose empirical foundation it calls into question.

The "rice prices" line in figure 1 is based on the series of Suzhou-prefecture annual rice prices calculated by Wang Yeh-chien from monthly price reports (see table 8, column B). Use of Suzhou data is appropriate not only because the original campaign against the granaries was in the name of Lower-Yangzi price stability, but also because Suzhou was the nation's central rice market. Its prices both reflected those of its upstream supply regions and strongly influenced those of other towns and cities that consumed the vast quantities of rice re-exported from it. Wang goes so far as to claim that prices in the Yangzi Delta (of which Suzhou was the leading city) "reflected conditions of demand and supply in the national, not just regional, market."[91] The "granary reserves" line in figure 1 shows the *minshu gushu* totals (table 8, column A), expressed in units of 10 million *shi*. The

---

90. On the price report system, see, e.g., Marks, "Rice Prices, Food Supply, and Market Structure," pp. 66–69.

91. Wang, "Secular Trends of Rice Prices," pp. 36–38; for the quotation, see p. 36.

minshu gushu figure for 1743, the initial moratorium year, is obviously unreliable, being identical with that for 1742.

The numerate official would have found in figure 1 no *prima facie* encouragement to believe that high ever-normal storage levels directly caused high grain prices. If anything, he might have been enticed towards the contrary position (Li Qingfang's) that high storage levels were needed for controlling prices through large-scale stabilizing sales. The peaks in annual rice prices in Suzhou correspond with troughs in storage levels; until 1754–55 (which does not fit the pattern), rice prices fell as storage levels rose, and *vice versa*. The one exception is the final price dip of 1746, which Li Qingfang might have explained as a delayed reaction to the 1745 peak storage level.

There is a measure of compatibility between the data shown in figure 1 and the notion that what raised grain prices was not necessarily high storage levels, but rather certain features of official buying. Anning might have taken the 1748 price peak as a dramatic vindication of his warning that reversion to large-scale buying as the main means of restocking would undo the good of the restrained approach of 1743–45. Official buying might have seemed so inflationary that its ill-effects were manifested even when the size of the reserves declined. However, the figures for 1752, when an unprecedented peak in prices coincided with the lowest storage level since before the *minshu gushu* started, should have proved too stark a vindication even for Anning. If prices surged while total stocks were at a twelve-year low, then, to the extent that the decreased reserves reflected lower acquisition levels, the allegedly inflationary features of the buying process could have accounted for the rise in prices only if these features operated more intensely as the quantity acquired fell.

It would be rash to present figure 1 as a reproach to present-day historians who swallow whole the mid-eighteenth-century belief that high ever-normal storage levels in themselves contributed significantly to rising grain prices.[92] For one thing, notwithstanding Wang Yeh-

---

92. Cf. Gao Wangling, "Yige wei wanjie de changshi," pp. 27–28. Gao moderated his views in the revised version of this article that appeared in his 1995 book. Although now accepting the *minshu gushu* data as indicating the actual storage levels of the 1740s, Gao was able to preserve the notion of an inflationary increase in reserves by suggesting, with limited evidence, that actual storage levels prior to

chien's opinion as to the national significance of Yangzi Delta rice prices, the comparison should arguably have been between grain prices at Suzhou and granary storage levels in the Yangzi Valley provinces alone. Unfortunately, complete series of *minshu gushu* data for the years in question are not available for any of these provinces, the figures for Jiangsu and Jiangxi being especially sparse. There are also major problems of consistency: *minshu gushu* totals for Jiangxi, Hunan, Hubei, and Sichuan should probably be assumed to include community granary stocks, those for Jiangsu and Anhui to exclude them.[93] Nonetheless, such Yangzi Valley provincial storage totals as are available fit the national pattern rather well, albeit with exceptions (see table 9 and figure 2). During 1741–55, there was generally an inverse correlation between annual Suzhou rice prices and total storage levels in the Yangzi Valley provinces. Should we be so audacious as to believe that actual storage levels at the time of greatest fullness in the ever-normal cycle rose nationwide from some 28 million *shi* in ca. 1738 to some 41 million between 1744 and 1748, it would become harder than ever to explain the 1746 price trough, if high storage levels *per se* caused high grain prices. The trough of 1746 would be especially puzzling because policy conditions for rapid reserve growth were at their best precisely in the previous two years (from April 1744 until November 1745).

Dare one speculate as to the more likely cause and effect relationships between Suzhou rice prices and Yangzi Valley storage levels? Suffice it to note that it was presumably the improved supply conditions reflected in the lower Suzhou prices that made possible the higher storage levels with which the latter were associated. To the extent that increased storage levels exerted upward pressure on grain prices, a self-correcting mechanism may then have come into play. As prices began to rise, officials were forced to increase the depletion rate and exercise restraint in post-harvest restocking. Only when grain prices had fallen could storage levels rise again. The degree of the responsibility of ever-normal storage for Suzhou rice price fluctuations cannot be read from figures 1 and 2, which only indicate a possibility too

Qianlong's reign did not reach 20 million *shi*. Idem, *Shiba shiji Zhongguo*, pp. 136, 152–54.

93. Will and Wong, *Nourish the People*, pp. 250–52.

Table 9
Total Granary Holdings in the Yangzi Valley Provinces
According to the *Minshu Gushu* Data, Compared with Annual Rice Prices
in Suzhou Prefecture, 1741–55

	Reported granary reserves (millions of *shi*)						
Year	Jiangsu	Anhui	Jiangxi	Hunan	Hubei	Sichuan	Suzhou price (tls/shi)
1741						2.5	1.34
1742	2.2	0.9	0.9	1.1	0.7	2.8	1.53
1743	1.9	0.7		1.1	0.8	2.5	1.60
1744		0.9		1.6		2.6	1.55
1745		1.2		1.6		2.7	1.42
1746		1.3		1.3	1.1	2.7	1.37
1747		1.1	1.9		1.1		1.61
1748	1.2	0.7[a]	1.5[a]		1.1[a]	1.8[1]	2.04
1749		0.9				2.0	1.69
1750		1.0		1.6	1.0	2.1	1.64
1751			1.3	1.0	0.6	2.2	1.93
1752	0.8	0.6	1.2	1.1	0.8	1.7	2.31
1753	1.0	0.7	1.7	1.3	0.8	1.4	1.73
1754	1.1	1.2		1.1	1.2	1.4	1.64
1755			1.7	1.3	1.4	1.7	1.89

[1]The incomplete copy of CC, Bandi, QL 13/11/22 at Academia Sinica implies a total of only 1.6 million.
SOURCES: Unless otherwise stated, Will and Wong, *Nourish the People*, appendix, table A.1, rows for the stated provinces (data transcribed by Will, Wong, and their collaborators from archival sources); Wang, "Secular Trends of Rice Prices," table 1.1, the "annual price" column. The *minshu gushu* data are correct to one decimal place.
[a] CC, Namin, QL 13/11/29; Peng Jiaping, QL 13/12/24; Peng Shukui, QL 13/12/8.

strong to be ignored that, during 1741–54, there were reciprocal influences between grain prices and grain storage levels. The latter may have combined with other influences that acted in the same direction on grain prices. All this is a very different proposition from the simplistic claim that high grain storage levels caused high grain prices. Such a claim is now untenable.

The Qing court, on the other hand, cannot be blamed for failing to perceive, in 1747 and 1748, a pattern that was then less clear than it became by 1754—or would have become, had Qing officials possessed

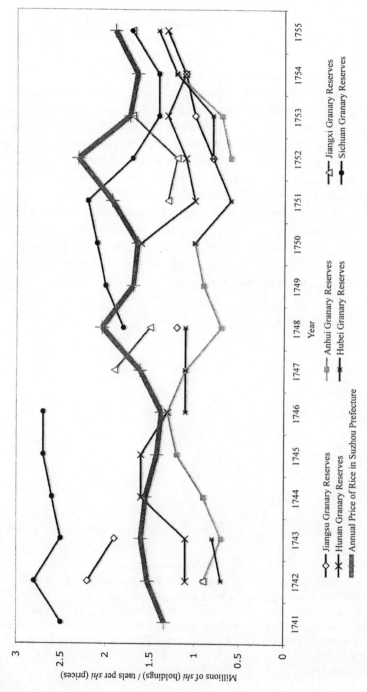

Figure 2 Total Granary Holdings in the Yangzi Valley Provinces According to the *Minshu Gushui* Data, Compared with Annual Rice Prices in Suzhou Prefecture, 1741–55

Jiangsu Granary Reserves
Hunan Granary Reserves
Annual Price of Rice in Suzhou Prefecture

Anhui Granary Reserves
Hubei Granary Reserves

Jiangxi Granary Reserves
Sichuan Granary Reserves

modern habits of depicting data. Qianlong's court, let us recall, received stimuli of various kinds and reacted to them in ways that are understandable, if not always informed by deep and accurate reflection. Stimuli reaching the court in 1747 and, more especially, 1748 included news of sharply rising grain prices, grain riots, demonstrations, and collective actions by the poor against grain merchants. Buying for the granaries was taking place on a considerable scale (and, apparently, across provincial boundaries in many cases); the targets nominally in force totalled 48 million *shi*. As we have seen, adherents of extreme antigranary positions had earlier questioned the wisdom of keeping reserves even at 28 million.[94] In light of the whole story told so far, it should occasion no surprise that Qianlong responded favorably when yet another investigating censor suggested, in November 1747, that excessive buying for the granaries might be to blame for the inexorably rising prices. The action Qianlong took, and the resulting flurry of renewed debate, are examined in chapter 7.

94. Quan, "Qianlong shisan nian," pp. 550–52; Will, *Bureaucracy and Famine*, p. 215; KYQRFDZ, vol. 2, pp. 564–69, 580–84, 591–94; and chap. 5 above. That interprovincial buying had resumed can probably be inferred from the fact that four respondents to the 1748 imperial questionnaire referred to it in terms suggesting that it was a current problem. CC, Zhang Yunsui, QL 13 (cat. no. 1142-024; quoted in chap. 4 above); CC, Yue Jun, QL 14/3/28; LFZZ, Shulu, QL 13/3/22 (d.r.); QSL/QL, *juan* 323:48a.

7

The Grand Discussion: 1748–49

This chapter examines what previous scholarship has represented as the great ever-normal granaries debate: the episode of 1748–49 in which the provincial governors and governors-general gave the court their explanations of the rising grain prices, at imperial command. To be sure, the emperor chose a radical course of action in August 1748, ignoring the multiple nuances and caveats in the provincial memorials, several of which were yet to arrive when he aborted this phase of the consultation process. Thus was much thoughtful effort by more than a score of senior officials largely wasted.

In fact, the emperor was receiving more or less the answer that he wanted. Majority opinion identified the demands of the ever-normal system as an inflationary factor second only to population growth, and amenable to governmental action in a way that population growth was not. Qianlong could therefore claim justification for his radical solution: slash the storage targets. But was such action really in accord with well-informed opinion from the provinces? In this chapter, I examine selected provincial discussions in some depth, beginning with defences of the granaries and distinguishing two sharply different categories of anti-granary memorials. On one hand are hard-line attacks; on the other, responses that, while ostensibly toeing the court's line, betray some reservations about the view—hereafter termed "the granary hypothesis"— that high grain storage levels were substantially responsible for the inflation.

Why devote a chapter to a grand rehearsal of arguments that must generally have been quite stale by 1748, given that there had already been a decade of controversy about the granaries? One reason is that the exercises in multicausal analysis that arrived from the provinces provide a superb window on the general economic consciousness of mid-Qing regional administrators. They are also suggestive about the moral qualities (political courage, intellectual independence) represented in this crucial stratum of the mid-Qing government. They are thus valuable documents for historians of Sino-Manchu economic thought and political culture—and use of the originals (or best available archival copies), rather than the more familiar *Shilu* summaries, enables us to capture points that otherwise would have been lost. Equally important, however, is the need to clarify the exact content of the advice Qianlong received, so that his decision can be evaluated in relation to it. Here was a policy departure that the statistical hindsight used in chapter 6 shows to have had a weak empirical foundation. If it was also more radical than the most iconoclastic provincial proposals, we have, perhaps, a choice between emphasizing Qianlong's rashness, or looking for some motivation other than that stated. Discussion of what this motivation may have been, and why it has not left clearer traces in the Chinese-language historical record, will be found in chapter 8.

The Quest for Wisdom on the Sources of Inflation

The 1748 discussions originated with a memorial from the investigating censor Ou Kanshan, a man of Lechang county on the Guang-dong-Hunan border. He had obtained his *jinshi* degree in 1737 and thus belonged to a different scholastic generation from the Chinese anti-granary radicals of 1739–43, all of whom had graduated in the Yong-zheng period. There is no obvious reason to suspect that he was an associate of theirs.[1] On 15 November 1747, Ou revived the notion of a link between official buying for the granaries and the rising price of grain. His arguments were variants on a familiar theme, and his main proposals were identical with others that had been rejected earlier in the decade. They were to be rejected in their turn. The court, however, drew upon Ou's preamble in preparing the edict that launched the 1748 inquiry.

---

1. Zhu and Xie, comps., *Ming Qing jinshi*, vol. 3, pp. 2,267 and 2,708. For another contribution to an economic policy debate by Ou Kanshan, see Dunstan, "'Orders Go Forth,'" pp. 129–30.

Despite their fate, Ou's views are just interesting enough to warrant summary. He claimed that in the major rice producing provinces—even Sichuan—the price of grain was "multiple times" higher than it had been under Kangxi and Yongzheng. He noted three possible explanations—population growth, natural disasters, and hoarding—favored, he said, by other analysts and raised an objection to each. He blamed the high Middle- and Upper-Yangzi prices on the "wind of official buying," especially the convergence of buyers from other regions on provinces that had enjoyed good harvests. Then, changing tack to consider cases in which magistrates bought locally, he echoed Wei Tingpu in tracing the alleged inflationary impact to the discrepancy between the maximum approved replacement cost for grain used in famine relief, and actual post-harvest market prices. When a magistrate bought grain forcibly from rich households at the low permitted price, his victims were driven to resort to speculation to make good their losses. The magistrate, guiltily conscious of the reason for such misconduct, would turn a blind eye. "It is because of this that each year, after the restocking of the granaries, the price of rice is bound to rise, and in the spring and summer surges daily."

Somewhat like Yang Eryou in 1742, Ou depicted the stabilizing-sales process as useless to most people and beneficial only to the antisocial and corrupt. Official grain was sold at prices calculated on the basis of a small reduction from the "surging" market price. The only people who could conveniently attend the sales were those who lived in or near the county seat. Such people preferred commercial grain, which was less coarse and only slightly more expensive, and which could be obtained without long waits. Seeing that the general public did not want official grain, brokers serving the commercial rice shops purchased country-dwellers' door placards (the proof of identity used to establish entitlement to buy the daily household ration). Thus equipped, they bought up the official rice stocks. Within about ten days, "half" the granary grain would have fallen into the hands of commercial rice dealers. While this was going on, the market price rose daily, dragging the official price up in its wake. By the time that the official stocks were running out, the market price was higher than ever.

Echoing Li Qingzhi and Yang Eryou, Ou advocated that in future, grain should be bought for the granaries only when the price was actually low, and that ever-normal stocks should be sold at the cost price, with a small supplement to cover wastage. Grain raised by selling titles should be sold at the original valuation rate, plus an adjustment for wastage. These measures would suffice, Ou thought, to restore prices to a lower level after a few years. The grand secretaries and Board of Revenue could easily reject these notions by citing the responses given to the proposals of Bulantai and Xu Yisheng in (lunar) 1739, and Yang Eryou in 1742. That buying for the granaries should take place only when prices were low was already the policy in force; provincial chief administrators already had orders to determine appropriately large reductions from the current price when selling grain during food shortages; and a policy of always selling at cost price would make it impossible to use the profits realized in some years to offset the deficits incurred in others.[2]

So perished Ou's proposals, but the concern inspiring them was to be reborn, in flesh transported from his preamble. Already in late November, Qianlong ordered that, despite its rejection, Ou's memorial be circulated to the provincial governors and governors-general, "so that they might recognize the cause of the high price of grain" (*ling qi zhi mi gui shoubing zhi you*) and take measures to eliminate it. A lengthier, more rhetorical edict was released for circulation to the provincial chief administrators on 12 January 1748. This latter document was presented as the emperor's tangential reflections on a general ban on speculative hoarding and on buying grain futures from peasants.[3] The ban had been promulgated only the day before, on Grand Council advice, but Qianlong was already voicing reservations as to its prospects of reducing grain prices. A more searching inquiry into the causes of the inflationary trend of recent years was needed.

Representing the inflation as a serious, bewildering phenomenon, the edict listed five possible causes and commented on each. The first (mentioned by implication) was excessive interregional exportation of

---

2. CC, Ou Kanshan, QL 12/10/13, Grd. Secs. and Bd. Rev., QL 12/10/25. On the earlier memorials cited, see chaps. 4 and 5 above.

3. QSL/QL, *juan* 304:14b–15a, 16a; cf. Wang Xianqian, comp., *Donghua xu lu*, *juan* 26:11b, and chap. 3 above. The November edict is transcribed, with date, in LFZZ, Nasutu, QL 13/2/10; see also CC, Yue Jun, QL 14/3/28. Yue Jun, at least, received the November and the January edict on the same day, along with his copy of Ou's memorial.

grain by merchants; the last was excessive stockpiling in the ever-normal granaries. In between came speculative hoarding, population growth, and natural disasters, as in Ou's memorial. The objections that the edict stated to each explanation were more elaborately worded than those in Ou's memorial, the order was different, the import was not entirely identical, and a simpler version of this rhetorical format had already been used in the 1743 moratorium edict.[4] Nonetheless, there still seems to be a certain family relationship between Ou's rhetoric and the edict's.

As Kishimoto and Rowe have noticed, one cannot read this edict without forming the impression that the emperor wished most attention paid to the fifth possibility, that is, the granary hypothesis.[5] Qianlong implied that none of the other explanations was convincing, whereas he set out the case against the granaries at relative length. His expressed reservations focused more on the practical implications of convicting the granaries than on the tenability of the hypothesis. He noted that only in a small minority of cases had the 1743–44 targets been reached, and that more buying for the granaries was urgently needed everywhere; but he hastily moved on to comment on the importance of the purchase system for emergency preparedness, as if to stop the reader noticing that the widespread depletion of reserves cast doubt on the suggested explanation. To make a point of showing awareness of the granaries' importance was astute, as it preempted strident reassertions from the pro-granary censors. The fact that the edict acknowledged the care with which the targets had been reset may be interpreted in the same way.

Was the emperor sincere in expressing bewilderment, and in professing concern about the future of the granaries were purchasing to be suspended? At the end of the edict, after much verbiage (including allegations of a generally negligent attitude among provincial chiefs), he ordered all governors and governors-general to carry out a whole-hearted investigation and report their findings. At this point, he did invite respondents to mention any further factors of which they were aware. This suggests some degree of open-mindedness. However, the

---

4. Lü Xiaoxian, comp., "Qianlong sannian," part 2, p. 12.
5. Kishimoto, *Shindai Chūgoku no bukka*, p. 303; Rowe, "State and Market," pp. 27–28, *Saving the World*, p. 260.

hint in the first part of the edict as to the expected answer seems so strong that few provincial chiefs are likely to have missed it. As their responses show, few did.[6]

How the Vote Went

At least twenty-seven responses were submitted, of which two have been excluded from the following content analysis because only an abstract or brief reference is available to me.[7] Most of the responses were written in 1748, but three date from the following year, after the final decision on the granaries' new storage targets. The last memorial, submitted in June 1749, made one of the most radical proposals of the whole debate, as discussed in chapter 9. The known responses represent the views of twenty-six provincial chiefs: the Shanxi governor, Zhun-tai, wrote two memorials in order to distinguish his discussion of conditions in his present jurisdiction from his views on why grain prices were rising in "southeastern" China. There were two responses for Anhui and three for Guizhou. Manchu respondents greatly outnumbered Chinese (nineteen to seven), and of the Chinese respondents, two were Chinese bannermen. Manchus were represented all along the spectrum of opinion on the granaries, including both

6. The edict (QSL/QL, *juan* 304:16a–18b) is quoted in full in several of the answering memorials and translated (minus the first paragraph) in Dunstan, *Conflicting Counsels*, pp. 279–82. Cf. the long, discursive essay question (written in Qianlong's name) for the 1748 palace examination, held in May. Candidates were to address a number of contemporary issues, including the high price of grain. Three possible courses of action were suggested: suspending buying for the granaries, sterner measures against merchant hoarders, and forbidding rich landed families to hoard grain. The text gave close attention only to the suggestion about the granaries—incorporating the truism that became the standard cliché of 1748 edicts on that subject. "There is only a certain amount of grain produced; it stands to reason that if it is accumulated in official hands, there must be shortage for the people." QSL/QL, *juan* 313:33b–34a.

7. The abstract is of the response of the Zhili governor-general, Nasutu. It suggests that he blamed the high grain prices chiefly on the extensive interregional movement of supplies necessitated when natural disasters struck several regions at once. He mentioned official buying for the granaries as a cause of Zhili's present high post-harvest millet prices, but made clear that this was only one of the pressures on the new millet supply. Aibida, the incoming Guizhou governor, had submitted a response by 28 September. CC, Nasutu, QL 13 (cat. no. 1142-003); YFD, QL 13/8/6 (7:1616).

spectrum of opinion on the granaries, including both extremes. However, no Chinese respondent took a hard-line antigranary position. There is evidence in two memorials of consultation of immediate subordinates in the provincial hierarchy; in one of these cases (a Manchu response) it is likely that much of the memorial's content was contributed by the (Chinese) provincial administration commissioner.[8] The possibility of ghostwriting in other memorials cannot be excluded. A few of the responses conform to a provincial policy tradition. For example, the Henan governor remained interventionist, while the relatively new Fujian governor continued the Fujian tradition of stressing the potential of selling *jiansheng* titles for grain.[9]

Numerical analysis of the replies is complicated by the fact that, although many of them work through the edict's list of possible causes, they do not follow a standard format. Opinions were often nuanced, and some authors' perceptions are too complex to be captured in broad categories. Some respondents wrote with reference to their own jurisdictions, some to the situation nationwide, and some to both in turn. While the best-crafted memorials are a pleasure to read, one or two responses go off at lengthy tangents or frustrate the analyst with seeming contradictions. As a set, the documents deserve close study because although the consensus was broadly as the court had directed, and although a few of the discussions seem somewhat perfunctory, by and large the content fails to support an image of provincial chief administrators as sycophants and yes-men. Apart from a common and possibly culpable silence on one issue (to be addressed in chapter 8), intellectual honesty and independence seem to characterize many of the responses.[10] In only one case (that of the Yunnan governor and

---

8. LFZZ, Aligun QL 13/8/6 (d.r.); Jie Xizhou, QL 13/4/23 (d.r.).

9. The Sichuan response is an exception. As Sichuan governor in the early 1740s, Shise (now in Henan) had been zealous in trying to amass more stocks through title sales (CC, Shise, QL 8/7/4). By contrast, Jishan, Sichuan governor from mid-1743 until September 1748, was one of the few respondents who identified the expanded granary system as the central cause of the inflation. References to this and all other available 1748–49 responses cited here are supplied in notes to the next three sections.

10. Cf. Rowe's comments on Chen Hongmou's "courageous" resistance to Qianlong's "broad hint" about the ever-normal stockpiles ("State and Market," p. 30; *Saving the World*, p. 261). Chen was indeed one of the granaries' more

Yunnan-Guizhou governor-general) is there noticeable overlap between the views expressed by a governor and those of his immediate superior. With the 1748–49 debate, for the first time, almost all the top provincial administrators appear in our story speaking for themselves, and not as the generalized butt of imperial accusations. The spectacle is quite impressive, even though not one respondent suspected a link between the inflow of foreign silver and domestic price behavior.

There was a wide range of opinions on the granary hypothesis and on granary-related remedies for the inflation. Among those who accepted the hypothesis, some expressed a quantitative understanding of why ever-normal stockpiling should be inflationary, others stressed the unintended consequences of the annual purchase system, and others again invoked both types of argument. In the discussion that follows, I group the respondents into three categories: defenders of the granaries, payers of lip-service to the granary hypothesis, and accusers of the granaries. The last group comprised both moderates and hard-liners. Broadly speaking, opinion divided along geographical lines. As expected, there was considerable, albeit nuanced, opposition from the northern and southwestern provinces to Qianlong's preferred view and the policy implications likely to be drawn from it. Surprisingly, however, three of the responses from downstream Yangzi Valley provinces were lukewarm in endorsing the granary hypothesis, or even subtly protective of the granaries.

All but a few respondents agreed that there was a phenomenon to be explained, and that the rising prices were unwelcome. Only Shanxi and Gansu were stated to be free of the inflationary trend, while two respondents for Yunnan and Guizhou indicated that these provinces had limited price problems. The Guangxi governor wrote neutrally of the inflation in his province, which he represented as a predictable consequence of Guangxi's mutually beneficial trade with adjacent Guangdong. The Guangdong governor, in turn, acknowledged the role of imported Guangxi grain in sparing Guangdong as sharp an inflationary trend as that experienced elsewhere. However, he, like the great majority of the respondents, accepted that explaining the general inflation was a valid task. There was consensus that the answer lay in a combi-

---

"staunch" defenders, but, for the present author, his response does not particularly stand out for either courage or interest.

nation of causes, and many and various were the factors invoked. But, overall, population growth and buying for the granaries were the two factors assigned a major role by most respondents.

Seventeen respondents mentioned population increase as a factor in its own right, whether nationwide or specifically in their own province or a neighboring jurisdiction. In addition, the Sichuan governor cited population growth as making it dangerous to store so much grain in the granaries. One Guizhou respondent, having explicitly excluded population pressure as an inflationary factor in Guizhou, mentioned the influx of immigrants from other provinces (drawn by the mining industry and associated commercial boom), and the wasteful habits that they had brought with them. One governor-general cited figures that must have looked alarming indeed, especially as he took them to be representative of nationwide demographic growth. According to Kaerjishan, Fujian's population had risen from over 1.4 million at the beginning of the Kangxi period (1661) to over 7.5 million in 1747. These figures imply more than a fivefold increase over less than ninety years and an annual growth rate of some 5 percent.[11]

At first sight, it does not appear that, overall, the respondents thought the state's large-scale stockpiling a more important cause of the inflation than population growth. Seventeen of the memorials cite the expanded granary system as a factor; these include the three lukewarm responses. Two further memorials expound the view that buying for the granaries caused price rises, but one points out the short-term nature of such rises, while the other exonerates the size of the reserves. Thus even on a crude numerical "vote," the granary system emerges only marginally ahead of population increase as the factor blamed by most respondents. More significantly, at least ten memorials tend to identify population growth as the central underlying cause, while only four accord first place to the granary system or state intervention generally. However, several respondents discerned a relationship between these leading factors. For at least three respondents, population increase was the fundamental cause, state stockpiling the chief aggra-

---

11. Cf. the 0.8 percent per year cited by Susan Naquin and Evelyn S. Rawski as the peak population growth rate experienced under the Qing (*Chinese Society*, p. 107). More loosely, if the Chinese population rose from 100–150 million in 1650 to 410 million in 1850 (ibid., p. 25), this implies an average annual growth rate of 0.86–1.55 percent.

vating factor. Kaerjishan, in an interesting attempt at integrated analysis, represented natural disasters and the granary system as interacting to ensure that prices raised by population growth would remain high. There was a broader tendency to see the two key factors as products of forces that were radically different in kind. Population increase was assumed to be either the work of "Heaven" or an outcome of the reigning dynasty's good government. Not one respondent suggested that anything could or should be done to check it.[12] By contrast, the granary system was like the "waste" of land or grain in reflecting flawed human action. Here was a proper sphere for governmental effort.

What of the factors seen as less important? Most respondents at least touched on grain speculation. Two argued that it was a major factor, at least for short-term surges in grain prices; another eight either advocated measures against hoarding and deliberate price manipulation, or indicated that such measures were already in place in their jurisdictions. However, there were considerable reservations as to the seriousness of the problem. Thirteen respondents opined that speculative hoarding was not a particularly significant factor (either in general, or in their own jurisdictions), or that it could cause high prices but was not a fundamental cause of the inflation. Several respondents subscribed to the view that speculators sold before the end of the *soudure* period, whether because their only motive had been to await the rise of prices, or because they would need capital to restock in the autumn. A few indicated that the existing bans served to deter such speculative activity as could be harmful to the public. More interestingly, as we saw in chapter 3, half a dozen of the memorials argued (or, at least, reflect awareness of the argument) that, so far from being harmful, speculation served the interests of communities in which it occurred.

The last two possible factors mentioned in the January edict were natural disasters and the interregional export of grain. The former aroused little interest, probably because it was clear to most respondents that natural disasters caused short-term crises but could not in any obvious way be blamed for long-term inflation. Kaerjishan was

---

12. Cf. Li Bozhong's claim that Jiangnan literati had a rudimentary grasp of the need for population control by the mid-eighteenth century ("Kongzhi zengzhang," p. 54). Such consciousness is not reflected in any document considered here, despite the authors' general concern with population pressure on resources.

alone in arguing that disasters aggravated the inflationary trend that resulted from demographic growth. He suggested that they created a sort of deficit, in that "one harvests the new [only to use it to] make up the old." Thus prices stayed up even when good harvests were restored, a process that Kaerjishan probably thought cumulative, as he went on to note that even given normal harvests, places with an overall food surplus were outnumbered by those with overall food shortage. Most of the other respondents who mentioned natural disasters fall into three categories: those who found the state of the harvests irrelevant to explaining long-term inflation, those who did not clearly distinguish between long-run and short-run effects, and those who wrote from fairly unsophisticated regional economies, in which the state of local harvests was of greater relative importance than was the case elsewhere.

Response to the idea that the interregional export of grain might be a factor was similarly mixed and no more enthusiastic. One or two respondents noted that commercial grain transfers spread the effect of natural disasters well beyond the stricken region, as merchants drew on the limited surplus of zones A and B to profit from the famine prices of zone C. The Sichuan governor attributed the rise of prices in Sichuan to its increased commercial exports—exports brought about by the yet higher prices that expansion of the granary system had induced in the importing provinces. However, other replies reflected the accepted view that, in smoothing interregional price differences, commerce played a beneficial role. The Yunnan-Guizhou governor-general invoked the price-mechanism argument: commercial exportation could not cause progressive price increases because merchants stopped buying on markets where price rises jeopardized their profit margins.

Only Xinzhu, acting governor-general of Hunan and Hubei, expressed any animus against merchants whose exports had pushed up prices anywhere in his jurisdiction, and he discussed the group he had in mind as antisocial hoarders rather than legitimate interprovincial traders. The Hankou retail market in cereals, like that of any other major Yangzi Valley city, was highly sensitive to commercial shipments, the presence of numerous merchants buying for Lower Yangzi markets being enough, Xinzhu observed, to cause sharp price increases. Although he paid lip-service to the doctrine of the beneficial role of commerce, it must have been convenient for him to allege that certain individuals whose recent large-scale exports had caused a sudden rise in Hankou rice prices were not genuine merchants, but "profit-cravers who have borrowed the name of merchant to engage craftily in hoarding."[13] Xinzhu seems to have thought it obvious that hoarding was injurious, although he did not blame such misconduct for the long-term inflationary trend and regarded it as less pernicious than the illegal export of grain by sea. He was one of three respondents who mentioned the latter problem—a surprisingly small number, in view of the intensity of the suspicions, amounting almost to panic, expressed by some official authors on this topic.[14]

Numerous possible factors that the emperor had not suggested were cited by one or a few respondents. Several respondents mentioned what we would consider aspects or by-products of increased sophistication of the economy or other socioeconomic change, including population growth. Suggestions included the growth of nonfarming groups within society, increasing luxury, the use of land for nonfood crops, increasing concentration of landownership, a rise in land prices (mentioned chiefly by the Middle Yangzi governors), and the interest of producers in high grain prices. Two respondents remarked on farming households' increased dependence on the market for staple foods; for this, one blamed the spread of extravagant habits, while the other blamed increasing rural poverty caused by demographic growth. As the size of landholdings shrank, so did the prospects of farmers having surplus grain, or even grain enough for their own families' subsistence needs.

---

13. Xinzhu's concern was about exports of rice from Hankou in departing salt boats. He claimed that, during several days, such exports had raised Hankou rice prices by over o.i tl./*shi*. For Xinzhu, what made the exporters hoarders was the contrast between their massive out-shipments of grain (made possible by the large size of the salt boats), and the characteristic merchant pattern of smaller shipments spread over time. He advocated measures—such as immediate forced sales under official supervision—against "hoarders" who hired salt boats to ship rice by the "full thousands and heaped tens of thousands" of *shi*.

14. Xinzhu's denunciation of the maritime export of grain grows out of his discussion of hoarding. He alleged that intending exporters dodged surveillance by taking small amounts of grain to coastal "engrossers" (*wohu*), on whose premises they accumulated hoards until the New Year holiday. They then took advantage of relaxed surveillance to smuggle the grain out to sea. Cf., for other expressions of the fear that Chinese grain was being shipped to foreigners or offshore evildoers, Will, *Bureaucracy and Famine*, pp. 216–17; Ye, comp., "Qianlong chao miliang maimai shiliao," part 1, pp. 26–29, part 2, pp. 29–30.

Quite a few respondents pointed out what they considered flawed behavior patterns. The Liang-Guang governor-general and the Jiangxi governor blamed not only the granary system, but also official interference or ineptitude more generally. The Fujian governor alleged waste of the land's potential as a result of peasant laziness, adding that folk in Jiangsu, northern Anhui, Henan and Shandong (a list probably referring to the environmentally problematic Huaibei region) were too prone to desert the land in times of hardship.[15] Their negligence as farmers aggravated the subsistence problem. In the same moralistic vein, several respondents commented on this or that form of "waste" of land or grain. Such memorialists proposed official action against the making of grain-based liquor, the growing of tobacco, the excessive use of land for graves, or the irresponsibility of wealthy families whose parks and gardens swallowed too much arable.[16]

Perhaps better economic thinking was shown by the one respondent who mentioned a monetary factor, or the three who observed that the inflation was general and was not confined to grain. However, enough has been said to show that, collectively, the respondents were fertile in suggesting factors. What the above summary could not do was convey the richness and sophistication of many responses, the variety of policy proposals offered to the court, or the extent to which opinions differed on the central issue of the granaries. To remedy these shortcomings is the task of what follows. Selected responses will be examined in sufficient detail to bring out their distinctive features. Because the granaries' defenders were a minority and on the losing side (at least in 1748–49), let me first try to rescue their views from historical obscurity.

---

15. On the ecology of the modern Huaibei region (Jiangsu and Anhui north of the River Huai plus the adjacent parts of Henan and Shandong), see Perry, *Rebels and Revolutionaries*, chap. 2. On the environmental and social problems of modern southwest Shandong, see Esherick, *Origins of the Boxer Uprising*, pp. 17–28, and Pomeranz, *Making of a Hinterland*, esp. chap. 3.

16. It was Tuerbing'a, the Yunnan governor, who was concerned about the size of graves. He alleged a recent tendency, widespread in the lower and middle Yangzi provinces (especially Jiangxi), to ignore government restrictions on grave size.

The Granaries' Defenders

The granaries' defenders were administrators of northern or south-western provinces. The list goes as follows: Shise (Henan); Huang Tinggui (Gansu); Echang (Guangxi); and Zhuntai, in his capacity as Shanxi governor only. Chen Hongmou (Shaanxi) and Aligun (Shandong) thought the annual buying process inflationary but denied that the amounts kept off the market were inordinately high. Chen argued positively for large ever-normal stockpiles. Hengwen (Guizhou) did not explicitly defend the granaries but seems to have found their role more positive than negative in the Guizhou context of limited price problems. His colleague Jie Xizhou had still less time for the granary hypothesis as far as Guizhou was concerned.[17]

Gansu and Shanxi: no inflationary trend, official stockpiling essential. Huang Tinggui and Zhuntai denied that their rugged and commercially isolated northern jurisdictions were undergoing an inflationary trend. Experience in Gansu, indeed, had been the opposite. Freak high prices (6.0 to 9.0 taels per *shi*) caused by military demand under Yongzheng had given way to gradually stabilizing prices after the cessation of hostilities (1735), and then to positively low ones (by Gansu standards) because of successive good harvests beginning in 1742. Huang cited examples from different parts of Gansu to argue that, while prices varied because of such local circumstances as the proximity of large troop concentrations, or the special vulnerability of parts of Lanzhou and Gongchang prefectures to drought, there were no relatively high regional prices that could not be easily explained. He concluded: "The level of grain prices in Gansu depends generally on the condition of the harvests." Zhuntai told the court that, on first arrival in the Shanxi capital at harvest-time the year before, he had been amazed by the prevailing high grain prices. After consulting the price records for the

---

17. The references for the memorials considered in this section are as follows: CC, Shise, QL 13/1/23; Zhuntai, QL 13/4/18, first mem. (cat. no. 1142-035); Huang Tinggui, QL 13/4/24; Chen Hongmou, QL 13 (cat. no. 1143-013); Echang, QL 13/5/22; Hengwen, QL 13/6/10; and LFZZ, Jie Xizhou, QL 13/4/23 (d.r.) (cf. QSL/QL, *juan* 311:46b–49a); Aligun QL 13/8/6 (d.r.) (cf. QSL/QL, *juan* 323:45b–49a).

last twenty-nine years, however, he had realized that in Shanxi such high prices were normal.

Thus for Huang and Zhuntai, there was no phenomenon to be explained, as far as their own jurisdictions were concerned. Huang accepted that the official buying process was inflationary in grain-surplus provinces linked by water transport to large markets, but the contrast between such conditions and those prevailing in Gansu could not have been more absolute. In Gansu, "for the level of [grain] prices to be kept in balance must depend precisely on official buying." This was not simply because this poor and arid province needed large reserves in case of catastrophic droughts. Gansu's commercial isolation cut the province off from outside help in times of famine and also rendered real the danger of "disasters caused by plenty" (glutted grain markets). As we saw in chapter 3, Huang defended the role of Gansu's petty speculators in providing demand for grain. *A fortiori*, he could not but uphold the value of state intervention buying that was carried out responsibly, giving the private customer priority (if Huang can be believed), and whose purpose was to manage the problematic Gansu market in the interests of the public and the military forces on the border.[18]

Zhuntai opined that in Shanxi, poor agricultural conditions, commercial isolation and exceptionally severe transport difficulties made granary reserves "the scheme of prime importance" for avoiding famine. So far from advocating a further reduction of Shanxi's storage target, he advised the court as to the help the province needed to meet that target. His request took a familiar form: let Shanxi *jiansheng*-title buyers be debarred for two years from paying in silver at the Board of Revenue. The Board had been mistaken in rejecting such a proposition the previous year: to require Shanxi's would-be *jiansheng* to pay in grain within Shanxi offered the only realistic hope of meeting the compromise target, from which the current shortfall was some 750,000 *shi* (27 percent).

---

18. Huang claimed that his new rule of 1742 requiring official buyers to hold back until midday had protected the Gansu public from the ill-effects of granary restocking practices elsewhere. CC, Huang Tinggui, QL 6/11/28, and chap. 4 n. 56 above. Cf. Dunstan, *Conflicting Counsels*, p. 215 for another reference to the complementary action of official and private buying in assuring demand for surplus grain: in 1738, the Shaanxi governor noted that any risk of a glutted market was being averted by the combined effect of speculative hoarding and official buying.

Zhuntai did not confine himself to defending the principle of serious grain storage in Shanxi. Official storage, he suggested, addressed only the problem of emergency relief and could not reduce the prevailing high grain prices in the province. To moderate grain prices, Shanxi's administrators should adopt two goals: increasing grain production and facilitating commerce. In putting forth ideas for boosting grain production, Zhuntai was typical of several 1748–49 respondents for whom the granary system was not the only major cause of elevated prices. Indeed, pursuit of what I elsewhere call "defensive expansion" (as opposed to *per capita* growth) was the standard response of court and bureaucrats in high-Qing China to the worsening ratio between population and resources. P-É. Will has written much about mid-Qing "productivist adventures," those manifestations of government preoccupation with boosting food supply; there is no need to pile up examples here.[19] However, Zhuntai's program for enhancing food security in Shanxi is worth summarizing, not only because it was already being implemented, but also because of his engagement with the obstacles that the province's geography laid in the way of commerce. As we shall see, Zhuntai believed in the efficacy of Yangzi Valley commerce; in advocating road improvement in Shanxi, he tried to bring this northern province closer to the southern model. Yet the Qing redrawing of far-northern boundaries gave Zhuntai opportunities that were not available to Yangzi Valley governors. He offered both an integrated blueprint for frontier development and a commercial solution to the problem of transporting frontier grain surpluses to the southwest Shanxi cities.

Zhuntai assumed that the Shanxi authorities faced a situation in which there was "almost no [cultivable] land left uncultivated" within the province's traditional borders. Such was the state of affairs in most of China proper as commonly perceived by mid-Qing civil servants. Zhuntai was conventional in seeking higher productivity on the existing acreage through irrigation projects wherever the potential existed. But not every governor could so readily envisage literal expansion of

---

19. For the terms "defensive expansion" and "productivist adventures," see (respectively) Dunstan, "Official Thinking," pp. 596-97, and Will, "Clear Waters," p. 309. For a rich examination of "productivism" in action, as well as the broader issue of expansion versus growth in late imperial China, see Will, "Développement quantitatif."

Han-style agriculture in transborder territories. Zhuntai cited a recently inaugurated survey of reclaimable land in the Guihua Cheng region of southern Inner Mongolia; this, although regarded as "beyond the frontier" (*kouwai*), lay administratively within Shanxi province under the Qing dynasty. The survey would be the first stage of a systematic effort to expand grain cultivation north of the Great Wall, in areas that had not traditionally been part of China proper, and to generate a surplus large enough to feed others besides the local garrisons that underpinned Manchu control. Previous central government policy had tended to encourage the use of Inner Mongolian land to absorb surplus Chinese labor—labor typically set loose by the famines that prompted authorizations of seasonal migration across the Great Wall.[20] By contrast, Zhuntai's colonial vision was of grain to feed the Shanxi urban resident at home.

Zhuntai was not the first Shanxi governor to be fascinated by the prospect—glimpsed already by Yongzheng in 1725—of using agricultural surpluses from the Guihua Cheng region to reduce urban grain prices in the interior. Two of his immediate predecessors, Liu Yuyi and Aligun, had been involved in an experiment to find out whether grain could be transported cheaply from Mongolian Shanxi to the populous southwestern quarter of the province by using ox-hide floats to travel down the Yellow River with the current.[21] This experiment having been reported unsuccessful, the provincial administration had turned to more conventional approaches. Zhuntai did mention the possibility of having grain moved overland from Guihua Cheng southwest to Tuoketuo, and then shipped down the Yellow River to the port of Cangtou Zhen, whence shipping up the lower reaches of the River Fen was easily arranged. Shipping grain down the Yellow River was feasible, if only one knew how; commercial interests were already doing it.[22]

---

20. On Chinese agricultural expansion in Mongolia in the first century of Manchu rule, see Ma Ruheng and Cheng Chongde, *Qingdai bianjiang*, vol. 1, pp. 273–85, esp. p. 281 for the pace of reclamation and Han Chinese settlement in the Ordos region flanked by Guihua Cheng.

21. Zhang, "Liangshi xuqiu," p. 41; Dunstan, *Conflicting Counsels*, pp. 27–28, 48–52.

22. Later in 1748, the prefect of Tongzhou (Shaanxi) told his provincial governor how private traders overcame the challenge of the Yellow River's current. The letter is translated in Dunstan, *Conflicting Counsels*, pp. 53–56.

Perhaps, however, because his advisors were still overchastened by the failure of the ox-hide float experiment, Zhuntai seems to have adopted road improvement as the prime task for facilitating commerce in Shanxi.

Zhuntai's response to the January edict on grain prices describes the extensive roadworks that were in progress south of the Yanmen Pass in Daizhou near the inner loop of the Great Wall, at Hanxin Ling in Pingyang in the southwest of the province, and on the east-west road from Pingding to the Zhili border. He wrote of repairs and improvements to difficult tracts, of strategic stretches being opened to cart traffic from the north or south.[23] The promotion of overland commercial transport from the new agricultural regions north of the Great Wall (and from Zhili, Henan, Shaanxi, and the former defence zone between the inner and the outer loops of the Great Wall) was central to his vision. What one misses in his comments is any estimate of how far the most ambitious road improvement project could reduce the proverbially high transport costs incurred in mountainous Shanxi. Commercialism had its limits in north China.

Henan: let speculation remain the prime target!   Shise, as Henan governor, remained true to the interventionist tradition that he had inherited from his predecessors, Yin Huiyi and Yaertu.[24] While identifying population growth as the fundamental cause of the inflation, Shise saw legitimate and illegitimate commercial activity as the main reason for those upward fluctuations that could not be explained simply by local harvest failures. Indeed, he took a cliché of the antigranary position and turned it against unregulated private commerce. For Shise, the point was not that each *shi* in the granaries meant one *shi* less for sale, but rather that "when [private] hoarders add one *shi* to their stockpiles, the folk lose one *shi* from their food supply." He interpreted

---

23. Besides mentioning plans to have the road through Hanxin Ling widened to take cart traffic from the south, Zhuntai noted that the mountain road through the Yanmen Pass was now "broad and level throughout. It is apparent to the eye that large cart traffic from beyond the frontier will all be able to pass without obstruction."

24. Cf. chap 4 above, and, for the vigor with which Yin Huiyi and Yaertu suppressed yeast manufacture in Henan (in order to root out the "waste" of grain in liquor-making), Dunstan, *Conflicting Counsels*, pp. 217–19.

the seasonal pattern of speculative activity in the opposite way from those provincial chiefs who claimed that hoarders played a positive role in their communities. As we have seen, for governors such as Chen Dashou, it was a defence of the speculator that he sold in the *soudure* period, when prices reached their peak.[25] For Shise, by contrast, it was sufficient condemnation of the speculator that he awaited the *soudure*'s high prices before selling.

In Shise's view, spatial variations in a province's grain prices reflected differences in harvest quality, whereas post-harvest price rises were explicable by trade and hoarding. Commercial exports from zones of plenty were, of course, stimulated by the high prices of less fortunate areas in a process of redistribution that Shise accepted as inevitable. Prohibition of speculative hoarding, by contrast, ought to be the first priority of territorial officials who cared about assuring popular subsistence. Such prohibition had just shown its value in Henan, where a firm ban had sufficed to bring about a gradual decline of prices that had surged to 1.2 or 1.3 tael per *shi* (unhusked) in regions where the harvest had been moderate to good. Official buying for the ever-normal granaries, on the other hand, was simply necessary. It did not cause price rises, because the rule was to buy only while grain remained cheap.

Shaanxi and Shandong: the purchase system inflationary, the amounts stored not too high. As governor of the drought-prone, northern province of Shaanxi, Chen Hongmou maintained his earlier belief that buying for the granaries pushed up market prices. As we have seen, he had, as Jiangxi governor in 1742–44, been one of those promoting use of title sales as a potentially complete substitute for the annual buying process.[26] If his role in that episode raises questions about his commitment to the ever-normal system, there is no trace of disrespect for this ancient institution in his 1748 memorial. To the contrary, he defended the principle of large-scale state stockpiling. The publicity attending official buying did indeed, he thought, cause sudden price increases, the effect being so strong that it was manifest even when the amounts

25. See chap. 3 above.

26. See chap. 6 above. The account that follows may be compared with that in Rowe, *Saving the World*, pp. 261–62.

bought were small. However, given the ways in which granary stocks were restored to the public, conventional ever-normal practice meant that grain was "dear at first but not dear later." Such a pattern was different from the progressive price inflation, which he attributed primarily to population growth.

Chen's prescription for the empire's overall food shortage focused on encouraging the cultivation of marginal land in remote areas. This should be done, he thought, by publicizing, properly implementing, and, if possible, extending the existing policy of permanent tax exemptions on small parcels of reclaimed land (with reasonably generous *mu* conversion rates for larger parcels).[27] However, he also wrote at length about the ever-normal system. He asserted the necessity of *soudure*-period stabilizing sales even in normal years, expatiated on the transport costs that could have been saved in recent famine relief operations had more grain been on hand in local granaries, and rejected the idea that the existing storage targets were too high. Targets should be high, but, in order to reach them, one should require payment for both *jiansheng* and *gongsheng* status to be made locally in kind, while giving poor landowners the option of paying their land tax in grain. Chen dismissed the notion that boosting the state's stockpiles in these ways would deprive the market. The fact was that the realm's chronic overall food stringency was periodically aggravated by seasonal shortages and major subsistence crises; large grain reserves, acquired, as far as possible, in ways that did not cause price surges, provided the best means for addressing these problems. Cost-effectiveness could be enhanced if branch stockpiles were created along navigable waterways.[28]

The response submitted in the name of Aligun, the Shandong governor, but perhaps largely the work of his colleague Tang Suizu, was one of the more thorough and original memorials of the whole set. It was written after Qianlong's decision to reduce the storage targets, a move that the author had no choice but to praise. Yet the brief, con-

---

27. *Mu* conversion was the practice of compensating for differences in soil fertility by letting areas larger than a *mu* count as one *mu* for fiscal registration purposes. In the simplest case, two *mu* of poor land could be deemed equivalent to one *mu* of fertile land. Some local *mu* conversion schedules were far more complicated than this. See Ho, *Studies*, pp. 103–16.

28. For developments in Shaanxi later in 1748 that would have seemed to vindicate Chen's views, see Dunstan, *Conflicting Counsels*, pp. 29–30, 53–55.

ventional plaudits are undermined by suggestions elsewhere in the memorial that, to the extent that the granaries were the problem, the aspect that required reform was the purchase system, not the amount stored. The Shandong explanation took population growth as fundamental, while noting high land prices and the increased sophistication of the economy as derivative factors. Population growth had raised the number of "those pursuing parasitic trades" (a stock designation for merchants of all kinds), leading in turn to a general price rise across the entire range of textile raw materials and products, for example. Aggravating factors included the high value of "copper" (brass) coin relative to silver, and the effects of granary restocking as at present implemented. As to the former, the author explained that when dealers bought grain from the producers using coin, and then converted their cost price into silver at the current rate, the effect was to inflate the price by 20 to 30 percent. This was because a tael of silver was now worth only between 70 and 80 percent of its theoretical value in terms of brass coin.[29]

As for the granaries, the Shandong memorial gives an account of why official purchasing should be inflationary, but it implies that large-scale state stockpiling *per se* could not be blamed for the high prices, because it was not really taking place. The amounts of grain being bought did not keep pace with those used for relief, for which reason very few of the provincial storage targets had been met. "This means that much of the grain bought is still dispersed among the people. It would seem inappropriate to overdo the criticism that 'half the population's output goes into the granaries.'" The hyperbolic internal quotation is from the January edict.[30] It is dismissed with a deft understatement.

---

29. Cf. the fragmentary provincial exchange rate data collected by Wang Guangyue and Hans Ulrich Vogel. These data suggest that, while coin was notably "dear" throughout the first twenty-eight years of Qianlong's reign, 1748 may have been the worst year in much of northern and eastern China, with the exchange rate reaching lows of 600 cash/tl. in Xi'an and 700 to 710 cash/tl. in Shandong and some other eastern provinces. Wang Guangyue, "Qianlong chunian qianjia," pp. 96–97; Vogel, "Chinese Central Monetary Policy," pp. 19–20, 27, 30 (cf. ibid., pp. 33, 35, 38); see also Chen Zhaonan, *Yongzheng Qianlong nianjian*, figure 1 (facing p. 20).

30. QSL/QL, *juan* 304:17a–b.

The Shandong proposals for reform of the annual purchase system focused on the need for sensitivity to market conditions and (where interprovincial purchasing was necessary) means to prevent news of impending purchases from reaching distant target markets in advance. In the context, such proposals, which aimed only at adjusting current practice, implied defence of the stockpiles. It was measures for increasing agricultural production that had pride of place among the Shandong recommendations, and one of these was premised on the continuing operation of the ever-normal system. To Aligun (or Tang), the central challenge in agriculture, at least in northern China, was to boost labor inputs. One way of doing this would be to help poor farmers with the cost of hiring labor in the crucial weeding season. When granary reserves were sold during the spring, interest-free loans could be offered to farmers out of the proceeds. As the loans would be repayable in unhusked grain after the autumn harvest, this scheme had the potential to reduce the annual grain purchase requirement. As we saw in chapter 3, however, Aligun did not match his support for the granary system with a strongly interventionist approach towards grain speculation. In this, he was akin to Huang Tinggui and different from Shise.

Guangxi and Guizhou: limited price problems, granaries not to blame. Not all the responses from southwestern provinces defended the granaries. One of the most coherent expositors of the antigranary view was the Yunnan-Guizhou governor-general Zhang Yunsui, one of whose subordinates, the Yunnan governor Tuerbing'a, seconded him on crucial points. But Zhang and Tuerbing'a were mainly generalizing about the system nationwide, whereas the authors considered here wrote specifically of conditions within their own jurisdictions.[31] The most interesting discussion of southwestern conditions is by Echang,

---

31. Zhang and Tuerbing'a turned to the situation in their own jurisdictions towards the end of their memorials. Both claimed that in that context, population growth (particularly in connection with the mining industry) was the basic cause of rising prices. While Zhang stressed that maintaining granary reserves was essential in border provinces (such as Yunnan), he also suggested that, in certain circumstances, to restrain buying for the granaries might be as necessary in Yunnan as it was elsewhere.

whose jurisdiction (Guangxi) was an economically undeveloped grain-producing province. Echang pointed out that Guangxi grain prices had nearly doubled, but he exonerated the granaries for this increase, regarding it rather as the byproduct of a necessary—indeed, mutually beneficial—relationship with Guangdong.[32] His memorial shows one Qing administrator consciously seeking to establish a more objective understanding of Guangxi's economic situation than that which had previously guided action in this province.

To Echang, large-scale interprovincial export was the reason for the rise of Guangxi grain prices. However, this was not a situation for which callous merchants or voracious neighbors should be blamed, but an expression of economic interdependence between Guangdong and Guangxi. Substantial demographic growth in Guangdong—Echang instanced the expansion of Foshan, whose population, formerly numbered in five figures, was now "in the hundreds of thousands"— necessitated increased imports of Guangxi rice.[33] Guangxi producers benefited from the resulting cash income, while Guangxi's imports of Guangdong commodities represented commercial opportunities for Guangxi people in their home province's internal distribution network. To a modern mind, these points may be too elementary to merit exposition, but Echang was aware of combatting a less enlightened, "supply protectionist" mentality in which an attitude of blame was freely taken.[34] His policy was to forbid attempts to block the flow of

---

32. Echang indicated that the price of husked rice had risen from its "former" level of some 0.8 tl./*shi* to between 1.4 and 1.7 tl./*shi*. On the economic relationship between Guangxi and Guangdong in Qing times, and the environmental implications of that relationship, see Marks, *Tigers*, chaps. 8–10.

33. Marks (ibid., p. 238) cites 500,000 as a likely estimate of the population of Foshan (a commercial and industrial town near Guangzhou) "by the end of the eighteenth century." A mid-eighteenth-century estimate taken by David Faure to include "outsiders" is 30,000 households (Faure, "What Made?," pp. 13–14). Even assuming an average household size of five persons for a town with many immigrants, sojourners, and artificers, 30,000 households implies a total population of only 150,000 individuals, whereas Echang's wording suggests at least 200,000. His estimate may include merchant visitors who did not stay in Foshan long enough to be perceived as residents.

34. On "supply protectionism," see chap. 3 above, and on the Guangxi authorities' recent "protectionism" regarding coin supply, Dunstan, "'Orders Go Forth,'" pp. 108, 110–11.

grain to Guangdong, while reminding Guangxi farmers of the importance of keeping ample reserves for their own household consumption.
This approach presumably reflects a background in which the interests
of many, if not most, Guangxi residents were well served by high grain
prices, but the temptations of a booming market and the vagaries of the
climate left a powerful undercurrent of subsistence anxiety.

There were two voices from Guizhou. In July, the acting governor
Hengwen wrote a short memorial in which he conceded that grain
prices in Guizhou had risen because of population increase, but indicated that the upward movement had been limited.[35] In Guizhou, the
state of the harvests remained the primary determinant of grain prices.
Hengwen admitted that state purchases of grain for military uses could
cause localized price rises. However, his one brief reference to Guizhou's ever-normal granaries was couched in positive terms. It was
because these granaries now held large stocks (by Guizhou standards)
that they could be effective in combatting subsistence crises.

Jie Xizhou, the provincial surveillance commissioner, cited his long
experience of service in Guizhou as justification for venturing to submit his views directly to the throne. Writing in April, he in turn denied
that in Guizhou "half the population's output goes into the granaries."
On Jie's first arrival in Guizhou in 1726, husked rice had cost only 0.45
to 0.5 or so tael per *shi*; more recently, the price had ranged from 0.7 to
0.9 tael per *shi* in good years, and from 1.1 to 2.0 in bad. Jie accepted that
the increase was a phenomenon to be explained. To do so, he invoked
the growing sophistication of the economy, which he attributed largely
to immigration from other provinces, much of it in connection with
the mining industry. It was the immigrants who had brought commercialization, a taste for "luxury" and ostentation, and a grain-based
liquor industry that had spread to rural areas. To address the problem
of inflation, Jie recommended a ban on "luxury" and the restriction of
the liquor industry, to which he added proposals for promoting water
conservancy and pushing the frontiers of cultivation up the hillsides
and into bamboo forests. The social obstacles to reclamation by poor

---

35. Hengwen noted that maximum husked-rice prices in Guizhou in 1746–48 had
ranged from 0.8 to about 1.00 tl./*shi*—levels that he did not find particularly high.
Jie Xizhou's testimony (below) indicates that famine prices in Guizhou reached
higher levels.

cultivators were a challenge that would require careful handling by the territorial bureaucracy. Rethinking the granary system would have been beside the point in Guizhou.

Ambivalence Where Least Expected

Three of those responses that pay lip-service to the granary hypothesis prove, on close examination, to be ambivalent about it. All were written by (or in the name of) Manchu provincial chiefs. It is surely significant that one spoke for a grain-rich Middle Yangzi province (Jiangxi), one for a major importer of Yangzi Valley surpluses (Zhejiang), and one for a trio of provinces that included both grain-exporting Jiangxi and grain-importing Jiangsu. Had there been consensus among mid-eighteenth-century provincial leaders that, geography permitting, the grain market's workings were beneficent and sufficient, one would have expected these authors to have endorsed the granary hypothesis without much hesitation. They should, presumably, have pressed for a major reduction of the state's commitment to stockpiling grain that, given the efficient water-transport networks covering the lowland, "core" parts of their jurisdictions, could have been more rationally distributed by grain merchants. This is not what we find.[36]

Zhejiang: limited interest in the granary hypothesis.   Zhejiang had the realm's fifth-highest compromise storage target (3.48 million *shi*), and its second-highest basic target (2.8 million *shi*). Nonetheless, Guzong, the Zhejiang governor from October 1747 until April 1748, did not evince much perturbation about the possible impact of buying for Zhejiang's ever-normal granaries on local market prices. In his preamble, he expressed mechanical respect for Qianlong's thoroughness in identifying causes of the high grain prices—causes that, of course, included state stockpiling. Having indicated formulaically that his master's list was altogether pertinent, Guzong addressed three further factors that he thought relevant specifically to Zhejiang's case. It was

---

36. The ambivalent responses are as follows: CC, Guzong, QL 13 (cat. no. 1142-020); Yinjishan, QL 13/7/2; Kaitai (cat. no. 1142-026). Guzong's superior, Kaerjishan (governor-general for Zhejiang and Fujian), although a moderate accuser of the ever-normal system, evinced only weak interest in reforming it.

only after a fairly substantial exposition of these other factors that he turned to the question of the granaries.

Heading Guzong's list was the problem created for a major food importer like Zhejiang now that the flow of grain from its usual, Middle Yangzi suppliers was reduced to a trickle. Guzong, who had been in post for only a few months since the dismissal of the over-zealous Chang'an, offered the explanation that in recent years, Jiangxi and Huguang grain prices had been "incomparably" higher than in the past, with the result that merchants no longer found it profitable to import grain to Zhejiang. This implausible statement may be interpreted (at least for the time being) against the background of the developing supply crisis in Hangzhou that Guzong's successor, Fang Guancheng, would attribute to Chang'an's ban on warehousing.[37] Devoid, apparently, of the wit to hypothesize a link between the ban on warehousing and the diminishing appeal of the northern Zhejiang market to grain merchants, Guzong also lacked the guile to divert attention from his own complicity in Chang'an's blunder by scapegoating the granaries for the rise in Middle Yangzi grain prices (which he did not try to explain). It is no wonder that he was soon transferred back into a specialized branch of government—the Grand Canal administration—in which he had more experience.[38]

In expounding his first point, Guzong emphasized the high proportion of the rural Zhejiang population whose livelihood was based on crops other than staple foodstuffs. In his second point, he drew attention to the numerous outsiders who drew on Zhejiang's food supply without contributing to grain production. This group included the indigo growers, paper makers, and iron smelters from Jiangxi and Fujian who worked in Zhejiang's mountainous peripheries. Also significant were the food needs of the "continuous procession" of merchants who passed along the major trade route linking the southern stretches of the Grand Canal with mountainous Quzhou, the gateway to Jiangxi and thence Fujian, Guangdong, and Huguang. Third on Guzong's list of factors was the outflow of grain by sea, whether on fishing vessels or

---

37. See chap. 3 above. I return to the causation of the 1748 supply crisis in chap. 8.

38. For Guzong's career as director-general of the Grand Canal (Zhili), director-general of Grain Transport, and, in 1748–54, director-general of the Grand Canal (Henan and Shandong), see Qian, comp., *Qingdai zhiguan nianbiao*, vol. 2, pp. 1,401–13.

merchant craft. This, while technically illegal, was very hard to stop, in his brief experience. In fact, he did not think that there was much that could or should be done about any of the three factors, apart from exemplary punishment for one or two longtime maritime grain smugglers.

Guzong was similarly noncommittal about the need for reform of the granary system or for a cutting of reserves. He referred, with apparent approval, to the dismissal of the four oft-cited requests—those by Bulantai, Xu Yisheng, Ji Huang, and Yang Eryou—that buying for the granaries be halted, and pointed out that the benefits of annual stabilizing sales could be realized only if there were post-harvest buying to replace the sold-off grain. All that was needed was flexibility and restraint, with buying carried out exclusively in years of plenty. Guzong suggested, judiciously, that "considered reductions" could be made in the compromise targets, and pointed out that unexpended purchase funds could be used in relief distributions. However, he devoted as much space to discussing the best approach for handling grain speculators as he did to proposed adjustments to the ever-normal system. He stopped far short of portraying official grain stockpiling as a harmful practice calling for immediate reform.

Jiangsu-Jiangxi-Anhui: hostile rhetoric belied.   Yinjishan, as Liang-Jiang governor-general, had his headquarters in Jiangsu and was responsible for Jiangsu, Anhui, and Jiangxi. He presided over a granary system that had rather modest compromise targets (2.1 million *shi* for Jiangsu, 2 million for Anhui, and 1.6 million for Jiangxi). However, in Qing administrative parlance, Jiangsu in particular was a "southeastern" province, and it was the "daily rising" rice prices in the "southeastern" provinces that had fuelled the agitation of the early 1740s. Writing in late July, 1748, Yinjishan had recently been engaged in pacifying Suzhou after a mishandled popular disturbance occasioned by the sharply rising price of grain. Whether or not he was there when the cost of living peaked, he had every reason for concern about the soaring prices in that central rice emporium.[39] If Yinjishan accepted the granary

---

39. QSL/QL, *juan* 314:32a–33a; cf. table 8 and figure 1 above for the alarming sharpness of the 1748 price rise. Yinjishan's memorial was written after the exposure of the putative link between Chang'an's ban on warehousing and the supply

hypothesis, vehement assertion on his part would have been unsurprising.

At first sight, vehemence against the granaries is found in Yinjishan's memorial. The opening of his discussion of the granary system suggests almost rabid adherence to the antigranary position. As one reads on, however, one gains the impression that the initial forceful statement of the case against the granaries was a rhetorical ploy, designed to clear the way for an oblique defence of the time-honored institution. Once one had shown (with just a hint of sarcasm) that one understood the attractions of a policy of scattering the uselessly immobilized official stocks among the people for commercial distribution, one was in a good rhetorical position to raise reservations.

It is not that Yinjishan believed adjustments to the ever-normal system to be unnecessary. To the contrary, he proposed that the rapidity of turnover be limited so as to reduce the need for buying. Springtime sales should be made only insofar as they were justified by acute *soudure*-time shortages, and silver should replace grain in relief distributions during localized disasters whose severity was not extreme. Administrators whose storage targets had been reached should preserve their stocks carefully, without seeking to add to them. Those with unmet targets should buy only in years of good harvests, replacing purchases with *jiansheng* title sales if market conditions remained unfavorable for buying grain. Yinjishan did not specify whether by "targets" he meant the compromise or basic targets. Either interpretation would be tenable. What can be affirmed is that he asserted the importance of the granaries, refrained from explicitly proposing a retreat from the targets deemed appropriate in 1743–44, and set out to formulate a policy that would cut official buying without a general moratorium. This was not quite the approach to be expected of a market-conscious "southeastern" provincial chief (and Yinjishan's discussion of the use-of-silver option shows that he was not devoid of market-consciousness).

---

crisis in Hangzhou and other Jiangnan cities. While he quoted a few lines from the edict that repudiated the ban, it does not seem to have occurred to him to accept the latter as an explanation for the rising prices. The body of the memorial was written as if the ban had never come to Yinjishan's attention.

Not only were Yinjishan's reform proposals modest, but he also made it clear that he did not think the granaries should bear too much of the blame for the inflation. In his preamble, he mentioned buying for the granaries fourth in a list of five inflationary factors. He pointed out that the inflation had been general and affected all sorts of commodities that were not the objects of official purchase. From this he reasoned explicitly that official buying could not be the whole explanation. He devoted less space to the granaries than he did to denouncing the preparation of rice wine, expounding his ideas for the suppression of large-scale cultivation of the glutinous rice that was its chief ingredient, and advocating similar measures against the diversion of paddy land to growing sugar, tobacco, and luxury aquatic vegetables such as lotus-root. If, as he estimated, the wine industry's annual consumption of glutinous rice in the three Liang-Jiang provinces was indeed in the "millions" of *shi*, and so was the consumption of wheat in yeast-making for the wine industry, his space-allocation was not necessarily disproportionate.[40]

Jiangxi: the need to see mere numbers in proportion.   Finally, there was the ambivalent report of Kaitai, the Jiangxi governor. Since, from the beginning of the debate, a major focus of the case against the granaries had been professed concern about the effects on Middle Yangzi grain markets of buying for the Lower Yangzi granaries, one might have expected those who spoke for Hunan, Hubei, and Jiangxi in 1748 to take an especially hard-line antigranary position. This is, of course, assuming that the Middle Yangzi governors paternalistically favored the interests of poor consumers, rather than identifying with those of wealthy landowners who stood to benefit from high grain prices. A cynic might suggest that it was precisely because these governors' true sympathies lay with the landowning interest that none of them attacked the ever-normal system very strongly—even though the Hunan and Hubei respondents must be listed among its attackers. Kaitai, for his part, not only opined that present granary restocking practices

---

40. Yinjishan estimated that the number of commercial wine-makers in the three provinces was at least in the thousands and growing daily. He alleged that there were counties in which the acreage devoted to glutinous rice exceeded that devoted to regular paddy.

tended to provoke price rises, but also made proposals whose effect would have been to protect Jiangxi from buying for the granaries of other provinces. To this extent, his response conformed with reasonable expectations of a Middle Yangzi governor's approach. What makes his memorial interesting, however, is his near ridicule for the idea that too much grain was being bought for Jiangxi's own reserves.

For Kaitai, the root cause of the inflation was population growth, whose effects were compounded by inept administrative responses to the whole range of problems generated by food shortages. Official behavior in such contexts was typically alarmist on one hand and superficial on the other; as a result, the antisocial profit-maximizing tendencies of grain dealers were encouraged and not checked. The characteristic market response to official desperation to meet granary restocking quotas—intensification of speculative activity—was but one manifestation of this broader pattern. Officials who would proceed calmly when they had small amounts to purchase were apt to resort to panic buying when the shortfalls to be filled were large. But the official propensity for ill-considered action was not confined to such occasions. Rather, officials too pusillanimous to implement proper surveillance against hoarders responded to minor subsistence problems with empty, self-important gestures, such as putting up large notices. Such fuss served only to exacerbate popular insecurity and thereby give unscrupulous grain dealers a pretext for raising prices arbitrarily.

Having argued that, ineptly managed, the granary restocking process caused price increases, Kaitai duly suggested reform. His proposal, while intended for nationwide application, was in the Jiangxi tradition established by Chen Hongmou: it sought to protect consumers from the inconveniences of official buying through partial reliance upon title sales. In future, Kaitai recommended, when shortfalls in the granary reserves were small and the local harvest was at least a 70 percent good one, buying should be done "as appropriate" within provincial boundaries.[41] When these favorable conditions did not obtain, the provincial authorities should request a temporary order that their province's aspirants to *jiansheng* status buy the title in the province in exchange for

---

41. For discussion of how percentage harvest ratings were determined, how they were used, and how they should be interpreted, see Marks, "'It Never Used To Snow,'" pp. 423–26.

grain. This order would remain in force until the storage target had been reached. Up to a point, this proposal represents the Jiangxi governor helpfully commending successful Jiangxi experience as a model for other provinces. However, as he noted that a virtue of such arrangements would be provincial self-sufficiency in grain for stockpiling, it is reasonable to suspect that he was still more interested in protecting Jiangxi consumers from thoughtless buying by the emissaries of other provinces.

Yet Kaitai did not opine that Jiangxi's own granary system was an unnecessary impediment to the workings of commerce in this relatively grain-rich province. To the contrary, he pointed out that the total amount now held in Jiangxi's granaries (which he put at over 1.7 million *shi*, some 100,000 *shi* more than Jiangxi's compromise target) did not, at most, greatly exceed half the annual output of one large, productive county in the province.[42] This was judging by the annual output of the two counties administered from the provincial capital, which he estimated at 3 and 4 million *shi* (unhusked) respectively. But not all of the 1.7 million *shi* reflected recent buying. Allowing, said Kaitai, for pre-existing stocks, reallocated tribute grain, and the proceeds of title sales, the cumulative total bought since 1743–44 had been less than 700,000 *shi*. This was not even 30 percent, at most, of the annual output of one large productive county. Jiangxi's experience was atypical, and Kaitai did not suggest that similarly minuscule proportions of total provincial output were being bought elsewhere. Nor did he hazard an estimate of the total amounts being bought on Jiangxi markets for the granaries of other provinces. However, given Qianlong's pronouncement that "half the population's output goes into the granaries," Kaitai's figures sounded a strong note of skepticism. Jiangxi, it appears, was a province whose compromise target had been overfulfilled without unduly straining locally-grown staple food supplies.

Kaitai explicitly argued against drastic measures based on the assumption that buying for the granaries was to blame for the inflation. Both commercial circulation and official storage were important for combatting famine, he said, and although they might raise grain prices, "one really should not blame them deeply." If granary reserves were to

---

42. Cf. Will and Wong, *Nourish the People*, p. 304, table 9.4, which gives the Jiangxi granary system's "year-end balance" for 1747 as 1,736,000 *shi*.

be ample, there would always have to be buying. The point was to prevent the adverse consequences of buying inappropriately done. Adjustments such as those that he proposed were surely preferable to a moratorium, which would only create the need for major buying later. Kaitai may have taken the less than noble attitude that Jiangxi's grain supplies should be protected from the granaries of other provinces, leaving his subordinates with optimal conditions for the relatively unchallenging task of managing Jiangxi's low-target stockpiles successfully. But he did not attack the ever-normal granaries more than he defended them.

The Granaries' Accusers

All the remaining responses indicate unambiguous acceptance of the granary hypothesis, at least as a partial explanation for the rise in grain prices. However, the authors varied greatly in the weight that they attached to the granary system as compared with other factors, and in the degree of radicalism shown in their reform proposals. Hallmarks of moderate responses include dispassionate tone, multicausal explanation, and interest in remedies other than drastic curtailment of buying for the granaries. Prime examples of such moderation include the thoughtful analyses of Kaerjishan, already cited, and Yang Xifu, whose discussion has long been well known among Qing specialists.[43] Some of the remedies proposed by moderates were in the tradition of "defensive expansion" or its conventional accompaniment, avoiding "waste." Yang's memorial provides a good example. By way of reform of the granary system, he advocated selective reductions of the compromise targets by 10 to 20 percent and greater flexibility about the annual 30 percent rotation norm. However, he followed these proposals with a

---

43. E.g., Zelin, *Magistrate's Tael*, pp. 294–97, and, for an almost complete translation, Dunstan, *Conflicting Counsels*, pp. 282–89. The moderate and less than hard-line antigranary memsorials are as follows: CC, Peng Shukui (Hubei), cat. no. 1142-023; Zhang Yunsui (Yunnan and Guizhou), cat. no. 1142-024; Yang Xifu (Hunan), cat. no. 1142-025; Namin (Anhui), QL 13/5/16, first mem. (cat. no. 1143-004); Tuerbing'a (Yunnan), QL 13/6/9; Pan Siju (Fujian), QL 13/6/25; Kaerjishan (Zhejiang and Fujian), QL 13/6/26 (fragment); Xinzhu (Hubei and Hunan), QL 14/2/28; and Yue Jun (Guangdong), QL 14/3/28.

lengthy disquisition calling for a nationwide water-conservancy campaign in order to boost grain production.[44]

The line between moderate and extreme is sometimes hard to draw. One borderline respondent was the Yunnan-Guizhou governor-general Zhang Yunsui, whose explanation of why official buying for the granaries should push up grain prices was excerpted in chapter 4. Zhang regarded population growth as the fundamental cause of the inflation, with immoderate, ubiquitous, and quota-driven buying for the granaries the one severe exacerbating factor. Recognizing that the granaries played an essential role in frontier provinces, he stressed that the moratorium approach was suitable only for "southeastern" provinces, where commerce was well developed. Yet he was unsparing in his arguments against the granaries, even challenging the assumption that state stockpiling was needed because the ordinary, thriftless people could not keep their own reserves. As he put it:

One *shi* more in the official stores means one *shi* less for the folk's use, and yet the folk cherish grain more than do the authorities. It is not necessarily true that grain held by the authorities will be carefully preserved, without losses, while grain held by the people will be wasted, with none left over.

For the "southeastern" provinces, Zhang favored a two-to-three-year moratorium on buying for the granaries. In his case, recognition that expansion of the granary system was not the sole or fundamental cause of the inflation did not mean lack of zeal for radical restraints on buying. There is nonetheless a gap between his thorough, somewhat nuanced exposition and the strident, essentially monocausal or extremist discussions that I call hard-line responses. Three of these are examined here.[45]

----

44. The comments of Namin (Anhui) contrast with other respondents' generally conventional "productivist" and antiwaste proposals. Namin went beyond the consensus that virtually all of China proper's readily cultivable land was already under cultivation, suggesting that it would be ill-advised to open up new land in the interior. Any new reclamation would either encroach on river courses or provoke disputes. Namin, like Zhuntai, supported reclamation outside China proper.

45. For the hard-line memorials, see CC, Celeng, QL 13/3/28; Zhuntai, QL 13/4/18, second mem. (cat. no. 1142-036); Jishan, QL 13/int.7/6; Yaerhashan, QL 14/4/25; and LFZZ, Shulu, QL 13/3/22 (d.r.) (cf. QSL/QL, *juan* 311:28b–29b). Jishan and Yaerhashan wrote as the Sichuan and acting Jiangsu governors respectively.

Guangdong-Guangxi: official interference is the problem. The most single-mindedly anti-interventionist of all the twenty-six replies was by Celeng, governor-general of Guangdong and Guangxi. His memorial has two main parts, one dealing with the granaries, and one with other kinds of state intervention in the grain trade, as we saw in chapter 3. Celeng represented these other forms of intervention as aggravating factors, the opposite of what was needed to correct the disequilibria caused by state buying for the granaries.

The main faults that Celeng saw in the granary management practices of territorial officials were impatience and excessive zeal. Provincial authorities whose insistence on respect for deadlines was blind to actual supply conditions were partially responsible, he hinted, for the behavior of those county magistrates who forced members of the local gentry or wealthy commoners to buy grain for the granaries at less than market prices. Nor was this all:

There is, besides, [a disposition to] vie in pursuit of singularity, setting up other categories besides the ever-normal and pre-empting merchant grain, [which is] either reserved for helping out adjacent jurisdictions or stored for the whole province's relief. The provincial, regional, and brigade commanders [in the Green Standards Army] likewise join their tongues in talk of grain reserves and set up separate brigade granaries (*yingcang*).[46]

Even in the best of years, the combined, insistent pressure of demand from civil and military officials, gentry, and aspirants to *jiansheng* status was bound to send prices up sharply, when concentrated on "one or two" productive areas.

Celeng's economically liberal prescription was "that those things that impede the grain [should] all be done away with; that, with official purchasing knowing restraint, commercial transportation may flow freely; and that, with grain among the populace becoming day by day more plentiful, in two or three years' time a great reduction may be

---

46. On brigade granaries, see QCWXTK, vol. 1, *juan* 35, pp. 5,179, 5,182 (1726, 1729, Guangdong), 5,185 (1733, Sichuan); *juan* 36, pp. 5,187 (1736, Guangdong), 5,190–91 (1739, Zhejiang, Fujian, Sichuan; 1736, 1740, waterways brigades), 5,193 (1744, Henan), 5,194 (1746, Shandong, waterways brigades); QSL/QL, *juan* 73:21a–b (Guangdong, 1738). In the Guangdong model, brigade granary stocks were lent to the soldiers in the *soudure* period. The granaries were replenished after harvest through deductions from the soldiers' pay. The brigade granaries established later in Henan were intended to operate like ever-normal granaries.

looked for in the price." He called not only for the elimination of the various interventionist practices, of *jiansheng* title sales in favor of the granaries, and of brigade granaries, but also for reform of official buying practices, a moratorium on buying, the systematic use of silver in relief distributions, and the freezing of the nationwide grain storage target at the level of present reserves. As Celeng understood it, a target so determined would have been relatively low. He believed present total holdings to be "not less than" 30 million *shi*, comprising as much of the old 28-million *shi* target as was currently in stock, community granary reserves, and the accumulated proceeds of *jiansheng* title sales. Some 30 million *shi*, including (as was *not* usual) community granary stocks, ought to be ample, he suggested.

Anhui: the people's expectations should be checked. The message from Anhui was similarly uncompromising and somewhat more radical. It is true that the governor Namin's response, submitted in June, devoted comparatively little space to the granary hypothesis, despite unambiguously endorsing it. Even Namin, however, sent out weak signals of support for liberal orientations in economic policy.[47] More significantly, the provincial administration commissioner Shulu had replied earlier (as acting governor), arguing that the ever-normal system was ineffective as well as inflationary. While the buying phase aggravated the anxieties and greed that led to hoarding, the subsequent sales could have a favorable impact on market prices only at excessive cost to public funds, and even then would not reach all the needy. If, on the other hand, official buying were suspended, those now tempted to hoard would realize that there was no point and sell their grain before it rotted. Not only would hoarding thus be eliminated without prohibition; with grain released for circulation, "real merchants" would "do business" in their proper "quest for tiny profits," thereby keeping

---

47. Namin mentioned currency supply as a further area in which one should *ting qi ziran* (leave things to take their course)—by which he meant eschewing the proliferation of provincial minting operations. On the same day, he wrote a very brief memorial to acknowledge receipt of the late May edict chiding Chang'an for excessive zeal in suppressing hoarding. Here Namin described Qianlong's dictum that "with the affairs of the market-place . . . one should let the people carry out the circulation for themselves" as "truly a sound rule unchanged throughout ten thousand ages." CC, Namin, QL 13/5/16 (cat. nos. 1143-004 and 1143-005).

prices down in areas of good and poor harvests alike. For the time being, therefore, official buying should be done only for those granaries whose storage level was more than 50 percent below the basic target. Such buying should be local, and it should await a good harvest. When stocks were rotated, the replacement grain should also be bought locally, and sales intended to assist the public should be made only after "real" harvest failures.

So far, Shulu's proposals were not different in kind from others that had gone before, although he was probably the first to suggest explicitly that the minimum tolerable storage level could be as low as half the basic target (apart from Wu Wei, for whom the tolerable minimum would have been zero).[48] However, Shulu's discussion introduced a new and harsh note, suggesting that too much was being done to help the Jiangnan poor, and that Jiangnan's inhabitants were being spoiled with too readily granted relief. Relief, Shulu indicated, was supposed to be only for major disasters; it had never been annual in the past. He claimed that it was in Jiangnan, where at most 20 to 30 percent of households were engaged in agriculture, that the most relief was given (whereas the conventional ideology of famine relief saw it as specifically for peasants).[49] He listed some other provinces in such a way as to suggest that relief activity was concentrated in eastern and north-central China and tapered off towards the remote southwestern provinces. Why so? Not, as one might suppose, because of climate and/or relative population density, but because folk in the distant provinces "have never been accustomed [to expect relief] and . . . do not dare indulge in wanton hopes." In Jiangnan and the adjacent provinces, by contrast, "the habituation [of the people] is complete, and no sooner is there some climatic abnormality than . . . they gaze with outstretched necks." The munificence of recent famine relief measures (imperial bounty "without precedent in history") contrasted, on the people's side, with an "insatiable" lust for gain—a lust that was expressed in troublemaking and attempts to constrain the authorities when the latter disappointed overweening expectations of relief.

"I in my foolishness," advised Shulu, "am of the opinion that the presumptuousness (*jiao*) of the populace's spirit should . . . be gradually

---

48. See above, chap. 5.
49. Will, *Bureaucracy and Famine*, p. 134.

repressed." In future, localized or minor dearths should be met only with measures appropriate to the occasion, not standard relief operations. Appropriate measures apparently meant leaving the people to "exchange what they have for what they lack," that is, buy food from the market. Shulu probably envisaged that the authorities would help them by providing doles of silver—an approach that he had claimed to be effective. However, the tone of his remarks was such as to suggest that perhaps even this expenditure should be begrudged.[50]

How the Shanxi respondent minded the business of China's "southeast." We come finally to the one respondent who, in 1748, fully expressed that confidence in market forces for which one looks in vain in the submissions for the Middle and Lower Yangzi provinces by Guzong, Yinjishan, and Kaitai. This outspoken official was Zhuntai, the Shanxi governor, in his separate memorial on the situation in China's "southeastern" provinces. Zhuntai made very clear the strength of his conviction that, in the "southeast," excessive buying for the granaries was the major cause of the inflation. Most striking in his fervent but generally unoriginal denunciation is the following abstract discussion:

It is an essential characteristic (*qing*) of material things that they are cheap when plentiful and expensive when in short supply. It is their inherent tendency (*shi*) that they are plentiful when circulating (*tong*) and in short supply when they stagnate (*zhi*). It is their proper pattern (*li*) that they circulate when each [individual] takes thought for himself, and transfers [of goods] are made among the people (*ge zi wei mou er zhuanyi zai min*), but that they stagnate when one sole method is adhered to, and exchanges take place [under the control of] the authorities (*shou qi yi fa er jiaoyi zai guan*). If, now, the established method of the ever-normal [system] is adhered to in pursuit of circulation and withal abundance, failure seems inevitable.

To Zhuntai, who had high regard for the efficacy of private commerce, and for whom avid official buying was objectionable partly because it squeezed the merchants out, economic individualism (as represented in the formula *ge zi wei mou*, "each takes thought for himself") yielded superior results to those obtainable from unitary state planning.

---

50. The Grand Council copy of Shulu's memorial, which is the only full version I have found so far, is hard to read in places. It is fair to note the possibility of errors of interpretation. Such errors are, I think, unlikely to be major.

Zhuntai's proposals were daring—to the point that he was almost courting rejection for excessive radicalism, or so one would have thought. His ideas reflected the opinion that the private grain trade in the Yangzi Valley provinces was so well developed, and rice output so high, that officialdom would normally not need to have recourse to grain stockpiles. During natural disasters, distributions in the form of silver, coupled with the merchant tendency to gravitate towards high selling prices, would normally suffice to save the poor. Even if relief in kind were needed, the grain could easily be bought from growers in adjacent jurisdictions, if only those jurisdictions did not have to buy grain for their own ever-normal stockpiles.

Zhuntai envisaged what, by the standards of his day, would have been a virtual free-trade zone in the seven Yangzi Valley provinces (from Sichuan east to Jiangsu and Zhejiang). His proposals would have largely freed this huge and grain-rich area from official competition in the storage and redistribution of grain surpluses. He advocated that, except in areas like Huizhou prefecture (where geographical conditions were unfavorable for the rapid importation of emergency grain stocks), sizable cuts should be made from the *basic* ever-normal storage targets, which should be reduced to the four-figure numbers of the Kangxi period.[51] Grain held in excess of these low-level targets should be sold in "stabilizing sales," with the proceeds deposited in circuit and prefectural treasuries until required for direct monetary doles for famine victims. Zhuntai did not say how (or indeed whether) the disbursed funds would be replaced. His proposal had the same rationale as Wu Wei's older and yet more extreme idea of selling off the granary reserves in their entirety. The extraordinary release of ever-normal grain onto the market would inaugurate a new regime of cheapness and abundance, the state having renounced large-scale purchasing and stockpiling of grain. A four-figure grain reserve was not large by the standards of merchant inventories or hoards kept for speculative gain.

Did Zhuntai really court rejection? His memorial is dated 14 May, which means that it was written long before Qianlong was ready to

---

51. Cf. QCWXTK, vol. 1, *juan* 34, p. 5,173, which gives the standard target for "large" county-level jurisdictions in ca. 1700 as 10,000 *shi*. Zhuntai had perhaps seen and misinterpreted Kangxi-period targets expressed in husked grain (e.g., those recorded under 1691 in ibid., *juan* 34, p. 5,170). Such targets would have been half of the corresponding figures for unhusked grain.

make a decision. The plan was to wait until all the provincial responses had arrived and then refer them to the Grand Council for confidential deliberation.[52] The interesting fact remains that on 12 August, the emperor decreed a policy departure that was both less and more radical than Zhuntai's proposal. It was less radical in that it allowed for the possibility of cutting targets only to Yongzheng levels, but more radical in that it was to be implemented in all provinces, without distinction between the highly commercialized "southeast" and the rest of the country. What had the emperor in mind, and why did he choose a crude solution when so many nuanced proposals were available? Chapter 8 looks beyond the granaries debate for a likely partial answer.

---

52. LFZZ, Shulu, QL 13/3/22 (d.r.).

8

The Slashing of the Targets

As we have seen, Qianlong interrupted the flow of discussions from the provinces in August 1748 with an edict signalling a radical reversal of his previous expansionary policy on state stockpiling. There followed a period of fact-finding and preliminary implementation; it was not until January 1749 that the responsible committee transmuted his orders into a recommendation for a 30 percent cut in targets. The central issue addressed in this chapter is whether the perverse crudity (as it must seem with hindsight) of the August decision is likely to have had causes other than, on one hand, peak rice prices and widespread unrest, and, on the other, the monarch's personality and state of mind. Should the newly resolute rejection of expansionary ambitions be seen, essentially, as a panic reaction, to be expected of one prone to hastiness and vacillation? Or can a close reading of the committee's report and some associated documents, combined with attention to their broader context, suggest another rationale for the decision?

I argue below that these texts give ample grounds for declining to take the stated rationale completely at face value. The significance of the 30 percent cut was, I think, more complex than is generally assumed. While the ostensible justification was probably more than a pretext, my contention is that the events of the late summer of *1745* remind the historian to look westward, to Sichuan, to complement that explanation. The Board of Revenue's maneuvers in 1745 had shown that it was not unthinkable to seek to divert granary restocking funds to military finance. By 1748, the Qing state was again embroiled, much more deeply, in a military adventure to the west of Sichuan.

The Options for Reform

Before examining Qianlong's response to the diverse analyses submitted to him, let us recapitulate the policy options suggested by the fifteen or so provincial chiefs who agreed that the granary system was at least partly responsible for the inflation, and who submitted their responses during 1748, before the final decision on new storage targets. There were basically five prescriptions, put forward on their own or in different combinations. These were: (1) suspension of buying until prices fell (that is, a second moratorium); (2) reduction of the storage targets; (3) greater flexibility, and other administrative adjustments to the ever-normal system; (4) continued use of *jiansheng* title sales; and (5) the substitution of silver for grain in relief distributions. There was a sizable body of opinion in favor of firm action to curb the inflationary impact of buying for the granaries; however, the support for drastic measures was not very strong. Neither the moratorium nor the target-reduction option was advocated by more than half of these respondents, although a majority (ten) did advocate at least one of these approaches. Correspondingly, nine of these respondents expressed interest in the use-of-silver option, whose point was generally agreed to lie in the mitigation of any adverse consequences of a moratorium or target-reduction order.

Of the seven advocates of a moratorium, three envisaged that suspension of buying should last for "two or three years," while one spoke only of temporarily "going slow" on buying. Two preferred conditional suspension: the local authorities should do no buying as long as the county granary held a specified proportion of its basic target in the form of grain. For Shulu, as we have seen, that proportion should be 50 percent; the acting Hubei governor suggested 60 percent. Zhang Yunsui (echoed by his subordinate Tuerbing'a, the Yunnan governor) favored a moratorium but thought that strategic frontier provinces should be exempted from it.

Advocates of reducing the storage targets were even less numerous than proponents of a moratorium, and in only one memorial (Zhuntai's second submission) were truly drastic cuts envisaged. As we have seen, Guzong spoke of "considered reductions" from the compromise targets, while Yang Xifu thought that, where appropriate, these targets should be cut by 10 to 20 percent only. Jishan, the Sichuan governor, wanted a moratorium tried first. If, after a year or two, the moratorium seemed effective in reducing prices, provincial chiefs should be ordered to reconsider their storage targets and cut any that were too high. Celeng's relatively radical proposal (freeze maximum holdings at the level of present reserves, on the assumption that the nation's granaries currently had 30 million *shi*) still implied a global storage target 2 million *shi* higher than the basic target (28 million *shi*). Zhuntai himself made clear that his ideal of reversion to the four-figure county-level targets of the Kangxi era applied only to the seven Yangzi Valley provinces, and even in that zone was intended to exclude jurisdictions that lacked convenient water transport. Limiting the scope of his proposals to the Yangzi Valley meant improving on the cruder binary division of the nation into frontier "northwest" and commercialized "southeast." Zhuntai explicitly noted that the large, more-or-less "southeastern" zone comprising Fujian, Guangdong, and Guangxi needed large reserves because of its commercial isolation from the rest of China. He also requested special accommodation to help Shanxi, his current, northern jurisdiction, to reach its compromise target.

Just over half of those who, in 1748, expressed acceptance of the granary hypothesis saw at least part of the solution in adjustments to the system. The need for flexibility about the annual 30 percent rotation norm attracted the most comment, with respondents stressing that one should not sell off more grain than necessary to reduce *soudure* prices and forestall a real risk of rotting. Also mentioned were the importance of buying only in good years, or only while prices were low, and the desirability, in jurisdictions where the compromise targets were already met, of annually selling any extra grain brought in by sales of *jiansheng* titles. Kaerjishan elevated the concept of flexibility into a grand, overarching principle that should govern all aspects of granary policy. He argued that there were too many variables even within individual provinces for any panacea to be possible, and pointed out that it might make sense to overfulfil the local targets when grain was abundant. His sense of relevant variables was well developed: the best course of action might depend not only on supply conditions and the prospects for relief through commerce, but also on the circumstances of any given natural disaster. It would make a difference whether the disaster followed a run of bad years or of good ones, as well as whether the adjacent jurisdictions had enjoyed good harvests.

There was a tendency to see the fourth and, more especially, fifth prescriptions (*jiansheng* title sales and the use-of-silver option) not as solutions that could stand alone, but as ancillary to one of the other three approaches. Advocacy of title sales as a serious perennial alternative to buying was confined to respondents who were, or had been, associated with the relatively successful experiments in Jiangxi and Fujian. Thus, on one hand, the Sichuan and acting Hubei governors proposed the use of title sales for counteracting the depletion that a moratorium would bring. For Yinjishan, they offered a way of reconciling oneself to the need to keep buying suspended for the duration of adverse market conditions: if the titles found buyers, the granaries could be replenished gradually. Chen Hongmou and (probably) Kaitai apart, only Pan Siju, the Fujian governor, regarded sale of *jiansheng* titles as an approach in its own right. Pan's proposals are worth examining as a final note on the progress and significance of the Fujian experiment.

Pan reminded the court of the established view that, because of Fujian's commercial isolation, official granary reserves played an essential role, being needed even in the annual *soudure* period. Although the province was duly awaiting the fulfillment of its 2-million *shi* contribution target before proposing a new overall target, it was now less than 400,000 *shi* short of the contribution target, while total holdings exceeded 2.3 million *shi*. This success, however, had its problematic side: it was because Fujian was simultaneously buying grain and selling *jiansheng* titles for grain that the province had suffered a progressive rise in cereal prices. It is no surprise, in view of what we have seen of the Fujian approach, that Pan chose the grain-buying method for relegation to supplementary status. He suggested that when, in due course, Fujian's overall target was established, the province should continue to accept grain in return for *jiansheng* titles. If the title sales yielded enough, annual buying would become superfluous. Pan no doubt envisaged that the future target would not greatly exceed present holdings, which he described as "ample." We saw in chapter 6 that there is reason to suspect his predecessor, Zhou Xuejian, of having sought to manipulate the central government into letting Fujian more or less substitute a contribution target for the compromise one required by the policy of 1742, and thus substantially eliminate the purchase principle. This objective must now have seemed close to realization. As if to consolidate the gains already made, Pan held out a fiscal inducement—or rather, revised the inducement that Zhou had offered in December 1744. When annual buying was rendered unnecessary, he suggested, the authorities should report the proceeds of the past spring's stabilizing sales to the Board of Revenue for use in army pay.

In his proposals for the realm at large, Pan extrapolated from the Fujian model. He realized that Fujian had enjoyed atypical success with title sales but did not pause to discuss the applicability of this experience elsewhere. If only other provincial bureaucracies used effective techniques of exhortation, he suggested, they should become able to rely essentially on title sales to meet and then maintain their targets (compromise targets, to judge by the context). Buying should become a secondary approach, to be used only with caution.

For most respondents, the main attraction of the fifth prescription (using silver in relief distributions) was that it made possible lower storage levels than would have been needed for completely literal feeding operations. The existence of the use-of-silver option could therefore justify advocacy of either the moratorium approach or a reduction of the storage targets. However, the rationale for issuing silver to famine victims was premised on the operation of a highly effective and responsive private commerce. It was not obvious that the required degree of responsiveness could be expected in north Chinese conditions. In 1748–49, accordingly, the ten respondents who expressed interest in the use-of-silver policy were based in, or prescribing specifically for, the Yangzi Valley or "southeastern" provinces. The policy was mentioned or recommended by the governors-general of Jiangsu-Jiangxi-Anhui and Guangdong-Guangxi, the Zhejiang and Sichuan governors, the acting governors of Anhui and Hubei, and the acting Jiangsu governor appointed in October 1748. Three respondents from "frontier" provinces favored it for economically developed regions of the "interior," or, to use Zhang Yunsui's vivid phraseology, for "the southeast, that land of swamp, where boat and oar pass everywhere, and commercial rice comes to the rescue in unbroken stream."

While most supporters of the use-of-silver option were aware that its success depended on a lively private grain trade, those based in the "southeast" proper (as opposed to the southwest and far south) tended to restrain their professions of faith in the efficacy of commerce. They typically reserved the policy for minor, localized disasters, in which sufficient inflows of commercial grain from nearby unaffected areas could be expected with a fair degree of confidence. The acting Hubei governor recommended the use of a mixture of silver and grain in such disasters, while Celeng and probably Shulu and Yinjishan envisaged distributions made entirely in silver. Celeng took an extreme position. The Guangdong-based hard-liner wished to see a silver-grain combination used even in "great disasters" and was dogmatic on the use-of-silver policy's success record. Contradicting Chen Hongmou, who mentioned substantial shipments of relief grain in recent years to stricken regions of Jiangsu north of the Yangzi, and Namin, who was still more explicit, Celeng wrote as follows.[1]

In recent years, . . . the prefectures of Luzhou and Fengyang [in northern Anhui], and Huai'an and Xuzhou [in northern Jiangsu] have undergone rather severe disasters, and Your Majesty . . . did not begrudge funds in the tens of millions to relieve them. Over a period of four or five years, how can [the sum devoted] have been only a hundred million? In general, [the relief was] consistently distributed in silver, and there is now none of the disaster victims who does not repose secure. It may be seen that once one has silver, one can buy food at one's convenience.

The use-of-silver option could be represented (as it was by Yinjishan) as a more cost-effective and efficient way of delivering relief than the established practice of transporting supplementary stocks when ever-normal grain reserves ran short. It was, of course, also a labor-saving option, compared with the burden of keeping the granaries well stocked. Was the policy's tempting simplicity associated with a certain thoughtlessness—a certain indifference towards the fate of famine victims—on the part of its adherents? This may have been true of radicals such as Shulu and Celeng, but not necessarily of all supporters. Yinjishan addressed the possibility of local markets too depleted for the use-of-silver policy to work without adjustment, or indeed at all. If, he indicated, the problem were that market prices were too high, the rate at which victims' grain allowances were commuted into silver could be revised *ad hoc*. However, in the event of extreme shortage, officialdom "ought naturally" to bring in grain supplies from other jurisdictions (if,

---

1. Referring to widespread 1747 food shortages that had not spared Jiangsu, Namin noted that Qianlong had not only authorized the diversion of tribute grain to relief purposes, but also allocated extra food relief. This was because, with four contiguous provinces smitten, His Majesty had "truly feared that if relief were issued only in the form of silver, [the recipients] would have no place to purchase [grain]." For references to this and other 1748 responses, see notes to chap. 7.

presumably, the county's own reserves had been used up). Yinjishan, who advocated neither a moratorium nor reduction of the storage targets, was more able than other supporters of the use-of-silver option to assume that, were his proposals followed, adequate reserves would be available when needed.

It is fair to say, in short, that the majority opinion from the provinces was that buying for the granaries should be at least somewhat restrained. However, those respondents who shared this view offered Qianlong a fairly wide range of proposals as to method. It would be going too far to claim that there was *consensus* that the targets set in 1743–44 should be repudiated. Arguably, the principle that should have been seen to emerge most strongly from the twenty-six memorials was that different policies should be applied in northern and southern China, or in "border" and "southeastern" provinces. However, true to form, the emperor preferred a bold, across-the-board solution.

Let There Be Cuts!

Qianlong announced his decision on 12 August 1748, without awaiting the last of the responses from the provinces.[2] Presumably, he thought it necessary to move before the autumn buying season started. His edict represented the granary hypothesis as, after all, entirely reasonable, for "only a certain amount of grain is produced. It . . . naturally follows that if too much is concentrated in official hands, there will necessarily be a shortfall in that left [among] the people." The edict renounced the policy of adding to "the old targets of the Kangxi and Yongzheng periods" and ordered that all holdings in excess of these targets be gradually sold. Alternatively, surplus holdings could be redistributed across provincial borders, if there were neighboring provinces whose stocks fell short of their "old" targets. The grand secretaries and Board of

---

2. As of 6 August, replies from fifteen "places" (governorships or governor-generalships) had been received, while nine were outstanding. Apart from the three responses written in 1749, the missing ones were probably Tuerbing'a's, Pan Siju's, Kaerjishan's, Yinjishan's, Jishan's, and Aligun's. Those by Hengwen and Aibida, although probably not yet received, may not have been expected, given that Jie Xizhou had replied for Guizhou. YFD, QL 13/7/13 (7:1616); cf. ibid., QL 13/8/6, and CC, undated note, cat. no. 1142-014.

Revenue were to work out a redistribution plan, as well as ascertaining the "original" targets and associated stock rotation method.[3]

The edict, which was fairly brief, did not mention the use-of-silver option. It neither elaborated on the rationale for reverting to "the old targets of the Kangxi and Yongzheng periods," nor offered guidance as to which of its pre-Qianlong targets any given jurisdiction was to choose. It is possible that the emperor was attracted by Zhuntai's vision and wanted lower, Kangxi-period targets adopted in the Yangzi Valley provinces, and higher, Yongzheng ones retained elsewhere. It is equally possible that the only significance of the inclusion of the word "Kangxi" was to emphasize the thoroughness of the repudiation of Qianlong's earlier, expansionary policy. It may be that in ordering investigation of pre-Qianlong stock rotation principles, the emperor was taking up the notion that there might be lessons in the putative Kangxi approach of not insisting upon physical reserves of grain.[4] The historian can only guess; contemporary senior officials must have been left guessing too, unless they had access to inner court "sources" who could interpret the imperial intentions for them.

It was not until the end of January 1749 that the grand secretaries and their fellow deliberators were ready to present recommendations. In the meantime, implementation and development of the new policy were pushed on apace. On 5 September, the emperor directed the provincial chiefs to submit swift and accurate statements of their provinces' "Kangxi and Yongzheng targets" and provide full details of the

---

3. QSL/QL, *juan* 319:5b–6b.

4. As we saw in chap. 5, Li Qingzhi and Sun Hao had claimed in 1743 that under Kangxi, magistrates had not been punished for keeping granary reserves at least partly in silver. The January 1748 edict adduced the notion that "in the Kangxi period, the granary reserves were kept in silver, not in grain" without explicitly endorsing it; it was Zhang Yunsui who told Qianlong dogmatically that "in the Kangxi period, [the granaries] held silver and not grain, but there was never any question of relief not being carried out." For a less sanguine view of late-Kangxi granary management, including the substitution of silver for grain, see Zelin, *Magistrate's Tael*, pp. 4 and 83. Huang Liuhong's advice on famine relief administration (1694) is inconsistent with any notion of mid-Kangxi granaries normally containing silver only (cf. Dunstan, *Conflicting Counsels*, pp. 289–90).

the present state of their reserves.[5] He had ordered that the Jiangsu authorities buy only in those jurisdictions whose current holdings fell short of the "old" targets. On 7 September, this instruction was made applicable nationwide in an edict prompted by reports of generally good harvests. On 23 September, Qianlong rebuked Kaerjishan, the Zhejiang-Fujian governor-general, for having set a deadline for completion of the buying needed to restore Zhejiang's reserves to their "old" target level.[6] Consideration of the state of the market was to take precedence over attaining even the "old" storage norms. This was the third of these autumn edicts to reiterate some version of the truism that more grain in the authorities' hands meant less among the people. It was also the second to ask rhetorically whether, rather than accumulating the fruits of the good harvests in official granaries, it would not be better to "let [them] circulate within the villages."[7] Here was a striking reversal of the previous assumption that the right time for official buying was, precisely, following good harvests.

One could say that the emperor had done little more than finally renounce an overambitious policy adventure of his early days as ruler. However, even to command reversion to the basic targets would have been to select a policy more radical than was advocated by any of the provincial chiefs except Zhuntai and, arguably, the half-dozen respondents who favored a definite moratorium on buying. To decree that targets earlier and lower than the basic targets also be considered was probably to fly a kite, that is, to see how far responsible opinion was prepared to follow Zhuntai and the earlier apostles of a grain market as free as possible of state competition. To urge that a year of

---

5. QSL/QL, *juan* 320:21a–b. On 15 October, Qianlong complained that many of the governors and governors-general had not yet reported. He found this "very dilatory." Ibid., *juan* 323:16a–b.

6. The edict quotes the shortfall from the "old" Zhejiang target as 800,000 *shi*, but the detailed figures later supplied by the Zhejiang administration put the deficit much higher, at over 1.8 million (see table 10 below). As the edict referred to Zhejiang's deficit as large, there may be a transcription error. An 800,000-*shi* shortfall would have been only the approximate amount to be bought annually assuming (a) Zhejiang's "Yongzheng" target, and (b) exact application of the 30 percent rotation norm (see table 2 above).

7. QSL/QL, *juan* 318:44a–b, 320:23a–24a, 322:4a–5a. The edict quoted in *juan* 318 was clearly issued after the 12 August edict (to which it refers), although it precedes the latter edict in this source.

plenty be seen as an opportunity to make grain on the marketplace abundant was to start conditioning officialdom for a sea-change in political economy. But how much had political economy really to do with the matter by this stage? Is it possible that considerations of another order were again at work?

The Conservative Settlement of Early 1749

The kite, when finally hauled down, was positioned a short way in the opposite direction from that in which Qianlong was looking. The new total target that emerged from the early 1749 deliberations was not 28 million *shi* or less, but about 33.8 million (33,792,335 to be precise). Had the deliberative committee wished to adopt the suggestion of at least a partial return to Kangxi targets, the figures supplied by fifteen or more provinces, although not, in the majority of cases, actual targets, would have given it a preliminary basis. However, perhaps deterred by the thought of reserves of under 500,000 *shi* in Anhui, or not much more than 200,000 in Hubei, the committee passed quickly over its Kangxi-period data. Some provinces, noted the report, had not set targets under Kangxi; elsewhere the targets had been very low; elsewhere again, records were incomplete. It would be better to reinstate "the old Yongzheng-period targets." The committee refrained from pointing out that rather few of the available Yongzheng figures clearly represented actual targets either.[8]

As Will has noted, the committee proposed six exceptions to the still-drastic cutback. Shaanxi, Gansu, and Yunnan should be allowed to retain targets set under Qianlong because specific Yongzheng-period targets had not been established for them, and all three were on the frontier. The Shaanxi and Gansu reserves were stated to have military as well as civilian functions; the former was to keep its 1743 compromise target, while the latter was to keep the high-level target that had

---

8. Cf. table 2 above. The main source for the account that follows is the deliberative committee's full report, CC, Zhang Tingyu et al., QL 13/12/12, with its statistical appendix, "Ge sheng changping cang gu ding'e qingdan" [List of Established Provincial Targets for Ever-normal Granary Grain Holdings] (fragment, n.d., dated 1749 by present author; cat. no. 1132-016). For summaries, see QCWXTK, vol. 1, *juan* 36, p. 5,195; QSL/QL, *juan* 330:33b–35b; DQHDSL, vol. 9, *juan* 190:4a–5b (pp. 7,590–91).

gone uncut in 1743. Yunnan, however, was to revert to its Qianlong-period basic target (minus 100 *shi*).[9] Also worthy of special consideration were Guangdong, whose geography did not permit abundant
grain production, and Fujian and Guizhou, where food deficits were
not easily relieved by private commerce. These three provinces' present
storage levels, which either fell well short of the "Qianlong-period targets" or were "barely" up to them, should be adopted as new targets. To
be sure, questions arise when one compares these provinces' 1749 targets as stated in later sources (2,953,661 *shi* for Guangdong; 2,566,449 for
Fujian; 507,010 for Guizhou) with 1748 estimates of current storage
levels (2,901,700 *shi* for Guangdong; 2.3 million for Fujian in July 1748,
achieved partly through continuing title sales; between 1.2 and 1.4 million for Guizhou).[10] I address these problems later.

The committee also adjusted the Zhili and Fengtian targets upward
to allow for changes in administrative geography that had entailed the
foundation of new ever-normal granaries. It was the above major and
minor concessions that, in combination, raised the revised nationwide
target to almost 33.8 million *shi*. Despite Zhuntai's advocacy, the
committee had not looked favorably upon Shanxi's claims to special
treatment, nor did it propose exceptions for the last two northern
provinces (Henan and Shandong). Unlike Qianlong, however, it had
expressed some recognition of the need to take into account such factors as strategic importance and commercial isolation.

Up to this point, the committee seems to have been somewhat
supportive of the granary system, given the radicalism of the August
edict. However, when we look at its handling of the statistical information sent in by the provinces, we find a rather different picture. The
approach was formally correct, but not entirely solicitous about the
real level of reserves. The provincial chiefs had been required to submit
figures for the following: grain actually in store; grain sold and not yet
replaced; grain on loan to local people; and unexpended proceeds of

---

9. Cf. tables 3, 6, and 7 above. For Will's account of the 1749 cuts, see *Bureaucracy and Famine*, pp. 192–94.

10. CC, Pan Siju, QL 13/6/25, Zhang Yunsui, QL 13 (cat. no. 1142-024), Hengwen, QL 13/6/10; LFZZ, Jie Xizhou, QL 13/4/23 (d.r.). For the 1749 targets, see
DQHDSL, vol. 9, *juan* 190:4b–5a (pp. 7,590–91), and QCWXTK, vol. 1, *juan* 36,
p. 5,195. The latter source preserves a variant of 2,566,409 *shi* for Fujian, but this
commonly cited figure is almost certainly inaccurate.

past sales. It made sense for Qianlong to specify these categories because he was asking for the information in early September, close to the point of maximum depletion in the annual cycle.[11] The committee's report suggests that it was from late December on that most of the statements arrived; it is therefore likely that some of them reflect at least partial restocking. Nonetheless, the statistical appendix to the committee's report shows that the provincial statements mainly followed the suggested format. Although the appendix, being torn, lacks information for five provinces, the missing data can generally be supplied from the original provincial statements and/or their statistical appendices. Only in Gansu's case must we calculate back from the *minshu gushu* figure, reported three months later.

To be sure, the data represent a situation in flux, especially for those provinces that were drawing on their stocks during the autumn. This was true of Shandong, Shaanxi, Guangdong, and, above all, Sichuan, where continuing appropriations of ever-normal grain for military rations made it meaningless to submit any information beyond Sichuan's "theoretical holdings for the current year" (*xiannian yingcun gu*), plus the statement that, having habitually replaced all its sold and lent grain, the province had no unexpended proceeds of past sales.[12] The nation-wide totals calculated in tables 10 through 14 are marred by these realities and by other problems mentioned in the notes. Ignoring these flaws in order to gain a preliminary overview, we may say that about 27 million *shi* were reported to be in store in the autumn of 1748; that grain sold or otherwise distributed and not yet replaced totalled 7 million *shi*; and that about 5 million *shi* were probably on loan (tables 10 and 12). Nationwide, the actual post-harvest holdings reported to the center were short of the effective current basic target (30,755,542 *shi*) by almost 3.9 million *shi*. They were short of the new "Yongzheng-period" or substitute targets (33,792,335 *shi* in total) by over 6.9 million (tables 10 and 11). The committee's proposals for filling the 6.9-million *shi* gap do much to expose the limits of its commitment to the antifamine stockpiles.

---

11. QSL/QL, *juan* 320:21a–b.
12. CC, Bandi, QL 13/9/26 and (LFZZ) appendix.

Table 10
Reported Actual Holdings in the Autumn of 1748, Compared
with the Basic Targets in Force as of That Year
(Units: *shi* of unhusked grain. Figures for husked grain have been converted to
unhusked by doubling. Bold type is used to indicate provinces whose actual
holdings exceeded their basic targets. Rounding is consistently to nearest integer.)

Province	A Basic target*	B Reported actual holdings, autumn 1748	C B compared with A (B as a percent- age of A)
Shandong	2,959,386	2,185,892[1]	−773,494 (74%)
Zhejiang	2,800,000	943,343	−1,856,657 (34%)
Henan	2,310,999	1,132,302[2,a]	−1,178,697 (49%)
Fujian	(2,150,000)[3]	2,052,411[3,a]	−97,589 (95%)
Shaanxi	**2,061,741**	**2,477,003[a,b]**	**+415,262 (120%)**
Zhili	1,996,216	1,628,607[4]	−367,609 (82%)
Guangdong	**1,925,685**	**2,901,700[5,a,b]**	**+976,015 (151%)**
Anhui	1,832,000[6]	691,956[6]	−1,140,044 (38%)
Jiangsu	1,568,000	1,134,399[7,a]	−433,601 (72%)
Shanxi	**1,550,000**	**1,933,583[8]**	**+383,583 (125%)**
Guangxi	1,413,398	1,322,596[9]	−90,802 (94%)
Jiangxi	**1,370,713**	**1,506,609[10]**	**+135,896 (110%)**
Gansu	**1,228,571**	**(2,107,403)[11,a]**	**+ 878,832 (172%)**
Hunan	**1,202,133**	**1,256,415[a]**	**+54,282 (105%)**
Fengtian	1,120,000[6,12]	401,812[6]	− 718,188 (36%)
Sichuan	**1,100,000**	**(1,458,642)[13,a]**	**+358,642 (133%)**
Hubei	1,070,000	617,284[14]	− 452,716 (58%)
Yunnan	701,500[15]	604,154[14]	−97,346 (86%)
Guizhou	**395,200**	**507,013[16,a,b]**	**+111,813 (128%)**
TOTAL	30,755,542	26,863,124	−3,892,418 (87%)

NOTES: *From table 7, column B, unless otherwise stated.

[1] Comprises 899,994 *shi* of ever-normal grain plus 1,285,898 *shi* (predominantly husked converted here to unhusked) of special supplementary stocks (tribute grain plus interprovincial
transfers, including 300,000 *shi* from Zhili to help Shandong restock). QSL/QL, *juan* 323:1a–b,
23a–b, 31a–32a. The "actual holdings" fig. theoretically represents stocks as of late September
plus the 300,000 *shi* sent later from Zhili. The supplementary stocks sent earlier are described
as *yingcun* (here, "should be left over"), implying that the full amount may not have been
present even in September.
[2] Fig. corrected on the basis of provincial statement. Excludes 570,895 *shi* remaining in the
separate granaries that had been established using tribute grain.
[3] Col. A: contribution target (see chap. 6). Col. B: theoretical reserves, minus grain sold over
several years and not replaced, minus grain supplied to military. Excluded are the target

Table 10, cont.

(400,000 *shi*) and current holdings (120,838 *shi*) of a stockpile recently established on Taiwan. These figs. are reported separately in the Fujian statement.

[4] Excludes 300,000 *shi* transferred to Shandong (see n. 1 above).

[5] Excludes 92,786 *shi* held outside the ever-normal targets by the granary of the Guangzhou Assistant Prefect for Grain (cf. CC, Yue Jun, QL 13/10/28).

[6] Fig. stated in husked grain and converted here to unhusked.

[7] Includes 596,358 *shi* from the Middle Yangzi (196,358 left from a transfer from Jiangxi's granaries; 200,000 each bought for Jiangsu by Jiangxi and Hunan).

[8] Includes an unstated quantity of beans and husked grain.

[9] Excludes 70,604 *shi* unhusked replacing an unused allocation of tribute grain (sent for relief sales in 1742–43). The stocks had been kept for making loans; the interest, paid in kind, was to be sold for provincial public purposes. These reserves were not reported until May 1749, when Shulu proposed to sell them and allocate the proceeds to the military. CC, Shulu, QL 14/4/12.

[10] Excludes 200,000 *shi* transferred to Jiangsu (see n. 7 above). LFZZ, appendix to Kaitai, QL 13/8/6.

[11] Calculated as follows from Gansu's 1748 *minshu gushu* data, which are expressed in standard *shi*: opening balance of 2,950,351 *shi* minus 842,948 *shi* issued in that year. However, the fig. reported in the missing statistical appendix to CC, Huang Tinggui QL 13/9/20 (i.e., 10 Nov.) will have been higher if it reflected any post-harvest restocking.

[12] Although this fig., adopted in 1743, is stated in tables 6 and 7 as Fengtian's compromise target, it is best understood as a revised basic target comprising the original basic target (1,080,000 *shi*) plus 40,000 *shi* for a jurisdiction that had been raised to county status at the end of Yongzheng's reign.

[13] Theoretical holdings. In late August, Sichuan's reserves had been reported as 1,479,000+ *shi*, a figure that excluded stocks delivered to the army. CC, Jishan, QL 13/int.7/6.

[14] Includes some husked rice and grain of other kinds (for Hubei, cf. CC, Peng Shukui, QL 13/12/8).

[15] Round fig. adopted by 1748; see table 7, n. 2.

[16] Fig. stated as 505,759 *shi*, including some husked rice and grain of other kinds. 507,013 *shi* is the total obtained by converting these minor categories into their unhusked equivalent.

SOURCES: Unless otherwise noted, CC, "Ge sheng changping cang gu ding'e qingdan" (fragment; catalog number 1132-016). All other statistical appendices are in the LFZZ collection.

[a] CC, Yang Xifu, QL 13/8/18; Kaerjishan and Pan Siju, QL 13/8/28 plus appendix, LFZZQZ (QL 13), 3257; Shise, QL 13/9/8 plus appendix, LFZZQZ (QL 13), 3209; Aibida, QL 13/9/12 first mem. (cat. no. 1144-036); Yue Jun, QL 13/9/13, QL 13/10/28; Chen Hongmou, QL 13/9/20 third mem. (cat. no. 1144-046); Bandi, QL 13/9/26 plus appendix; Celeng and Yaerhashan, QL 13/11/15; Hubao, QL 13/12/17.

[b] LFZZ, Aibida, QL 13/9/12 plus appendix; Yue Jun, QL 13/9/13 plus appendix; Chen Hongmou, QL 13/9/20 plus appendix.

Table 11
Reported Actual Holdings in the Autumn of 1748, Compared with the
"Yongzheng-Period" or Substitute Targets Determined in Early 1749
(Units: *shi* of unhusked grain. Rounding is consistently to nearest integer. Bold type
indicates provinces whose actual holdings exceeded their "Yongzheng-period" or
substitute targets. Upper case indicates provinces whose "Yongzheng-period" or
substitute target exactly matched their table 10 basic target.)

Province	A Yongzheng-period or substitute target	B Reported acutal holdings, autumn 1748[*]	C B compared with A (B as a percent- age of A)
Gansu	3,280,000[1,a]	(2,107,403)	–1,172,597 (64%)
SHANDONG	2,959,386	2,185,892	–773,494 (74%)
Guangdong	2,953,661[a]	2,901,700	–51,961 (98%)
ZHEJIANG	2,800,000	943,343	–1,856,657 (34%)
Shaanxi	2,733,010[a]	2,477,003	–256,007 (91%)
Fujian	2,566,449[2,a]	2,052,411	–514,038 (80%)
HENAN	2,310,999	1,132,302	–1,178,697 (49%)
Zhili	2,154,524[3]	1,628,607	–525,917 (76%)
Anhui	1,884,000[4]	691,956[4]	–1,192,044 (37%)
Jiangsu	1,528,000	1,134,399	–393,601 (74%)
JIANGXI	**1,370,713**	**1,506,609**	**+135,896 (110%)**
Shanxi	**1,315,837**	**1,933,583**	**+617,746 (147%)**
Guangxi	**1,274,378**	**1,322,596**	**+48,218 (104%)**
Fengtian	1,200,000[3,4,5]	401,812[4]	–798,188[5] (33%)
Sichuan	**1,029,800**	(1,458,642)	**+428,842 (142%)**
Hunan	**702,133**	**1,256,415**	**+554,282 (179%)**
YUNNAN	701,500	604,154	–97,346 (86%)
Hubei	**520,935**	**617,284**	**+96,349 (118%)**
Guizhou	**507,010[a]**	**507,013**	**+3 (100%)**
TOTAL	33,792,335[6]	26,863,124	–6,929,211 (79%)

NOTES: [*] From table 10, column B.
[1] Not clear whether this fig. was intended to represent granary or standard *shi*. It is likely that the committee ignored the distinction.
[2] Variant: 2,566,409 *shi*. QCWXTK, vol. 1, *juan* 36, p. 5,195.
[3] "Yongzheng-period target" adjusted upward to allow for recently established jurisdictions and/or recent additions to provincial territory.
[4] Fig. stated in husked grain and converted here to unhusked.
[5] There are two problems with the Fengtian figs. (1) The adjusted target (1,200,000 *shi*) can be correct only on the assumption that a newly added county-level target was to be in husked grain, not unhusked as stated. (2) A digit is missing in the committee's figure for the current shortfall from this target. This has been corrected in the table (col. C).
[6] Calculated fig. The committee stated the total as "33,792,330 *shi* odd."

Table 11, cont.
SOURCES FOR COLUMN A: Unless otherwise noted, CC, "Ge sheng changping cang gu ding'e qingdan."
ᵃ DQHDSL, vol. 9, *juan* 190:4b–5a (pp. 7,590–91). For Guizhou, the col. A and col. B figs. differ only because the committee ignored decimals when converting husked to unhusked, etc.

Given that restocking funds were generally available—if not sales proceeds, then allocations to replace free emergency relief and stocks transferred to other provinces—it should theoretically have been possible to plug most of the gap by replacing the sold-off and otherwise distributed reserves through purchase. Of course, relative prices would have determined the exact proportion of the gap that could have been so plugged. But had the approach chosen been, in principle, both to recover all outstanding loans and to replace all sold, distributed and transferred grain, there would have been a safety margin (potential surplus) of up to about 5 million *shi* (tables 12 and 13). A combination of dunning and buying was, in fact, the method recommended; in those few cases where there was a choice, however, the committee envisaged dunning as the primary approach, with buying to be used only if necessary to plug remaining shortfalls.

Before exploring the implications at provincial level of this and other preferences of the committee, let us scrutinize the figures with which it was operating. This statistical inquiry, however tedious, is essential if we are both to understand those implications realistically, and to come as close as possible to satisfying curiosity as to the highest level ever reached by the reserves before the target cuts of 1749.

The data scrutinized. We begin with the Fujian data, which, as before, are—paradoxically—both atypical and revealing of temptations and tendencies that existed elsewhere. The Fujian authorities calculated their current actual (*xiancun*) holdings (2,052,411 *shi*) as follows: theoretical holdings (3,537,327 *shi*) minus unreplaced grain sold in 1748 and previous years (970,876 *shi*) minus grain issued to the military in previous years (514,040 *shi*). The theoretical holdings comprised accumulated "contributions" from official and private sources (categories that, together, had accounted for about 300,000 *shi* since Kangxi times), "old" contributions in exchange for *jiansheng* titles (a category that had shrunk from 1.4 million *shi* under Kangxi to about 1.08 million in 1748),

Table 12

Theoretically Possible Holdings by the Winter of 1748–49

If All Missing Grain Replaced

(Units: *shi* of unhusked grain; rounding is consistently to nearest integer.)

Province	A Reported actual holdings, autumn 1748*	B Grain sold or otherwise used and not yet replaced	C Grain on loan	D Theoretically possible winter holdings (A+B+C)
Gansu	(2,107,403)	842,948(-)[1,2,a]	—[2]	(2,950,351)[1]
Shandong	2,185,892	1,472,124[3]	1,200,727	(4,858,743)[3]
Guangdong	2,901,700	140,763[4,a,b]	—	3,042,463
Zhejiang	943,343	940,931[2,5,b]	—[2]	1,884,274
Shaanxi	2,477,003	156,603[6,a,b]	549,614[6,a,b]	3,183,220
Fujian	2,052,411	970,876[7,a]	—	(3,023,287)[7]
Henan	1,132,302	205,563[8]	675,704[8]	2,013,569
Zhili	1,628,607	—	1,377,439	3,006,046
Anhui	691,956[9]	985,520[9,10]	214,120[9,10]	1,891,596
Jiangsu	1,134,399	453,343[11,a]	314,545[11,a]	1,902,287
Jiangxi	1,506,609	25,160[b]	4,834	1,536,603
Shanxi	1,933,583	28,340[12]	72,706[12,b]	2,034,629
Guangxi	1,322,596	11,019	31,061	1,364,676
Fengtian	401,812[9]	381,632[9]	118,410[9]	901,854
Sichuan	(1,458,642)	0[a]	0[a]	(1,458,642)
Hunan	1,256,415	218,681[a]	59,307[13,a]	1,534,403
Yunnan	604,154	25,834[14,a]	154,079[14]	784,067
Hubei	617,284	450,157[15]	8,574	1,076,015
Guizhou	507,013	(1,987+)[16]	—	(509,000+)[16]
TOTAL	26,863,124	7,311,481	4,781,120	38,955,725

NOTES: * From table 10, column B.

[1] Col. B fig. (in standard *shi*) is from Gansu's 1748 *minshu gushu* report. Col. D fig. is identical with the 1748 *minshu gushu* opening balance.

[2] Sales (etc.) fig. includes loans.

[3] Col. B. fig. comprises 1,084,330 *shi* of Shandong ever-normal grain and 387,794 *shi* (husked converted to unhusked) from other sources. Relief operations were still in progress, and 800,000 tls. out of the 1,097,177 tls. of sales proceeds were earmarked for purposes other than granary replenishment. The col. D fig. is therefore not meaningful.

[4] Further sales expected, pending the completion of the harvest. Provincial statement notes unexpended purchase funds corresponding to a *total* of 460,042 *shi* sold during 1742 and 1745–48 and not replaced.

[5] Includes unstated amounts sold/lent before 1748.

[6] Further loans, sales and other drawings on reserves expected. Provincial statement also notes arrears of 297,211 *shi* from loans made before 1748.

Table 12, cont.

[7] Col. B fig. (a) *includes* unreplaced grain sold over several previous years (probably the whole period 1741–47); (b) *excludes* 514,040 *shi* issued to the military over successive years. Assuming all this grain to be replaceable, the Fujian authorities stated the province's theoretical maximum holdings as 3,537,327 *shi* (variant: 3,537,325 *shi*). If we estimate the amount sold in 1748 alone as 450,000 *shi* (cf. CC, Yong Ning, QL 13/8/21), a col. D fig. somewhat more consistent with the others in this table might be 2,502,411 *shi*. Excluded from this table are additional data (cf. table 10, n. 3) for the new, nominally 400,000-*shi* stockpile on Taiwan: 120,498 *shi* sold in 1748; 76,680 *shi* allocated to cover 1747 military rations; notional col. D fig. of 318,017 *shi*.

[8] Figs. (a) *include* grain sold or lent in previous years and not replaced; (b) *exclude* (i) 190,000 + *shi* of ever-normal grain sent to Shandong in 1748 and (ii) 44,220 and 160,029 *shi* sold and lent (respectively) from the tribute grain reserves, as well as an unspecified amount sent to Shandong from these reserves.

[9] Fig. stated in husked grain and converted here to unhusked.

[10] Col. B fig. (a) *includes* (i) 288,730 *shi* used in famine relief or sent outside Anhui in 1745–46 and (ii) (probably) an unstated amount of grain sold before 1748; (b) *excludes* 250,000 *shi* (sent to Shandong in 1748) whose replacement was agreed to be superfluous. Col. C fig. *includes* an unstated amount of grain lent before 1748. LFZZ, Namin, QL 13/9/11 (appendix).

[11] Col. B fig. includes 132,102 *shi* notionally corresponding to the unspent balance of a wheat-purchase allocation. Col. C fig. includes 175,351 *shi* owed by northern Jiangsu taxpayers (postponed levy of tribute grain).

[12] Col. B fig. includes 441 *shi* unreplaced since 1746. Col. C fig. includes 35,161 *shi* lent in 1748, 24,724 lent in 1747, 4,689 lent in 1746, 1,050 lent in 1745, 1,254 advanced to the military mainly in 1747, etc. LFZZQZ (QL 13), 2772.

[13] Includes grain issued/advanced to the military.

[14] Col. B fig. comprises 17,491 *shi* sold in 1748 (of which 10,570 were "extra-target grain") plus 8,343 used during 1743–47 and not yet replaced. Col. C fig. comprises 144,479 *shi* lent in 1748 plus 9,600 advanced to the community granary system.

[15] Fig. labelled as "grain to be bought." As the combined amount sold and lent in 1748 is elsewhere stated as 161,844 *shi* (CC, Peng Shukui, QL 13/12/8), 296,887 *shi* out of the col. B fig. must have been sold or distributed in previous years (unless part of it represented grain never yet held).

[16] CC, Zhang Yunsui, QL 13/9/19 states 509,000 + *shi* as Guizhou's theoretical holdings for 1748. As, however, the appendix to LFZZ, Aibida, QL 13/9/12 records almost 2,000 tls. of unexpended proceeds of past sales, the col. B fig. (1,987 *shi*) must be too low.

SOURCES: Unless otherwise noted, CC, "Ge sheng changping cang gu ding'e qingdan." All other statistical appendices are in the LFZZ collection.

[a] CC, Yang Xifu, QL 13/8/18; Kaerjishan and Pan Siju, QL 13/8/28 plus appendix, LFZZQZ (QL 13), 3257; Shise, QL 13/9/8 plus appendix, LFZZQZ (QL 13), 3209; Yue Jun, QL 13/9/13; Chen Hongmou, QL 13/9/20 third mem. (cat. no. 1144–046); Tuerbing'a, QL 13/9/23 plus appendix; Bandi, QL 13/9/26 plus appendix; Celeng and Yaerhashan, QL 13/11/15; Hubao, QL 13/12/17.

[b] LFZZ, Yue Jun, QL 13/9/13 plus appendix; Chen Hongmou, QL 13/9/20 plus appendix; appendix to Kaitai, QL 13/8/6; LFZZQZ (QL 13), 2772, 2940.

Table 13
Theoretically Possible Holdings by the Winter of 1748–49, Compared
with the "Yongzheng-Period" or Substitute Targets
(Units: *shi* of unhusked grain. Rounding is consistently to nearest integer. Bold type
indicates provinces whose theoretically possible winter holdings *fell short of* their
"Yongzheng-period" or substitute targets.)

Province	A "Yongzheng-period" or substitute target*	B Theoretically possible winter holdings†	C B compared with A (B as a percentage of A)
Gansu	**3,280,000**	**(2,950,351)**	**−329,649 (90%)**
Shandong	2,959,386	(4,858,743)	(+1,899,357) (164%)
Guangdong	2,953,661	3,042,463	+88,802 (103%)
Zhejiang	**2,800,000**	**1,884,274**	**−915,726 (67%)**
Shaanxi	2,733,010	3,183,220	+450,210 (116%)
Fujian	2,566,449	(3,023,287)	+456,838 (118%)
Henan	**2,310,999**	**2,013,569**	**−297,430 (87%)**
Zhili	2,154,524	3,006,046	+851,522 (140%)
Anhui	1,884,000	1,891,596	+7,596 (100%)
Jiangsu	1,528,000	1,902,287	+374,287 (124%)
Jiangxi	1,370,713	1,536,603	+165,890 (112%)
Shanxi	1,315,837	2,034,629	+718,792 (155%)
Guangxi	1,274,378	1,364,676	+90,298 (107%)
Fengtian	**1,200,000**	**901,854**	**−298,146 (75%)**
Sichuan	1,029,800	(1,458,642)	(+428,842) (142%)
Hunan	702,133	1,534,403	+832,270 (219%)
Yunnan	701,500	784,067	+82,567 (112%)
Hubei	520,935	1,076,015	+555,080 (207%)
Guizhou	507,010	(509,000)	+1,990 (100%)
TOTAL	33,792,335	38,955,725	+5,163,390 (115%)

NOTES: * From table 11, column A. † From table 12, column D.

"new" (presumably, since 1738) contributions in exchange for *jiansheng* titles (1.7 million), and a bewildering array of minor categories, ranging in size from 100 to 174,000 + *shi*, of which some had originated in the misdemeanors of named individuals, and some dated from Yongzheng times. If the 2.3 million *shi* that Pan Siju reported for Fujian in July 1748 were real, they presumably represented grain corresponding to the 1.7 million *shi* raised through title sales since 1738, plus about 600,000 *shi* remaining from all the other categories, which thus appear very theoretical indeed.[13]

The Fujian statistics enable us to reconcile the claim that Fujian's new (1749) storage target (2,566,449 *shi*) was the same as its current storage level with the fact that the storage level that Fujian reported in the autumn was only 2,052,411 *shi*. As a later report from the Fujian provincial chiefs makes clear, subtracting the total sold over the years from the theoretical holdings was taken to yield the amount "that should still be present" (2,566,450 *shi*; minor discrepancies here and elsewhere reflect rounding of decimals). The 514,040 *shi* that had been issued to the military in previous years *might as well* still have been present, presumably, because there were funds to replace them; the same applied to the grain issued in 1748, a figure for which was not yet available. One could, therefore, add the 514,040 *shi* back to the 2,052,411 *shi*, yielding the 2.5-million *shi* target.[14] Whether Fujian had ever really had 2.5 million *shi* in store all at one time is unclear. The province's cumulative "new" contributions total had risen steadily, reaching 1,660,000 *shi* before the end of (lunar) 1747, and 1,739,000 *shi* by summer's end in 1748. Fujian's holdings might have peaked at that point but for the ongoing annual sales, which the new contributions only partially offset. If we take the autumn actual holdings (2,052,411 *shi*) and add 450,000 *shi* as a plausible estimate of sales in 1748 (see below), we reach 2,502,411 *shi* as a hypothetical post-restocking winter total for Fujian (cf. table 12, column D, note 7). However, to obtain the 1747 year-end balance, we must deduct the 78,664 *shi* realized through title sales in the first half of 1748. In any case, the 1748 autumn figure was itself theoretical—that is, derived from calculation, not stocktaking. In October, Yong Ning, the acting provincial administration commissioner, put total holdings only at "not below" 1.9 million *shi*.[15]

The 1748 statistical report from Fujian is unlike all others in the series, revealing the unique depth and strength of that province's tradition of reliance on title sales. It also warns, however, of flaws that may

---

13. CC, Kaerjishan and Pan Siju, QL 13/8/28 plus appendix, LFZZQZ (QL 13), 3257; CC, Pan Siju, QL 13/6/25; LFZZQZ (QL 13), 3258.

14. Cf. CC, Kaerjishan and Pan Siju, QL 13/10/28 (which gives 970,404 *shi* as the amount of unreplaced sold grain, and 2,566,920 *shi* as the total "that should still be present"); CC, Kaerjishan and Pan Siju, QL 13/8/28 plus LFZZQZ (QL 13), 3257.

15. LFZZQZ (QL 13), 3258; CC, Yong Ning, QL 13/8/21.

be hidden in less detailed reports. The understanding that what was required was a statement of assets rather of real grain stocks was apparently widespread. Some provinces' actual holdings figures may be theoretical even where this is not explicitly noted. Figures for sold and lent grain may silently include grain sold or lent in earlier years than 1748. As Fujian's case shows, the implications of such unmarked inclusiveness may not be trivial. Given that Yong Ning indicated that over 1 million *shi* of grain sold in Fujian during 1741–48 were unreplaced, and that he estimated the Fujian population's annual need for stabilizing sales grain at 400,000 to 500,000 *shi*, it is likely that about half of the 970,876 *shi* reported in the statistical account as unreplaced sold grain represents sales conducted during 1741–47.[16] Had we possessed for Fujian only the summary data that survive for some other provinces, we might have estimated Fujian's 1747 year-end balance as 3,023,287 *shi*—the sum of 2,052,411 and 970,876 *shi* (cf. table 12). The true figure may have been as low as 2.3 million. In 1749, a committee uninformed that a given sales total represented grain sold over several years might have overestimated the ease with which that grain could be replaced by purchase. A committee unaware of (or choosing to ignore) the fact that a given *loans* total included arrears might have underestimated the difficulty of using debt recovery to bring reserves to their new target level.

Let us look at a few more provinces. Guangdong's data seem straightforward: the 1748 reported actual holdings figure (2,901,700 *shi*) constitutes the 1747 year-end balance (3,042,463 *shi*) minus sales for 1748 alone. The discrepancy between the actual holdings figure and the supposedly identical 1749 target (2,953,661 *shi*) is explained by the close similarity between the latter and Guangdong's 1748 *minshu gushu* total (2,953,680 *shi*), which was reported in mid-January 1749, reflected post-harvest restocking, and included community granary and other extraneous stocks. There is, however, risk of misreading the fact that 41 percent of the 1747 final balance comprised title sales proceeds. This does not necessarily imply that the 1747 total can safely be accepted as Guangdong's top 1740s storage level, as suggested in table 14. Will and Wong cite higher Guangdong *minshu gushu* totals for 1741, 1745, 1746, and, in particular, 1744, when the compromise target, identical with Guangdong's peak 1740s *minshu gushu* total (3,359,767 *shi*, no doubt

---

16. Ibid.

reported some months later), supposedly represented "the old hold-ings" (perhaps meaning the basic target) plus subsequent proceeds of title sales. As these amounts apparently included unreplaced sold grain from previous years, the 1744 total must be taken as the theoretical, rather than actual, holdings for that year. On present evidence, we may assume that the reported breakdown of the 1747 year-end balance (1,786,550 *shi* of ever-normal grain, 1,255,913 of title sale proceeds) indi-cates the amount still held within each category after downward fluc-tuations from a peak that probably exceeded 3.1 million *shi*.[17] In 1749, therefore, the committee resolved to cut Guangdong's reserves by more than 3 percent compared with their peak level, while upholding future state stockpiling in Guangdong (as in Fujian) through a generous in-terpretation of "current storage level."

The Guizhou case was different. On one hand, it was the October actual holdings figure reported by Governor Aibida that was adopted as the new target; on the other, this figure was *lower* than the estimates, ranging from 1.2 to 1.4 million *shi*, that Jie Xizhou, Hengwen, and Zhang Yunsui offered in 1748 for Guizhou's current storage level.[18] The discrepancy reflects the existence of reserves of husked rice that had been accumulated out of surplus uncommuted-land-tax proceeds. In the autumn of 1748, there were over 600,000 *shi* left in this category, plus 260,000 *shi* of purchased grain. If one adds these numbers to Guizhou's 500,000 *shi* of ever-normal grain, ignoring the need to convert husked to unhusked by doubling, the result is indeed 1.36 million *shi*. In a memorial of the same date as his ever-normal reserves statement, Ai-bida reckoned correctly. If, as he recommended, one cut the 860,000 *shi* (husked) of tax proceeds plus bought grain to 750,000 *shi* and then added the 250,000 *shi* that the ever-normal stocks represented, one would have 1 million *shi* (husked) to meet both military and civilian needs in this frontier province.[19] Since Guizhou's total stockpiles in 1748 were thus equivalent to over 2.2 million *shi* unhusked, the com-mittee had no need to add to the October actual holdings figure in setting a new target for the ever-normal stocks alone.

---

17. LFZZ, Yue Jun, QL 13/9/13 plus appendix; CC, Yue Jun, QL 13/11/28; Will and Wong, *Nourish the People*, appendix, table A.1, p. 528; QSL/QL, *juan* 214:9b.

18. For references, see n. 10 above.

19. Aibida, QL 13/9/12 second mem. (cat. no. 1144-037).

With Gansu's new target, the committee probably overlooked the distinction between granary and standard *shi*. As table 11 shows, they cannot have allowed for that distinction in calculating the new nationwide total target as some 33,792,330 *shi*. It was noted in 1752 that Echang, the previous Gansu governor (since early 1749) had assumed the Gansu target to be in standard *shi*, with the result that when the granaries were notionally full with 3,280,000 standard *shi*, they in fact had only 2,296,000 granary *shi* (984,000 granary *shi* short of the real target). It was Yang Yingju, governor in 1751–52, who took action to restore the Gansu target to a granary-*shi* basis.[20] Ignoring the distinction was convenient in 1749, because it let the committee suppose that, after restocking, Gansu's reserves would be only some 300,000 *shi* below their new target (table 13). With the distinction recognized, the projected shortfall would have been 1.7 million standard *shi*.

In two of the four cases explored so far, the committee was at best somewhat cavalier in its approach to data that bore crucially on prospects of meeting the new provincial targets. Some provinces' data were so crude as to have made it impossible to assess those prospects accurately even had more zeal been brought to the task. This may be illustrated by comparing the Shaanxi figures with those for Zhejiang. Chen Hongmou reported the Shaanxi granaries' assets as 3,323,827 *shi* of grain in store or on loan, plus funds corresponding to 156,603 *shi* of sold grain. The theoretically possible total holdings as of early 1749 could therefore have been stated as over 3.48 million *shi* (ignoring, for argument's sake, the drought that made such calculations academic for Shaanxi in 1748–49). Chen also noted, however, that 297,211 *shi* of the total on loan represented arrears from 1747 or before; as these would normally have been harder to reclaim, we can deduct them from the theoretical total, yielding a more realistic projection of less than 3.2 million for the post-restocking level (see table 12). As Shaanxi's reserves had grown progressively through title sales since the mid-1740s, we can *provisionally* take this lower figure as a proxy for Shaanxi's likely pre-1748 peak holdings (table 14).[21]

---

20. Wu Shiduan, QL 16/11/22, repr. GZD/QL, vol. 2, pp. 25–26.

21. Cf. JS, Qing Fu, QL 12/3/15; also below, esp. n. 25, for the possibility that the Shaanxi peak was earlier (1746) and higher (by up to some 160,000 *shi*).

For Zhejiang, by contrast, the committee was given only the single figure of 940,931 *shi* for sales and loans made over more than one year, including 1748. As the Zhejiang opening balance (1,884,274 *shi*: theoretical holdings at the end of 1747 plus title sales proceeds from the first quarter of 1748) also included an unstated volume of loans and sales from previous years, it would be impossible to do more than estimate Zhejiang's real holdings as of early 1748, using a breakdown of the available replacement funds (404,000 + taels from 1748; 142,000 + from previous years) provided in a slightly later document.[22] The vagueness would have done nothing to help the committee gauge the difficulty of restoring Zhejiang's stocks even to 1.88 million *shi*, let alone the "Yongzheng" target of 2.8 million. Two other provinces whose theoretically possible holdings (as of 1748–49) include unstated amounts that had been sold and/or lent in previous years are Anhui and Henan.

The data of 1748 and early 1749 provide our best means of estimating the maximum likely ever-normal holdings in the 1740s, but they must be used with caution. Table 14 is an attempt to determine the peak holdings that would be implied by these data alone, on the heuristic (but probably counterfactual) assumption that continuing title sales resulted in a net progressive rise in total storage during 1745–48. Had that been so, the nearest possible approximation to peak holdings would have been the 1748 opening balance plus subsequent (preferably net) gains through title sales. In table 14, I use the available 1748–49 data to reconstruct this figure as closely as possible. The aim is to obtain a generally realistic total, with upward biases preferred in cases of uncertainty. The more problematic provincial totals, such as those for Shandong and Sichuan, have been recalculated using the best data available, as detailed in the notes.[23] Interprovincial transfers made in 1748 and reflected in tables 10–13 are reversed in table 14, while specified amounts of grain that had been unreplaced since before 1748 have been

---

22. CC, Fang Guancheng, QL 13/10/17.

23. The Sichuan *minshu gushu* figures used in table 14 are stated in *cangdou* (granary measure) *shi* (CC, Bandi, QL 13/11/22). In the absence of evidence that these were oversized measures like their Gansu namesakes, I have left them unconverted. The Sichuan granary *shi* seems indeed to have been only half the Sichuan market *shi*. CC, Gao Yue, QL 14/3/14; cf. Will and Wong, *Nourish the People*, pp. 236–38.

Table 14

Maximum Probable Holdings Implied by the 1748–49 Data Alone,
Compared with the Compromise Targets of 1743–44

(Units: *shi* of unhusked grain. Corrections to nearest integer have been made as appropriate. Bold type indicates provinces whose maximum probable holdings exceeded their compromise targets.)

Province	A Compromise target*	B Maximum probable holdings†	C B compared with A (B as a percent- age of A)
Gansu	4,685,714	2,950,351[1]	–1,735,363 (63%)
Shandong	3,975,200	3,185,051[2]	–790,149 (80%)
Guangdong	3,359,767	3,042,463	–317,304 (91%)
Zhejiang	3,480,000	1,884,274[3]	–1,595,726 (54%)
Shaanxi	**2,733,010**	**3,183,220**[4]	**+450,210 (116%)**[4]
Fujian	**(2,150,000)**[5]	**(2,552,411)**[5]	**+402,411 (119%)**
Henan	3,573,800[6]	2,203,569[6]	–1,370,231 (62%)[6]
Zhili	4,370,000	3,306,046[7]	–1,063,954 (76%)
Anhui	2,000,000	1,852,866[8]	–147,134 (93%)
Jiangsu	2,111,000	1,705,929[9]	–405,071 (81%)
Jiangxi	**1,606,000**	**1,736,603**[10]	**+130,603 (108%)**[10]
Shanxi	2,736,000	1,996,644[11]	–739,356 (73%)[11]
Guangxi	1,413,398	1,364,676[12]	–48,722 (97%)
Fengtian	1,120,000	901,854	–218,146 (81%)
Sichuan	2,929,459	(2,393,654)[13]	–535,805 (82%)
Hunan	1,757,354	1,534,402[14]	–222,952 (87%)
Yunnan	941,600	775,724[15]	–165,876 (82%)[15]
Hubei	1,017,844	(779,128)[16]	–238,716 (77%)
Guizhou	**498,460**	**(509,000)**[17]	**+10,540 (102%)**[17]
TOTAL	(48,110,680)[18]	37,857,865	–10,252,815 (79%)
Henan tribute granaries		775,144	
ADJUSTED TOTAL	(48,110,680)[18]	38,633,009	–9,477,671 (80%)

NOTES: * From table 7 unless otherwise indicated. † From table 12, column D unless otherwise indicated.

[1] The 1748 *minshu gushu* opening balance; in standard *shi*.

[2] Calculated as follows: sales from Shandong's own reserves in 1748 (and perhaps earlier) up to the time of the provincial statement (1,084,330 *shi*) *plus* loans (1,200,727 *shi*) during the same period *plus* the balance of Shandong's reserves remaining at the time of the statement (899,994 *shi*). All grain explicitly stated to have been from sources other than Shandong's ever-normal stocks has been excluded; it is, however, not unlikely that 872,132 *shi* (husked converted to unhusked) of the loaned grain were from outside the Shandong ever-normal system.

[3] Theoretical holdings at the end of 1747 (including unreplaced lent and/or sold grain) plus title sales proceeds from the first quarter of 1748.

Table 14, cont.

[4] Will and Wong, *Nourish the People*, appendix, table A.1, p. 528, quote 3,185,393 *shi* for the 1747 Shaanxi *minshu gushu* fig. Adoption of this fig. would mean adding 2,173 *shi* in col. C.

[5] Col. A: contribution target. Col. B: reported 1748 autumn holdings (2,052,411 *shi*) plus upward-biased estimate of grain sold during 1748 (500,000 *shi*).

[6] Col. B fig. includes 190,000+ *shi* of ever-normal grain sent to Shandong in 1748, and an unknown amount of grain sold / lent in previous years and not replaced. The 1749 Henan *minshu gushu* fig. (3,089,797 *shi*) stated by Will and Wong (ref. as in n. 4) must include the tribute grain reserves. With the 1748–49 tribute reserves data added, the Henan line in table 14 reads: col. A: 5,010,000 *shi*; col. B: 2,978,713 *shi* (plus an unspecified amount sent to Shandong in 1748); col. C: -2,031,287 *shi* (59%).

[7] Includes 300,000 *shi* transferred to Shandong in 1748.

[8] Col. B fig. (a) *includes* 250,000 *shi* sent to Shandong in 1748; (b) *excludes* 288,730 *shi* used in famine relief or sent outside Anhui in 1745–46 and not yet replaced. It also includes unstated amounts that either (a) had been lent or (probably) sold before 1748, or (b) had been missing since 1745–46 and were to be replaced through title sales.

[9] Jiangsu's reserves were being continually depleted by natural disasters in the late 1740s. Its theoretically possible holdings by winter 1748–49 (table 13) include at least 771,709 *shi* that originated outside the Jiangsu ever-normal system. To ensure that any bias in the col. B fig. is upward, I deduct from the table 13 fig. only 196,358 *shi* supplied from Jiangxi granaries. It is in fact unlikely that the Jiangsu granaries held as much as 1.7 million *shi* at any one time in the late 1740s.

[10] Col B: 1748 opening balance, which includes 200,000 *shi* later transferred to Jiangsu. Will and Wong (ref. as in n. 4) quote 1,942,767 *shi* for the 1747 Jiangxi *minshu gushu* fig. Adoption of this fig. would mean adding 206,164 *shi* in col. C.

[11] Col. B: 1748 opening balance plus 4,139 *shi* of spring-quarter title sales proceeds (fig. excludes 37,985 *shi* of arrears and other unreplaced grain from previous years). Will and Wong (ref. as in n. 4) quote 2,242,089 *shi* for the 1748 Shanxi *minshu gushu* fig., but this includes community granary stocks. That the Shanxi holdings were about 27 percent short of the compromise target in 1748 is corroborated in Zhuntai, QL 13/4/18, first mem. (cat. no. 1142-035).

[12] Excludes 70,604 *shi* corresponding to unused relief grain (sent to Guangxi in 1742–43) that had been retained for making loans.

[13] 1748 *minshu gushu* opening balance (2,355,236 *shi*) plus 1748 title sales proceeds and other receipts (208,418 *shi*) minus some 170,000 *shi* of community granary stocks (cf. CC, Jishan, QL 13/int.7/6, which puts *shecang* stocks at 176,700+ *shi*). The 2.39 million total (col. B) can be reconciled with the theoretical fig. of 1,458,642 *shi* (tables 10–13) if the latter represents notional holdings as of the time of the provincial statement. 1,458,642 *shi* plus the 936,199 issued for military (etc.) uses in 1748 yields some 2.39 million. CC, Bandi, QL 13/11/22 (*minshu gushu* report). The 1748 Sichuan *minshu gushu* fig. stated by Will and Wong (ref. as in n. 4) is less easily reconciled with these data.

[14] 1748 opening balance.

[15] Col. B fig. excludes 8,343 *shi* unreplaced since 1743–47. Will and Wong (ref. as in n. 4) quote 1,007,430 and 1,107,753 *shi* respectively for the 1747 and 1748 Yunnan *minshu gushu* figs. Adoption of the latter would mean adding 332,029 *shi* in col. C.

[16] 1748 reported autumn holdings, plus total sold and lent in 1748 as stated in the *minshu gushu* report. The reported *minshu gushu* opening balance for 1748, exclusive of community granary stocks, was only 610,237 *shi*. CC, Peng Shukui, QL 13/12/8.

[17] Col. B fig. excludes 860,000 *shi* (husked) of accumulated tax grain and bought grain, as these were seen (in principle) as outside the ever-normal system. If these stocks are included, the col. B and C data are 2,229,000 and +1,730,540 *shi* (447%) respectively.

[18] Total as stated in the committee's report, CC, Zhang Tingyu et al., QL 13/12/12.

excluded. The unavoidable inclusion of unstated and hidden amounts of chronically missing grain provides a built-in upward bias, as does the impossibility of stating the net gains from title sales had the normal annual cycle been completed.

With all their imperfections, the table 14 data imply that, had 1740s actual ever-normal holdings reached their highest nationwide level in 1748, that peak would still have been below 38 million *shi*. In order to compare this total with the post-1744 nationwide target, we must add a figure for the Henan tribute granaries, since a target for the latter was probably included in the 48 million *shi* (cf. table 6). Thus adjusted, the hypothetical peak 1740s holdings rise to about 38.6 million, nearly 9.5 million *shi* short of the target in force in 1748. The official 1748 *minshu gushu* total (31 million) constitutes 80 percent of this 38.6 million, which can serve as an upwardly biased proxy for real holdings at the point of greatest fullness in the 1748–49 cycle had it not been broken by the August edict.

But 1740s ever-normal holdings probably peaked earlier than 1748. The decision, in November 1745, to re-open sales of *jiansheng* titles for silver at the Board of Revenue made most unlikely any subsequent progressive rise in storage, except in individual provinces that enjoyed, or were able to negotiate, unusually favorable conditions. According to the *minshu gushu* data, as we have seen (table 8 and figure 1), nationwide holdings peaked in 1745 and then fell progressively until 1748, their second-highest level being in 1746. The available *minshu gushu* totals for individual provinces are perhaps more reliable; they suggest provincial peaks in various years, generally pre-1748. Sichuan in particular achieved an early peak and avoided any significant decline in storage until the Jinchuan campaign.[24]

The 1745 nationwide *minshu gushu* total was only about 35.6 million *shi*. As argued in chapter 6, it is not certain that the entire difference between that figure and the corresponding total for 1744 (32.1 million) represents a net addition to the stockpiles. The apparent rise in holdings may reflect the fact that title sales proceeds realized in the first two quarters of the year were captured in statistics that normally excluded autumn-purchased grain. Assuming, nonetheless, that 1745 was the peak year, what must be added to the maximum likely holdings for 1748–49

---

24. Will and Wong, *Nourish the People*, appendix, table A.1, p. 528.

to yield an upward-biased but broadly realistic estimate of the 1745–46 post-restocking level? In their survey of *minshu gushu* reports from the 1740s, Will, Wong and their collaborators found twelve pre-1747 provincial totals (referring to eight provinces), in addition to those for Guangdong and Sichuan, that are higher than the corresponding "maximum probable holdings" calculated in table 14.[25] Granted, the pre-1749 provincial peaks quoted by Will and Wong refer to various years, must generally be assumed to have been lower than the corresponding year-end balances, and probably do not constitute a complete set. They are also likely to include community granary stocks (a fact reflected in Will and Wong's six 1747 or 1748 provincial *minshu gushu* totals that exceed the corresponding maxima in table 14).[26] They therefore do not provide a basis for calculating the putative 1745–46 nationwide peak. However, if we look both at the overall pattern and at the size of the gaps between the peak provincial *minshu gushu* data and the lower corresponding maxima in table 14, it becomes hard to imagine that more than 3 million *shi* should be added to the "maximum probable" nationwide total shown in table 14 (38,633,009 *shi*).

I therefore estimate peak actual ever-normal holdings in the 1740s as unlikely ever to have exceeded, or even reached, 41.6 million *shi* (43.1 million hectoliters). The 1745 *minshu gushu* total (nearly 35.6 million) constitutes some 85 percent of this figure. This percentage is broadly consistent with those *minshu-gushu* to year-end-holdings ratios that can be estimated for the early 1740s, as shown in chapter 6. It is, however, likely that a smaller proportion than usual of the 1745 restocking was accomplished through post-harvest buying. Greater proportional use of title sales was central government policy between April 1744 and November 1745, and, presumably, the preference of some territorial officials. Spring and summer title sales proceeds would have inflated the

---

25. For 1746, for example, these totals are (in *shi*): Shaanxi, 3,345,355; Gansu, 3,199,482; Hubei, 1,069,259; Yunnan, 1,039,770. Sichuan's peaks were in 1742 (2,764,546) and 1746 (2,713,289). Henan's tribute grain reserves may have peaked in 1736 at some 1,436,200 *shi*, after which 660,000+ were used over the years, presumably on a no-replacement basis, as well as the 204,249 reported as replaceable in 1748. Ibid.; CC, Shise, QL 13/9/8.

26. Ten provinces usually included community granary reserves in their *minshu gushu* reports, and four more may have. Will and Wong, *Nourish the People*, table 8.3 (p. 251).

1745 *minshu gushu* total to the extent that they replaced post-harvest buying. The lower the proportion of buying and post-harvest title sales in the 1745 restocking mix, the higher the ratio of the *minshu gushu* total to the post-restocking peak. It seems permissible to cut the estimate of the maximum likely 1740s peak to 41 million *shi*, which still leaves that ratio under 87 percent. Actual 1740s holdings in the ever-normal granaries, I suggest, never exceeded about 85 percent of the 1744–49 nationwide target, and probably never reached even that level.

Implications for the provinces of the committee's approach. Let us return to the deliberative committee in early 1749 and its approach to filling the 6.9-million *shi* gap between reported actual holdings and proposed new total target. As we have seen, theoretically there were assets available to plug the gap, with, potentially, a 5-million *shi* margin. The committee's ideal—if only the outstanding loans had been more help-fully distributed among the provinces in deficit—would have been to recover the not quite 4.8 million *shi* of lent grain, and to replace the remaining 2.1 million by buying grain with some of the available re-stocking funds. While the preference for loan recovery was justifiable in narrow fiscal terms, questions arise when we consider what it would have meant for individual provinces. Further doubts arise from the committee's preference for silver deposits in provincial treasuries over grain transfers to fill resistant shortfalls.

Table 11 compares, province by province, the reported actual hold-ings with the newly recommended "Yongzheng-period" or substitute targets. It shows that six, mostly southern, provinces (excluding Si-chuan) already had enough grain to meet their relatively (or, indeed, very) low new targets. Shanxi and Hunan each had a surplus exceeding 500,000 *shi*. Table 13 compares the "Yongzheng-period" targets with the maximum possible holdings for each province had all sold, lent or otherwise used grain been replaced. Excluding famine-stricken Shan-dong as well as Sichuan, the number of provinces with surplus grain now rises to thirteen.[27] Four provinces would have been below target;

---

27. As Shandong had suffered repeated natural disasters, including autumn floods in 1748, its reserves had been supplemented with tribute grain and grain transfers from other provinces. Relief operations, still in progress at the time of the committee's report, necessitated continued drawing on the replenished stocks. The

of these, Zhejiang would have been short by over 915,000 *shi* (nearly 33 percent). Three more provinces (excluding Guizhou) would have had very narrow margins. These assessments may be pessimistic, as low post-harvest prices might have enabled some provinces to buy more grain than they had sold. However, since my focus is on the committee's thinking, I shall continue to use its accounting principles.

Table 13 implies that, assuming all loaned grain to be recoverable, and all replacement funds sufficient, given current prices, to replace the missing grain of other categories, two-thirds of the provinces would have been able to meet their reset targets, with margins ranging from 0.4 to 118.5 percent. While the first of these assumptions was probably the more dubious, the committee had fiscal rationality on its side in preferring loan recovery where possible. Lending grain, for sowing or consumption, was a recognized alternative way of helping the peasantry at difficult times of year and in emergencies.[28] Loans were supposed to be repaid after the autumn harvest, and an (agricultural) year of plenty such as 1748–49 should have offered generally good prospects for debtor compliance with these terms—and perhaps, even, for clearance of arrears. It would be redundant to spend state funds on buying grain that should have been reclaimed during the autumn. In the extreme case of Zhili, which did not report a figure for sold grain, the amount of grain reported as on loan approached 1.4 million *shi*. As Zhili needed only some 500,000 *shi* to meet its "Yongzheng" target, it made fiscal sense to deem this province not only free of deficit, but actually in surplus. Why waste Zhili's unspent sales proceeds (silver and brass coin to a value of about 160,000 taels) on buying extra grain? Why, indeed, waste Fujian's 621,519 taels of unspent sales proceeds when, in order to assure attainment of that province's new storage target, its granary administrators had but to disburse the funds for replacing the grain that had been issued to the military in past years?[29]

Yunnan's 97,000-*shi* deficit could be removed by the assumption that the province had reclaimed, or could reclaim, the grain that peasants owed its granaries. As full loan recovery would leave a surplus

---

acting governor had warned that buying for the Shandong granaries should be suspended for the current cycle. QSL/QL, *juan* 323:1b.

28. Will, *Bureaucracy and Famine*, pp. 204–6.

29. LFZZ, Pan Siju, QL 14/6/3 confirms that such were the orders to Fujian.

of some 56,700 *shi*, Yunnan's replacement funds (proceeds of selling a
mere 25,800 *shi*) could be deposited in the provincial treasury. The
Jiangsu deficit, by contrast, could theoretically have been filled entirely
by purchase, and buying was already taking place. However, recovery
of the outstanding loans would have eliminated all but 20 percent of the
deficit. The committee recommended that the Jiangsu authorities be
instructed to reclaim the loans and take stock when the bought grain
was delivered to the granaries. Any bought grain that was surplus
should be sold, while any surplus unexpended purchase funds should be
deposited in the provincial treasury.

That loan recovery from vulnerable, poor, and, sometimes, crafty
peasants would be a straightforward process is too daring an assumption for the modern scholar. Will has adduced much evidence to the
contrary, from an only slightly later period.[30] The governors even of
Yunnan and Jiangsu no doubt had their misgivings when orders based
on the above recommendations reached them. Still more problematic
were the cases of Anhui and Henan, in which the grain to be recovered
included arrears from before 1748 (true probably also in Jiangsu) *and*
the deficits were larger. In Anhui, to be sure, only some 18 percent of
the deficit could have been plugged through the recovery of loans an
unknown percentage of which were in arrears. In Henan, by contrast,
57 percent of a deficit exceeding 1.1 million *shi* consisted of both old
(pre-1748) and new (1748) loans.

Zhejiang's deficit, which represented two-thirds of its "Yongzheng"
target, was even larger than Anhui's and Henan's. However, as grain on
loan probably accounted for only 8 percent of this deficit, doubts about
the deliberators' commitment to stockpiling in Zhejiang must rest on
grounds other than suspected indifference to loan recovery problems.[31]
As we have seen, full replacement of Zhejiang's missing grain would
still have left a shortfall of over 915,000 *shi* (almost 33 percent). This
could have been more than halved by transporting the surplus holdings
of Hunan (over 554,000 *shi*); indeed, it could theoretically have been 90
percent eliminated had all of Hunan's surplus assets (including grain on

---

30. Will and Wong, *Nourish the People*, pp. 178–85.

31. A report of April 1749 implies that Zhejiang's 940,931 *shi* (about half the
deficit) reported as replaceable in 1748 comprised 790,004 *shi* of sold or transferred
grain, and 150,927 of grain on loan. CC, Fang Guancheng, QL 14/3/9.

loan and grain replacement funds) been used in Zhejiang's favor. Unless Hunan's surpluses were concentrated in upland peripheries, it should not have been unduly costly to ship them to Zhejiang. The expenditure should not have been begrudged, by previous standards; in August, indeed, Qianlong had envisaged interprovincial redistribution precisely for such circumstances.

The committee, however, showed no interest in this possibility. Hunan's surplus grain was to be sold, as was the grain recovered from the peasant debtors; the proceeds of these sales were to be reported to the Board of Revenue, as were the unneeded grain replacement funds. Zhejiang, the granaries of whose capital (Hangzhou) were virtually empty at the time of the provincial statement, was to restock to the theoretically possible 1.88-million *shi* level, and then content itself with gradual rebuilding through *jiansheng* title sales.[32] The committee justified the temporary *de facto* cut by pointing out that Zhejiang's "Yongzheng" target (2.8 million *shi*) was a generous one.[33]

The slow, cheap, unreliable approach of selling *jiansheng* titles was imposed on two of the three other provinces that were not even theoretically able to restock to "Yongzheng" target level. The excuse given for not using interprovincial transfers—the less than ideal location of these provinces relative to those that had surplus grain already in store—was convincing for Gansu and the fourth province, Fengtian. The committee stated that Fengtian was moving towards its target gradually though a grain levy on farmland (a process expected to take three or four years); that Henan was already selling *jiansheng* titles for grain, while its deficit after loan recovery and use of the available restocking funds (a shortfall of 297,430 *shi*, that is, nearly 13 percent of the "Yongzheng" target) would be a very small one; and that Gansu's re-

---

32. Hangzhou's metropolitan counties, Renhe and Qiantang, each had a storage target of 60,000 *shi*. Their theoretical holdings at the start of 1748 had been 37,970 and 40,006 *shi* respectively. By autumn, all of Renhe's stocks had been sold, lent or transferred; Qiantang had 1,729 *shi* left. LFZZQZ (QL 13), 2940. The depletion presumably resulted from Hangzhou's early-summer price crisis (see chap. 3 above).

33. Although the Zhejiang target eventually reverted to 2.8 million *shi*, a 1752 memorial assesses the province's current holdings against a target of only 1.6 million. Yaerhashan, QL 17/8/21, repr. GZD/QL, vol. 3, pp. 634–35. Zhejiang storage levels were, at best, substantially below 2.8 million *shi* for most of the period 1749–68, according to the limited available data. Will and Wong, *Nourish the People*, tables 8.7 and A.1 (pp. 284, 528–29).

serves, like those of Zhejiang, were at least at a level embodying "preparedness."

The committee noted that drawings were still being made on the reserves of three provinces that, by its accounting methods, did not have deficits. Continuing famine relief in Shandong and Shaanxi plus army supply work in Sichuan (theater of the Jinchuan campaign) made it unrealistic to calculate the balances. However, leaving all seven problem provinces aside, and, for the other twelve, adding the theoretically purchasable or recoverable grain to that in store, the committee determined that there was a surplus ("extra-target grain," *yi e gu*) of 3,219,107 *shi*. Unexpended grain-sales proceeds that were now superfluous amounted to 1,428,127 taels plus 36,203 strings of cash. The committee recommended that all the extra-target grain (both that in store and that to be acquired through loan repayments) be gradually sold, and the figures reported to the Board of Revenue. The surplus purchase funds should be deposited in the provincial treasuries and the sums reported to the Board for reallocation—the committee did not specify to what.[34]

It is true that the committee proposed some accommodation for provinces that had difficulty in recovering enough loaned grain to restock to "Yongzheng" target level. Provided that local market conditions were suitable, and that they reported the matter to the central government, they should be allowed to "retain" an appropriate sum out of the funds earmarked for reallocation. This sum would be used for buying.[35] The committee also spared the miscellaneous granaries whose existence Celeng had decried. From the widespread state-sponsored

---

34. That the Board, not the provincial authorities, would do the reallocation is not explicit in the committee's formulae, viz., *bao bu zhuo bo* (literally, "report to the Board and allocate [after consideration =] appropriately") and *zaobao zhuo bo* ("report and allocate appropriately"). However, the sequence of the two phrases suggests that such is the correct interpretation. I interpret *bao bu zhuo bo* in light of the formula used in the 1745 instruction to desist from buying, *xiangxi zaobao yi bian zhuochou banli* ("report [the quantities of unexpended purchase funds] in detail so that [the Board] can make a plan for their disposal"; CC, Chen Dashou, QL 10/8/16). I thus read *bao bu zhuo bo* as *bao bu yi bian zhuo bo*, "report [the sums] to the Board so that [the latter] can reallocate appropriately."

35. Fujian was authorized to draw on 150,000 *shi* of husked rice retained from the 1748 tribute grain of Jiangsu and Zhejiang if necessary to fill shortfalls in its granaries. See memorandum quoted in LFZZ, Pan Siju, QL 14/6/3.

"community granaries" to the anomalous-sounding "granary of the Yuhuan subprefectural magistrate" off the southern Zhejiang coast, all were outside the ever-normal category and should be left alone (apart from a demand that detailed figures on their operations be submitted to the Board of Revenue).[36] Finally, whatever Qianlong may have meant by asking about earlier stock rotation principles, the committee proposed no revision of existing policy on this subject. Rather, it stressed the importance of flexibility, reasserted that buying should be done only as long as prices were low, and indicated that the general intent was to keep the granaries as well-stocked as was compatible with avoiding undesirable price rises.

Despite these gestures, the report gives the continuing impression of a committee anxious, on one hand, not to weaken the granary system excessively, but at the same time not averse to finding opportunities of freeing funds for other purposes. It is not only that even the basic targets were no longer sacred. The basic targets, after all, had been treated with no more respect in May 1743—or, more to the point, in August 1745, at a time of incipient fiscal stringency associated with a military campaign. Still more suspicious is the fact that, working from statistics some of which were patently dubious or misleading, the committee made cavalier assumptions about the replaceability of stocks that might have been quite problematic to replace in practice, as members no doubt realized. As well as, probably, ignoring the customary use of extra-large measures in Gansu, it represented Sichuan's theoretical (*ying cun*) holdings as grain "actually" in store at the time of writing (*xianzai shi cun*). It even anticipated that famine-stricken Shandong would have surplus funds to report to the Board of Revenue when the accounts for 1748 were closed. That province, after all, had 1.2 million *shi* of grain on loan to put towards its "Yongzheng" target.[37]

The committee might have been expected to recommend abolition of the sale of *jiansheng* titles for grain, except in provinces with admitted recalcitrant deficits or, perhaps, famines or military entangle-

---

36. Only the fate of a 20,000-*shi* stockpile on Chongming Island in the Yangzi estuary was left open, pending consideration of the Jiangsu governor's eventually successful request that these stocks be retained. Cf. the refs. to this stockpile in CC, Zhang Tingyu et al., QL 14/8/25.

37. CC, Bandi, QL 13/9/26 plus (LFZZ) appendix; CC, "Ge sheng changping cang gu ding'e qingdan," entries for Sichuan and Shandong.

ments. After all, as previously used, this practice had given every province a free share in a revenue source that was quite valuable to the central government. Why let the deficit-free provinces keep this privilege, now that the goal of larger stockpiles had been abandoned? The committee's approach was subtler, again combining gesturing to the ideal of well-stocked granaries with an unobtrusive fiscal consciousness. The deficit-free provinces should be allowed to keep their title-selling programs as extra insurance against harvest failure, but their access to this resource would no longer be gratis. Grain realized through title sales should be recorded in separate accounts and used either for famine relief, or to replace sold grain at times when restocking could not be done by purchase. In the latter case, the unexpended purchase funds should be reported for reallocation. This would presumably have put them under Board of Revenue control.

Why Did the Committee Cook the Books?

What exactly did "reallocation" mean? The expression *zhuo bo* ("allocate [after consideration =] appropriately") is used repeatedly in the statistical appendix, always referring to the fate of unexpended purchase funds. However, no hint is given anywhere in the report as to the kind of use envisaged. Perhaps this silence is significant. In October, Qianlong had rather hesitantly directed that purchase funds rendered superfluous by the decision to restore the "Kangxi" and "Yongzheng" targets should generally be placed in the provincial treasury to prevent embezzlement. The county magistrates would be able to apply for allocations from these funds for necessary expenditures.[38] This, while vague, at least permitted readers to assume that the monies would remain dedicated to socially beneficial purposes within the province, if not necessarily to the maintenance of grain reserves in the particular counties that had deposited the funds. For the committee to recommend that the remittances be reported to the Board of Revenue was to propose that ultimate control over the funds be handed to the central government. Although Board allocation could have been to civil uses within the home province, the bare formula "allocate appropriately"

---

38. QSL/QL, *juan* 323:15b–16a.

left open the possibility of diversion to quite other purposes, across provincial borders.

We saw in chapter 6 that, in the mid-1740s, a reasonable use for supposedly redundant purchase funds was taken to be army pay. Indeed, the Board's 1745 attempt to gain control of "surplus" monies from the granaries was in the context of an unsuccessful military campaign on Sichuan's western marches. In the spring of 1747, several months before Ou Kanshan submitted the memorial that sparked the 1748 debate, the Qing court had launched new military operations northeast of the territory where it had been engaged in 1745. Thus was inaugurated the still more costly and, until the unexpected end, humiliating first Jinchuan campaign. By early 1749, Qianlong had fully accepted that, if victory could not be won within the next few months, the attempt to subdue his disorderly vassal, a lamaist local potentate known in Chinese-language sources as the *Shaluoben*, must be abandoned. [39] Prominent among the considerations underlying his willingness to admit defeat was the great cost of the campaign.

The hope in January 1749, when the committee was preparing its report, was that a final sharp offensive, planned for May and early June, would secure a victory that was recognizable enough for the court to end the war without projecting an image of weakness. It was with this intent that an extra 35,000 troops had been committed to the struggle, and that Qianlong's new right-hand man Fuheng, recently designated as director of military operations in Sichuan (and as leader of the central-government Grand Council), had been sent out in overall command of a crack Manchu force in late December. [40] The committee's report, dated 30 January 1749, was concluded thirteen days after Qianlong issued an edict, to be communicated secretly to Fuheng, expressing doubt as to whether funding for the war could be continued. The edict foreshadowed that if success were not clearly in sight by the end of the fourth month (mid-June), Qianlong would be inclined to declare an end to hostilities. This was one step in a progressive withdrawal of imperial commitment to the war. The next step came within a few days of the

---

39. On the 1747–49 Jinchuan campaign and its background, see Zhuang, *Qing Gaozong shi quan*, pp. 109–28, Dai Yi, *Qianlong di*, pp. 174–82, and Woodside, "The Ch'ien-lung Reign," pp. 261–62.

40. Dai Yi, *Qianlong di*, p. 178; Guo, comp., *Qingshi biannian*, vol. 5, pp. 312, 314, 316–17; Bartlett, *Monarchs and Ministers*, pp. 174–75.

report's completion, with edicts variously indicating that Qianlong was resolved to have hostilities concluded by mid-June or the end of May, and that if the offensive had not succeeded by mid-May, the aim should be reduced to securing the *Shaluoben*'s surrender.[41] Such is the context within which the fiscal consciousness showing between the report's lines must be interpreted. We should recall that the years 1746–48 had seen a sharp temporary fall in annual government income, owing to the one-year remission of the land tax announced in 1745. Originally intended as an act of grace to be enjoyed throughout the realm in 1746, the remission had in fact been spread over the three-year period.[42]

The cost of military containment of the *Shaluoben*'s aggression towards neighboring tribes had been estimated in 1747 as 3,000 to 4,000 taels per day. In mid-January 1749, Qianlong predicted that, even if the final offensive were successful, the total cost would be 10 million taels; at that time, the cumulative total that had been allotted from public funds was over 8.6 million, excluding 0.77 million later stated to have been drawn from the Sichuan treasury.[43] While the central government was spared the experience, reported from the front, of boiling the leather of saddles and buff-coats for food, it had been forced repeatedly to authorize new appropriations for the campaign.[44] It is worth tracing the details of these allocations (table 15), not only to suggest the extent of the budgetary difficulties caused by the war, but also to establish how the projected "savings" from the ever-normal system would have looked in comparison with the sums that had been committed to the war on separate occasions.

---

41. Guo, comp., *Qingshi biannian*, vol. 5, pp. 318, 322; QSL/QL, *juan* 329:55a–56b, *juan* 330:48b–49a, *juan* 331:3a–4a; cf. *juan* 330:38a–41a on the cancellation of mobilization orders for 9,000 troops, which did not necessarily reflect diminished commitment to the war. For confirmation that the date of 2 Feb. under which one of these edicts is recorded was probably its own, not that of the memorials abstracted first in the same entry, compare ibid., *juan* 330:46b with *juan* 331:4a–5a.

42. QSL/QL, *juan* 242:9a–10b, 243:13b–14a; cf. chap. 6 above.

43. PDJCFL, *juan* 3:22b–23a (quoted in Guo, comp., *Qingshi biannian*, vol. 5, p. 269); QSL/QL, *juan* 329:55a; and below. While estimates vary (depending partly on what is included), it is probably safe to say that although the war itself ended earlier than expected, it actually cost at least 7 to 8 million taels in public funds alone. E.g., Guo, op. cit., p. 337; Zhuang, *Qing Gaozong shi quan*, p. 128; Chen Feng, *Qingdai junfei*, pp. 259–64.

44. For the leather-boiling episode, see QSL/QL, *juan* 319:13a.

Table 15
Appropriations of Public Funds for the Jinchuan Campaign, 1747–48
(Units: taels of silver)

Date	Amount	Provenance	Cumulative total
First half of 1747	400,000	Jiangxi, Hubei[1]	400,000
June 1747	200,000	Jiangxi[1]	600,000
July 1747	600,000	Guangdong[1]	1,200,000
December 1747	300,000	Hunan	
	200,000	Jiangxi[2]	1,700,000
March 1748	1,000,000	Board of Revenue[3]	2,700,000
Not clear	200,000	Shaanxi[5]	2,900,000
By July 1748	1,000,000	Probably Jiangxi, Hubei[4,5]	3,900,000
August 1748	200,000	Shaanxi[5]	
	100,000	Gansu	
	200,000	Jiangxi	
	200,000	Zhejiang	
	1,000,000	Board of Revenue[5]	5,600,000
November 1748	1,011,100+	Hubei, Hunan, Jiangxi[6]	6,611,100+
December 1748	1,000,000	Guangxi, Shanxi	
	1,000,000	Board of Revenue[7]	8,611,100+

SOURCES: [1] QSL/QL, *juan* 292:16a–b.
[2] PDJCFL, *juan* 4:14b–15a.
[3] Ibid., *juan* 5:22b–23b.
[4] QSL/QL, *juan* 316:9a.
[5] PDJCFL, *juan* 9:25a–26b.
[6] QSL/QL, *juan* 327:25b; LFZZ, Peng Shukui, QL 13/12/22 (d.r.); cf. JF, Peng Shukui, QL 13/12/8.
[7] Ibid., *juan* 327:11b; JF, Shulu, QL 13/12/17.

In accordance with standard procedure, Jiangxi and Hubei had first been called upon to send a total of 400,000 taels to Sichuan. A further 200,000 taels were requisitioned from Jiangxi in late June 1747; shortly afterwards, the central government responded to a plea from the Sichuan governor by allocating 600,000 taels from Guangdong. After 500,000 taels had been allocated from Hunan and Jiangxi in December, the next million (March 1748) was sent from the treasury of the Board of Revenue (that is, the central government).[45] By this time, an osten-

---

45. QSL/QL, *juan* 292:16a–b; PDJCFL, *juan* 4:14b–15a, *juan* 5:22b–23b; cf. Luo, *Lüying bing*, pp. 368–69, and QHDSL, vol. 9, *juan* 169:14b–15a (pp. 7,307–8), which suggest that Guangdong would not normally have been called on to send military

sibly desperate Sichuan governor had requested the sale of official ranks in exchange for grain deliveries to the army, with a *shi* of husked rice valued at the extraordinary rate of 30 taels. His request was granted, although his immediate superior, finding the valuation rate far too high even after a 16 percent cut, pushed successfully for a switch to payment in silver.[46] In early July 1748, a request, endorsed by the Board, for another million taels prompted Qianlong to express secret reservations as to whether the mounting expenditure was worthwhile. Meanwhile, the Shaanxi treasury provided 200,000 taels, probably before July; in August, the Shaanxi governor, Chen Hongmou, drew on the funds for paying Shaanxi's troops to send the same amount again. But the Sichuan governor wanted another 1.5 million; 1 million of this sum was sent from the Board's reserves, with Gansu, Jiangxi, and Zhejiang directed to supply the rest. Shaanxi and Gansu were normally recipients, not sources, of interprovincial subsidies.[47]

The last few months of 1748 were dominated by planning for the final offensive scheduled for 1749. Accordingly, some 1.01 million taels from Jiangxi and the Huguang provinces were earmarked for Sichuan during the 1748 autumn allocations, while 2 million more were made available from Guangxi, Shanxi, and the Board treasury. This brought the total budgeted direct cost to at least 8.6 million taels, excluding monies from the Sichuan treasury, 340,000 taels for military salaries later appropriated in advance from Zhejiang's 1749 tax revenue, and 100,000 taels from the Imperial Household Department coffers (the privy purse) for bounties to the soldiers.[48]

The campaign was not to be financed from public funds alone. In Confucian terms, additional wartime taxation, direct or indirect, was an expedient fit only for periods of early-dynastic consolidation or

---

subsidies to other provinces. I owe the refs. to PDJCFL in this par. and table 15 to Guo, comp., *Qingshi biannian*, vol. 5, pp. 272, 281–82, 303.

46. Guo, comp., *Qingshi biannian*, vol. 5, p. 281; QSL/QL, *juan* 309:57b–59b; JS, Bandi et al., QL 13/5/11.

47. QSL/QL, *juan* 316:9a–b; PDJCFL, *juan* 9:25a–26b; cf. DQHDSL, vol. 9, *juan* 169:14b–15a (pp. 7,307–8).

48. Zhuang, *Qing Gaozong shi quan*, p. 125; Guo, comp., *Qingshi biannian*, vol. 5, pp. 306, 310, 312, 314; QSL/QL, *juan* 327:11b, 25b; JF, Fang Guancheng, QL 14/1/25. On the autumn allocations, see Luo, *Lüying bing*, p. 368; Iwai, "Shindai kokka zaisei," pp. 137–38, 141–42.

late-dynastic decline—not for a triennium in which ten years of sagely rule were being celebrated with a rolling universal respite from the land tax. There could, however, be morality all round if men of property and the state's merchant clients were given opportunity to show their gratitude—for the tax remission and/or commercial patronage—by making large donations to the war effort.[49] The appeal looked successful: by April 1749 or so, nearly 3.3 million taels had been pledged by salt merchants, southern Shanxi gentry (*shenshi*, that is, persons qualified for, currently engaged in, or retired from high-status careers in bureaucratic service), and two merchant contractors, including the son of the famous Fan Yubin, who were engaged in army supply work in western Sichuan (table 16). The southern Shanxi gentry, who pledged the largest share, presumably had connections with the financial and commercial circles for which their province was renowned. While the final results of the appeal were not yet known on 30 January 1749, the court was probably aware that over 1.5 million taels had been promised. Further pledges were expected.[50]

Pledges, however, did not necessarily mean extra, business-sector cash for the coming offensive. The Guangdong merchants offered contributions spread over three years (1749–51), while monies promised by two groups of Lianghuai merchants were advanced out of official funds. The debt was still being managed through an annual repayment plan in 1751—and these, as shown below, were not the only cases.[51] In early 1749, the court could still be fairly confident of funding a cam-

---

49. For an obsequious reference to the tax remission in one donor petition, see JS, Aligun, QL 14/2/20. Chen Feng, *Qingdai junfei*, pp. 293–310 confirms that, under the Qing, wartime taxation was used mainly before 1685 and after 1790. Chen's scant material on wartime levies between these dates (including during one or both Jinchuan campaigns) suggests that they were usually regional and not necessarily approved. The heyday of the merchant contribution as a source of wartime finance was 1748–1814 (ibid., pp. 302–3, 331–35).

50. Guo, comp., *Qingshi biannian*, vol. 5, p. 335; below, table 16 and refs. there cited. On the two contractors' involvement in the Jinchuan campaign, see Dai Yingcong, "Qing State," p. 69.

51. JS, Shise, QL 14/2/3, Jiqing, QL 15/12/27; cf. LFZZ, Tang Suizu, QL 14/3/8 (d.r.). Wang Tang and Fan Qingzhu were already in debt to the state—indeed, Wang's assets were under official scrutiny. KC, Zhuntai, QL 13/7/15, Aligun, QL 13/12/20; cf. Dunstan, "Safely Supping," esp. pp. 71–72.

Table 16
Sums Pledged by Private Contributors for the Jinchuan Campaign
(Units: taels of silver)

Pledges by Shanxi-based merchants and gentry	
Pingyang and Fenzhou gentry	1,102,000
Army supply contractors Fan Qingzhu and Wang Tang	350,000
Hedong sector salt merchants	140,000
Zezhou gentry	400,000[a]
SUBTOTAL	1,992,000
Pledges by Lianghuai salt merchants	
"Huainan" and "Huixi" merchants	200,000
Northern Zhejiang and southern Jiangsu merchants	100,000
Jiangxi merchants	100,000
Huguang merchants	200,000
Other Lianghuai merchants	200,000
SUBTOTAL	800,000
Pledges by other salt merchants	
Changlu sector salt merchants	300,000
Fujian sector salt merchants	100,000
Guangdong sector salt merchants	100,000
SUBTOTAL	500,000
GRAND TOTAL	3,292,000

SOURCES: Guo, comp., *Qingshi biannian*, vol. 5, p. 335; JS, Shise, QL 14/2/3; Aligun, QL 14/2/20; Jiqing, QL 15/12/27; KC, Peng Shukui, QL 14/1/19; LFZZ, Tang Suizu, QL 14/3/8 (d.r.); Xu, *Qingdai juanna zhidu*, p. 41.
[a]Guo, loc. cit., says 100,000.

paign whose cumulative cost remained within 10 million taels; but what if the war dragged on into the autumn? In mid-February, the emperor admonished Fuheng, who was showing disconcerting signs of zeal, that the war must be concluded by 25 May. It was in this context that he raised the specter of the conflict entirely consuming the 27 million taels or so that the Board of Revenue had left in its reserves.[52] Hyperbole apart, he had reason to worry. While the Board's reserves had twice before dipped below 30 million taels in the eighteenth century, neither

---

52. QSL/QL, *juan* 331:49b–50a, 52b.

previous dip had coincided with so steep a fall in silver's value relative to grain and other goods.[53]

In fact, the war formally ended on 22 March when the *Shaluoben* surrendered, and with it perished any likelihood of the court incurring the opprobrium of commanding that "redundant" ever-normal purchase funds, conveniently assembled in provincial treasuries, be rushed to Sichuan.[54] It is, however, virtually inconceivable that this expedient never occurred to those examining the assets of the ever-normal network in the winter of 1748–49. After all, military finance was an accepted use of excess ever-normal purchase funds. Subventions to the troops of the home province may have been the norm, but, as we have seen, some 135,000 taels of Jiangxi and Zhejiang ever-normal savings had been sent to the Yunnan-Guizhou military. Memorials of June and August 1747 envisage the allocation of specific items of unneeded ever-normal purchase funds to army pay.[55] There is, admittedly, no evidence that the newly redundant purchase funds of 1748 were being earmarked for Sichuan in Chinese-language documents concerning the October push to have these monies placed in the provincial treasuries.[56] However, by early February 1749, the Hubei authorities had decided to include 50,000 taels of local grain-purchase funds in a 300,000-tael

---

53. In 1723, the Board had held only 23.7 million tls., but the annual price of rice in Suzhou prefecture had been 1.00 tl./*shi*; in 1743, the corresponding figures had been 29.1 million tls. and 1.6 tl./*shi*. In 1748, by contrast, the Suzhou prefecture annual rice price had reached 2.04 tls./*shi*. Lü Jian, comp., "Kang Yong Qian Hubu," pp. 19–20; Wang, "Secular Trends of Rice Prices," table 1.1, p. 42; cf. fig. 1 above.

54. On the negotiation of the *Shaluoben*'s surrender (which proceeded while orders for immediate cessation of hostilities were in transit to Sichuan), see Zhuang, *Qing Gaozong shi quan*, pp. 127–28; Dai Yi, *Qianlong di*, p. 180; Guo, comp., *Qingshi biannian*, vol. 5, pp. 330–35.

55. JS, Saileng'e and Chen Hongmou, QL 12/4/27; Kaerjishan and Chen Dashou, QL 12/7/6; and chap. 6 above. JS, Chen Dashou, QL 12/7/6 cites a recent imperial endorsement of the idea of reporting such funds to the Board of Revenue for reallocation.

56. See the proposal (CC, Shulu, QL 13/8/10) used by Qianlong to inaugurate this push, and the provincial responses (archived under CC and KC for QL 13/9 to 14/3; for refs., see table 17). Governor Aibida proposed to allot 26,400+ tls. of redundant sales proceeds from Guizhou's stockpiled tax grain to the military, but he did not mention Sichuan and had planned this six weeks earlier. CC, Aibida, QL 13/9/12 2nd mem. (cat. no. 1144-037), QL 13/10/28.

emergency loan to Sichuan. Although it is not certain that these were "redundant" ever-normal sales proceeds, we need not doubt that such funds would have been pressed into service had the war continued.[57]

In early 1749, the Sino-Manchu government faced acute cash-flow problems, aggravated by the time-lag in communications between Beijing, Chengdu, and the subsidizing provinces. On 1 February, Qianlong sent Aligun, now Shanxi governor, urgent orders to advance to the depleted Sichuan treasury the second half of the 1,000,000 taels so far pledged by Shanxi gentry. Advancing the first half had left a mere 190,000 taels in the Shanxi treasury. It took the Shanxi administration commissioner nearly three weeks to work out how to scrape together the required sum: 140,000 taels from the provincial treasury, a 100,000-tael first installment from the gentry, and 260,000 taels of military funds from Suiyuan, north of the Great Wall. Shanxi, like Hubei, presumably had no land-tax income in 1748 because of the universal tax remission.[58] Hubei's 300,000 taels was the most it could (or would) spare in response to an appeal for a 1,000,000-tael loan; Hunan could (or would) add only 200,000. Both Hunan and Shaanxi (which had been asked to lend 500,000) were bearing a full share of war-related costs already.[59]

With such difficulties looming, it would have been extraordinary had the committee been uninterested in the 3.3 million taels of unspent ever-normal sales proceeds that the provinces reported (table 17). The committee, looking mainly at the aggregate provincial balances, sometimes reached different conclusions as to the amounts redundant than did governors who distinguished between local stockpiles that already met pre-Qianlong targets, and others for which buying was still needed. Some discrepancies between provincial and committee figures for redundant funds (table 17, columns B and C) reflect the time-lag between the provincial statements, the provincial responses on the funds' in-

---

57. LFZZ, Peng Shukui, QL 13/12/22 (d.r.); cf. LFZZ, Kaitai, QL 14/1/16 (d.r.), KC, Peng Shukui, QL 14/1/19. While the first two sources refer to these funds as "unhusked grain funds (*gu jia*) held by circuits, prefectures and counties," the last uses the wording "unhusked-grain funds returned (*jiaohuan*) by the circuits and prefectures." The standard term for depositing unspent purchase funds in the provincial treasury was *tijie* (to forward).

58. KC, Aligun, QL 14/1/8; QSL/QL, *juan* 243:14a.

59. LFZZ, Peng Shukui, QL 13/12/22 (d.r.), Kaitai, QL 14/1/16 (d.r.).

terim placement, and the committee's report. All things considered, it says much for the committee's moderation that it identified only 1.4 million taels as definitely surplus at the time of its report.

What was the membership of this committee? By Qianlong's original instructions, it was to comprise the grand secretaries and senior Board of Revenue officials. However, it would be no more inaccurate to describe the body that reported as a joint session of the Grand Council and senior Board representatives. This may seem unremarkable, given Bartlett's point that the term "grand secretaries" in early Qianlong documents often "signified the topmost echelon of grand councillors," implying, she suggests, that acts attributed to the grand secretaries were in many cases actually the work of the Grand Council. I have pointed out elsewhere, however, that although the leading "inner-court grand secretaries" also led the Grand Council, this does not preclude the possibility that contemporaries saw a distinction between referring a matter to the grand secretaries and referring it to the Grand Council.[60] Still more pertinent is Bartlett's evidence that the first Jinchuan campaign occasioned an important "burst" of Grand Council "expansion."[61] While individual grand councillors had surely been involved, if only as edict-writers, in the formation of imperial policy on the ever-normal granaries throughout the debate, it was precisely in the Jinchuan war that there occurred a clear relative shift from "outer" to "inner court" in the locus of key deliberations on grain storage targets.[62]

In April 1748, Qianlong, rescripting Shulu's reply to his call for opinions on the cause of the inflation, had ordered that once all the provincial answers had arrived, they should be forwarded to the Grand Council for secret discussion.[63] Although he ordered in September that the provincial statements of granary assets go to the grand secretaries for joint consideration with the Board, in mid-October he referred to

---

60. Bartlett, *Monarchs and Ministers*, p. 174; Dunstan, "The 'Autocratic Heritage,'" p. 89 n. 41.

61. Bartlett, *Monarchs and Ministers*, pp. 172–73.

62. On the distinction between inner- and outer-court institutions, the dual character of the grand secretaries as "high-ranking dignitaries of both the outer- and inner-court worlds," and the edict-drafting duties of grand councillors, see ibid., pp. 3–7, 18–19, 32–33, and 217–19.

63. QSL/QL, *juan* 311:29b.

Table 17
"Redundant" Ever-Normal Purchase Funds (Winter, 1748–49)
(Units: taels of silver [correct to nearest integer in cols. A and B]. "N.d." indicates that the provincial response to the October edict [or most similar available document] quotes no figure for *redundant* purchase funds. A dash indicates a simple lacuna.)

Province	A Gross purchase funds reported in autumn statement	B Sum reported as "redundant" after October edict re. deposit in provincial treasuries	C Sum assumed "redundant" under the recommendations of January 1749 (reconstructed)
Fujian	603,878[1,i]	621,519[2,i]	621,519[a,ii]
Zhejiang	529,029[1,ii]	N.d.[i]	Zero[b]
Guangdong	318,339[3,ii]	310,724[4,i]	318,338[c]
Anhui	317,233[1]	N.d.[7,ii]	Negligible at best[b]
Shandong	297,177[5]	N.d.[i,iii]	Hard to predict[d]
Shaanxi	206,758[5,ii]	206,758[5,6,i]	Hard to predict[d]
Jiangsu	184,362[1,3,i]	N.d.[7,i]	Hard to predict[e]
Henan	173,614[3,i]	32,751[4,7,i]	Zero[b]
Hubei	164,652[1]	N.d.[i]	164,652[f]
Zhili	120,252[1,3]	—	128,105[g]
Hunan	118,925	N.d.[7,i]	118,925[f]
Fengtian	103,526	N.d.[i,iii]	Zero[b]
Gansu	101,800[1,3,iii]	74,964[1,2,iii]	Zero[b]
Shanxi	34,858[ii]	9,794[2,iii]	34,857[f]
Jiangxi	17,393[ii]	N.d.[i]	17,392[f]
Yunnan	15,936	5,477[8,iii]	15,936[g]
Guangxi	6,404	6,160[7,iii]	6,404[f]
Guizhou	2,000[3,ii]	(26,400+)[9,i]	1,999[3,f]
Sichuan	Zero[ii]	Zero[ii]	Zero
TOTAL	3,316,136	1,294,547	1,428,127

[1] Excludes sum in brass coin, as follows (in strings, correct to nearest integer). Col. A: Fujian, 48,654; Zhejiang, 8,917; Anhui, 46,827; Jiangsu, 12,726; Hubei, 3,559; Zhili, 31,664; Gansu, 15,351. Col. B: Gansu, 14,849.

[2] Reversion to the "Kangxi target" was assumed (with explicitly justified exceptions in the cases of Gansu and Shanxi). Cf. CC, Kaerjishan and Pan Siju, QL 13/10/28, 1st mem. (cat. no. 1145-018) for Fujian.

[3] Excludes sum(s) not regarded as proceeds of ever-normal sales, as follows: Guangdong, 3,384 tls., sales proceeds from non-ever-normal stockpile; Jiangsu, 66,051 tls., special allocation for buying wheat, plus 8,499 tls., sales proceeds from Chongming Island stockpile; Henan, 42,275 tls., sales proceeds from the tribute granaries; Zhili, 7,853 tls. (and 980 strings), loans for purchasing seed grain; Gansu, 12,602 tls. (and 238 strings), miscellaneous; Guizhou, 26,400+ tls., sales proceeds from stocks of surplus tax grain.

Table 17, cont.

[4] Includes non-ever-normal purchase funds, as follows: Guangdong, 3,384 tls. from a non-ever-normal stockpile in Guangzhou; Henan, 1,133 tls. from the tribute granaries.

[5] Excludes sum otherwise allocated, as follows: Shandong, 800,000 tls. for famine relief; Shaanxi, 10,912 tls. for loans to support transfrontier cultivation under an approved regional scheme.

[6] Province whose autumn holdings were in surplus even if the "Yongzheng target" was assumed (cf. table 10).

[7] Reversion to the "Yongzheng target" was assumed.

[8] Retention of the early Qianlong basic target was assumed.

[9] Proceeds of sales from stocks of surplus tax grain.

Reconstructed rationale for column C entries

[a] Shortfall from the reset target to be filled using other funds.

[b] Province with recalcitrant shortfall or marginal potential surplus (table 13).

[c] Reset target supposed to be identical with actual holdings as most recently reported.

[d] Famine relief in progress; reserves being depleted even if, as in Shandong, more sales proceeds being generated (cf. CC, Zhuntai, QL 14/3/3).

[e] Balance unclear until action taken to recover monies spent on grain that could have been obtained through dunning.

[f] Province whose reported autumn holdings exceeded or met the reset target (table 11).

[g] Shortfall from the reset target could theoretically be fully met by reclaiming loaned grain (tables 12 and 13). For Zhili, fig. assumes recovery of 7,853 tls. lent for buying seed grain.

Qing rounding conventions are followed in col. C so that the committee's arithmetic can be reconstructed precisely.

SOURCES: for col. A, CC, "Ge sheng changping cang gu ding'e qingdan" unless otherwise noted. For col. B, as noted.

[i] CC, Kaerjishan and Pan Siju, QL 13/8/28, QL 13/10/28 (2nd mem., cat. no. 1145-019); Shise, QL 13/9/8 plus appendix, LFZZQZ (QL 13) 3209, QL 13/9/17; Chen Hongmou, QL 13/9/20 2nd mem. (cat. no. 1144-045); Kaitai, QL 13/9/26 (cat. no. 1145-002); Su Chang, QL 13/10/12; Fang Guancheng, QL 13/10/17; Wen Fu, QL 13/10/24; Aibida, QL 13/10/28; Yue Jun, QL 13/10/28; Celeng and Yaerhashan, QL 13/11/15; Zhuntai, QL 14/3/3; Peng Shukui, QL 14/3/7.

[ii] LFZZ, appendix to Kaitai, QL 13/8/6; Yue Jun, QL 13/9/13 plus appendix; Aibida, QL 13/9/12 plus appendix; Chen Hongmou, QL 13/9/20 plus appendix; Namin, QL 13/9/11; Bandi, QL 13/9/26 plus appendix; Tang Suizu, QL 13/11/14 (d.r.); Pan Siju, QL 14/6/3; LFZZQZ (QL 13), 2772, 2940.

[iii] KC, Huang Tinggui, QL 13/9/28 (8 days later than the provincial statement, which lacks the col. A fig.); Shulu, QL 13/11/20; Aligun, QL 13/12/2; Su Chang, QL 13/12/10; Tuerbing'a, QL 13/12/18; cf. Zhang Yunsui, QL 13/12/20.

the discussion that these data would inform as a Grand Council function. This shift occurred in the edict in which he indicated that redundant purchase funds should generally be deposited in provincial treasuries rather than retained at county level.[64]

---

64. Compare ibid., *juan* 320:21a–b with ibid., *juan* 323:16a–b; see also the transcriptions in the committee's report.

The twelve-man committee that reset the ever-normal storage targets in late January 1749 comprised three overlapping groups: the
available grand secretaries, available grand councillors, and the team of
senior officials from the Board. The report's list of signatories suggests
that all those grand secretaries who were still in the capital took part,
including two (Shi Yizhi and the assistant grand secretary Akedun)
who were not members of the Grand Council. Those attending as
grand secretaries were listed first, in order of precedence, whether or
not they were also grand councillors. However, half of the committee
comprised Grand Council members, and all those grand councillors
who were still in the capital were signatories, including three (Shuhede,
Wang Youdun, and the Mongol Nayantai) who were not also grand
secretaries. Shuhede's participation is explained by his recent appointment as Manchu president of the Board of Revenue; but Wang
Youdun and Nayantai, whose outer-court positions were, respectively,
president of the Board of Justice and president of the Court of Colonial
Affairs, must have been present solely as grand councillors. Shuhede
apart, the Board of Revenue had four representatives: the Chinese
president (Jiang Pu, a former grand councillor) and three vice-
presidents, including Ji Huang.[65]

Gone were the days when major departures in granary policy were
referred to joint sessions of the grand secretaries and Nine Ministries
Assembly—a body that, even if subject to grand-councillor management, still represented the entire outer-court bureaucracy.[66] With war
being waged on China's western borders, the fate of the civilian antifamine stockpiles was decided by a small committee composed mainly
of grand councillors and senior Board of Revenue officials. While numerical Manchu preponderance was not an issue (only two of the grand

---

65. Compare the list of signatories to CC, Zhang Tingyu et al., QL 13/12/12 with
the information for QL 13 in Qian, comp., *Qingdai zhiguan nianbiao*, vol. 1, pp. 51
and 137–38. Ji Huang, a Board of Works vice-president, had been assigned concurrent vice-presidential duties at the Board of Revenue.

66. Cf. Bartlett, *Monarchs and Ministers*, pp. 154, 188, and chap. 5 above. Chang
Lu's 1737 proposal for massive stockpile expansion was referred to the Regency
Council and Nine Ministries Assembly for joint consideration. Sun Hao's 1742
proposal for target reduction and the 1743 moratorium initiative were referred to
joint sessions of the grand secretaries and Nine Ministries Assembly—whose role,
in 1743, of working out the details of an imperial policy decision paralleled that
entrusted to the smaller, substantially inner-court committee in 1749.

councillors present were Manchus), the Grand Council belonged to the inner court and worked directly with the emperor. The fact that the literal meaning of its name (*Junji chu*) was "Office of Military Strategy" may not have been significant as late as 1749.[67] What numerous and often lengthy edicts make quite clear, however, is that the Jinchuan campaign was occupying a large share of its attention. As writers and recipients of Qianlong's wartime pronouncements, the grand councillors who served on the committee would have been thoroughly *au fait* with his latest thoughts on the campaign and its funding.

On 10 March 1749, by which date Qianlong had decided to end the war immediately, an edict suggested in passing that the high price of rice in Zhejiang and Jiangsu was due to the diversion of Sichuan grain to feeding the Qing forces in the Jinchuan area.[68] Is it possible that the Jinchuan war was already disrupting the normal, crucial flow of Sichuan rice to lower-Yangzi markets by mid-1748? As Dai Yingcong has pointed out, the provisioning demands of this adventure were greater than the bare troop numbers would suggest. Over the campaign as a whole, soldiers were probably outnumbered more than 2:1 by "military laborers" engaged in transportation and other auxiliary work, including construction.[69] Although the campaign's impact on the Sichuan grain market should have been limited by the large-scale use of ever-normal stocks, any skewing of the normal spatial distribution of demand for grain may have produced some unfamiliar price behavior.[70] The resulting insecurity would have conduced to supply protectionism.

---

67. The name had had its broader connotation of "Office of Affairs of State" for about a decade by 1749. Bartlett, *Monarchs and Ministers*, p. 173.

68. QSL/QL, *juan* 333:25a.

69. Dai Yingcong, "Qing State," pp. 37, 40–45, and, e.g., PDJCFL, *juan* 7:1a (report, June 1748, of the hiring of over 12,000 porters to carry rations for the 13,000 soldiers and support staff just arriving from Shaanxi, Gansu, Yunnan, and Guizhou). Cf. Lai, *Qianlong zhongyao zhanzheng*, p. 205 for manpower estimates that Dai, p. 37, cites not quite accurately, and p. 206 for estimated food requirements.

70. Undocumented material in Lai, *Qianlong zhongyao zhanzheng* (p. 205) illustrates how use of granary reserves probably only *limited* the war's impact on Sichuan's commercial grain supplies. The quota of husked rice to be appropriated from granary stocks was allegedly levied from local people, who were repaid with unhusked from the granaries. Some people had to buy rice to meet the levy, despite the high prices to which their exigency no doubt contributed. In some cases, repayment took the form of silver, so that granary stocks were not involved at all.

The earliest unambiguous evidence of an official embargo on Sichuan grain exports in the first Jinchuan war refers to a ban for which Gao Yue, as acting Sichuan administration commissioner, asked imperial approval in the tenth month (21 November to 19 December) of 1748. Whether or not he really waited for authorization (dated 19 February 1749) before implementing it, this ban was not lifted until the provincial authorities felt fully safe to do so, that is, late in April 1749.[71] Perhaps anticipating such a ban, Hubei's administration commissioner Yan Ruilong proposed sometime before mid-February that in future when grain prices rose in the great river port of Hankou, 30 percent of the commercial rice arriving from upriver be reserved for sale to Hankou consumers. In the quoted text of his memorial, there is wording suggestive of a previous embargo.

Yan noted that in the fifth and sixth months of 1748 (that is, between 27 May and 24 July), very few rice boats had been arriving from Sichuan because "the water [= river] was blocked at the gorges." The term that I translate as "blocked" (*fengbi*) probably connotes closure by administrative fiat. These dates are probably roughly correct, given that grain shipments through the Hankou conurbation's main customs station were reportedly proceeding normally as of 7 April.[72] The episode thus seems too late to explain the starvation of Lower Yangzi markets throughout May—although the *ad hoc* action Yan took *that summer* to divert Sichuan rice to Hankou consumers would have worsened the shortage further downstream. However, disruptions of Sichuan rice exports (caused in part by army supply needs) had a well-documented impact on Jiangnan grain prices in 1731–33. We need not yet dismiss the notion that a pre-June contraction of the flow of Sichuan rice was a key reason for the 1748 Jiangnan grain shortage

---

CC, Bandi, QL 14/3/9, Shuhede et al., QL 14/3/1 and Gao Yue, QL 14/3/14 confirm that by war's end at latest, a large proportion of the grain requirement was being purchased on the market.

71. CC, Shuhede et al., QL 14/3/1, Bandi, QL 14/3/9, Gao Yue, QL 14/3/14.

72. While Peng Shukui discerned a long-term downward trend in rice flows into Hubei from Sichuan and Hunan, he cited the 1.15 million *shi* (mainly husked, converted here to unhusked) of Jiangnan-bound grain recorded at the customs station from 4 October 1747 to 7 April 1748 as evidence that there was relatively little hoarding in Hubei. CC, Peng Shukui, QL 13 (cat. no. 1142-023; memorial written in April—cf. QSL/QL, *juan* 311:33b–34b).

blamed on Chang'an's alleged ban on warehousing (which must have begun before his dismissal in October 1747).[73] Perhaps, by June, the lure of high prices in the war zone, coupled with supplementary official procurements, had both reduced the flow of grain down the Yangzi and made Sichuan officials nervous about civilian food supply, thus provoking a ban that reinforced, rather than counteracting, the effects of market forces, to the detriment of food supply in Lower Yangzi cities.[74]

It is at least as plausible to posit military concerns as the cause of a May-to-July export ban. The granary reserves were finite, and the war was dragging on. Why risk food draining out of Sichuan in expectation of, and response to, the normal summer peak of grain prices on Lower Yangzi markets?[75] Whatever the precise dates and rationale, a summer export ban would not have been surprising. The term "conspiracy of silence" may be fair comment on the failure of China's provincial chiefs to take advantage of the call for explanations of the abnormal grain prices to warn the court of the war's dangers with regard to food supply in Jiangnan cities. Even—or especially?—Jishan, the Sichuan governor, did nothing but follow his master's hint that this discussion was about the impact of the ever-normal system.

The most cynical reading possible of the ever-normal granaries debate of 1748–49 is that, from the autumn of 1748 at latest, it was a smokescreen for an attempt to wrest resources from the antifamine granaries to subsidize a military campaign. The war was not to be mentioned as a source of high food prices until it was convenient to do so. As long as the campaign was the priority, concern about inflation was to be channelled into fiscally expedient attacks on public welfare institutions. One must suspect, the cynical view continues, that it was precisely the disappointing findings on the ever-normal system's assets that finally made Qianlong set a firm limit on the duration of the war.

---

73. Yan's proposal is excerpted in YFD, QL 13/12/24 (d.r.) (7:1616). See also Abe, *Shindai shi*, pp. 505–8; Qian, comp., *Qingdai zhiguan nianbiao*, vol. 2, p. 1,598; chap. 3 above.

74. Sources of March and May 1748 imply that the price of cereal foodstuffs at the front was at least 8 to 9 tls./*shi*, and could rise as supply lines lengthened. Private vendors seemingly found it worthwhile to take grain to the army despite high transport costs. QSL/QL, *juan* 309:58a–b; PDJCFL, *juan* 6:26a–b; cf. Dai Yingcong, "Qing State," pp. 63–68.

75. Cf. Chuan and Kraus, *Mid-Ch'ing Rice Markets*, pp. 20–21.

The committee had shown that the amount of grain replacement funds that could be deemed redundant after a responsible resetting of the targets was some 1.4 million taels, while the amounts of grain made surplus and now actually in store totalled less than 2 million *shi* un-husked (tables 11 and 17). The figure of 1.4 million taels lay only about midway in the range of the sums that the court had injected into the war at different times in 1748 (table 15). It was not enough to underwrite a major prolongation of the conflict. The report was submitted for Qianlong's consideration on 30 January; by 3 February, he had declared the middle of the fourth month (late May) to be the deadline for the termination of hostilities. In the meantime, implementation of the report's recommendations would create a contingency reserve com-prising the 1.4 million taels plus proceeds of the sale of up to 3.2 million *shi* (unhusked) of "extra-target grain," the exact amount depending partly on the success of dunning operations. Such a contingency reserve could be worth having, given the uncertainties inherent in armed con-flict. There was merit in keeping fiscal options open until the outcome of the war was clearer and the forces were withdrawn.

The above interpretation is probably too stark. Qianlong's remarks about the termination of another public welfare initiative suggest a more nuanced understanding. Since 1742, the court had sought to di-minish the effect of indirect taxation on the price of staple foodstuffs by cancelling one major transit tax on grain and beans. It had seemed that one should be able to reverse some upward price movements by re-moving the tax that was their cause. Since, on the contrary, the price of grain had been rising dramatically, it was easy to allege that the ex-periment had failed. Little resistance was to be expected when an in-ternal customs superintendent called Tula proposed reimposition of the tax to supplement the funding for the Jinchuan war. The grand secretaries endorsed this notion about three weeks before the report on the granaries was submitted. Thus ended the "permanent" remission of the tax. In his reimposition edict, Qianlong claimed that he was not actuated "solely" by considerations of military finance. Ten weeks later he denied that they had weighed with him at all. Rather, he suggested, there were public-interest grounds for ending a fruitless experiment.[76]

---

76. QSL/QL, *juan* 329:26a–27a, 334:10b–11a; Wang Xianqian, comp., *Donghua xulu, juan* 29:11b; Kōsaka, "Kenryū-dai zenki," pp. 66, 76–77; LFZZ, Tula, QL

Naive as it would be to take these protestations at face value, the flu-idity of his justification for the *volte-face* offers a clue for interpreting the 1748–49 decisions on the granaries. The Jinchuan situation was in flux; so was the thinking of those trying to manage it from distant Beijing.

We should probably recognize a complex interplay of motives in the granaries debate of 1748–49. Of course it was potentially useful that, with a war in progress and revenue reduced by the land tax remission, Ou Kanshan had revived the allegation that the ever-normal system did more harm than good. However, it may indeed have been concern about the renewed inflationary trend that inspired the debate's launch. As noted in chapter 6, the mid-Qing court probably lacked the statis-tical sophistication to realize how poorly the available data supported the idea that larger granary reserves meant higher grain prices. The surge of Lower Yangzi rice prices in 1748, unprecedented since 1679–80, must have been alarming, although the court chose to perceive a partial explanation in Chang'an's excessive zeal. The accompanying riots and demonstrations would have imparted urgency to the search for a cure.[77] Nor did the determination to curb ever-normal stockpiling subside once the Jinchuan war was over. To the contrary, a high-level report of October 1749 dismissed a few brave efforts to raise the reset provincial targets by taking advantage of an intraprovincial target-redistribution exercise.[78]

Despite all this, one cannot ignore the fiscal attractions of the target-reduction strategy—which, as we have seen, had only weak provincial support in 1748. The notion of a second moratorium received more support, but where would the fiscal advantages have been? A second moratorium could at best have released funds for intragovernmental borrowing. Intense fiscal concerns during the summer of 1748, while the Jinchuan war dragged on, would, furthermore, explain the coarseness of the policy announced in August. This policy ignored the distinction, so strongly stressed in the provincial responses, between

---

13/11/4. Qianlong cited different public-interest grounds for discontinuation in each pronouncement. On the transit tax experiment, see Kōsaka, op. cit., pp. 59–66; Dunstan, *Conflicting Counsels*, pp. 170–72; He, "Qianlong nianjian," pp. 90–91.

77. See chap. 3 above and Wang, "Secular Trends of Rice Prices," table 1.1, pp. 40–42.

78. CC, Zhang Tingyu et al., QL 14/8/25 and below.

commercialized and commercially isolated parts of China. All were to
see their storage targets cut to the "old" levels "of the Kangxi and
Yongzheng periods." Why the reference to Kangxi targets, whose restoration had been advocated by Zhuntai alone? Zhuntai's memorial on
the "southeast" may have directly inspired the 12 August edict, for there
is reason to suspect that Qianlong had just reread it.[79] However, the
chief attraction may not have been Zhuntai's vision of a basically free
grain market, but rather the prospect of deriving maximal revenue
from the existing stockpiles. As the court awaited the next call for
military funds, it was not in a position to be overnice about the differences between China's regional economies. Peter Perdue has recently argued that in late imperial China, "both civilian and military
provisioning played a role in state policies. Sometimes they complemented each other, and sometimes one was sacrificed to the other."[80] If
the interpretation I pursue here is correct, it would illustrate his point
from a new angle.

Qianlong's mind may not have been firmly set in the late summer
and autumn of 1748. His implicit promise, in October, that, after their
transfer to provincial treasuries, redundant purchase funds would remain available for local use may have been intentionally misleading.
Alternatively, it may reflect vacillation. Only with great reluctance
could an ostensibly Confucian monarch milk a public welfare institution for a military campaign. Rather than seeing the whole 1748–49
debate as a sophisticated plot to gain acceptance for the ransacking of
granary resources, it is probably best to imagine the court engaged with
contingency planning and worst-case scenarios. By January 1749,
Qianlong's military resolve was weakening. In reporting, the committee both completed the unfinished business created by past orders
and helped him to clarify his options. Its findings did not alone pre-

---

79. On 6 August, at Qianlong's behest, the Grand Council secretariat began
submitting copies of the provincial responses for his perusal at the rate of two per
day, in order of receipt. While I do not have dates for all fifteen responses received
by then, comparison of the placement of their *Shilu* abstracts with the documents'
sequence in the archives suggests that Zhuntai's memorials were approximately nos.
10 and 11. Assuming that the submissions were on consecutive days, Qianlong
probably scrutinized Zhuntai's memorials on 10 or 11 August. YFD, QL 13/7/13
(7:1616); cf. ibid., QL 13/8/6.
80. Perdue, *China Marches West*, p. 531.

cipitate his decision that the war must be concluded by mid-June or late May, but they may well have been one influence.[81] In any case, the committee's recommendations suited the predicament of a government fighting a costly war with reduced annual income. Even if it envisaged that, for appearances' sake, the "savings" from the granaries would be applied to uses other than war finance, the committee was contributing to budgetary planning for a year in which a war must be concluded, and the other contingencies of empire met, out of straitened resources. Any improvement in the finances of a belligerent government strengthens its war-fighting capacity.

Who were the granaries' friends on the committee? Why, apart from Qianlong's diminishing commitment to the Jinchuan war, was the system protected from the full radicalism of his original orders? What signs are there of resistance to universal target-reduction from a bureaucracy conditioned to associate substantial stockpiles with social responsibility? The committee members who seem most likely to have advocated prudence in resetting targets are Chen Dashou and Jiang Pu. Chen, now Chinese president of the Board of Personnel and a grand councillor, had been governor of Anhui in 1739–41, Jiangsu in 1741–46, and Fujian in 1746–47. As we have seen, notwithstanding his keen insight into market processes, in 1743 and 1745 he had taken steps to protect the Jiangsu stocks from central government decisions that threatened to erode them. Jiang, now Chinese president of the Board of Revenue, had been a grand councillor from early 1746 until May 1748. As Hunan governor in 1743–45, he had ignored the 1743 moratorium to the extent of proposing to encourage neighboring provincial administrations to buy grain in Hunan for granary restocking. The answers that he and governor-general Emida submitted in 1745 to a central government circular on monetary policy suggest a generally interventionist stance in economic matters.[82] Most pertinent of all, in the autumn of 1748, Jiang had taken an initiative to moderate Qianlong's radical, across-the-board approach.

After the September edict ordering that buying be restricted to that needed to restore reserves to the "old" target levels, Jiang submitted a

---

81. Cf., e.g., QSL/QL, *juan* 330:45b–51a, *juan* 331:1b–4a.

82. Qian, comp., *Qingdai zhiguan nianbiao*, vol. 1, pp. 137–38, vol. 2, pp. 1,592–98; above, chaps. 3, 5, and 6; Dunstan, "'Orders Go Forth,'" pp. 86–116.

memorial tactfully drawing attention to the relevant respects—degree of commercialization, proximity to external frontiers, and so on—in which jurisdictions differed from each other, even within provinces. He astutely pointed out that disregard for this diversity would jeopardize the goal of stabilizing market prices. He implicitly proposed criteria for setting storage targets for subprovincial units; these criteria generally reflected a consensus that was clear in the 1748 provincial responses and had been building for a decade. Jurisdictions that did not need large stocks were, first, those in the vicinity of provincial capitals or with good water transport, and, second, fertile ones with high grain output. Places that, on the contrary, should have their "old" targets raised were mountainous and remote jurisdictions, jurisdictions that were prone to natural disasters, places of military importance, and places (such as Linqing in Shandong and Tongguan in Shaanxi) whose location—on or near provincial boundaries—was convenient for dispatching supplementary relief stocks to other provinces.

In the context of the stated imperial policy current at the time, the natural interpretation of Jiang's proposal was that it envisaged intra-provincial *redistribution* of the restored Yongzheng or Kangxi targets. A rationalized sharing-out of these lower targets would minimize the impact of the cuts on the more vulnerable jurisdictions. On 5 November 1748, no doubt assuming that only redistribution was in question, Qianlong cautiously acknowledged that there was sense in Jiang's proposals and ordered the provincial chiefs to consider how his ideas might be applied in their own provinces. Most responses were probably still pending when the committee reported.[83] But Jiang had in effect suggested that county-level storage targets be revisited to ascertain which jurisdictions needed larger stockpiles than under their "old" targets. He thereby opened an avenue of resistance for provincial chiefs who thought the cuts unwise. He had, perhaps unwittingly, given them an opportunity to argue that their aggregate provincial targets should be higher than the "old" ones.

There were provincial chiefs who toed the redistribution-only line or recommended minimal adjustments. Chen Hongmou, indeed, had no need to resist, because he had already argued successfully for reten-

---

83. CC, Huang Tinggui, QL 14/2/9 (which quotes Jiang's memorial); QSL/QL, *juan* 324:34a–b; CC, Zhang Tingyu et al., QL 13/12/12.

tion of Shaanxi's 1743 target by the time that he responded.[84] Huang Tinggui, by contrast, wrote before the committee reported, offering cuts in twenty-seven Gansu jurisdictions in exchange for retention of the post-1738 targets elsewhere in the province (and creation of three new stockpiles). The result would have been a reset target of 2,790,000 granary *shi*, compared with a Kangxi and Yongzheng target of 860,000. Shanxi's Yongzheng target was 1,315,837 *shi*; Aligun unsuccessfully proposed that it be raised to 1,808,000. Kaitai, now moved to Hunan, resisted subtly. It took him two memorials to secure agreement, in October 1749, that Hunan might keep over half its extra-target grain for helping other provinces or even for use in Hunan, with the proviso that this grain would not be replaced and thus did not represent an increase of the reset target. Strategic invocation of Jiang Pu's memorial contributed to the rhetorical effectiveness of Kaitai's first submission, written in April.[85]

There were probably other cases of resistance, but let us conclude by focusing on that offered for Jiangxi—like Hunan, a province in which contraction of the granary system should, theoretically, have seemed attractive (except from a landowner viewpoint).[86] Jiangxi's spokesman was its administration commissioner Peng Jiaping, who had already tried abortively to have the Jiangxi target reset at some 1.5 million *shi*.[87] It is true that, on the question of where large stockpiles were needed, Peng stood Jiang's reasoning on its head. In grain-rich Jiangxi, suggested Peng, the remote, mountainous jurisdictions did not need extra reserves. Their commercial isolation protected them from losing grain to the interregional market, and the routine *soudure* sales of old granary stocks met with little enthusiasm from local consumers. Furthermore, while two prefectures on Jiangxi's northern borders seemed well-placed

---

84. LFZZ, Nasutu, QL 13/10/9; material relating to Zhili, Jiangsu, and Anhui in CC, Zhang Tingyu et al., QL 14/8/25; CC, Chen Hongmou, QL 13/9/20 1st mem. (cat. no. 1144-044), QL 14/5/19.

85. CC, Huang Tinggui, QL 13/10/24 plus appendix, LFZZQZ (QL 13) 2772; material relating to Shanxi in CC, Zhang Tingyu et al., QL 14/8/25; CC, Kaitai, QL 14/2/29; Bd. Rev., QL 14/9/8, repr. MQDA, vol. 160, pp. B89,649–53 (doc. no. 024486).

86. Henan may have been resistant (CC, Zhang Tingyu et al., QL 14/8/25); see also the general ref. to resistant provinces cited in Bd. Rev., QL 14/9/8, repr. MQDA, vol. 160, p. B89,651.

87. CC, Zhang Tingyu et al., QL 14/8/25.

for shipping stocks to other provinces, they did not produce much grain and could not support expanded stockpiles for interprovincial relief transfers.

In Jiangxi's case, Peng argued, the places where extra reserves were needed were precisely the vicinity of the provincial capital (Nanchang) and other jurisdictions with good water transport. This, presumably, was partly because, although not near provincial borders, Nanchang and its fertile neighbors west and south of Lake Boyang were the best positioned to maintain stocks for transfer elsewhere. More importantly, Peng pointed out that in Jiangxi, the annual influx of merchants after harvest meant that "wherever boat and oar can penetrate, if the price [offered] is at all reasonable, the farmers vie to sell their surplus grain. They lack the sense to save it. Whenever the *soudure* arrives, many of the people are in difficulty over food." In grain-surplus territories, in other words, good water transport meant not the relief of local scarcity, but its creation.[88]

Although Peng thus had differences with Jiang, he took full advantage of the opportunity that Jiang had provided. He noted the population's growth since targets were set in 1699, and the repeated grain-transfers from Jiangxi granaries to other provinces. He envisaged that while jurisdictions that had seen little change since the last two reigns should abide by their "old" targets, jurisdictions in the hinterland of the provincial capital with rising populations and good water transport should have increases of up to 10,000 *shi* compared with their "old" targets. There should also be prefectural stockpiles ranging in size from 8,000 *shi* for small prefectures to 30,000 *shi* for the provincial capital. Although he conceded that the "old" targets of remote, mountainous jurisdictions could be cut, the net implication of his county-by-county proposals was a considerable increase over Jiangxi's "Yongzheng" target (1,370,713 *shi*). In forwarding his discussion on 26 March 1749, Huang Tinggui, now Liang-Jiang governor-general, cited 1,519,000 *shi* as the proposed provincial target. The "old" target would be raised by almost 11 percent, yielding a figure only 87,000 *shi* (some 5 percent) short of Jiangxi's 1743 target (1,606,000 *shi*).

---

88. Peng had articulated broadly similar principles in 1742. Cf. above, chap. 5, n. 40.

26 March was too late. The committee's recommendations had been accepted at the end of January; the Jiangxi counterproposal was dismissed with others in October.[89] Huang's memorial may have helped provoke a final meeting of the grand secretaries to reach official closure on the reasons for the rising price of grain. Their report, presented in early May, acknowledged the wide range of opinions in the provincial submissions but affirmed that "the majority" had advocated a slackening of activism in buying for the granaries. This only served to justify the previous decision to revert, in principle, to the "Yongzheng" targets. This decision should be upheld; it should be complemented with prudence in restocking practices and such other measures as provincial chiefs had reason to believe might moderate grain prices in their jurisdictions.[90] In the wake of a near-disastrous military adventure, it was time to consolidate the court's authority through unwonted inertia in public welfare policy.

Peng's resistance was futile but not insignificant. It adds to the evidence that in 1748–49 there was no consensus of responsible opinion that the medium-high targets of 1743–44 must be brought down to stabilize grain prices. When Qianlong requested provincial advice on how to explain and control the rising prices, only a minority of the respondents advocated even mild or selective target-cuts. The command for sweeping cuts aroused resistance first from the Chinese president of the Board of Revenue, and then, building on his initiative, from two experienced senior administrators of Middle Yangzi provinces, as well as at least two northern governors. Qianlong and his committee were not implementing the considered wisdom of the territorial   bureaucracy. Rather, they were forcing through a policy for which there seemed to be an economic rationale, but which probably reflected counsels of fiscal expediency.

---

89. CC, Huang Tinggui, QL 14/2/9; CC, Zhang Tingyu et al., QL 14/8/25; QSL/QL, *juan* 330:33b–35b (entry for 30 January 1749). Rowe's statement (*Saving the World*, pp. 260, 513 n. 53) that the decision to cut the targets was taken in late spring is perhaps based on confusion of this entry with that of, as he puts it, "QL 14/3" (mid-April to mid-May) cited in n. 90 below.

90. QSL/QL, *juan* 337:13a–b.

9

Of Loose Ends and
Parallel Developments

It was never likely that closure on the impact of the ever-normal granaries would be achieved by one or two reports in 1749. Prices would continue to fluctuate, while maintaining an upward trend, and officials would continue to have their opinions. This final chapter does not recount the vicissitudes of the ever-normal system after the great debate, a task that has been ably accomplished by Will and Wong and their collaborators.[1] Rather, it finishes the story of the debate, in which there were fresh bursts of radicalism yet to come. The story is then put in a broader perspective by surveying other developments of the "long 1740s" that are consistent with it. The abolition of the banner grain bureaus for controlling grain speculation in Beijing; the withdrawal of financial aid to famine refugees; the one-year suspension of the land tax; and harsh sentencing for leaders of food riots—all these, in different ways, complement the picture of diminishing imperial commitment to problematic and demanding public welfare programs. They invite us to return to, and problematize, the theme of liberalization. What were the social implications of the relative shifts from interventionism towards more market-oriented approaches that occurred in the "long 1740s"? And what were the broader ideological concomitants of a rudimentary economic liberalism whose clearest 1748 expression (Zhuntai's memorial) may have tempted Qianlong to subordinate popular subsistence to military adventurism?

---

1. Will and Wong, *Nourish the People*, chaps. 3 and 4 and passim.

While the approach adopted in this chapter perforce stresses breadth over depth, it also maintains this book's consistent emphasis on the interest and significance of specific initiatives, specific arguments, and specific decisions at the specific points in time when they were made or taken. It is partly because, in this chapter, I am not concerned with later trends in granary administration that my reading of the evidence contrasts radically with R. Bin Wong's.[2] My view is that scrutiny of individual moments is crucial to a securely-founded understanding of the politics and ideology of any period. Examination of a few related policy developments towards the end of the "long 1740s" will help prepare the ground for exploration of this period's significance in the political history of Qianlong's reign—an ongoing project about which I raise a few ideas in the conclusion to this book.

Let us return to prices and the ever-suspect granaries. When, in 1752, the price of rice in Suzhou reached a level that was practically unprecedented since the Ming-Qing transition, calls for more radical repudiation of activist grain storage sounded once again.[3] This time, they were partially translated into policy. Yet, as in 1745, the court withdrew from the brink of near-total suspension of the ever-normal system. The first step in the gradual build-up of reserves that characterized the ensuing decades was taken in 1753.[4] 1753 thus marked the great debate's conclusion. Even in 1749, however, there was unfinished business. Three last responses to the edict of 12 January 1748 arrived in the late spring and early summer of 1749. While two of these were simply

---

2. Wong, citing a 1983 paper of mine, denies that the late 1740s changes in granary policy spelled a diminution of direct state commitment to "supply stability." He sees, instead, a tendency to adopt alternative strategies, such as *jiansheng* title sales and promotion of community granaries, to circumvent the problems of the ever-normal system. Ibid., pp. 95–96, 38–40, 63–66, etc. I have shown above that the significance of title sales was variable and problematic (among other details on which I differ from Wong). More basically, his project was to reconstruct the broad patterns of the granary system's history over two centuries. *Prima facie*, he was justified, from that perspective, in viewing the 1748–49 cutback as a temporary check in a longer process of expansion.

3. Among the Yangzi Delta annual rice prices calculated by Wang Yeh-chien for 1663–1747 ("Secular Trends of Rice Prices," table 1.1, pp. 40–42), only the exceptional Shanghai peak of 1680 (2.30 tls./*shi*) rivalled the Suzhou peak of 1752.

4. Will, *Bureaucracy and Famine*, p. 194; Will and Wong, *Nourish the People*, pp. 277–79, 281–85, and appendix, table A.1.

overdue, the third, and most interesting, was largely gratuitous.[5] The grand secretaries had submitted their vindication of the target cuts a month before Yaerhashan, the acting Jiangsu governor, replaced his earlier, interim response with a long discussion of the ever-normal system's impact on grain prices. More radical than Zhuntai's unsolicited proposals for the Yangzi Valley provinces, it will refocus our attention on "grain-centered liberalism" and the obstacles to its fulfillment in mid-eighteenth-century China.

Knowing Where to Stop

It is not that Yaerhashan envisaged total state withdrawal from famine relief endeavors, including precautionary storage. On the contrary, reserves of 40,000 to 50,000 *shi* (unhusked) should be kept in every prefecture and independent subprefecture (*zhili zhou*) for relief in major famines. Distribution of grain should be a last resort; it could be supplemented by distribution of silver and by public works projects. Silver should also be distributed in those minor and localized disasters that merited relief. This may sound no more radical than the prescriptions of Celeng and Shulu, but in fact key features of the ever-normal system were completely missing from Yaerhashan's proposals.

Yaerhashan's blueprint rejected "stabilizing sales" as inconsistent with the principle that only in severe subsistence crises should grain be issued to assist the people. The prefectural and independent subprefectural granaries were not to supplement the county granaries but to replace them. Their intended stockpiles would not have been equivalent to the combined holdings of the average prefecture's subordinate counties, even under the "Yongzheng" targets. In Jiangsu, for example, the pre-1738 targets had ranged from 16,000 *shi* for small county-level jurisdictions to 30,000 *shi* for large ones. A prefectural reserve of 50,000 *shi* would theoretically have been equivalent to the combined Yongzheng-period stocks of one large and one medium-sized

---

5. The acting Huguang governor-general Xinzhu, instructed to make good his dismissed predecessor's negligence, responded in mid-April. The Guangdong governor Yue Jun, who replied in mid-May, sought to excuse his tardiness by claiming that he had been systematically examining conditions in Guangdong. CC, Xinzhu, QL 14/2/28; Yue Jun, QL 14/3/28.

Jiangsu county.[6] Moreover, one looks in vain, in Yaerhashan's proposals, for that careful discrimination between commercialized and hard-to-commercialize regions that marked even Zhuntai's ideas. Yaerhashan did his best to argue that no part of the nation needed sizable reserves of grain. Another central feature of the ever-normal system that he wished to see abolished was the annual buying process. The open market would be spared the pressures of official buying because the prefectural granaries would be restocked (annually or biennially, at the prefect's discretion) through barter of the tired stocks with fresh grain from the fields of substantial local landowners.

Could this unequal exchange have worked without the prefect using powers that far exceeded those thought proper at the time? It would be difficult to hail the proponent of such barter as a champion of free market economics. It nonetheless remains the case that Yaerhashan objected strongly to government control of grain. This was, for him, the central cause of the inflation. The annual buying process and the sale of *jiansheng* titles for grain both represented "official acquisition" (*guanshou*) and were harmful for that reason. "Commodities have always circulated among the people, in which respect antiquity and the present do not greatly differ. Once they undergo official acquisition, without exception they [commodities] become expensive." The evidence for this was the cheapness of goods that escaped "official acquisition," such as firewood (still free for the taking in some places), Fujian sweet potatoes (a reliably cheap standby for most of the province's poor), and Zhangzhou oranges (dramatically cheaper when not subject to official purchase). As to the mechanism, or rather "inevitable tendency," through which "official acquisition" made prices soar, Yaerhashan invoked only the belief that the "empty commotion" attendant on official buying provoked the antisocial wiles of those in a position to raise market prices artificially. The result was an impact on prices out of all proportion to the quantities acquired, resulting in price levels that in no way reflected actual supply. Supply, indeed, was not a problem: continuing agricultural expansion meant that there should be no question of shortage.

Yaerhashan did not offer a positive argument for leaving the market to take care of prices. In expounding the view that large reserves were

---

6. HHCC, Bundle 88, Chen Dashou, QL 8/3/10.

nowhere needed, he cited the prevalence of commerce, even in much of north China, but only as one factor among others. He seems to have thought that leaving almost all the grain "among the people" would suffice to control speculation, because speculation took place only after prices were already high, which they would cease to be, once "official acquisition" was abjured.[7] Such theoretical underdevelopment, by the standards of his day, may have contributed to his failure to convince Qianlong's advisors. His memorial, dated 9 June 1749, was considered on 15 July together with a follow-up memorial in which, echoing Shulu, he suggested that habituation to the availability of large welfare stockpiles risked making the folk "presumptuous." Having no longer any reason to do otherwise, the deliberators (the Grand Council and senior Board of Revenue officials) sounded the voice of social responsibility. The ever-normal system was a good and necessary institution, and the established guidelines were flexible enough to stop the annual buying process from being inflationary. Yaerhashan must see to it that the stocks held in Jiangsu under the Yongzheng target were properly managed according to existing policy. Especially for a member of the Manchu royal lineage like Yaerhashan, this must have seemed a snub.[8]

Was there a section of the Manchu and, so to speak, peri-Manchu elite that thought the court did too much for the overweening populace and would therefore have welcomed drastically reduced stockpiling? In 1751–52, the titular grand secretary Gao Bin became a leading advocate of termination of bulk official buying for the granaries. Gao was the ethnically Chinese father of one of Qianlong's concubines and "a member of the Manchu Bordered Yellow Banner." As Zhili governor-general during the famine of 1743–44, he had stressed the profit motive's efficacy in guaranteeing the release of private stocks onto dearth-stricken markets.[9] Was it out of fidelity to long-held beliefs that, late in 1752, he put forward a proposal, more radical than Zhuntai's, for substituting market mechanisms for the ever-normal process? Or was he

----

7. CC, Yaerhashan, QL 14/4/25.

8. CC, Grd. Coun. and Bd. Rev., QL 14/6/2. Only Yaerhashan's suggestion that *jiansheng* titles be sold exclusively for silver interested the deliberators. They said that, before making recommendations, they would await reports from Fujian and Sichuan on the effectiveness of selling the titles for grain.

9. See Li Man-kuei's biography of Gao Bin in *Eminent Chinese*, ed. Hummel, vol. 1, pp. 412–13; and chap. 3 above.

pandering to welfare-weariness within a faction that may have come to include Qianlong? The gross mismatch, in 1751–52, between grain prices and the storage levels invoked to explain them suggests that the latter possibility should not be dismissed.

In 1751, the annual price of rice in Suzhou prefecture, as calculated by Wang Yeh-chien, was 1.93 taels per *shi*. In 1752, it rose to 2.31 taels per *shi*. These were crisis levels by contemporary standards and were presumably reflected in high prices elsewhere. The *minshu gushu* nationwide storage figure for 1751 was some 27.3 million *shi*; this was the lowest such total for any year from 1741 through the end of Qianlong's reign, save for the 1752 total of just under 26.7 million. The average *minshu gushu* total for 1741–50 had been almost 32.3 million. The inverse correlation between prices and reported granary reserves was glaring.[10] The court was probably aware of it, but, after all, the argument that official buying was intrinsically inflationary had a long pedigree by 1752. An edict of mid-August 1752 rehearsed this argument and the judiciously adapted truism that "If there is less bought by officialdom, there will be more sold on the markets." Having noted the "ubiquitously" elevated prices and Gao's 1751 proposal to end official bulk-buying for good, it announced the following decision:

Those who take thought for the price of grain all speak of halting purchasing, and this is not without discernment. Although it is not possible explicitly to set up law perpetually abolishing it, if we take this year's situation, provincial granary reserves in fact afford [an adequate] provision in most cases. Even if there should arise the need [to supplement them], it will surely be possible to make allocations from nearby. If the actual amount in store attains three or four tenths [of the target], there is no need to rush to have recourse to buying. As for issuing funds and delegating personnel to buy [in other provinces], it would appear that this should be completely stopped.

The governors and governors-general were to ascertain the state of the harvests in their jurisdictions, deliberate, and report. If it was appropriate to desist from buying they should issue proclamations to inform

---

10. Wang, "Secular Trends of Rice Prices," table 1.1, p. 42; QSL/QL, *juan* 405:19b, 429:34a; Will and Wong, *Nourish the People*, appendix, tables A.1 and A.2; cf. chap. 6, figure 1 above.

the merchant community of this decision straight away, without awaiting imperial approval.[11]

In view of the low level of reported granary reserves in 1751–52, this was an odd departure. It is fair to point out that, ten weeks later, Qianlong authorized the retention of 700,000 *shi* of tribute grain (equivalent to 1.4 million unhusked) for restocking in three central provinces.[12] Also, the suggestion that 60 to 70 percent depletion rates might be tolerated was surely made on the assumption that most granaries were substantially fuller. Nonetheless, the pronouncement arguably implied a *de facto* global storage target, after a few years, of only 10 to 13.5 million *shi* (30 to 40 percent of the 1749 nationwide target). This would have done much indeed to meet the views of those who thought society best served by leaving "the people" in control of their own grain.

What was the intent of the order that those provincial administrations that decided to abstain from official buying should announce the fact to the merchant community? Presumably, however heavily the notices were larded with appeals to morality, they would effectively have told the merchants that their collective market share had been enlarged. This swing towards the private sector must have encouraged Gao to greater radicalism. Why not definitively transfer almost the entire waterborne grain business to merchant hands not only in the Yangzi Valley, as Zhuntai had proposed, but also in parts of northern China? As Will has noted, in discussing Gao's memorial, the grand councillors argued supportively that it did not matter how much or how little grain was bought for the granaries: as soon as an official emissary stationed himself at a "place where grain masses together or grain boats in transit moor," the local brokers used the news of his arrival as a pretext to raise prices. Gao's proposal, as the grand councillors cited it, was that there was no need to change the ways of provinces, such as Shanxi, Shaanxi, Guangdong, and Guangxi, that did not draw on Yangzi Valley surpluses, but:

---

11. QSL/QL, *juan* 418:13b–14b—a ref. that I owe to Will's account of this episode (Will and Wong, *Nourish the People*, pp. 143–47). For Gao's 1751 proposals, see YFD, QL 16/7/6 (d.r.) (8:1618-2).

12. QSL/QL, *juan* 423:13b–14a.

From now on, as regards those county-level jurisdictions of Zhili, Henan, Shandong, Hunan, Hubei, Jiangxi, Anhui, Jiangsu, and Zhejiang that are riverine and boat-frequented, it would be best to let the merchants themselves carry out transport and circulation (*bu ruo ting shangfan zi xing zhuanyun liutong*); there is no point in official buying.

This did not mean that granary reserves would be neglected altogether. Territorial officials whose jurisdictions had experienced a good harvest would be expected to take advantage of the low prices to do some strictly local buying. If a jurisdiction faced a subsistence crisis for which it had inadequate reserves, the provincial chiefs should have the necessary buying done *ad hoc*.

The idea was not without appeal. However, the grand councillors noted that it required further deliberation and recommended that it be sent out for provincial comment. Qianlong assented on 19 November.[13] But opinion at court was moving too fast for the practical administrators in the provinces. As Will has shown, both Gao's proposal and the August edict met with a mixed response from the provincial chiefs. These initiatives were not to shape the future. The latest known case of a provincial governor adducing the principle that buying be not seen as urgent once granaries had 40 percent of their targets dates from February 1754.[14] By then, Hubei had been granted a 77 percent target increase. This development, which took place in 1753, signalled the end of retrenchment. *Minshu gushu* storage totals quickly resumed their previous norm (the average for 1753–62 being just under 31.9 million *shi*) before embarking on a gradual climb. Moreover, the Hubei target was increased precisely to provide for grain transfers to other provinces. Together with the 1740s, the 1750s were probably the heyday of the interprovincial transfer of ever-normal grain. The provinces involved were typically those "located along the principal axes of the navigable waterway system," that is, those in whose case the choice between state and commercial distribution was most real.[15] Gao Bin had posed this choice starkly, but to no avail. The court had renounced expansionist

---

13. YFD, QL 17/10/14 (d.r.) (9:1622-2); Yongchang and Hengwen, QL 17/12/5, repr. GZD/QL, vol. 4, pp. 513–14; cf. Will and Wong, *Nourish the People*, p. 144, to which I owe the latter ref.

14. Will and Wong, *Nourish the People*, pp. 143–45 and 147 n. 15; see also YFD, QL 17/11/29 (d.r.) (9:1622-2).

15. Will, *Bureaucracy and Famine*, pp. 194, 281–82.

ambitions that would have squeezed the merchants' market share, but it finally drew back from the free-market alternative. The upward trend of grain prices continued in the years ahead, but the state retreated no farther from precautionary stockpiling than was decided during 1748–49.[16]

Why, given that Gao Bin had the backing of the August edict, was his radicalism ultimately less influential than Zhuntai's? A large part of the answer may surely be found in the post-August interactions between court and provinces, which repeated a familiar pattern. Some provincial chiefs resisted the latest extremism from the center, while Qianlong was soon undermining his own orders by making exceptions in response to provincial reports. A further factor was that harvest conditions turned out to be suitable for buying grain in many places. It is true that the August edict elicited eight compliant responses. These represented a geographically wide spread of provinces, with overall reserve levels ranging from 30 to 90 percent of target. The Anhui and Shandong provincial chiefs even agreed to limit purchases to those required to restore all county-level stockpiles to 40 percent of target (with the buying local and subject to price signals, promised the Anhui governor). Acceptance of 60 percent depletion was thus not unthinkable in the territorial bureaucracy in 1752.

But nine still more scattered provincial administrations resisted or (in two cases) made compromise proposals. These provinces had a roughly similar range of storage levels, relative to target, to that of the first group. No matter how limited the depletion, the spokesmen for all these provinces opined that buying should proceed, or at least argued its importance. Most interesting were the responses for Fengtian and Jiangsu. In the former, which had only 30 to 40 percent of target, state purchasing was still thought necessary to supplement demand. The dearth of local buyers reportedly created risk that grain would drain out of the region if not purchased by the state. In this case, it was state hoarding that was to conserve stocks for the localities that had produced them. The Jiangsu respondents accepted the edict's rationale, and

---

16. Will and Wong, *Nourish the People*, p. 277 n. 73 and appendix, table A.1; and, e.g., Wang, "Secular Trends of Rice Prices," table 1.1, pp. 42–43, and figs. 1.1 and 1.2; L. M. Li, "Grain Prices in Zhili Province," figs. 2.1 to 2.3; and Marks, "Rice Prices, Food Supply, and Market Structure," pp. 72–73.

also the principle of a minimum percentage holding past which buying should be halted, but asked that, for Jiangsu, the percentage should be 50. Yet again, the guardians of the "presumptuous" urban populace of China's most commercialized province were not enthusiasts for major state withdrawal from the grain market. They preferred the traditional argument that a densely populated region had especial need of "full and abundant" official reserves.[17]

As had happened before, a radical initiative was losing momentum in the face of perceptions of a need to guard against subsistence problems in the tried and trusted way. As early as September, Qianlong made an exception of Henan, whose northwestern neighbors, Shanxi and Shaanxi, were reportedly in the early stages of a severe drought. Henan's harvest had been rated 80 percent successful, and its reserves stood at 50 percent of target level. Cautious buying for the Henan granaries was to be undertaken after all. Qianlong also approved the concessions that Chen Hongmou requested for Fujian in response to the August edict. Fujian's reserves were to be brought up to a minimum of 50 percent of target throughout the province; careful buying beyond the 50 percent level was to proceed as long as prices remained favorable.[18] With even the August policy so easily eroded, there was little hope for Gao's more extreme proposal in the court of official opinion. It too transparently entailed a rapid running down of the reserves of the affected provinces.[19]

In 1752, there was nothing other than the high preharvest prices to push the government towards the leap into the dark that radicals from Wu Wei to Gao Bin had advocated for more than ten years. Apart from inattention to the inverse correlation between granary stock sizes and Suzhou grain prices, key features of the background to the adoption of a watered-down and coarsened version of Zhuntai's proposals in 1748–49 were absent in 1752. First, in 1752 there was not even the ghost of an interventionist excess (the 1738–43 high-level storage chimera) to be renounced. Second, and more important, in 1752 the state was not

---

17. QSL/QL, *juan* 418:14b–19a (ref. from Will and Wong, *Nourish the People*, p. 143 n. 4).

18. QSL/QL, *juan* 420:16a–17a, 418:18b–19a.

19. Cf. the remarks of the Hubei governor and governor-general. Yongchang and Hengwen, QL 17/12/5, repr. GZD/QL, vol. 4, p. 514 (ref. from Will and Wong, *Nourish the People*, p. 144).

involved in any military adventure comparable to the Jinchuan war. It was not under unusual fiscal strain. The next major military campaign began in 1755; the next universal remission of the land tax was in 1770. Central government treasury reserves (those controlled by the Board of Revenue) had more than recovered, exceeding 38 million taels at year's end.[20] In the absence of abnormal fiscal pressure, bureaucratic common sense, abetted by climatic hazard, triumphed over welfare-weariness, which had in any case found other targets, and/or proto-liberalism. We historians could choose to stress the inertia of the system, but to what purpose? It is not clear that the radicals were right, and the circumstances in which changes did occur are far more interesting.

Let Able-Bodied Famine Refugees Fend for Themselves!

On 1 April 1748, Wubai, the Manchu Director-general of the Capital Granaries reported on his management of 3,420 poor people of both sexes and all ages who had drifted towards the capital because of hardship in their home region. In accordance with procedures of early 1744, they had been sheltered in temporary mat-sheds at nearby Tongzhou and fed altogether 1,086.67 *shi* of *suomi* from the Tongzhou granaries. Night and day surveillance had ensured that there were no fire hazards or disturbances. 196 persons had either expressed a wish to seek a livelihood away from home or fallen sick and died (coffins were provided); this had left 3,224 to be issued with travel allowances and sent home in the second month (28 February to 28 March). Officialdom had been mobilized to donate for important extras: warm clothing (over 1,500 padded cotton garments); carts and donkeys for the elderly and very young. Veracious or not, the report is simple: an unpretentious record of a responsibility acquitted satisfactorily.[21]

---

20. Lü Jian, comp., "Kang Yong Qian Hubu," p. 21 and below. On the campaign against the Zunghars (1755–57), see Perdue, *China Marches West*, pp. 272–89; Crossley, *Translucent Mirror*, pp. 319–20; Zhuang, *Qing Gaozong shi quan*, chap. 2; Dai Yi, *Qianlong di*, pp. 182–223.

21. Wubai, QL 13/3/4, repr. MQDA, vol. 152, pp. B85,239–40 (doc. no. 020400). The Qing state's metropolitan welfare operations are surveyed in Naquin, *Peking*,

Perhaps Wubai's report affords a glimpse of ordinary humanitarianism in the Qing bureaucracy. The same seems true of a January 1744 memorial by the investigating censor Li Qingfang, whose moralistic instincts we observed in chapter 5. Li was opposing a recent decision to protect the capital from a further influx of fugitives from the dearth-stricken counties of Zhili and Shandong by intercepting them and assisting them firmly home. It was because others had already argued that this was impractical that it had been agreed to deflect the flow to Tongzhou and a county southwest of Beijing.[22] Li, by contrast, undertook an advocacy role. It was inhumane and futile to force famine victims back to homes that only desperation could have made them leave. His own lodgings were surrounded by the shanties of such victims, and he could testify to their tranquillity, good order, and gratitude for state relief. Not one had made trouble.[23]

It is common knowledge in today's democracies that images are central in the politics of welfare and humanitarianism. I have begun with images of Qing "economic refugees" that stress their law-abiding nature because these contrast radically with accusations used in 1748 to justify the abolition of the system under which those 3,224 persons were helped home. This system, whose history Will traces at least to the late Ming, was known as *liuyang zisong*. The key principles were that local authorities in whose jurisdictions famine refugees arrived were required to "harbor and nourish" (*liuyang*) them over the winter and then "send them home with monetary assistance [and/or grain rations]" (*zisong*) in time to plant the new year's crops.[24]

As Will has shown, this system had its problems. A major goal of antifamine policy was to encourage peasants to stay at home and wait for such relief as they were eligible to receive. And yet, there may have

---

pp. 638–51. For a fuller version of the present section, with direct quotation from primary sources, see Deng (Dunstan), "Shilun liuyang zisong."

22. E'ertai et al., QL 8/11/30 (d.r., see QSL/QL, *juan* 205:20a–b), transc. NGDKDA, Office of the Gendarmerie, QL 8/12/3 (communication, doc. no. 093970).

23. Li Qingfang, QL 8/12/9 (d.r.), transc. NGDKDA, Office of the Gendarmerie, QL 8/12/15 (communication, doc. no. 099025). On the reception of famine refugees in Beijing in 1743–44, see Will, *Bureaucracy and Famine*, pp. 234–35.

24. For substantial discussion of the *liuyang zisong* system, see Will, *Bureaucracy and Famine*, pp. 226–40, and, for a snapshot of its operation under Yongzheng, Xu Ben, YZ 11/4/4, repr. MQDA, vol. 055, pp. B31,557–64 (doc. no. 010676).

been some truth in allegations that the prospect of the monetary assistance grants tempted peasants to desert their stricken fields unnecessarily. This was so especially when the grants were generous, and perhaps especially in Zhili, where the presence of the imperial capital may have magnified tendencies that were less prevalent elsewhere. There were probably even cases of deliberate abuse. For example, one might draw one's relief entitlement at home and then take to the roads so as to qualify for refugee assistance. Making multiple requests for travel funds, perhaps using false names, was another frequently reported trick. There may have been seasonal migrants who saw no need to disabuse officials who provided for them under the *liuyang zisong* rules.[25] Concern to deter gratuitous migration or avoid unnecessary use of state resources might prompt administrators to withhold aid from visitors who could be deemed to have other ways to survive. In 1741, Chen Hongmou, as Jiangxi governor, warned that indiscriminate aid to all arrivals in the Jiujiang area from flood-affected north Anhui would, as word spread, provoke a mass influx of refugees "from near and far." He directed that assistance be denied not only to those coming from unaffected jurisdictions, but also to those who "[had] been in Jiujiang for a while, [had] relatives to whom to turn, or who [could] earn their food as hired laborers." Those who had relatives in the adjacent Huguang provinces and wished to join them should not be detained. These orders anticipated key provisions of the abolition edicts.[26]

It is hard to believe, however, that the abuses and frauds were remotely as common and systematic as implied in the following passage from an edict of 1 June 1748—the second of the two that ended the *liuyang zisong* policy in its established form. Having described how the groups into which returning refugees had been divided, in accordance with the rules, invariably caught up with each other on the way, the text continues:

---

25. Ibid., pp. 47–49, 226–31, 237; LFZZ, Namin, QL 13/10/26. Further allegations that the system was exploited by persons for whom it was not intended are cited in Deng, "Shilun liuyang zisong."

26. PYTOCG, *juan* 12:15a–16a. The ecologically problematic north Anhui countryside was a perennial source of seasonal migrants who were later alleged to be capable of improperly accepting *liuyang zisong* benefits. LFZZ, Namin, QL 13/10/26; cf. Perry, *Rebels and Revolutionaries*, pp. 54–56.

Massed together in their hundreds and thousands, [the returnees] demand at will, even going so far as to ransack shops, revile the *yamen* personnel escorting them and defy senior officials, finding a hundred pretexts for disputes. As soon as they have entered their home jurisdiction, their one fear being investigation on the part of the authorities, they raise a final clamor and disperse. The two or three escorting runners cannot stop them. After they have scattered, they again depart the jurisdiction and claim to be famine refugees. They travel back and forth and are [each time] sent back with monetary help, so that it is an endless cycle. They finally rely upon this as a lasting strategy for the support of life. Those who genuinely settle and resume their occupation are not one or two out of a hundred. Such are the problems with the assisted return home.

Later in the edict comes the final denunciation:

The cost to neighboring provinces is incalculable, and those who are assisted home are in the last analysis not real members of the poor and needy. It is a detraction from munificence and the service of an empty name; it is in no way consonant with proper government.[27]

In a later edict (1753), the "wicked commoners" who had been encouraged by the system to gain allowances by fraud and to plunder in gangs on their way home are contrasted with "genuine famine refugees," who may be either taking refuge with relatives or supporting themselves as hired laborers.[28]

The style of rhetoric is familiar from attacks on welfare clients in Western societies. In fact, the able-bodied adult male beneficiaries of the *liuyang zisong* system were to some extent being stigmatized for the limitations of regular relief. As Will has pointed out, peasants would see a need to go and look for food during those periods of hunger, usually early in a crisis, that were not adequately covered even by the rather careful provision for preliminary distributions that the rules prescribed. Still more to the point, a household that was classified, during disaster assessment surveys, as only "moderately poor" would find its able-bodied adult males ruled ineligible for assistance. Records survive of individual peasants claiming that it was the relief system's failure to meet the needs of the whole family that had driven them onto the roads. However, these underclass voices were to be silenced first, as Will has

---

27. QSL/QL, *juan* 314:16a–b. For discussion and full translation, see Dunstan, *Conflicting Counsels*, pp. 72–74, 93–97.
28. QSL/QL, *juan* 450:9b–10b.

shown, by the local authorities who "systematically" disputed the travellers' assertions, and later, on a grander scale, by Qianlong's rhetorical damnation.[29] In 1748, the court lost interest in the available countermeasures to abuses of the *zisong* system.[30] Rather, it abolished the provision except as it applied to the absolutely destitute and those obvious and canonically-sanctioned objects of state charity, "the old, the very young, and the crippled or infirm."

The first abolition edict (19 April 1748) breathes a responsible reformism that leaves one ill-prepared for the intemperate accusations of the second. The April edict argued that in the case of prolonged famines resulting from repeated harvest failures, there was no point in sending people home. Confronted by starvation, they would only take to the roads again. In future, while the *zisong* policy should be applied in mild natural disasters, in cases of repeated harvest failure officials should differentiate between genuinely helpless and ordinary adult refugees. The former should, as before, be fed and housed by the host jurisdiction until conditions back home were suitable for their return. The latter might well be able to find help from friends or relatives, or to support themselves by hiring out their labor. The tone here is not hostile to able-bodied refugees. To the contrary, the ostensible purpose is to provide appropriately for the genuinely needy while not imposing upon those who might be better left to find their own solutions, at least in the short term.[31] On 26 April, Qianlong chided the Huguang governor-general for having let his subordinates provide inadequate travel allowances for all the 1,314 refugees from Shandong and Jiangsu who were still in the Hankou conurbation, rather than weeding out those who could be self-reliant and (presumably) recognizing that this was no time to be returning refugees to the disaster-stricken region straddling the Shandong-Jiangsu border. Here too, the spirit was one of responsible relief administration.[32]

---

29. Will, *Bureaucracy and Famine*, pp. 129–30, 236–39.

30. On countermeasures, see ibid., pp. 230–31; QSL/QL, *juan* 239:38a–b.

31. QSL/QL, *juan* 311:15a–16b; DQHDSL, vol. 11, *juan* 288:22b–23b (pp. 8,947–48).

32. The criticism was perhaps unfair in some respects, as the offending report mentions refugees who were making their own return arrangements, while the administrative actions in question had been taken before the 19 April edict. QSL/QL, *juan* 311:27b–28b; cf. LFZZ, Saileng'e, QL 13/3/13.

Was it because the April 19 edict was insufficiently blunt that its June sequel was needed? Or was Qianlong shifting his stance out of frustration with the "presumptuous" poor? The June edict cited one acting governor who had failed to grasp Qianlong's intent. This second edict detailed the alleged abuses of the *liuyang zisong* system, as illustrated above, and then intoned that while appropriate arrangements should be made to assist the genuinely helpless, including poor people bereft of all means of survival by truly severe disasters, in general:

It would be better to let [able-bodied famine refugees] seek their own food and contrive their own livelihood, and to issue clear and incisive proclamations so that [the people] understand that there is nothing to be gained by drifting and by taking to the roads, and will not lightly leave their neighborhood or forsake their old source of livelihood.[33]

The *coup de grâce* came in the autumn, probably in late September. An investigating censor had made allegations of refugee unruliness—a recognized danger if rations ran short or groups of refugees became too large. In response, the Board of Revenue secured approval for a recommendation that *liuyang* provision be reserved for the genuinely helpless (with officialdom instructed not to extend it indiscriminately to sturdy refugees), and that the *zisong* system be replaced with grants of food to support women, children, the elderly and the disabled on their journey home.[34] Thus ended the *liuyang zisong* system in its previous form—as wide-scope social security for the peasantry in time of famine. A 1752 memorial shows the Shaanxi governor Zhongyin assuming that current imperial policy was to leave all except people in those four categories to fend for themselves. He had directed that peasants be warned that *liuyang zisong* had been "discontinued." In fact, Zhongyin was firmer than the court, which in 1751 approved arrangements, including *zisong*, for Zhejiang drought victims who had crossed into Fujian, and which in 1752 directed the Zhejiang authorities to plan *zisong* provision for their own famine refugees. In November 1753,

---

33. QSL/QL, *juan* 314:16b–17a.

34. The new instructions are quoted in LFZZ, Namin, QL 13/10/26. See also LFZZ, Saileng'e, QL 13/3/13; NGDKDA, Bd. Rev., QL 13/8/4 (doc. no. 120095, fragment). The new policy may have been approved by a short-term regency committee on Qianlong's behalf. QSL/QL, *juan* 322:10b.

however, one edict admonished the Anhui governor that there was no place for the harmful *liuyang zisong* system in the dynasty's principles of governance, while another represented this system as one that had been implemented in the past and whose use was now again being advocated— an idea that the court rejected emphatically. While references to *zisong* in the sense of helping famine victims home punctuate the Qing *Veritable Records* for the first five decades of the eighteenth century, especially the 1740s, they disappear for the remainder of the Qianlong period after 1753, apart from two records of court acceptance of such action in Henan in 1757–58, and a final denunciation of the practice in 1763.[35]

The drastic curtailment of *liuyang zisong* provision should not be seen as a simple act of social vandalism by China's Manchu occupiers. As illustrated below, vilification of beneficiaries of this and other welfare systems was not a solely Manchu vice. It may, indeed, have had greater insidious force when perpetrated by elite Chinese. As to motivation, the cutback may reflect the fiscal strains created by the Jinchuan war and universal tax remission. After all, other expenses were entailed besides the victims' rations and allowances—for example, payments to the escorting personnel and cart drivers or boatmen could reportedly come to a considerable amount.[36] However, as contemporary experience reminds us, once governments start asking which refugees are "genuine" and which are not, they risk committing disproportionate resources to upholding the rules. Even without a war, restriction of provision to those whose helplessness was obvious would have been a tempting pragmatic alternative to the multiplication of controls. The curtailment also represented a less sharp break with some past practice than appears at first sight. For example, the arrangements for which Kaerjishan sought approval as Shandong governor in 1743 envisaged that *zisong* assistance would be channelled to those who most

---

35. Zhongyin, QL 17/8/10, repr. GZD/QL, vol. 3, p. 575; QSL/QL, *juan* 394:4b, *juan* 410:8b–9a, *juan* 449:9b–10a, *juan* 450:9b–10b, *juan* 547:29b–30b, *juan* 555:40b, *juan* 680:24a–25b; cf. DQHDSL, vol. 11, *juan* 288:23b–25b (pp. 8,948–49). I thank Professor Lai Hui-min for using Academia Sinica's searchable electronic version of the *Qing shilu* to find me all occurrences of the term *zisong* in that work for the whole Qing dynasty.

36. Cf. LFZZ, Saileng'e, QL 13/3/13. For further discussion of this point, see Deng, "Shilun liuyang zisong."

needed it, that is, the elderly and sick.[37] And, as discussed below, the idea of liberating able-bodied peasants to pursue their own solutions was less innovative than it was convenient to make it seem in the abolition edicts.

The *zisong* system could have a coercive face, and this indeed could be rhetorically exploited. In September 1742, the Shandong governor assumed that strict adherence to the rules implied that Jiangsu flood victims should be sent home as soon as they were found on Shandong territory (although Qianlong agreed that such action would be inappropriate).[38] The edict of April 1748 noted the state's "generosity" in "dispatching official runners to escort" those "foolish people" who had "lightly" abandoned their homes and fields, helping them home and "causing them to resume their old source of livelihood"; but the guidelines in use in early 1744 made clear that, once resettled, the wanderers were to be told not to depart again. Li Qingfang, for his part, objected that the refugees at risk of being forced home that winter included persons who had come to look for work or planned to stay with kin. But Li's concern was with the timing: one should not send peasants home until the second lunar month, the whole point being to enable them to sow the new year's crop. He did not advocate a termination of assistance.[39] The edict of April 1748, on the other hand, may not have been quite innocent in repudiating the idea of thoughtlessly "driving" famine victims back to their home neighborhoods regardless of conditions there. It took the second edict to clarify that the flexibility for which the case was built in April was really partial abolition. The

---

37. QSL/QL, *juan* 197:25a. For a 1746 example of the exclusion from *liuyang zisong* provision of able-bodied refugees who had arrived without dependents, see Anon., *Zhen'an shigao*, p. 149.

38. QSL/QL, *juan* 173:39a–b. The *li* (regulation) to which the governor referred may have been a recent supplementary article that seemed to reserve *liuyang* at the expense of the host jurisdiction for those "solitary and poor" refugees who were over 1,000 *li* (units of distance) from home. The rest should be sent back and cared for in their home jurisdiction. Shen Zhiqi, comp., *Da Qing lü jizhu* (1746 revised ed.), vol. 1, "Da Qing lü xuzuan tiaoli," p. 120.

39. QSL/QL, *juan* 311:15a–b; E'ertai et al., QL 8/11/30 (d.r.) and Li Qingfang, QL 8/12/9 (d.r.), transc. NGDKDA, Gendarmerie, QL 8/12/3 and QL 8/12/15 (docs. nos. 093970 and 099025); see also Will, *Bureaucracy and Famine*, pp. 228–29, and, for pre-Qianlong texts in which at least some coercion seems implied, DQHDSL, vol. 11, *juan* 288:20a–21b (pp. 8,946–47).

second edict of November 1753 crowned its vindication of the curtailment by arguing that "genuine famine refugees" would be impeded in their quest for livelihood if the authorities of host jurisdictions insisted on "detaining and placing them one by one" under the *liuyang* rules. The Shaanxi governor had meanwhile done his bit to represent the new policy as supportive of the sturdy famine refugee by noting that "one should not hinder and detain" him.[40]

It is doubtful whether any significant liberation was really taking place. Not only were most rural dwellers free to migrate in normal times; there were certainly already cases, before 1748, of letting famine refugees who seemed to have their own plans for survival (for example, casual employment, or migration beyond the Great Wall) do as they saw fit. There was probably indeed, as Will suggests, a preference for flexibility towards such people, not least because voluntary "repatriation" of famine refugees had arguably been imperial policy since 1742.[41] A partial parallel to the court's hypocrisy on this occasion might be its claim to be liberating from economic restraint those Chinese servicemen who were dismissed from the Eight Banners in the ethnically motivated purge of 1754–79.[42] In reality, the abolition of the full *liuyang zisong* system was Janus-faced. Removal of the putative incentive to migration represented by the travel grants was expected to encourage peasants to await state assistance in the communities where they were registered. Receipt of regular relief would enable them eventually to resume agricultural production and contribute to state income through the land tax. In this sense, the abolition favored continuing state control of the peasantry.

---

40. QSL/QL, *juan* 311:15b; QSL/QL, *juan* 450:10b; Zhongyin, QL 17/8/10, repr. GZD/QL, vol. 3, p. 575.

41. In April 1748, the Huguang governor-general cited guidelines excerpted from a September 1742 edict that would have gone at least to several provinces. The edict specifies that flood refugees who do not want to go home should not be forced; the quoted principles make clear that *zisong* is for those wishing to return. The 1742 edict may have been only a precedent, but it is excerpted in such a way as to look like a rule, and the full text was eventually codified. Compare LFZZ, Saileng'e, QL 13/3/13, QSL/QL, *juan* 172:37b–38a, and DQHDSL, vol. 11, *juan* 288:22a–b (p. 8,947). See also Will, *Bureaucracy and Famine*, pp. 227–28; the 1741 example cited above; QSL/QL, *juan* 197:25a, etc.

42. Elliott, *Manchu Way*, pp. 333–34, 337–42.

At the same time, however, to decline to escort wandering peasant males home was to remove an occasional check on the mobility of labor, freeing more famine victims to survive or die as migrants. Able-bodied males who chose not to await, or were ineligible for, official relief were to accept responsibility for their own subsistence. Unless their relatives could help, they would be thrown upon the mercy of the labor market, somewhat as recipients of relief doles in the form of silver were thrown on that of the grain market (although the latter had their own position strengthened). As shown in chapter 5, the substitution of silver for grain in relief distributions was, to its theorists, partly a way of helping famine victims stand on their own feet. It would, if fully implemented, have represented one step from dependency to self-reliance as the basis of the welfare system from the client's viewpoint. The abolition of the *liuyang zisong* system went a step farther: self-reliance but no help.

Can the abolition of full *liuyang zisong* provision be seen as a practical adaptation to demographic change? This depends in part on how one views certain pronouncements as to the refugees' identity—and thereby hangs the tale of competing images with which this section started. As we have seen, the edicts of June 1748 and 1753 constructed a dichotomy between "genuine famine refugees" and "wicked" abusers of the system. The abusers came to be stereotyped as disorderly vagrants, or, more objectively, country folk who had no land. The humanitarian impulses of officials could alternatively be read as bids to buy off troublemakers. A contribution to establishing the unruly vagrant / genuine victim dichotomy was made by the investigating censor Huang Dengxian in a memorial of August 1748. Huang depicted a class of "vagabonds" (*youshou zhi min*) who exploited the *liuyang zisong* system to fare better during natural disasters than they did in years of plenty, thereby tempting real peasants to action (flight from famine) that they would otherwise have taken only as a last resort. Huang's central concern was the risk of disorder if bands of returnees were allowed to be too large. In this connection, he criticized some local officials in Henan for supplementing the statutory cash allowances of a throng of Shandong natives—presumably the vagabondish sort—in an attempt at appeasement that had (allegedly) only provoked incidents of plunder in remote villages along their path. In fact, these were probably some of the unfortunates who had been dispatched from Hankou with inadequate allowances and, probably, inadequate supervision. It was

Huang's memorial that provoked the September abolition of *zisong* provision, as described above.[43]

Zhongyin, the Shaanxi governor, and his immediate subordinate, the administration commissioner, echoed Huang in 1752. The Qishan county magistrate had understood that there were "poor people in search of food" moving westward in groups of two and three plus family dependents towards Longzhou, presumably from the drought-stricken eastern Wei valley. He wanted to lend grain from the community granaries to those wishing to move on, while encouraging the rest to go home, aided by grants of coin. The provincial administration commissioner, ordered to investigate by a suspicious Zhongyin, had reported that a large proportion of these folk were landless. He went on: "There are always such people, even in a year of plenty. They are vagabondish (*youduo*) to begin with. When the price of grain goes up to any extent, they are in difficulties over food and take their families and go elsewhere." This report raised two issues. The question Zhongyin answered—in the negative—was whether such feckless folk deserved support. It was undesirable, he assured Qianlong, that a wish on the part of magistrates to curry favor with the populace should result in "the thick-flowing grace of kindly nourishment being conferred on vagabonds."[44] The issue he did not address was what, objectively, was the point of treating landless people as if they were landed.

As Will has mentioned, the court took up this latter issue in 1763 by enunciating a new doctrine: except perhaps in truly exceptional circumstances, all so-called famine refugees were landless. An edict that was written to justify the rejection, on other grounds, of a proposal to revive *zisong* to deal with the many country folk who had come to Beijing because of floods explained that previous authorizations of this measure had been intended to help farmers to preserve their foothold in society. However:

Now, with the experience of many days, [it proves] that those of the roving folk who go afar to seek their livelihood are all persons entirely devoid, at home, of fields and farmsteads on which to rely. If, nonetheless, one insists on

---

43. Huang Dengxian, QL 13/7/30 (d.r.), transc. NGDKDA, Bd. Rev., QL 13/8/4 (doc. no. 120095, fragment); cf. LFZZ, Saileng'e, QL 13/3/13, Namin, QL 13/10/26.

44. Zhongyin, QL/17/8/10, repr. GZD/QL, vol. 3, pp. 574–75.

compelling their return, then even once they have gone back to their old neighborhood, they will still be persons without occupation.[45]

One was therefore justified in denying them resettlement assistance.

What sort of social science was this? Alexander Woodside would perhaps propose a charitable interpretation, given his reference to "proto-sociological investigations"—a "survey," no less—serving to justify imperial instructions, in 1792, that famine refugees be urged to seek food through employment north of the Great Wall, rather than massing at Beijing's gruel kitchens. Suffice it to note, first, that the edict cited is mute on the inquiry's methodology, and second, that Qianlong's approach to sociology was perhaps not infallible. In 1814, the Jiaqing emperor was so unfilial as to contradict his father's 1763 opinion. Jiaqing authorized *zisong* in response to a specific request, commenting that: "The roving folk in question are not all fellows without occupation, and some of their acres at their places of registration are already sown with wheat."[46] The rationales conveyed in edicts are, in short, an insufficient basis on which to view the abolition of the *liuyang zisong* system as a response either to solid information or to population growth and increased peasant landlessness.

What mattered was perhaps not so much the actions and economic status of the famine victims as the way in which these were viewed. Li Qingfang assumed that some of the refugees in Beijing in early 1744 were landless, but that they would earn their keep by labor once assisted home. In 1720, a provincial governor reported calmly that over 1,000 recipients of *zisong* grants had absconded *en route* to eastern Shandong from Beijing or central Zhili. Thus vanished more than half the famine victims whom "civil and military" Shandong personnel had rounded up and tried to shepherd home. The governor inferred that the absconders were landless and houseless but opined that they must have decided to seek a living elsewhere and should be left to do as suited them. Even allowing for a certain laxity under the ageing Kangxi em-

---

45. QSL/QL, *juan* 680:24a–25b; DQHDSL, vol. 11, *juan* 288:24b–25b (pp. 8,948–49); cf. Will, *Bureaucracy and Famine*, p. 230 n. 13. For the edict's background, see Bd. Rev., QL 28/2/12 (d.r.), transc. NGDKDA, Bd. Rev., QL 28/2 (communication, doc. no. 093237), and Deng, "Shilun liuyang zisong."

46. Woodside, "The Ch'ien-lung Reign," p. 308; QSL/QL, *juan* 1,408:5a–7a; DQHDSL, vol. 11, *juan* 288:25b–26a (p. 8,949); Will, *Bureaucracy and Famine*, p. 230 n. 13.

peror (whose comment was "Noted"), it is striking that the governor neither criticized the absconders' conduct nor suggested that their travel grants were funds ill-spent. Nor did he express concern about the fact that some refugees who went all the way home were landless. He reported that seeds had been issued to those returnees who had land, while the local authorities had been directed to find ways of succoring the rest.[47]

How could there have been only one truth about the motley crowds that took to the roads during subsistence crises? The historian is not obliged to choose between the representations offered by contemporaries. The 1720 episode illustrates that Qianlong did not necessarily misread his times in assuming that there was a large pool of surplus labor that might be best left free to find employment where it could. Indeed, references (in, for example, the abolition edict of June 1748) to famine refugees crossing the Great Wall into southern Manchuria or Mongolia suggest that famine could act as a spur to permanent re-settlement of individuals who could not be supported by the finite arable at home. It is surely significant that references to *zisong* as a popular-assistance measure in *Veritable Records* entries for the 1760s and 1770s are concerned with grants to help the Gansu poor migrate to the newly conquered Xinjiang, thereby becoming tools of colonization policy.[48] All this said, however, one cannot miss the kinship between the defamatory rhetoric of the edict of June 1748 and Qianlong's previous denunciations of a supposed proclivity to indolence on the part of the potentially expensive poor. In 1748, he alleged that able-bodied male refugees were willfully becoming permanent state pensioners; in 1744, while promoting the haphazard method of using *jiansheng* title sales for granary restocking, he had imputed a dependency mentality to society at large.[49] Although his implausibly harsh image of *liuyang zisong*

---

47. Li Qingfang, QL 8/12/9 (d.r.), transc. NGDKDA, Gendarmerie, QL 8/12/15 (doc. no. 099025); Li Shude, KX 59/3/26, repr. *Kangxi chao Hanwen zhupi zouzhe huibian*, vol. 8, pp. 664–65.

48. QSL/QL, *juan* 314:16b and, e.g., *juan* 716:5b–7a, *juan* 1,010:23b–26b; cf. Will, *Bureaucracy and Famine*, pp. 44–46 (which also notes the importance of seasonal migration) and Perdue, *China Marches West*, pp. 333–53, esp. p. 344.

49. See chap. 6 above and, for an earlier (1740) and less extreme example, QSL/QL, *juan* 120:1a–3a.

beneficiaries no doubt had provocations in reported cases of abuse and other misbehavior, the edict is a highly suspect text.

Even in the middle decades of the Qianlong reign, the imperial abolition of the full *liuyang zisong* system may not have prevented every individual official throughout the length and breadth of China from quietly supplying displaced peasants with assistance to go home. Still less did it prevent a comeback of this system in the nineteenth century.[50] Viewed, however, as a deliberate change of policy at a specific point in time, the abolition constituted a relative shift from paternalist and, to some extent, coercive care towards economic individualism and state indifferentism. It was liberalizing in principle but did not mean discontinuation of state interest in a stable rural social order; it invoked the labor market but did not rest on assessment of demand for migrant labor. As an event (or sequence of events) specifically of 1748, it was consistent with the economic and social views of the most extreme, Manchu opponents of the ever-normal system. The June abolition edict probably helped build the ethos in which fiscally expedient cuts in ever-normal targets would soon prove politically acceptable. It also expressed an impatience with unruly commoners that, as shown below, came to a head in a yet harsher edict issued on the same day.

To the extent that territorial officialdom complied with the abolition orders, what were the likely effects? Among the populace, the removal of state assistance to return to the "ancestral" lands that represented a peasant's security may have increased both vagrancy and distrust of the established order, thus weakening society's cohesion and stability. Dare we posit a link between the curtailment of the *liuyang zisong* system and the pervasive economic, social and psychological insecurity that so impresses the reader of Philip Kuhn's account of the "soulstealing" panic of the late 1760s, or Matthew Sommer's of the sexual anxieties of high Qing China? Why exactly was there a "growing

---

50. For some 1810 provincial guidelines that specified no criterion for eligibility to receive a daily *zisong* grain ration other than lack of means to return home, see Nayancheng, *Zhen ji*, p. 739. A book reflecting 1831 relief work in the Wuchang area expounds an adaptation of classic *liuyang zisong* procedures, while *liuyang zisong* was implemented on a massive scale in flood relief operations near the end of the Qing dynasty. Zhou Cunyi, *Jiang yi jiuhuang biji*, pp. 576–77; Horichi, "1906 nen Kōhoku," pp. 7–8.

crowd" of "rootless rascals" lurking on the margins of society and menacing the chastity of the good girls and boys of peasant households? The trends described by Sommer were established before the late 1740s, but what of the suppurating wounds and broken bones of those unhappy mendicants who, in 1768, suffered judicial torture because of hysterical accusations by people with homes? Can these be traced to a decline in social trust in which the court's desertion of the sturdy famine refugee had been a contributory factor?[51]

Exit the Banner Grain Bureaus

We turn now to the abolition, in 1752, of the Beijing banner grain bureaus discussed in chapter 2. The bureaus, created out of paternalism towards the bannermen alone, had come to be seen as effective stabilizers of grain prices in Beijing's Inner City. Intended to counter speculation by means of stabilizing sales, they operated on a year-round basis. Grain sold from the bureaus when market prices rose could be replaced through theoretically compulsory purchases from the stipend grain that the Beijing bannermen received three times per year under Yongzheng, and four times per year from about 1737. For residents of Beijing's Outer City, sales at the bureaus complemented, and were probably of secondary importance to, direct stabilizing sales of tribute (and other non-stipendiary) grain. There were twenty-four bureaus in the capital and two in nearby Tongzhou, plus (from the late 1730s) three bureaus for the bondservants of the Imperial Household Department.

Lillian M. Li and Alison Dray-Novey have argued that the bureaus were abolished for two reasons: first, that they "had not actually kept prices stable, in officials' view," and second, that their administration was subject to abuse—specifically, "the danger of forced purchases" and possible corruption. Hosoya Yoshio has also represented the bureaus as unsuccessful in stabilizing Beijing grain prices, attributing the failure partly to the power of merchant magnates such as Fan Yubin.[52] But may not the bureaus' overall performance have been a matter of in-

---

51. Kuhn, *Soulstealers*, esp. pp. 41–48 and 105–18, and accounts of mendicant experience of suspicion and torture in chaps. 1, 4, 8, etc.; Sommer, *Sex, Law, and Society*, pp. 13–14, 96–101.

52. L. M. Li and A. Dray-Novey, "Guarding Beijing's Food Security," pp. 1,008–9; Hosoya, "Hakki beikyoku kō," pp. 200–2.

terpretation in the early 1750s? The pronouncement that they had been ineffective was Qianlong's. The previous year, by contrast, a high-level report had represented the design as worthy of implementation on the original bold scale, albeit with more streamlined management. I prefer to reserve judgment on the bureaus' effectiveness and focus instead on the meaning of their abolition. It was clearly liberalizing, for it removed a government-imposed constraint on the free circulation of stipend grain. Close examination of its immediate context shows that it does not necessarily amount to evidence of a decline in imperial commitment to popular well-being even in Beijing (where pragmatic motivations for paternalist assistance were exceptionally compelling). Rather, there was a change of means towards the goal of price stability. The change itself was radical and sensible, but the process through which it emerged was a haphazard one. The story does not contradict the thesis of diminishing commitment on the emperor's part.

The 1752 abolition was not the first move against the banner grain bureaus. The story of the previous attack, which took place in the first three years of Qianlong's reign, draws attention to the kinds of issues—about management and scope of service, for example—that may need to be considered before an indigenous complaint of ineffectiveness can be upheld. I therefore review that story here, along with evidence that the bureaus were still taken quite seriously over the decade and a half before their abolition.

As Hosoya has shown, the first threat came from certain senior Manchus, including Yinlu, the young emperor's uncle and chief regent. Already in the spring of 1736, the number of the Beijing bureaus was cut from twenty-four to eight (plus one, instead of the recently approved three, for the Household Department bondservants). The initial capitalization of the main bureau network had been 120,000 taels; now, the retention of the original allocation rate (5,000 taels per bureau) implied a two-thirds reduction in the network's funded operations. What happened at Tongzhou was similar: the two Tongzhou bureaus were amalgamated, and their total capital was cut by 62.5 percent. The scaled-down system was to be tried out for a year or so and then reviewed, with an eye to making further cuts if they were warranted.[53]

---

53. Hosoya, "Hakki beikyoku kō," pp. 193–95 and 206 n. 23. According to CC, Yong Xing, QL 9/6/12, both the Tongzhou and the Beijing amalgamations took

The sequence of complaints against the bureaus suggests a plan to ensure that more cuts or, preferably, abolition would emerge as the obvious decision. If there was such a plot, it almost worked. In the first round of allegations (as quoted by Hosoya), it was claimed that too much grain was lying unsold in the bureaus, and that the wages paid for extra hulling of the rice were wasted. An aspect of the 1736 cuts that Hosoya does not mention was the discontinuation of this hulling service.[54] This might have been calculated to engender one problem mentioned in the second round of allegations (late 1737 to early 1738): bannermen who needed to buy grain preferred to buy it from the private hulling shops (*duifang*), since most private grain was fully husked. Useless to the bannermen, the stipend grain accumulated in the bureaus. Non-banner buyers turned out to be "wicked merchant profiteers" who hoarded the incompletely processed bureau grain. But how much grain was really piling up? Another second-round allegation was that bannermen preferred to sell stipend grain to merchants so as to avoid the heavy cost of moving it from granary to bureau. This problem may have been exacerbated by the reduced number of bureaus; it must have limited the amount of grain available for sale to profiteers.[55]

Yinlu and his associates enjoyed a brief success. The grain bureaus were abolished in early 1738. Grain speculation in Beijing would simply be prohibited; it was in this context (that is, during the discussions that led to the abolition) that private dealers were forbidden to hold more than 50 *shi* at a time—a prohibition that was not rescinded when the bureaus were restored.[56] But opposition to the cutting of the network

---

place in Yongzheng 13. That lunar year included a period (early October 1735 to mid-February 1736) when Yongzheng had died. However, the *Shilu* entry cited by Hosoya suggests that the Beijing bureau network was cut later in the spring of 1736.

54. QSL/QL, *juan* 13:17b–18a (ref. from Hosoya, "Hakki beikyoku kō," p. 206 n. 23). On the stages of decortication needed to produce white rice, see Chuan and Kraus, *Mid-Ch'ing Rice Markets*, p. 93.

55. Hosoya, "Hakki beikyoku kō," pp. 194–95; cf. L. M. Li and A. Dray-Novey, "Guarding Beijing's Food Security," p. 998 (map) for the granaries' location. Most of the granaries were on the eastern (Tongzhou) side of the palace compound, and either within the Inner City wall or only just outside it.

56. QSL/QL, *juan* 56:9a–b; Hosoya, "Hakki beikyoku kō," p. 195; YFD, QL 16/9/1 (d.r.) (8:1619); cf. chap. 1 above. For an example of short-term use of coercive practices (surveillance, enforcement of bans on hoarding and export of grain from

had already been expressed. The arguments of the investigating censor Ma Chang'an, presented in November 1737, supply context for the reports of rising prices that prompted reinstatement of the entire bureau network in the late spring of 1738.

Ma was in no doubt as to the vital role that had been played by the full set of bureaus. The prices of all commodities in Beijing were governed by the price of grain, he pointed out. The bureaus had been effective in countering merchant speculation; prices had, in consequence, been generally stable, a success that had been enhanced by letting bannermen have bureau grain on credit during upward fluctuations. The stability had benefited all the city's residents, not the bannermen alone. However, after the Beijing bureaus' total capitalization was cut to 40,000 taels, their managers had been unable to buy much of the stipend grain. As a result, sales to private buyers had soon been occurring "in the open," rice prices had burst out of the pattern of recent years, the bannermen had undergone subsistence difficulties, and the general price level had risen, as had the "price" of coin (exchange value relative to silver).[57]

The litany was predictable, the reading of developments to be expected of a partisan of state intervention trading. However, in his own eyes, Ma was trying to prevent a crisis, not writing a treatise on political economy. Grain prices in the capital in the autumn of 1737 were obdurately high despite repeated stabilizing sales to counteract a disappointing harvest. In Ma's view, such perverse price behavior was clear evidence of private hoarding, whose ill-effects, already felt, would be acute in the 1738 *soudure* period. It was urgent to re-establish the full complement of bureaus in time to prevent large-scale speculative buying from the next issue of stipend grain. The old level of capitalization should be restored; there should be strict surveillance to ensure that no stipend grain was sold to private buyers; and the operations of the bureaus should be extended to black beans, which served as fodder for the banner horses. The high demand for black beans in the capital

---

the surrounding countryside) in the days of the grain bureaus, see Shuhede, QL 16/7/23, repr. GZD/QL, vol. 1, p. 231.

57. On the concept of the "price" of coin in Qing official discourse and the reasons why high coin prices were thought undesirable, see Dunstan, "'Orders Go Forth,'" pp. 69–72.

made them a natural target for speculators, especially following poor harvests such as that of 1737. In a final challenge to the abolitionists, Ma recommended that each bureau be allotted a second capital sum of 5,000 taels for buying black beans.[58]

Ma's views must have seemed vindicated by the persistence of high prices after the remaining bureaus were abolished. In the late spring of 1738, the censors Shuhede and Zhu Fengying submitted memorials blaming recent price rises on the unrestrained speculative buying of stipend grain. A response by the imperial prince Hongzhi and others reasserted the interventionist understanding of the bureaus' *raison d'être* and recommended that they be restored. Explicitly restated was the expectation that the bureaus would resell stipend grain in such a way as to abate high market prices. Qianlong assented, and the original twenty-four bureaus were re-established, plus three for the Household Department bondservants. In early May, it was decided to issue the bureaus' capital half in the form of grain, thus expediting the resumption of stabilizing sales. By mid-August, at least one bureau manager saw need to request extra stocks for all the bureaus, because the stipend grain that they had bought was running out. Only with such supplementation would the network be able to meet the demand for cut-price grain until the next issue of stipend payments. The request was granted, although the bureaus were allocated only 1,000 *shi* apiece (half the amount requested). This episode, if we dare take it at face value, belies the accusation that the bureaus were redundant. It was the influx of busy country folk since late July to buy food in the city that was reported to be putting extra strain on Beijing's grain supplies.[59]

In Tongzhou, restoration of the second bureau had to wait until 1744, in which year the total capitalization of the Tongzhou operations was raised to 20,000 taels. This was 25 percent higher than the original (1728) grant. The successful record of the twenty-seven Beijing bureaus was cited in support of the proposal to revive the Tongzhou system.[60] Thus the banner grain bureaus were not unanimously thought to have out-

---

58. CC, Ma Chang'an, QL 2/10/3. For brief samples of Ma's rhetoric, see chap. 2 above.

59. QSL/QL, *juan* 64:17b–19a, 65:8b, 226:10b–11a; CC, Bd. Rev., QL 3/7/8. Cf. Hosoya, "Hakki beikyoku kō," pp. 195–97.

60. CC, Yong Xing, QL 9/6/12 and chap 2 above.

lived their usefulness in the inflationary 1740s. To the contrary, short-term challenges to Beijing's price stability furnished new opportunities for them to serve the city's population.[61]

A Board of Revenue memorial of mid-September 1743 yields a glimpse of bureau operations during one such challenge. Qianlong had launched the measures at the end of July, blaming for the unusually high prices not only inadequate rainfall, but also the role of the hot summer in delaying the arrival of commercial grain, and the intercalary (extra) month that there had been during May-June. Special stocks had been allocated, and most of these were being channelled to the market via the banner bureaus. Only 10,000 *shi* of tribute grain were issued, in installments, to separate sales venues in the Outer City. By contrast, the bureaus received 40,000 *shi* of tribute grain (an average of 1,481 *shi* per bureau) plus 27,000 *shi* of black beans. As in August 1738, the special stocks issued to the bureaus were intended to supplement the stipend grain that the bureaus had purchased earlier in the quarter. Perhaps because of the intercalary fourth month, the bureaus' holdings of stipend grain were quite depleted at the beginning of the operation, with the fullest having less than 2,000 *shi*, and the others less than 1,000.

The next installment of stipend and salary grain was issued half a month early, beginning on 2 September, and by mid-month the cut-price sales were seen as having served their purpose. Admittedly, the reported falls in current market prices may not all look dramatic. "Coarse granary rice" was down from 1,000 to 800 standard cash per *shi*, "coarse *suomi*" from 1,150 to 1,000, and "coarse old rice" from 1,200 to 1,100, while the price of black beans had not changed. However, the Board officials noted with satisfaction that the gradual reduction in grain prices should now induce a corresponding stabilization of the price of coin (presumably because demand for coin ought to be falling). With the new harvest in prospect, they were ready to agree that de-

---

61. Li and Dray-Novey's suggestion ("Guarding Beijing's Food Security," p. 1,009) that the bureaus faced a lesser challenge in the Yongzheng period than later is a valuable one. However, their claim that "when prices were higher in the 1740s and 1750s, there seemed no benefit for any party in trying to restrict stipend sales to government-run bureaus" (ibid.) seems to me to oversimplify the issues.

liveries to the bureaus and Outer City sales venues be suspended for the time being.[62]

The bureaus played a less crucial, but still strategic role in protracted special stabilizing sales in the spring of 1751, which makes their final abolition the next year seem a sharp reversal.[63] The abolition was, however, presaged by a short-term suspension of bureau purchases of grain in the winter of 1750–51. The ostensible purpose of this measure was to avoid exacerbating the rather high prices that already prevailed in Beijing. Should stabilizing sales be necessary in the spring, the bureau managers were to arrange for tribute grain to be issued directly from the metropolitan granaries. Before long, the bureaus were ordered to hold stabilizing sales with the grain that they already had, with supplementary issues from the granaries if needed.[64] Implicit in the suspension of buying was a choice as to who should manage the surplus stipend grain that bannermen would presumably sell as usual—perhaps in reduced volume, if some had the wit and the resources to keep this more than usually appreciating asset for their future profit. Moreover, the court was now applying to the bureaus the principle—long established in the ever-normal system—that price conditions might necessitate postponement of restocking. Avoiding extra strain on markets now had priority over maintaining the wherewithal to combat merchant speculation.

It is not that consensus had been reached that Beijing's private shopkeepers had changed their ways, or that their propensity to speculate had been exaggerated or was positively useful. To the contrary, later in 1751, Zhu Lunhan, who, as a Chinese bannerman, was now vice commander-in-chief of one of the Chinese banners, denounced both the commercial abuse of grain sold by the bureaus, and merchant

---

62. CC, Sanhe et al., QL 8/8/4; QSL/QL, *juan* 194:14b–15b, 199:8b. QSL/QL, *juan* 203:4a–b (December 1743) refers to plans for further sales of black beans through the bureaus.

63. In 1751, much stress was placed on sales outside Beijing, which were credited in April with having lowered the city's grain prices by 0.1 tl./*shi* (by checking an influx of rural buyers). These extramural sales were continued (indeed, expanded) after the urban sales were cut back in early May. YFD, probably QL 16/2/28–30 (8:1618-1, frames 147–58), and ibid., QL 16/3/14, 16/3/28, 16/4/3, 16/4/16 (8:1618-1), QL 16/5/3, 16/5/10 (8:1618-2) (all d.r.).

64. QCWXTK, vol. 1, *juan* 37, p. 5,197.

profiteering in stipend grain more generally. He alleged that a certain proportion of the stipend grain was still flowing directly from its original recipients to private-sector purchasers, who would speculate as merrily as ever. Using the accustomed trick of fabricating statements about harvest prospects, they would draw the market price down just before the bannermen received their grain, buy the grain up cheap, and then make prices soar. To make matters worse, the city's hulling-shops were sending a succession of individuals to buy grain from the bureaus, thereby evading the rule that limited such purchases to 0.1 *shi* per person and accumulating substantial stocks of stipend grain (perhaps with the help of corruption at the bureaus). Zhu asked that all such parasitic profiteering be forbidden, and that an officially set price should henceforth govern all private transactions in stipend grain.[65]

Qianlong had already noted that those in charge of the bureaus were "suffering wicked persons to go to the bureaus and buy privily, [so as to] hoard [the grain] and fish for profits." This was in an edict of October 1751 in which he alleged mismanagement and suggested organizational reforms, including amalgamations. As one possible model, he envisaged a regime of one bureau per group of three banners (Manchu, Chinese, and Mongol), with the resulting eight bureaus grouped into two "wings" under a senior director. The grand ministers of the Eight Banners were instructed to prepare recommendations; when Zhu's memorial arrived, they were told to respond to it as part of their deliberations, and the grand councillors were brought into the discussion.

The joint report of the two groups of advisors was at partial variance with Qianlong's ideas, although he endorsed it at the time. They accepted the need for more specialized and integrated management but did not agree that the number of bureaus should be cut. The size of the population in the city and its environs, they said, required that the bureau system should control large, broadly distributed stocks of grain. The premises of individual bureaus were too small to store large quantities, besides which they were liable to overcrowding by customers. The resulting confusion only served the purposes of those who wanted to abuse the system. While the division into two "wings" was desirable to enhance administrative control, the twenty-four regular banner bureaus should all be retained. Each bureau should have the

---

65. QCWXTK, vol. 1, *juan* 37, p. 5,197.

flexibility to hold more or less than its "original target" of 5,000 *shi*, according to the local population density.

In response to Zhu's memorial, the grand ministers and councillors estimated that of the grain issued to the bannermen on any one occasion, 30 to 40 percent was retained by the recipients for their own consumption, 20 to 30 percent was bought by the bureaus, and the remainder (30 to 50 percent) would all "circulate outside" and feed the populace. Zhu's request for a fixed price for alienated stipend grain was premised on the notion that, since such grain was originally public sector grain, acquired through taxation, and since it had a discrete market, its price could be determined independently of private sector mechanisms. The grand ministers and councillors found this fallacious. Because, they pointed out, stipend grain accounted for only a portion of the capital's supply, its price was bound to rise and fall according to total supply conditions. A fixed price would be unenforceable. The new, more integrated managerial arrangements should, however, make it possible to end speculative buying from the bureaus, and measures should be taken to achieve this. The new management structure (grouping of the bureaus into two directorates, or "wings") was indeed implemented by mid-February 1752.[66]

Was it the implicit admission that the bureaus were controlling only about 30 to 50 percent of the grain sold by bannermen that subsequently made Qianlong feel justified in declaring the system ineffective? If so, the justification need not have been regarded as compelling. Admittedly, the bureaus were not fulfilling the early intention that they would buy 100 percent of the alienated stipend grain. As suggested in chapter 2 above, this was probably true from the beginning, although less true in 1728 than it later became. However, the ever-normal model for stabilizing sales envisaged the use of a limited quantity of

---

66. QCWXTK, vol. 1, *juan* 37, pp. 5,197–98; QSL/QL, *juan* 397:27a–28b (ref. from Hosoya, "Hakki beikyoku kō," p. 200); YFD, QL 16/12/26, 16/12/27 (d.r.) (8:1619). In the autumn of 1751, the Grand Council was quite open to interventionist schemes in favor of Beijing. In November, it secured Qianlong's assent to the "expedient" of committing 24,000 taels from the Imperial Household Department to eight-year interest-free loans to private carters to enable them to buy large mule- or horse-carts. While this proposal had more than one purpose, the winning rationale was the claim that a cart shortage was the cause of Beijing's recent high grain prices! YFD, QL 16/10/3 (d.r.) (1619).

public-sector grain to regulate a larger private sector. If the bureaus controlled only 30 percent of the sold stipend grain, this was already a substantial quantity. Using a 1752 statement that the rank-and-file bannermen received over 600,000 *shi* per quarter (2.4 million per year), we may estimate that the grain annually passing through the bureaus totalled between 480,000 and 720,000 *shi* (20 to 30 percent of the total issued, and considerably more than the 360,000 *shi* implied by the original design).[67] While rising population in the city as a whole, together with price changes, may have necessitated the special supplements exemplified above, the bureaus should usually have controlled enough grain to make a difference, if indeed the ever-normal theory had validity.

The edict that, presumably in the first half of 1752, abolished the bureaus is quite short. It declared that "The original purpose of setting up the grain bureaus was to serve the bannermen's convenience. Since the bureaus were established, the price of grain has really not attained stability, besides which the coercive buying of their grain is an actual burden to the banner people." The bureaus were therefore to close. If stabilizing sales were necessary in future, the Board of Revenue should consult the throne and make arrangements—presumably drawing grain directly from the metropolitan granaries. The Tongzhou bureaus were closed down a little later. There was a clearer rationale for closure of the Tongzhou bureaus: as salary grain for two years had been issued to the high-status recipients, it would be a long time before normal patterns of bureau activity could be resumed.[68] As to the motive for closing the Beijing bureaus, the edict notes only the obvious fact that they had not kept grain prices stable in an absolute sense. As they may well have kept prices more stable than they would otherwise have been, it is pertinent to ask whether the real reason for the abolition lay elsewhere.

Desire for a radical solution to continuing abuses and mismanagement would seem one possibility. However, the strongest evidence to date for such an interpretation comes from Tongzhou, where circum-

---

67. YFD, QL 17/2/10 (d.r.) (8:1622-1).
68. QCWXTK, vol. 1, *juan* 37, p. 5,198, and below. I follow previous authors in assuming this record's validity. While QCWXTK lacks the authority of archival sources, I have not previously found it unreliable.

stances were different from those in Beijing. The stipendiaries were typically of higher status in the former case, and the grain stipends were therefore larger. In 1745, a Guards Brigade commander-general defended the administration of one Tongzhou bureau at great length against charges of mismanagement and malfeasance.[69] Whether these charges were justified or not, the issue aroused court attention and may have raised questions as to the standard of administration at the Beijing bureaus. Then, in March 1752, the grand councillors and others considered allegations that, in order to save haulage costs, Tongzhou stipendiaries had been selling their grain stipends to the Tongzhou bureaus without removing them from the state granaries. The "official bureaus" were reportedly consolidating such purchases inside the granaries before selling them to the very "private bureaus" whose profiteering they were supposed to counteract. The alleged abuse was probably part of a broader pattern of mismanagement at the Tongzhou granaries, which were under investigation at the time. It did not lead immediately to the abolition of the Tongzhou banner bureaus, which did not happen before June.[70]

Mismanagement could take less opprobrious forms and might be partially a matter of opinion. Pricing policy required a delicate balance between different goals. Considerations on the side of lower prices were the need to ensure real benefit to poor consumers and avoid all appearance of profiteering; those on the side of higher prices were the risk of operating at a loss and/or provoking the very behavior that the system was designed to counteract. It is likely that by the time when Zhu Lunhan wrote his 1751 memorial, bureau grain was being underpriced. Not only did five bureaus make losses ranging from 61 to 488 taels between May 1750 and December 1751;[71] there is evidence that

---

69. CC, Qingtai, QL 10/8/30.

70. CC, Grd. Coun. et al., QL 17/2/16; QSL/QL, *juan* 408:23b, 24b–25a; Wu Jianyong, "Qingdai Beijing de liangshi gongying," pp. 181–2. In saying that this abuse was "without doubt . . . the real reason why the Qing court abolished the banner grain bureaus" (p. 182), Wu omits to mention that this source refers specifically to the Tongzhou bureaus. See also QCWXTK, vol. 1, *juan* 37, p. 5,198, and, e.g., QSL/QL, *juan* 408:5b–7b, 14a, 16a–b.

71. YFD, QL 16/12/27 (d.r.) (8:1619). The remaining bureaus had made profits ranging from 2 to 422 taels.

principles designed to minimize the risk of undesired merchant responses were being contravened.

A norm of the ever-normal system (albeit one that Qianlong had undermined in 1742 by ordering more flexibility) was that price reductions during stabilizing sales should not exceed 0.1 tael per *shi* compared with the current market rate. Overgenerous price cuts not only encouraged the hoarding of private-sector grain but also tempted shopkeepers to buy state-sector grain for hoarding. Selling grain of excessively good quality was also likely to provoke abuse.[72] As an ex-vice-president of the Board of Revenue understood the issue in October 1751, whatever the price of grain on Beijing markets, the price of grain sold from the banner bureaus should be slightly lower, drawing the market price down through stepped reductions or keeping it down once it had fallen. Of "recent years," however, a new pricing principle had been adopted: limitation of the bureaus' profit—eventually to a flat rate of 0.1 tael per *shi*. The cost price of bureau grain thus replaced the current market rate as the basis of pricing. As the bureaus bought when grain was cheap, they could no longer sell at prices high enough to deter speculative buying.[73]

The vice-president's information was not fully correct. It is true that in mid-1750, Qianlong had expressed a carefully nuanced concern about the danger of encouraging excessive profit-mindedness in bureau managers.[74] However, in the spring of 1751, the prices charged at Beijing's stabilizing sales outlets, including the bureaus, were indeed set on the basis of reductions from the current market rate. The problem was that in late March, quite large cuts were substituted for the normal 0.1 tael per *shi* that had been ordered in December. For *suomi* and the low-grade "granary rice" there was to be a 0.35 tael per *shi* reduction from the current price (1.55 tael per *shi*). These cereals were seen as "quite" expensive and in high demand. Even for the better-quality "old rice" there was to be a 0.25 tael per *shi* cut, although, at 1.65 taels per *shi*, this kind of grain was not seen as extremely dear, nor was demand for it high. Whatever the precedents for Beijing—a 0.34 tael per *shi* cut for

---

72. Will, *Bureaucracy and Famine*, pp. 183–85; QCWXTK, vol. 1, *juan* 36, pp. 5,189–91; CC, Celeng and Anning, QL 2/6/1, Qingtai, QL 10/8/30; and chap. 4 above.

73. YFD, QL 16/9/1 (d.r.) (8:1619).

74. YFD, QL 16/12/27 (d.r.) (8:1619).

suomi in 1748 was thought the most relevant—Will notes in a general way that after 1742, 0.3 tael per *shi* became the maximum cut normally allowed in serious subsistence crises. Beijing grain prices were not perceived to be at real crisis levels in March 1751. Especially as those prices were brought down sharply around the end of April by early release of stipend grain—and that this early release did not, as in 1743, *follow* an intercalary month but *precede* one—the complaints, later that year, of speculative buying should not come as a surprise.[75]

If indeed the problem with the bureaus in the early 1750s was more mismanagement than flawed design, the reform plan submitted by the grand ministers and councillors might have been at least as good a choice as abolition—in the absence of other change. However, on 30 March 1752 Qianlong decided to try to discourage speculation by staggering the issues of stipend grain to ordinary bannermen, so that the men of two or three banners would receive grain each month. This simple step to smooth the flow of grain onto the Beijing market was surely preferable to maintaining a complex state grain-trading system to manage the consequences of releasing vast amounts three or four times per year. As the grand councillors put it the next day, the measure's likely outcome would be to cause "hoarding to cease spontaneously, without prohibition."[76] Yet here was another sharp change of direction, in view of the decision, six days earlier (24 March), to give the high-status payees of the Tongzhou granaries two years' grain stipends all at once, in order to expedite an audit of the stocks. It was predicted that this measure also would conduce to greater price stability on Beijing's grain market. Stability would be enhanced, Qianlong (or his ghost-writer) opined, because the "princes, dukes, grand ministers and the rest" would all "have surplus stocks at home." They would therefore not need to compete with poorer consumers in the markets. The grand councillors, commenting the next day, preferred a quantitative ration-

---

75. YFD, probably QL 16/2/28–30 (8:1618-1, frames 147–58); ibid., QL 16/4/3, 16/4/16 (both d.r.) (8:1618-1); QSL/QL, *juan* 382:17b; Will, *Bureaucracy and Famine*, p. 185.

76. YFD, QL 17/2/16 (d.r.) (8:1622-1); QSL/QL, *juan* 409:2a–3a (ref. from Wu Jianyong, "Qingdai Beijing de liangshi gongying," p. 178; see also L. M. Li and A. Dray-Novey, "Guarding Beijing's Food Security," p. 1,006. Neither essay links the staggering of stipend issues with the closing of the bureaus).

ale. The extraordinary issue would add over 615,000 *shi* to the 205,000 normally payable; the unusual abundance would induce a great fall in the price of grain, which would be reflected in lower prices for all other commodities.[77]

If the rationale for staggering the rank-and-file stipend issues was valid, the predominant effect of large-scale salary advances from the Tongzhou granaries should have been to aggravate the instability of metropolitan grain prices. Qianlong recognized the risk that, far from prudently conserving their grain at home, Tongzhou stipendiaries would sell it to exporters (merchants planning to remove it from the metropolitan area), speculators, or liquor manufacturers. Tightened surveillance to prevent the loss of grain through export or distillation was subsequently recommended. The grand councillors had meanwhile noted the risk that overabundance in the months to come might mean shortage even by the end of 1752. But, after all, six times as much grain annually became available through payments to the rank and file as through salaries to their superiors. It was not as though the city's grain supply depended entirely on the salaries, they reasoned.[78] Did they convince themselves? Would speculative buying cease as prices plummeted? The court had taken an extraordinary step and would now have to face the consequences of progressively pouring grain into the metropolitan market throughout the three months or more that it would take to clear 0.82 million *shi* from the Tongzhou stockpiles.[79]

Was it this new danger that impelled the court's sudden enlightenment? Its reversal of direction was radical indeed. In moving from a single, massive issue from the Tongzhou granaries to staggered, reduced issues in Beijing, the court was no doubt seeking to counteract the excess it had just committed. But did that excess itself induce an overdue and fundamental questioning of customary practice? Was it in this moment of policy crisis that the court realized that a more consistent flow of stipend grain onto the city's markets might reduce the risk of speculation in the first place? If so, we have here something more than

---

77. QSL/QL, *juan* 408:16b–17a; YFD, QL 17/2/10 (d.r.) (8:1622-1).

78. QSL/QL, *juan* 408:17a–18a; CC, Grd. Coun. et al., QL 17/2/16; YFD, QL 17/2/10 (d.r.) (8:1622-1).

79. CC, Yinlu, QL 17/2/27 (d.r.); cat. no. 1152-002, date corrected from transcription in YFD, QL 17/2/27 (8:1622-1).

"zigzagging" around a golden mean.[80] In quantitative terms, excess prompted a reversion that considerably overshot the previous norm. In terms of policy conception, the court did not so much retreat to moderation as strike out on a new path.

When exactly were the Beijing banner grain bureaus abolished? The odd omission of the abolition edict from the *Veritable Records* removes, for the time being, any basis for accusing Qianlong of deciding to close the bureaus before a viable alternative had been identified. Methodological responsibility prescribes the charitable assumption that the decision to close the bureaus followed the breakthrough on staggering of stipend issues. The bureaus were still operating on 13 April, when Qianlong temporarily halted stabilizing sales because grain prices in Beijing had fallen. The remnants of the 40,000 *shi* specially issued from the metropolitan granaries in February were to be stored in the bureaus along with any previously purchased stipend grain. As these were probably the sales after whose completion the abolition edict said the bureaus should be closed, we cannot exclude the possibility that this edict antedated 30 March. With ever more grain from the Tongzhou granaries expected to reach Beijing markets, there was nothing else to do with the leftover bureau grain but store it.[81]

Staggering the stipend issues did not quell speculation permanently. In the summer of 1787, the discovery, on shopkeepers' premises, of minor hoards totalling some 66,000 *shi* refocused the absent court's attention on ways to prevent speculation in Beijing and Tongzhou.[82] It was in the context of attempts to manage the situation through forced sales, posted prohibitions, surveillance, and threats (in short, the techniques of coercion) that a vice censor-in-chief proposed the reestablishment of banner grain bureaus. In his response, Qianlong expatiated at some length on why such action would be vain. But, at the end of the edict, he forwarded the proposal for serious consideration by no less a forum than a conference of his regents in the capital, the grand secretaries, the Nine Ministries Assembly, and the banner commanders-

---

80. Cf. chap. 3 above.

81. QSL/QL, *juan* 406:2a, 409:11a; YFD, QL 16/12/26 (8:1619); QCWXTK, vol. 1, *juan* 37, p. 5,198.

82. QSL/QL, *juan* 1,280:11b–13a, 19b–20b, 26a–28a; *juan* 1,281:4b–7a.

in-chief.[83] It is not as though state trading were an infantile disorder that the Sino-Manchu establishment had outgrown.

What, in conclusion, was the significance of the twin measures of 1752: the abolition of the banner grain bureaus and the staggering of stipend payments to the rank and file? Let us consider these simply as public policy decisions, without reference to their background of empiricism. In reducing the need for complex anti-speculation mechanisms by reforming its own stipend-payment practices, the court was moving towards the ideal of "maximum effect with minimum direct involvement" that Will once posited as a generic goal of much Qing policy formation.[84] The state would be directly involved in Beijing's provisioning for as long as the grain tribute system lasted, but the extra layer of involvement that had been the banner bureau network would now be removed. The change of 1752 can further be called a relative liberalization of Beijing's grain market. The edict that abolished the bureaus described the "coercive buying" of stipend grain as a "burden" to the banner population. Now the bannermen would be free to sell more of their grain to whomever they pleased. Paternalistic fears lest they sell cheap but buy dear were out-of-date: with reduced amounts of grain released at a time in the new, staggered stipend issues, prices would be kept up and speculative buying rendered problematic. Market forces would not necessarily rule unchecked in the Inner City, as the stocks in the metropolitan granaries would still be available (once normality had been restored after the audit) for stabilizing sales when needed. The key change would be that, every year, some hundreds of thousands of *shi* of grain would escape temporary impounding in the bureaus. Instead, this grain would enter the market, in a relatively even flow, and become available for retail, storage, or—despite the price deterrents—hoarding.

As the episode of 1787 reminds us, the abolition of the bureaus would not have been liberalizing in the long run if it contributed to a regrowth of speculative activity that provoked renewed state intrusion with the traditional battery of coercive techniques. A firm liberaliza-

---

83. Ibid., *juan* 1,281:11a–12b; ref. from Wu Jianyong, "Qingdai Beijing de liangshi gongying," p. 180; see also L. M. Li and A. Dray-Novey, "Guarding Beijing's Food Security," p. 1,009.

84. Will, "State Management," p. 81.

tion policy could have been built only on an application to the Beijing grain market of a theoretical defence of speculation such as those explored above in chapter 3. It has yet to be demonstrated that any eighteenth-century official argued that speculation in Beijing was a functional response to objective conditions, and that it served the public interest. The awareness of market processes that had been frequently articulated in the 1740s had the rhetorical power to justify liberalizations but lacked the systematization that might have helped them take root. In the meantime, the changes of 1752 made possible a responsible management strategy at reduced governmental effort. An emperor who was now less charmed by tireless commitment to assuring lower-class subsistence could have been pleased with his accomplishment.

The Landowners' Tax Holiday

A state that aspires to do less presumably needs less income. It can noisily repudiate a "tax and spend" approach, emphasizing instead the wisdom of letting society retain the wealth to find its own solutions to social and economic problems. The third development that was consistent with diminishing commitment to state welfare activism was the universal land and labor-service tax remission proclaimed in 1745. Although spread over the three years 1746 through 1748, it was originally intended to glorify the tenth anniversary of Qianlong's accession in a single burst of munificence in 1746. This was not the only universal land and labor-service tax remission in the eighteenth century. Others were declared in 1710, 1770, 1777, 1790, and 1795.[85] It was, however, the only one declared when reserves in the central government treasury were at so low a level.

As shown in chapter 6, the remission edict, issued on 5 July 1745, coincided with the court's experiment with promoting *jiansheng* title sales as a potential substitute for annual buying for the ever-normal

---

85. DQHDSL, vol. 11, *juan* 265:10a–11a, *juan* 266:18b–19a, 26a–27a, 34a–b, 41b–42a (pp. 8,590, 8,605–6, 8,609–10, 8,613, 8,617); *Qinding Hubu zeli*, *juan* 83:1a–b, 6a–7b, 8b–12a; Will, *Bureaucracy and Famine*, p. 292 n. 50. General remissions of the grain tribute (staggered over longer periods than the three years that was standard for universal land and labor-service tax remissions) were proclaimed in 1766, 1778, and 1794. DQHDSL, *juan* 266:16a–b, 27b–28a and 37a–b (pp. 8,604, 8,610, 8,615).

granaries. The edict probably preceded the Board of Revenue directive that could have led to total breakdown of the ever-normal system, that is, the order to refrain from restocking through purchase in the coming autumn. Thus, shortly after the edict's promulgation, the state indeed seemed poised to start doing less for popular subsistence. The remission edict cited a version of the truism that punctuated court rhetoric on the ever-normal granaries in 1748. Just as more grain in the hands of the authorities meant less for the people, so, more positively, ". . . the realm has only so much wealth. If it is not accumulated with the sovereign, it will be dispersed among the subjects."[86] Assumed here was something every good Confucian knew: "storing wealth among the people" was a wise and virtuous principle of government. When there was a surplus in the treasury and an imperial anniversary to celebrate, why not conspicuously honor such a doctrine?

When, later in July, Qianlong accepted the recommendation that the remission be spread over three years, he took the opportunity to make his liberality more thorough. Suppose a natural disaster struck a region in the year in which its taxes were to be remitted. How would the stricken farmers feel the bounty of the universal tax remission, given that the disaster would have brought them tax exemptions anyway? The answer was to let them have their extraordinary remission the next year instead. How would tax debtors know that their imperial parent loved them if the dunning went on just as usual in the remission year (when, of course, they might have found it easier to pay)? There was to be a moratorium on dunning until the year after.[87] Meticulous concern indeed, but could the treasury afford it? The budget surplus did not greatly exceed one year's income from the land and labor-service tax alone, and it cannot be considered large by eighteenth-century standards. Let us compare the total reported holdings of the Board of Revenue treasury in 1745 with those for 1710 and 1770, that is, the first two other years in which a universal land and labor-service tax remission was declared during the high Qing period. In 1745 the treasury held

---

86. QSL/QL, *juan* 242:9b–10a.

87. QSL/QL, *juan* 243:13b–15a; cf., on tax exemptions as disaster relief, Will, *Bureaucracy and Famine*, pp. 241–46, esp. table 18, which shows the standard percentages of tax remitted for specific levels of disaster. Full exemptions were sometimes granted.

only some 33.2 million taels of silver; in 1710, by contrast, it had held 45.9 million, and in 1770 it held 77.3 million. As to the last three re-mission years (1777, 1790, and 1795), incomplete figures suggest that reserves probably peaked in the late 1770s at just over 80 million taels and did not fall much below 60 million until the late 1790s.[88]

The picture of Qianlong's imprudence would probably not greatly fade if these reserve totals were adjusted to allow for changes in the buying power of silver. Wang Yeh-chien has put the annual rate of increase in Yangzi Delta rice prices between "the 1680s" and ca. 1820 at only 0.7 percent.[89] Dangerous as it would be to extrapolate from his Suzhou and Shanghai data to a national inflation rate, we can claim that the quoted totals understate the degree by which the Board of Revenue was poorer in 1745 than in 1710 in real terms. Although they overstate the degree by which the Board was richer in 1770 than in 1745, it re-mains true that a sum of even 60 million taels during the period 1770–1800 was worth substantially more, in real terms, than 33 million taels in the mid-1740s. Qianlong in 1745 was fiscally rash compared both with his grandfather, the Kangxi emperor, and with his older self.

I suggested in chapters 6 and 7 that, already in 1745 and again in 1748–49, the three-year loss of revenue entailed by the tax remission helped push the central government to consider mitigating its war fi-nance problems at the expense of the ever-normal system. Although its moves in this direction were checked in 1745 and circumscribed in 1748–49, they illustrate how careless munificence could jeopardize routine government activities. To broaden the discussion, let us recall that a substantial proportion of land and labor-service tax income was earmarked for local and provincial purposes, whether in the province of collection or through subsidies beyond its borders. A limited surplus

---

88. Lü Jian, comp., "Kang Yong Qian Hubu," pp. 20–21; Kishimoto, *Shindai Chūgoku no bukka*, p. 491, fig. 13.1. The 1777 remission edict notes that Board re-serves exceed 70 million taels. *Qinding Hubu zeli, juan* 83:8b. The annual revenue quota for the land and labor-service tax was stated by the grand secretaries in July 1745 as about 28.2 million, whereas total tax income (excluding surcharges) for 1753 has been estimated at some 56 million. QSL/QL, *juan* 243:13b; Wang, *Land Taxa-tion*, p. 72.

89. Wang's 31-year moving averages for Yangzi Delta rice prices show the fol-lowing: for 1710, 0.98 tl./*shi*; for 1745, 1.58 tl./*shi*; for 1770, 1.88 tl./*shi*; for 1795, 1.91 tl./*shi*. Wang, "Secular Trends of Rice Prices," p. 67 and table 1.1, pp. 41–43.

in the national exchequer was no guarantee that local and provincial governments could do without their staple source of income for one year.

The Board of Revenue did call, in the late summer or early autumn of 1745, for detailed provincial statements of the funds available for meeting costs in the remission years. However, close consultation between court and provinces did not take place until late autumn and winter. On 23 October, Qianlong ordered that provincial chiefs quickly send the central government details of all surplus monies accumulated over previous years. They were to indicate which of these funds could be made available to cover the shortfalls that the remission would create. It is not clear whether the court planned only an assessment of the need and prospects for extraordinary interprovincial transfers to plug short-term provincial deficits, or whether it was now also tempted to milk provincial treasuries in favor of the central government (or war effort). There is a sentence in the edict that possibly betrays intent to milk, but it is too ambiguous to serve as evidence.[90]

While the management of the remission at provincial level must await further research, a preliminary survey of the governors' responses suggests that many provinces had substantial disposable accumulated revenue with which to offset their own remission-created deficit, at least in part—whether or not there would be funds to spare for transfer elsewhere. For example, of the provinces whose remission year was imminent, Hunan currently had over 900,000 taels disposable, of which it would need some 700,000 in 1746. Jiangsu had 1.08 million taels in the main provincial treasury with which to meet expenditures in 1746 of 1.73 million; as of the November cut-off for the figures, it was unclear whether the 650,000-tael gap would be fully plugged by funds not yet received (although the 125,000 disposable taels in circuit treasuries would probably have helped).[91] From these documents, one infers that the deficits in provincial and, presumably, local budgets would normally be managed by drawing on reserves (perhaps including those of other provinces where necessary). Diversion of funds, further short-term revenue-sacrifices by the central government, and the reduc-

---

90. QSL/QL, *juan* 249:18a–b.
91. KC, Yang Xifu, QL 10/10/27; Chen Dashou, QL 11/1/8. This set of memorials is archived under KC and JF for QL 10/10 to 11/2.

tion or postponement of expenditure would have been other options. In early 1746, indeed, the court sent the provincial chiefs secret letters reasserting previous orders to postpone public works (such as city wall restoration) wherever possible because of the remission. It was in this context that—at the least—some 198,000 taels of presumably redundant Jiangxi, Zhejiang, and Guizhou stabilizing-sales proceeds were transferred to the Yunnan-Guizhou military, while over 500,000 taels of such funds in Fujian were reported for allocation to annual military or administrative costs. Such also is the background to the swift depletion of certain provincial treasuries by the Jinchuan war of 1747–49.[92]

A crucial category of provincial revenue in which the court already knew that deficits would be created was income from the wastage (*huohao* or *haoxian*) surcharge. *Huohao* was a percentage added to land and labor-service tax bills, nominally to cover the loss of metal that occurred when the odd weights of uncoined silver received from taxpayers were recast into standard ingots. Following its regularization by Yongzheng, *huohao* had provided both the supplementary salaries "for nourishing integrity" that enabled territorial officials to meet their operating costs, and funds for various governmental expenses and projects.[93] The grand secretaries' original recommendation was that the wastage surcharge be not remitted. On 21 August, about a month after receiving this advice, Qianlong asked his leading grand secretaries, Zhang Tingyu and Nuoqin, to reconsider secretly. Reporting in mid-September, Zhang and Nuoqin upheld their former view. The annual nationwide *huohao* quota amounted to less than 4.44 million taels (including certain other monies), while the annual requirement for supplementary salaries and public expenses totalled some 4.41 million. The margin of surplus was thus narrow to begin with; if the *huohao* were remitted, there would be no income for these essential costs. Use of the surplus *huohao* from past years and surplus proceeds of stabilizing sales would leave recalcitrant deficits totalling nearly 1.39 million taels. Zhang and Nuoqin therefore recommended that *huohao* be levied as usual. Qianlong assented at the time, but early in 1746 he ordered

---

92. QSL/QL, *juan* 254:24a–b; KC, Saileng'e, QL 10/10/25, Maertai and Zhou Xuejian, QL 10/12/7, Zhou Xuejian, QL 10/12/7; Bd. Rev. communication transc. NGDKDA, Zhang Guangsi, QL 11/5/26 (doc. no. 074841).

93. Zelin, *Magistrate's Tael*, pp. 119–20 and ff.; note also pp. 269–72, 284–88.

that collection of *huohao* in each province's remission year be postponed until the following year.[94]

Presumably, at least in provinces that did not pay grain tribute, collecting *huohao* without the basic tax would have been a daunting, uneconomic proposition. The concern for taxpayer convenience expressed in the postponement edict can possibly be read as a disguised acknowledgment of this fact.[95] However, tribute-paying provinces were expected to collect not only the basic tribute, but also a surcharge, payable in silver, known as *caoxiang*. This obligation would not be suspended in the remission year. In Jiangsu and Zhejiang at least, the *caoxiang* had been amalgamated into the basic land and labor-service tax and did not appear as a separate item on tax bills. Much labor would be involved in re-establishing *caoxiang* assessment rates, communicating them throughout the countryside, and recalculating individual households' liability. While calculating and communicating *huohao* liabilities would require labor too, assessing and collecting both these minor taxes would have been less wasteful if undertaken as a single process (as the Jiangsu governor had suggested).[96] Collection of *caoxiang* would have been less uneconomic had there been *huohao* revenue as well.

Was Qianlong being obstinate? He was certainly not interested in playing the heedful recipient of censorial remonstrance. Soon after the promulgation of the universal tax remission, a censor called He Tai suggested that this action was imprudent, as it contravened the principle of building reserves in case of later need. If revocation was not possible, perhaps the court could substitute complete remission of arrears. The unchastened emperor denounced He for "giving rein to his private intelligence and petty cleverness to engage in reckless discussion of the court's weighty governmental matters." Qianlong stigmatized He as being perversely unlike all his other subjects, who were supposedly delighted with his munificence. The Board of Personnel, ordered to consider how He should be disciplined, advised dismissal. By

---

94. QSL/QL, *juan* 243:14a, 245:15a, 247:2a–b, 256:5a–6a; TF, Zhang Tingyu and Nuoqin, QL 10/8/19; cf. TF, Chang'an, QL 11/2/7, Pan Siju, QL 11/3/16.

95. Cf. TF, Chen Dashou, QL 10/7/24; QSL/QL, *juan* 256:5b.

96. TF, Chen Dashou, QL 10/7/24, Pan Siju, QL 11/3/16. On *caoxiang*, see Li Wenzhi and Jiang Taixin, *Qingdai caoyun*, p. 113.

this time, Qianlong had moved on. The overweening censor was demoted and transferred.[97]

How universal would the rejoicing have been in reality? Wealthy landlords would clearly have benefited from the tax remission; so should every poor peasant who owned a plot of land. Even smallholders who rented more land than they owned should have derived some benefit. Millions of people presumably enjoyed a one-year windfall, whose magnitude depended on the size, quality, and hence tax category of their landholdings and the probity of local government administration. This windfall would have improved their position, although its benefits would have been offset by any rise in the oppressiveness of government or decline in the usefulness of government to taxpayers—two possible results of budget stringency. But what of tenant farmers, who paid rent, not tax? In a generally negative assessment of tax remissions as a famine relief measure, Will has claimed that these "mainly benefited landowners, especially the great landlords of gentry status, who could always count on help from the administration when it came to recovering their full rents."[98] The key question was whether landlords would pass the tax remissions on to tenants by lowering their rent. In July 1745, Qianlong followed recent precedent. In the remission years, magistrates should exert their best persuasive powers to make the local landlords joyfully respond to conscience.[99]

Two censors realized that this would be problematic. They were Wei Tingpu, original proponent of the 1743 moratorium on buying for the granaries, and Sun Hao, perhaps the leading agitator in the early 1740s movement to reduce the pressure of the ever-normal system.[100] Wei submitted a memorial that stressed the presumptuousness of rent-resisting tenants. He advocated a fixed rate for rent reductions chiefly as a protection for landlords. Sun proposed that the benefit of the remission be shared equally between landlord and tenant. However, his concern likewise was less with fairness to the tenant than with dispute prevention. His notion of fairness illustrates the pro-landlord bias of tax remissions as a form of governmental generosity. Of the 28 mil-

---

97. QSL/QL, *juan* 243:7a–8b.
98. Will, *Bureaucracy and Famine*, pp. 241–44; quotation from p. 242 n. 40.
99. QSL/QL, *juan* 243:14a–b.
100. Chap. 5 above.

lion taels of revenue forgone by the state, the landlord and the tenant sides would each receive 14 million; this was fair. However, tenants outnumbered landlords. Given Sun's model, the lower the proportion of landlords, the more regressive would the non-taxation be.

But Sun's model was generally not given. Responding, in mid-August, to Qianlong's instructions to consider both memorials, the grand secretaries and Board of Revenue reiterated that rent concessions were a matter of landlord morality and responsiveness to public feeling. A legal approach, which the setting of rates or proportions would imply, was inappropriate. The report quoted the precedent that Qianlong had invoked when ordering that landlords be exhorted. This was an edict of early 1736 that had made clear how refractory tenants should be treated. It had also overridden a "permanently" applicable enactment of Qianlong's sainted grandfather, Kangxi. Kangxi had required that landlords pass on 30 percent of the benefit of tax remissions to their tenants; Qianlong had recommended 50 percent but ruled out coercion.[101] In August 1745, the emperor's advisors found their assignment simple. His Majesty had already given his instructions. Both censors' proposals could be dismissed as impractical and likely only to provoke disputes or tempt tenants to importune their landlords. The emperor assented.[102] This time, however, censorial concerns were not necessarily discordant with provincial experience. Later that month, the Jiangsu governor, Chen Dashou, invoked the rent-resisting tendencies of Jiangnan tenants to advocate the same solution as Sun Hao. Qianlong's response to this and Chen's other proposals (on *caoxiang* and *huohao*) was noncommittal, neither forbidding Chen to act nor vouchsafing the support of an explicit order.[103]

---

101. QSL/QL, *juan* 9:2b–4a, or DQHDSL, vol. 11, *juan* 265:21b–22a (pp. 8,595–96). On the contrast between Kangxi's and Qianlong's approaches to landlord tax remissions, see Kondō, "Shinchō kenryoku," pp. 171–72, and Bernhardt, *Rents*, pp. 38–39.

102. TF, Grd. Secs. and Bd. Rev., QL 10/7/17 (which transcribes the two censors' memorials). Wei made one suggestion that found favor: landowners with taxes in arrears should be exhorted to frugality in the remission year so that they could pay on demand when collection resumed.

103. TF, Chen Dashou, QL 10/7/24; QSL/QL, *juan* 245:23a–b. Chen's memorial seems to refer to the practice of specifying a guaranteed minimum rent and then basing the actual amount due in any given year on the quality of the harvest.

No doubt, in the event, there were landlords who rose to the call to manifest a "trend of benevolent sacrifice." Others probably did not, leaving the poorer of the poor to pay as usual. To him that had was given not only the tax break, but also the freedom to choose whether to be generous—a freedom that, if Wei and Sun were right, may not have been in his best interests. However, in confirming it, Qianlong weakened the position even of assertive tenants. Tenant aspirations to share in the benefits of his munificence would have no legal basis.[104]

Beat the Presumptuous to Death!

What if the poor—not necessarily tenants, but any poor people afflicted with a sense of righteous grievance—were so overweening as to take the law into their own hands? This final section notes the harshness, by the standards of the day, of the treatment of food rioters and other demonstrators in the late 1740s. Contemporaries were aware that there was a choice as to how clamorous plebeians should be regarded. Victories for harshness might reflect an intensification (perceived or real) of the challenge that mob action posed to government, not to mention fear of the consequences of being seen as soft. A shift towards intolerance was nonetheless consistent with reduced commitment to welfare assistance. Both could be justified in the same way.

Shulu's call, in 1748, for the "presumptuousness" of Jiangnan relief claimants to be "gradually repressed" was a renewal of some hard-line intrabureaucratic lobbying by which Qianlong had declared himself convinced in 1746. In the autumn of 1745, Qin Huitian cited relief client rowdiness as but one indication of a growing "spirit of perversity" among the masses. The unruliness took such forms as raiding villages and market towns, or making a commotion at the local *yamen* when expected food relief was issued "slightly late." On Qin's advice, local officials were forbidden to encourage such misconduct by showing any leniency towards offenders. About a year later, the fears of Sun Hao

---

Bernhardt (*Rents*, p. 23) was apparently unable to find evidence of this practice before 1760.

104. On tenant assertiveness in eighteenth-century Jiangnan and its basis in contract and custom, see Bernhardt, *Rents*, pp. 21–39. As Bernhardt notes (p. 28), such conditions did not prevail throughout China—especially not in regions in which sharecropping was common.

and Wei Tingpu came true in western Fujian. Some tenants resorted to violence to back demands for rent cuts in view of the universal tax remission. In condemning their behavior in October 1746, Qianlong noted that this incident, together with a market shutdown in Jiangsu, had changed his mind about censorial warnings that popular presumptuousness should not be left to "flare up daily higher"—language that he had previously thought exaggerated. The shutdown was allegedly intended to put pressure on the local magistrate to report total natural disaster, thereby entitling the poor to an indiscriminate relief distribution. Besides ordering heavy punishment for the Fujian tenants, Qianlong remarked on the need for parents to chastise "unworthy" sons severely, just as they cared lovingly for "worthy" ones. He ordered more attention to the disciplinary side of governance throughout the territorial bureaucracy.[105]

Was "presumptuousness" fact or artifact? In 1745, about a month after the Board of Justice had endorsed Qin's memorial, Qianlong had noted an allegation that clamorous behavior by relief clients typically resulted from bad official management. The real culprits might be those administrators who gave the populace unrealistic expectations by letting them imagine that the disaster report could be exaggerated, who created panic among legitimate recipients by delaying pre-relief procedures, or whose poor choice of personnel resulted in misappropriation of supplies that should have gone to famine victims. It was when local officials panicked at situations that they could not properly control that they shifted the blame to the people's "presumptuousness." In 1745, Qianlong emphasized the need for correction of any such incompetence.[106] Whether or not he really believed that his subjects were generally placid and appreciative, he was doing what any responsible bureaucratic head would have done in the circumstances. We may well ask whether, given the 1745 warning of the unreliability of allegations of "presumptuousness," every responsible head would have changed his rhetorical tune as thoroughly as Qianlong did in the autumn of 1746. To be sure, representations from what one is tempted to call the Chinese law-and-order lobby continued intermittently thereafter. While specific cases of unrest and suppression might have ethnic

---

105. QSL/QL, *juan* 248:12a–b, 273:26b–28a.
106. QSL/QL, *juan* 250:23b–25a.

overtones, certain Chinese censors offered the Manchu court unsolicited support for harshness or advocated greater pressure on the territorial bureaucracy to warn potential troublemakers and nip disorder in
the bud.[107]

After 1746, did Qianlong practise critical reading of hostile reports
on the "presumptuous" poor? The divergent accounts of a demonstration in Suzhou on 20 May 1748 help us to recognize not only the tragic
consequences of an intensified imperial preference for uncharitable
readings, but also the establishment's need to repudiate anything that
smacked of fraternization between officials and rioters. A city resident
called Gu Yaonian, possibly a market stall-holder, had gone to the
yamen of the acting provincial governor, Anning, to request official
action to force down the price of rice. He cut a dramatic figure—arms
bound, sharp blade clenched between teeth, a banner or placard carried
behind his back, perhaps even a heroic slogan painted on his bare
chest—and he had a following. The situation grew out of hand during
his questioning by the magistrate of Changzhou county, which had
jurisdiction over part of the city, with fellow demonstrators eventually
rescuing him from arrest.[108] Some damage was done, first at the county
yamen (a broken partition, for example) and then at the governor's
headquarters (at least a knocked-down fence). Thirty-nine arrests were
made. This information comes from three accounts: two reports to the
throne (one each by the provincial surveillance commissioner, Weng
Zao, and the Lianghuai salt administration commissioner, Jiqing), and a
private version transcribed in a nineteenth-century edition of the prefectural gazetteer.[109]

---

107. In addition to Huang Dengxian's mem. (August 1748) cited above, see LFZZ,
Zhang Weiyin, QL 13/int.7/15 (September 1748) and Li Wenju's 1747 memorial
excerpted in Wu Renshu, "Chengshi liangshi baodong," pp. 345, 348.

108. In Ming times, it was the poorer side of town that was administered by
Changzhou. Clunas, *Fruitful Sites*, p. 68. This may still have been so after 1724,
when Changzhou was divided to create the new county of Yuanhe.

109. See transcriptions in, respectively, KYQRFDZ, vol. 2, p. 583; Wu Renshu,
"Chengshi liangshi baodong," pp. 357–58; 1883 *Suzhou fuzhi, juan* 149:6a–b (ref. from
KYQRFDZ, vol. 2, p. 584); cf. Santangelo, "Urban Society," pp. 104–5. The gazetteer account had been transcribed from an earlier gazetteer-style work compiled in
1803. Wu quotes a second private account from *Danwu biji* (Notes by Danwu), a
collection of anecdotes by Gu Gongxie, a Suzhou literatus. As part of an unflat-

It is, of course, the two official reports that use derogatory language about the demonstrators, mention damage to official property, and/or give Gu a quarrelsome, disreputable, perhaps even seditious character. Between them, they construct local authorities who had done what they could about the price of grain through stabilizing sales, a firm Anning, and an incompetent Chinese subordinate, the acting prefect Jiang Shunjiao. The private account, by contrast, emphasizes the harshness of Anning's response, representing him as taking a hard line from the beginning. At the end of the incident, he is shown angered by a crowd "crying and lamenting" outside his *yamen*, and ordering troops with firearms to drive the people off.

Gu Yaonian would probably have been executed even had it been the private account that reached Qianlong. However, it was Anning's report that sealed his fate, leading to a repression that was intentionally harsh by previous standards. Matters were not helped by Anning's accompanying impeachment of acting prefect Jiang, who is depicted by the private account as knowing how to talk to the people, and as calming them somewhat by undertaking to put their request to Anning. What Anning had seen was a noisy crowd outside his headquarters and a Chinese prefect who had not only advocated appeasement, but also ignored orders to subdue the riot. Anning's Jiang was a useless coward, but we cannot exclude the possibility that the real Jiang was sympathetic to the rioters. At least, the court worried that the Suzhou populace would see him as a martyr to their cause. Anning had sent a signal with potential ethnic import. Any hint that the Chinese, as opposed to just the lower classes, might become ungovernable could only intensify the court's response.[110]

What makes it likely that, even granted a sympathetic representation of his actions, the demonstration leader would have faced the death

---

tering story about a joke that Anning supposedly made eight years later, this is probably the least reliable account of the four.

110. LFZZ, Anning, QL 13/4/25; QSL/QL, *juan* 314:25b–26b; Wu Renshu, "Chengshi liangshi baodong," pp. 349–50. Gu Gongxie's anecdotal version of the incident (quoted by Wu) notes that Jiang had previously "won the people's hearts." As punishment for his role in the riot, Jiang was assigned to wall repair or military "grain station" construction, but he bought himself free by "contributing" 10,000 taels, presumably to the war effort. YFD, QL 13/9/13, 13/11/12 (d.r.) (7:1616); cf. Dai Yingcong, "Qing State," pp. 41–42.

penalty is the fact that a harsh, new supplementary article on popular disturbances had been added to the penal code in 1745 or 1746, perhaps as a direct result of Qin Huitian's memorial. This new legislation provided for sentencing according to the "Supplementary Article on Scoundrels" for all "lawless elements in Zhili and the provinces" who "take advantage of local harvest failures to gather in bands to plunder, and disturb and harm the virtuous, or intimidate the senior officials," or who "plunder the villages or markets or make a commotion at the official chamber because relief or loans come slightly late, or gather a crowd and close the market or revile the authorities on account of private indignation."[111] The "make a commotion at the official chamber" criterion was arguably applicable in Gu's case, at least by analogy. Sentencing according to the "Supplementary Article on Scoundrels" meant "immediate" decapitation for the principal offender and provisional condemnation to strangling for accomplices. While an "immediate" decapitation could not be carried out until the mandatory review process had been completed, the person so sentenced had no chance of having his punishment commuted, unlike those whose sentences were qualified with the words "pending the assizes."[112] Another new article of 1746—the response to representations from a certain regional commander—empowered local officials to take with them troops and militiamen carrying firearms when going to the arrest of armed demonstrators who were offering resistance. The legislators made clear that this did not entitle such forces to open fire on unarmed crowds, even if the latter were offering resistance.[113]

---

111. According to DQHDSL (1899 edition), the new article was created in QL 11 (approx. 1746). However, unlike the 1746 article mentioned immediately below, it is included in a list of recent legislative innovations in the 1746 version of Shen Zhiqi's edition of the penal code. That list was intended to include material added up to the end of QL 10 (approx. 1745). Some of the wording in the new article appears to draw on Qin's memorial. Compare DQHDSL, vol. 19, *juan* 788:1b (p. 15,064), Shen, *Da Qing lü jizhu* (1746 revised ed.), vol. 1, "Da Qing lü xuzuan tiaoli," *fanli* 1a, *juan* 4:2a (pp. 33, 129), and QSL/QL, *juan* 248:12a–b.

112. DQHDSL, vol. 19, *juan* 771:7a, 794:7b–8a; vol. 20, *juan* 825:8b (pp. 14,902, 15,120, 15,417); Sommer, *Sex, Law, and Society*, pp. 99, 327–28. On the terms "immediate" and "pending [or "after"] the assizes" (a loose translation), see Bodde and Morris, *Law in Imperial China*, pp. 92–93, 131–43.

113. DQHDSL, vol. 19, *juan* 771:10b (p. 14,903); QSL/QL, *juan* 277:11b–12b. The regional commander had suggested that if a crowd resisted, the responsible official

On 1 June 1748, the day of his denunciation of the *liuyang zisong* system's beneficiaries, Qianlong decided that riot leaders should pay a heavier penalty even than "immediate" (noncommutable) decapitation. A report from Anning of lawlessness elsewhere in Jiangsu had convinced him that the people had grown overbold and must be taught a lesson. The latest outrage, at Qingpu county in the province's southeast, had involved the destruction of property by a group trying to block the export of grain from the locality, and—more heinously—the throwing of stones at civil and military personnel who had come to quell the violence. A long, wide-ranging edict complained that the delay imposed by the review procedure for death sentences weakened their deterrent force. Qianlong therefore ordered the Board of Justice to design a harsher supplementary article that perhaps might be repealed once the populace was cowed. The Board proposed new legislation, to apply in cases in which officials were struck and the size of the crowd was at least "forty to fifty persons." The main refinements were exposure of the principal offender's head, "immediate" decapitation for any particularly close accomplices (and strangulation "pending the assizes" for the others), heavy beatings for those coerced into joining the affray, and the public posting, throughout the jurisdiction, of the principal offender's name, with an account of his offence. This felon's execution was to be more literally "immediate" than usual. It would take place on the basis of a swift investigation only. The governor and governor-general were to report the case to the emperor, but the time-honored procedure of review of formally pronounced death sentences by the highest judicial authorities would not be followed. Qianlong assented, and a supplementary article along these lines was added to the penal code.[114]

But were even these measures draconian enough? Four days after ordering that the new article be drafted, Qianlong sent down an edict

---

should be permitted to order the troops to open fire, with no questions asked if anyone was killed. The Board of Justice, however, argued that it was important to distinguish between armed and unarmed crowds. KYQRFDZ, vol. 2, p. 596 truncates the *Shilu* entry, omitting all reference to the Board's move to protect unarmed crowds.

114. QSL/QL, *juan* 314:12b–15a; cf. DQHDSL, vol. 19, *juan* 771:7b–8b (p. 14,902). The new article survived until 1788, when it was amalgamated with two similar articles (DQHDSL, *juan* 771:8b–9b).

ordering that "the real instigator and the chief offender" in the Suzhou demonstration be beaten to death immediately. Beating to death was not a statutory punishment and thus could not have been prescribed in a formal supplementary article. Five men were beaten to death in Jiangnan before the Board's recommendation was received: three in Suzhou, and two in Qingpu, the latter by Anning's decision.[115] These premature brutalities were to prove embarrassing. On 9 July, after the Board had reported, Qianlong issued a rationalizing edict to explain that while beating ringleaders to death in front of a mob would have a salutary effect, once a ringleader had been arrested and tried one could proceed only according to the penal code. Genuinely immediate decapitation was to be the thing in future.[116] This was all very well, but Qianlong's order that the central figures in the Suzhou incident be beaten to death had been issued sixteen days after the event and cannot have been received for at least another five.[117] There was no question of the purpose of that punishment being to quell the riot.

The treatment of the Jiangnan demonstration leaders formed part of a pattern, with the emperor demanding harsher sentences than would otherwise have been imposed. Without the benefit of the Board of Justice's deliberations, Anning had sentenced the more guilty Qingpu accomplices to penal servitude. This was a punishment that, in its most severe degree, would have lasted for three years only, unless imposed as a reduced death sentence, in which case it would have been for five. Ostensibly for reasons of practicality (what if the convicts fled their servitude?), Qianlong ordered on 9 July that both the Suzhou and the Qingpu accomplices should wear the cangue for the rest of their days. This was a sentence to lifelong discomfort and humiliation, restriction of movement, and, therefore, constraints in earning livelihood.[118] The

---

115. QSL/QL, *juan* 314:25b–26a, 315:5a–b, 316:19a–b.

116. Ibid., *juan* 316:19a–20a.

117. Cf. Fairbank and Teng, *Ch'ing Administration*, pp. 10 and 16. The order to beat the Suzhou ringleaders to death was given on 5 June; according to 1883 *Suzhou fuzhi* (*juan* 149:6b), it reached Suzhou on 22 June. While this part of the gazetteer account is not fully reliable, the dates of the edicts likewise suggest that the reports from Suzhou to Beijing were not being sent at the fastest rate.

118. QSL/QL, *juan* 315:5a–b, 316:20a; *Suzhou fuzhi, juan* 149:6b; Shen, *Da Qing lü jizhu* (1746 revised ed.), vol. 1, *juan* 1:1b (p. 2 of repaginated main text; cf. Bodde and Morris, *Law in Imperial China*, pp. 77–78).

emperor opined that Anning had been overlenient in two other cases. In mid-August he rebuked Aligun, the Shandong governor, for his charitable attitude towards persons who had resorted to plundering for food after a run of famine years. He insisted that the norm be merciless deterrent sentencing and subsequently transferred Aligun to a "simpler" post. Later, he expressed satisfaction with the work of Zhuntai, Aligun's successor, who ordered his subordinates to be more diligent in apprehending robbers, prepared new guidelines for "rewards and punishments," and reactivated the *baojia* mutual surveillance scheme.[119]

Meanwhile, faced with the problem of how best to quell the unrest in Suzhou, Qianlong had been concerned to prevent the governor-general, Yinjishan, from succeeding Jiang Shunjiao in the role of popular champion. As we saw in chapter 7, in replying to Qianlong's questionnaire about the cause of the inflation, Yinjishan showed a thoughtfulness about the ever-normal system that would have been consistent with a sympathetic attitude towards the poor. Sympathy was perhaps what the Suzhou poor expected of him.[120] In early June, Qianlong received reports of a ditty circulating in the streets of Suzhou that showed a certain ethnic open-mindedness: Anning was implicitly likened to the Tang-dynasty foreign troublemaker An Lushan (a military governor turned rebel), Yinjishan to a Buddha whose arrival in Suzhou would put things right. Yinjishan was indeed Anning's superior, but Qianlong's response, conveyed in a series of three edicts, made clear that it was Anning's line, perceived as harsh in Suzhou, that was to prevail. Yinjishan was to go to Suzhou. He was to work with Anning to conclude the criminal proceedings against the leading demonstrators and subdue the city. To guard against the risk that Yinjishan would court popularity by being lenient, the emperor instructed Anning to report on his superior's performance. Consistent with this repressive approach, Qianlong reflected that it might be sensible, as a

---

119. QSL/QL, *juan* 316:20a, 315:5b, 319:9a–10b, 325:41b, 329:66a. For 1747 examples of Qianlong insisting on harsher sentencing than was proposed, see KYQRFDZ, pp. 564–65, 567–69.

120. Cf. the image of Yinjishan perpetuated by Fang Chao-ying, who claims that "The people of Kiangsu [Jiangsu] whom he ruled, intermittently for some twenty years, loved him for his justice and his friendliness." See Fang's biography of Yinjishan in *Eminent Chinese*, ed. Hummel, 2:921.

long-term precaution, to add a Manchu garrison to the Green Standards (Chinese) forces stationed in the city.[121]

It is easy to see the emperor's point of view. Historians of "high Qing" China usually do. Weighing with, or on, him in the summer and early autumn of 1748 were putative indications of a widespread, growing trend of "savagery and violence," signs of tension between the conquered and their Manchu masters, suspicion of an overweening, manipulative Chinese populace, frustration at a military adventure that was going badly and the inflation that it may have sharpened, grief at his empress's untimely death, worry about lax officials, and concern lest a high-ranking Manchu like Yinjishan attempt to curry favor not only with the Chinese elite but also with the populace.[122] To recognize that his harshness was arguably more a sign of weakness than of strength is still to privilege the emperor as an object of consideration. It is time to shift the focus to his actions.

In a study of the political ideology of the three high Qing emperors, Gao Xiang presents statistics for the number of convicts whose death sentences were confirmed at the annual autumn assizes in the first twenty-four years of Qianlong's reign. He shows that during 1736–47, a total of 2,316 prisoners (193 per year on average) had their names checked for death by strangling or decapitation. During 1748–59, by contrast, 4,302 prisoners (358.5 per year) suffered the same misfortune. There were seven general reprieves (one-year postponements of death-sentence confirmation) in the first period, but only four, of which two were partial, in the second. Even so, the average number of confirmed death sentences per year of normal procedure was greater in the second period than in the first (537.75 compared with 463.2).

Gao suggests, furthermore, that in the second period (1748–59), Qianlong was increasingly inclined to order summary or even secret executions for what he chose to view as serious affronts against the state's security or authority. Gao cites the following examples. In 1748, the emperor ordered the Fujian-Zhejiang governor-general to have four

---

121. QSL/QL, *juan* 314:31a–35a.

122. For further examples of Qianlong's concern about the savage, violent, manipulative populace, see QSL/QL, *juan* 314:13b, 316:19b. On the death of the Xiaoxian empress (April 1748) and Qianlong's displeasure at Yinjishan's perceived tendency to identify with the Chinese elite, see Kutcher, "Death of the Xiaoxian Empress," pp. 710–11, 719–20.

Christian missionaries secretly killed in prison and report that they had died of illness. In separate incidents in 1752 and 1753, without adducing any statute or article of the penal code, he ordered summary decapitation for those recently captured would-be rebels who were deemed especially guilty on the basis of immediate proceedings. As Kuhn has shown, summary decapitation also befell the magistrate who was blamed for letting the 1752 "conspiracy" develop in his jurisdiction. Finally, in 1755, faced with a reported disturbance over the height of a building in a *huiguan* (native place association) headquarters, Qianlong ordered the summary beating to death of a few ringleaders of a protest action. The commotion had grown out of anger that the *huiguan* leadership had accepted money from the local authorities to reduce the building's height without consulting the ordinary members, who had all contributed to the construction costs.[123] Qianlong's response was of a piece with his treatment of the Suzhou demonstration leaders in 1748.

His approach to popular disorder during 1746–48 thus seems to have foreshadowed a trend of heightened imperial violence, of both sanctioned and unsanctioned kinds, culminating in genocide to clinch the subjugation of the Zunghars in 1757.[124] As for the domestic realm, Gao opines that after Qianlong abandoned his early experiments with playing the lenient emperor, he grew even harsher than Yongzheng. Which was in fact the harsher may be difficult to say, and perhaps not important. Wu Renshu suggests that the Yongzheng and Qianlong periods should be bracketed together as a time when severity prevailed in the handling of food riots, in contrast with the late Ming and the Kangxi eras, when there was more tendency to try to "pacify" the rioters without resorting to suppression. In Yongzheng's time, supplementary articles providing for "immediate" (not summary) decapitation for the leaders of various types of popular protest (and heavy beatings for coerced followers) were added to the penal code. Suzuki Hidemitsu lists cases of Yongzheng approving or even ordering sum-

---

123. Gao Xiang, *Kang Yong Qian*, pp. 300–2; Kuhn, *Soulstealers*, p. 63; Huang Tinggui, QL 20/3/12, repr. GZD/QL, vol. 10, pp. 883–85. The correct reference for Gao's 1752 material is QSL/QL, *juan* 413:20a, not *juan* 412 as stated in his footnote. For the 1753 edict, see QSL/QL, *juan* 432:14b–16a.

124. Perdue, *China Marches West*, pp. 283–87; cf. Lewis, *Sanctioned Violence in Early China*.

mary beatings to death for various offences (although not leadership of a food riot).[125] With the new article of 1748, Qianlong took Yong-zheng's harshness a step farther, enlarging the scope of summary justice in a bureaucracy in which, granted certain circumstances, extrajudicial, fatal beatings were already tolerated. In 1748, indeed, the righteous anger of the little folk who wanted something done about the price of grain was crushed beneath Qianlong's indignant lawlessness even while a more draconian law was being drafted.

---

125. Gao Xiang, *Kang Yong Qian*, p. 302; Wu Renshu, "Chengshi liangshi baodong," p. 348; DQHDSL, vol. 19, *juan* 771:7a–b (p. 14,902); Suzuki, "Jōhei kō," pp. 150–53, 156 (but cf. p. 155 for an example of the beating to death of ringleaders of collective raiding for food in the supposedly lenient Kangxi era).

CONCLUSION

Political Economy or

Political Process?

Let me start with some conclusions about mid-eighteenth-century Sino-Manchu ideas of political economy, as reflected in discussions about popular subsistence policy. At the most general level, my findings endorse those of earlier studies.[1] Although many administrators often thought in simple, literal ways about popular subsistence problems and their management, there was also a good deal of consciousness of the workings of market forces in the mid-Qing bureaucracy. This bureaucracy was rather highly numerate, in the sense that the importance of statistical data was well understood. It is true that mid-Qing officialdom lacked techniques of statistical analysis, just as it had a limited range of economic insights available to guide its discussions. However, mid-Qing officials operated in a world that knew not modern social science. Perhaps, granted that constraint, ability to view large numbers in relative terms and apply basic economic concepts logically may be accepted as a mark of policy discussion quality. A number of senior eighteenth-century Chinese and Manchu officials (or ghost-writers) deserve posthumous appreciation for their intelligent, indeed sophisticated, discourse on the likely economic outcomes of specific governmental choices.

In chapter 3, I argued that, by drawing together fragmentary statements from a number of policy discussion documents, we can build a

---

1. See, e.g., Will, "Discussions about the Market-Place," pp. 326–29 and refs. there cited.

coherent model of how, in the minds of market-conscious Qing officials, the eighteenth-century Chinese grain market would have operated without state intervention. I suggested that, to understand the issues as such officials saw them, we should posit two planes: a horizontal (spatial) plane, in which consuming communities competed for the available supplies of grain, and a vertical (temporal) plane, in which the central question was the timing of the release of private stocks that were intended for the local market. On the horizontal plane, a community experiencing shortage could compete successfully for commercial deliveries to the extent, first, that its current prices were higher than those that merchants could obtain elsewhere, and, second, that the local people had enough purchasing power to project an image of effective demand. I showed that one Chinese official (Fang Bao) argued rather explicitly that the relative pull of the different market prices current at prospective destinations ensured that grain flowed in a rational sequence to the areas of greatest need. It followed that the normal operation of the profit motive could do much, on the horizontal plane, to distribute surplus stocks to the communities that really needed them.

On the vertical plane, the focus was on hoarded stocks. Here, the market-conscious argument was that the selfish intentions of landlord and merchant hoarders worked in the best interests of the communities to whom they planned to sell their grain. By withholding it from the market until prices peaked in the *soudure* period, they ensured that there would be supplies available at that hungry time. They also did what anxious consumers were not allowed to do: they safeguarded their target community's reserves against would-be exporters. In urban contexts, behavior that seemed typical of speculative hoarders could be viewed instead as careful management of the available stocks to protect consumers from severe price fluctuations. Few if any authors shared Adam Smith's confidence that the most skilful speculators timed their release of stocks so well as to give the client community the best possible outcome from deficient harvests. To the contrary, the majority opinion was that it was advisable for local authorities to encourage speculators to sell earlier than they might otherwise have done. However, one Manchu official (Kaerjishan) suggested that merchant hoards that were accumulated in years of plenty provided valuable insurance against future famine. To him, presumably, it was acceptable if some reserves were not sold in the *soudure* period but carried forward into the next agricultural year.

This reconstructed model, as I left it in chapter 3, was marred by one unresolved tension and two uncertainties, of which one concerned exactly when hoarders would sell if there were no official pressure. The unresolved tension was between the claims of the vertical and horizontal modes of distribution. It would have been difficult even for the most market-conscious mid-eighteenth-century officials to construct a theory that the market spontaneously ensured the best possible allocation of supplies between communities on whose behalf reserves were hoarded, and communities elsewhere that depended on commercial imports. Discussion of this problem seems to have been confined to positing a second mechanism by which consumer interests in exporting communities were supposedly protected, that is, the deterrent function of high local cost-prices. Here was a second constraint on belief in market forces in mid-eighteenth-century China.

On the second uncertainty identified in chapter 3 there is now more to say. The question, which referred to the horizontal mode of distribution, was as follows. How much trust could be placed in combinations of high prices and existing levels of purchasing power to draw grain into severely dearth-stricken communities? More precisely, could such combinations be trusted to draw in enough supplies to reduce local prices to levels at which the majority of famine victims could afford the grain they needed? Although the common-sense answer was "no," different levels of trust were shown by different participants in the ever-normal granaries debate. The "vote" of the eighteenth-century bureaucracy as a whole would have been for little trust: the state would always have to supplement the market by maintaining stockpiles of grain to sell, lend, or give, as necessary, to poor consumers. This conventional position was upheld by various provincial chiefs in an unbroken relay throughout the ever-normal granaries debate. It survived the most radical challenges of that debate and re-emerged as bureaucratic orthodoxy in the early 1750s. But what were the most radical challenges? What was the highest level of trust in market forces evinced by any radical opponent of state stockpiling during 1738–53?

Broadly speaking, I accept Will's point (which is intended to apply to the horizontal plane) that the highest trust in market forces in the eighteenth-century Sino-Manchu bureaucracy stopped short of a belief that the state could stand back and do nothing in the face of serious subsistence crises. The radicals who wanted precautionary state stockpiling minimized (or ended) pressed for the creation of what Will calls "a government-supported artificial market" in dearth-stricken areas through the issuing of doles of silver as a substitute for grain.[2] Their most important contribution was to supply the rudiments of a theoretical foundation for this practice, which was already used as an expedient before they wrote. As shown in chapter 5, Li Qingzhi and Wu Wei argued that merchants would respond to the perception that ordinary people had the money to buy grain by "com[ing] running" to restock disaster-stricken markets. Fang Bao's failure to mention purchasing power in his otherwise sophisticated treatment of the functioning of price incentives had been a regrettable omission. While neither Li nor Wu offered a synthesis or used abstract language, they unintentionally pointed the way to a more complete theoretical understanding of the influences guiding merchant choices.

Li and Wu wrote in a context in which the question "state or merchant?" was being posed quite sharply. In the late 1730s and early 1740s, officials such as Yang Eryou, Anning, and Wu Wei himself were asking, occasionally in abstract terms, whether state precautionary stockpiling was as superior to merchant management as was commonly supposed. Against state stockpiling were allegations of malpractice (such as acquiring grain, through hapless surrogates, at less than market prices), the supposed inflationary impact of the annual buying process, and the image of state granaries as unnaturally concentrating resources that should have been dispersed. In favor of commercial management were the evident success of the grain trade in feeding major cities, the experience, commitment, and skill that merchants brought to their *métier*, and the perceived tendency of commerce to set grain flowing in a free and natural way. Unlike merchants, who were at liberty to respond to price signals appropriately, bureaucratic buyers operated under pressure. Their visibility and their predicament caused undesirable reactions. Brokers and speculators exploited their presence in the market; consumers and long-distance traders rushed to defend themselves against the threat that bureaucratic competition posed for them. All these responses tended to raise prices. The benefits of so-called stabilizing sales did not outweigh the harm of this inflation; to the contrary, official sales could exacerbate it. The state claimed to protect society from hoarders, but an impartial observer might have seen with

---

2. Ibid., p. 353.

difficulty wherein lay the difference between state granary and private hoard. Such, in brief, was the radical case against the ever-normal granaries; more moderate critics endorsed part of it.

The purpose of Sun Hao, Wu Wei, and, to a lesser extent, Li Qingzhi in creating arguments for issuing famine relief at least partly in silver was to persuade the court that there was an alternative to the granary system's evils. In other words, for Sun and Wu at least, the motivation was predominantly negative. Wu in particular was driven by an animus against the ever-normal system; he thus wrote rhetoric, not theory. His rhetoric, like Sun's and Li's more sober expositions, contained theoretically interesting ideas, but the ideas were not the point. The point, for all three, was to persuade the court to reduce the scale of stockpiling, whether by moderating rigid expectations (Sun and Li) or abolishing the ever-normal system altogether (Wu). An intentional shift from maintaining grain reserves to issuing monetary doles would have meant the adoption of more purely market-oriented relief policies. In Sun's eyes at least, it would also have signified a healthy transfer of responsibility from state to society, including disaster victims.

Much sense was written on both sides of the ever-normal granaries debate, and still more in the middle. My purpose is not to adjudicate—although, far from admiring the granaries' opponents, I suspect that those who sought to protect the ever-normal system by advocating moderate, market-sensitive reforms were probably the most in tune with mid-eighteenth-century Chinese realities. It is one thing to appreciate the economic insights of market-conscious Qing officials, quite another to hail them as proto-antisocialists, as if the postcommunist world had all the answers. Assessment ought to take a different tack. For an intellectual historian, the public-policy discussions of mid-Qing officials provide a rich hunting ground, but at some point one must acknowledge limitations. Individuals of varying persuasions argued intelligently within the constraints of the memorial format, and yet, when one considers the debate's main outlines, the image it conveys is not a wholly favorable one. All in all, the events of 1738–53 do not reflect especially well on the mid-Qing governmental apparatus.

In my opinion, the tragicomedies recounted in this book should not be blamed primarily on intellectual failures. Although it may be sad that the Sino-Manchu potential for what we call social science, or even political economy, did not produce an Eastern Adam Smith, officials who presented cogently argued cases to the throne were contributing appropriately in their context. What more could have been asked of them? It does not necessarily follow, from the constraints they faced as servants of a bureaucratic state, that the root problem lay in institutional deficiencies. Although the amount of power that Qianlong enjoyed was surely dysfunctional in the events narrated here, there was little fundamentally unsound about the structure of the mid-Qing governmental system. To the contrary, in comparative perspective, that system offered rather good conditions for careful arguments to have a real chance of influencing policy. There was no ban on challenging conventional administrative wisdom or on putting forward radical ideas. Nor did the institutionalized Confucianism of the late imperial state act as a straitjacket. One of the most refreshing aspects of the economic discourse studied in this book is its relative autonomy from the Confucian scriptural tradition.[3] While freedom of expression was certainly not absolute in the mid-Qing governing elite, the eighteenth-century Sino-Manchu state had its own provision for serious and stimulating policy discussion that sometimes touched on fundamental issues.

Despite the policy failures and betrayals recounted in this book, we may remain confident both of the basic validity of the mid-Qing governmental system and of the intelligence of many senior officials. In what follows, I seek to understand the undistinguished decision-making that characterized Qianlong's role in the granaries debate in terms of political factors. More specifically, the themes will be imperial ambition and naivety, competing government priorities, the role of interest groups, and a possible backlash against Chinese-style paternalism in certain Manchu quarters. The first of these themes demands immediate

---

3. My findings qualify Benjamin Elman's remarks about "the centrality of [Confucian] classical studies . . . for political discourse in imperial China." It is true that in premodern China, government action in support of popular subsistence was ideologically premised on the Confucian doctrine of kingly responsibility for popular well-being. It is also true that the Confucian scriptural and historical traditions provided resources from which practicing political economists could draw rhetorical support. However, in the early Qianlong period, the core arguments about market function and how state involvement could affect it were technical and economic, not Confucian. Their scholar-official authors were not "forced to articulate their political views through the controlled medium of state ritual, classical sanction, and historical precedent," nor did they necessarily bother with "the language of the Classics or the Dynastic Histories." Cf. Elman, *Classicism*, p. 74.

comment. Qianlong's wilfulness has emerged throughout this study as a strong negative influence on policy. Ultimately, the responsibility for what went wrong was his. He was the principal decision maker, and he was capable of overruling his advisors. His role must and will be stressed—but in due course. It is important to narrow the focus gradually. Otherwise, we risk a trite conclusion (the obvious dangers inherent in ultimately autocratic political systems). We have indeed watched Qianlong act in ways that tended to frustrate the potential for wise governance held by mid-Qing institutions and procedures. My aim is not to emphasize this observation but to put it in context.

It may be objected that the best-known decision of the whole debate, that is, the 1748–49 decision to revert, in principle, to the so-called "Yongzheng" targets, was, on the contrary, a wise and prudent one. The attempt, begun in 1738, to double granary reserves by selling *jiansheng* titles had been an understandable mistake by a well-meaning but inexperienced young ruler. The reduction in the nationwide storage target during 1743–44 had been insufficient to correct this excess. An appropriate balance between state and merchant participation in managing the national grain surplus was achieved only through further cuts in 1749. In 1738–43, the state had sought too much control; in 1748–49, it properly curtailed its ambitions.[4] My position, by contrast, is that if we focus exclusively on the content of decisions, we risk being overinfluenced by our own, contemporary, political opinions in assessing their wisdom. Of course, content matters greatly, and outcomes matter even more. However, we cannot fully understand, still less evaluate, decisions unless we attend to process, asking why and how their makers reached them. To probe the politics behind decisions on state stockpiling whose wisdom was expounded at great length is to refuse to take the Qianlong court on its own terms. With the help of edict-drafters, Qianlong posed as paragon. It is a historian's task to show wherein his governance was ordinary, that is, not wholly guided by professed ideals, cogent reasoning, or endorsed principles of action.

---

4. To judge by his evaluation of the early Qianlong shifts in ever-normal storage policy (*Shiba shiji Zhongguo*, pp. 157–67), Gao Wangling would endorse this objection. Gao's evaluation is stimulating and provocative, but it lacks the depth that comes from systematically attempting to penetrate the rhetoric of edicts and the *Shilu* abstracts of memorials.

Let us briefly suppose—against my own views, and purely for the sake of argument—that minimal direct state participation in the grain trade was the objectively "right" answer for mid-eighteenth century China. Let us both identify the officials who urged the most radical disengagement from state stockpiling, and review the moments when the central government made, or seemed poised to make, the most significant "progress" towards disengagement. Do we see straightforward triumphs of "enlightened" argument, or is the picture murky? In showing that the latter is the case, we begin with the junior censors and others who attacked the granaries in the early years of the debate (1739–42). As discussed in chapter 4, some of these critics had a common Lower Yangzi background and are likely to have known each other. Wu Wei, the earliest and most strident radical, had connections with Huizhou, famed as a place of origin of influential merchants. Although conspiracy to represent a Yangzi Valley grain trade lobby cannot be proved, these censors wrote in such a way as to defend the interests of grain merchants, whose market share was threatened by moves to expand state holdings. As shown in chapter 5, a 1742 memorial by Wu Wei's fellow Hangzhou resident and *tongnian jinshi*, Sun Hao, led to the central government directive that provincial administrations propose lower, more realistic storage targets than the chimerical ones of 1738–39.[5] Sensible as this decision was, it may have been precipitated by vicarious pressure from a grain trade lobby.

When, in 1743, the grand secretaries and Nine Ministries Assembly recommended a moratorium on buying for the granaries, the suggestion they were following was from another junior censor, Wei Tingpu. Two years later, Wei and Sun advocated similar amendments to Qianlong's plans for universal land and labor-service tax remission; on that occasion, both censors wrote from a propertied class perspective, although the type of property was land, not merchant capital. Wei was not a native of the Lower Yangzi region, but he was a *tongnian jinshi* of Xu Yisheng, one of the Zhejiang antigranary radicals. He may have been part of a coterie, including Xu and Sun, that discussed policy issues and tended to agree about them. Meanwhile, censors of differing

---

5. *Tongnian jinshi* were persons who passed the metropolitan examination in the same year (1730, in Sun's and Wu's case). The bond thus formed was deemed important in traditional Chinese society.

persuasions had led the emperor in these early years of the debate. Even the original idea of doubling reserves had been a censor's. By 1747, when Ou Kanshan wrote the memorial that presaged the great 1748 review of ever-normal policy, Qianlong may have learned to use representations from officialdom to pursue agendas of his own. At the beginning of his reign, however, he seems to have been both more dependent and less firm. He was persuaded to adopt radical policy lines (and indeed *volte-faces*) but did not necessarily uphold them when the view from practical provincial government began to reach him.[6]

Despite appearances, the 48-million-*shi* nationwide target that resulted from the call for lower storage targets did not represent a simple cut. The available statistics show that significantly reduced targets were typically adopted for those provinces that reported in 1743. However, a new shift of policy in 1744 gave other provinces the opportunity to gain approval for targets that were not greatly reduced from (or even higher than) the ambitious ones of 1738–39. The policy change, suggested by Anning, involved reviving the campaign to sell *jiansheng* titles for grain as a potential substitute for restocking the granaries through purchase. This notion had not originated with Anning but with two of his seniors in the bureaucracy of the Liang-Jiang region. It probably reflected the interest of officialdom in minimizing its commitment to the onerous and problematic annual buying process. There is reason to suspect that, from 1744, the leadership of one province was scheming to become officially expected to refill its granaries entirely by selling *jiansheng* titles. Each of the high targets set in 1744 may reflect one of three lines of thinking: genuine belief that a high target was needed, expectation that proposing a high target would be seen as bespeaking devotion to the people, and hope that the subtarget for grain acquired through title sales could be made gradually to supplant that for grain acquired by purchase.[7]

There was, therefore, some arbitrariness about the targets set in 1744, and this requires comment. The interest in precise quantification that pervades much of the documentary record of high Qing government was the product of a long tradition that Alfred Crosby, for example,

---

6. See chaps. 5, 6, and 8 above; Zhu and Xie, comps., *Ming Qing jinshi*, vol. 3, p. 2,691.
7. See chap. 6 above.

could have done more to recognize.[8] The criteria that provincial chiefs were told to use in drawing up new county-level storage targets were sensible: county size, population density, distance from navigable waterways. We know, from extant schedules mainly in routine memorials, that these criteria were applied systematically and thoughtfully at provincial level (sometimes with adjustments to suit regional conditions). Similar criteria had been used in 1738–39. To be sure, the bureaucracy could possibly have done still better. Trade-flow data culled from brokers' records could have been used to estimate the average marketed grain surplus; such estimates might have been useful in assessing proposed targets not solely in relation to potential need for granary reserves, but also in terms of their compatibility with flourishing commercial distribution. The sudden policy change of 1744 highlights the vulnerability of the Qing civil service's capacity for rational quantitative planning. Political intervention resulted in an inconsistent set of targets reflecting such extrinsic factors as the date of their submission. This arbitrariness may have decreased confidence that quantitative work was practically worthwhile. This would have been unfortunate, as more attention to available statistics might have offered some protection against intuitive, capricious, or self-interested judgments that existing storage levels were too high and caused inflation.

In 1745, the Board of Revenue effectively ordered that local administrations rely entirely on *jiansheng* title sales to restock their granaries that year. No grain was to be bought. Such a policy, if continued for a few years, would have eliminated the ever-normal system altogether. If the suspicions of a certain censor were correct, the motive was to save funds for the military—perhaps for a campaign west of Sichuan. Shortly after launching this campaign, Qianlong had declared a universal one-year suspension of the government's main source of revenue, the land and labor-service tax. The moment was doubly inauspicious: not even his grandfather had been so munificent at a time when central government reserves were so low. The attempt to wrest compensatory savings from the ever-normal system was probably pushed by the

---

8. Compare the tokenism of the references to China in Crosby, *Measure of Reality*, pp. 230–31 with, for example, the evidence of precocious (fourth century B.C.) Chinese awareness of the possibility of government statistics reflected in Herforth, trans., "*Guoyu*," pp. 127–28.

Board of Revenue. Not only had the Board to meet new funding challenges; the latest experiment with selling titles for grain would have reduced its income. Qianlong frustrated the Board's move by allowing certain governors to disregard its orders. However, he also capitulated to the Board by restoring its power to sell the titles for silver. This seems to have sufficed to save the granaries. The Board now had no option but to lift the pressure to desist from buying.[9]

By 1748, when ever-normal policy was systematically reviewed, enough data may have been available for close observers to notice that the relationship between ever-normal storage levels and Suzhou rice prices (at least) was probably inverse. However, the bureaucracy lacked the techniques to establish this clearly. It is not surprising that the court-led discussions that took place in 1748 were premised on the opposite assumption. It was convenient that they should be. There was another war to fight in the far west of Sichuan, and 1748 was the last of the three years over which the universal tax remission had been spread. Protection of supplies to feed the troops may have contributed to the high grain prices that led to popular unrest in distant, downstream Suzhou. Consulted about the cause of the widespread inflation, most provincial chiefs expressed at least some concern about the impact of the ever-normal system. Few, however, advocated reduction of the storage targets, and fewer still suggested drastic cuts. There were, however, some radical critiques of the granary system, of which the most strident were by Manchus. Celeng objected to busybody government in general; Shulu thought that Jiangnan folk were too "presumptuous" in their expectations of relief, and that less should be done for them; Zhuntai considered private trade so well-developed in the Yangzi Valley that the state need keep only token reserves in that vast region.[10]

In one way, Zhuntai's view was moderate compared with Qianlong's decision. Zhuntai favored drastic stockpile reduction only in those parts of the realm, and indeed of the Yangzi Valley, where well-developed trade was a conspicuous reality. Qianlong's demand, in August 1748, was for universal reinstatement of the supposed Kangxi and Yongzheng targets. The reference to the low targets of the Kangxi

9. Chap. 6 above.
10. See above, chaps. 6 (figs. 1 and 2), 7, and 8.

period presumably signalled that radical reduction was to be considered. The committee that recommended the new targets in January 1749 obtained a compromise: reversion to the Yongzheng targets would be the norm, and the exceptions would allow for larger stockpiles than in the Yongzheng period. However, a close reading of the committee's report suggests that it was balancing two goals: preservation of the ever-normal system and the creation of savings. While it would be too cynical to suggest that the sole purpose of cutting the storage targets was to help finance the Jinchuan campaign, it would have been strange if such a use for the newly redundant granary restocking funds did not occur to the committee. Because the campaign ended in March 1749, there is no point in seeking evidence that monies from the granaries were applied to the war effort. If my reading of the sources is correct, however, the cutting of the ever-normal storage targets in 1748–49 was a reflection not only of economic policy concerns, but also of wartime fiscality.[11]

By 1752, the evidence for an inverse correlation between granary storage levels and Suzhou rice prices should have been clearer, even to contemporaries. However, when prices peaked during that year, Qianlong responded by suggesting that grain need not be bought, as long as granaries had 30 to 40 percent of their target holdings. This striking (if fiscally shrewd) departure fell chronologically between two further radical proposals, both from persons close to the imperial house, that the granary system be cut yet again. In the summer of 1749, Yaerhashan both advocated abolition of key features of the ever-normal system, such as county granaries and stabilizing sales, and raised the specter of the popular "presumptuousness" that, he suggested, was fostered by the upkeep of large welfare stockpiles of grain. For Yaerhashan, a move against the ever-normal system would be, in part, an attack on "presumptuousness." We may discern a parallel with the attitudes and actions of his Manchu sovereign, whose cuts to welfare institutions were associated both with negative stereotyping of famine refugees and demonstration leaders, and with a growing tendency, from 1746, to meet "presumptuous" and "perverse" conduct with intensified judicial harshness.[12]

---

11. Chap. 8 above.
12. Chap. 9 above.

The second antigranary memorial, by Gao Bin, was from 1752. It proposed that the state withdraw substantially from precautionary storage in those Yangzi Valley and north China jurisdictions in which commerce could be trusted to distribute grain supplies effectively. To judge from an earlier memorial, Gao may have had an abstract notion of the power of the profit motive to draw supplies to areas that needed them, even in north China. Thus his radical proposal may have been theoretically informed. It would be hard to say the same of the 1753 decision to abolish Beijing's banner grain bureaus. What seems to have removed the bureaus' *raison d'être* was the decision to stagger the issues of the bannermen's stipendiary grain. By smoothing the flow of grain onto the Beijing market, the state reduced its previous provocations to speculative behavior. This much was understood. However, the decision to stagger the stipend issues was almost accidental. The Tongzhou granaries were being cleared by issuing two years' worth of stipend payments all at once. It was necessary to do something to counteract the extraordinary flow of grain onto the Beijing-Tongzhou market.[13]

The stories that have been told in this book reflect more complex political processes than are suggested by the word "autocracy"—or even by the term "monarchical-conciliar form of government" that Bartlett posits for the Qianlong reign.[14] At least during the ever-normal granaries debate, many others besides Qianlong and his grand councillors influenced public-policy decision-making. The role of junior censors is especially interesting. Study of the various contributors and reflection on their motives is essential if we are to gain a realistic understanding of economic policy formation in Qing China. Policy revisions were not simple translations into practice of the rather sophisticated economic insights that undoubtedly existed in the Qing bureaucracy. To the contrary, pressure to reduce the state's commitment to stockpiling was maintained despite growing *prima facie* evidence that the assumption used to justify this pressure was untrue. The scaling down of state welfare provision during 1742–52 resulted from a range of influences and considerations. At different times, these included: the need to retreat from a chimerical expansionary program; the need to fund a

---

13. Chap. 9 above.
14. Bartlett, *Monarchs and Ministers*, p. 199.

costly military campaign at a time when normal state income had been voluntarily reduced; a shift in imperial priorities from "nourishing the people" to state security and foreign and colonial policy; overt suspicion, in some Manchu quarters, that the conquered populace was being spoiled; and, very possibly, indirect and covert pressure from a grain trade lobby. Important stages in the scaling down appear to have reflected complex tussles between competing policy ideas and bureaucratic interests. The Board of Revenue could find ways of defending fiscal interests, while astute provincial governors could scheme for the replacement of the annual-purchase system with less taxing means for granary restocking. Arguably, the most impressive players were those provincial chiefs who successfully negotiated restraints on the more radical moves against the granary system. Whether right or wrong in terms of economic theory, they were defending an institution that experience and "common sense" taught them to think essential for the people's well-being.

We come, finally, to the role and character of Qianlong—a "puzzle" and "enigma" in Woodside's words, inseparable from the issue of Qing dynastic decline.[15] Qianlong had his successes in his six decades of power. As an imperialist ruler, the butcher of the Zunghars can hardly be called amiable, but, as Crossley has shown, he grew adept at manipulating constructs of ethnocultural identity to facilitate control of his expanding, far-flung empire.[16] Kuhn, in his study of the 1768 "soulstealing" scare, paints a more troubling picture of an obsessively suspicious monarch who needed careful handling to make him end a disgraceful witch-hunt in which he had been "chief prosecutor, from first to last."[17] At the time, Qianlong was in his late fifties and thus lacked the excuse of senility. It is impossible to think Qianlong an able ruler after reading *Soulstealers*—even taking into account Kuhn's suggestion that the inner content of the campaign to track down sorcerers was Qianlong's concern with bureaucratic discipline (in other words, that the campaign was functional for an emperor who needed opportunities to harangue, if not chastise, his senior territorial officials for the perennial failings of which he accused

---

15. Woodside, "The Ch'ien-lung Reign," p. 231.
16. Crossley, *Translucent Mirror*, pp. 221–22 and chap. 6, esp. pp. 312, 320–27.
17. Kuhn, *Soulstealers*, pp. 173–81 (the quotation is from p. 173).

them).[18] Norman Kutcher has suggested that the evolution of what he calls the "political campaign strategy" (use of "campaigns" to reassert monarchical power over the bureaucracy) can be traced back to 1748. In that year, Qianlong was outraged by the "disrespect" shown by officials, Chinese and, worse, Manchu, who shaved their heads as usual during the hundred days of state mourning for his beloved empress. Not only did the flood of reports of offenders create an embarrassing dilemma, given that death sentences had been passed on the first shavers to reach the court's attention; the deluge was also profoundly disillusioning for Qianlong. If Kutcher is right, Qianlong was learning for the first time that his officials did not feel deep personal loyalty to him. It was the cynicism that this discovery engendered, together with new realizations "about the limitations of his power," that increasingly inclined him towards "the political campaign, based . . . on a model of coercion and arbitrary power."[19]

The idea that midcentury saw a transition in Qianlong's style of governance is found also in Gao Xiang's work. Gao focuses on the polarity between *kuan* (leniency) and *yan* (severity), identifying 1741, 1748, and 1751 as landmarks in Qianlong's trajectory from embracing leniency to accepting the need for harshness. Gao picks these years because of episodes that he takes as especially strong provocations to a hardening of the imperial heart (corruption scandals in 1741, personal tragedy and military frustration in 1748, unacceptable criticism aimed directly at the throne in the "bogus memorial case" of 1751).[20] Key aspects of the new trend, in Gao's view, were an insistence on absolutism as Qianlong broke free of the ascendancy of E'ertai, Zhang Tingyu, and their protégés; stricter control of the bureaucracy; and a tendency towards severity in carrying out the law.[21] It is true that Gao views the emerging relationship between Qianlong and influential grand councillors such as Fuheng from a different perspective from Bartlett (and

---

18. Ibid., pp. 220–22. Kuhn carefully notes (p. 221) that there is no positive evidence that Qianlong was consciously using the antisorcery campaign "to whip his bureaucracy into line."

19. Kutcher, "Death of the Xiaoxian Empress," pp. 709–18, 722–23 (the quotations in the last sentence are from p. 723).

20. Gao, *Kang Yong Qian*, pp. 289–91. On the "bogus memorial case" (Kuhn's translation), see Kuhn, *Soulstealers*, pp. 60–62.

21. Gao, *Kang Yong Qian*, pp. 291 ff., 296 ff., and 299 ff.

the present author). However, the idea that Qianlong showed a growing ideological commitment to autocracy in these years is compatible with Crossley's exposition of his claims to semimystical, transcultural centrality as ruler of a multiracial empire. Also consistent with the suggestion of a harsher, more assertive Qianlong from about 1750 is the fact that this emperor's aspirations to martial achievement were first glimpsed in the late 1740s.[22]

The stories told in this book support the notion that 1748 and the following years were a watershed in the political history of Qianlong's reign. The decline of active imperial interest in boosting state preparedness for famine, the subordination of famine relief objectives to fiscal and military priorities, decreased commitment of governmental effort and resources to solving popular subsistence difficulties, a tougher stance towards food rioters and demonstration leaders—all these fill out the picture of a relative shift from ostentatious pursuit of "benevolence" to a disciplinarian, militaristic ethos more in keeping with Manchu tradition. Assessment of these developments will inevitably reflect the historian's own political values and opinions. As argued above, however, it may be easier to transcend our own leanings to left or right if we focus on outcomes where possible, but in any case on process: the ways in which decisions were reached and the real reasons underlying those decisions.

This book has focused on decision-making process regarding state intervention in the grain trade throughout the period 1738–52. A key implication of its findings is that, whatever the scope and nature of the midcentury shift, the continuities are just as worthy of attention. It had, after all, been the supposedly "lenient" young Qianlong who, in November 1735, inaugurated the proceedings that, according to Crossley, changed Yongzheng's pardon of a poor and bookish would-be rebel called Zeng Jing to the ultimate judicial cruelty, death by slicing.[23] Qianlong's propensity for willful self-entrapment in politically embarrassing predicaments was new neither with the antisorcery campaign of 1768 nor with the prosecution of "disrespectful" head-shavers

----

22. Ibid., pp. 295–96 (cf. Bartlett, *Monarchs and Ministers*, pp. 269–78); Crossley, *Translucent Mirror*, p. 221 and chap. 5, esp. pp. 270–71; Dai Yi, *Qianlong di*, p. 168; cf. Waley-Cohen, "Commemorating War," pp. 869–73 and passim.

23. Crossley, *Translucent Mirror*, pp. 253–59.

twenty years earlier. It was presaged in his adoption of Chang Lu's proposal for a major expansion of the ever-normal granary reserves (1738), and it was confirmed by his perversely thorough generosity to taxpayers in the early stages of a military campaign (1745). While the impracticality of the granary expansion project was revealed only gradually, the wild swings of policy during 1743–45 revealed the suggestibility and lack of firmness that were the flip-side of Qianlong's self-will. Bartlett reports that a consistent inspiration of her work on the institutional history of high Qing China has been the question "What had happened to the imperial power" by the reign of his successor.[24] That question is a good and important one, but we should supplement it with another. What happened to imperial *authority* while Qianlong was on the throne?

Qianlong as political person hid behind the persona created by his edict-writers, in a process that was functional for his mystique but misleading for the gullible historian. In this book, I have followed the convention of presenting edicts issued in his name as emanations of a collective personality whom, for convenience's sake, we call "Qianlong"; but I have also sought to identify an individual monarch using his prerogative through varying responses to advice from different quarters. Of course, we do not see a sage (a sage was not to be expected), but neither do we see a leader on a par with the Yongzheng the fiscal reformer (Yongzheng the reluctant militarist was unimpressive).[25] In the realm of civil governance, the young Qianlong did not establish strong credentials as one capable of harnessing the Sino-Manchu bureaucracy's considerable intellectual, moral, and professional resources. Could it have been inability to lead the bureaucracy that forced him into battle with it? And is it possible that analysis of political decline under Qianlong should start from the year of his accession?

---

24. Bartlett, *Monarchs and Ministers*, p. xi.
25. Perdue, *China Marches West*, pp. 240–55.

Appendix

APPENDIX

Chronology of the Granaries Debate

Late 1737 — Chang Lu's proposal that the ever-normal stockpiles be doubled through sale of *jiansheng* titles for grain.

Mar. 1738 — Provincial chiefs ordered to consider whether building extra reserves through *jiansheng* title sales would benefit their jurisdictions.

1738–39 — With "basic targets" totalling some 28 million *shi*, provincial chiefs propose additional contribution targets totalling some 32 million.

Ca. 1739–42 — Radical critiques of official buying and the ever-normal system by Wu Wei, Lu Zhuo, Bulantai, Xu Yisheng, Ji Huang, Yang Eryou.

Mar. 1741 — As concession to Board of Revenue, Qianlong restores the option of buying *jiansheng* titles through payment in silver at the Board.

Jun. 1742 — Grand Secretaries and Nine Ministries Assembly respond to memorial from Sun Hao by recommending lower provincial storage targets. Qianlong agrees.

1743 to ca. Mar. 1744 — At least ten provinces set new storage targets, most of which represent substantial cuts.

May 1743 — Perhaps responding to memorial by Wei Tingpu, Qianlong orders moratorium on: (1) selling *jiansheng* titles for granary contributions; (2) restocking through interprovincial purchase. Grand Secretaries and Nine Ministries Assembly recommend halt even to local buying (as well as in-kind title sales) until prices fall.

Qianlong assents, but declares one-year exemptions for the Jiangxi and Fujian cut-rate title-sale programs (responding to memorial by Li Qingfang).

Jun.–Nov. 1743   Qianlong authorizes careful local buying in several provinces, thereby declining to support hard-line interpretation of the moratorium. Sophisticated arguments for hard-line approach offered by Sun Hao, Wu Wei, Li Qingzhi.

Jan. 1744   Chen Hongmou and Yinjishan (1) advocate cut-price title sales as potential substitute for restocking through purchase; (2) mention possibility of saving granary restocking funds for military uses.

Apr. 1744   Invoking arguments developed by Anning, Qianlong revives title sales for grain, with reduced title-prices and as potential substitute for restocking through purchase. Sales for silver at Board of Revenue suspended. Board instructs provincial chiefs to set new contribution targets.

Ca. Apr.– Dec. 1744   New storage targets set for most provinces that had not finalized their targets earlier. These targets typically represented relatively minor cuts or even increases compared with the high-level targets.

Feb.–Mar. 1745   Qianlong deciding on a military campaign west of Sichuan.

Jul. 1745   Qianlong announces universal remission of the 1746 land tax; a later decision to spread the remission over 3 years will still mean no tax income in 1746 from several fiscally strategic provinces. By mid-July, signs of court awareness that the Sichuan campaign will be costly.

By mid-Aug. 1745   Board of Revenue issues orders against buying for the granaries this harvest season. Unexpended purchase funds to be reported for reallocation; only title sales to be used for granary restocking.

Sept.–Oct. 1745   Qianlong declines to uphold the ban on buying for the granaries when some provinces resist.

Nov. 1745	Qianlong re-opens title sales for silver at Board of Revenue, thereby ending the attempt to rely entirely on title sales for granary restocking.
Apr. 1747	Launch of the first Jinchuan campaign.
Nov. 1747	Qianlong orders circulation to the provinces of memorial by Ou Kanshan blaming high grain prices on granary restocking.
Jan. 1748	Qianlong orders provincial chiefs to submit explanations of the rising price of grain.
Ca. Feb. 1748–Jun. 1749	At least 27 provincial explanations of the rising grain prices submitted, of which about 15 arrived by Aug. 1748.
Spring–Early Summer, 1748	Intensifying crisis of high grain prices in Lower Yangzi cities.
Aug. 1748	Qianlong orders reversion to "the old targets of the Kangxi and Yongzheng periods."
Sept. 1748	Provincial chiefs ordered (1) to report their granary networks' old targets and current assets; (2) to permit buying only where needed to restock to the "old" target levels.
Oct. 1748	Qianlong orders deposit of redundant granary restocking funds in the provincial treasuries.
Jan. 1749	With final offensive planned for May–June, Qianlong expressing doubt about the continuity of funding for the Jinchuan war after mid-June.
30 Jan. 1749	*Ad hoc* committee recommends (1) provincial storage targets totalling 33.8 million *shi*; (2) loan recovery as the preferred means of restocking to the reset target levels; (3) sale of surplus grain; (4) toleration of subtarget holdings in 4 provinces; (5) report of redundant purchase funds to Board of Revenue for reallocation. Qianlong assents.
Feb.–Mar. 1749	Qianlong showing decreasing commitment to the Jinchuan war, which he had already decided to abort when it ended in Qing victory on 22 Mar.

May 1749	Grand Secretaries' report endorsing the reversion to the Yongzheng targets and its rationale.
1751–52	Peak in Suzhou grain prices coincides with trough in nationwide ever-normal storage levels; Gao Bin advocates termination of bulk-buying for the granaries.
Aug. 1752	Qianlong permits suspension of buying where stockpiles are at 30–40% of target level.
1753	The Hubei storage target is raised; end of the debate.

Reference Matter

Bibliography

Abe Takeo. *Shindai shi no kenkyū* (Studies in Qing history). Tokyo: Sōbunsha, 1971.

Anon. *Zhen'an shigao* (Draft directives from a relief casebook). 1746–47. Abridged and reprinted from ms. held by the Chinese Academy of Social Sciences in *Zhongguo huangzheng quanshu* (Complete collection of Chinese works on famine relief), ed. Li Wenhai and Xia Mingfang (Beijing: Beijing guji chubanshe, 2003–), vol. 2, part 2, pp. 103–74.

Atwell, William S. "Notes on Silver, Foreign Trade, and the Late Ming Economy." *Ch'ing-shih wen-t'i* 3, no. 8 (1977): 1–33.

Ban Gu et al. *Hanshu* (A history of the Han dynasty). 12 vols. Beijing: Zhonghua shuju, 1975.

Bartlett, Beatrice S. *Monarchs and Ministers: The Grand Council in Mid-Ch'ing China, 1723–1820.* Berkeley: University of California Press, 1991.

Bernhardt, Kathryn. *Rents, Taxes, and Peasant Resistance: The Lower Yangzi Region, 1840–1950.* Stanford: Stanford University Press, 1992.

Black, Alison Harley. *Man and Nature in the Philosophical Thought of Wang Fu-chih.* Seattle: University of Washington Press, 1989.

Bodde, Derk and Clarence Morris. *Law in Imperial China Exemplified by 190 Ch'ing Dynasty Cases (Translated from the* Hsing-an hui-lan*) with Historical, Social, and Juridical Commentaries.* Cambridge, Mass.: Harvard University Press, 1967; reprint, Philadelphia: University of Pennsylvania Press, 1973.

Braudel, Fernand. *The Structures of Everyday Life.* Vol. 1 of *Civilization and Capitalism, 15th–18th Century.* Trans. Siân Reynolds. London: Collins, 1981.

———. *The Wheels of Commerce.* Vol. 2 of *Civilization and Capitalism, 15th–18th Century.* Trans. Siân Reynolds. London: Collins, 1982.

Bray, Francesca. *Technology and Gender: Fabrics of Power in Late Imperial China.* Berkeley: University of California Press, 1997.

CC. First Historical Archives (Beijing). *Zhupi zouzhe, Caizheng, Cangchu* (Re-scripted palace memorials, Fiscal matters, Granary reserves).

Chang Chung-li. *The Chinese Gentry: Studies on their Role in Nineteenth-Century Chinese Society.* Seattle: University of Washington Press, 1955.

Chen Dongyou. "Kangxi chao mijia zhong de shangren xingwei" (Merchant behavior and rice prices in the Kangxi period). *Zhongguo shehui jingji shi yanjiu* (Studies in the social and economic history of China) 53 (1995, no. 3): 46–58.

Chen Feng. *Qingdai junfei yanjiu* (A study of military expenditure in the Qing dynasty). Wuhan: Wuhan Daxue chubanshe, 1992.

Chen Zhaolun. *Zizhu shanfang shiwen ji* (Collected poetry and prose of Chen Zhaolun). Edition of ca. 1800.

Chen Zhaonan. *Yongzheng Qianlong nianjian de yin/qian bijia biandong (1723–95)* (The fluctuations in the silver/cash exchange rate in the Yongzheng and Qianlong periods). Taibei: Zhongguo xueshu zhuzuo jiangzhu weiyuanhui, 1966.

Ch'ü T'ung-tsu. *Local Government in China under the Ch'ing*. Cambridge, Mass.: Harvard University Press, 1962.

Chuan, Han-sheng. See under Quan Hansheng.

Clunas, Craig. *Fruitful Sites: Garden Culture in Ming Dynasty China*. London: Reaktion Books, 1996.

Crosby, Alfred W. *The Measure of Reality: Quantification and Western Society, 1250–1600*. Cambridge: Cambridge University Press, 1997.

Crossley, Pamela Kyle. *Orphan Warriors: Three Manchu Generations and the End of the Qing World*. Princeton: Princeton University Press, 1990.

———. *A Translucent Mirror: History and Identity in Qing Imperial Ideology*. Berkeley: University of California Press, 1999.

Dai Yi. *Qianlong di ji qi shidai* (The Qianlong emperor and his times). Beijing: Zhongguo Renmin Daxue chubanshe, 1992.

Dai Yingcun. "The Qing State, Merchants, and the Military Labor Force in the Jinchuan Campaigns." *Late Imperial China* 22, no. 2 (2001): 35–90.

Deng Hailun. See under Dunstan, Helen.

DQHDSL. *Qinding Da Qing huidian shili* (Imperially authorized collected statutes of the great Qing dynasty: precedents and regulations). Reprint of the 1899 edition. Taibei: Xin Wenfeng chuban gongsi, 1976.

DQHDZL. *Qinding Da Qing huidian zeli* (Imperially authorized collected statutes of the great Qing dynasty: precedents and regulations). 1767.

Dray-Novey, Alison. "Spatial Order and Police in Imperial Beijing." *Journal of Asian Studies* 52, no. 4 (1993): 885–922.

Dunstan, Helen. "Safely Supping with the Devil: The Qing State and its Merchant Suppliers of Copper." *Late Imperial China* 13, no. 2 (1992): 42–81.

———. *Conflicting Counsels to Confuse the Age: A Documentary Study of Political Economy in Qing China, 1644–1840*. Ann Arbor: The University of Michigan, Center for Chinese Studies, 1996.

———. "'Orders Go Forth in the Morning and Are Changed by Nightfall': A Monetary Policy Cycle in Qing China, November 1744–June 1745." *T'oung Pao (International Journal of Chinese Studies)* 82 (1996): 66–136.

———. "The 'Autocratic Heritage' and China's Political Future: A View from a Qing Specialist." *East Asian History* 12 (1996): 79–104.

———. "Official Thinking on Environmental Issues and the State's Environmental Roles in Eighteenth-Century China." In *Sediments of Time: Environment and*

Society in Chinese History, ed. Mark Elvin and Liu Ts'ui-jung (New York: Cambridge University Press, 1998), pp. 585–614.

——. "Tunhu yu jihuang: shiba shiji gaoji guanliao zouzhe zhong suo fanying tunhu de juese" (Famine and the hoarder: the role of hoarders as reflected in the memorials of eighteenth-century senior officials). In *Ziran zaihai yu Zhongguo shehui lishi jiegou* (Natural disasters and social structure in Chinese history), ed. Fudan Daxue Lishi dili yanjiu zhongxin (Shanghai: Fudan Daxue chubanshe, 2001), pp. 211–33.

——. "Shilun liuyang zisong zhidu zai Qianlong chao de yishi feichu" (On the Qianlong-period discontinuation of the system of reception centers and assisted passage home for famine refugees). In *Tian you xiongnian: Qingdai zaihuang yu Zhongguo shehui* (Heaven sends some bad years: natural disasters and Chinese society in the Qing dynasty), ed. Xia Mingfang (Beijing: Sanlian shudian, 2006), forthcoming.

E'ertai et al., comps. *Baqi tongzhi chuji* (Gazetteer of the Eight Banners: original edition). 1739. Reprint, Taibei: Taiwan xuesheng shuju, 1968.

Elman, Benjamin A. *Classicism, Politics, and Kinship: The Ch'ang-chou School of New Text Confucianism in Late Imperial China*. Berkeley: University of California Press, 1990.

Elliott, Mark C. *The Manchu Way: The Eight Banners and Ethnic Identity in Late Imperial China*. Stanford: Stanford University Press, 2001.

Elvin, Mark. "The Gentry Democracy in Shanghai, 1905–1914." Ph.D. diss., University of Cambridge, 1967.

Esherick, Joseph W. *The Origins of the Boxer Uprising*. Berkeley: University of California Press, 1987.

Fairbank, John K. and Teng Ssu-yü. *Ch'ing Administration: Three Studies*. Cambridge, Mass.: Harvard University Press, 1960.

Fang Bao. *Fang Bao ji* (Collected works of Fang Bao). 2 vols. Shanghai: Shanghai guji chubanshe, 1983.

Faure, David. "What Made Foshan a Town? The Evolution of Rural-Urban Identities in Ming-Qing China." *Late Imperial China* 11, no. 2 (1990): 1–31.

Fu Yiling. *Ming Qing nongcun shehui jingji* (Rural society and economy during the Ming and Qing). Beijing: Sanlian shudian, 1961.

GCQXLZ. Li Huan, comp. *Guochao qixian leizheng* (Classified biographies of venerable and distinguished personages under the present dynasty). 1890.

GZD/KX. *Gongzhong dang Kangxi chao zouzhe* (Secret palace memorials of the Kangxi period). Taibei: National Palace Museum, 1976.

GZD/QL. *Gongzhong dang Qianlong chao zouzhe* (Secret palace memorials of the Qianlong period). Taibei: National Palace Museum, 1982–89.

Gao Wangling. "Yige wei wanjie de changshi: Qingdai Qianlong shiqi de liangzheng he liangshi wenti" (An incomplete experiment: provisioning policy and grain supply problems in the Qianlong period of the Qing dynasty). *Jiuzhou xuekan* (The nine provinces journal) 2, no. 3 (1988): 13–40.

——. *Shiba shiji Zhongguo de jingji fazhan he zhengfu zhengce* (Economic development and government policy in eighteenth-century China). Beijing: Zhongguo shehui kexue chubanshe, 1995.

Gao Xiang. *Kang Yong Qian san di tongzhi sixiang yanjiu* (A study of the ideology of rulership of the Kangxi, Yongzheng, and Qianlong emperors). Beijing: Zhongguo Renmin Daxue chubanshe, 1995.

Gujin tushu jicheng (Complete collection of written texts and illustrations, past and present). (1726). Shanghai: Zhonghua shuju, 1934.

Guo Chengkang, comp. *Qingshi biannian* (An annalistic history of the Qing dynasty), vol. 5, *Qianlong chao, shang* (The Qianlong reign, part one). Beijing: Zhongguo Renmin Daxue chubanshe, 1991.

Guo Songyi. "Qingdai liangshi shichang he shangpin liang shuliang de guce" (The Qing grain market: an estimate of the quantity of grain traded). *Zhongguo shi yanjiu* (Journal of Chinese history) 64 (1994, no. 4): 40–49.

HCJSWB. He Changling and Wei Yuan, comps. *Huangchao jingshi wenbian* (A statecraft anthology of our august dynasty). 1827. Reprint of the 1873 edition. Taibei: Shijie shuju, 1964.

HHCC. First Historical Archives (Beijing). *Huke hongben, Cangchu* (Copies of routine memorials made for the Office of Scrutiny for Revenue, Granary reserves).

HQZY. "Renhe Qinchuan Jushi," comp. *Huang Qing zouyi* (Memorials of the august Qing dynasty). N.d.

Han Guanghui. *Beijing lishi renkou dili* (The historical population geography of Beijing). Beijing: Beijing Daxue chubanshe, 1996.

Hangzhou fu zhi (Gazetteer of Hangzhou prefecture). 1923 edition.

Hartwell, Robert. "A Cycle of Economic Change in Imperial China: Coal and Iron in Northeast China, 750–1350." *Journal of the Economic and Social History of the Orient* 10, no. 1 (1967): 102–59.

He Benfang. "Qianlong nianjian queguan de mianshui cuoshi" (Exemptions from internal customs duties in the Qianlong period). *Lishi dang'an* (Historical Archives) 28 (1987, no. 4): 87–93.

Herforth, Derek D. "An Annotated Draft Translation of the *Guoyu*: I, *Zhouyu* A." *Suzugamine Joshi Tanki Daigaku jinbun shakai kagaku kenkyū shūhō* (Collected studies in the humanities and social sciences at Suzugamine Junior College for Women) 30 (1983): 117–46.

Ho Ping-ti. *Studies on the Population of China, 1368–1953.* Cambridge, Mass.: Harvard University Press, 1959.

———. *The Ladder of Success in Imperial China: Aspects of Social Mobility, 1368–1911.* New York: Columbia University Press, 1962.

Hommel, Rudolf P. *China at Work: An Illustrated Record of the Primitive Industries of China's Masses, Whose Life Is Toil, and Thus an Account of Chinese Civilization.* New York: John Day, 1937; reprint, Cambridge, Mass.: M.I.T. Press, 1969.

Horichi Akira. "1906 nen Kōhoku no suigai, kikin to kyūsai" (Flood, famine and relief in Jiangbei in 1906). Paper presented at the International Conference on Qing-Dynasty Natural Disasters and Chinese Society organized by the Institute of Qing Dynasty History, Renmin University of China and the State Committee for the Compilation of the History of the Qing Dynasty, Beijing, 2005.

Hoshi Ayao. *Chūgoku shakai fukushi seisaku shi no kenkyū—Shindai no shinsaisō o chūshin ni* (A history of social welfare policy in China, with special reference to the relief granary system under the Qing dynasty). Tokyo: Kokusho kankōkai, 1985.

Hosoya Yoshio. "Hakki beikyoku kō—Shinchō chūki no Hakki keizai o megutte" (A study of the Banner grain bureaus with special reference to the economy of the Eight Banners in the mid-Qing period). *Shūkan Tōyōgaku* (Papers in Oriental studies) 31 (1974): 181–208.

Hsiao Kung-chuan. *Rural China: Imperial Control in the Nineteenth Century*. Seattle: University of Washington Press, 1960.

Hu Jizhuang. *Zhongguo jingji sixiang shi* (A history of Chinese economic thought). 3 vols. Shanghai: Shanghai Renmin chubanshe, 1983.

Huang Liuhong. *Fuhui quanshu* (A comprehensive treatise on felicity and kindness). 1699. Facsimile of 1850 Japanese edition, with foreword and index by Yamane Yukio. Tokyo: Kyūko shoin, 1973.

Huang Liu-hung (Huang Liuhong). *A Complete Book Concerning Happiness and Benevolence: A Manual for Local Magistrates in Seventeenth-Century China*. Djang Chu, trans. Tucson: University of Arizona Press, 1984.

Hucker, Charles O. "Governmental Organization of the Ming Dynasty." *Harvard Journal of Asiatic Studies* 21 (1958): 1–66.

——. *A Dictionary of Official Titles in Imperial China*. Stanford: Stanford University Press, 1985.

Hummel, Arthur W. ed. *Eminent Chinese of the Ch'ing Period (1644–1912)*. 2 vols. Washington: United States Government Printing Office, 1943–44.

Hymes, Robert P. "Moral Duty and Self-Regulating Process in Southern Sung Views of Famine Relief." In *Ordering the World: Approaches to State and Society in Sung Dynasty China*, ed. Robert P. Hymes and Conrad Schirokauer (Berkeley: University of California Press, 1993), pp. 280–309.

Iwai Shigeki. "Shindai kokka zaisei ni okeru chūō to chihō—shakuhatsu seido o chūshin ni shite" (Center and provinces in fiscal administration in the Qing dynasty, with special reference to the *zhuobo* [allocation] system). *Tōyōshi kenkyū* (Studies in Eastern history) 42, no. 2 (1983): 126–54.

JF. First Historical Archives (Beijing). *Zhupi zouzhe, Caizheng, Jingfei* (Rescripted palace memorials, Fiscal matters, Expenses).

JS. First Historical Archives (Beijing). *Zhupi zouzhe, Caizheng, Juanshu* (Rescripted palace memorials, Fiscal matters, Contributions).

Jing Junjian. "Legislation Related to the Civil Economy in the Qing Dynasty." Trans. Matthew H. Sommer. In *Civil Law in Qing and Republican China*, ed. Kathryn Bernhardt and Philip C. C. Huang (Stanford: Stanford University Press, 1994), pp. 42–84.

Johnson, Linda Cooke. *Shanghai: From Market Town to Treaty Port, 1074–1858*. Stanford: Stanford University Press, 1995.

KC. First Historical Archives (Beijing). *Zhupi zouzhe, Caizheng, Kuchu* (Rescripted palace memorials, Fiscal matters, Treasury reserves).

KYQRFDZ. Zhongguo Renmin Daxue, Qingshi yanjiusuo and Dang'an xi Zhongguo zhengzhi zhidu shi jiaoyanshi, comps., *Kang Yong Qian shiqi chengxiang renmin fankang douzheng ziliao* (Materials on the resistance struggle of the people in town and countryside during the Kangxi, Yongzheng, and Qianlong periods). 2 vols. Beijing: Zhonghua shuju, 1979.

Kahn, Harold L. *Monarchy in the Emperor's Eyes: Image and Reality in the Ch'ien-lung Reign.* Cambridge, Mass.: Harvard University Press, 1971.

Kaplan, Steven L. *Bread, Politics and Political Economy in the Reign of Louis XV.* 2 vols. The Hague: Martinus Nijhoff, 1976.

Kishimoto Mio. "Kōki nenkan no kokusen ni tsuite—Shinsho keizai shisō no ichi sokumen" (On the Kangxi depression: some aspects of early Qing economic thought). *Tōyō Bunka Kenkyūjo kiyō* (Annals of the Research Institute for Oriental Culture) 89 (1982): 251–306.

——. "Shinchō chūki keizai seisaku no kichō—1740 nendai no shokuryō mondai o chūshin ni" (The tone of mid-Qing economic policy as seen in the 1740s food grain crisis). *Chikaki ni arite—Kin-Gendai Chūgoku o meguru tōron no hiroba* (Being nearby: discussions on modern China) 11 (1987): 17–35.

——. *Shindai Chūgoku no bukka to keizai hendō* (Prices and economic change in Qing China). Tokyo: Kenbun shuppan, 1997.

Kondō Hideki. "Shinchō kenryoku no seikaku—Chūgoku ni okeru zettai ōsei" (The character of Qing dynastic power: absolute monarchy in China). In *Iwanami kōza sekai rekishi* (The Iwanami course on world history) (Tokyo: Iwanami shoten, 1971), pp. 161–95.

Kōsaka Masanori. "Kenryū-dai zenki ni okeru kanzei shukoku-zei menjo-rei ni tsuite" (On the suspension of internal customs duties on staple foodstuffs in the early Qianlong period). *Bunka* (Culture) 32, no. 4 (1969): 42–78.

Kuhn, Philip A. *Soulstealers: The Chinese Sorcery Scare of 1768.* Cambridge, Mass.: Harvard University Press, 1990.

Kuroda Akinobu. "Shindai bichiku kō: shisan keitai yori mita keizai kōzō ron" (Grain storage under the Qing dynasty: an economic structural approach in terms of asset forms). *Shirin* (Historical studies) 71, no. 6 (1988): 1–28.

Kutcher, Norman. "The Death of the Xiaoxian Empress: Bureaucratic Betrayals and the Crises of Eighteenth-Century Chinese Rule." *Journal of Asian Studies* 56, no. 3 (1997): 708–25.

LFZZ. National Palace Museum (Taibei). *Junji dang, Lufu zouzhe* (Grand Council archives, Palace memorial copies).

LFZZQL. National Palace Museum (Taibei). *Qingzhe* or *qingdan* (statistical statements) in the *Lufu zouzhe* (palace memorial copies) collection of the *Junji dang* (Grand Council archives).

Lai Fushun. *Qianlong zhongyao zhanzheng zhi junxu yanjiu* (A study of military supply in Qianlong's major military campaigns). Taibei: Guoli Gugong Bowu-yuan, 1984.

Leftwich, Richard H. *The Price System and Resource Allocation.* Revised edition. New York: Holt, 1961.

Leong Sow-Theng. *Migration and Ethnicity in Chinese History: Hakkas, Pengmin, and Their Neighbors.* Ed. Tim Wright. Stanford: Stanford University Press, 1997.

Lewis, Mark Edward. *Sanctioned Violence in Early China.* Albany: State University of New York Press, 1990.

Li Bozhong. "Kongzhi zengzhang, yi bao fuyu—Qingdai qian zhongqi Jiangnan de renkou xingwei" (Controlling population growth in order to protect prosperity: the demographic behavior of Jiangnan people in the early and mid-Qing). *Xin shixue* (New history) 5, no. 3 (1994): 25–70.

Li Chainong. *Huangzheng zheyao* (Essentials of famine relief administration). 1833. Reprinted in *Zhongguo huangzheng quanshu* (Complete collection of Chinese works on famine relief), ed. Li Wenhai and Xia Mingfang (Beijing: Beijing guji chubanshe, 2003–), vol. 2, part 4, pp. 505–56.

Li, Lillian M. "Grain Prices in Zhili Province, 1736–1911: A Preliminary Study." In *Chinese History in Economic Perspective*, ed. Thomas G. Rawski and Lillian M. Li (Berkeley: University of California Press, 1992), pp. 69–99.

———and Alison Dray-Novey. "Guarding Beijing's Food Security in the Qing Dynasty: State, Market, and Police." *Journal of Asian Studies* 58, no. 4 (1999): 992–1,032.

Li Wenzhi and Jiang Taixin. *Qingdai caoyun* (The Qing grain tribute system). Beijing: Zhonghua shuju, 1995.

Li Yuandu, comp. *Guochao xianzheng shilüe* (Brief lives of eminent personages under the present dynasty). 1866. Punctuated ed. with subtitle *Qingdai 1108 ren zhuanji* (1,108 Qing-dynasty biographies), ed. Yi Mengchun. 2 vols. Changsha: Yuelu shushe, 1991.

Liang Qizi. *Shishan yu jiaohua: Ming Qing de cishan zuzhi* (Philanthropy and moral transformation: charitable organizations in the Ming and Qing dynasties). Taibei: Lianjing chuban shiye gongsi, 1997.

Liu Shijiao. *Huangzhu lüe* (Famine plans in brief). 1608. Reprinted from a 1911 ed. of Yu Sen, comp., *Huangzheng congshu* (Collected works on famine relief) (1690) in *Zhongguo huangzheng quanshu* (Complete collection of Chinese works on famine relief), ed. Li Wenhai and Xia Mingfang (Beijing: Beijing guji chubanshe, 2003–), vol. 1, pp. 483–98.

Liu Ts'ui-jung. "A Reappraisal of the Functions of the Granary System in Ch'ing China (1644–1911)." In *Les techniques de conservation des grains à long terme: leur rôle dans la dynamique des systèmes de cultures et des sociétés*, ed. Marceau Gast, François Sigaut and Corinne Beutler, vol. 3, part 1 (Paris: Éditions du CNRS, 1985), pp. 305–21.

Lu Zengyu. *Qinding kangji lu* (Imperially authorized record of soothing and succoring), ed. Ni Guolian, re-edited E'ertai et al. 1740. Reprinted from a Japanese ed. (preface 1794) in *Zhongguo huangzheng quanshu* (Complete collection of Chinese works on famine relief), ed. Li Wenhai and Xia Mingfang (Beijing: Beijing guji chubanshe, 2003–), vol. 2, part 1, pp. 225–456.

Luo Ergang. *Lüying bing zhi* (The Green Standards Army). Beijing: Zhonghua shuju, 1984.

Lü Jian, comp. "Kang Yong Qian Hubu yinku linian cunyin shu" (Figures for the annual level of reserves in the silver vault of the Board of Revenue during the Kangxi, Yongzheng, and Qianlong periods). *Lishi dang'an* 16 (1984, no. 4): 19–21.

Lü Xiaoxian, comp. "Qianlong sannian zhi sanshiyi nian nagu juanjian shiliao" (Materials on the selling of *jiansheng* titles for grain, 1738–1766). Part 1, *Lishi dang'an* 44 (1991, no. 4): 3–17; part 2, *Lishi dang'an* 45 (1992, no. 1): 12–27.

MQDA. Zhang Weiren, ed. *Zhongyang Yanjiuyuan Lishi yuyan yanjiusuo xiancun Qingdai Neige Daku yuancang Ming Qing dang'an* (Ming and Qing documents from the archives of the Qing Grand Secretariat preserved at the Institute of History and Philology, Academia Sinica). Taibei: Academia Sinica, Institute of History and Philology, 1986–95.

Ma Feibai, ed. *Guanzi Qingzhong pian xinquan* (A new exegesis of the "Light and heavy" chapter of the *Guanzi*). 2 vols. Beijing: Zhonghua shuju, 1979.

Ma Ruheng and Cheng Chongde. *Qingdai bianjiang kaifa* (Frontier development in the Qing dynasty). 2 vols. Taiyuan: Shanxi Renmin chubanshe, 1998.

Marks, Robert B. "Rice Prices, Food Supply, and Market Structure in Eighteenth-Century South China." *Late Imperial China* 12, no. 2 (1991): 64–116.

———. *Tigers, Rice, Silk, and Silt: Environment and Economy in Late Imperial South China*. Cambridge: Cambridge University Press, 1998.

———. " 'It Never Used To Snow': Climatic Variability and Harvest Yields in Late-Imperial South China, 1650–1850." In *Sediments of Time: Environment and Society in Chinese History*, ed. Mark Elvin and Liu Ts'ui-jung (New York: Cambridge University Press, 1998), pp. 411–46.

Metzger, Thomas A. "The State and Commerce in Imperial China." *Asian and African Studies* 6 (1970): 23–46.

———. *The Internal Organization of Ch'ing Bureaucracy: Legal, Normative, and Communication Aspects*. Cambridge, Mass.: Harvard University Press, 1973.

Miller, Judith A. *Mastering the Market: The State and the Grain Trade in Northern France, 1700–1860*. Cambridge: Cambridge University Press, 1999.

Min Erchang, comp. *Beizhuan ji bu* (A supplement to "Collected biographical inscriptions"). Beijing: Yenching University, 1932.

NGDKDA. Institute of History and Philology, Academia Sinica. Digitized document from the *Neige Daku dang'an* (Archives of the Grand Secretariat).

Naquin, Susan. *Millenarian Rebellion in China: The Eight Trigrams Uprising of 1813*. New Haven: Yale University Press, 1976.

———and Evelyn S. Rawski. *Chinese Society in the Eighteenth Century*. New Haven: Yale University Press, 1987.

———. *Peking: Temples and City Life, 1400–1900*. Berkeley: University of California Press, 2000.

Nayancheng. *Zhen ji* (An account of relief operations). 1813. Reprinted in *Zhongguo huangzheng quanshu* (Complete collection of Chinese works on famine relief), ed. Li Wenhai and Xia Mingfang (Beijing: Beijing guji chubanshe, 2003–), vol. 2, part 2, pp. 671–804.

Oberst, Zhihong Liang. "Chinese Economic Statecraft Ideas in the Song Period (960–1279)." Ph.D. diss., Columbia University, 1996.

PDJCFL. Lai Bao and the Qing Military Archives. *Pingding Jinchuan fanglüe* (The strategies by which Jinchuan was pacified). 1752. Reprinted by Xizang Shehui Kexue Yuan, Xizangxue Hanwen wenxian bianjishi. Sanhe, Hebei: Quanguo tushuguan wenxian suwei fuzhi zhongxin, 1991.

PYTOCG. Chen Hongmou. *Peiyuan Tang oucun gao: wenxi* (Chance survivals from the Peiyuan Hall: directives). N.d.

Perdue, Peter C. "The Qing State and the Gansu Grain Market, 1739–1864." In *Chinese History in Economic Perspective*, ed. Thomas G. Rawski and Lillian M. Li (Berkeley: University of California Press, 1992), pp. 100–25.

———. *China Marches West: The Qing Conquest of Central Eurasia*. Cambridge, Mass.: Belknap Press of Harvard University Press, 2005.

Perry, Elizabeth J. *Rebels and Revolutionaries in North China, 1845–1945*. Stanford: Stanford University Press, 1980.

Pomeranz, Kenneth. *The Making of a Hinterland: State, Society, and Economy in Inland North China, 1853–1937*. Berkeley: University of California Press, 1993.

———. *The Great Divergence: China, Europe, and the Making of the Modern World Economy*. Princeton: Princeton University Press, 2000.

QCWXTK. Ji Huang et al., comps. *Qingchao wenxian tongkao* (Comprehensive scrutiny of documents: Qing dynasty) (1786). Reprint of the 1936 *Shitong* edition. Taibei: Xinxing shuju, 1965.

QSL/KX. *Da Qing Shengzu Ren Huangdi shilu* (Veritable records of the Kangxi period). Reprint, Taibei: Huawen shuju, 1970.

QSL/QL. *Da Qing Gaozong Chun Huangdi shilu* (Veritable records of the Qianlong period). Reprint, Taibei: Huawen shuju, 1970.

QSL/YZ. *Da Qing Shizong Xian Huangdi shilu* (Veritable records of the Yongzheng period). Reprint, Taibei: Huawen shuju, 1970.

Qian Shifu, comp. *Qingdai zhiguan nianbiao* (Chronological tables of high officeholders in the Qing dynasty). 4 vols. Beijing: Zhonghua shuju, 1980.

Qianlong tingji (Court letters of the Qianlong period). N.d. 10 vols. Reprint, Taibei: Guangwen shuju, 1974.

Qinding Hubu zeli (Imperially authorized precedents and regulations of the Board of Revenue). 1865.

Qingshi liezhuan (Biographies for the standard history of the Qing dynasty). Shanghai: Zhonghua shuju, 1928.

Qiu Pengsheng. "You shichan lüli yanbian kan Ming Qing zhengfu dui shichang de falü guifan" (The evolution of the market offenses laws and Ming-Qing legal norms for commerce). In *Shixue: chuancheng yu bianqian xueshu yantaohui lunwenji* (History: papers from a conference on continuity and change) (Taibei: Guoli Taiwan Daxue lishi xuexi, 1998), pp. 291–333.

Quan Hansheng. "Meizhou baiyin yu shiba shiji Zhongguo wujia geming de guanxi" (On the connection between silver from the Americas and the eighteenth-century Chinese price revolution). 1956; reprinted in Quan Hansheng, *Zhongguo jingji shi luncong* (Collected papers on Chinese economic history) (Hong Kong: Chinese University of Hong Kong, New Asia Institute, 1972), pp. 475–508.

———. "Qing zhongye yiqian Jiang Zhe mijia de biandong qushi" (The trend of rice price changes in Jiangsu and Zhejiang during the early Qing). 1964; reprinted in Quan, *Zhongguo jingji shi luncong*, pp. 509–15.

———. "Qianlong shisan nian de mi gui wenti" (The problem of high grain prices in 1748). 1964; reprinted in Quan, *Zhongguo jingji shi luncong*, pp. 547–66.

—— and Richard A. Kraus. *Mid-Ch'ing Rice Markets and Trade: An Essay in Price History*. Cambridge, Mass.: Harvard University, East Asian Research Center, 1975.

Rawski, Evelyn Sakakida. *Education and Popular Literacy in Ch'ing China*. Ann Arbor: University of Michigan Press, 1979.

——. *The Last Emperors: A Social History of Qing Imperial Institutions*. Berkeley: University of California Press, 1998.

Reed, Bradly W. *Talons and Teeth: County Clerks and Runners in the Qing Dynasty*. Stanford: Stanford University Press, 2000.

Ren Yuanxiang. *Minghe Tang wenji* (Collected writings from the Minghe Hall). N.d.

Ritsurei kenkyūkai (Society for the Study of Premodern Law), ed. *Kumamoto han kunyaku hon Shin ritsurei isan* (The *Da Qing lüli huizuan* as annotated for reading in Japanese under the auspices of Kumamoto Domain). Ca. 1837; Chinese original 1793, comp. Shen Xiangnan. Tokyo: Kyūko shoin, 1981.

Roth, Gertraude. "The Manchu-Chinese Relationship, 1618–1636." In *From Ming to Ch'ing: Conquest, Region, and Continuity in Seventeenth-Century China*, ed. Jonathan D. Spence and John E. Wills (New Haven: Yale University Press, 1979), pp. 4–38.

Rowe, William T. *Hankow: Commerce and Society in a Chinese City, 1796–1889*. Stanford: Stanford University Press, 1984.

——. "State and Market in Mid-Qing Economic Thought: The Case of Chen Hongmou (1696–1771)." *Études chinoises* 12, no. 1 (1993): 7–40.

——. *Saving the World: Chen Hongmou and Elite Consciousness in Eighteenth-Century China*. Stanford: Stanford University Press, 2001.

Santangelo, Paolo. "Urban Society in Late Imperial Suzhou." In *Cities of Jiangnan in Late Imperial China*, ed. Linda Cooke Johnson (Albany: State University of New York Press, 1993), pp. 81–116.

Sasaki Masaya. "Shindai kanryō no kashoku ni tsuite" (On money-making by Qing bureaucrats). *Shigaku zasshi* (Journal of history) 63, no. 2 (1954): 22–57.

Sen, Amartya. *Poverty and Famines: An Essay on Entitlement and Deprivation*. Oxford: Oxford University Press, 1982.

Shangyu dang (Archive of imperial edicts). Microfilm.

Shangyu qiwu yifu (Edicts concerning endorsed proposals on Banner affairs). N.d. Reprint, Taibei: Taiwan xuesheng shuju, 1976.

Shexian zhi (Gazetteer of She county). 1937 edition.

Shen Xiangnan. *Da Qing lüli huizuan* (Penal code of the great Qing dynasty with collected annotations). 1793. See under Ritsurei kenkyūkai.

Shen Zhiqi. *Da Qing lü jizhu* (Penal statutes of the great Qing dynasty with collected annotations). 1715. Punctuated edition by Huai Xiaofeng and Li Jun. 2 vols. Beijing: Falü chubanshe, 1998.

——. *Da Qing lü jizhu* (Penal statutes of the great Qing dynasty with collected annotations). 1715. Revised edition by Hong Gaoshan, 1746. Reprint (3 vols.), Beijing: Beijing Daxue chubanshe, 1993.

Shigeta Atsushi. *Shindai shakai keizai shi kenkyū* (Studies of Qing social and economic history). Tokyo: Iwanami shoten, 1975.

Skinner, G. William. "Regional Urbanization in Nineteenth-Century China." In *The City in Late Imperial China*, ed. G. William Skinner (Stanford: Stanford University Press, 1977), pp. 211–49.

Smith, Adam. *An Inquiry into the Nature and Causes of the Wealth of Nations*. Fifth edition, 1789. Ed. Edwin Cannan, 1904. Reprint (2 vols. in 1), with a preface by George J. Stigler, Chicago: University of Chicago Press, 1976.

Smith, Thomas C. *Native Sources of Japanese Industrialization, 1750–1920*. Berkeley: University of California Press, 1988.

Sommer, Matthew H. *Sex, Law, and Society in Late Imperial China*. Stanford: Stanford University Press, 2000.

Sun Jiagan. *Sun Wending Gong zoushu* (The memorials of Sun Jiagan). N.d. Reprinted in *Jindai Zhongguo shiliao congkan* (Taibei: Wenhai chubanshe, 1966–73), no. 541.

Suzhou fuzhi (Gazetteer of Suzhou prefecture). 1883 edition.

Suzuki Hidemitsu. "Jōhei kō: Shindai chūki shikei anken shori no ichi kōsatsu" (On death by beating: an inquiry into the implementation of the death penalty in the mid-Qing period). *Chūgoku: shakai to bunka* (Chinese society and culture) 17 (2002): 149–73.

TF. First Historical Archives (Beijing). *Zhupi zouzhe, Caizheng, Tianfu* (Rescripted palace memorials, Fiscal matters, Land tax).

Thaxton, Ralph. "On Peasant Revolution and National Resistance: Toward a Theory of Peasant Mobilization and Revolutionary War with Special Reference to Modern China." *World Politics* 30, no. 1 (1977): 24–57.

Tongzhou zhi (Gazetteer of Tongzhou department). 1879 edition.

Vogel, Hans Ulrich. "Chinese Central Monetary Policy, 1644–1800." *Late Imperial China* 8, no. 2 (1987): 1–52.

von Glahn, Richard. "Community and Welfare: Chu Hsi's Community Granary in Theory and Practice." In *Ordering the World: Approaches to State and Society in Sung Dynasty China*, ed. Robert P. Hymes and Conrad Schirokauer (Berkeley: University of California Press, 1993), pp. 221–54.

———. *Fountain of Fortune: Money and Monetary Policy in China, 1000–1700*. Berkeley: University of California Press, 1996.

Waley-Cohen, Joanna. "Commemorating War in Eighteenth-Century China." *Modern Asian Studies* 30, no. 4 (1996): 869–99.

Wang Fuzhi. *Du Tongjian lun* (On reading the *Comprehensive Mirror for Assistance in Government*). 3 vols. Beijing: Zhonghua shuju, 1975.

Wang Guangyue. "Qianlong chunian qianjia zeng'ang wenti chutan" (A preliminary investigation of the rise in coin prices in the early Qianlong period). *Lishi dang'an* 14 (1984, no. 2): 95–102.

Wang Xianqian, comp. *Donghua xu lu* (Further records from within the east gate of the palace compound). 1887.

Wang Yeh-chien. "The Secular Trend of Prices during the Ch'ing Period (1644–1911)." *Journal of the Institute of Chinese Studies of the Chinese University of Hong Kong* 5, no. 2 (1972): 347–68.

———. *Land Taxation in Imperial China, 1750–1911*. Cambridge, Mass.: Harvard University Press, 1973.

———. "Food Supply in Eighteenth-Century Fukien." *Late Imperial China* 7, no. 2 (1986): 80–117.

———. "Secular Trends of Rice Prices in the Yangzi Delta, 1638–1935." In *Chinese History in Economic Perspective*, ed. Thomas G. Rawski and Lillian M. Li (Berkeley: University of California Press, 1992), pp. 35–68.

Whelan, T. S. *The Pawnshop in China, Based on Yang Chao-yü*, Chung-kuo tien-tang yeh *(The Chinese Pawnbroking Industry), with a Historical Introduction and Critical Annotations*. Michigan Abstracts of Chinese and Japanese Works on Chinese History, no. 6. Ann Arbor: University of Michigan Press, 1979.

Will, Pierre-Étienne. *Bureaucratie et famine en Chine au 18ᵉ siècle*. Paris: Mouton Éditeur, 1980.

———. *Bureaucracy and Famine in Eighteenth-Century China*. Trans. Elborg Forster. Stanford: Stanford University Press, 1990.

———. "On State Management of Water Conservancy in Late Imperial China." *Papers on Far Eastern History* (Canberra) 36 (1987): 71–91.

———. "Développement quantitatif et développement qualitatif en Chine à la fin de l'époque impériale." *Annales: Histoire, Sciences Sociales* 1994, no. 4: 863–902.

———. "The 1744 Annual Audits of Magistrate Activity and Their Fate." *Late Imperial China* 18, no. 2 (1997): 1–50.

———. "Clear Waters versus Muddy Waters: the Zheng-Bai Irrigation System of Shaanxi Province in the Late-Imperial Period." In *Sediments of Time: Environment and Society in Chinese History*, ed. Mark Elvin and Liu Ts'ui-jung (New York: Cambridge University Press, 1998), pp. 283–343.

———. "Discussions about the Market-Place and the Market Principle in Eighteenth-Century Guangdong." In *Zhongguo haiyang fazhan shi lunwen ji* (Collected essays on the history of Chinese maritime development), ed. Tang Xiyong, vol. 7 (Taibei: Academia Sinica, Sun Yat-sen Institute of Humanities and Social Sciences, 1999), pp. 323–89.

——— and R. Bin Wong. *Nourish the People: The State Civilian Granary System in China, 1650–1850*. Ann Arbor: The University of Michigan, Center for Chinese Studies, 1991.

Wong, R. Bin. "Food Riots in the Qing Dynasty." *Journal of Asian Studies* 41, no. 4 (1982): 767–88.

——— and Peter C. Perdue. "Grain Markets and Food Supplies in Eighteenth-Century Hunan." In *Chinese History in Economic Perspective*, ed. Thomas G. Rawski and Lillian M. Li (Berkeley: University of California Press, 1992), pp. 126–44.

Woodside, Alexander. "The Ch'ien-lung Reign." In *The Cambridge History of China*, vol. 9, part 1, *The Ch'ing Dynasty to 1800*, ed. Willard J. Peterson (Cambridge: Cambridge University Press, 2002), pp. 230–309.

Wu Jianyong. "Qingdai Beijing de liangshi gongying" (Grain supply in Qing Beijing). In *Beijing lishi yu xianshi yanjiu* (Studies on Beijing, past and present), comp. Beijing Shi Shehui Kexue Yuan, Beijing Shehui Hanshou Daxue, and Beijing Shi Yanjiuhui (Beijing: Yanshan chubanshe, 1989), pp. 167–86.

Wu Qiyan. "Qingdai qianqi yahang zhi shishu" (The brokerage system in the first half of the Qing dynasty). *Qingshi luncong* (Collected essays on Qing history) 6 (1985): 26–52.

Wu Renshu. "Mingmo dao Qing zhongye de chengshi liangshi baodong" (Urban grain riots from the late Ming to the mid-Qing). *Shiyuan* (Historical inquiry) 20 (1997): 317–61.

Wu Tao. "Qingdai Jiangnan shequ zhenji yu difang shehui" (Neighborhood relief and local society in Qing Jiangnan). In *Ziran zaihai yu Zhongguo shehui lishi jiegou* (Natural disasters and social structure in Chinese history), ed. Fudan Daxue Lishi dili yanjiu zhongxin (Shanghai: Fudan Daxue chubanshe, 2001), pp. 259–94.

Xu Daling. *Qingdai juanna zhidu* (The sale of offices and titles in the Qing dynasty). Beijing: Yanjing Daxue, Hafo-Yanjing xueshe, 1950. Reprint, Hong Kong: Longmen shudian, 1968.

Xu Dixin and Wu Chengming, eds. *Zhongguo ziben zhuyi fazhan shi* (A history of the development of capitalism in China), vol. 1, *Zhongguo ziben zhuyi de mengya* (Nascent capitalism in China). Beijing: Renmin chubanshe, 1985.

Xu Guangqi. *Nongzheng quanshu jiaozhu* (An annotated edition of Xu Guangqi's "Comprehensive Treatise on Agronomy"). Ed. Shi Shenghan, with the assistance of Xibei Nongxue Yuan, Gu nongxue yanjiushi. 3 vols. Shanghai: Shanghai Guji chubanshe, 1979.

Yamamoto Susumu. "Shindai zenki no heichō seisaku: saibai, sōcho seisaku no suii" (The stabilizing sales policy in the first half of the Qing dynasty: the shift from purchasing to granary storage). *Shirin* 71, no. 5 (1988): 38–70.

Yan Sisheng. *Chumeng shanfang ji* (Collected works of Yan Sisheng). 1745.

Yang Lien-sheng. *Money and Credit in China*. Cambridge, Mass.: Harvard University Press, 1952.

Yao Siren. *Da Ming lü fu li zhujie* (Annotated edition of the penal statutes of the great Ming dynasty, with the supplementary articles appended). 1585 or later. Reprint, Beijing: Beijing Daxue chubanshe, 1993.

Yao Yuxiang and Hu Yangshan, comps. *Da Qing lüli xing'an xinzuan jicheng* (A new comprehensive edition of the penal code of the great Qing dynasty, with precedents). 1873. Reprinted in facsimile under its alternative title, *Da Qing lüli huitong xinzuan* (A new comprehensive edition of the penal code of the great Qing dynasty). 5 vols. Taibei: Wenhai chubanshe, 1964.

Ye Zhiru, comp. "Qianlong nianjian Jiangnan shusheng xing jin xiqu shaojiu shiliao" (Materials on the yeast and liquor prohibitions in certain Yangzi Valley provinces in the Qianlong period). *Lishi dang'an* 25 (1987, no. 1): 13–20.

——, comp. "Qianlong nianjian Jiangbei shusheng xing jin xiqu shaojiu shiliao" (Materials on the yeast and liquor prohibitions in several northern provinces in the Qianlong period). Part 1, *Lishi dang'an* 27 (1987, no. 3): 27–35; part 2, *Lishi dang'an* 28 (1987, no. 4): 16–21, 59.

——, comp. "Qianlong chao miliang maimai shiliao" (Materials on the grain trade in the Qianlong period). Part 1, *Lishi dang'an* 39 (1990, no. 3): 23–30; part 2, *Lishi dang'an* 40 (1990, no. 4): 29–37, 53.

Yuxing qiwu zouyi (Memorials on Banner affairs imperially approved for action). N.d. Reprint, Taibei: Taiwan xuesheng shuju, 1976.

Zelin, Madeleine. *The Magistrate's Tael: Rationalizing Fiscal Reform in Eighteenth-Century Ch'ing China.* Berkeley: University of California Press, 1984.

Zhang Yongjiang. "Liangshi xuqiu yu Qingchu Nei Menggu nongye de xingqi" (The demand for grain and the rise of agriculture in Inner Mongolia in the early Qing period). *Qingshi yanjiu* (Studies in Qing history) 51 (2003, no. 3): 30–42.

Zhao Ersun et al., comps. *Qingshi gao* (Draft history of the Qing dynasty). 1928. Reprint, 48 vols., Beijing: Zhonghua shuju, 1977.

Zhao Hong'en. *Yuhua Tang Liang Jiang shi gao* (Proclamations of the Liang-Jiang governor-general, from the Yuhua Hall). Contained in the same author's *Yuhua ji* (The Yuhua collection). 1734.

Zhaolian. *Xiaoting za lu* (Notes from the Whistling Pavilion). Completed ca. 1815; first known publication 1880. Reprint, Beijing: Zhonghua shuju, 1980.

Zhongguo Diyi Lishi Dang'an Guan, comp. *Kangxi chao Hanwen zhupi zouzhe huibian.* (Collected Chinese-language imperially endorsed palace memorials of the Kangxi period). 8 vols. Beijing: Dang'an chubanshe, 1984–85.

———. *Zhongguo Diyi Lishi Dang'an Guan guancang Qingdai zhupi zouzhe caizheng lei mulu* (Catalog of Qing palace memorials on fiscal matters held by the First Historical Archives of China). Vol. 3, *Ku chu, cang chu* (Treasury and granary reserves). Beijing: Zhongguo caizheng jingji chubanshe, 1992.

Zhou Cunyi. *Jiang yi jiuhuang biji* (Notes on famine relief in Jiangxia county). 1834. Reprinted in *Zhongguo huangzheng quanshu* (Complete collection of Chinese works on famine relief), ed. Li Wenhai and Xia Mingfang (Beijing: Beijing guji chubanshe, 2003–), vol. 2, part 4, pp. 557–81.

Zhu Baojiong and Xie Peilin, comps. *Ming Qing jinshi timing beilu suoyin* (An index to Ming and Qing lists of successful candidates for the *jinshi* degree). 3 vols. Shanghai: Shanghai guji chubanshe, 1980.

Zhuang Jifa. *Qing Gaozong shi quan wugong yanjiu* (A study of the "ten complete martial victories" of the Qianlong emperor). Taibei: Guoli Gugong Bowuyuan, 1982.

ZPYZ. *Yongzheng zhupi yuzhi* (Edicts of the Yongzheng emperor issued in the form of rescripts). 1732, 1738.

Character List

A'ersai 阿爾賽
Aibida 愛必達
Akedun 阿克敦
Alantai 阿蘭泰
Aligun 阿里袞
An Lushan 安祿山
Anning 安寧
Anxi 安溪

bachi hangshi lü 把持行市律
Baigou 白溝
bao bu zhuo bo 報部酌撥
baojia 保甲
baoquan shen jia xingming 保全身家
   性命
Baqi miju 八旗米局
Batu 巴圖
ben zhe jian shou 本折兼收
bi bu ke shao zhi shu 必不可少之數
Boyang 鄱陽
bu ruo ting shangfan zi xing zhuanyun
   liutong 不若聽商販自行轉運流通
bu tongshang 不通商
bu ying wei lü 不應為律
Bulantai 布蘭泰
buyi zhi yi 不抑之抑

Cai Maode 蔡懋德
caimai zhi fan 採買之煩
caimai zhi lei 採買之累
cangdou 倉斗
cangmi 倉米

Cangtou Zhen 倉頭鎮
caoxiang 漕項
ce 冊
Celeng 策楞
Chang Lu 常祿
Chang'an 常安
Changlu 長蘆
changping benfa 常平本法
changping cang 常平倉
Changsha 長沙
changsui 長隨
Changzhou 長洲
Chaozhou 潮州
Chen Dashou 陳大受
Chen Hongmou 陳弘謀
Chen Qining 陳其凝
Chen Zhaolun 陳兆崙
chengse mi 成色米
Chenzhou 陳州
chi tiao 遲糶
Chongming 崇明
ci mi zhong suo gong zhi 此米眾所
   共知

da xueshi 大學士
Daizhou 代州
Dajian Lu 打箭爐
dakō shitsutsu 蛇行しつつ
Deqing 德清
dian 典
diaomin 刁民
difang fuhu 地方富户

difang ji gu bu yan qi duo 地方積穀不厭其多

ding shu 定數

Dong Wei 董煟

dongbo 冬撥

dongbo guxiang ce 冬撥估餉冊

duifang (hulling shop) 碓房

duifang (warehouse) 堆房

e 額

Echang 鄂昌

E'ertai 鄂爾泰

edi 遏糴

Emida 鄂彌達

en 恩

E'rongan 鄂容安

Fan Can 范璨

fan jian lü 犯姦律

Fan Qingzhu 范清注

Fan Yubin 范毓馪

Fang Bao 方苞

Fang Guancheng 方觀承

feifen 非分

feng 豐

fengbi 封閉

Fengyang 鳳陽

Fenzhou 汾州

Foshan 佛山

Fuheng 傅恆

fukanshō ron 不干涉論

Fumin 福敏

Fuzhou 福州

gaicang 蓋藏

Gan Rulai 甘汝來

Gao Bin 高斌

Gao Heng 高珩

Gao Wangling 高王凌

Gao Xiang 高翔

Gao Yue 高越

gaotai 高擡

ge zi wei mou er zhuanyi zai min 各自爲謀而轉移在民

Gongchang 鞏昌

gongsheng 貢生

gu (sedentary merchant) 賈

gu 穀 (unhusked grain)

gu jia 穀價

Gu Gongxie 顧公燮

Gu Yaonian 顧堯年

guan miju 官米局

guan ru mijia zhi zhong 貫入米價之中

guanggun li 光棍例

Guangzhou (Guangdong) 廣州

Guangzhou (Henan) 光州

guanshou 官收

guanwang 觀望

Gubei Kou 古北口

Guide 歸德

Guihua Cheng 歸化城

Guo Songyi 郭松義

Guzong 顧琮

Haiwang 海望

Haizhou 海州

Hangzhou 杭州

Hankou 漢口

Hanxin Ling 韓信嶺

hao mi 好米

haoxian 耗羨

He Tai 赫泰

Hedong 河東

Henan 河南

Hengwen 恆文

Hengzhou 衡州

Hong Taiji 洪台吉

Hongzhi 弘旺

Hosoya Yoshio 細谷良夫

Hu Baoquan 胡寶瑔

Hu Jitang 胡季堂

Huai'an 淮安

Huainan 淮南

Huaiqing 懷慶

Huang Dengxian 黃登賢

Huang Liuhong 黃六鴻

Huang Tinggui 黃廷桂

Huang You 黃祐

Hubu zeli 戶部則例

Huguang 湖廣

Hui Shiqi 惠士奇

huiguan 會館

Huixi 徽西
Huizhou 徽州
Hunan shengli cheng'an 湖南省例
　成案
huohao 火耗
huohao guigong 火耗歸公
huo ji jia luo 貨集價落
Huzhou 湖州

Ji Huang 嵇璜
Ji Zengyun 嵇曾筠
jian 奸/姦
Jiang Pu 蔣溥
Jiang Shunjiao 姜順蛟
Jiangnan 江南
Jiangning 江寧
jiansheng 監生
jiao 驕
jiaohuan 繳還
Jiaxing 嘉興
Jie Xizhou 介錫周
jiemai 截買
Jinchuan 金川
Jingde Zhen 景德鎮
Jining 濟寧
Jiqing 吉慶
jiquan zi mu 計權子母
Jishan 紀山
jiu qing 九卿
Jiujiang 九江
juan 捐
jueluo 覺羅
Junji chu 軍機處

Kaerjishan 喀爾吉善
Kaifeng 開封
Kaitai 開泰
Kishimoto Mio 岸本美緒
kouwai 口外
kuan 寬

Lang Tingji 郎廷極
Lanzhou 蘭州
Lechang 樂昌
leling chutiao 勒令出糶
li (supplementary article, etc.) 例

li (proper pattern) 理
Li Guangdi 李光地
Li Qingfang 李清芳
Li Qingzhi 李清植
Li Wei 李衛
Liaodong 遼東
ling qi zhi mi gui shoubing zhi you
　令其知米貴受病之由
lingdi zhengtun 零糴整囤
Lingnan 嶺南
Linqing 臨清
Liu Fang'ai 劉方藹
Liu Yuyi 劉於義
liutong tiaomai 流通糶賣
liuyang 留養
liuyang zisong 留養資送
longduan gaotai 壟斷高擡
Longxi 隴西
Longzhou 隴州
Lu Zhuo 盧焯
luyin 路引
Luzhou 盧州
lü 律

Ma Chang'an 馬昌安
Ma Hongqi 馬宏琦
Ma Jing 馬熉
Malan Zhen 馬蘭鎮
maoyi zhi chang 貿易之常
Mei Gucheng 梅轂成
mi 米
mi hang 米行
min qian 民欠
minshu gushu 民數穀數
minshu gushu zouzhe 民數穀數奏摺
minju 民局

Namin 納敏
Nanchang 南昌
Nankang 南康
Nanyang 南陽
Nasutu 那蘇圖
Nayantai 納延泰
nianzhong dabo 年終大撥
Ningbo 寧波
Nuoqin 訥親

Ou Kanshan 歐堪善

Pan Siju 潘思榘
pandang 盤當
Peng Jiaping 彭家屏
Peng Shukui 彭樹葵
Pingding 平定
Pingyang 平陽
pingtiao 平糶

qi huo 奇貨
qi huo ke ju 奇貨可居
qianfa lü 錢法律
qianju 錢局
Qiantang 錢塘
Qiao Xueyin 喬學尹
qihang yijia 齊行議價
Qin Huitian 秦蕙田
qing 情
Qingpu 青浦
Qishan 岐山
quan 權
quan fen 勸分
Quzhou 衢州

Raoyang 饒陽
Raozhou 饒州
Ren Yuanxiang 任源祥
Renhe 仁和
Runing 汝寧
Ruzhou 汝州

Saileng'e 塞楞額
Shaluoben 莎羅奔
shangfan bi yingyun er lai 商販必營運而來
shangmi wenfeng er zhi 商米聞風而至
Shanzhou 陝州
shao 少
shecang 社倉
She (county) 歙
Shen Maohua 沈懋華
Shen Tingfang 沈廷芳
Shen Zhiqi 沈之奇
shengshi 聲勢
shenshi 紳士

shi 勢
shi min zi yang 使民自養
Shi Yizhi 史貽直
Shise 碩色
shisi ping wujia lü 市司評物價律
shiyong 使用
shizai ke xing zhi shu 實在可行之數
shou qi yi fa er jiaoyi zai guan 守其一法而交易在官
Shuhede 舒赫德
shuhuang 熟荒
Shulu 舒輅
shuqu 贖取
Songjiang 松江
sui mai, sui mai 隨買隨賣
Suiyuan 綏遠
Sun Hao 孫灝
suomi 梭米
Suzhou 蘇州

tanfeng 貪風
Tang Menglai 唐夢賚
Tang Pin 湯聘
Tang Suizu 唐綏祖
Tang Ying 唐英
Tian Mao 田懋
tiaoju 糶局
tiben 題本
tijie 提解
ting cong min bian 聽從民便
ting mai gujia 停買穀價
ting minjian zi wei liutong 聽民間自為流通
ting qi ziran 聽其自然
tingzhi caimai 停止採買
tong 通
Tongguan 潼關
tongnian jinshi 同年進士
tongshang 通商
Tongzhou (Shaanxi) 同州
Tongzhou (Zhili) 通州
Tuerbing'a 圖爾炳阿
Tula 圖拉
tun 囤
tundang 囤當
tunfa 囤發

tunhu 囤戶
tunji 囤積
tunji juqi 囤積居奇
Tuoketuo (Shanxi) 托克托

Wan Nianmao 萬年茂
Wang Chengyao 王承堯
Wang Fuzhi 王夫之
Wang Jian 王檢
Wang Pilie 王丕烈
Wang Rou 王柔
Wang Tang 王鐺
Wang Youdun 汪由敦
wei ling lü 違令律
Wei Tingpu 衛廷璞
Weihui 衛輝
Weng Zao 翁藻
wohu 窩戶
wu ren qi ziran zhi li 無任其自然之理
Wu Wei 吳煒
Wuchang 武昌
Wuxi 無錫

Xi'an 西安
xiancun 現存
xiang 餉
xiangbao 鄉保
xiangshi 鄉市
Xiangtan 湘潭
xiangxi zaobao yi bian zhuochou banli
    詳細造報以便酌籌辦理
xiannian yingcun gu 現年應存穀
xianzai shi cun 現在實存
Xie Min 謝旻
xingshi 行使
Xinzhu 新柱
Xu Qi 徐杞
Xu Rong 許容
Xu Yisheng 徐以升
Xue Cheng 薛澂
xunhuan bushan 循環簿扇
Xuzhou (Henan) 許州
Xuzhou (Jiangsu) 徐州

Yaerhashan 雅爾哈善
Yaertu 雅爾圖

yan 嚴
Yan Ruilong 嚴瑞龍
Yan Sisheng 晏斯盛
Yang Eryou 楊二酉
Yang Xifu 楊錫紱
Yang Yingju 楊應琚
yanglian 養廉
Yanmen Guan 雁門關
yi bian 以便
yi buzhi zhi zhi 以不治治之
yi e gu 溢額穀
yi jia 抑價
yi min yang min 以民養民
yi yin dai zhen 以銀代賑
yicang 義倉
yin gu jian zhen 銀穀兼賑
Yin Huiyi 尹會一
ying de zhi zui 應得之罪
yingcang 營倉
yingcun 應存
yinhao 銀號
Yinjishan 尹繼善
Yinlu 胤(允)祿
Yong Xing 永興
you bei wu huan 有備無患
youduo 游惰
youshou zhi min 游手之民
yuanqi 元氣
Yue Jun 岳濬
Yuhuan 玉環
Yuyao 餘姚

zaliang 雜糧
zaobao zhuo bo 造報酌撥
Zeng Gong 曾鞏
Zeng Jing 曾靜
Zezhou 澤州
zhantun 棧囤
Zhang Kai 張楷
Zhang Shizai 張師載
Zhang Tingyu 張廷玉
Zhang Yunsui 張允隨
Zhangde 彰德
Zhangjia Kou 張家口
Zhangzhou 漳州
Zhao Hong'en 趙宏恩

Zhao Shenqiao 趙申喬
Zhaolian 昭槤
Zhengzhou 鄭州
Zhexi 浙西
zhi 滯
zhili zhou 直隸州
zhishu you wei lü 制書有違律
zhong (middle) 中
zhong ("all") 眾
zhong dao 中道
Zhongyin 鐘音
Zhou Xuejian 周學健
Zhu Fengying 朱鳳英
Zhu Lunhan 朱倫瀚
Zhu Xi 朱熹

zhuang 庄
Zhuang Yougong 莊有恭
Zhuntai 準泰
zhuo bo 酌撥
zhuo ying ji xu 酌盈劑虛
zhuoji 酌劑
Zichuan 淄川
ziran 自然
zisong 資送
zouxiao an 奏銷案
zouxiao ce 奏銷冊
zu 租
Zu Kefa 祖可法
zuoling 佐領
zuzhi 阻滯

Index

Harvard East Asian Monographs
(* out-of-print)

Harvard East Asian Monographs

Harvard East Asian Monographs

Harvard East Asian Monographs

Harvard East Asian Monographs

Harvard East Asian Monographs

Harvard East Asian Monographs

Harvard East Asian Monographs

Harvard East Asian Monographs

Harvard East Asian Monographs